ONE

THE MOST POWERFUL NUMBER

Textbook for Students Preparing to be Elementary Arithmetic Teachers and Secondary Mathematics Teachers

AUTHOR: TIMOTHY W. YOUNG

THIS BOOK IS A MATHEMATICS TEXTBOOK FOR COLLEGE JUNIORS AND SENIORS PREPARING TO BECOME ELEMENTARY ARITHMETIC TEACHERS OR SECONDARY MATHEMATICS TEACHERS.

EVERYONE INVOLVED IN ARITHMETIC AND MATHEMATICAL EDUCATION REALIZES THE IMPORTANCE OF TEACHING/ILLUSTRATING CONCEPTS FIRST WHEN INTRODUCING MATHEMATICAL TOPICS. THIS IS A FACT WHICH 99.999...% OF ALL TEACHERS UNDERSTAND. IF YOU ARE PREPARED TO TEACH ARITHMETIC OR MATHEMATICS, YOU KNOW THAT 99.999...% EQUALS 100%, NOT CLOSE TO 100% BUT EQUAL TO 100%.

TEACHING CONCEPTS IS THE FIRST STEP, BUT IT IS NOT THE LAST STEP WHEN STUDENTS ARE LEARNING TO SOLVE ARITHMETIC AND MATHEMATICAL PROBLEMS. EVEN THOUGH TEACHING CONCEPTS IS THE FIRST STEP, IT IS ONLY THE BEGINNING OF THE PROCESS AND NOT THE END IF YOU ARE GOING TO BUILD A MATHEMATIC'S SKYSCRAPER.

THERE ARE NO PICTURES IN THIS TEXTBOOK, IT IS A SERIOUS MATHEMATICS TEXTBOOK **WHICH CONCENTRATES ON HOW TO TEACH RULES AND PROCEDURES, PLUS HOW TO INCLUDE NUMBER SENSE IN YOUR DAILY/WEEKLY LESSONS**.

STEP ONE, UNDERSTANDING CONCEPTS: WHEN LEARNING ANYTHING IN MATHEMATICS, UNDERSTANDING CONCEPTS IS IMPORTANT. BUT IF THE STUDENTS DO NOT MEMORIZE SPECIFIC NUMBER FACTS AND "LEARN AND REMEMBER" THE ARITHMETIC RULES/PROCEDURES WHICH NEED TO BE LEARNED/MASTERED IN ARITHMETIC, STUDENTS WILL STRUGGLE IN ALGEBRA AND ADVANCED MATHEMATICS CLASSES.

THIS TEXTBOOK WILL EXPLAIN AND ILLUSTRATE HOW TO TEACH RULES AND PROCEDURES TO STUDENTS, SO THEY CAN MASTER THE REQUIRED RULES AND PROCEDURES, AND HAVE A GREAT CHANCE TO BE SUCCESSFUL IN HIGHER-LEVEL MATH CLASSES BY USING THE SAME RULES IN ARITHMETIC WHICH THEY WILL USE IN ALGEBRA AND HIGHER-LEVEL MATH CLASSES.

IN THE PROCESS, WE WILL INTRODUCE AND ILLUSTRATE HOW TO USE TWO NEW COMMON-SENSE THEOREMS WHICH NO ONE HAS EVER NAMED AND FEW TEACHERS EMPHASIZE. THESE TWO NEW THEOREMS WILL HELP STUDENTS SOLVE A VARIETY OF ARITHMETIC AND MATHEMATICAL PROBLEMS. BOTH THEOREMS ARE SIMPLE, BUT POWERFUL.

READ AND STUDY THIS TEXTBOOK. READ AND STUDY MANY OF THE RESEARCH PAPERS INDICATED IN THIS TEXTBOOK, AND ALSO SOLVE ALL THE PROBLEMS INDICATED AT THE END OF EACH CHAPTER. THEN, YOU SHOULD BE PREPARED TO BE AN EXCELLENT ELEMENTARY ARITHMETIC TEACHER AND/OR AN EXCELLENT SECONDARY MATH TEACHER. STUDY AND DIGEST EVERY COMMENT INDICATED IN THIS TEXTBOOK. EVERY SENTENCE, EXPLANATION, EXAMPLE PROBLEM, AND COMMENT IS IMPORTANT.

ONE

The Most Powerful Number

College Textbook for Students Preparing to be Elementary

Arithmetic Teachers and Secondary Mathematics Teachers

TIMOTHY W. YOUNG

www.timyoungbooks.com

About the Author | One the Most Powerful Number

A short biography about the author, Timothy W. Young, is contained near the end of the book to include his webpage information and contact information.

ISBN: 978-1-960757-63-0 Paperback

978-1-960757-64-7 Hardcover

The focus of this college textbook is to help prepare college students, who plan to become an elementary arithmetic teacher and/or secondary mathematics teacher, to be knowledgeable and confident on the first day students enter their classroom.

The teaching procedures discussed and illustrated throughout this textbook can be used starting early in elementary school, but the illustrations and examples contained in this textbook focus on teaching students ways to **'Learn and Remember'** how to simplify and solve all types of fraction problems (rational numbers). Math education researchers from many countries agree the biggest indicator in 5th-grade arithmetic to predict success in algebra and higher-level math classes is a solid understanding of fractions, decimals, and percentages, known as rational numbers.

I assume that 100% or close to 100% of arithmetic and mathematics teachers believe the first step when students are going to work with any arithmetic or math topic is to illustrate and explain the concepts surrounding the topic of interest. **Understanding concepts in arithmetic and mathematics is the first step,** but not the last step in the learning process in an arithmetic or mathematics classroom.

I assume over 90% of current arithmetic and math teachers took a course in college which involved teaching math concepts. This textbook concentrates on the next step in the college process to prepare future arithmetic and math teachers to teach students how to **'Learn and Remember'** rules and procedures to work with all types of fraction problems starting in third, fourth, or fifth grade when students are learning how to find equivalent fractions and concluding by emphasizing the same rules/procedures to simplify and solve algebra rational expression problems, trigonometric identities, and calculus limit problems.

I am sure 100% of my readers will not agree with all my teaching suggestions, but I am also confident 100% of my readers will learn something new about ways to teach rules and procedures in arithmetic and mathematics.

Tribute and Thank-You to Dr. Siegler for inviting me to attend your research meetings. I met Dr. Siegler in the summer of 2012 after an article was published in the Pittsburgh Post-Gazette, Tuesday, June 19, 2012, Vol. 85, NO. 324 1/19/12 pages 1 & 3, titled "Learning fractions and division early will help America's students as they tackle tougher problems ahead, a research study finds **Formula written for math success**," by Mary Niederberger, piqued my interest.

Here are some quotes from this article: 1. "Mastery of fractions and early division is a predictor of students' later success with algebra and other higher-level mathematics, based on a study done by a team of researchers led by a Carnegie Mellon University professor." 2. "Everyone is aware that overall U.S. math achievement isn't very good in relative terms or compared to other parts of the world." 3. "**Mr. Siegler said the changes in math education need to take place at the universities that train teachers, in professional development programs for current math teachers, and in the elementary classrooms where students are learning fractions and early division concepts.**" The title of the research article referenced in the newspaper article is "Early Predictors of High School Mathematics Achievement," published in *Psychological Science*, the flagship journal of the Association for Psychological Science (Siegler, Duncan, Davis-Kean, Duckworth, Claessens, Engel, Susperreguy, & Chen. 2012).

I retired after almost thirty-eight years in the Pennsylvania Public Education System in 2009. I worked in three different school districts. For ten of those years, I served as either a high school principal or assistant principal, and for the other years, I was a secondary math teacher. I mention this comment now because when I was a principal in two different school districts, I frequently found myself answering questions from parents who were frustrated with a high school teacher. I did not keep track of the number of times when I responded to parents regarding their frustration with high school teachers in general, but I did notice a strong pattern that spiked my interest. The pattern I noticed regarding negative parent phone calls was probably over 60% or maybe closer to 75% of the parent complaints focused on high school math teachers. In addition to the negative phone calls, I had parent meetings that focused on the parents' frustrations with high school mathematics teachers. Since I was a secondary math teacher for most of my career, I became obsessed with finding reasons and solutions to the question, "Why are secondary math teachers frequently under attack by parents in the United States?" I thought the reason might have something to do with fractions, but I had no evidence to back up my beliefs.

Here is a **condensed** biography about Dr. Siegler, the professor and math education researcher. "Dr. Siegler is a Schiff Foundation Professor of Psychology and Education at the Teachers College, Columbia University." Dr. Siegler spent over 40 years working at Carnegie Mellon University in the Psychology Department, with much of his research at that time focused on student learning as it relates to arithmetic and mathematics before retiring from CMU and accepting a similar position indicated above in 2018 at Columbia University. "Dr. Siegler has published more than 250 articles and chapters, written 13 books, and edited 4 others. His books have been translated into numerous languages, including Japanese, Chinese, Korean, German, Spanish, French, Greek, and Portuguese."

"Much of Dr. Siegler's research focuses on how theoretical understanding of mathematical development can be applied to improving children's math learning. His studies examine how children's representations of numbers influence their ability to learn whole number arithmetic, fractions, and other mathematics topics."

Dr. Siegler's research has been recognized in numerous ways. The following is a partial list. "He has been awarded the American Psychological Association's Distinguished Scientific Contribution Award, been selected to the National Academy of Education, and been chosen as one of the 40 most distinguished graduates of the State University New York at Stoney Brook."

Remember, the above comments are only a few of the comments from his website. The comments enclosed in quotation marks in a previous paragraph are direct quotes from his website indicated below. There is much more I could say about Dr. Siegler, the professor, the researcher, one of my mentors, and a friend. If you want to learn more about Dr. Siegler, his research, his colleagues, students he has worked with, and specific articles and books he has written, refer to the website below to learn about this amazing professor and individual, (https://siegler.tc.columbia.edu).

When I read the article in the Pittsburgh Post-Gazette, I finally had an expert, Dr. Siegler, who could explain why my fixation on fraction problems, might be the number one reason why students struggled in secondary math courses, and I had to find out more.

I contacted Dr. Siegler, and he invited me to have lunch with him at CMU. After an hour of lunch and discussion, he must have sensed I was strongly interested in his research, and he invited me to attend his weekly math research discussions with his team of eight to twelve like-minded people at Carnegie Mellon University. I learned so much about problems the students encountered in elementary school regarding fractions, other basic arithmetic concepts, and rules which I should have learned prior to entering my first classroom as a mathematics teacher. Since I learned so much from Dr. Siegler and his research, I started to think about how elementary arithmetic teachers and secondary math teachers could apply his research findings to help all students "Think, Learn, and Remember" arithmetic and mathematics concepts, rules, and procedures with the goal to be successful throughout their high school math classes, college math classes, and solving math problems they might encounter anytime during their professional career or as a parent.

Since I learned so much about the problems students experienced in arithmetic prior to entering an Algebra 1 class later in their math education career, I constantly reminded myself about the quote indicated above in bold print from the Pittsburgh Post-Gazette article, where Dr. Siegler indicated, "*change needs to occur at the universities where students learn to teach arithmetic and mathematics and change also needs to occur with professional development for all elementary arithmetic teachers and secondary math teachers.*" Since I had the opportunity to meet many of Dr. Siegler's students/colleagues and attend around 200 research discussion meetings, I was inspired to write two books. The books are similar; this book is a college textbook, "One; the Most Powerful Number", which is the first of the two books to be published, written for students to study as a fifteen-week, 3-credit, college course prior to entering an arithmetic or mathematics classroom for the first time. The second book titled "The Most Powerful Number 1", is written with the objective of being a professional development book for experienced teachers.

If you read and study either of the books, I strongly recommend you also read and study many of the research articles referenced in both books, which will give you background information to help you prepare to teach arithmetic and mathematics classes/courses.

Dr. Siegler is the person who gave me ideas regarding what to emphasize in arithmetic, he motivated me without knowing it, and he taught me a lot about how to teach and what to teach as an elementary arithmetic teacher and secondary math teacher. Dr. Siegler was and still is a friend and someone I greatly admire. Much of the research I reference in this textbook are research articles in which Dr. Siegler was the main author or personally involved with the publication of the article with many authors who were part of his research teams at Carnegie Mellon University, Columbia University, and/or other Universities.

I have posted several questions and comments on the NCTM blog website over the past couple of years and received some great feedback. Here are two specific comments I posted: **1.** What Arithmetic Topic is the biggest indicator of success when students enter an Algebra class? My comments after several individuals responded were posted on the website blog on December 8, 2020. **2.** Three (3) Important Questions (plus 1) for all arithmetic and mathematics teachers from Kindergarten through Grad School. Here are two of the three questions: 1. When you were an undergraduate student prior to student teaching or entering the classroom for the first time, "Did you ever take an arithmetic or mathematics course which helped you learn how to introduce and teach **concepts** focused on arithmetic or math problems?" 2. When you were an undergraduate student, prior to student teaching or entering the classroom for the first time, "Did you ever take an arithmetic or mathematics course which helped you learn how to introduce and teach **procedures** focused on arithmetic or math problems?" The original 3 (plus 1) questions were posted on the website on Aug 26, 2021. Take a moment and think about how you would respond to the two questions indicated that I posted. In the second post, I personally believe understanding concepts is the first step when learning arithmetic, the second step includes students memorizing and learning facts and procedures, and finally, students need to put all the knowledge gained using concepts, definitions, facts, rules, and procedures to **think**, if they are going to solve a wide variety of arithmetic and mathematics problems in the future.

PREFACE

A SPECIAL TRIBUTE TO THE
MOST AMAZING TEACHERS.

TEACHERS WHO CREATE MIRACLES
IN THE CLASSROOM EVERYDAY.

I AM TALKING ABOUT
EARLY ELEMENTARY TEACHERS

(KINDERGARTEN – THIRD GRADE).

Preface

I am in awe when I think about the magic every kindergarten, first, second, and third-grade teacher creates every day in their classroom. I cannot imagine how any of these teachers start with 20-30 youngsters who come from 20-30 different backgrounds and ability levels. Some of these students might not know the first thing about the numbers from 1 to 10 and the 26 letters in the alphabet. Some of these students may be able to count and recognize the numbers from 1 to 100 and already have some reading skills. Many students begin kindergarten less prepared than their classmates, and immediately, they need more help. These students will come from a wide variety of different home situations with different values and belief systems.

Some parents are so demanding and want to help their child succeed and be ready for everything they will encounter in the early elementary school years. All parents want their child to succeed, but due to issues beyond the control of the teacher, some students do not have the same support system at home. Some students may come from a single-parent family, and the parent must work in addition to being a parent, or the child is raised by a grandmother and/or grandfather. Some students may come from a home life where they may not get 2 or 3 well-balanced meals daily, or they are raised by an older sibling. Not all students are given the same opportunities for success when they are not in school, but the teacher must overcome all the situations with the goal of helping all students reach their maximum potential.

There are so many challenges for every teacher and every student in these early elementary grades, including learning to read, learning to write, and learning to socialize.

Wow, it is a miracle to me how early elementary teachers accomplish so much. They are real miracle workers, and they lay the foundation for the educational careers of all their students.

Since this is an arithmetic/mathematics book, lest I forget, these teachers must also lay the foundation for mathematics, starting with the basics of arithmetic.

Rather than look at the NCTM standards for kindergarten, 1st, 2nd, and 3rd grade, allow me to summarize the arithmetic learning outcomes expected when students' complete 3rd grade in Pennsylvania. I use the Pennsylvania standards only to indicate basic examples, not as a final factual report for all states. Do not simply think about this abbreviated list for 3rd-grade end-of-the-year arithmetic goals which need to be learned but take the time to think about all the preliminary steps which must be accomplished: concepts which students need to understand and facts that must be "learned and remembered", by all students who are going to be successful in 4th grade and beyond.

The following summarized list is taken off the following website: https://www.education.pa.gov on January 21, 2022. I do not think this is much different from other states and from the NCTM standards. I used this website because I am familiar with the site, and I feel it is easy to access and understand, but not necessarily the standard for all states. (I googled Pennsylvania Third Grade Math Standards to get to the correct website.)

Numbers and Operations: General comments indicate to focus on Place Value Properties of Operations regarding multi-digit addition and subtraction problems and rounding off whole numbers to the nearest ten or hundred. <u>Develop an understanding that a fraction is a number, and a fraction can be represented on a number line as one point. The students</u>

should also be able to generate equivalent fractions and compare fractions with the same numerator or denominator.

More specifically: 1. Understand place value properties to solve multi-digit addition and subtraction problems. 2. Explore and develop an understanding of fractions as a number.

Algebra: Demonstrate an understanding of the relationship between multiplication division problems by concentrating on multiplication notation and concepts first. Students need to demonstrate some fluency, identify, and explain patterns in arithmetic. The students should recognize whether a problem is solved using multiplication or division and understand the relationship between multiplication and division. Students will recognize and explain patterns with numbers and solve problems using the four basic arithmetic operations.

Geometry: Partition two and three-dimensional shapes into equal parts and express the area of the partitioned shape into a unit fraction as part of the whole (Examples: $\frac{1}{2}$ *of the shape, or* $\frac{1}{6}$ *of a circle, or* $\frac{1}{8}$ *of a rectangle, etc.*). Understand how to partition a geometric shape into equal parts and recognize how to represent one section as a unit fraction.

Measurement, Data, and Probability: This involves working with simple measurements, translating simple charts and line plots, finding the area of basic geometric shapes (ex. squares and rectangles) using both addition and multiplication, and working with estimations involving temperature, liquid volume, mass (what they really mean for a 3rd grader is the weight of an object), and length. The objectives include telling and writing time accurately within one minute, understanding and estimating temperature, liquid volume (ex. gallon of milk), mass/weight (mass is the more proper word to use), and length of an object. Additionally, interpret basic tally charts, tables, pictographs, line graphs, and bar graphs. Lastly and very importantly, the students will find the area of a rectangle using both addition and multiplication to explain the answer.

The Pennsylvania standards add three additional comments which must be emphasized by all arithmetic and mathematics teachers in every classroom situation.

1. Students must use their knowledge and experiences involving arithmetic and mathematics to interpret how to solve problems. At the end of 3rd grade, the goal is specifically focused on determining whether to multiply or divide to find a solution.
2. Work with students and have the students work with each other to develop opportunities for sharing student work, student thinking, and solutions.
3. Establish protocols, so students have peer-to-peer mathematical discourse, which supports active listening and respect for different ideas and values.

I was a secondary mathematics teacher and the youngest students I ever worked with were already young adults when they entered my seventh-grade arithmetic class. I admit in my 38-year educational career, I only worked with seventh and eighth graders for a total of 5 or 6 years when I taught two or three classes per year of seventh and eighth grade arithmetic classes. I also taught a few classes with gifted 7th and 8th graders mixed in with my high school algebra and geometry classes. I was named the math department head at Tyrone Area Jr./Sr. High School at the beginning of my eighth year of teaching. I taught at Tyrone for almost 21 years at the beginning of my career. I felt it was important for me to teach all the different courses offered in the math department, so I had the experience of teaching the very best students and the students who needed the most help from grades 7-12. Throughout my entire teaching career, I always believed if I was a good teacher, then the students who needed me the most were the students who struggled with arithmetic and math. (Comment: Wow, did I mature as a teacher.) Nonetheless, by the time I taught these students in 7th and 8th grade, they had already developed an understanding of many arithmetic and mathematics concepts, rules, and procedures. I did not start from scratch like the miracle teachers in grades K-3; I built on what other teachers had already started.

Thank you for all the miracles you perform daily to prepare students to enter their secondary math classes. You lay the foundation for students to become successful for the rest of their mathematical careers and the rest of their lives.

The arithmetic concepts developed in elementary school, the arithmetic facts which are memorized in elementary school, the arithmetic definitions which are used in elementary school, and the arithmetic rules and procedures which are introduced and then learned in elementary school are the same concepts, facts, definitions, rules, and procedures which are used to develop more advanced concepts, facts, rules and procedures in higher-level high school and college math classes. Notice, I did not include the word definitions when I mentioned the higher-level high school and college math classes in the previous sentence. Students will learn new math definitions when they enter higher-level math classes, and they will be required to reference the definitions which they already learned in their elementary arithmetic classes. The rules and procedures learned in arithmetic are the foundation to build and develop new rules and procedures in Algebra, Geometry, Trigonometry, Pre-Calculus, Calculus, etc. Elementary teachers build the foundation in arithmetic for the superstructure which will be built on top when students continue their careers in future mathematics classes.

Early elementary teachers are the most amazing teachers in the education process especially the math education process.

I personally thank-you for your hard work and dedication with our students. You create miracles in your classroom every day.

Table of Contents

Chapter 1 Are Arithmetic Rules And Procedures Really Necessary? Page 1

First Assignment Page 9

Chapter 2 Introduction Two Amazing Theorems: Young's Equation/Ratio

Theorem & Young's Conversion Theorem Page 16

Second Assignment Page 48

Chapter 3 Adding And Subtracting Simple Fractions:

Rules And Procedures Are Important Page 65

Third Assignment Page 129

Chapter 4 Challenging Addition And Subtraction Fraction Problems:

"Without Rules These Problems Will Seem Impossible" Page 146

Fourth Assignment Page 212

Chapter 5 Begin To Learn How To Convert Thousands Of Mathematics

Expressions Into Equivalent Expressions Page 237

Fifth Assignment Page 271

Chapter 6 Unit Conversions In Arithmetic Page 298

Sixth Assignment Page 334

Chapter 7 Other Arithmetic Conversion Procedures Page 344

Seventh Assignment Page 377

Chapter 8 Work With More Advanced Mathematics Problems Using "Young's Equation/Ratio Theorem" And "Young's Conversion Theorem" – The Power Of One (1) Is Amazing Page 388

Eighth Assignment Page 486

Chapter 9 Important – Three Phrases You Will Encounter In Other Textbooks Page 495

Ninth Assignment Page 499

References Page 518

Suggested Future Mathematics Education Research Topics (FRT) Page 523

Solutions to Assignment Questions Page I

Short Autobiography Page xvii

Acknowledgments and Influential Friends In My Life Page LI

CHAPTER 1

ARE ARITHMETIC RULES AND PROCEDURES REALLY NECESSARY?

WE NOW START WITH FOURTH AND FIFTH GRADE ARITHMETIC TOPICS, FOCUSING ON RULES AND PROCEDURES REQUIRED TO SOLVE ALL TYPES OF ARITHMETIC PROBLEMS INVOLVING FRACTIONS. WE ASSUME YOU ALREADY KNOW THE BASIC RULES AND PROCEDURES, SO LET'S BEGIN.

Chapter 1

My dream as a mathematics teacher was to have all students earn an "A" in all my classes. It never happened, but I found if I raised my standards, a higher percentage mastered the concepts, rules, and procedures. In fact, all students demonstrated significant improvement. If our intention as teachers is to have our students master the concepts, rules, and procedures in the mathematics curriculum by embracing The Textbook as a teaching template, some students may temporarily reach mastery, but few will "learn and remember" the concepts, rules, and procedures two, three, or four months later.

When I taught mathematics in the 1970s and 1980s, I found if I applied a guesstimated scale of "1-10" in my mind (with 10 representing full mastery of a specific topic), 40% to 60% of the students understood the topic a few months after it was taught. Sadly, when students are required to work with fractions in middle school and beyond, usually fewer than 50% of the students remember the procedures and concepts necessary to solve basic fraction problems with 80% accuracy, using only a pencil and paper. These guesstimates reflect the findings in empirical research studies (Kloosterman, 2010; Siegler & Pyke, 2013; Braithwaite, Tian, & Siegler, 2018). These results are discouraging to everyone involved in the learning process.

The responsible question should be: "What can I do better to ensure 70%-95% of my students "learn and remember" the topics which I present in my classroom?" As you read and study this textbook, you may find the teaching approaches discussed in this book to be iconoclastic compared to "From-the-Text" teaching practices. Here are **five principles** I often utilized and frequently mention in this textbook:

1. Illustrate and emphasize how to use the rules to solve challenging problems related to specific topics.
2. Emphasize minor concepts which teachers often assume the students understand, but frequently the students still have some confusion.
3. Show students how to use the present topic to solve future mathematics problems.
4. Introduce new topics in short, 2-4 minute segments starting one or two months before assigning homework problems from the textbook involving the new topic.
5. Review previously learned topics in short, 2-4 minute segments for 1-2 months after the topic was presented in the textbook.

   (Future Research Topic (FRT) 1a: If teachers use these "Five Teaching Principles", we believe students will demonstrate improvement in all their arithmetic skills. All FRTs mentioned in this book are listed at the end of the textbook.)

The goal is not to have students reach level "10" on my more-or-less intuitive "1-10" scale in all classes but to have them reach levels "13", "14", or "15" for every topic taught and thus go beyond the curriculum requirements. Toward this end, this textbook focuses on two important topics which textbooks and teachers begin to emphasize in fifth and sixth grade:

1. Solving/Simplifying all types of fraction problems.
2. Converting units of measurement into *equivalent* units of measurement and converting arithmetic expressions into *equivalent* arithmetic expressions.

Throughout this textbook, I demonstrate how to use the five principles to teach these two focal topics, utilizing many examples to illustrate how to solve problems. Several problems illustrated in this textbook are basic, while others are more challenging than typical textbook problems. When I gave homework problems from the textbook, I frequently assigned a couple of problems that were more challenging than standard textbook fare. Prior to assigning the challenging problems, I illustrated how to use all the rules and explained how to solve similar challenging problems in the classroom. My goal was to make sure the students could solve the simple textbook problems with a high degree of accuracy and stretch them to solve more challenging problems involving the same topic.

Teaching students how to simplify all types of <u>fraction</u> problems involves unique procedures. Most students, probably over 90% of them, cannot master all the concepts in one year. Some students may need more than four years to become proficient solving all types of problems involving fractions. Yet, if one follows the five principles indicated above, one will discover many students demonstrate significant improvement compared to students who were taught using conventional teaching methods.

The fourth teaching procedure indicated above is paramount. Introducing new topics using correct procedures in short segments prior to assigning the homework problems for a specific topic is pedagogically special. When students do textbook homework problems for the first time, they feel like they already know how to solve the problems; the textbook problems are simple compared to some of my examples. There is a phrase in education which goes somewhat like this, "Practice does not make perfect--it makes permanent." I agree, which is why it is important to ensure all students are prepared to solve the problems correctly when they complete their first homework assignment. The worst thing that can happen when students attempt a new homework assignment is the reinforcement of incorrect procedures. If this occurs, the person responsible for the student's failure could be the teacher, not the student.

Early in Chapter 3 is a section with 15 lists of basic fraction example problems. These 15 sets are the types of problems I suggest you use to introduce fraction operations for a few minutes, two or three times per week, prior to assigning homework problems from the textbook involving fractions. These example lessons can be used at the end of the year in fourth grade for many students or at the beginning of the year in fifth grade. I will discuss some of the specific benefits of using these 2-3 minute introductions in Chapter 3 after discussing the 15 lists of basic fraction example problems.

Here are some results discovered when I continually challenged my students to solve advanced arithmetic problems focusing on fractions and conversions after I used the five teaching principles listed above:

1. The best students achieved at the "13" to "15" level, which I emphasized.
2. The good students consistently achieved at the "10", "11", or "12" level.
3. The poor students improved significantly and often achieved at the "8" or "9" level.
4. All students realized the rules for adding and subtracting fractions were different from the rules for reducing, multiplying, and dividing fractions.
5. All students realized when they needed to add and subtract fractions and find a least common denominator (LCD) first; they needed to convert the fractions into equivalent fractions with the LCD.
6. All students thought reducing, multiplying, and dividing fractions were easier to simplify than adding and subtracting fractions.
7. The low-achieving students illustrated significant improvement in multiplying natural numbers and working with exponents.

8. All students considered the textbook addition and subtraction fraction problems easy because they could almost always find the LCD in their head and convert the given fractions into equivalent fractions with relative ease.
9. Over 90% of the students were proficient when they were required to reduce, multiply, and divide fraction problems from the textbook and the additional challenging problems I continually assigned as homework.
10. Over 90% of the students were able to compute the answers to conversion problems with 90% accuracy.

    (Future Research Topic (FRT) 1b: These are our nonscientific findings which we observed after using the "Five Teaching Principles" previously mentioned.)

I was a secondary mathematics teacher who taught all levels of arithmetic and mathematics, 7th-grade math through calculus, during my 38 years in public education. At the end of my career, I frequently taught the entire gamut of abilities in grades 9-12. My satisfaction was piqued when my students commented about how easy the test problems were after taking mid-year and final tests written by other teachers. My joy multiplied when students shared how well they did the next year in their math classes. The ultimate gratification occurred when the teachers who had my students the following year indicated my students remembered what they had learned in my class. Math teachers who had my students a year after they were in my class frequently commented that my students remembered (at a much higher rate than did students who were not in my class) how to solve problems taught the previous year. These teachers were also impressed with the level of understanding my students expressed and often used them to assist other students who were having difficulty.

I wish I could identify specific research articles to support my findings, but I am not aware of any study or studies which have thoroughly investigated them. I base my assumptions on the hard-scrabble, dog-eared gradebook variety of results my students achieved when they were in my class. As anecdotal as they may seem to the hard-core researcher, my four decades of classroom experience and observation may provide an interesting set of topics for curious researchers interested in math topics to investigate. As you read this textbook, I hope you understand why I feel so strongly that the five principles are paramount for all mathematics teachers.

My two major goals when I was teaching were:

1. Make sure the students mastered the problems required for the present grade/course.
2. Make sure the students were prepared to use the rules and procedures needed to solve more difficult problems in future arithmetic and mathematics classes.

Toward these dual pedagogical ends, the major purposes of this textbook are to help math educators understand the importance of the number 1 when solving a variety of arithmetic (algebra) problems and how to use two special theorems introduced herein: "Young's Equation/Ratio Theorem" and "Young's Conversion Theorem". Both theorems focus on the Power of the Number One (1).

The topics discussed in this textbook, the problems presented in this textbook, the illustrations to solve the problems in this textbook, and the nine assignments contained in this textbook are designed to help prepare college students who plan to be elementary arithmetic teachers or secondary mathematics teachers. The goal after you read and study this textbook is for you to master all the procedures illustrated to solve all fraction problems and a wide variety of conversion problems, plus to have some new ideas on how to teach fraction and conversion problems when you enter the classroom. This textbook is also written for present elementary teachers and secondary mathematics teachers who are searching for ideas and methods which may help students "learn and remember" arithmetic and mathematics concepts and better prepare students for success in future arithmetic and math classes. We also think educators who are in graduate school preparing to be education administrators along with present education administrators should read and study this textbook, so they have some knowledge about the challenges all arithmetic and mathematics teachers face on a day-to-day and year-to-year basis. The assignments are designed for teachers and young adults who are preparing to be teachers, not the 5th and 6th graders and beyond which you are going to instruct. There will be a second book published for experienced teachers to use as an in-service book discussion. The second book is the same as the textbook, without the questions listed at the end of each chapter. This book will be less expensive, and if a school is going to use this book as an in-service book discussion, we suggest the leader of the in-service presentation purchase one textbook and non-textbooks for the experienced teachers to read and study.

We hope the example problems, the illustrations, and the new theorems which we introduce, along with the assignments, gives everyone involved with arithmetic and mathematics education, some ideas to better present information in class and thus better prepare students to be successful in your class this year and future arithmetic and mathematics classes in the years to come.

First Assignment

FRACTIONS

A. Think about how you would *illustrate* to 4th, 5th, and/or 6th-grade students the procedures/rules to find the answer for the following fraction addition/subtraction problem. Understanding concepts is important! $\frac{7}{12}+\frac{1}{12}-\frac{3}{12}$

1. Now that you have taken a few moments to think about how you would *illustrate* how to find the simplified answer "$\frac{5}{12}$" in problem "A.", write "1, 2, or 3 paragraphs", to summarize the rules and procedures you would emphasize to students, so they can solve future fraction addition and/or subtraction problems with identical denominators. (Notice: this problem does not require the students to reduce the final answer. Therefore, do not worry about explaining how to reduce fractions when solving these problems. Reducing fractions will be illustrated and emphasized later in this textbook.)

B. If the paragraph(s) to explain how to add and subtract fractions with identical denominators are written well in question "1", then over 90% of your students should be able to solve the following problems based on your written explanation. Solve the following 10 problems using mental math, *copy the problems as written* and place the solutions to the right of the equal relationship symbols.

2. $\frac{5}{9}-\frac{1}{9}=$

3. $\frac{4}{7}+\frac{2}{7}=$

4. $\frac{3}{12}+\frac{1}{12}-\frac{2}{12}+\frac{5}{12}=$

5. $\frac{7}{53} + \frac{4}{53} + \frac{1}{53} - \frac{5}{53} - \frac{2}{53} =$

6. $\frac{2}{x} + \frac{3}{x} - \frac{1}{x} =$

7. $\frac{5}{301} - \frac{2}{301} + \frac{11}{301} + \frac{9}{301} =$

8. $\frac{15}{xyz} + \frac{2}{xyz} + \frac{10}{xyz} + \frac{1}{xyz} - \frac{3}{xyz} =$

9. $-\frac{5}{k^3m} + \frac{7}{k^3m} + \frac{9}{k^3m} - \frac{3}{k^3m} =$ (You may rearrange the fractions to solve this problem.)

10. $\frac{11}{10.79} - \frac{5}{10.79} - \frac{4}{10.79} - \frac{2}{10.79} + \frac{0}{10.79} =$

11. $+\frac{9}{(x+y)} + \frac{11}{(x+y)} + \frac{0}{(x+y)} + \frac{10}{(x+y)} - \frac{5}{(x+y)}$

Again, notice, none of the answers to these initial problems will reduce. Do you think your better students at the end of the year in 4th grade and all (over 90%) of your students in 5th grade can solve these problems early in the school year?

C. In problems 2-11, you were told to *copy the problems* and write the solutions to the right of the given problems. The reason you were asked to copy the problems was to find out if you wrote the fractions using slanted lines or horizontal lines. The given problems and almost all the problems illustrated in this textbook use the horizontal line notation. The reason we use the horizontal line (vinculum) notation is because we found students in 7th grade and higher who used the slanted line notation seemed to have more difficulty working with fraction problems than students who used the horizontal line fraction notation. **Think** about this comment and why some students may have problems working with fraction problems if they use slanted line fraction notation.

12. Write five example problems to illustrate why the slanted line fraction notation may be more confusing than the horizontal line fraction notation. All the problems written above were written using the horizontal line (vinculum) notation.

13. You may also ask, "Why do we write the majority of the fraction problems in the horizontal format left to right, as indicated above, versus the up and down format, which is frequently used in early elementary arithmetic textbooks for addition and subtraction fraction problems?" Write your answer to this question, and we will answer this question later in the textbook.

Here is one example to illustrate the two different notations used to add or subtract two fractions:

$$\begin{array}{r} \frac{2}{5} \\ +\frac{1}{5} \\ \hline \end{array}$$ (Early elementary vertical notation) or (Horizontal notation): $\frac{2}{5}+\frac{1}{5}=$

CONVERSIONS

D. **Think** about how you would *illustrate* to young students how to convert "$48\ inches\ into\ 4\ feet\ or\ 48\ in.\ into\ 4\ ft.$". Students must always understand concepts and in this type of problem, students must also know basic facts, such as "$1\ foot\ equals\ 12\ inches$" or "$1\ ft. = 12\ in.$".

14. After thinking about conversion problem D. above, write "1, 2, or 3 paragraphs" to summarize the rules and procedures you would emphasize to students so they can solve future unit conversion problems using the same rules which you wrote about. Of course, if the students are supposed to convert feet into inches, or miles into feet, or tons into pounds, or quarts into gallons, etc., they will have to know the required facts (conversion factors) related to the specific units they are asked to convert.

Therefore, do not go into detail about the different units and the equivalent units with the appropriate numbers involved. Your explanation should concentrate on the general rules and procedures students need to use to convert from one unit of measurement into an equivalent unit of measurement, once they know the number involved with the conversion of the two units.

E. If your paragraphs are written well in response to question "14", where you explained the rules and procedures you would emphasize when teaching students to solve unit conversions problems, then over 90% of your students should be able to solve the following problems.

15. Convert 2 feet into inches (Remember "12 inches = 1 foot").
16. Convert 15,840 feet into miles (Remember "1 mile = 5280 feet").
17. Convert 10,000 pounds into tons (Remember "1 ton = 2000 pounds").
18. Convert 3 hours into seconds (Remember 3600 seconds = 1 hour").
19. Convert 5 days into hours (Remember "1 day = 24 hours").

Notice all 5 conversion problems are one-step conversion problems. Later in this textbook, the conversion problems will involve more than one step to complete.

20. Convert 150 centimeters into meters (Remember "1 meter = 100 centimeters).
21. (Make believe problem.) Convert the volume measurement "*lippos*" into "*ninos*". We know the following made-up fact "$7\ lippos = 15\ ninos$". If we have 28 *lippos*, how many *ninos* will you have? You may write the answer as a mixed number or a repeating decimal. Based on your explanation above, does this problem seem impossible? Do you think 90% of your students in 6th grade can compute the correct answer? If you read and study this textbook, we guarantee you that 90% of your 6th

graders will consider this type of problem to be a basic conversion problem, if you emphasize the procedures illustrated throughout this textbook.

F. Step 1. Look at the following two conversion problems and make sure the given answers are correct. (Nothing to write, just think.) Step 2. Answer the *italicized* questions in problems "22" and "23" below. (Write your explanation.) Step 3. As you solve questions "22" and "23" ask yourself the following question, "Did I sufficiently explain the procedures in my explanation in question "14" to find the correct numerical answer to each question? (Nothing to write, just think and reflect on your written answer in problem 14.)

22. Convert 60 inches into feet (Remember "12 inches = 1 foot"). When you get the answer 5 feet, "*How do you illustrate to your students why you mathematically changed the label from inches to feet?*" Maybe it is magic? Maybe it is just something you do when converting between units of measurement?

23. Convert 100 meters into centimeters (Remember "1 meter = 100 centimeters"). When you get the answer 10,000 centimeters, "*How do you explain to your students why you mathematically changed the units from meters to centimeters?*" This must be a mathematical trick which seems to always work.

Make sure your written answer explaining the procedures required to convert inches to feet in problem "22" and meters to centimeters in problem "23." is written so an average 5th grader will understand the reason(s) why the number and the units changed to get an equivalent measurement.

Converting units of measurement into equivalent units of measurement is a difficult mathematical procedure to explain to students, so spend some time thinking about how you need to word your explanation to ensure that 90% of your students are competent when they are required to solve all types of conversion problems. Remember the two focal points of this book are:

1. Solving/Simplifying all types of fraction problems. (The introductory fraction questions indicated in the assignment above only involved adding and subtracting fractions with identical denominators, which should be easy for all college juniors and beyond.)
2. Converting units of measurement into *equivalent* units of measurement and converting arithmetic expressions into *equivalent* arithmetic expressions.

Thus, we start our discussion about fractions for students at the end of 4th grade and the beginning of 5th grade, when students begin to learn the rules to add, subtract, reduce, multiply, and divide fractions. This means the teachers in the earlier elementary grades must teach the meaning of the fraction notation (concept), $"\frac{a}{b}"$ *which could equal* $\frac{1}{2}, or\ \frac{7}{12}, or\ \frac{91}{100}, or\ \frac{3}{x}, or\ \frac{y}{10}, etc.$

Prior to students entering 5th grade, previous elementary teachers should have illustrated and required students to solve problems by measuring the length of objects using both "feet and inches" or "feet and yards", or measuring time using "days and hours", or measuring volume "quarts and gallons", etc. If your students did not experiment with different ways to express the same measurement using different labels prior to arriving in your 5th grade classroom, you must spend time helping your students to understand why there is more than one way to express how much something weighs, or how much liquid a container will hold, or the length and width of your classroom, etc. Students must understand concepts prior to attempting to use the rules to find solutions to *all* arithmetic problems. Students will never remember the rules if they do not understand the concepts and why the rules work.

Comment: Concepts, procedures, and rules which are illustrated, practiced, and *learned* in previous classes are the most critical factor if students are going to be successful in your class this year. When we used the word *learned* in the previous sentence, what we really mean is the word "*remembered*". *Learning* how to solve problems using rules and procedures in one grade and *remembering* how to use the same rules and procedures the next year is not the same thing. If students do not *remember* what they should have *learned* in previous grades, then it sets into motion a series of new problems for you in your class this year.

A marketing executive for a large corporation in the United States told me about the following advertising principle when producing a television commercial: MAKE SURE THE MAIN POINT IS STATED AT LEAST THREE TIMES DURING THE AD. Watch the ads on television and think how many times they repeat a phone number in a commercial or they mention a specific comment like the following phrase, "It's my money and I want it now".

I made the point in the last sentence with the goal to make all arithmetic teachers and secondary mathematics teachers take a moment to think about how important it is to restate important comments in the classroom. If repeating a specific point three times is considered the minimum standard in advertising, "What do you think is the minimum number of times it will take all students (over 90% of your students) to understand math concepts which are often presented using visual representations?" The question just presented in the last sentence is the easy part about teaching arithmetic and many math concepts, but the next question is the challenging question which everyone needs to consider, "What is the minimum number of times an arithmetic teacher and/or mathematics teacher needs to explain rules and procedures to solve challenging problems in arithmetic and mathematics?" Maybe explaining how to solve mathematics problems using rules and procedures three times is not enough to ensure over 90% of your students master the required rules and procedures involving challenging math problems, especially, when the problems involve several steps to derive the solution. Wow, something to think about.

In this textbook we illustrated the rules and procedures required to solve all the problems at least three times and probably more times than you want to think about. Our goal is to ensure that over 90% of all the people who study the problems illustrated in this textbook will "Learn and Remember" the rules and procedures to solve the simplest of problems and the most challenging problems. If you are going to master the rules and procedures emphasized in this textbook, you may need to be introduced to the rules and procedures at least five or more times and then you may need to practice using the rules and procedures to solve problems many more times. Repetition is a teaching strategy all great arithmetic and mathematics teachers use on a regular basis.

CHAPTER 2

INTRODUCTION

TWO AMAZING THEOREMS: YOUNG'S EQUATION/RATIO THEOREM & YOUNG'S CONVERSION THEOREM

YOU WILL DISCOVER AN AMAZING LITTLE SECRET AS YOU STUDY THIS TEXTBOOK. THE RULES STUDENTS NEED TO LEARN IN ARITHMETIC ARE THE SAME RULES THEY WILL USE IN ALGEBRA AND HIGHER-LEVEL MATH CLASSES.

Chapter 2

As indicated in the preface and contents pages, this book focuses on the Power of the Number One (1) and two corresponding theorems, which illustrate several amazing rules related to 1. The two theorems, "Young's Equation/Ratio Theorem" and "Young's Conversion Theorem", have been employed for centuries by mathematicians and scientists, but very few teachers emphasize their importance. Furthermore, to date, no one has formally named the two theorems. (Refer to Chapter 8 for clarification.) Amazingly, many math teachers do not realize the theorems exist. As a result, many students have difficulty converting mathematical expressions into equivalent mathematical expressions. Once teachers understand the power of these two theorems, they will understand why they make a wide range of confusing mathematics problems easier for many students to simplify or solve. Prepare to be amazed. The theorems are simple yet powerful.

There are two important arithmetic topics textbooks and teachers begin to discuss starting in 4th or 5th grade. All students should master these topics before they enter an algebra class. Unfortunately, many students never master the rules related to either topic, which creates difficulty for many of them when they begin their journey into advanced mathematics and science classes (Bailey, Hoard, Nugent, & Geary, 2012; Siegler & Lortie – Forgues, 2017). The two topics can best be expressed as questions:

1. Why is it often necessary to convert from one number, expression, or unit into an equivalent number, expression, or unit, and how should people do so?
2. How should people solve/simplify fraction problems which involve adding, subtracting, reducing, multiplying, and dividing?

Both arithmetic topics just mentioned involve an understanding of advanced arithmetic rules and procedures, which are not emphasized by most elementary arithmetic teachers. If students are going to master the rules and procedures, teachers must emphasize them for two or three years--and in some cases, four. Teachers need to apply the same rules and procedures in all grade levels when they explain these topics. If teachers continually refer to the two theorems titled – "Young's Equation/Ratio Theorem" and "Young's Conversion Theorem", which are introduced and illustrated throughout this textbook, students will "learn and remember" the procedures necessary to master the topics indicated.

Both Theorems focus on the "Power of the Number One (1)".

Students need to convert measurements from one unit into another in 5th or 6th grade using rules and procedures. Hopefully, elementary teachers ask students to measure the length of different shapes, so students realize "12 inches" is equivalent to "1 foot" and "36 inches = 1 yard". Additionally, students need to recognize "24 inches = 2 feet" and "3 ft. = 36 in.". When students are asked to convert from one unit of measurement involving magnitude into another equivalent unit of measurement involving magnitude, many students know there is a specific number for each type of conversion problem which they must use.

The question many students frequently struggle with is: "Should I multiply or divide by the special number which is appropriate for the two units indicated in the problem?"

Example problem: If a United States dollar is equal to 1.09 Canadian dollars, convert 25 Canadian dollars to United States dollars.

Many people ask, "Should I multiply or divide the number 25 by 1.09 to figure out the answer? The answer is, "You should divide 25 by $1.09 to get the answer: $22.936." Later, in this textbook, we will explain how to solve this problem and illustrate how to convert expressions into equivalent expressions using the same procedures for a wide variety of conversion problems. The procedures/rules emphasized herein will help students understand how to solve a wide range of mathematics and science problems for the rest of their lives. (Refer to your written response to the three questions, 14, 22 and 23, in the first assignment and think about your explanation to convert from one unit of measurement into an equivalent unit of measurement. Were you able to quickly solve the conversion problem above regarding 25 Canadian dollars, with confidence based on your explanation?)

Many students remember getting confused when they converted feet into inches and inches into feet in elementary school. They knew to solve one conversion; they should multiply by 12, and to do the other, divide by 12. How would one solve the following problem: "Convert $\frac{1}{24}$ of an inch into feet?" Do we multiply by 12 or divide by 12? We should divide by "12" when solving this conversion problem, and the answer is "$\frac{1}{288}$ ft.". Did anyone guess the answer was "$\frac{1}{2}$ ft." or just say this question makes no sense? (Refer to your written response to the three questions, 14, 22 and 23, in the first assignment and think about your explanation to convert from one unit of measurement into an equivalent unit of measurement. Were you able to quickly solve the conversion problem, "Convert $\frac{1}{24}$ of an inch into feet?" with confidence based on your explanation?) The secret to why you should divide by the number "12" is a teaching focus point in this textbook.

There is no rule or property which says if we multiply by "12" or divide by "12", we will be able to convert back and forth among all types of units. The number "12" does work for feet and inches, but the number "12" is worthless when converting between meters and centimeters, ounces and pounds, or days and weeks. The following statement may seem absurd to many people: "There is one universal number by which we can always multiply to complete all unit conversion problems." (The universal number will be revealed in the next three pages—and most readers have likely already surmised it.) Illustrate to students how to multiply by this number sometime by the end of October in 5th grade. In fact, teachers should insist students multiply by this number in 3rd or 4th grade when they begin to find equivalent fractions. (Examples: $\frac{3}{4} = \frac{6}{8}$ or $\frac{1}{2} = \frac{2}{4}$ or $\frac{1}{2} = \frac{5}{10}$ etc.) Prior to teaching the correct procedures to convert fractions into equal fractions, elementary teachers spend months illustrating that the indicated fractions just mentioned are equal by using a wide variety of graphs, charts, line segments, and computer illustrations. After the students have discovered the fractions just mentioned are equal by using graphs, charts, line segments and computer illustrations, teachers should illustrate the second fraction can be derived by multiplying the first fraction by the number <u>1</u> in 3rd or 4th grade.

It may not be important when teaching 3rd, 4th, or 5th grade students to refer specifically by name to the two theorems discussed in this textbook, but it is important for students to know the proper procedures to convert a fraction into an equivalent fraction using the theorems. If students use the simple and obvious procedures discussed and illustrated in this textbook when they begin to convert a fraction into an equivalent fraction in 3rd or 4th or 5th grade, they will be prepared for success in 5th, 6th, 7th grade and beyond. Every teacher thinks he/she knows how to multiply by this number, but few fully understand The Power of the Number One (1). Repetition at each grade level and across grade levels is pivotal for the retention and transfer of any mathematical skill, so much so we must forewarn readers this textbook intentionally overstates the simplest concepts and repeats itself many times. Stylistically, this textbook would be quite simple and entertaining to parody! We do this on purpose because, too often, the first time we make a statement, the full meaning of the statement is not fully understood. When we first try to explain a mathematical procedure in this textbook or to students, frequently, many little concepts contained in the procedure or statement are not fully understood the first time we illustrate a procedure or make a statement. If you are going to be a great mathematics teacher, you will repeat yourself and restate the obvious many times for almost all the topics you want the students to master. We call it "purposeful redundancy." It is the style of all great math teachers. May the parody writers have their fun!

It seems too easy to multiply by 1 every time we want to convert a unit or an arithmetic expression into an equivalent expression, but this is exactly what "Young's Conversion Theorem" suggests. If one multiplies a term, expression, or number by a ratio or fraction equal to 1, one will get an answer equivalent to the term, number, or expression with which one started. This does not mean the ending unit of measurement, or the ending arithmetic expression will look *identical* to the starting unit of measurement or expression, but what it does mean is the ending unit of measurement or expression is *equivalent* to the beginning unit of measurement or expression. If the starting and ending terms look identical, then one arrives at a special type of equation referred to as an *identity* or, more specifically, a property referred to as the Reflexive Property. Consider the previous instance when "$\frac{1}{24}$ of an inch is equivalent to $\frac{1}{288}$ of a foot". These two measurements indicated may not look *identical,* but we guarantee they are *equal.* This means that "$\frac{1}{24}\ in. = \frac{1}{288}\ ft.$". Throughout this textbook, the number 1 will manifest itself in a thousand different ways as we illustrate how to multiply by the number 1 written as a ratio or fraction.

Fourth or fifth grade is when teachers usually teach simple conversion problems and when students are required to use their knowledge of measurement facts to decide whether to multiply or divide by a specific number based on the units involved. Prior to 4th or 5th grade, students should solve different types of conversion problems using pictures and measuring different objects and shapes. The first goal is to make sure students understand the concept that there are multiple ways to write the same measurement using different units. In 4th, 5th, or 6th grade, students must learn to solve conversion problems using correct procedures to convert from one unit of measurement into a matching unit of measurement, such as feet to inches, meters to centimeters, seconds to hours, quarts to gallons, or ounces to pounds.

In 6th, 7th, and/or 8th grade, students typically begin to perform more difficult unit conversions, such as miles per hour to feet per second, cubic yards to cubic inches, or meters to inches. The simple conversions taught in 4th, 5th, and 6th grade are usually one-step conversions, while conversions taught beyond these early years are sometimes two, three, or four-step conversions. However, if instructors teach the one-step conversions using both "Young's Equation/Ratio Theorem" and "Young's Conversion Theorem", the more difficult conversions are simple to teach. "Young's Equation/Ratio Theorem" along with "Young's Conversion Theorem" helps students to convert between different types of currency; to change percentages to decimals and decimals to percentages; to master all types of measurement conversions (feet to miles, miles to yards, meters to centimeters, tons to ounces, pints to gallons, radians to degrees, square miles to square yards); and to calculate many algebra, chemistry, physics, and engineering conversions.

It is necessary to keep in mind, mathematically, it is only possible to convert from one unit of measurement involving magnitude into another equivalent unit of measurement involving magnitude, if the two units both measure the object in question the same way. For example, it is possible to convert feet to inches because they both measure a linear length; to convert tons to pounds because they both measure the weight of an object; to convert pints to gallons because they both measure how much a three-dimensional object will hold, or to convert cubic meters into liters because they both measure the volume of a three-dimensional object.

It is not normal to convert dollars into feet because the two units mentioned do not measure the same thing. There is no specific relationship between money and feet unless you lay dollar bills next to each other and decide how many dollar bills placed in a line make exactly one foot. Likewise, it is impossible to convert a cubic meter into a yard because a cubic meter measures volume and a yard measures length. Further, it is impossible to convert days into kilograms because one type of measurement entails time and the other mass. In the metric system using the procedures discussed in this textbook, it is possible to convert a metric ton into liters of water, but this may be beyond the scope of a normal 6th or 7th-grade arithmetic class. Converting a metric ton into liters of water is a conversion that students should be able to explain at some time when they are in high school math or science class.

When students are in 4th and/or 5th grade (or even earlier), they begin to realize pairs of fractions like ("$\frac{1}{2} = \frac{2}{4}$", "$\frac{1}{2} = \frac{4}{8}$", "$\frac{1}{2} = \frac{3}{6}$", and "$\frac{3}{4} = \frac{6}{8}$") are equivalent. This is an excellent time to teach students how to multiply by the number (fraction) 1, to convert the first fraction into the second equivalent fraction. In fact, teachers in the 3rd or 4th grade should introduce this procedure. Multiplying a fraction by a fraction equal to 1, such as "$\frac{4}{4}$", or "$\frac{2}{2}$" or "$\frac{3}{3}$" is a procedure which can easily be taught when students begin to work with equivalent fractions.

All four of the simple equivalent fraction examples listed in the previous paragraph, can be illustrated as true by using picture graphs, number lines, or computer graphics.

Examples: $\frac{1}{2} = \frac{1}{2} \times 1 = \frac{1}{2} \times \frac{4}{4} = \frac{1 \times 4}{2 \times 4} = \frac{4}{8}$ and $\frac{3}{4} = \frac{3}{4} \times 1 = \frac{3}{4} \times \frac{2}{2} = \frac{3 \times 2}{4 \times 2} = \frac{6}{8}$

Even more importantly, when students begin to add and subtract fractions, they must learn how to find LCDs and convert fractions into equivalent fractions. Since adding and subtracting fractions frequently involves converting them into equivalent expressions, introduce both "Young's Equation/Ratio Theorem" and "Young's Conversion Theorem" at this juncture. The most difficult set of procedures students must master in arithmetic occurs when students are required to add and subtract fractions with unlike denominators. When students encounter these problems, they must find LCDs, convert fractions into equivalent fractions, and then add and subtract the fractions with identical denominators.

This textbook devotes a great deal of time to explain the required steps for adding and subtracting a wide variety of fraction problems. *Most of the arithmetic textbooks in the United States and around the world concentrate on simple fraction addition and subtraction problems--and the rules are not emphasized in the arithmetic textbooks. Therefore, students rarely have a chance to master the rules to find all types of LCDs and to add and subtract all types of fractions.* **Our goal is to prepare students to work with rational expressions**

(algebraic fractions) by teaching the basic rules in arithmetic. This means as soon as possible, in 5th, 6th or 7th grade, arithmetic teachers need to illustrate how to use the procedures/rules mentioned in the arithmetic textbooks but are never required when the students solve the textbook problems. It will be a challenge, but the rewards for the students will be worthwhile when they enter Algebra 1, Algebra 2, Precalculus, and Calculus classes in high school. If the students begin to learn the necessary rules mentioned in arithmetic textbooks and emphasized in this textbook for working with semi-challenging and difficult arithmetic fraction problems, they will be prepared for their advanced high school mathematics classes. Consider "Young's Conversion Theorem", the simple form of the Theorem is fine when converting a fraction into an equivalent fraction:

> This is the elementary version of "**Young's Conversion Theorem**": If one multiplies a fraction by another fraction equal to 1, then the ending fraction is equivalent to the starting fraction, but it will look different.

The starting and ending fractions will be equivalent, but the numerators and the denominators of the two fractions will be different. The main fact to emphasize is, the magnitudes of the two fractions are equal. This is another way of saying the two fractions represent the same point on a number line. Note the use of "Young's Conversion Theorem" illustrating why the fractions "$\frac{1}{2} = \frac{4}{8}$" and "$\frac{3}{4} = \frac{6}{8}$" in the two examples previously mentioned.

Many readers may be pondering the meaning of "Young's Equation/Ratio Theorem". Eventually, this basic theorem and how the two theorems work together will help students convert mathematics expressions, fractions, and units of measurement into equivalent expressions, fractions, and units of measurement. Both "Young's Equation/Ratio Theorem" and "Young's Conversion Theorem" apply to the two example problems illustrated above, but it is fruitless at this time to parse "Young's Equation/Ratio Theorem" as we initially focus on "Young's Conversion Theorem" and understand how to use the procedures indicated to convert fractions and expressions into equivalent fractions and expressions.

Teaching Point: A fraction represents a single number or magnitude on a number line. A fraction is a single number which frequently represents a part of a whole. It takes two numbers to write a fraction, but the line between the numerator and the denominator represents a division operation. Most people will agree that the fraction, "$\frac{8}{4}$", represents the number, "2" because they realize the line between the numerator "8" and the denominator "4" means to divide the number "8" by "4" to find the quotient, "2". This means the fraction, "$\frac{8}{4}$" is a single number and a single point on a number line. It is normal to represent a number as two or more numbers, but it is often so obvious few people consider the fact that the number "34" really translates into the following arithmetic problem: "$3 \times 10 + 4 \times 1$" or "$30 + 4$". We are so familiar with natural numbers and whole numbers it seldom occurs to us that numbers like "34, or 235, or 4,589" really are a combination of arithmetic operations. We know arithmetic textbooks in the 1970's and 1980's, contained a section to illustrate this concept. Our hope is new arithmetic textbooks emphasize the following fact, a fraction and a natural number or whole number are all single numbers derived by using basic arithmetic operations and represent a single point on a number line.

The natural numbers are often referred to as the counting numbers, "$N = \{1, 2, 3, 4, 5, \dots\}$". This is the normal or natural way to teach a child to count. The whole numbers, "$W = \{0, 1, 2, 3, 4, 5, \dots\}$", include the number *zero (0)*. This may seem like a minor difference, but it is significant when referring to different objects. If you have three fresh pizza pies, you have three whole pies. If you eat one piece of pizza, you only have two whole pies and pieces of a third pie. When you have one whole pie remaining, and you eat one slice of pizza, you have "0" whole pies. You just have part of a pie remaining.

To summarize, what do the following two numbers have in common: the rational number (fraction) "$\frac{3}{4}$" and the natural number "34"? (Interesting fact: The number "34" and the equivalent fraction "$\frac{34}{1}$" are also both rational numbers.)

1. Both the numbers "$\frac{3}{4}$" and "34" are written using the same two digits.

2. Both numbers can be translated into a basic arithmetic problem. You can convert the number "34" into a combination of two multiplication problems which are added, a concept which is not discussed often and not emphasized. When converting the fraction, "$\frac{3}{4}$" into a decimal, it must be emphasized the fraction is a division problem.

3. Both the numbers "34" and "$\frac{3}{4}$" have a major property in common that many teachers do not emphasize. Thus, many students never really understand that the fraction, "$\frac{3}{4}$" stands for a single number, just like the number "34". This concept can be emphasized another way: both the numbers represent exactly one point on a number line. Each of the points, when placed on a number line, represents a magnitude or distance from the number "0". It may seem so simple to some elementary teachers that both the fraction, "$\frac{3}{4}$" and the natural number "34" represent exactly one point on a number line, but it is critical that students early in their elementary careers understand every fraction represents a single number. Research indicates many students look at a fraction as two distinct numbers and never fully grasp the fact a fraction represents a single number (Braithwaite & Tian et al., 2018; Vukovic, Fuchs, Geary, Jordon, Gersten, & Siegler, 2014, Siegler & Pyke et al., 2013, Siegler, Thompson, & Schneider, 2011; Booth & Siegler, 2008; Ni & Zhou, 2005).

Before students are required to change a fraction into a decimal, teachers must first illustrate and emphasize the following fractions represent division problems: "$\frac{12}{6} = 12 \div 6 = 2$"; "$\frac{25}{5} = 25 \div 5 = 5$", "$\frac{40}{2} = 40 \div 2 = 20$", "$\frac{315}{15} = 315 \div 15 = 21$" and then "$\frac{1}{2} = 1 \div 2 = .5$" or "$\frac{3}{4} = 3 \div 4 = 0.75$". Of course, students will have to be proficient with long division procedures and how to use long division to convert a fraction into a decimal when the denominator is greater than the numerator, when the divisor is greater than the dividend, or when the quotient of a division problem contains a remainder.

One possible reason why many students may consider a fraction two separate numbers and not a single number could be the way fractions are introduced in preschool and kindergarten. Fractions are usually introduced as two numbers, requiring students to concentrate on the denominator, which indicates the total number of parts, and then on the numerator, which indicates the number of parts which are being considered. This type of discussion is really focusing on a special fraction called a ratio. For instance, the teacher may talk about a pizza pie and indicate there were four pieces and one piece of pizza remains. What part of the pie is left? The answer: One piece of pizza out of four pieces of pizza written as a ratio with a label in both the numerator and the denominator, "$\frac{\text{1 piece of pizza}}{\text{4 pieces of pizza}}$". Alternatively, write a fraction with only one label "$\frac{1}{4}$ of the pie or $\frac{1}{4}$ pie".

Thus, students are taught to focus on two separate things: the number of pieces of pizza remaining and the total number of pieces in the whole pie. Teachers should embrace the process of introducing fractions using this two-number scenario, but as soon as possible, elementary teachers must start to emphasize a fraction represents a single number, just like the number, "5". Emphasize a fraction is a single point on a number line in 1st or 2nd grade by getting the students to mark off the total parts indicated by the denominator on a number line between the numbers 0 and 1, and then use the numerator to determine where to place a point on the number line by counting the number of line segments starting at "0". This means the number of line segments between 0 and 1 is equal to the number in the denominator.

There are two ways to illustrate and explain to the students how to mark a point on a number line to represent a fraction:

1. The first method involves placing hash/tick marks on the number line. This does not mean teachers should place hash/tick marks between 0 and 1 equal to the denominator. The goal is to get the correct number of line segments between 0 and 1. In order to accomplish the goal, place one less hash mark than the number in the denominator. The reason there is one less hash mark between 0 and 1 than the number in the denominator is because the last hash mark is where the number 1 is already located. The objective is to make sure the number of line segments between 0 and 1 is equal to the number in the denominator, not to the number of hash marks. The hash marks must be as evenly spaced as possible between the numbers 0 and 1. Once the students have marked the line between 0 and 1 with the correct number of line segments, then the students can count the segments starting at "0" using the numerator as the guide to find the point which is represented by the given fraction. Here is an example to illustrate the directions: If the given fraction is "$\frac{3}{8}$", then start at the number "0" at the far left of the line segment and indicate the placement of the number 1 to the right of the number "0". The placement of the number 1 is arbitrary based on how big the teacher wants the segment to be. Then, evenly space seven hash

marks between 0 and 1 on the number line, which will create eight small line segments between 0 and 1. Next, count from left to right three hash marks based on the numerator "3" and mark the third hash mark with a dot to indicate the placement of the fraction, "$\frac{3}{8}$". One must use both numbers to find the indicated point, but the fraction and the point represent exactly one point and one number. The distance from the "0" point to the fraction point is referred to as the magnitude of the fraction (Fazio, DeWolf, Siegler, 2016; Fazio, Kennedy, & Siegler, 2016). The length of the line segment indicated by placing the point between the two end points 0 and 1 represents the fraction "$\frac{3}{8}$". This is the method we prefer teachers demonstrate to students when they are determining the placement of the point on a number line for the fraction "$\frac{3}{8}$". The reason is, when students are asked to place a point on a number line, the numbers 0 and 1 are often already indicated.

Teaching Point: When the denominator in the given fraction is an even number, such as the denominator "8" in the fraction, "$\frac{3}{8}$" it might be beneficial to explain where the hash/tick mark for the fraction "$\frac{1}{2}$ & $\frac{4}{8}$" should be placed and then illustrate with this particular type of problem where the fractions "$\frac{1}{4}$ & $\frac{2}{8}$" and "$\frac{3}{4}$ & $\frac{6}{8}$" are plotted. These types of problems should be used initially to introduce how to graph points on a number line to represent the magnitude of a fraction. In the future, students will be required to plot fractions such as ($\frac{3}{5}, \frac{4}{7}, \frac{8}{9}, \frac{1}{11}, etc.$) on a number line with odd-numbered denominators. Fractions with odd-numbered denominators might create more difficulty when finding the middle of the number line versus working with even-numbered denominators. When you are working with "8*ths*", and you place a hash/tick mark in the middle of the line segment to represent the fraction "$\frac{1}{2}$", emphasize the single hash mark creates two segments. When you place the hash marks for the fractions "$\frac{1}{4}$", "$\frac{3}{4}$", and "$\frac{1}{2}$" the three hash marks create four short line segments.

2. The second method also requires the students to place hash/tick marks evenly spaced between the numbers 0 and 1, again to make sure the number of line segments between the two numbers equals the denominator. A slight difference in the directions for this explanation is the learner should start at the number "0" and evenly space the hash marks to the right equal to the denominator. The hash mark at the right end of the line segment represents where the number 1 must be placed. Using the same example problem, "$\frac{3}{8}$", this time, start at "0" and evenly space eight hash marks to the right. Make sure the eighth hash mark is where the number 1 is located. Using this method to place hash marks, the hash mark indicating the number 1 is the eighth hash mark based on the denominator "8". After placing all the hash marks between 0 and 1 on the number line, go to the number "0" at the far left and count to the right "3" hash marks based on the numerator. Place a dot on the third hash mark.

Teaching Point: Do not discuss both explanations with your students in the early elementary grades. Instead, emphasize one method until the students have mastered the concept based on the first explanation. Then illustrate a second or third method to attack the same problem. Over 90% of the students will continue to use the method the teacher initially emphasized. We underscored the previous sentence because when one first teaches any concept, we believe students have a strong tendency to remember the initial explanation more than they do the follow-up discussion. This is the reason we believe it is so important to illustrate the rules and procedures as early as possible when teaching any mathematics concept and make sure the first explanation is worded and presented correctly. While specific research articles about "the first method learned" phenomena are scant, students regularly solve problems using the method they best remember, later in their math careers. A few research articles imply this effect but are not explicit. *(FRT 2: The "First Learned Method" is the method students rely on most frequently.)*

A *ratio* is a special fraction where we want to concentrate on the numerator and the denominator separately. When we posed a previous problem in the form "$\frac{\text{1 piece of pizza}}{\text{4 pieces of pizza}}$", it was written in a special format, called a ratio. In a ratio, we are supposed to concentrate on both the numerator and the denominator separately as they both have a label. In this example problem, the final answer may be written as a fraction because it refers to a part of a whole. When working with a fraction, we may have one label or no label. The final answer, "$\frac{1}{4}$ of the pie or $\frac{1}{4}$ pie", has only one label to the right of the fraction, "$\frac{1}{4}$". Special point of interest: A fraction is frequently written as a decimal or a percent, but a ratio is usually NOT written as a decimal or a percent.

When students are first taught to divide using the long division process, the number outside the division box, the divisor, is usually smaller than the number inside the division box, the dividend. In the first problems most students encounter, the dividend is a multiple of the divisor. This means the answer, the quotient, will not have a remainder. The quotient will be a natural number.

This is the same way we illustrated in previous examples that a fraction is a different way to write a division problem, prior to having students convert a fraction into a decimal. As students become more proficient with the division process, problems will be presented in which the divisor will not divide evenly into the dividend, and the quotient can be written as a natural number with a remainder. However, the preferred way to write the quotient will be as a mixed number or a decimal (ex. "$\frac{6}{5} = 1\frac{1}{5}$" or "1.2"). It is important students master the long division process in a methodical way.

First, they must master division when the divisor and the quotient are natural numbers, and later the students should learn how to solve a division problem when the divisor is a decimal, and the quotient is a rational number—that is, any number written as a fraction, mixed number, or a repeating or terminating decimal. The students need to understand that many times the divisor will not divide perfectly into the dividend, and there will be a fractional remainder. Initially, students should write the quotient as a mixed number when the divisor does not perfectly divide into the dividend. The next goal is to have the students write the quotient as a decimal if the quotient is not a Natural Number. In the four example problems listed below, the divisor in every division problem is smaller than the dividend. This means the quotient is always greater than 1.

Examples: $8\overline{)24}$ $25\overline{)175}$ $5\overline{)22}$ $7\overline{)24}$

Here are the same four problems written as fractions: "$\frac{24}{8}, \frac{175}{25}, \frac{22}{5}, \frac{24}{7}$".

Students must then learn how to convert fractions which are less than 1 into decimals. This means they must learn how to solve long division problems when the number inside the division box (dividend) is smaller than the number outside the division box (divisor). Once students have mastered this procedure, it is a great opportunity to again emphasize a fraction and a decimal number both represent exactly one point on a number line, and the fraction and/or decimal represents exactly one number. (Example: Convert the fraction "$\frac{3}{4}$" into the decimal "$.75$". To convert the fraction into the equivalent decimal, students must place the smaller number "3" inside the division box and the larger number "4" outside the division box. The point on the number line represented by the decimal "$.75$" is the same point as the point represented by the fraction, "$\frac{3}{4}$").

When elementary students first encounter a division problem like "$4 \div 3$ or $\frac{4}{3}$", it does not make much sense to them because they have only encountered division problems where the divisor is smaller than the dividend. This presents a teaching challenge every elementary arithmetic teacher will encounter. The way the teacher explains this problem may determine the math success or failure many students will experience when they move on in their math careers. Before students convert a fraction into a decimal, students must be able to solve long division problems for the following situations. 1. When both the divisor and dividend and the quotient are natural numbers. 2. When the divisor and dividend are both natural numbers and the quotient is a natural number with a remainder indicated. 3. When the divisor and dividend are both natural numbers and the quotient is a mixed number. Students must then extend their division skills and work with even more challenging division problems involving a divisor which is a decimal, then a dividend which is a decimal and then when both the divisor and dividend are decimals. If students struggle to solve long division problems, continue to review the procedures, and regularly assign division problems as additional homework and quiz/test questions. Continually encourage students to feel confident solving long division problems by giving them easy problems they can solve and mix in more challenging problems. Solving all types of long division problems in elementary school is a key indicator of success for students when they enter algebra in later grades (Siegler, Duncan et al., 2012). Prior to assigning homework problems involving long division problems, use short, 2-3 minute mini-lessons and always remember to focus on the five teaching principles mentioned earlier. We recommend illustrating how to divide the smaller number "3", by the larger number "4, 2-3 months prior to assigning homework problems involving a divisor (the number outside the division box) which is larger than the dividend (the number inside the division box). We know from experience weak math students will frequently place the smaller number outside the division box when a division problem is written in the following form: "$3 \div 7,\ 8 \div 10,\ or\ \frac{5}{9}$".

If teachers do not constantly remind students that a fraction is a single number written as a division problem involving two numbers, many will fail to fully understand this basic concept. If we want students to recognize fractions represent single numbers, not two numbers, it is imperative in the early elementary grades to encourage students to place points on a number line indicating where different whole numbers are positioned and, most importantly, where simple fractions and mixed numbers appear on the number line. Before emphasizing a fraction like "$\frac{3}{4}$ or $\frac{13}{16}$" represents a single point on a number line, it would probably be easier to emphasize the following types of fractions ("$\frac{6}{2}, \frac{12}{6}, \frac{20}{5}, \frac{7}{7}$, or $\frac{20}{20}$") each represents one point on a number line as previously discussed (Fazio, Kennedy et al., 2016).

> Reminder: A fraction represents a single point on a number line, which indicates the magnitude of the fraction.
> A ratio is not usually represented as a single point on a number line.

If you use "Young's Conversion Theorem" in arithmetic, you can quickly change any fraction into an equivalent fraction by multiplying by a fraction equal to 1. Here are a few more examples to illustrate how to convert a fraction into an equivalent fraction by multiplying by 1: "$\frac{3}{4} \times 1 = \frac{3}{4} \times \frac{5}{5} = \frac{15}{20}$, therefore, $\frac{3}{4} = \frac{15}{20}$" and "$\frac{7}{8} \times 1 = \frac{7}{8} \times \frac{\mathbf{11}}{\mathbf{11}} = \frac{77}{88}$, therefore $\frac{7}{8} = \frac{77}{88}$". Later, in this book, we will give detailed explanations about the power of multiplying by a fraction equal to 1, plus we will explain how to add and subtract fractions and convert units of measurement into equivalent units of measurement. Remember, if the second fraction is "$\frac{N}{N}$" and one multiplies by this fraction, the ending fraction will be equal to the starting fraction. (Here are some examples of fractions in the "$\frac{N}{N}$" format: $\frac{8}{8}, \frac{11}{11}, \frac{3}{3}, \frac{77}{77}, \frac{6.99}{6.99}, etc.$) If one multiplies by the fraction "$\frac{1}{1}$", the beginning and ending fractions will be identical, which is how many people interpret the following property. This is what everyone thinks the Multiplication Identity Property for One (1) says:

"$a \times 1 = a$" or "6 × 1 = 6" or "11 = 11 × 1" or "1 × 6788.4 = 6788.4" or "$\frac{11}{16} \times 1 = \frac{11}{16}$".

Notice, in these examples, the number multiplied by "1" is identical to the ending number. "Young's Conversion Theorem" focuses on the advanced meaning of the "Multiplication Identity Property for One (1)" and the "Power of One (1)" in arithmetic and higher-level mathematics courses. The Multiplication Identity Property for One (1) means much more than a simple arithmetic interpretation which implies we end up with the identical answer with which we started.

When students first learn to convert fractions into equivalent fractions in 3rd, 4th, or 5th grade, teachers need to teach the procedures which will work for simple fraction conversions and for the more difficult conversions they will encounter in high school and college. If students learn the correct procedures in the beginning of their arithmetic careers, there is a high probability they will master the procedures forever. *(FRT 2: The "First Learned Method" is the method students rely on most frequently.)* There are at least three times when students work with fractions, and they must convert fractions into equivalent fractions. Some textbooks may not begin to convert fractions into equivalent fractions until 5th grade, but many students starting in 3rd grade could master converting fractions into equivalent fractions using "Young's Conversion Theorem".

The first addition and subtraction fraction problems for which students are asked to find the sum or difference usually have identical denominators, so there is no need to convert any of these given fractions into equivalent fractions.

1. Students must convert fractions into equivalent fractions when they add and subtract fractions with denominators which are not identical. Once students learn they can only add and subtract fractions with identical denominators, it is time for the students to add and subtract fractions with different denominators and make sure all the fractions in the problem have been converted into equivalent fractions with identical denominators (Braithwaite & Tian et al., 2018).
2. The second type of situation when students should convert fractions into equivalent forms is when they are comparing two or more fractions to determine which fractions are larger or smaller. Several examples which follow will illustrate how to use "Young's Conversion Theorem" to add and subtract fractions and to determine which fractions are larger or smaller.
3. The third time students are required to find equivalent fractions is when they learn to reduce a fraction. The rules to reduce fractions do not require students to use "Young's

Conversion Theorem". This book will discuss how to reduce simple fractions using standard procedures illustrated in arithmetic textbooks and taught by most elementary arithmetic teachers. We will also illustrate how to reduce all types of fractions (challenging arithmetic fractions and algebra fractions) using factor trees which are discussed in arithmetic and factoring rules in algebra.

Students must initially learn how to convert fractions into equivalent fractions by using "Young's Conversion Theorem", as explained above. It is important that students realize fractions can be equivalent, even though the numbers in the numerator and the denominator of one fraction are larger compared to those in another fraction. You can find an infinite number of fractions equivalent to an initial fraction simply by multiplying by an infinite number of fractions which equal 1. Remember, any time we multiply by 1 or a fraction equal to 1, we will get a fraction equivalent to the initial fraction.

Work with the random fraction "$\frac{4}{5}$". The fractions below are all equivalent to

"$\frac{4}{5}$": "$\frac{4}{5} \times 1 = \frac{4}{5} \times \frac{2}{2} = \frac{8}{10}$"; "$\frac{4}{5} \times 1 = \frac{4}{5} \times \frac{3}{3} = \frac{12}{15}$"; "$\frac{4}{5} \times 1 = \frac{4}{5} \times \frac{4}{4} = \frac{16}{20}$"; "$\frac{4}{5} \times 1 = \frac{4}{5} \times \frac{5}{5} = \frac{20}{25}$".

Realize, we used "Young's Conversion Theorem" when we multiplied the fraction "$\frac{4}{5}$" by the fractions "$\frac{2}{2}, \frac{3}{3}, \frac{4}{4}$, and $\frac{5}{5}$", and mathematicians universally agree that all four fractions equal 1 because the numerators and the denominators are identical. Remember, "Young's Conversion Theorem" states, "When you multiply a fraction by another fraction equal to 1, you get an equivalent fraction." This means the following fractions are all equivalent (same magnitude on a number line): $\{\frac{4}{5}, \frac{8}{10}, \frac{12}{15}, \frac{16}{20}, \frac{20}{25}, \frac{24}{30}, \frac{28}{35}, \ldots\}$ (Schneider & Siegler, 2010). One can determine an infinite number of equivalent fractions by simply multiplying the original fraction "$\frac{4}{5}$" by other fractions which equal 1, such as "$\frac{9}{9}, \frac{10}{10}, \frac{11}{11}, \frac{12}{12}, \ldots$". The set of equivalent fractions which can be derived using "Young's Conversion Theorem" is infinite. When one learns how to multiply by the number 1 when the number 1 is written in different forms, the amazing world of arithmetic and mathematics becomes boundless. Note, mathematicians will normally write a *set* of numbers or terms enclosed in a pair of braces, "{" and "}". This means when one sees a group of letters or numbers or words enclosed with braces, the mathematician is indicating the objects enclosed in the braces have something in common, and the *set* notation is appropriate. Notice the use of braces when we listed the *set* of fractions equivalent to "$\frac{4}{5}$" above: $\{\frac{4}{5}, \frac{8}{10}, \frac{12}{15}, \frac{16}{20}, \frac{20}{25}, \frac{24}{30}, \frac{28}{35}, \ldots\}$.

Students must know how to convert fractions into equivalent fractions prior to learning how to add and subtract fractions. Without the basic understanding of the procedures already illustrated in this chapter to convert fractions into equivalent fractions, students will already be behind in their knowledge of the procedures required to add and subtract fractions. Imagine you are learning how to solve the most difficult problems you will encounter in arithmetic, adding and subtracting fractions, and almost immediately, on day one or day two, you are behind in your knowledge of the procedures required to complete one of the basic steps. If a problem involves adding and/or subtracting fractions, "The fractions must have a common denominator, preferably a least common denominator (LCD)." There is a process all students must master when they are required to find a least common denominator (LCD) and when the denominators are large numbers or algebra expressions. The process of finding challenging LCDs involves factor trees. Once the LCD is determined, then the students can find the sums and differences between two or more fractions and compare the magnitudes of fractions.

If you know how to find the least common multiple (LCM) for the numbers indicated in this paragraph using factor trees, you probably had an excellent arithmetic teacher or mathematics teacher at some point in your educational career, one who taught the rules and procedures to find LCDs and LCMs for all types of arithmetic and the most difficult trigonometric problems. One of the goals when readers finish studying the topics discussed in this book is for them to be able to compute the least common multiple (LCM) for all types of numbers and algebraic expressions without trial and error. Here is an example problem discussed in Chapter 4: "Find the LCM for the following three numbers using factor trees: "88, 96, and 112". If a teacher does not know how to use factor trees to illustrate how to find the least common denominator, then he/she really does not know the correct way to find a least common denominator for all types of fractions. This is an arithmetic procedure many elementary teachers mention, but few elementary teachers emphasize it. Knowing how to find LCDs in arithmetic is a requirement when students simplify algebra fractions, referred to as rational expressions.

> The rules taught in arithmetic are the foundation for student success in advanced math classes.

At this point, we must know how to convert a fraction into an equivalent fraction using the elementary form of "Young's Conversion Theorem", not to find LCDs and LCMs, but simply to be knowledgeable of the importance and definition of both expressions. We will tell you, the LCM for the three numbers indicated is computed by multiplying the following numbers: "$2^5 \times 3 \times 7 \times 11 = 7{,}392$". Here are a few quick questions. How will you illustrate to your students that "7,392" is really the LCM for the three given numbers? What is the difference between an LCD and an LCM? Where did the numbers "2^5", "3", "7", and "11" come from? We will answer all these questions as you continue to read the explanations and study the solutions.

One of the problems discussed in Chapter 3, "$\frac{1}{2}+\frac{1}{4}$", is a simple addition problem involving two fractions. The common denominator is easy to compute in your head if you have already memorized standard multiplication facts. Use "Young's Conversion Theorem" when teaching students to add and subtract simple addition and subtraction fraction problems which require the students to convert at least one fraction into an equivalent fraction with the same denominator. Ironically, when we solve simple problems, the rules required to solve more challenging problems are sometimes difficult to understand because we have already developed a set of tricks/procedures which we know will work for us when we solve standard textbook problems. Maybe this is the reason why teachers never get to the point where they need to teach the rules. They never get beyond the basic problems written in the textbooks (Braithwaite & Siegler, 2018).

There are two important words used well over a hundred times in this book. Many teachers use them interchangeably, but there are differences between what they mean mathematically: fractions and ratios.

What are the similarities? They both have a numerator and a denominator. They are often both written in the same format. To some people, they mean the same thing. Sometimes when we write a ratio, it is written in the same form as any other fraction. When performing arithmetic operations with fractions and ratios, all the operations are performed using the same rules.

What are the differences? A fraction represents part of a whole. The denominator represents the number of parts in the whole, and the numerator represents the parts you are working with or focused on. A ratio requires a person to refer to both the numerator and denominator separately. At one instant, we need to focus on the numerator and the next instant on the denominator.

When you write a fraction, the two numbers are frequently written in a vertical form with a horizontal line, vinculum, between the two numbers. The number on top is referred to as the numerator, and the bottom number as the denominator, but the two numbers with the horizontal line represent one number. Teachers must emphasize to their students that a fraction is a single number represented by two numbers related by a division operation symbol. It is a teaching point which students must understand as early in elementary arithmetic as possible.

On the other hand, a ratio is often written in the same format as a fraction with a numerator and a denominator, but when we work with a ratio, we focus on the numerator and the denominator as two numbers because both numbers represent something which is important when interpreting the meaning of the ratio. A ratio may be written with a colon between the two numbers, such as the notation, "1 : 3" or the phrase, "1 to 3", but if we are going to perform any arithmetic operations with a ratio, we must write it using the fraction notation.

A fraction represents one point on a number line. The point on the number line represents the magnitude (distance) from the starting point, "0" on the number line. In contrast, a ratio is <u>not</u> normally written as a point on a number line.

A fraction will sometimes have a label to the right of the fraction. If there is a label to the right of a fraction, there is usually only one label, such as "$\frac{1}{2}$ of a candy bar or $\frac{1}{2}$ bar". When a student wants to indicate the fraction "$\frac{3}{4}$" on a number line, he/she places a point on the number line, which indicates the magnitude of the fraction compared to the number "0" on the number line. If he/she is working with a fraction and wants to place a point on a number line to represent the fraction, the fraction will probably not have a label indicated to the right of the fraction. A fraction will sometimes have one label to the right of the fraction or no label. If he/she is measuring a specific length within a number line, he/she could write the measurement as "$\frac{3}{4}$ in. or $\frac{3}{4}$ *of* an in.". In this example, the fraction "$\frac{3}{4}$" has one label to the right of the fraction. If the teacher is asking students to find "$\frac{3}{4}$" of a number such as "$\frac{3}{4}$ *of* 8" the fraction, "$\frac{3}{4}$" has no label. There may or may not be a label with the number "8", depending on the way the problem is stated.

A ratio usually has two labels indicated. One label usually goes with the number in the numerator, and the other label goes with the number in the denominator. Here are two examples to illustrate a ratio will often have two labels indicated: "$\frac{\text{3 red dots}}{\text{4 blue dots}}$" and "$\frac{\text{55 miles}}{\text{1 hour}}$". A ratio may not appear to have any labels, but in these cases, the two labels were cancelled because they were identical. Therefore, the indicated ratio looks just like any other fraction. A great example to illustrate this concept is to refer to the slope of a line in algebra. The slope of a line is frequently written in the fraction format "$\frac{3}{4}$", but one must realize, there is a linear measurement label in the numerator and usually the same linear measurement label in the denominator. If the labels in both the numerator and the denominator appear to be missing, you must realize they cancelled because they were identical. Perhaps it is better to say they are not required. The definition of a slope of a line or the pitch of a roof is written as a ratio such that the "slope $= \frac{\text{rise}}{\text{run}}$". Here are several ratios which represent the slope of a line, with the labels indicated, and then with the labels cancelled: "$\frac{3 \text{ ft.}}{4 \text{ ft.}} = \frac{3}{4}$", "$\frac{3 \text{ in.}}{4 \text{ in.}} = \frac{3}{4}$", "$\frac{3 \text{ cm}}{4 \text{ cm}} = \frac{3}{4}$".

> In the paragraph above, I used the word cancelled. I do not like to use the word cancel or cancelled when dividing identical terms in a fraction or subtracting two identical terms. The wise person will realize the two identical terms in a fraction both become "1's" because a fraction is a division problem. When one combines a positive and a negative number which are identical, they combine to become "0". I do not like to use the word cancel or cancelled in either situation but too many people/teachers use these two words in both situations. Please realize what the words really mean in both situations.

For individuals who are not familiar with the definition of the slope of a line, the word "rise" represents a linear measurement between two points on a line, written with one of these types of labels: inches, feet, yards, miles, centimeters, meters, squares on graph paper, etc. The length of the line segment is measured based on a vertical length. The word "run" represents the length of the horizontal line segment between the same two points on the line. Usually, the length of the "rise" and the length of the "run" are measured using the same units of measurement as indicated in the examples in the last paragraph. If the units are identical, as indicated in the example problems which appear above involving the slope of a line, we cancel both labels, and the slope is written without any labels. Once we know we are working with the slope of a line, we realize we are working with a ratio, and the labels have been removed because they cancelled. When working with the slope of a line, it is usually important to deal with the numerator and the denominator separately. In other situations, when working with the slope, use the same rules which apply to any fraction.

It is possible to write the slope of a line using two different types of linear measurement units, but this is not typically mentioned in high school algebra textbooks. Think about this example problem. A group of workers is required to lay railroad tracks on a mountain side. In this situation, the slope of the railroad tracks may be indicated by the following ratio: "10 feet per mile = $\frac{10\,feet}{1\,mile} = \frac{10\,ft.}{mi.}$".

This example below is an unusual situation regarding slope. Reference the 2nd rectangle comment on page 47 regarding the definition of slope.

A ratio is often considered a more advanced word to use instead of the word fraction, but a ratio is a special type of fraction where the goal is to focus on both the numerator and the denominator separately. The most advanced way to refer to either fractions or ratios is to discuss the set of rational numbers. Look at the first five letters in the word "**ratio**nal". What do you notice? When mathematicians refer to the set of rational numbers, they usually define the set of rational numbers as any number which is written as a fraction using either positive or negative whole numbers: $\{\ldots, -4, -3, -2, -1, 0, 1, 2, 3, 4, \ldots\}$ plus the fact the denominator cannot equal "0". The *set* of positive and negative whole numbers $\{\ldots, -4, -3, -2, -1, 0, 1, 2, 3, 4, \ldots\}$ is referred to as the *set* of integers. A rational number is a fraction written, so the numerator is an integer, the denominator is an integer, and the denominator is not "0" or equal to "0".

Finally, people frequently use the two words fraction and ratio interchangeably and realize there are some special features regarding the two words which make them slightly different when working with mathematics terms. A comment for the mathematical purist and secondary mathematics teachers: Here is the mathematical shorthand notation for the definition of a "Rational Number = $\mathrm{Q} = \{\frac{\mathrm{x}}{\mathrm{y}}: \forall\, \mathrm{x} \,\varepsilon\, \mathrm{I}$ and $\forall\, \mathrm{y} \,\varepsilon\, \mathrm{I}, \mathrm{y} \neq 0\}$".

The mathematical notation is not important for all students to understand. If you are going to write the shorthand notation indicated above, then you need to explain to your students how to interpret the symbols. High school mathematics teachers who teach advanced math classes probably already explain the notation to their students. Every little symbol in the notation means something special to mathematicians. The capital letter, "*Q*" is the mathematical abbreviation for Rational Numbers when referring to number systems and the capital letter, "*I*" is the abbreviation for Integers. The braces are used to indicate the numbers enclosed in the braces are a *set* of numbers. The notation, "$\frac{x}{y}$" refers to all the numbers in the *set* and indicates all the numbers are fractions with the letter/variable "x" representing the numerator and the letter/variable "y" representing the denominator. The symbol "∀" is a mathematics shorthand abbreviation for the word, "*all*", and the other mathematics abbreviation symbol, "ε", represents the two words, "contained in". Therefore, this section of the abbreviation in the notation, "∀ x ε I and ∀ y ε I" means <u>*all*</u> the "x" and "y" values in the fraction, "$\frac{x}{y}$" must be contained in the <u>*set*</u> of Integers. Finally, the notation "$y \neq 0$" indicates the denominator "y" can never equal <u>0</u>.

Answer to a question that we proposed earlier: "Why do we write fractions with horizontal lines, not slanted lines?" The reason is simple: "When students are working with several fractions, and they use slanted lines, it becomes difficult to distinguish between the numerators and denominators, and it creates confusion." *(FRT 3: Compare the difference between students' performance if they use horizontal line fraction notation versus slanted line notation.)*

> The fourth teaching principle which was mentioned earlier was: "Introduce math concepts in short mini lessons 2 or 3 times a week for 2 or 3 months before a topic is discussed in the textbook or problems are assigned for homework the first time." The mini lessons should last between 2-5 minutes. An unbelievable situation occurs when you do this. You may think you are losing time when you take 2-3 minutes and sometimes 5 minutes out of your daily lessons to introduce math concepts, but by the end of the school year you will save a lot of time and be able to cover more topics and your students will 'learn and remember' the concepts at a much higher rate than you ever imagined.

Plotting points on a horizontal number line starting in kindergarten is an excellent tool to help students begin to understand magnitude and concepts involving greater than and less than. Obviously, in kindergarten students would work with either Natural Numbers or Whole Numbers.

In 2nd or 3rd grade, students should start to plot points on horizontal number lines which represent fraction magnitudes. Once students are successful plotting Natural Numbers, Whole Numbers, and Fractions on horizontal number lines you can introduce the students to vertical number lines and graph the same types of numbers as points on vertical lines.

Eventually, you will want the students to graph mixed numbers on both horizontal and vertical lines along with decimals. As students' progress with their number line graphing abilities, they should be able to graph points on number lines when the starting number is not zero and when the number line involves negative numbers.

Number line graphs are an excellent teaching tool, and they help students' development mental knowledge about all types of numbers and in the process, you are preparing the students to work with two-dimensional algebra graphs.

Comment for secondary math teachers: The algebra definition of the slope of a line is "$m = \frac{rise}{run}$". There are times in engineering and other professions when the meaning of the two numbers may switch, such as the grade of a hill where the first number represents the horizontal length, and the second number represents the vertical length. Always look up the exact definition when referring to a synonym for the word slope involving specialized situations, to ensure you understand exactly what each number represents. Interesting special situation, but something you need to be aware of, as a math teacher.

In a previous light blue rectangle with a red border, I mentioned I do not like to use the two words **cancel** or **cancelled**. The reason I do **not** like to use the word cancelled when reducing identical factors in a fraction is, the identical factors in the numerator and the denominator technically represent a division problem. Consider the fraction, "$\frac{30}{35}$" written in factored form, "$\frac{2 \times 3 \times 5}{5 \times 7}$". The horizontal line in a fraction is a division operation symbol. When we rewrite this fraction as "$\frac{2 \times 3 \times 1}{1 \times 7}$" we really did not cancel the "5" in the numerator with the "5" in the denominator, we technically divided the "5" in the numerator and the "5" in the denominator and the quotient became "1". It would be acceptable to rewrite the fraction above "$\frac{2 \times 3 \times 1}{1 \times 7}$" in the equivalent form, "$\frac{2 \times 3}{7} X 1$" which equals "$\frac{2 \times 3}{7}$" and then equals "$\frac{6}{7}$". The normal way to write the solution for this problem indicating all the steps is: $\frac{30}{35} = \frac{2 \times 3 \times 5}{5 \times 7} = \frac{2 \times 3 \times 1}{1 \times 7} = \frac{2 \times 3}{7} = \frac{6}{7}$. This is a great example to emphasize the importance of the number "1" and many teachers refer to the process as cancelling both the "5" factors in the numerator and denominator, but really it is a division problem and teachers frequently use the slang word cancel when explaining the solution.

The other situation where people/teachers use the word cancel is when they solve the following simple arithmetic problem: "$+16 - 16 = 0$" Technically the two "16's" did not cancel each other out, we simply preformed a subtraction problem.

I dislike the words cancel and cancelling but these two words are used because no one to my knowledge has come up with a SHORT phrase to explain the process for either the dividing process or the subtraction process.

Therefore, reluctantly, I will continue to use the two words cancel and cancelling in this manuscript until someone comes up with two short easy to understand phrases which mathematicians agree is a better way to refer to the two different situations.

Second Assignment

DEFINITIONS

A. In your own words, write what you think is the best definition for the words indicated below. The words indicated below are all words which apply to elementary arithmetic concepts. After you write all your definitions, look up the definition of each word on the internet or in a dictionary and write the internet or dictionary definition for each word. In arithmetic and mathematics, definitions are extremely important, and a minor change in a definition may change the entire meaning of the word. We assume the wording in your initial definition will be different than the internet/dictionary definition. After you write both definitions, think about your definition and decide if your definition covers all the specific points indicated in the definitions found on the internet or in a dictionary. There are other arithmetic words which we could include in our word list, but these arithmetic words are seldom used in higher-level math courses: Addend, Minuend, Subtrahend, Multiplicand, and Multiplier. Therefore, we will not include these words in any of our written assignments.

1. A. Write the definition of the word, "Numerator". B. Give five examples and indicate which number is the numerator.
2. A. Write the definition of the word, "Denominator". B. Give five examples and indicate which number is the denominator.
3. A. Write the definition of the word, "Divisor". B. Give five examples and indicate which number in each example is the divisor.

4. A. Write the definition of the word "Dividend". B. Give five examples and indicate which number is the dividend.
5. In questions 1-4 which two pairs of words are basically synonyms to each other?
6. What word represents the answer in a division problem?
7. A. Write a definition of the word "Fraction". B. Explain what the three parts of a fraction mean.
8. A. What does a mathematician mean when they use the word "Multiple" or "Multiples"? B. Write five examples using "set" notation to illustrate the definition of multiples.
9. A. Write the mathematical definition of the word, "Factor(s)". B. Write five examples using "set" notation to illustrate the definition of factors. C. "Factors" and "multiples" both have something to do with multiplication, "Do these two words mean the same thing?
10. A. Write the mathematical definition of the word, "Set". B. Write 10 examples of different types of sets and use proper notation. Five of the 10 sets should have nothing to do with numbers. (Interesting Fact: Sometimes mathematicians refer to the definition of the word "set" as an undefined word.) After you look up the definition of the mathematical definition of the word "set" on the internet, ask Google the following question, "Why do some mathematicians refer to the word "set" as an undefined word"? C. What did you find?

B. Write the definitions of the following numbers.

11. Natural Numbers – A. Write the definition using words. B. Use mathematical notation to illustrate what the definition means.
12. Whole Numbers – A. Write the definition using words. B. Use mathematical notation to illustrate what the definition means.
13. Integers – A. Write the definition using words. B. Use mathematical notation to illustrate what the definition means.
14. Rational Numbers – Write the definition using words. (Comment: The mathematical shorthand notation was indicated in this chapter for the definition of the set of Rational Numbers, but we do not expect you to fully understand the shorthand notation unless you are majoring in mathematics.)
15. What do you say to your students to help them understand the difference between Natural Numbers and Whole Numbers? How do you get your students to understand why mathematicians refer to the one set as Natural Numbers and the other set as Whole Numbers?
16. Why would mathematicians pick the word "Rational" when they refer to Rational Numbers?

PLOTTING POINTS ON A NUMBER LINE (Horizontal and Vertical Lines)

C. Using horizontal lines (left to right), which all are equal in length (approximately 6 inches long) for problems 17-26. No numbers should be indicated on the ten number lines. We want you to *estimate* where a point should be placed on the number line, which will indicate the magnitude of the given number in problems 17-26. We suggest the left-hand end point should equal the number "0", but this is not a requirement. The number to the far right may change, based on the given number. The number indicated at the right-hand end of each number line must be an integer larger than the given number for that problem.

17. $\frac{3}{5}$ 18. $2\frac{3}{5}$ 19. $\frac{7}{11}$ 20. $7\frac{7}{11}$ 21. $\frac{3}{13}$

22. $702\frac{3}{11}$ 23. $\frac{1}{6}$ 24. $1999\frac{1}{6}$ 25. $\frac{41}{8}$ 26. $\frac{51}{100}$

D. Using vertical lines (bottom to top), which all are equal in length (approximately 6 inches long) for problems 27-36. No numbers should be indicated on the ten number lines. We want you to *estimate* where a point should be placed on the number line, which will indicate the magnitude of the number in problems 27-36. We suggest the bottom end point should equal the number "0" but this is not a requirement. The number at the top may change, based on the number given. Use an integer greater than the given number to represent the number at the top of the line.

27. 0.6 28. 2.6 29. 0.636363... 30. 7.636363 ... 31. 0.23

32. 702.23 33. 0.1666 ... 34. $1999\frac{999}{1000}$ 35. 5.125 36. 0.50999 ...

A FRACTION REPRESENTS A DIVISION PROBLEM

E. Find the quotient for each division problem (fraction). Write the quotients as a natural number or a mixed number (a natural number with a fraction). Notice, in all these problems; you divide a larger number by a smaller number.

37. $\frac{6}{2} = ?$ 38. $\frac{55}{11} = ?$ 39. $? = \frac{18}{7}$ (Write the answer as a mixed number.)

40. $\frac{11}{5} = ?$ 41. $\frac{52}{25} = ?$ 42. $\frac{7{,}361}{1} = ?$

EQUIVALENT FRACTIONS

F. Find several equivalent fractions in problems 43-48 by multiplying the fractions by the following fractions, which all equal 1: $\{\frac{2}{2}, \frac{3}{3}, \frac{7}{7}, \frac{12}{12}, and\ \frac{27}{27}\}$. To find the equivalent fractions, multiply the 6 fractions below, problems 43-48, by the 5 fractions, which equal 1 contained in the last sentence. Illustrate in your work how you multiply each fraction below by the number 1 and then indicate you are multiplying each fraction below by a fraction which equals 1. (Here is an example of a solution: "$\frac{7}{9} = \frac{7}{9} \times 1 = \frac{7}{9} \times \frac{2}{2} = \frac{14}{18}$".) We like this illustration because the example emphasizes, one must multiply the given fraction by 1 and use "Young's Conversion Theorem".

43. $\frac{3}{4}$ 44. $\frac{5}{6}$ 45. $\frac{9}{10}$

46. $\frac{13}{10}$ 47. $\frac{13}{16}$ 48. $\frac{41}{43}$

WHAT QUALITIES DO THE FOLLOWING PAIRS OF NUMBERS HAVE IN COMMON?

G. The following pairs of numbers consist of an Integer and a fraction (Both are Rational Numbers). The two numbers are different, but what qualities do they have in common?

49. $38\ and\ \frac{3}{8}$ 50. $216\ and\ \frac{21}{6}$ 51. $3101\ and\ \frac{101}{3}$

LESS THAN, EQUAL, OR GREATER THAN

H. Copy the problem and place one of the following relationship symbols $\{<, =, or\ >\}$ between the two given numbers to make a truthful mathematical statement.

52. $\frac{3}{8}$? $\frac{5}{8}$ 53. $5\frac{4}{11}$? $5\frac{1}{11}$ 54. $\frac{7}{15}$? $\frac{7}{16}$ 55. $7\frac{7}{99}$? $7\frac{7}{9}$

56. $702\frac{3}{11}$? $99\frac{10}{11}$ 57. 0.16099 ? 0.161616 ... 58. 10.25 ? $10\frac{1}{4}$

59. $\frac{4}{88}$? $\frac{1}{22}$ 60. $\frac{3}{13}$? $\frac{30}{130}$ 61. 0.727272 ... ? 0.727272

LCMs, LCDs, and GCFs

I. The next section of problems focuses on LCMs, LCDs and GCFs. You will have to know the definitions of the three phrases, the differences between the three phrases, and how to explain these phrases to students in arithmetic.

62. If you refer to the abbreviation "LCM", you must understand the definitions of the three words – Least, Common, and Multiple. Using the three words just indicated, write 1 or 2 paragraphs to explain what an LCM means when you are working with a "set" of numbers. You may use a couple of "sets" of numbers to illustrate the meaning of the abbreviation LCM.

63. If you refer to the abbreviation "LCD" you must understand the definitions of the three words - Least, Common, and Denominator. Using the three words just indicated, write 1 or 2 paragraphs to explain what an LCD means when you are working with numbers. Make sure you clarify what type of numbers you are working with when you are required to find an LCD. You may use a couple of "sets" of numbers to illustrate how to work with LCDs when simplifying arithmetic problems.

64. A. There are some similarities between an LCM and an LCD; what are they? B. What is the difference or differences between an LCM and an LCD?

65. Write a 1 or 2-paragraph summary about the method and or procedures you tell your students to follow: A. To determine an LCM for a set of numbers. B. To determine an LCD for two or more fractions.

66. If you refer to the abbreviation "GCF", you must understand the definitions of the three words – Greatest, Common, and Factor. Using these three words just indicated, write 1 or 2 paragraphs to explain what a GCF means when you are working with numbers. You may use sets of numbers to illustrate the meaning of the abbreviation, GCF.

67. You may be required to find a GCF when you are working with a list of natural numbers, fractions (rational numbers), or when you are simplifying or solving problems involving rational numbers (fractions). Write at least 6 examples where the directions or the procedure to solve a problem will require you to find a GCF.

J. A. Find both the LCM and GCF for the following "sets" of numbers. B. Explain why your answers represent the LCM for the given numbers. We suggest you write 2, 3, or 4 sets of multiplication tables, depending on whether you are working with 2, 3, or 4 numbers, to illustrate why you are positive you determined the correct LCM for the given sets of numbers. C. Explain why your answers represent the GCF for the given numbers. We suggest you write sets of factors for each number in each problem to illustrate why you are positive you determined the correct GCF for each set of numbers. Here is an example set of factors for the number "16" in problem 71. - $\{1, 2, \mathbf{4}, 8, 16\}$. Remember, factors are numbers or terms written in a multiplication problem and the number "16" can be written in several ways as a multiplication problem: $16 = 1 \times 16$ or $16 = 2 \times 8$ or $16 = 4 \times 4$.

68. $\{6, 4\}$ 69. $\{6, 10\}$ 70. $\{6, 10, 4\}$

71. $\{8, 12, 16\}$ 72. $\{3, 9, 12\}$ 73. $(3, 5, 9, 15\}$

K. Illustrate why we know the given LCM or LCD is the Least Common Multiple or Least Common Denominator for the given sets of numbers. We suggest you use multiplication tables for the numbers indicated to justify why the given number is the correct LCM or LCD.

74. $LCM = 90$ $\{15, 30, 5, 45\}$

75. $LCM = 7{,}488$ $\{72, 64, 78\}$

76. $LCM = 75$ $\{ 15, 75, 25\}$

77. $LCD = 1470$ $\{70, 98, 42\}$

L. Illustrate why we know the given GCF is the Greatest Common Factor for the given sets of numbers. We suggest you write the factors for all the indicated numbers to illustrate why the indicated number is the correct GCF. (Example: Here is the set of factors for the number "24" {1, 2, 3, 4, 6, 8, **12**, 24})

78. $GCF = 12$ $\{24, 12, 48\}$

79. $GCF = 12$ $\{60, 48, 36\}$

80. $GCF = 6$ $\{90, 24, 12, 60, 48, 36\}$

81. $GCF = 17$ $\{51, 85, 34\}$

SOLVE LONG DIVISION PROBLEMS USING A DIVISION BOX WITH THE DIVISOR TO THE LEFT OR THE RIGHT OF THE DIVISION BOX AND THE DIVIDEND INSIDE THE DIVISION BOX.

(In the United States, we usually place the divisor to the left of the division box, but in some countries, the divisor is placed to the right side of the division box. Use the same mental procedures whether the divisor is to the left or to the right of the division box.)

M. This section involves long division problems. Write all the steps. If the quotient involves a remainder, write the remainder as a decimal rounded off to two decimal places, round off to the nearest hundredth. Do not use a calculator.

82. $\frac{64193}{23}$ 83. $22523000 \div 1010$

84. $\frac{73}{151}$ *or* $73 \div 151$ 85. $7 \div 691$ *or* $\frac{7}{691}$

BASIC EXPLANATION HOW TO GRAPH A LINE IN A RECTANGULAR COORDINATE SYSTEM

(Technically, you only need **two points** to graph a straight line.)

We want you to graph the six problems below 86.-91., which all involve a point and the slope. We start with these types of problems because the definition of the slope of a line was a topic of interest in this chapter.

Graph the problems 92.-97., which all involve at least two points. These problems should be easier to graph than the previous six problems.

Use a minimum of 4 points to graph the lines indicated below in problems 86.-91. involving a point and the slope of the line. We suggest you use graph paper to illustrate/write the solutions to these problems, but it is not a requirement. On the graph paper, draw six (6) different preliminary graphs, with one line going left to right and the second line going from bottom to top. The two lines need to intersect at a right angle. (If the lines form a right angle, the lines are referred to as perpendicular lines.) The graphs may be small or large, but you should have at least 10 units to the right of the point of intersection and 10 units above the point of intersection of the two intersecting lines. The mathematical definition of the slope of a line is: "*slope equals rise divided by run*" using words, or "$m = \frac{rise}{run}$" using a ratio, or "$m = \frac{y_2 - y_1}{x_2 - x_1}$" using a formula.

If you graph a line represented in each of the six problems indicated below, you will have to plot the given point first. The procedure to plot the point is to start at the point of intersection of one of your drawings involving the two lines. The point of intersection of the two lines is written using the notation, (0, 0), and this point is referred to as the origin. Use the six blank preliminary graphs to graph problems 86.-91. The first number (left hand number) tells you to begin at the origin, (0, 0) and move to the right the indicated number of spaces or blocks based on the first number (do not make a mark and do not lift your pencil yet), then reference the second number (right hand number) and count in the upward direction the number of blocks indicated by the second number. This is where you need to place a dot/mark to indicate the given point. The second part of the problem refers to the slope of the line you are going to draw. Your next objective is to find a second point if you want to draw the line required for the problem. Without lifting your pencil or pen from the point you just indicated on the graph paper, use the numerator of the slope fraction (ratio) and count upward the number of blocks or spaces indicated by the numerator. Without making a mark, when you count in the upward direction the required number of blocks, refer to the denominator and count to the right the number of blocks or spaces indicated by the denominator. Now, make a second mark or dot. You now have two marks/dots on the graph paper. You may draw a straight line by connecting the two points/dots you just indicated on the graph paper. We prefer you find a third point on the line before you connect the first two points by starting at the second point and following the same directions using the slope which you used to find the second point after you plotted the first point. Using the third point, you will be able to find a fourth point using the same directions you used to find the third point, but you must realize you are starting at the third point, not the second point. Once you have all the required points indicated on the graph paper (in the upper right section of the graph), then use a straight edge (ruler) and connect the points to form a straight line. (We would like you to extend the line you draw in both directions to indicate the line does not really begin at one point and end at another point.)

The normal notation to represent a point when there are two lines involved in the graph (one horizontal line and one vertical line) is to use parentheses with two numbers inside the parentheses, and a comma between the two numbers. (The word parentheses implies that both the left and right parentheses symbol is written. The notation just described involving parentheses and two numbers separated by a comma is referred to as an "<u>ordered pair</u>".) If you are just representing a point on a single number line, which was indicated earlier in Chapter 2, then there is not a specific notation, just written directions. The first number, as indicated in the previous paragraph, represents the units moving to the right from the point of intersection of the two perpendicular lines and the second number, as indicated in the previous paragraph, represents the units moving upward from the point of intersection of the two perpendicular lines. We have used the most basic terminology and examples to illustrate how to place a point on a graph when both numbers in the <u>ordered pair</u> are positive, and the slope is positive. (Technically, the first number in an <u>ordered pair</u> indicates whether you should move left or right from the origin, and the second number indicates whether you should move up or down. Also, when you are working with a slope, the numerator tells you to move either up or down, and the denominator tells you to move either left or right. We believe you should mention these additional comments after you initially discuss how to graph a line using a point and a slope, but on the first day, keep the examples simple. Over the next few weeks, you will have the opportunity to discuss situations where you move either left or right and up or down.)

Important Note: We wrote the previous two paragraphs regarding a point and the slope of a line and how to graph the line defined by the two given pieces of information. Notice how difficult it is to write about a simple concept in algebra and the procedures to solve the problem correctly. We did this for two reasons. The first reason is to emphasize how important it is to write lesson plans and study how you plan on explaining specific topics in arithmetic and mathematics. The second reason is to illustrate why it is important to introduce concepts over a period of a couple of weeks or months in short segments to help students completely digest the rules, prior to solving problems in a homework assignment regarding a specific topic the night after you introduced the new concept that afternoon.

Additional information: The two pairs of lines which you should have drawn to graph the six problems below are normally referred to as the "x" axis and "y" axis. The "x" axis is the horizontal line, and the "y" axis is the vertical line. When you prepare your graph using the horizontal "x" axis and the vertical "y" axis and the lines are perpendicular, the setup of the lines in this format is referred to as the "Cartesian Coordinate System" or the "Rectangular Coordinate System". As indicated above, the two numbers in parentheses are referred to as an "ordered pair". Here are several examples of ordered pairs: "$(6,1), (0,7), (5,11), (2,2), \left(\frac{1}{3},5\right), (0.28, 0.5), (0,0), (-2,1), \left(-\frac{4}{5}, 0.7\right), (-11,-3), (4,-4)$".

The reason mathematicians refer to the notation as "ordered pairs" should be obvious, there is a definite order to the numbers, and there are two numbers. The notation when writing an ordered pair is important. Therefore, we will repeat the universal mathematical notation explanation. An ordered pair is always written using parentheses with a comma between the two numbers. The first number always represents the number of spaces/units to move on the "x" axis, and the second number always represents the number of spaces/blocks to move on the "y" axis. If the first number in the parentheses, which represents the value of "x", is positive, you should start at the origin, the point of intersection of the two perpendicular lines, then count by moving to the right the number of spaces indicated by the number. If the first number in the parentheses, which represents the value of "x" is negative, you should start at the origin and count the required number of times by moving to the left. The second number, which is the "y" value, represents a position on the vertical line. If the "y" value is positive, then count upward, and a negative "y" value means to move down the required number of times indicated by the number.

In all the given problems below, the two numbers are all positive. This means when you graph all 12 problems below, reference problems 86. through 97., you must start at the origin and move to the right the number of indicated spaces and once you move to the right without making a mark, move up the number of spaces indicated by the second number. Eventually, you will be required to work with negative numbers, including fractions and decimals, but not the problems indicated below. This is a beginning exercise for arithmetic students, not a lesson for Pre-Algebra or Algebra students. (Comment: The small letter "m" is the variable used universally in algebra to represent the word slope when referring to the slope of a line or the slant of a line. The slope of a line is always a ratio even when there are no labels indicated.)

N. The six problems you are required to graph below, starting with problem 86. all involve a point and a slope. The six problems you are required to graph below, starting with problem 92. all involve 2, 3, or 4 points. When you connect the points in all 12 problems, the graph must be a straight line.

86. Point = (2, 3) $m = \frac{1}{2}$ - The slope could be written as "$m = \frac{1\ space}{2\ spaces}$", or "$m = \frac{1\ in.}{2\ in.}$", or "$m = \frac{1\ mile}{2\ miles}$", or etc. (Remember, the identical labels in the numerators and denominators will cancel (divide and both become "1"); therefore, the labels in this special situation are not required.) Graph the line indicated by the point and the slope. Use a straight edge or ruler to connect all the points you indicated on the graph, and you should form a straight line.

87. Point = (3, 2) $m = \frac{2}{1}$ (Note: Normally, if the denominator in a fraction or the denominator of a slope is "1", the number "1" is NOT written, BUT when working with a slope of a line, the number "**1**" in the **denominator** is **important** and you will probably have to encourage some students to write the invisible "1" in the denominator.) The slope for this problem is normally written without the number "1" indicated. Therefore, when the slope is "$m = 2$", the recommended way to write the ratio representing the slope is "$m = \frac{2}{1}$". Use a straight edge or ruler to connect all the points you indicated on the graph, and you should form a straight line.

In the four remaining problems, always use a straight edge or a ruler to connect the points to form a straight line on the graph paper.

88. Point = (1, 4), $m = \frac{2}{5}$ All the slopes equal "$\frac{2}{5}$". $m = \frac{2\ steps}{5\ steps}$ & $m = \frac{2\ cm.}{5\ cm.}$

89. Point = (4, 1), $m = \frac{5}{2}$ All the slopes equal "$\frac{5}{2}$". $m = \frac{5\ blocks}{2\ blocks}$ & $m = \frac{5\ yds.}{2\ yds.}$

90. Point = (2, 5), $m = \frac{1}{3}$ All the slopes equal "$\frac{1}{3}$". $m = \frac{1\ miles}{3\ mi.}$ & $m = \frac{1\ km}{3\ km}$

91. Point = (2, 5), $m = 3$ All the slopes equal "$\frac{3}{1}$". $m = \frac{3\ feet}{1\ foot}$ & $m = \frac{3\ km}{1\ km}$

Important Note: All slopes are ratios because both the numerator and the denominator may or may not have a label, and when you use the slope ratio to find the second point on the graph, you must refer separately to both the numerator and the denominator. Also, notice when the labels cancel (divide each other out), as in these examples, the slope looks just like any other fraction you will encounter.

O. The following six problems all involve at least two points. Technically, you only need two points to graph a line, but we encourage beginners to use at least four points when they graph lines. Draw six preliminary graphs involving the two perpendicular lines referred to as the "x" axis and "y" axis using the same rules to solve problems 86.-91.

When plotting the points indicated in problems 92.-97., you must always focus on the origin, "(0, 0)" as your starting point. When plotting the first point, focus on the first number in the parentheses and move to the right the indicated number of spaces, DO NOT lift your pencil, then count upward the number of spaces indicated by the second number to the right in the parentheses. This is where you place your first point/dot. Repeat the process for the second point and again start at the origin. If there is a third or fourth point, always return to the origin and move to the right the number of times indicated by the first number and then up the number of times indicated by the second number. After you place the 2 points or 3 points or 4 points, use a straight edge to connect all the points to form a straight line. (We want you to extend your line in both directions when you draw the line.)

92. Point 1 = (2, 3), and Point 2= (3, 6). Use a straight edge or ruler to connect the two points you indicated on the graph, and you should form a straight line.

93. Point 1= (3, 2), Point 2= (5, 3), and Point 3= (7, 4). Use a straight edge or ruler to connect all the points you indicated on the graph, and you should form a straight line.

In the four remaining problems, always use a straight edge or a ruler to connect the points to form a straight line on the graph paper.

94. Point 1= (1, 8) and Point 2= (2, 7) and Point 3= (3, 6) and Point 4= (4, 5)

95. Point 1= (4, 1) and Point 2= (5, 3) and Point 3= (6, 5)

96. Point 1= (6, 2) and Point 2= (5, 4) and Point 3= (4, 6) and Point 4= (3, 8)

97. Point 1= (2, 5) and Point 2= (4, 3) and Point 3= (6, 1)

P. Based on the limited information already given regarding the definition of the slope of a line, find the slopes of the lines for the points indicated in two previous problems, which are also indicated below. (Here is an example solution using problem "95." above. You only need two points to find the slope of a line. In problem "95." we will focus on the two points (4, 1) and (6, 5). The choice of points is irrelevant. The definition of slope, using words, indicates you should focus on the rise of the line first in the numerator; therefore, we will focus on the two "*y*" values "5" and "1" in the two given points. The order of the two "*y*" values is also not important, but in this problem, it is easier to focus on the two numbers, "5" and "1" in the order they are indicated. If you want to find the numerator of the slope (the rise) you need to subtract the two "*y*" values. If you want to find the denominator (the run) of the slope, you must focus on the two matching "x" values "6" and "4" in the two given points. Again, subtract these two numbers to find the denominator of the slope. The two "x" values/numbers are selected in the same order as the two "y" values/numbers. The slope for problem "96." is therefore found by using the following ratio (fraction): "$\frac{5-1}{6-4} = \frac{4}{2} = \frac{2}{1} = 2 = m$". If we switch the order of the two "y" values and the two "x" values, we get the fraction "$\frac{-4}{-2} = \frac{4}{2} = \frac{2}{1} = 2 = m$", but we will avoid using negative integers at this time and keep it simple. Eventually, students will have to work with negative numbers, but is not a major point of interest at this time. Again, we encourage teachers to mention how to work with the numbers when the order of the two pairs of numbers is switched.)

98. Find the slope of the line for problem "92." above.

99. Find the slope of the line using the points indicated in problem,"93." above.

(Comment: In the selected problems 92., 93., and 95., we wanted to keep the solutions simple. Therefore, we made sure the slopes for these three problems are all positive. If you want to discuss lines which have a negative slope, we suggest you work with the three other problems in this section.)

Every minute in an arithmetic or mathematics classroom is important! Always try to introduce or review some arithmetic or mathematics topic versus allowing valuable time to be wasted. There is always too little time and so much more for the students to learn. We use this same type of principle continually throughout this textbook. Whenever you encounter a colored rectangle inserted in this textbook in a place where the information contained in the rectangle is a comment which might not be directly related to the information contained in a specific section, it is our way of introducing and or reviewing a comment, rule, fact, or procedure which we believe is important for you to understand. We intentionally try to fill every little space with something for you to read and study because there is so much information which you need to understand, if you are going to be an amazing arithmetic or math teacher, which we hope is your goal. Read and study all the comments contained in these rectangles. Everything in arithmetic and mathematics is important!

CHAPTER 3

ADDING AND SUBTRACTING SIMPLE FRACTIONS: RULES AND PROCEDURES ARE IMPORTANT

STUDENTS MUST KNOW THE RULES TO SIMPLIFY FRACTION PROBLEMS IN ARITHMETIC IN ORDER TO BE SUCCSSFUL IN ALGEBRA AND OTHER ADVANCED MATHEMATICS COURSES.

Chapter 3

Teaching Point: Whenever we discuss the procedures for comparing, adding, subtracting, reducing, multiplying, and dividing fractions throughout this textbook, we focus on how to explain arithmetic problems involving fractions, so students will understand the rules required to simplify algebra fraction problems (referred to as rational expressions). Always focus teaching efforts for every mathematics topic on how students will be required to solve problems when they enter a more advanced arithmetic or math class later in their math careers (Bailey, Zhou, Zhang, Cui, Fuchs, Jordon, Gersten, & Siegler, 2015; Siegler & Lortie – Forgues, 2015; Siegler & Pyke et al., 2013). Great teachers illustrate how to solve problems which require students to understand the concepts and then use rules and procedures to solve the simple basic problems from the textbook plus slightly more challenging problems which might not be included as part of the textbook assignments. Great teachers ensure students will be able to solve all textbook problems along with slightly more challenging problems to make sure the students will be successful in future math classes. At times it may seem problems which involve rules and procedures not normally emphasized are beyond the scope of the class, but this is the challenge, and it is also how to develop growth. If students are going to be prepared to simplify fractions in algebra and beyond, they need to be exposed as soon as possible to the rules when they are solving arithmetic problems. If we try to teach to a level which is beyond what the textbook expects kids to accomplish, we will find many of the students will learn how to solve the more challenging problems, and they will think the textbook problems are easy. *(FRT 4: Teach to a level beyond the textbook expectations.)*

This chapter involves several simple problems which can be used to illustrate how to convert fractions into equivalent fractions and eventually add and/or subtract fractions. The solutions for many of these problems can be illustrated easily using graphs, charts, number lines, or computer graphics. One of the example problems discussed in this chapter, "$\frac{1}{2}+\frac{1}{4}$", is supposed to be easy. The students should have already solved this problem in an earlier grade by using pictures, graphs, line segments, or computer illustrations to find the solution "$\frac{3}{4}$".

The main goals in this chapter are to illustrate how to convert fractions into equivalent fractions, and then add and subtract two or more fractions with the same denominator. We also want to find the least common denominator, referred to as the LCD, if two or more fractions do not already have the same denominator. The two expressions, least common denominator (LCD) and least common multiple (LCM), almost mean the same thing. The minor difference between an LCM and an LCD is, an LCD is a special type of LCM. An LCD is an LCM specifically referring to the denominators of two or more fractions. A least common multiple (LCM) refers to a group of numbers. The group of numbers might be a list of denominators from two or more fractions, or the set of numbers might be from a group of numbers written for a specific problem.

This textbook will continue to use "Young's Conversion Theorem" to convert a given fraction into an equivalent fraction. "Young's Conversion Theorem" emphasizes the following truth: "When we convert a fraction into an equivalent fraction, we must multiply by the number 1." The textbook will always indicate we are multiplying a given fraction by the number 1 when we are performing the conversion process, and we will always substitute a special form of the number 1 into our example conversion problems derived from previous steps in the process.

To illustrate how to add and subtract fractions, we will also have to find LCDs when necessary. We will then convert some fractions into equivalent fractions with the correct LCD prior to adding and subtracting the fractions with the same LCD. In this chapter, the addition and subtraction problems are simple, and students must be able to find the correct LCD using their knowledge of the multiplication and division tables. We will also introduce the rules to find LCDs for a few of the example problems in this chapter, but students should be able to find the LCDs in this chapter by using mental math.

In Chapter 4, we will explain and illustrate the rules necessary to work with challenging addition and subtraction problems when we need to find LCDs which are much larger than the denominators in this chapter. In Chapter 4, the conversion process to find equivalent fractions with the same LCD is the same process we will introduce when we solve simple addition and subtraction problems in this chapter. Some of the examples discussed in this chapter are typical 5^{th,} and 6th-grade fraction problems students already encounter in classroom textbooks. Others are more challenging than the typical 5th and 6th-grade textbook problems. Remember, it will normally take two or three years for most students to master all the rules and procedures involving fractions. Do not feel you must rush the students to learn all the rules in a short amount of time. The more time the students are exposed to the rules and procedures to work with fractions, the more positive the teaching and learning situation will be. *(FRT 5: If students are exposed to rules in mathematics over a longer time frame, then their long-term memory will improve.)*

If students are going to be successful in subsequent mathematics courses, solving these addition and subtraction fraction problems is essential. If students are going to be successful in algebra, we must ensure that 90% of students can solve these types of problems with 90% accuracy before they move on to any type of algebra class. Understanding fractions, solving problems involving fractions, and grasping number sense with fractions are essential concepts students must master if they are going to be successful in advanced mathematics courses (Bailey et al., 2012; Bailey, Siegler, & Geary, 2014; Booth & Newton, 2012; Heller, Post, Behr, & Losh, 1990; Siegler et al., 2012; Siegler, Fazio, Bailey, & Zhou, 2013; Torbeyns, Schneider, Xin, & Siegler, 2015; Watts, Duncan, Siegler, & Davis-Kean, 2014).

We will initially solve the problems below using terminology teachers normally employ when they teach 4th or 5th graders. In many of these example problems, we explain the rules which are necessary to solve more challenging addition and subtraction problems. The procedures discussed in this chapter to solve most of the problems are the same procedures many people already use when they do mental math, and they do not need to write all the steps to properly solve the problems. The goal is to emphasize the mental steps we do not normally write when we solve problems and clarify why the mental tricks many people use work, based on sound mathematical rules. When students are required to write all the mathematical steps used to solve a problem, they develop an understanding of the steps and become more proficient with the process of solving the problems.

The more teachers insist students write specific steps which lead to the solution of a problem, the more the steps become automatic and the more the students' math skills improve. We want students to improve their math skills in a variety of ways which include some of the following areas: Number understanding; Short term comprehension; Long term comprehension; Mental math skills; etc. *(FRT 6: The more students write the steps to solve problems, the better their long-term memory will be.)*

Teaching Point: The following examples are problems a teacher should begin to introduce a couple of months before the students are expected to add and subtract fractions. Use these types of problems as introductory problems to be discussed for a few minutes, a few days per week. The problems can be introduced before class begins, at the end of class, or if possible, anytime during the school day when there is a short break in the routine. Assign these types of problems as additional homework problems for several weeks prior to teaching the section involving adding and subtracting fractions. Also, use these examples as discussion problems when the main objective is to begin to work with fractions. Many of these example problems are a little different from the regular textbook problems. We consider it important for teachers to challenge their students to simplify slightly more challenging problems than the textbook requires. Emphasize all the necessary steps and teach the rules and procedures necessary to solve future problems involving fractions.

The first fifteen sets of example problems could be used at the end of fourth grade or immediately when students begin fifth grade. These problems involve simple mental math tasks. The goal is to get the students to understand the concepts, to learn the different rules required to add and subtract fractions, and to reduce and multiply fractions. Expect students to realize the rules for adding and subtracting fractions are significantly different from the rules for reducing, multiplying, and dividing fractions. Many students at the end of fifth grade, sixth grade, seventh grade and even college get the rules confused for the different operations when simplifying fraction problems (Bailey et al., 2012; Bailey et al., 2014; Booth et al., 2012; Heller et al., 1990; Jordan, Hanson, Fuchs, Siegler, Gersten, &

Micklos, 2013; Kloosterman et al., 2010; Siegler et al., 2012; Stigler, Givven, & Thompson, 2010). Make sure the students understand the rules are different. The first fifteen sets of fraction problems are for introduction, but it is imperative you emphasize early that the procedures when working with fraction operations are different. When the students do their first homework assignment from the textbook (addition of simple fractions), include a fraction reducing problem and a fraction multiplication problem.

Here are some thoughts prior to attempting to plan a mini-lesson sequence. The initial step is to decide what procedures you want the students to understand prior to getting to the chapter focused on fractions.

First, illustrate how to solve some of the following problems using graphs, charts, line segments, and computer illustrations.

1. Adding and subtracting fractions with identical denominators (Concepts and Procedures).
2. Why do these fractions equal one: "$\frac{2}{2}, \frac{8}{8}, \frac{5}{5}, etc.$"?
3. Why do the following fractions equal "0": "$\frac{0}{2}, \frac{0}{6}, \frac{0}{11}, etc.$"?
4. Explain that a fraction is a division problem. Simplify the following fractions: "$\frac{11}{11}, \frac{10}{5}, \frac{16}{4}, etc.$"
5. Find equivalent fractions by multiplying by fractions equal to <u>1</u>, such as: "$\frac{2}{2}, \frac{3}{3}, \frac{5}{5}, etc.$". This is actually "Young's Conversion Theorem", but it is not necessary to refer to the theorem by name. Emphasize that the rules to multiply fractions are not the same rules used to add and subtract fractions.
6. Find the biggest number, which divides into two different numbers. This number is referred to as the greatest common factor (GCF).
7. Reduce fractions by dividing both the numerator and the denominator by the biggest number (GCF), which divides into both the numbers.

8. Find an equivalent fraction to a given fraction when the denominator of the second fraction is given.

There are several other concepts students must become familiar with prior to doing homework problems focused on solving challenging fraction problems including: Improper fractions; Mixed numbers; Long division of all types of problems; Adding and subtracting several fractions; Multiplying several fractions; Invert and multiply the fraction to the right of a division operation symbol "÷", etc.

Here is an important question that elementary arithmetic teachers must find the answer to if they expect students to master all the operations involving fractions: Why do students learn about "prime numbers" and "factor trees"? We will discuss the importance of factor trees when students are required to add, subtract, reduce, multiply, and divide fractions continually throughout this textbook. Understanding how to work with factor trees is the key to success, for all students when they are working with fractions. Prior to asking the students to work with challenging addition, subtraction, multiplication, and division problems, use 2-3 minute mini-lessons and apply the rules discussed in this textbook to prepare students for success with challenging arithmetic fraction problems and rational expressions in algebra.

There are so many little steps students must be familiar with when working with fractions. It is unrealistic for average students to be able to learn and remember all the steps if they are supposed to learn them in a week, a month, or even two months (Braithwaite, Pyke, & Siegler, 2017; Lortie-Forgues, Tian, & Siegler, 2015; Vukovic et al., 2014). It takes at least two years for math-oriented students to master all fraction procedures and three or more years for average and below-average students to master all the rules necessary to solve fraction problems.

The following mini lessons not only help us remember what we have already introduced, but also focus on our objectives in future months October, November and/or December. If you put mini-lesson comments in your lesson plans and find you do not have enough time for execution, just keep them for the next day.

Day 1 Assume previous teachers already illustrated to your students how to solve these problems using graphs, geometric shapes, line segments, and or computer simulations. If this is not true, then you will have to illustrate the concepts and have the students focus on the solutions using graphs, line segments, geometric shapes, and or computer simulations.

1. $\frac{2}{5}+\frac{1}{5}$ Use a picture graph to illustrate the answer and then discuss the rule. Answer equals "$\frac{3}{5}$". Plot a point on a number line to represent the fraction "$\frac{3}{5}$".

2. $\frac{3}{7}+\frac{2}{7}$ Use an illustration and discuss the rule. Plot the point "$\frac{5}{7}$" on a number line.

3. $\frac{3}{7}+\frac{2}{7}-\frac{1}{7}$ Use the rules to add and subtract fractions. Answer is "$\frac{4}{7}$".

4. $\frac{3}{8}+\frac{5}{8}$ Use the rules. Answer is "$\frac{8}{8}$". What does the answer "$\frac{8}{8}$" mean?

Day 2 Which might be 1, 2, or 3 days after the first introductory lesson.

1. $\frac{3}{9}-\frac{1}{9}+\frac{2}{9}$ Use a diagram to illustrate the answer and then discuss the rule again. Answer is "$\frac{4}{9}$".

2. $\frac{3}{5}-\frac{1}{5}$ Emphasize the identical denominator rule when adding and subtracting these two fractions. Answer is "$\frac{2}{5}$".

3. $\frac{3}{5}+\frac{2}{5}=\frac{5}{5}$ You may want to discuss this problem. The answer is "1".

4. $\frac{7}{11}-\frac{2}{11}+\frac{4}{11}-\frac{1}{11}=\frac{8}{11}$ You may want to discuss different ways to solve this problem.

Day 3 Introduce a fraction greater than one. Emphasize, a fraction is a division problem.

1. $\frac{3}{8}+\frac{3}{8}-\frac{1}{8}=\frac{5}{8}$ Notice, none of the answers will reduce except the answers which equal one at this time.

2. $\frac{2}{7}+\frac{1}{7}+\frac{0}{7}+\frac{4}{7}=\frac{7}{7}=1$ Emphasize the rules and discuss the value of the fraction, "$\frac{0}{7}$".

3. $\frac{3}{5}+\frac{4}{5}+\frac{3}{5}=\frac{10}{5}=2$ This may require some discussion.

Day 4 Introduce Equivalent Fractions.

1. $\frac{2}{3}=\frac{4}{6}$ Use illustrations to emphasize the fractions are equal. Think about what we did to both the number "2" and the number "3" to get the new numbers "4" and "6".

2. $\frac{1}{2}=\frac{2}{4}$ Illustrate why the fractions are equal using picture graphs. Again, what did we do to both the numerator and denominator of the first fraction, to get the numerator and denominator in the second fraction?

3. $\frac{1}{2}=\frac{5}{10}$ Use pictures to illustrate. What did we do to the first two numbers this time to get the last two numbers?

4. $\frac{1}{3}=\frac{6}{18}$ Tell me what we did to the two numbers "1" and "3" to get "6" and "18"?

5. Solve the following problem: "$\frac{5}{6} = \frac{5}{6} \times 1 = \frac{5}{6} \times \frac{2}{2} = \frac{10}{12}$" Use a pie chart to illustrate the fractions, "$\frac{5}{6}$ & $\frac{10}{12}$", are equal but do not spend a lot of time explaining the procedure today. Allow the students a day or two to think about the process.

Day 5 Discuss the multiplication property for the number 1: ("$6 \times 1 = 6$", "$11 \times 1 = 11$", "$1 \times 4 = 4$", "$a \times 1 = a$", etc.). The last equation simply indicates no matter what number you use to replace the letter "a", you get an equivalent answer to the starting term. Find equivalent fractions by multiplying a given fraction by 1. The example problems below will be the first time, students encounter "Young's Conversion Theorem". It is not necessary to mention the name of the theorem but emphasize when you multiply a fraction by any fraction equal to 1; you get an equivalent fraction.

1. $\frac{1}{2} = \frac{1}{2} \times 1 = \frac{1}{2} \times \frac{2}{2} = \frac{2}{4} \quad \therefore \quad \frac{1}{2} = \frac{2}{4}$

2. $\frac{2}{3} = \frac{2}{3} \times 1 = \frac{2}{3} \times \frac{4}{4} = \frac{8}{12} \quad \therefore \quad \frac{2}{3} = \frac{8}{12}$

3. $\frac{5}{6} = \frac{5}{6} \times 1 = \frac{5}{6} \times \frac{?}{?} = \frac{??}{??}$ The students may find different fractions equal to "$\frac{5}{6}$".

Once students understand these three examples and know the rule to multiply by a fraction equal to one, it is time to point out the difference between the rules required to add and subtract two or more fractions and the rules to multiply two or more fractions.

Day 6 This is a review day for the first five introduction days. Give a two-minute quiz for bonus points. Solve the following five questions. You will have to decide how you want to handle bonus points or even if you want the students to earn bonus points. Students give their best effort when they believe correct work will be rewarded. You may not want to give these five problems as a "high-stakes" quiz because the students are just learning how to solve these problems. Do not make it a stressful situation. Make it fun.

1. $\frac{2}{7}+\frac{4}{7}=$ The answer is "$\frac{6}{7}$".
2. $\frac{3}{5}+\frac{3}{5}-\frac{2}{5}=$ The answer is "$\frac{4}{5}$".
3. $\frac{7}{10}+\frac{3}{10}=$ The answer is "$\frac{10}{10}$" which equals "1".
4. $\frac{7}{8}+\frac{5}{8}+\frac{5}{8}-\frac{1}{8}=$ This problem is more difficult than previous problems. We will be amazed if you get the right answer. The answer is "$\frac{16}{8}$" which equals "2".
5. Find the fraction equal to "$\frac{3}{5}$" by multiplying by the fraction "$\frac{4}{4}$". Remember, "$\frac{4}{4}=1$".

Day 7 Introduce the concept and how to work with Greatest Common Factors.

1. Illustrate how to solve the 5 questions from the quiz.
2. Answer the question, "What is the biggest number which divides into both "6" and "9"?" The answer, "3" is referred to as the GCF.
3. What is the largest number, which divides into both "12" and "16"? Answer is "4".

Day 8 Magnitude of fractions on number lines.

1. Find the answer: "$\frac{3}{5}-\frac{2}{5}$" Use a diagram to illustrate the solution and discuss the rules. You may also want to plot the three fractions on three different number lines to illustrate how the starting segment is larger than the second segment, and the answer is smaller than either of the two original segments. Answer is "$\frac{1}{5}$".

2. Find the answer: "$\frac{6}{7}+\frac{5}{7}+\frac{3}{7}-\frac{0}{7}$ Discuss the rules and procedures. Using a number line to explain/illustrate the solution might be beneficial. Answer is "$\frac{14}{7}=2$".

3. Find an equivalent/reduced fraction: "$\frac{6}{9}$" by dividing each number by "3". Use pictures and/or line segments to illustrate the fractions, "$\frac{6}{9}$ and $\frac{2}{3}$", are equal.

4. Find an equivalent/reduced fraction: "$\frac{12}{16}$" by dividing each number by "4".

Day 9 How to multiply by fractions equal to 1 to find equivalent fractions.

1. Find the missing numerator: "$\frac{3}{4}=\frac{?}{12}$" Some students will realize the missing number is "9". We want them to show the work starting with the 4th example problem, below.

2. Find the missing number: "$\frac{2}{5}=\frac{?}{10}$" Some students will realize the missing number is "4".

3. Do the following division problem and use a division box: "$\frac{165}{11}$". Remember, a fraction is a division problem written using a different notation.

4. Find the missing number: "$\frac{9}{11}=\frac{?}{99}$" We suggest you emphasize the notation illustrated next. $\frac{\text{Denominator of the second fraction}}{\text{Denominator of the first fraction}}=\frac{99}{11}=9.$ Use a division box to solve the division problem. "$99 \div 11 = 9$" and $\frac{9}{9}=1$.

   Now, multiply the first fraction by "$\frac{9}{9}$". Therefore, "$\frac{9}{11}=\frac{9}{11}\times 1=\frac{9}{11}\times\frac{9}{9}=\frac{81}{99}$"

Day 10 Continue the Day 9 discussion because example 4 was a challenging problem.

Remember, when you place a point representing two equal fractions on a number line, the two fractions are the same point even though the numerators and the denominators are different.

1. $\frac{25}{5}$ This is a division problem. The quotient is "5".

2. Reduce: $\frac{10}{15}$ Hint: What is the biggest number which divides into both "10 and 15"?

3. $\frac{9}{11} = \frac{?}{99}$ The same problem as yesterday.

4. $\frac{26}{35} = \frac{?}{105}$ $\frac{\text{Denominator of the second fraction}}{\text{Denominator of the first fraction}} = \frac{105}{35} = 3$

We know: $\frac{3}{3} = 1$ $\frac{26}{35} = \frac{26}{35} \times 1 = \frac{26}{35} \times \frac{3}{3} = \frac{26 \times 3}{35 \times 3} = \frac{78}{105}$

5. Try this problem with a partner. $\frac{23}{25} = \frac{?}{150}$ $\frac{150}{25} = 6$ We know $\therefore \frac{6}{6} = 1$

$\frac{23}{25} = \frac{23}{25} \times 1 = \frac{23}{25} \times \frac{6}{6} = \frac{23 \times 6}{25 \times 6} = \frac{138}{150}$

Emphasize if you want to determine the specific fraction by which to multiply the first fraction, we must divide the denominator of the second fraction by the denominator of the first fraction. The way we explain this procedure is important. If you think you know how to solve all the problems using the present terminology you use in your classroom, find the numerator for this fraction problem: "$\frac{3x}{10y^2z} = \frac{?}{30y^3z^2}$. This type of question was not illustrated as part of the author's short introductory lessons for 4th and 5th graders, but it is a question readers will be able to simplify after they study this textbook.

Day 11 What is the smallest number, which is a multiple of both "2 and 5"? Here is the same question worded differently, "What is the smallest number that both "2 and 5" divide into without a remainder?" The answer is "10". Now, we want students to begin using mental math to determine the least common multiples and least common denominators.

1. Find the LCM for 2, 4, and 8. Answer is "8".
2. Find the LCM for 2, 4, and 5. Answer is "20".
3. $\frac{7}{13}+\frac{11}{13}-\frac{6}{13}-\frac{0}{13}$ Answer is "$\frac{12}{13}$".
4. Reduce $\frac{5}{15}$. Answer is "$\frac{1}{3}$". What is the "GCF" for the two numbers "5" and "15"?

Day 12 These questions are a review of the first quiz. Our goal is to ensure students get a chance to revisit the concepts, rules, and procedures which were previously discussed.

1. $\frac{2}{11}+\frac{4}{11}=$ Answer $=\frac{6}{11}$
2. $\frac{4}{5}+\frac{3}{5}-\frac{4}{5}=$ Answer $=\frac{3}{5}$
3. $\frac{7}{15}+\frac{8}{15}=$ Answer $=\frac{15}{15}=1$
4. $\frac{7}{9}+\frac{7}{9}+\frac{5}{9}-\frac{1}{9}=$ Answer $=\frac{18}{9}=2$
5. Find the fraction equal to "$\frac{3}{5}$" by multiplying by the fraction, "$\frac{7}{7}$". Remember, "$\frac{7}{7}=1$".

Day 13 This is the second (bonus) quiz.

1. $\frac{91}{103}+\frac{6}{103}-\frac{89}{103}+\frac{14}{103}$ Answer $=\frac{22}{103}$
2. Reduce the fraction, "$\frac{6}{9}$" (Hint: What is the GCF for the two numbers, "6" and "9"?)
3. $\frac{30}{6}$ Simplify: What does the line in a fraction problem represent?) Answer =5

4. Find the equivalent fraction to "$\frac{7}{8}$" by multiplying by the fraction "$\frac{4}{4}$". (Remember, "$\frac{4}{4} = 1$".) Answer = "$\frac{28}{32}$".

5. Find the missing number: $\frac{4}{5} = \frac{?}{25}$ Did you remember to divide the second denominator by the first denominator to determine which form of the number 1 to multiply the first fraction? Solution - $\frac{4}{5} \times 1 = \frac{4}{5} \times \frac{5}{5} = \frac{20}{25}$ We skipped some steps.

The goal of the quizzes, used as introductions, is to get the students to attempt to solve the problems on their own and write down the steps to find the solutions.

Day 14 Illustrate concepts and mention rules when multiplying fractions.

1. Go over the 5 quiz questions. Remember, these are bonus questions only! You do not want the students to be nervous or concerned about missing a question; you want them to learn.

2. Illustrate how to multiply "$\frac{2}{5} \times \frac{1}{2}$" using graphs, line segments or charts. Point out to the students that the rules to multiply two fractions are the same rules they used to convert fractions into equivalent fractions when they multiplied by a fraction equal to 1. They should know how to reduce the fraction "$\frac{2}{10}$" using the rules and determine the final answer "$\frac{1}{5}$".

3. Multiply "$\frac{1}{4} \times \frac{4}{7}$" Use graphs and charts to help students discover the correct procedures. The initial answer is "$\frac{4}{28}$", which reduces and becomes "$\frac{1}{7}$".

4. $\frac{4}{7} = \frac{?}{14}$ $\frac{\text{Denomiantor second fraction}}{\text{Denominator first fraction}} = \frac{14}{7} = 2$ $\therefore \frac{2}{2} = 1$ $\frac{4}{7} = \frac{4}{7} \times 1 = \frac{4}{7} \times \frac{2}{2} = \frac{8}{14}$

Day 15 Here are more fraction multiplication problems.

1. $\frac{3}{4} \times \frac{4}{7}$ Use graphs and charts and the procedures to get the answer "$\frac{3}{7}$". Emphasize the rules are different for multiplying fractions than they are for adding and subtracting fractions. Plot the points for all three fractions on a number line. Notice the magnitude of the answer compared to the given two fractions (Siegler et al., 2015).

2. $\frac{25}{101} - \frac{4}{101} + \frac{17}{101} + \frac{49}{101}$ Continue to emphasize the rules for adding and subtracting fractions. The answer is "$\frac{87}{101}$".

3. $\frac{4}{7} + \frac{2}{7}$ The answer is "$\frac{6}{7}$".

4. $\frac{4}{7} \times \frac{2}{7}$ The product is "$\frac{8}{49}$". Students must master the correct procedures.

The previous fifteen mini lessons illustrate how to introduce concepts involving fractions in short segments a couple of months prior to students being required to solve problems in a homework textbook assignment. When writing a lesson plan for the day, always include mini lessons at the end of the plan. Many days we planned on discussing the mini-lesson topic, but some days the lesson of the day or a homework discussion dictated we delay the mini-lesson to the next day. You can design your own lessons to cover additional fraction concepts. For example, rewrite fraction addition and subtraction problems as <u>one big fraction</u> once the fractions all have the same denominator, then only focus on the numerators. Also, write fraction multiplication and division problems (after the fraction to the right of the division operation symbol is inverted and the division problem is changed to a multiplication problem) as <u>one big fraction</u>, and then multiply all the numerators together and all the denominators together. We suggest you use the one big fraction notation, so students do not confuse the different rules required for the four different arithmetic operations involved with fractions. We will illustrate the one big fraction notation frequently in future problems in this textbook.

Numerous positive student learning results will emerge from these quick, nonthreatening introductions in your classroom:

1. Students will be aware of the different rules when simplifying fraction problems. Only emphasize two sets of rules when students work with fractions. One set of rules focuses on adding, subtracting, and comparing fractions as they need to find the least common denominator. The second set of rules focuses on reducing, multiplying, and dividing fractions. Remember, a fraction division problem turns into a fraction multiplication problem.
2. Students will already know how to do the homework problems, and they will use the correct procedures. Seldom will you have a student use an incorrect procedure when they do their homework assignments for the first time on a specific topic. If they make a mistake on their homework assignment, it usually will be an arithmetic mental mistake.
3. Students will breeze through the textbook problems. They will consider the textbook problems joyrides in comparison.
4. If a student is absent on the day the main lesson is taught, the student will still know how to do the homework assignment from the textbook.
5. If a student misses a couple of mini lessons, he/she will still know how to do the homework problems on the first day an assignment involving fractions is given.

6. Students will have a better chance to learn the procedures since they are introduced to them over a period of months instead of days. *(FRT 5: If students are exposed to rules in mathematics for a longer time frame, then their long-term memory will improve.)*

Teaching Point: Teach students to use factor trees every time they encounter a slightly challenging fraction addition or subtraction problem for which they must find an LCD. Also, teach them to use factor trees every time they reduce a fraction or multiply or divide two or more fractions.

The following 14 examples are slightly more challenging addition and subtraction problems. Begin to introduce these problems one or two weeks prior to the students doing their first homework assignment from the textbook. Use one, two, or three of these example problems in a two-minute introduction, depending on the difficulty of each question.

Remember, these are only introductory lessons. You still will spend 2, 3, 4 or more weeks discussing the problems in the textbook and assigning homework problems. If you spend two months introducing fractions, more days and even weeks may be required to teach fractions, and then several months will be needed to review fractions for 2-3 minutes in short mini lessons. Your joy will come when you realize your students understand concepts and "learn and remember" more procedures than you ever imagined. *(FRT 5: If students are exposed to rules in mathematics for a longer time frame, then their long-term memory will improve.)*

If you are an elementary arithmetic teacher or a middle/high school math teacher, take the time during the summer to identify the five most difficult topics which are presented in all the courses you teach in the upcoming school year. Then use the procedures illustrated throughout this textbook to introduce, teach, and review those five topics all year.

Here are more example problems you may want to use when students begin to solve fraction problems from the textbook.

1. Simplify: "$\frac{1}{2}+\frac{1}{4}$"

This is a simple fraction addition problem, and it is easy to see the solution is "$\frac{3}{4}$". If you are proficient when working with fraction addition problems, you might write the following steps to illustrate how to simplify this problem:

$$\frac{1}{2}+\frac{1}{4}=\frac{2}{4}+\frac{1}{4}=\frac{3}{4}$$

The five steps listed below seem so simple because you are experienced, and you can mentally solve this problem without indicating much work, but when you are teaching young students, they need to understand all the basic steps and writing the hidden steps should help them master the procedures to solve simple problems and eventually more challenging problems.

1. Determine the LCD is "4" for the two denominators. You know the denominator "2" in the first fraction will divide into the number "4" and the quotient will be a whole number. You also know the number "4" in the second denominator will divide into the number "4". The first step when adding and subtracting fractions is to find the LCD. You know you need to find a number that both denominators will divide into with no remainder.
2. The second step you also do quickly in your head because you know the denominator of the first fraction "2", divides into the LCD "4" exactly "2" times. It is so easy to divide the LCD "4" by the denominator of the first fraction "2" and get the answer (quotient) "2".

There are a few words in the last sentence you need to focus on: you divided the LCD by the denominator of the first fraction and got a quotient.

3. In the third step, convert the fraction "$\frac{1}{2}$" into the equivalent fraction, "$\frac{2}{4}$" and add the two given fractions. You already divided the LCD "4" by the denominator "2" in your head, and you know you need to multiply the numerator "1" in the fraction "$\frac{1}{2}$" by the quotient "2" which you determined in step 2. That seems like a lot to do in your head if you are an average or below-average math student. (Questions: Why did you multiply the numerator "1" by the quotient "2"? Why does this trick work?)
4. Now both fractions have the same denominator "4", you know you can simply add the numerators of both fractions to get the final answer "$\frac{3}{4}$" and keep the LCD in the final answer.
5. Frequently, the final step when adding and subtracting fractions is to reduce the numerator and the denominator if possible. In this problem, the fraction "$\frac{3}{4}$" will not reduce.

When you first assign addition and subtraction fraction problems, make sure the answers in the initial problems will not reduce. If you are the teacher and you are satisfied that the students have learned the procedures necessary to solve fraction addition and subtraction problems based on the previous five-step explanation, then immediately skip to Chapter 4, and simplify the problems in that chapter using the five-step mental math explanation just described.

If you were a good arithmetic student, you learned the process and just repeated what the teacher told you; you could do all the mental steps in your head. Not all students are equal, though. The process to solve this simple problem is effective for many students when they solve the simple problems in this chapter, but some students never learn all the mental steps and have no written procedures to reference when they try to find the solution.

Let us now give a detailed explanation with respect to the first 4 steps listed above. This is a challenging section to write for two reasons:

1. The problem "$\frac{1}{2}+\frac{1}{4}$" is a simple problem, and many people can do this problem in their head or write a few steps to obtain the correct answer. When solving simple problems, the rules sometimes seem too complicated and unnecessary.

2. Most arithmetic teachers do not emphasize the rules explained in the next several paragraphs. Therefore, the rules will be new to many people who read this section but are necessary to solve challenging fraction arithmetic addition and subtraction problems and rational expressions (algebra fractions).

If we are required to add the two given fractions, we want to use the least common denominator (LCD) "4". The fraction "$\frac{1}{4}$" already has the denominator of "4" and there is no need to change the fraction "$\frac{1}{4}$" into an equivalent fraction. The fraction, "$\frac{1}{2}$" must be converted into an equivalent fraction with a denominator of "4". Everyone who understands the meaning of a least common denominator, should know the number "4" is the LCD for these two fractions. You <u>could</u> also use common denominators of "8" or "12" or "16", but the best denominator to use for these two fractions is "4" because it is the LCD, the smallest of the common denominators and thus requires less work to find the simplified answer.

When students begin to find equivalent fractions in elementary school, they must learn to multiply a fraction by 1. We know there are a million different fractions which equal 1, so how should we decide which fraction to multiply "$\frac{1}{2}$" by in this problem? The answer to this question is, to focus on the LCD "4" and the denominator of the fraction we want to convert into an equivalent fraction--in this case "2". In this problem, divide the common denominator "4" by the denominator "2" and get the quotient "2". (Math notation to illustrate the correct thought process: ("$LCD \div Denominator\ of\ interest$" or better yet. "$\frac{LCD}{Denominator\ of\ the\ fraction\ of\ interest}$"). The quotient "2", in this situation, indicates you must multiply the fraction "$\frac{1}{2}$" by the fraction "$\frac{2}{2}$" and get the equivalent fraction "$\frac{2}{4}$". My suggestion is to write the following steps to solve this problem:

"$4 \div 2 = 2$ or $\frac{4}{2} = 2 \therefore \frac{1}{2} \times 1 = \frac{1}{2} \times \frac{2}{2} = \frac{2}{4}$" then "$\frac{1}{2} + \frac{1}{4} = \frac{2}{4} + \frac{1}{4} = \frac{2+1}{4} = \frac{3}{4}$". (Note: The mathematical shorthand notation involving three dots written as a triangle "$\therefore$" indicated in the solution, simply stands for the word "therefore".) When we wrote the steps in the solution in this paragraph, we specifically indicated how we multiplied the fraction "$\frac{1}{2}$" by the number 1 when we wrote "$\frac{1}{2} \times 1$". In the next step, we wrote "$\frac{1}{2} \times \frac{2}{2}$". In these two steps, we indicated we multiplied the fraction "$\frac{1}{2}$" by the number 1 and then replaced the number 1 with the fraction "$\frac{2}{2}$" because we knew "$\frac{2}{2} = 1$". This is a simple application of "Young's Conversion Theorem".

We believe you should use graphs, charts, and/or number lines to illustrate the fraction "$\frac{1}{2}$" equals the fraction "$\frac{2}{4}$" and when adding the two fractions "$\frac{1}{2} + \frac{1}{4}$" the answer is "$\frac{3}{4}$". After you have repeatedly illustrated the concepts involved when converting fractions into equivalent fractions and adding and subtracting fractions, you must begin to emphasize the procedures required to solve simple fraction problems and then more challenging ones. If your students are going to be prepared for algebra and other advanced mathematics topics, the students must master the procedures, but the procedures will only make sense when the students understand the concepts.

Once the two fractions have identical denominators, it is easy to determine which fraction is smaller and which is larger. The two given fractions in this example are "$\frac{1}{2}$" and "$\frac{1}{4}$". The two equivalent fractions for the given fractions are "$\frac{2}{4}$" and "$\frac{1}{4}$". Since the denominators are identical, the key to which is larger or smaller is contained in the numerator. Therefore, the larger fraction is "$\frac{2}{4}$" because the numerator is "2", and the smaller fraction is "$\frac{1}{4}$" because the numerator is "1". This means the fraction "$\frac{1}{2}$" is greater than the fraction "$\frac{1}{4}$". Mathematically, this means "$\frac{2}{4} > \frac{1}{4} \therefore \frac{1}{2} > \frac{1}{4}$".

Here is the student work with all the steps indicated:

$\frac{1}{2} + \frac{1}{4}$ The students should quickly realize the LCD is "4".

$\mathbf{4 \div 2 = 2 \quad \therefore \quad \frac{1}{2} = \frac{1}{2} \times 1 = \frac{1}{2} \times \frac{2}{2} = \frac{2}{4}}$

$\frac{2}{4} + \frac{1}{4} = \frac{3}{4}$

You could also write the last step as one big fraction and then add the numbers in the numerator and get the final answer. $\frac{2}{4} + \frac{1}{4} = \frac{2+1}{4} = \frac{3}{4}$

If you study the solution to the previous problem with the steps just indicated, you should understand how to convert the fraction "$\frac{1}{2}$" into the equivalent fraction "$\frac{2}{4}$" using rules versus doing the arithmetic in your head. You should understand how to divide the LCM

"4" by the denominator of the fraction "$\frac{1}{2}$" to determine the quotient is "2". You then multiply the fraction "$\frac{1}{2}$" by the fraction "$\frac{2}{2}$" to convert the fraction "$\frac{1}{2}$" into the fraction "$\frac{2}{4}$". This step is bolded in the solution written above.

There is one major concept involved in the solution of the problem "$\frac{1}{2}+\frac{1}{4}$" which mathematicians solve in their head, and we did not explain how to find a least common denominator when it is difficult to determine by only using mental math. We will introduce the rules required to find LCDs in this chapter when we illustrate how to solve example problems "4", "8", and "13". Understanding the procedures required to find a least common denominator for more difficult denominators is essential when solving the problems in Chapter 4 and when solving fraction problems in algebra (rational expressions).

If you do not think you need to know the rules to find LCDs for all types of fractions, use your mental arithmetic fraction skills to add and subtract the following two example problems:

1. "$\frac{7}{12}-\frac{2}{15}+\frac{11}{20}-\frac{1}{30}$"
2. "$\frac{5}{8x^3y^2z}+\frac{5}{12x^2y^4z}$".

Problem 1 is a basic but challenging arithmetic problem, and the second problem is a rational algebra expression. The procedures required to find a least common denominator involving large denominators will take weeks or months for your students to master. If you want your students to master this process, introduce the procedures for 2-3 minutes at a time, 2-3 times per week, prior to working with fractions. The rules and procedures to find a least common denominator are identical to the rules and procedures required to find a least common multiple. Therefore, you can initially discuss how to find LCMs for a group of numbers without referring to fractions and least common denominators. Many students will not master the rules required to find LCDs and add and subtract challenging fractions in fifth grade. Mastering all the procedures for adding and subtracting fractions with challenging least common denominators will probably take most students at least two years.

If you continually introduce, review, and discuss fraction problems beyond the scope of the typical textbook problems, you can expect half of your sixth graders will be able to solve the problems discussed in Chapter 4. A higher goal is to make sure at least 90% of the students entering an algebra class in 7th or $8^{th,}$ or 9th grade can solve the problems discussed in Chapter 4 with a minimum of 80% accuracy. More importantly, over 90% of the students entering an algebra class should know the rules required to solve challenging arithmetic fraction problems and rational expressions (algebra fractions). You will never reach these levels of competency if you teach fractions for a month or two months during the school year prior to students entering algebra. Fractions need special attention. Once your students master all the concepts involving fractions, they will be prepared to work with other rational numbers and experience success beyond your imagination.

Once students understand fractions must have identical denominators to add, subtract, and compare the fractions, then you can begin to discuss the procedures required to add, subtract, and compare the remaining problems in this chapter and address the problems in Chapter 4. Prior to simplifying all the fraction problems in this chapter, it might be an interesting teaching point to ask the students to list the fractions from smallest to largest or vice versa. You can then ask them why they listed the fractions in the order they selected and listen carefully to their explanations. With time and practice, the students may develop a keen sense of numbers and fractions. This should be a major goal for all arithmetic teachers with all arithmetic topics.

2. Simplify/Add: $\frac{2}{5}+\frac{1}{5}$

If you already used the mini lessons previously discussed for 2-3 minutes, students should immediately determine the answer "$\frac{3}{5}$". It is easy to illustrate conceptually the answer is "$\frac{3}{5}$" using pie charts, graphs, or line segments. It is also easy to discuss the procedures to solve this problem by referring to concepts. We know the two fractions already have the same denominator, which can be referred to as the LCD, and all we need to do is add the numerators and keep the denominator in the final answer. Most teachers would simply tell the students to write the solution this way: "$\frac{2}{5}+\frac{1}{5}=\frac{3}{5}$" or in vertical form. Encourage students to write the two fractions as one fraction prior to adding the numerators. You might write the solution to the problem in the following manner "$\frac{2}{5}+\frac{1}{5}=\frac{2+1}{5}=\frac{3}{5}$". When you illustrate how to find the answer to this problem using the fraction "$\frac{2+1}{5}$" in the next to last step, it is easy to emphasize when you are adding or subtracting two or more fractions, you only add or subtract the numerators; the denominator does not change when you write the final answer.

You can also quickly determine the larger fraction is "$\frac{2}{5}$" because both fractions in the problem "$\frac{2}{5}$" and "$\frac{1}{5}$" have the denominator "5". The larger fraction has the bigger numerator: "2". You must realize the smaller numerator for the two fractions is "1".

Therefore, the smaller fraction is "$\frac{1}{5}$". Here is the mathematical notation used to indicate the fractions are written in increasing order (smallest to largest) is "$\frac{1}{5} < \frac{2}{5}$".

3. Simplify/Add: $\frac{2}{5} + \frac{1}{2}$

This fraction addition problem is on the same difficulty level as the first example problem: "$\frac{1}{2} + \frac{1}{4} = \frac{3}{4}$". There is one additional step: both fractions need to be converted into equivalent fractions with the same (LCD). Just like example problem 1 above, expect 90% of your 5th grade students to recognize both the numbers "5" and "2" divide evenly into the number "10" with no remainder. Teachers who teach 3rd and 4th graders must ensure these students mentally master multiplication and division facts. This is a topic every 3rd and 4th grade teacher should discuss 3, 4, or 5 times a week for 2-5 minutes. If students enter 5th grade and are not fluent with the multiplication and division facts, their success when working with fractions will be limited. *(FRT 7: Is knowledge of multiplication and division facts the major indicator of success when solving fraction problems?)* Some teachers feel there is no way 90% of 5th graders can determine the LCD for the two denominators "2" and "5" is 10 quickly in their head. Arithmetic is the one topic in elementary school where the failure of students to learn a specific topic in a previous grade creates a roadblock during the next year and future years on the students' ability to learn new topics. When you encounter this type of situation, you must develop methods to teach the procedures and concepts which were not learned last year and reteach the topics this year prior to broaching the topics required in your class. <u>This is the purpose of this textbook</u>. When history teachers pass a student from grade to grade with a weak understanding of history, this might not create a major problem the ensuing year, but when this occurs in arithmetic, it becomes a game breaker.

Here are the steps students are normally expected to write to solve this problem:

$$\frac{2}{5} + \frac{1}{2} = \frac{4}{10} + \frac{5}{10} = \frac{9}{10}$$

You may want your students to write the problem using the vertical form rather than using the horizontal format. That is fine. The solution would look like this:

$$\begin{array}{rcl} \frac{2}{5} & = & \frac{4}{10} \\ + \frac{1}{2} & = & \frac{5}{10} \\ \hline & & \frac{9}{10} \end{array}$$

Now, look at the two solutions written in either vertical or horizontal form, and we will explain how many teachers tell students to solve this type of problem.

Step 1: Find the least common denominator (LCD) in your head by figuring out what is the smallest number which is divisible by both "5" and "2". (The number you select must be a multiple of both numbers.) If you know your multiplication tables, you should recognize immediately the number "10" is the smallest number you want to work with. (Third and fourth-grade teachers need to start asking their students to determine the smallest number, which is a multiple of two or more numbers, so they are prepared to find LCDs using their mental math skills in 5th, 6th, 7th grade and beyond.)

> A Least Common Multiple is the smallest number which a group of numbers will all divide into perfectly. In the example fraction problem indicated above, the number "10" is the smallest number "5" and "2" will both divide into and there will be no remainder.

Step 2: When solving the problem in vertical form, tell the students to write the two fractions to the right of the given fractions and place the number "10" in the denominators of both fractions.

Step 3: Since the fractions are written next to each other, you should ask yourself the question, "How many times does the number, "5", *go into* the number "10"?" The answer to the question is "2". Now, you need to multiply the numerator in the first fraction "2" by the number "2" that you just determined to get the number "4", which is the numerator in the equivalent fraction to the right. You need to repeat the same process again for the fraction "$\frac{1}{2}$". You want the fraction to the right of the fraction "$\frac{1}{2}$" to have the denominator "10". If you want to find the correct numerator to place above "10", ask yourself the same question you did for the first fraction, but this time focus on the number "2" in the denominator. How many times does the number "2" *go into* the number "10"? The answer is "5", so multiply the number "1" in the second fraction by the number "5" to get the second numerator "5".

Step 4: Use the two fractions to the right with the same denominator and add the two numerators to get the final answer "$\frac{9}{10}$".

Realize, research indicates only approximately 50% of your students will be able to solve these types of problems two or three months after you teach this topic (Kloosterman et al., 2010; Siegler & Pyke et al., 2013). Continually reflect on the way you explain different concepts to students and ask, "How can I teach this or any concept differently so more students will 'learn and remember' the procedures to solve the problems?" Question the way you word your explanations. Reflect on how the present topic will be presented in higher-level arithmetic and math classes. One of the first changes you may have to make when illustrating how to solve these fraction problems is to write the problems in the horizontal format, which is the way algebra fraction problems (rational expressions) are written. This may seem like a small adjustment, but it helps students understand how to use "Young's Conversion Theorem" and how to multiply by the number 1 when you convert the fractions into equivalent fractions. Many of the fraction addition and subtraction problems in elementary arithmetic textbooks are written in the vertical form.

A second change you must make is to write every step in the illustration rather than just using words to explain the process. Look at the same problem when we solve it using "Young's Conversion Theorem" and think about how the notation illustrates all the arithmetic steps involved in the solution. At this time, assume the students can find the least common denominator in their head using their knowledge of the multiplication tables. Perhaps students struggle with fraction problems because they are not proficient with the multiplication and division tables involving the integers from 1-10? In the early elementary grades, emphasizing multiplication facts is a topic which must be emphasized by all teachers and mastered by all students. *(FRT 7: Is knowledge of multiplication and division facts the major indicator of success when solving fraction problems?)* If a skill is necessary, teachers must use a variety of methods to ensure the skill is mastered by all students (over 90% of all students) so when higher-level concepts are presented, students are not embarrassed and left behind. When students are first learning the multiplication and division tables, it is a great time to ask them to find the smallest number that two or more numbers will divide into. Start getting the students to answer questions which are a little more difficult than the typical textbook problems. The students might not initially call the answer the least common multiple, but they need to be able to answer these types of questions and develop a keen sense of numbers (number sense).

> We have no empirical evidence to justify the next comment, but many math researchers might agree, "The biggest indicator of success when working with fraction problems in elementary school is mental mastery of the multiplication and division facts for the numbers from 1-10".

Consider this problem: $\frac{2}{5}+\frac{1}{2}$

We know the LCD is "10" based on our knowledge of the multiplication tables.

$10 \div 5 = 2$ or $\frac{10}{5} = 2$ $\therefore$ $\frac{2}{5} \times 1 = \frac{2}{5} \times \frac{\mathbf{2}}{\mathbf{2}} = \frac{4}{10}$ (We know that "$\frac{2}{2} = 1$".)

$10 \div 2 = 5$ or $\frac{10}{2} = 5$ $\therefore$ $\frac{1}{2} \times 1 = \frac{1}{2} \times \frac{\mathbf{5}}{\mathbf{5}} = \frac{5}{10}$ (We know that "$\frac{5}{5} = 1$".)

We indicated the two basic division problems above using two different division notations, "$10 \div 5 = 2$ or $\frac{10}{5} = 2$ and $10 \div 2 = 5$ or $\frac{10}{2} = 5$". We prefer the fraction division notation for these types of problems, but we also want students to be comfortable working with both notations. The reason we prefer to write the division problems as fractions is because when students simplify rational expressions (algebra fractions), the fraction notation is much easier to work with.

In the previous two steps, we determined how many times the LCD "10" was divisible by the denominator, "5" in the first fraction, and we found the quotient when the LCD "10" was divided by the denominator "2" in the second fraction. We emphasized that we divided the LCD by the denominator of the fraction we were converting into an equivalent fraction. Some teachers use the phrase "*goes into*" rather than emphasizing the word "divide". It sounds like an unimportant change in the choice of words but using the word "divide" is more direct and removes any confusion some students might experience. Using the word "divide" also emphasizes the operation we illustrate in the math solution. We converted both fractions into equivalent fractions by multiplying by the number 1.

$$\frac{2}{5}+\frac{1}{2} = \frac{4}{10}+\frac{5}{10} = \frac{4+5}{10} = \frac{9}{10}$$

Notice, in the horizontal format we rewrote the two original fractions and then substituted the two equivalent fractions we previously determined. We also believe if you write fraction addition and subtraction problems as one big fraction it is easier to emphasize you need to add and subtract the numerators first, and the denominator does not change when we compute the final answer. Do you understand by looking at the notation, we divided the LCD "10" by both the denominators to get the quotients "2" and "5"? Do you understand by the notation we multiplied the two fractions by a special form of the number 1 to find the two equivalent fractions "$\frac{4}{10}$" and "$\frac{5}{10}$"? Finally, do you understand why we added the two numerators to get the final answer "$\frac{9}{10}$"?

There is one concern at this point in our illustrations we have not addressed. Somehow, we will have to introduce/explain how to multiply the fractions "$\frac{2}{5} \times \frac{2}{2}$" and "$\frac{1}{2} \times \frac{5}{5}$" prior to solving this problem. No matter which method we use to teach addition and subtraction with fractions, we will need to illustrate how to multiply a fraction by some number to find the required fraction with the correct LCD. When we use the mental math conversion method, we are simply teaching an arithmetic trick which works. When we teach the second method using "Young's Conversion Theorem", we are teaching a procedure based on sound mathematics principles. If we illustrate how to multiply by the number 1 using the special fractions equal to 1, when it is time to teach multiplying fractions, we can refer to these types of multiplication problems as examples. Isn't it ironic we have to teach students how to multiply two fractions prior to teaching students how to add two fractions with unlike denominators? It is amazing how many mathematics topics overlap! When we try to teach one simple topic, we end up discussing two or three additional concepts/procedures. Earlier, we discussed placing a point on a number line to indicate a fraction represents a number. This is an excellent time to review and have the student's plot (graph) points on a number line from <u>0</u> to <u>1</u> representing all three fractions: "$\frac{1}{2}, \frac{2}{5}$, and $\frac{9}{10}$". You will be amazed how challenging this task will be for some students. This would be a great topic to discuss and illustrate why the answer is, "$\frac{9}{10}$". (Booth, Newton, & Twiss-Garrity, 2014; Fazio, DeWolf et al., 2016; Fazio, Kennedy et al., 2016; Schneider et al., 2010; Stigler et al., 2010).

4. Simplify/Subtract: $\frac{3}{4} - \frac{1}{8}$ or

$$\begin{array}{r} \frac{3}{4} \\ -\ \frac{1}{8} \\ \hline \end{array}$$

Solution set up vertically:

$$\begin{array}{rcr} \frac{3}{4} & = & \frac{6}{8} \\ -\ \frac{1}{8} & = & -\ \frac{1}{8} \\ \hline & & \frac{5}{8} \end{array}$$

Many 5th graders immediately recognize the LCD is "8", but our learning goal is 90%. Many people will write the problem vertically, as indicated above, and determine the difference is "$\frac{5}{8}$". Encourage students to write the problem horizontally as indicated below.

$$\frac{3}{4} - \frac{1}{8} = \frac{6}{8} - \frac{1}{8} = \frac{6-1}{8} = \frac{5}{8}$$

(FRT 8: We believe writing fraction problems using the horizontal format versus the vertical format will lessen the confusion of the rules for adding, subtracting, multiplying, and dividing fractions. We also believe the horizontal fraction format will better prepare students to solve rational expression problems in algebra.)

We added the extra fraction/step "$\frac{6-1}{8}$" in the solution process because we want to emphasize it is acceptable to write the two fractions as one fraction. Now, subtract the numerators in the one fraction and keep the denominator. The steps indicated are simple, and they are the basic steps many people write when they are explaining how to solve this simple fraction subtraction problem. We are now going to review and discuss the following steps used to solve this simple problem:

Step 1: Determine that the LCD is equal to "8". Using mental math, we know the number "8" is a multiple of both "4" and "8" and "8" is the smallest number both "4" and "8" will divide into with no remainder; therefore, "8" is the LCD.

Step 2: In this step, we converted the first fraction "$\frac{3}{4}$" into the equivalent fraction "$\frac{6}{8}$" by using mental math. We knew to divide the LCD "8" by the denominator "4" and determine the answer is "2". We then multiplied the numerator "3" by the number "2" to get the new numerator "6" and use the LCD "8". The second fraction "$\frac{1}{8}$" already has the correct LCD, so there is no need to find an equivalent fraction with the LCD "8". We often assume mental math is so easy and everyone understands just by looking at the solution exactly how to compute each step, but probably less than 50% of seventh graders ever master this mental process (Heller et al., 1990).

Step 3: In this step, we may simply write the converted fraction "$\frac{6}{8}$" and subtract the fraction "$\frac{1}{8}$" using either horizontal or vertical notation. We prefer to write the two fractions horizontally as "$\frac{6}{8} - \frac{1}{8}$".

Step 4: Simply subtract the two numerators, keep the denominator, and write the final answer "$\frac{5}{8}$". Write the two fractions as one fraction to emphasize the rule, subtract the numerators, and the denominator remains the same: "$\frac{6-1}{8} = \frac{5}{8}$".

Up to this point, we used example problems where the least common denominator (LCD) was easy to compute by using mental math or where the fractions already had the same LCD. In this example problem "$\frac{3}{4} - \frac{1}{8}$", it should be simple to determine the LCD is the number "8" using mental math skills involving multiplication and division facts with the numbers from "$1 - 10$". The questions in Chapter 4 are not as simple as these examples, and most people will need to master the procedures to determine the LCDs, as they will later be required to work with rational expressions in an algebra class.

> Remember, a Least Common Denominator (LCD) is a special type of Least Common Multiple (LCM). An LCD concentrates on the denominators of two or more fractions.

In Chapter 4, we are going to use the rules/procedures to determine a least common multiple (LCM) or least common denominator (LCD) for difficult arithmetic fraction problems and for all rational expressions (algebra fractions). In this chapter, starting with this problem, "$\frac{3}{4} - \frac{1}{8}$", we will discuss the rules and procedures required to find any LCM or LCD. We will focus on how to find a least common multiple because an LCM can be determined from a group of numbers, and it is not necessary to work with fractions initially. We will list the multiplication tables for the number "4": "$1 \times 4 = 4,\ 2 \times 4 = 8,\ 3 \times 4 = 12,\ 4 \times 4 = 16,\ etc.$". Here is the list of multiples for the number "8": "$1 \times 8 = 8,\ 2 \times 8 = 16,\ 3 \times 8 = 24,\ 4 \times 8 = 32,\ etc.$". Notice, every number listed in the multiplication tables for the number "8" {8, 16, 24, 32, etc.} is divisible by both "8" and "4". Also, notice many numbers in the set of the multiplication tables for the number "4" {**4**, 8, **12**, 16, **20**, 24, **28**, 32, etc.} are not divisible by the number "8". This is a significant observation. Since we are trying to find a number that both "4" and "8" divide into perfectly without a remainder, we know there are many numbers in the *multiplication* tables for the number "4" which are not divisible by "8", such as (4, 12, 20, 28, etc.). Therefore, we must focus on the *multiplication* tables for the number "8". All the numbers in the list (set) of the *multiplication* tables for the number "8" {8, 16. 24, 32, 40, etc.} are divisible by both the numbers "4" and "8". This is the logic we use to explain why the word "*multiple*", is one of three words in the phrase, "least common *multiple*".

Now our objective is to find the <u>smallest</u> (<u>least</u>) number that is a multiple for both the number "4" and the number "8". If we look at the two sets of multiples for both "4" and "8" {4, **8**, 12, 16, 20. 24, 28, 32, etc.} and (**8**, 16, 24, 32, etc.}, we need to recognize the number "8" is the <u>smallest</u> number *common* to both sets of numbers. Thus, the number, "8" is the <u>least</u> *common* multiple (LCM) for the two numbers "4" and "8". The word "*common*" in both sets of numbers in this situation really means "contained in" both sets of numbers.

Most people refer to the LCD when they are working with fractions because it is more technically correct. Since we determined the LCM for the two numbers "4" and "8" is the number "8", the number "8" is the LCD for the two fractions "$\frac{3}{4}$" and "$\frac{1}{8}$".

Below are the rules to find the LCM or LCD for the two numbers or denominators "4" and "8" using factor trees. These rules are usually mentioned in most 5th and/or 6th-grade arithmetic textbooks and higher-level arithmetic textbooks, but teachers seldom emphasize them. The reason teachers do not usually encourage students to master the rules indicated in the arithmetic textbooks using factor trees is simple: the problems assigned for homework rarely require the students to use the rules because most problems in the textbooks are basic fraction addition and subtraction problems. We want students to be able to find the LCD for the problem "$\frac{3}{4} - \frac{1}{8}$" using their mental math skills, but we also want the students to know the rules to find the LCD for denominators involving numbers that are larger than 10 because many students, but far fewer than 90%, can find denominators involving two or three numbers smaller than 10 by using their mental math skills.

> Since an LCM and an LCD mean the same thing when working with fractions, the method to find an LCM and/or an LCD is the same.

The procedures/rules illustrated below to find the LCD for the fractions "$\frac{3}{4}$" and "$\frac{1}{8}$" are the same rules students must understand if they are going to work with fractions with larger denominators such as "$\frac{67}{88}+\frac{91}{96}-\frac{103}{112}$" or rational expressions such as "$\frac{3m}{(m+1)(m+2)}-\frac{5m}{m+1}$". We will simplify this arithmetic problem "$\frac{67}{88}+\frac{91}{96}-\frac{103}{112}$" in Chapter 4 and simplify the rational expression "$\frac{3m}{(m+1)(m+2)}-\frac{5m}{m+1}$" in Chapter 8. If you can solve simple fraction problems with your mental math skills and challenging fraction addition and subtraction problems using the rules indicated below, you will be prepared to simplify rational expressions in algebra. The rules required to simplify/solve algebraic expressions are the same rules which need to be mastered in arithmetic.

Step 1, to find the LCM/LCD for all types of numbers and expressions: use factor trees to find the LCM for a group of numbers or to find the LCD for two or more denominators. You were probably introduced to factor trees in 5th or 6th grade but never understood why they were mentioned at the beginning of the chapter involving fractions.

Factor Tree for the denominator	4	Factor Tree for the denominator	8
	2×2		2×4
			$2 \times 2 \times 2$

Step 2, when finding the LCM/LCD: after you have listed the *prime numbers* in the sets of factor trees for all the numbers or denominators, set up a multiplication problem with all the different *prime numbers.* In this problem, there is only one *prime number* indicated in both sets of factor trees. This means the only number you should list in your multiplication problem at this time is the *prime number* "2". Maybe the number "2" all by itself is the LCM/LCD. We know this is incorrect because we understand the concept of an LCM/LCD based on our knowledge of the multiplication tables for the two numbers/denominators "4" and "8". Here is the multiplication problem we have at this moment:

"2 $\times$ something maybe".

Step 3, when finding the LCM/LCD: refer to the sets of factor trees with the *prime numbers* indicated in step 1. At this point, you need to determine if the *prime number* "2" appears more than once in either set of factor trees. You must recognize the *prime number* "2" occurs twice in the set of factors for the denominator "4" and three times in the list of factors for the denominator "8". Now, you must use the number "2" three times in the multiplication problem we started to set up in step 2. The rule when referring to the sets of factor trees listed in step 1 is, "Use each prime number in the multiplication problem in step 2 the greatest number of times it appears in one of the sets of factors." This means the multiplication problem in step 2 above should now be written in the following form:

"$2 \times 2 \times 2$ or 2^3 or 8".

Expect students to be able to factor all composite numbers. (A *composite number* is a number which can be written as the product of two or more *prime numbers.*) The more you emphasize writing composite numbers using factor trees and prime numbers, the more all students will recognize perfect squares up to 144, perfect cubes up to 125, and $2^4, 2^5$, and 3^4. You want students to recognize immediately the composite number "8" is a perfect cube. You want students to identify quickly that 25 is a perfect square, and it can be written as " 5^2 or 5×5". You want students to recognize the three forms of the same number when you are working with perfect squares, perfect cubes, etc. After you introduce how to work with these types of problems 2-3 times per week for 2-3 minutes per session for a couple of weeks, then you may teach topics involving factor trees. Finally, when you review problems involving LCDs and factor trees (prime numbers), your students will understand perfect squares, perfect cubes, and $2^4, 2^5,$ and 3^4 can all be written in one of three forms: (Examples: $49 = 7 \times 7 = 7^2$; $3^3 = 27 = 3 \times 3 \times 3$, $2^4 = 16 = 2 \times 2 \times 2 \times 2$, etc.)

The three steps just illustrated to find the LCM/LCD "8" for this problem are the same rules required to find the LCM/LCD for more challenging problems encountered later in this textbook. We will explain the procedures again when we solve example problem number 8 below. Here are the steps most people usually write to solve the problem "$\frac{3}{4} - \frac{1}{8}$" using their knowledge of the multiplication tables and some mental math: "$\frac{3}{4} - \frac{1}{8} = \frac{6}{8} - \frac{1}{8} = \frac{5}{8}$". This is all the written work a good mathematician needs to write to solve this problem. Students who are considered average and low-achieving math students often have difficulty following the logic indicated in these steps. We suggest when you illustrate how to solve this problem, write the following steps.

> Since an LCM and an LCD mean the same thing when working with fractions, the method to find an LCM and/or an LCD is the same.

$\frac{3}{4} - \frac{1}{8}$ Off to the side, convert the fraction "$\frac{3}{4}$" into, "$\frac{6}{8}$" using "Young's Conversion Theorem". $8 \div 4 = 2$ $\therefore \frac{3}{4} \times 1 = \frac{3}{4} \times \frac{2}{2} = \frac{6}{8}$

Students must know "$\frac{2}{2} = 1$" and how to multiply the two fractions "$\frac{3}{4}$" and "$\frac{2}{2}$".

$$\therefore \frac{3}{4} - \frac{1}{8} = \frac{6}{8} - \frac{1}{8} = \frac{\mathbf{6-1}}{\mathbf{8}} = \frac{5}{8}$$

When 5th or 6th graders solve this problem, they must recognize the LCD is "8" based on their knowledge of the multiplication tables. It is important to mention to the students we multiply by the number 1 when we convert the fraction "$\frac{3}{4}$" into the fraction "$\frac{6}{8}$". Repeatedly emphasize that we need to multiply by a special form of the number 1, written in the form "$\frac{2}{2}$" in this problem, to finalize the conversion process. The fraction "$\frac{2}{2}$" was determined by dividing the LCD "8" by "4" to derive the quotient "2". There is no need to convert the fraction "$\frac{1}{8}$" into an equivalent fraction with the denominator "8" because it already is in the form we want. Once the fractions have the same LCD "8", the solution is found by focusing on the subtraction problem involving the numerators "6" and "1". We write the two fractions as one big fraction with the LCD written once, and the two numerators subtracted prior to finding the final answer "$\frac{5}{8}$". Some people will say this math explanation requires the students to write more steps. Agreed, but once the students get into the habit of writing the indicted steps, there is no guesswork. The steps are based on mathematics rules, and the students have a written blueprint to follow. Once the two fractions are written with the LCD "8", it is easy to determine the fraction "$\frac{6}{8} > \frac{1}{8}$". This means the fraction "$\frac{3}{4} > \frac{1}{8}$" because the two fractions "$\frac{3}{4}$ and $\frac{6}{8}$" are equal. Again, you may want the students to graph all three fractions "$\frac{3}{4}, \frac{1}{8}$, and $\frac{5}{8}$" on a number line with the numbers 0 and 1 indicated.

In the remaining example problems, we are going to shorten the written explanations. We will indicate the nuances which make some of these problems slightly different from a problem already discussed. Most importantly, we will discuss how to find the LCD using the rules and procedures just illustrated when we found the LCD "8" for the two fractions "$\frac{3}{4}$ and $\frac{6}{8}$". If you are going to understand how we solve/simplify the problems in Chapter 4, you must master the rules introduced in this chapter to find LCDs for challenging addition and subtraction fraction problems.

5. Simplify or (Add and Subtract): $\frac{5628}{7392} + \frac{7007}{7392} - \frac{7006}{7392}$

This problem looks like it is challenging, but our low-achieving 9th graders solved this type of problem without hesitation. You may use this type of problem to have students practice adding and subtracting large numbers. Plus, they need to understand when you add and subtract fractions, if the denominators are identical, you simply add and subtract the numerators and keep the denominator to find the final answer. This problem is not the type of problem for which you will use pictures or graphs to illustrate how to find the answer. The students simply must know the rules to find the solution. Here are the steps to illustrate the solution:

$$\frac{5628}{7392} + \frac{7007}{7392} - \frac{7006}{7392} = \frac{5628+7007-7006}{7392} = \frac{5629}{7392}$$

Off to the side:

$$\begin{array}{r} 5628 \\ \underline{+\,7007} \\ 12635 \\ \underline{-\,7006} \\ 5629 \end{array}$$

Will the solution "$\frac{5629}{7392}$" reduce? It will not. We will explain why when we illustrate how to use factor trees to reduce fractions later. Students must be able to work with factor trees and understand the Power of the Number One (1) when they reduce fractions with large numbers in both the numerator and the denominator. You may want to mention to students the two numbers "7007", and "7006" are close to each other. Some of your students should recognize the difference between "7007 and 7006" is "1" and they could then add the number "1" to the first numerator, "5628" to get the final numerator "5629". It is also easy to determine the fractions written from smallest to largest are "$\frac{5628}{7392} < \frac{7006}{7392} < \frac{7007}{7392}$". We only focused on the absolute value of each fraction and ignored the subtraction operation symbol (negative sign) when we compared the magnitudes of the three fractions. Hopefully, the students realize comparing the magnitudes of fractions is a simple process if they have the same denominators. In this problem, simply arrange the fractions from smallest to largest based on the numerators.

When students are first starting to work with fractions, it is important to require the students to graph fractions and mixed numbers on a number line to help them realize a fraction is a single point. Therefore, it is a single number and not two or three different numbers.

6. Simplify or (Add and Subtract): $\frac{3}{7} + \frac{2}{7} - \frac{1}{7}$

This problem and example problem 5. above are similar. The three fractions already have the same denominator LCD. Let us write the three fractions as one fraction. Notice, we incorporate slightly challenging problems with simple problems which the students should already know how to solve quickly in their heads.

$$\frac{3}{7} + \frac{2}{7} - \frac{1}{7} = \frac{3+2-1}{7} = \frac{4}{7}$$

This problem can be used to illustrate the concept of adding and subtracting three fractions using graphs, number line segments, and charts. It is also easy to illustrate the three

I just implied that the subtraction operation symbol and the negative sign are the same thing. They are not, one is a sign, and one is an operation symbol. There are only two signs in arithmetic and mathematics. One sign is a positive sign (+) and the other is a negative sign (−). Interesting!

fractions written without a positive or negative sign are already written from largest to smallest "$\frac{3}{7} > \frac{2}{7} > \frac{1}{7}$" or written from smallest to largest "$\frac{1}{7} < \frac{2}{7} < \frac{3}{7}$".

> Continually remind students, a fraction is written using two numbers and a division operation symbol, but the fraction represents one number. Encourage your students to plot points on a number line to indicate the magnitudes of the fractions illustrated in several example problems. The goal is to have students develop an understanding of fractions and develop a keen sense of numbers. When students begin to solve multiplication and division problems involving two fractions, graphing all three points on a number line with the starting point at "0", presents an opportunity to introduce surprising number sense facts. Example problems must include: **Two fractions both between "0" and "1"**, Two fractions both greater than "1", and *One fraction between "0" and "1" and One fraction greater than "1"*. Surprising results occur.

7. Simplify or (Add and Subtract): $\frac{3}{5} - \frac{1}{5} + \frac{3}{5} - \frac{4}{5} + \frac{0}{5}$

This problem and the previous example problem 6. are similar. We included the special fraction "$\frac{0}{5}$" on purpose. When students are first introduced to fractions in the early elementary grades, they are taught the number in the denominator is the number of parts in the whole thing. The number in the numerator is the number of parts they are working with. This means they have something which involves "5" parts, but they have none of them when they are working with the fraction "$\frac{0}{5}$". Therefore, they have "0" pieces, which means they have nothing. If you have nothing in arithmetic, then you have the number "0". The four remaining fractions already have the LCD "5". We will write all four fractions as one fraction to solve the problem.

$$\frac{3}{5} - \frac{1}{5} + \frac{3}{5} - \frac{4}{5} = \frac{3 - 1 + 3 - 4}{5} = \frac{1}{5}$$

If you have a class of 5th grade mathletes, you may want to encourage them to group the two positive numbers and the two negative numbers together and then subtract the two numbers "6 and 5". Illustrate little math mental tricks students could use to make a problem simpler. It is a way to help students develop number sense, which is a key indicator of success for all students when they enter higher-level math classes. You can easily illustrate the answer is "$\frac{1}{5}$" by using graphs or line segments. You can also indicate the first fraction "$\frac{3}{5}$" and the fourth fraction "$\frac{3}{5}$" are identical. If we ignore the positive and negative signs to the left of the fractions and just concentrate on the magnitude of each fraction, the five fractions listed from largest to smallest based on the values of the numerators are: "$\frac{4}{5} > \frac{3}{5} \geq \frac{3}{5} > \frac{1}{5} > \frac{0}{5}$".

FACT: When you multiply two fractions, both greater than zero and less than "1", the product is less than either fraction. Graphing the three points on a number line, will illustrate this number sense fact.

8. Simplify or (Add and Subtract): $\frac{11}{12} + \frac{5}{6} - \frac{3}{4}$

You should be able to determine the least common denominator for this problem is "12" and then convert the two fractions "$\frac{5}{6}$" and "$\frac{3}{4}$" into equivalent fractions with the LCD "12". Hopefully, you will have to write very few steps to determine the answer "1". Here are the steps you might write to quickly solve this problem.

$$\frac{11}{12} + \frac{5}{6} - \frac{3}{4} = \frac{11}{12} + \frac{10}{12} - \frac{9}{12} = \frac{12}{12} = 1$$

Here are the steps you did quickly in your head:

1. You determined the LCD was "12".

2. You converted the two fractions "$\frac{5}{6}$" and "$\frac{3}{4}$" into the equivalent fractions "$\frac{10}{12}$" and "$\frac{9}{12}$". You divided the denominator "6" into the LCD "12" to get the quotient "2" and then multiplied the numerator "5" by the quotient "2" to get the numerator "10" in the new equivalent fraction "$\frac{10}{12}$". You performed the same process with the fraction "$\frac{3}{4}$" by dividing the LCD "12" by the denominator "4" to get the quotient "3" then you multiplied the numerator "3" to get the

converted fraction "$\frac{9}{12}$". The process seems simple. However, if the process is so simple, then why do many students never master, "Learn and Remember", the indicated steps?

3. Once the three fractions all have the denominator "12", you then added and subtracted the numerators to get the answer "$\frac{12}{12}$".

4. Finally, you recognized the answer "$\frac{12}{12}$" is a type of division problem and the final answer is "1".

This process is simply amazing, and when you explain the step-by-step process, it should make sense to all students. Wishful thinking! Many students never master the process, which seems simple to good math students. Do not be discouraged. When you illustrate how to solve a problem, try to write every step, and justify each step with sound mathematics rules. Finding the LCD is a difficult procedure for students who have not mastered their multiplication/division facts. Elementary teachers must devote more time to help some students memorize the multiplication/division facts, the benefits will be amazing for those students who successfully master this skill. If we are going to teach adding, subtracting, reducing, multiplying, and dividing fractions to students who have not mastered the multiplication and division facts, our only chance of success is to review these tables constantly and use factor trees. *(FRT 7: Is knowledge of multiplication and division facts the major indicator of success when solving fraction problems?)* If factor trees are emphasized daily when working with fractions, low-achieving students who never mastered the multiplication and division facts will start to focus more on the factor tree process, and their knowledge of the multiplication and division facts will improve significantly. Initially, focus on reducing, multiplying, and dividing fractions using factor trees and on the simple types of addition and subtraction problems contained in this chapter.

The rules and procedures which work to find the LCD for all types of fraction denominators are listed in the following paragraphs. It will take your best students anywhere from one to twenty-four months to master the rules required to find challenging LCDs/LCMs using the rules. Begin to discuss the rules and procedures to find LCMs several months before you teach the chapter focusing on fractions. In this chapter, you should be able to determine all the LCDs in your head. When solving more challenging addition and subtraction problems in Chapter 4, you will have to use the rules introduced in this chapter to find the LCDs. The steps to find the least common denominator (LCD) using factor trees and the rules mentioned but not emphasized in arithmetic textbooks are illustrated next, for the denominators in the three fractions: "$\frac{11}{12}, \frac{5}{6}$, and $\frac{3}{4}$".

1. Write the set of prime factors for each denominator. Another way to say the previous statement is "write factor trees for each denominator." When you write factor trees for natural numbers, the factor trees turn out to be a multiplication problem using only prime numbers. The set of *prime factors* for the first denominator "12" is the product of the three prime factors "$2 \times 2 \times 3$". When you write the factors, which multiply to give you the denominator in the second fraction "6", you should list the factors as "2×3". You should also realize the *factor tree* for the denominator "4", is "2×2". (Note: The set of Prime Numbers is written like this – $\{2, 3, 5, 7, 11, 13, 17, 19, 23, 29, 31, 37, etc.\}$. We intentionally used braces as part of the notation. Do you remember why we used braces in our notation?)
2. Go back to the three different lists (sets) of prime factors for the three denominators: "$12 = \mathbf{2 \times 2 \times 3}$ and "$6 = \mathbf{2 \times 3}$" *and* "$4 = \mathbf{2 \times 2}$". When you look at the three lists of prime

factors (factor trees), you should immediately realize there are only two different prime numbers involved in this problem: "2" and "3". In this step, set up a multiplication problem with the two numbers to begin to find the LCD: The LCD might equal "2×3".

3. In this step, determine the LCD based on the numbers involved in the multiplication problems in step 2. In the three lists of prime numbers (factors) for "12, "6", and"4", ask, "Does the prime number "2" occur more than once in any one of the lists?" The *prime number* "2" occurs twice in the list of prime numbers used to multiply to get the denominator "12", once for the denominator "6" and twice for the denominator "4". The number "2" occurred a maximum of two times in the lists (sets) of prime factors. The same logic can be applied to the prime number "3". It does occur two times in the lists of prime numbers, but it only occurs once in each list. Therefore, the prime number "2" will occur twice in the product to find the LCD, and the prime number "3" will occur once in the product to find the LCD. This means the LCD is "$2 \times 2 \times 3$ or 12" when working with the three denominators "12", "6", and "4". We already knew that "12" was the LCD based on mental multiplication, but we need to understand the rules which will be necessary to solve the problems in Chapter 4 such as "$\frac{7}{12} - \frac{2}{15} + \frac{11}{20} - \frac{1}{30}$". We just determined the LCD for our problem is "12". Now, we need to use the LCD "12" and write all the steps we want the students to write to find the answer. We already know the first fraction has the denominator "12" and we do not have to convert the first fraction into an equivalent fraction. We must convert the second and third fractions into equivalent fractions with the LCD "12". When you convert the second fraction into an equivalent fraction, divide the LCD "12" by the denominator "6" to get the quotient "2". Use the quotient "2" to help determine the special form of the number <u>1</u> to multiply the fraction "$\frac{5}{6}$", to find the equivalent fraction with the LCD, "12".

$$\frac{\text{LCD}}{\text{Denomiator Second Fraction}} = \frac{12}{6} = 2 \quad \therefore \ \frac{2}{2} = 1 \ \text{ thus } \frac{5}{6} = \frac{5}{6} \times 1 = \frac{5}{6} \times \frac{2}{2} = \frac{10}{12}$$

The reason, we divided the LCD "12" by the denominator "6" is evident when we write all the math steps and multiply the given fraction "$\frac{5}{6}$" by the fraction "$\frac{2}{2}$" to find the equivalent fraction "$\frac{10}{12}$". If we focus on the illustration above where we converted "$\frac{5}{6}$" into "$\frac{10}{12}$", we realize we end up with the denominator "12" in the final fraction. We needed to determine a number by which to multiply the denominator "6" in the first fraction in order to end up with the LCD, "12". The best way to derive what number to multiply "6" by to get "12" is to divide "12" by "6". If we are going to multiply the denominator "6" by the quotient "2", we must also multiply the numerator "5" by the same number "2". The division process and the multiplication process should be repeatedly illustrated. Assume by this time, the students know the fraction $\frac{2}{2} = 1$ and when you multiply by 1 you get an equivalent answer. The students must also know how to multiply the two fractions "$\frac{5}{6}$" and "$\frac{2}{2}$". If students are taught this way, they will immediately realize the rules for adding/subtracting fractions and multiplying fractions are different, and they will practice the rules for both situations regularly when they solve these problems.

Let us repeat the process from the last paragraph with the third fraction and the denominator "4". We will divide the LCD "12" by the denominator "4" and get the quotient "3". Using our understanding of the number 1, we know we want to multiply the fraction "$\frac{3}{4}$" by the fraction, "$\frac{3}{3}$".

$$\frac{LCD}{Denominator\ Third\ Fraction} = 12 \div 4 = 3 \qquad \therefore \qquad \frac{3}{4} = \frac{3}{4} \times 1 = \frac{3}{4} \times \frac{3}{3} = \frac{9}{12}$$

We used "Young's Conversion Theorem" in each of the conversion problems just indicated when we multiplied by the number 1 written in a special form. Once the students determine the LCD is "12", the steps indicated below are the steps we expect all students to indicate in the solution when they simplify the problem. It does not matter if the students know how to solve the problem using mental math or whether they write all the steps. We want all the students to get used to writing all the indicated steps so they will be confident when they are required to solve arithmetic problems like the ones illustrated in Chapter 4. We assume you already know the LCD is "12" in this problem. Since the first fraction already has the LCD "12" in the denominator there is no need to convert the fraction, "$\frac{11}{12}$", into an equivalent fraction.

$$\frac{11}{12}+\frac{5}{6}-\frac{3}{4}$$

Off to the side: $\frac{12}{6}=2 \therefore \frac{5}{6}\times 1=\frac{5}{6}\times\frac{2}{2}=\frac{10}{12}$

$12\div 4=3 \therefore \frac{3}{4}\times 1=\frac{3}{4}\times\frac{3}{3}=\frac{9}{12}$

$$\frac{11}{12}+\frac{10}{12}-\frac{9}{12}=\frac{11+10-9}{12}=\frac{12}{12}=1$$

Remember, there are three ways to write a division problem in arithmetic. Continually illustrate to your students how to transform a division problem from one form into the other two forms.

In the notation off to the side when converting the fraction "$\frac{5}{6}$" into the equivalent fraction "$\frac{10}{12}$", we multiplied by the special from of the number 1, "$\frac{2}{2}$". To determine the special form of the number 1 to multiply by, we divided the LCD "12" by the denominator "6", to get the quotient "2". Notice, we used fraction notation "$\frac{12}{6}$" to indicate we divided "12" by "6". When we converted the fraction "$\frac{3}{4}$" into the fraction "$\frac{9}{12}$", we multiplied by the fraction "$\frac{3}{3}$", which equals 1. When we wrote the division problem "12" divided by "4", we used the division operation symbol "÷" to indicate we were dividing "12 ÷ 4". We want students to realize they need to divide the LCD by the respective denominator to help determine the special form of the number 1 to multiply the respective fraction. In Chapter 4, the denominators are much larger numbers; therefore, we will use the division box when we divide the LCD by the denominator. When working with rational expressions, encourage the students to write the division problem as a fraction. Once the fractions have the same denominator, we can list the fractions from smallest to largest or vice versa based on the magnitude of the numerators, "$\frac{9}{12} < \frac{10}{12} < \frac{11}{12}$" ∴ "$\frac{3}{4} \leq \frac{5}{6} \leq \frac{11}{12}$".

9. Simplify or (Add and Subtract): $\frac{65}{101} - \frac{37}{101} - \frac{0}{101} + \mid - \frac{22}{101} \mid$

If your students have been exposed to absolute values, they should be able to change the given problem into a simple addition and subtraction problem without the absolute value notation. Interweave (interleave) different concepts which the students already learned into the topics for the present week (Patel, Liu, & Koedinger, 2017; Richland, Bjork, Finley, & Linn, 2005).

$$\frac{65}{101} - \frac{37}{101} - \frac{0}{101} + \frac{22}{101}$$

Refer to previous examples in this chapter to help you determine the solution. The four fractions which are either added or subtracted already have the same denominator, so the LCD is "101". There are two facts you should identify quickly when simplifying this problem. First, once we have an LCD for two or more fractions we are adding and subtracting, we may write this fraction problem as one big fraction with the LCD written once. Second, the fraction "$\frac{0}{101}$" equals "0". We will write the four fractions as one big addition and subtraction fraction problem and include the number "0" from the third fraction in the numerator. It will not make any difference in the final answer. We can also use this type of problem when we want to review adding and subtracting large whole numbers or adding and subtracting decimals. If we focus on the numerators after we set up one fraction, we must add or subtract the following whole numbers: 65, 37, 0, and 22. Note the number "0" is a whole number, but it is not a natural number. *(FRT 9: We believe if students solve addition, subtraction, multiplication, and division problems as one big fraction prior to the final computations then much of the confusion with respect to different fraction rules will be eliminated.)*

$$\frac{65}{101} - \frac{37}{101} - \frac{0}{101} + \frac{22}{101} = \frac{65 - 37 - 0 + 22}{101} = \frac{50}{101}$$

This is a problem in which students should recognize the rules to add and subtract fractions with identical denominators are easy to solve. This problem is not one you would normally illustrate using graphs, charts, and line segments, but you could use computer graphics to illustrate the solution. This time the students must use the correct rules and procedures when adding and subtracting fractions with the same denominator. Note, this fraction will not reduce. Again, you should quickly be able to arrange the four fractions from largest to smallest based on the numerators because the denominators are identical. The fractions arranged from largest to smallest if we use the absolute value of each fraction is: "$\frac{65}{101} > \frac{37}{101} > \frac{22}{101} > \frac{0}{101}$". A great investigative learning exercise which you may want to try is, tell your students to plot the points on a number line for the four given fractions when they are given in the original order for this addition and subtraction problem.

10. Simplify or (Add and Subtract): $\frac{1376}{1003} + \frac{2661}{1003} - \frac{22}{1003} - \frac{1006}{1003}$

This problem can be solved the same way as example problem 9. We are going to write one fraction and focus on adding and subtracting the four numerators once we have written one big fraction.

> We frequently encourage teachers to require students to graph fractions on a number line, especially when the students are adding, subtracting, multiplying, and dividing two fractions.

$$\frac{1376}{1003} + \frac{2661}{1003} - \frac{22}{1003} - \frac{1006}{1003} = \frac{1376 + 2661 - 22 - 1006}{1003} = \frac{3009}{1003} = 3$$

> Graphing the points on a number line for these fractions will probably be a challenge for many students, but a discussion may prove beneficial for all students. In previous problems when we arranged the fractions from smallest to largest or vice-versa, we only considered the absolute values of all the fractions. We suggest you do the same thing when you graph the points on a number line for these four fractions.

We want the students to recognize all four fractions have the LCD "1003" and write the four fractions as one big fraction then add and subtract the numerators. In the final step, we want the students to realize a fraction is a type of division problem and "3009" is divisible by "1003". We should easily be able to write the fractions from smallest to largest based on the numerators because all the denominators are identical. Again, it is not easy to illustrate the correctness of the answers to example problems 5, 9, and 10 by using graphs, charts, or number line segments. The students must understand the concept of adding and subtracting the numerators of fractions when the denominators are identical based on earlier example problems and illustrations discussed continually since the students were introduced to fraction addition and subtraction problems in previous grades. The students are now forced to use the rules to add and subtract fractions and not rely on pictures to reinforce the answer. We still could use computer graphics to illustrate the answer, but eventually, the rules must be mastered.

> Graph on a number line the three fractions contained in these two example problems and compare the answer with the initial two fractions: "$\frac{3}{4} \times \frac{1}{2} = \frac{3 \times 1}{4 \times 2} = \frac{3}{8}$" and "$\frac{3}{4} \div \frac{1}{2} = \frac{3}{4} \times \frac{2}{1} = \frac{3 \times 2}{4 \times 1} = \frac{6}{4} = \frac{3}{2} = 1\frac{1}{2}$".
> Facts: When you multiply two fractions which are both between "0" and "1" the answer, product is smaller than either of the two fractions. When you divide two fractions which are both between "0" and "1", the answer, quotient, will always be greater than the first fraction in the problem.

11. Simplify/Add: $5\frac{5}{8} + (\frac{1}{2})^2$

This problem is probably more appropriate for 6th graders. Students must recognize the first objective when simplifying this problem is to work with the exponent and simplify the expression "$(\frac{1}{2})^2$" as follows: "$(\frac{1}{2})^2 = \frac{1}{2} \times \frac{1}{2} = \frac{1 \times 1}{2 \times 2} = \frac{1}{4}$" (Patel et al., 2017; Richland et al., 2005). (Notice, when we multiplied "$\frac{1}{2} \times \frac{1}{2}$" in the illustration, we used <u>one big fraction</u> "$\frac{1 \times 1}{2 \times 2}$" to compute the product, "$\frac{1}{4}$".)

Do not be afraid to include previously learned mathematics concepts into problems to help the students review procedures they may have forgotten. This technique is referred to as **interleaving.**

Now simplify this problem: $5\frac{5}{8} + \frac{1}{4}$

Convert the mixed number into an improper fraction for two reasons. The first reason is the normal rule when multiplying and dividing mixed numbers is to convert mixed numbers into improper fractions. For average and low achieving arithmetic students, the more standardized the procedures when working with fractions, the less confusing the problems become. High-achieving mathematics students should master converting mixed numbers into improper fractions and then adding and subtracting the fractions. They should also be able to add the fractions first and then add the whole numbers when working with mixed numbers.

High-achieving students should also be able to subtract mixed numbers by concentrating on the fractions first and then focusing on the whole numbers. This means the high achieving students should understand the borrowing process when the first/top number (minuend) in a subtraction problem, is a mixed number and the fraction with the top/first number (minuend), is a smaller fraction than the fraction in the bottom number (subtrahend).

The second reason we encourage students to convert mixed numbers into improper fractions is, when students encounter rational expressions in algebra, they will never encounter a problem written in this format: "$x\frac{3}{x}$" or "$2y\frac{3}{2}$". High achieving and motivated math students should be exposed to as many procedures as possible to allow them to develop several methods to solve problems.

You will probably have to explain how to convert the fraction "$5\frac{5}{8}$" into an improper fraction. The <u>trick</u> is simple, "Multiply the denominator "8" times the whole number "5" and add the numerator "5" to find the new numerator "45", then write the equivalent improper fraction "$\frac{45}{8}$" with the denominator of the original fraction." Notice, we used the word <u>trick</u> in our explanation. Do you realize the <u>trick</u> works because of the "Power of the Number One (1)? The mixed number could be written like this: "$1+1+1+1+1+\frac{5}{8}$". Next, rewrite the problem using this form: "$\frac{8}{8}+\frac{8}{8}+\frac{8}{8}+\frac{8}{8}+\frac{8}{8}+\frac{5}{8}=\frac{8+8+8+8+8+5}{8}=\frac{45}{8}$". This process can be illustrated to be true using graphs, line segments, and/or computer graphics.

> It is amazing when we try to explain why an arithmetic trick works, we frequently find the verbal explanation seems more complicated than we expected. Maybe verbalizing how we use a trick to solve a problem is not as simple as we expect the explanation to be. Do you think students who struggle with arithmetic really understand your verbal directions? We believe illustrating procedures and solutions using proven mathematics principles is the only way to help all students' master procedures to solve all types of arithmetic and mathematics problems.

The common denominator for the given problem "$5\frac{5}{8}+\frac{1}{4}$" is "8". Once we convert the mixed number "$5\frac{5}{8}$" into an improper fraction equivalent to "$5\frac{5}{8}$" the improper fraction equals "$\frac{45}{8}$". We can now write the problem as "$\frac{45}{8}+\frac{1}{4}$". If you know the procedures, you likely convert the fraction "$\frac{1}{4}$", into the fraction "$\frac{2}{8}$" in your head. You might skip some of the steps indicated and simply add the two fractions and then concentrate on the whole number "5".

We decided to use the improper fraction "$\frac{45}{8}$" rather than focus on the two simple fractions and work with the number "5".

$$5\frac{5}{8}+\frac{1}{4} = \frac{45}{8}+\frac{1}{4} = \frac{45}{8}+\frac{2}{8} = \frac{45+2}{8} = \frac{47}{8} = 5\frac{7}{8}$$

Ask students to write the steps indicating how they converted the fraction "$\frac{1}{4}$" into the fraction "$\frac{2}{8}$". Encourage them to write this extra step to the side of the main solution. The step may seem unnecessary, but it will be helpful when the problems become more difficult. That is why we insist on the conversion step using "Young's Conversion Theorem" and multiply by a special form of the number 1 to the right side of the problem. Here are the steps we want students to write when they solve this problem. *(FRT 6: The more students write the steps to solve problems, the better their long-term memory will be.)*

Convert "$\frac{1}{4}$" into "$\frac{2}{8}$" off to the side.

$5\frac{5}{8}+\frac{1}{4} = \frac{45}{8}+\frac{1}{4} = \frac{45}{8}+\frac{2}{8} = \frac{45+2}{8} = \frac{47}{8} = 5\frac{7}{8}$ $\qquad$ $\frac{8}{4} = 2 \quad \frac{1}{4}\times 1 = \frac{1}{4}\times\frac{2}{2} = \frac{2}{8} \;\therefore\; \frac{1}{4} = \frac{2}{8}$

We can still illustrate the answer using graphs, number line segments, or computer graphics. We will also get a chance to emphasize a fraction is a division problem when we convert the fraction "$\frac{47}{8}$" into the mixed number, "$5\frac{7}{8}$".

Students struggle to list the numbers from smallest to largest when some of the given numbers are mixed numbers, and some are simple fractions. Some students concentrate so much on the fractions in the problem they overlook the obvious. The mixed number is larger than the simple fraction. If the mixed number is converted to an improper fraction, then "$\frac{45}{8}$" is obviously greater than "$\frac{2}{8}$", or "$\frac{45}{8} > \frac{2}{8}$", or "$5\frac{5}{8} > \frac{1}{4}$". Never assume all the students understand the obvious. Therefore, constantly illustrate and emphasize the obvious so every student will be successful in class. We could also illustrate "$5\frac{5}{8} > \frac{1}{2} > \frac{1}{4}$" if we wanted to go back to the numbers given initially in this problem. This is a great problem to illustrate how to derive the answer using a number line with the number "0" indicated to the left, and the number "10" indicated to the right (Fazio, DeWolf et al., 2016; Fazio, Kennedy et al., 2016; Booth et al., 2014; Booth et al., 2008).

This problem is an excellent problem to illustrate that it is not necessary to convert the mixed number into an improper fraction first. This problem is simple to solve if you simply add the two fractions first "$5\frac{5}{8} + \frac{2}{8}$" after the fraction, "$\frac{1}{4}$" is converted into the fraction "$\frac{2}{8}$". It is easy to determine the answer is "$5\frac{7}{8}$". Keep in mind, not all mixed number addition and subtraction problems are as simple as this example.

> Amazing Facts: When you multiply two fractions which are both between "0" and "1", the product is smaller than both fractions, but using the same two fractions in a division problem the quotient is greater than the first fraction.

12. Simplify/Subtract: $7\frac{1}{4} - 2\frac{5}{8}$

We would solve this problem using the same procedures just indicated to solve the previous problem. Here are the steps we encouraged students to write to solve this problem.

Initially convert "$7\frac{1}{4}$" into the improper fraction "$\frac{29}{4}$".

Convert "$7\frac{1}{4}$" into "$\frac{58}{8}$" off to the side.

$$7\frac{1}{4} - 2\frac{5}{8} = \frac{29}{4} - \frac{21}{8} = \frac{58}{8} - \frac{21}{8} = \frac{58-21}{8} = \frac{37}{8} = \mathbf{4\frac{5}{8}} \qquad \frac{8}{4} = 2 \quad \frac{29}{4} \times 1 = \frac{29}{4} \times \frac{2}{2} = \frac{58}{8} \therefore \frac{29}{4} = \frac{58}{8}$$

If you tried to solve this problem without converting the mixed number "$7\frac{1}{4}$" into the improper fraction "$\frac{29}{4}$", you encountered a situation where you had to borrow from the mixed number "$7\frac{1}{4}$" and change it into the equivalent mixed number "$6\frac{5}{4}$", which is a concept many students struggle with.

After students become confident converting mixed numbers into improper fractions and then subtracting the two numbers, you can explain how to borrow 1 from the whole number to the left of the fraction and add a special form of the number 1 to the fraction with the mixed number. Both the whole number and the fraction change when this conversion rule is implemented. For many average and low-achieving students this is a mental trick which makes little or no sense. This is a procedure they will never encounter in algebra, and this is an arithmetic concept which does not need to be discussed in arithmetic if the original mixed number is converted into an improper fraction. The students still need to realize a fraction is a type of division problem when they convert the improper fraction "$\frac{37}{8}$" into the mixed number "$4\frac{5}{8}$". You can determine which of the two mixed numbers is larger based on the whole numbers "7" and "2" indicated in the two given mixed numbers. You may discuss with your class how to determine the larger number by looking at the two improper fractions "$\frac{58}{8}$" and "$\frac{21}{8}$", but that is up to you as the teacher. This is a great problem to illustrate that the three mixed numbers, the two given numbers and the answer all represent three separate single numbers on a number line. When concentrating on the mixed number "$7\frac{1}{4}$" you should always want your average math students and mathletes to work with the procedures to borrow 1 from the whole number, then add the special form of the number 1 to the fraction located on the right side of the whole number. You must realize this is a difficult concept for many students. Illustration: "$7\frac{1}{4} = 7 + \frac{1}{4} = 6 + 1 + \frac{1}{4} = 6 + \frac{4}{4} + \frac{1}{4} = 6\frac{5}{4}$".

13. Simplify or (Add and Subtract): $\frac{5}{8} + 2 + 1\frac{1}{2} - 2\frac{3}{4} - \frac{1}{6}$

If you are proficient with fraction addition and subtraction procedures, you may only write the following steps when you solve this problem. We converted all the mixed numbers to improper fractions, but you might prefer to work with the mixed numbers. One great thing about arithmetic and mathematics is - several methods can be used to solve the same problem.

$$\frac{5}{8} + 2 + 1\frac{1}{2} - 2\frac{3}{4} - \frac{1}{6} = \frac{5}{8} + \frac{2}{1} + \frac{3}{2} - \frac{11}{4} - \frac{1}{6} = \frac{15}{24} + \frac{48}{24} + \frac{36}{24} - \frac{66}{24} - \frac{4}{24} = \frac{15 + 48 + 36 - 66 - 4}{24} =$$

$$\frac{29}{24} = 1\frac{5}{24}$$

How many 5th and 6th grade students can find the correct answer for the problem just indicated? Probably less than 50%, since most 5th and 6th grade students are never challenged in their textbooks to solve this type of problem (Braithwaite & Tian et al., 2018). Imagine how easy textbook problems and standardized test questions will be if your students can solve this type of problem. The first step is to write all terms as fractions:

$$\text{“}\frac{5}{8} + \frac{2}{1} + \frac{3}{2} - \frac{11}{4} - \frac{1}{6}\text{”}.$$

The next step is to rewrite all five fractions with the LCD. The LCD is "24" based on our knowledge of the multiplication and division tables, but we want to compute the LCD "24" by using the procedures necessary to simplify more difficult arithmetic fraction problems. This involves looking at all the denominators and setting up a list of the prime factors for each denominator. The prime factors for each denominator are listed below. We did not list any prime numbers under the denominator 1 below because there is no way to write the number 1 using prime factors. The number 1 is a special number with unique properties, but 1 is not a prime number, and 1 is not a composite number. If we are required to find the LCD, we need to work with the prime numbers indicated in the denominators. Remember, the second step when finding an LCD is to write a multiplication problem involving all the prime factors. This may be the LCD, or it might not be the LCD, "2 × 3". The only two numbers indicated when we write the factor trees for the denominators, "8, 1, 4, 6, and 2" are "2" and "3" (refer to the factor trees below). Do you realize why we use the two phrases "prime factors" and "factor trees" when solving these problems? The real question we are focusing on is, "Why do we use the word "factor" in each phrase?" Remember, the word "factor" means you have a term, number, or expression which is part of a multiplication problem.

The third step when finding an LCD is to go back to all the sets (lists) of prime numbers and determine if any of the numbers occurred more than once in the lists of prime factors. If a number does appear more than once in a list of prime factors, always refer to the list where the prime number appears the most often and always use the prime number based on the most times it appeared in any one list (set). The prime number "2" appears in a couple of lists, but it occurs the most times in the list of prime factors for the denominator "8". The prime number "2" appears three times in the list of prime factors for "8". The rule states, when we find the LCD, multiply by the prime number "2" three times. The prime number "3" only appeared once in the list of prime factors for the number "6". This means the number "3" should only appear once in the list of factors to multiply to get the LCD.

8	1	4	6	2
$\{2 \; X \; 2 \; X \; 2\}$		$\{2 \; X \; 2\}$	$\{2 \; X \; 3\}$	$\{2\}$

The LCD might equal "2 X 3". We multiplied all the different prime numbers indicated in the four sets of factor trees. This is not the LCD.

The LCD is "$2 \times 2 \times 2 \times 3 = 2^3 \times 3 = 24$". We now need to convert all the fractions into equivalent fractions with the LCD "24". Divide the LCD "24" by each denominator, then multiply by the special form of the number 1 determined when we find the different quotients:

Convert the fraction, "$\frac{5}{8}$". $\frac{24}{8} = 3$ $\therefore \frac{5}{8} = \frac{5}{8} \times 1 = \frac{5}{8} \times \frac{\mathbf{3}}{\mathbf{3}} = \frac{5 \times 3}{8 \times 3} = \frac{15}{24}$

Convert the fraction, "$\frac{2}{1}$". $\frac{24}{1} = 24$ $\therefore \frac{2}{1} = \frac{2}{1} \times 1 = \frac{2}{1} \times \frac{\mathbf{24}}{\mathbf{24}} = \frac{2 \times 24}{1 \times 24} = \frac{48}{24}$

Convert the fraction, "$\frac{3}{2}$". $24 \div 2 = 12$ $\therefore \frac{3}{2} = \frac{3}{2} \times 1 = \frac{3}{2} \times \frac{\mathbf{12}}{\mathbf{12}} = \frac{3 \times 12}{2 \times 12} = \frac{36}{24}$

Convert the fraction, "$\frac{11}{4}$". $\frac{24}{4} = 6$ $\therefore \frac{11}{4} = \frac{11}{4} \times 1 = \frac{11}{4} \times \frac{\mathbf{6}}{\mathbf{6}} = \frac{11 \times 6}{4 \times 6} = \frac{66}{24}$

Convert the fraction, "$\frac{1}{6}$". $24 \div 6 = 4$ $\therefore \frac{1}{6} = \frac{1}{6} \times 1 = \frac{1}{6} \times \frac{\mathbf{4}}{\mathbf{4}} = \frac{1 \times 4}{6 \times 4} = \frac{4}{24}$

(Comment: We wrote each of the multiplication problems in the next to last steps above as one big fraction multiplication problems. We like to use the one big fraction illustration for adding, subtracting, reducing, and multiplying fractions.)

We will rewrite the original problem, write the problem using proper and improper fractions, and then write the problem with the equivalent fractions substituted for the original fractions. In the next to last step, we write one big fraction with the LCD "24" and then add and subtract the numbers in the numerator to find the numerator of the answer, which is an improper fraction:

$$\frac{5}{8} + 2 + 1\frac{1}{2} - 2\frac{3}{4} - \frac{1}{6} = \frac{5}{8} + \frac{2}{1} + \frac{3}{2} - \frac{11}{4} - \frac{1}{6} = \frac{15}{24} + \frac{48}{24} + \frac{36}{24} - \frac{66}{24} - \frac{4}{24} = \frac{15 + 48 + 36 - 66 - 4}{24} =$$

$$\frac{29}{24} = 1\frac{5}{24}$$

This is a challenging 5th or 6th-grade problem because it covers a lot of different topics involving fraction addition and subtraction. Each step is relatively easy, but if your students begin to try to solve these types of problems, eventually, they will learn all the rules and they will become proficient with simple textbook and standardized test questions.

> Interleaving (interweaving) concepts is a great teaching tool, which helps students focus on several different concepts in one problem (Patel et al., 2017; Richland et al., 2005).

A proficient arithmetic/math student only needs to write a few steps to correctly find the solution to this problem: "$\frac{5}{8} + 2 + 1\frac{1}{2} - 2\frac{3}{4} - \frac{1}{6}$". Look back to the steps we indicated when we first solved this problem. Notice the steps indicated when we listed only the basic steps in the beginning and when we illustrated all the steps on the previous two pages. The point of emphasis is, good students have learned the tricks well, but even good students sometimes do not realize all the steps they are not indicating. When all the steps are illustrated, less proficient students can refer to the example problems, and with practice, they will also understand exactly why all the little steps fit together to simplify the problem. Not only do the students who sometimes struggle with arithmetic become more proficient, but highly proficient mathematics students really understand why basic mental tricks work if they write a few extra steps to solve these problems. The magnitudes of the fractions listed from smallest to largest based on the numerators with the LCD "24" are "$\frac{4}{24} < \frac{15}{24} < \frac{36}{24} < \frac{48}{24} < \frac{66}{24}$". When we refer to the original five numbers, the numbers listed from smallest to largest are "$\frac{1}{6} < \frac{5}{8} < 1\frac{1}{2} < 2 < 2\frac{3}{4}$".

> 14. Simplify or (Add and Subtract): $\frac{3}{5} - \frac{4}{5} + \frac{0}{99} - \frac{1}{5} + \frac{3}{5}$

This problem is almost the same arithmetic problem as number 3. There are a few little curves which make this problem slightly different from example problem 3, but in the end, it is the same problem. The first thing the students must realize is the fraction "$\frac{0}{99}$" becomes the whole number "0" and the fraction can be completely ignored since this is an addition/subtraction problem. The problem really becomes: "$\frac{3}{5} - \frac{4}{5} - \frac{1}{5} + \frac{3}{5}$".

There are a few teaching points you may want to discuss with respect to this problem and problem 3. You can discuss whether rearranging the terms is acceptable when adding and subtracting numbers. You could also illustrate how to find the answer using line segments. This means after locating the point where the fraction "$\frac{3}{5}$" is placed, you move to the left because you would be subtracting the fraction "$\frac{4}{5}$" and end up to the left of the number 0. This might create an interesting discussion. Then move to the left again because you are supposed to subtract the fraction "$\frac{1}{5}$". Next, you would add the fraction "$\frac{3}{5}$" and move the point to the right to end up "$\frac{1}{5}$" to the right of 0. Given enough time, explain all the options, but if you just want the students to get the correct answer, rearrange the fractions like this using the communitive and associative properties for addition and find the solution:

"$\frac{3}{5} - \frac{4}{5} - \frac{1}{5} + \frac{3}{5} = \frac{3}{5} + \frac{3}{5} - \frac{4}{5} - \frac{1}{5} = \frac{3+3-4-1}{5} = \frac{1}{5}$".

Emphasize these types of addition and subtraction fraction problems constantly in your class involving least common denominators, which appear challenging but are not as difficult as they initially appear. The question is, "When will students learn the rules necessary to solve more challenging addition and subtraction problems involving challenging LCDs?" We introduced the procedures students must master if they are going to solve challenging arithmetic fraction problems and rational expressions. If you only discuss the textbook problems which involve simple addition and subtraction of two fractions and then use two simple fractions to teach multiplication and division of fractions, some of your students will get confused because these types of problems all look the same. However, we know the procedures to solve addition/subtraction fraction problems, and multiplication/division fraction problems are significantly different (Jordan et al., 2013). Perhaps we gave too many illustrations to emphasize how to add and subtract fractions, or perhaps the explanations looked too identical, but go back and look again. We purposefully emphasized the same rules for all the example solutions, but we also tried to vary the way we explained the procedures. The first time you explain a set of procedures to your students to solve a group of problems, not all students will understand all the steps. Try to use several illustrations to explain similar problems, and when you explain the solutions, emphasize the same rules but try to say the same thing in different ways.

We frequently encourage teachers to require students to graph fractions on a number line, especially when the students are adding, subtracting, multiplying, and dividing two fractions. The reason we want the students to graph all three numbers on a number line when they are working with fraction problems is because of the special situations which occur when two fractions are multiplied and divided. Number sense when you are working with two fractions between "0" and "1" is sometimes surprising (Siegler, Lortie – Forgues et. al. 2015). Even college graduates get confused when they multiply two such fractions and divide two such fractions. Reference example problems contained in the yellow boxes already discussed in this chapter.

A question all arithmetic and mathematics teachers constantly ask themselves and each other is, "How will we know when a student is ready to take a challenging academic algebra course?" We believe the simple answer is three-fold. 1. When they can solve all types of 5th and 6th grade textbook fraction problems with a minimum score of 90%. 2. When they understand and have demonstrated an understanding of the procedures discussed in this textbook in Chapters 1-7. 3. When the student can solve long division problems involving rational numbers (Including decimals and natural numbers) with divisors less than 1,000 and dividends less than 100,000 and earn a minimum score of 90%. We believe it is important to master arithmetic concepts and develop problem solving skills in arithmetic, prior to entering an algebra class which emphasizes algebra problems more challenging than the introductory algebra problems presented in this textbook.

Third Assignment

DEFINITIONS

A. In your own words, write what you think is the best definition of the words/phrases indicated below. The words indicated below are all words or phrases which apply to elementary arithmetic concepts. After you write your definition, look up the definition of each word or phrase on the internet or a dictionary and then write the internet/dictionary definition for each word or phrase. In arithmetic and mathematics, definitions are extremely important, and a minor change in a definition may change the entire meaning of the word. We expect your definitions might be slightly different than the internet/dictionary definition in many cases.

1. A. Write the definition of the two-word phrase, "Rational Number". You are not expected to give the definition using mathematical notation. Write sentences as if you are explaining the definition to a class of fifth graders. B. List at least ten examples of rational numbers, then list at least 10 examples of numbers which are not rational numbers. (Hint: The opposite of a Rational Number is an Irrational Number. An Irrational Number can never be written as a fraction using Integers.)

   If you are an elementary arithmetic teacher or secondary math teacher, you must be able to explain the definitions and the meanings of many arithmetic terms and phrases and use terminology appropriate for your respective grade level.

2. A. Definition - Least Common Multiple (LCM). B. Explain the importance of the three words as they apply to the definition. C. Write four examples which mathematically illustrate why the three words are appropriate based on the definition.

3. A. Least Common Denominator (LCD). B. Explain the importance of the three words as they apply to the definition. C. Write four examples which mathematically illustrate why the three words are appropriate based on the definition.
4. A. Greatest Common Factor (GCF). B. Explain the importance of the three words as they apply to the definition. C. Write four examples which mathematically illustrate why the three words are appropriate based on the definition.
5. A. Explain the definition of the word "Interleave" as it applies to arithmetic problems. B. Give a list of at least five example problems which illustrate the definition of the word interleave. In three of your five example problems, include two different arithmetic concepts to illustrate how to interleave concepts into one problem. In the other two example problems, interleave at least three different arithmetic concepts. The concepts you interleave in your five examples should all involve arithmetic concepts which the students should have already learned a week or a month or two months ago, or concepts they will be required to learn soon. Interleaving previously learned concepts into homework or classwork assignments today will help the students review and eventually, "learn and remember" concepts previously taught. (Examples: We want the five example problems to focus on fractions: interleave concepts involving both addition and subtraction, use numerators with 4 digits or 5 digits, add and subtract fractions with decimals in the numerators, in one problem add fractions, mixed numbers and whole numbers, or if you want to use examples involving concepts students will encounter later in the year include exponents, square roots, absolute values, labels, etc.) There are many ways to interleave

arithmetic concepts into fraction problems, be original and think of some forms of interleaving which we did not mention.

6. A. Write the definition of the phrase "Prime Numbers". B. After you write your definition in sentence format, write the definition using correct mathematical notation. We do NOT want you to mention negative numbers. When you look up the definition on the internet or in a dictionary, you need to realize based on the exact definition, negative numbers are <u>not</u> considered prime numbers, but we have seen some authors indicate negative integers are prime numbers. We personally do not consider negative integers to be prime numbers, but we do not get too concerned about this slight disagreement because, in this situation, mathematically, it makes little difference.
7. A. Write the definition of the phrase "Composite Numbers". B. After you write your definition in sentence format, write the definition using correct mathematical notation. We do NOT want you to mention negative numbers. Some authors allow for negative integers to be considered composite numbers, but we do not want you to consider this situation.
8. Use the definitions of the two, two-word phrases "Prime Numbers" and "Composite Numbers" to explain why the numbers zero (0) and one (1) do not fit into either of the two sets of numbers referred to as "Prime" and "Composite".
9. Write the definition of the two-word phrase "Mixed Number".
10. Write the definition of the two-word phrase "Improper Fraction".

11. A. What does it mean to find the "Absolute Value" of a number or a number expression? B. Write a statement problem or word problem such that the absolute value would be considered the appropriate answer.

SPEED AND ACCURACY PROBLEMS

B. See how fast you can mentally solve all the problems in the 12 groups (A-L) of problems listed below. Work with two friends. One friend should use a stopwatch to time you as you mentally solve these problems. The second friend should write down each answer to check for accuracy after you complete each set of questions. The twelve sets of questions below all use the concept of interleaving different types of problems but not necessarily interleaving in any one problem. Each of the three of you in your group should solve four different sets of problems and rotate who goes first, second, and third when solving the problems. Hopefully, two things will happen. First, your speed improves and second, your accuracy improves. The first exception to these two outcomes would be a person who is so quick and accurate that they cannot really improve. The second exception may be an individual whose mental fraction recall knowledge is weak, but they will hopefully improve over an extended period, but not by doing these 12 sets of problems one time. You can also perform this exercise with one person other than yourself if you record your responses and compare your answers with the other person. You can check your time based on the recording and the two of you should be able to agree on the correct answers when the time pressure is removed. You could also record yourself on your cell phone and check your time and then carefully check your answers for accuracy. Each of the 12 groups of problems contains 16 questions. You do not need to reduce fractions unless the answer turns out to be a whole number. The reason we made the last comment is because the goal for several of the problems is to find an equivalent fraction by multiplying by a fraction equal to 1 and if you reduce these fractions, you will end up with the original fraction and defeat the purpose of the problems.

12. Do your best to be accurate and fast when solving the following sets of problems. If you multiply a fraction by 1, there is no need to reduce the answer.

a. *i.* "$\frac{3}{7}+\frac{2}{7}=?$" *ii.* "$\frac{8}{79}+\frac{7}{79}-\frac{0}{79}=?$" *iii.* "$\frac{4}{7}\times\frac{5}{5}=?$" *iv.* "$\frac{3}{13}+\frac{5}{13}-\frac{3}{13}=?$"

v. "$\frac{8}{5}-\frac{4}{5}=?$" vi. "$\frac{9}{10}-\frac{5}{10}-\frac{4}{10}=?$" vii. "$\frac{4}{5}\times\frac{8}{8}=?$" viii. "$\frac{7}{8}-\frac{3}{8}+\frac{1}{8}=?$"

ix. "$\frac{6}{101}+\frac{2}{101}=?$" x. "$\frac{5}{7}\times\frac{2}{2}=?$" xi. "$\frac{5}{7}\times\frac{2}{7}=?$" xii. "$\frac{8}{11}+\frac{5}{11}-\frac{1}{11}-\frac{1}{11}=?$"

xiii. Find the LCM – $\{2,4,8\}$ xiv. Find the LCD – "$\frac{1}{3}+\frac{5}{6}-\frac{1}{12}$"

xv. Find the GCF – $\{2,4,8\}$ xvi. Find the LCM – $\{2,4,5,10\}$

b. i. "$\frac{5}{7}+\frac{1}{7}=?$" ii. "$\frac{7}{79}+\frac{0}{79}-\frac{1}{79}=?$" iii. "$\frac{4}{7}\times\frac{6}{6}=?$" iv. "$\frac{7}{13}+\frac{2}{13}-\frac{7}{13}=?$"

v. "$\frac{8}{9}-\frac{4}{9}=?$" vi. "$\frac{5}{6}-\frac{3}{6}-\frac{2}{6}=?$" vii. "$\frac{5}{6}\times\frac{7}{7}=?$" viii. "$\frac{5}{7}-\frac{4}{7}+\frac{2}{7}=?$"

ix. "$\frac{7}{203}+\frac{4}{203}=?$" x. "$\frac{5}{6}\times\frac{3}{3}=?$" xi. "$\frac{4}{5}\times\frac{3}{5}=?$" xii. "$\frac{7}{9}+\frac{5}{9}-\frac{2}{9}-\frac{1}{9}=?$"

xiii. Find the LCM – $\{3,6,12\}$ xiv. Find the LCD – "$\frac{1}{2}+\frac{5}{8}-\frac{1}{4}$"

xv. Find the GCF – $\{5,10,15\}$ xvi. Find the LCM – $\{2,3,4,6\}$

c. i. "$\frac{1}{7}+\frac{5}{7}=?$" ii. "$\frac{6}{79}+\frac{7}{79}-\frac{0}{79}=?$" iii. "$\frac{4}{7}\times\frac{4}{4}=?$" iv. "$\frac{9}{13}+\frac{4}{13}-\frac{9}{13}=?$"

v. "$\frac{4}{9}-\frac{2}{9}=?$" vi. "$\frac{8}{9}-\frac{5}{9}-\frac{3}{9}=?$" vii. "$\frac{4}{7}\times\frac{3}{3}=?$" viii. "$\frac{5}{9}-\frac{2}{9}+\frac{4}{9}=?$"

ix. "$\frac{8}{97}+\frac{7}{97}=?$" x. "$\frac{5}{8}\times\frac{4}{4}=?$" xi. "$\frac{3}{4}\times\frac{3}{4}=?$" xii. "$\frac{6}{7}+\frac{5}{7}-\frac{2}{7}-\frac{2}{7}=?$"

xiii. Find the LCM – $\{2, 6, 18\}$ xiv. Find the LCD – "$\frac{1}{6}+\frac{5}{12}-\frac{1}{2}$"

xv. Find the GCF – $\{6, 8, 12\}$ xvi. Find the LCM – $\{4, 6, 2, 8\}$

d. i. "$\frac{2}{7}+\frac{2}{7}=?$" ii. "$\frac{9}{79}+\frac{4}{79}-\frac{0}{79}=?$" iii. "$\frac{5}{6}\times\frac{5}{5}=?$" iv. "$\frac{3}{17}+\frac{6}{17}-\frac{3}{17}=?$"

v. "$\frac{8}{11}-\frac{2}{11}=?$" vi. "$\frac{5}{8}-\frac{2}{8}-\frac{2}{8}=?$" vii. "$\frac{3}{8}\times\frac{6}{6}=?$" viii. "$\frac{5}{9}-\frac{4}{9}+\frac{3}{9}=?$"

ix. "$5\frac{3}{55}+5\frac{6}{55}=?$" x. "$\frac{7}{1}\times\frac{4}{4}=?$" xi. "$\frac{2}{5}\times\frac{2}{5}=?$" xii. "$\frac{7}{11}+\frac{7}{11}-\frac{2}{11}-\frac{1}{11}=?$"

xiii. Find the LCM – $\{4, 5, 10\}$ xiv. Find the LCD – "$\frac{1}{5}+\frac{5}{6}-\frac{1}{2}$"

xv. Find the GCF – $\{6, 9, 15\}$ xvi. Find the LCD – "$\frac{2}{5}-\frac{1}{2}+\frac{3}{4}-\frac{1}{10}$"

e. i. "$\frac{3}{5}+\frac{1}{5}=?$" ii. "$\frac{8}{17}+\frac{0}{79}-\frac{7}{17}=?$" iii. "$\frac{6}{7}\times\frac{7}{7}=?$" iv. "$\frac{12}{13}+\frac{12}{13}-\frac{12}{13}=?$"

v. "$\frac{8}{9}-\frac{3}{9}=?$" vi. "$\frac{9}{14}-\frac{3}{14}-\frac{5}{14}=?$" vii. "$\frac{3}{7}\times\frac{10}{10}=?$" viii. "$\frac{7}{17}-\frac{7}{17}+\frac{17}{17}=?$"

ix. "$\frac{5}{1001}+\frac{8}{1001}=?$" x. "$\frac{8}{9}\times\frac{2}{2}=?$" xi. "$\frac{4}{5}\times\frac{3}{5}=?$" xii. "$\frac{5}{13}+\frac{5}{13}-\frac{2}{13}-\frac{2}{13}=?$"

xiii. Find the LCM – $\{4, 8, 12\}$ xiv. Find the LCD – "$\frac{1}{4}+\frac{5}{6}-\frac{1}{2}$"

xv. Find the GCF – $\{25, 10, 15\}$ xvi. Find the LCD – "$\frac{2}{3}-\frac{1}{3}+\frac{3}{5}-\frac{1}{2}$"

f. i. "$\frac{3}{8}+\frac{2}{8}=?$" ii. "$\frac{8}{83}+\frac{0}{79}-\frac{1}{83}=?$" iii. "$\frac{4}{11}\times\frac{5}{5}=?$" iv. "$\frac{5}{13}+\frac{11}{13}-\frac{5}{13}=?$"

v. "$\frac{10}{11}-\frac{10}{11}=?$" vi. "$\frac{7}{10}-\frac{4}{10}-\frac{0}{10}=?$" vii. "$\frac{5}{8}\times\frac{6}{6}=?$" viii. "$\frac{10}{11}-\frac{5}{11}+\frac{2}{11}=?$"

ix. "$\frac{6}{53}+\frac{8}{53}=?$" x. "$\frac{7}{9}\times\frac{3}{3}=?$" xi. "$\frac{7}{9}\times\frac{7}{9}=?$" xii. "$\frac{9}{17}+\frac{2}{17}-\frac{0}{99}-\frac{11}{17}=?$"

xiii. Find the LCM – $\{6, 4, 9\}$ xiv. Find the LCD – "$\frac{1}{4}+\frac{5}{8}-\frac{1}{12}$"

xv. Find the GCF – $\{27, 21, 9\}$ xvi. Find the LCD – "$\frac{2}{4}-\frac{1}{3}+\frac{3}{24}-\frac{1}{2}$"

g. i. "$\frac{6}{11}+\frac{2}{11}=?$" ii. "$\frac{9}{83}+\frac{0}{833}-\frac{2}{83}=?$" iii. "$\frac{5}{7}\times\frac{9}{9}=?$" iv. "$\frac{4}{19}+\frac{5}{19}-\frac{4}{19}=?$"

v. "$\frac{7}{17} - \frac{5}{17} = ?$" vi. "$\frac{7}{11} - \frac{4}{11} - \frac{1}{11} = ?$" vii. "$\frac{9}{10} \times \frac{10}{10} = ?$" viii. "$\frac{15}{17} - \frac{14}{17} + \frac{2}{17} = ?$"

ix. "$\frac{13}{17} + \frac{4}{17} = ?$" x. "$\frac{3}{5} \times \frac{5}{5} = ?$" xi. "$\frac{5}{7} \times \frac{4}{7} = ?$" xii. "$\frac{7}{13} + \frac{8}{13} - \frac{0}{72} - \frac{3}{13} = ?$"

xiii. Find the LCM – $\{6, 12, 9\}$ xiv. Find the GCF – $\{45, 18, 9\}$ xv. Find the LCD – "$\frac{1}{8} + \frac{5}{6} - \frac{1}{12}$"

xvi. Find the GCF for the numerator and the denominator – "$\frac{15}{25}$"

h. i. "$\frac{5}{14} + \frac{8}{14} = ?$" ii. "$\frac{8}{101} + \frac{7}{101} - \frac{0}{79} = ?$" iii. "$\frac{4}{11} \times \frac{3}{3} = ?$" iv. "$\frac{3}{13} + \frac{5}{17} - \frac{3}{13} = ?$"

v. "$\frac{10}{13} - \frac{5}{13} = ?$" vi. "$\frac{7}{10} - \frac{3}{10} - \frac{3}{10} = ?$" vii. "$\frac{8}{9} \times \frac{6}{6} = ?$" viii. "$\frac{7}{23} - \frac{2}{23} + \frac{0}{23} = ?$"

ix. "$\frac{5}{47} + \frac{6}{47} = ?$" x. "$\frac{2}{9} \times \frac{11}{11} = ?$" xi. "$\frac{2}{11} \times \frac{4}{11} = ?$" xii. "$\frac{7}{17} + \frac{10}{17} - \frac{1}{17} - \frac{1}{17} = ?$"

xiii. Find the LCM – $\{4, 12, 9\}$ xiv. Find the GCF – $\{54, 27, 9\}$ xv. Find the LCD – "$\frac{1}{10} + \frac{5}{6} - \frac{1}{2}$"

xvi. Find the GCF for the numerator and the denominator – "$\frac{27}{36}$"

i. i. "$\frac{5}{10} + \frac{2}{10} = ?$" ii. "$\frac{8}{80} + \frac{7}{80} - \frac{2}{80} = ?$" iii. "$\frac{2}{3} \times \frac{5}{5} = ?$" iv. "$\frac{6}{13} + \frac{7}{13} - \frac{3}{13} = ?$"

v. "$\frac{8}{25} - \frac{4}{25} = ?$" vi. "$\frac{9}{10} - \frac{3}{10} - \frac{6}{10} = ?$" vii. "$\frac{6}{11} \times \frac{2}{2} = ?$" viii. "$\frac{7}{17} - \frac{5}{17} + \frac{2}{17} = ?$"

ix. "$\frac{9}{42} + \frac{8}{42} = ?$" x. "$\frac{5}{6} \times \frac{3}{3} = ?$" xi. "$\frac{5}{8} \times \frac{3}{7} = ?$" xii. "$\frac{10}{19} + \frac{8}{19} - \frac{0}{19} - \frac{8}{19} = ?$"

xiii. Find the LCM – $\{6, 10, 5\}$ xiv. Find the GCF – $\{48, 16, 24\}$ xv. Find the LCD – "$\frac{1}{9} + \frac{5}{6} - \frac{1}{12}$"

xvi. Find the GCF for the numerator and the denominator – "$\frac{36}{48}$"

j. i. "$\frac{3}{10} + \frac{4}{10} = ?$" ii. "$\frac{8}{180} + \frac{7}{180} - \frac{2}{180} = ?$" iii. "$\frac{7}{8} \times \frac{9}{9} = ?$" iv. "$\frac{8}{17} + \frac{7}{17} - \frac{3}{17} = ?$"

v. "$\frac{11}{23} - \frac{4}{23} = ?$" vi. "$\frac{9}{100} - \frac{3}{100} - \frac{6}{100} = ?$" vii. "$\frac{7}{13} \times \frac{2}{2} = ?$" viii. "$\frac{5}{29} - \frac{2}{29} + \frac{7}{29} = ?$"

ix. "$\frac{11}{42} + \frac{6}{42} = ?$" x. "$\frac{5}{6} \times \frac{10}{10} = ?$" xi. "$\frac{5}{8} \times \frac{5}{7} = ?$" xii. "$\frac{8}{17} + \frac{10}{17} - \frac{8}{17} - \frac{0}{19} = ?$"

xiii. Find the LCM – $\{6, 20, 5\}$ xiv. Find the GCF – $\{48, 60, 24\}$ xv. Find the LCD – "$\frac{1}{8} + \frac{1}{12} - \frac{8}{9}$"

xvi. Find the GCF for the numerator and the denominator – "$\frac{22}{33}$"

k. i. "$\frac{7}{11} + \frac{2}{11} = ?$" ii. "$\frac{5}{60} + \frac{7}{60} - \frac{1}{60} = ?$" iii. "$\frac{5}{9} \times \frac{5}{5} = ?$" iv. "$\frac{9}{19} + \frac{7}{19} - \frac{3}{19} = ?$"

v. "$\frac{12}{25} - \frac{4}{25} = ?$" vi. "$\frac{19}{10} - \frac{3}{10} - \frac{6}{10} = ?$" vii. "$\frac{7}{11} \times \frac{3}{3} = ?$" viii. "$\frac{17}{17} - \frac{5}{17} - \frac{12}{17} = ?$"

ix. "$\frac{15}{42} + \frac{8}{42} = ?$" x. "$\frac{11}{12} \times \frac{3}{3} = ?$" xi. "$\frac{7}{8} \times \frac{3}{8} = ?$" xii. "$\frac{17}{19} - \frac{8}{19} - \frac{0}{19} + \frac{8}{19} = ?$"

xiii. Find the LCM – {6, 9, 3} xiv. Find the GCF – {32, 8, 48} xv. Find the LCD – "$\frac{1}{15} + \frac{5}{6} - \frac{1}{10}$"

xvi. Find the GCF for the numerator and the denominator – "$\frac{72}{81}$"

l. i. "$\frac{5}{50} + \frac{2}{50} = ?$" ii. "$\frac{18}{89} + \frac{7}{89} - \frac{6}{89} = ?$" iii. "$\frac{7}{9} \times \frac{7}{7} = ?$" iv. "$\frac{8}{11} + \frac{7}{11} - \frac{6}{11} = ?$"

v. "$\frac{18}{25} - \frac{14}{25} = ?$" vi. "$\frac{17}{10} - \frac{3}{10} - \frac{5}{10} = ?$" vii. "$\frac{8}{13} \times \frac{2}{2} = ?$" viii. "$\frac{7}{13} - \frac{6}{13} + \frac{2}{13} = ?$"

ix. "$\frac{19}{52} + \frac{8}{52} = ?$" x. "$\frac{50}{60} \times \frac{3}{3} = ?$" xi. "$\frac{3}{8} \times \frac{5}{11} = ?$" xii. "$\frac{15}{23} + \frac{8}{23} - \frac{0}{23} - \frac{8}{23} = ?$"

xiii. Find the LCM – {20, 10, 5} xiv. Find the LCD – "$\frac{1}{9} + \frac{3}{8} - \frac{1}{12}$" xv. Find the GCF – {48, 12, 4}

xvi. Find the GCF for the numerator and the denominator – "$\frac{22}{66}$"

Question to Ponder: Do you want your elementary teachers (especially 5th-grade teachers and beyond) who teach arithmetic to be able to solve all these problems with close to 100% accuracy, quickly? Everyone can be expected to make a mistake when solving these problems, especially if they are trying to solve the problems quickly. We expect all good mathematics teachers in grade 7 and beyond to be able to solve each set of questions in under a minute per set with less than one error per set of problems. We expect all elementary teachers in grades 4 through 6 to solve each set of questions in under 90 seconds with less than an average of 1 error per set of problems.

We used the phrase "with less than an average of 1 error per set of problems," which means when a person solves four of the sets of problems, he/she may have a maximum of 3 errors for the four sets of problems.

CONVERSION PROBLEMS

C. We want you to explain how you get a different number when you complete your conversions and why the label changes.

13. A. Convert 60 inches into feet. B. Write a paragraph to explain how you converted the given number 60 into a new number and why the label changed from inches to feet.

14. A. Convert 7 days to minutes. B. Write a paragraph to explain how you converted the given number 7 into a new number and why the label changed from days to minutes.

15. A. Convert the fraction "$\frac{5}{8}$" into an equivalent fraction with the denominator, "72.

B. Write your explanation using sound arithmetic principles and procedures required to complete the conversion process.

16. A. Convert the fraction "$\frac{8}{9}$" into an equivalent fraction with the numerator "64".

B. Write your explanation to complete the conversion process for this problem.

17. Use the procedures/directions that you wrote in problems "13. B." and "14. B." as your guide and convert 55 miles per hour to feet per minute.

18. Use the procedures/directions you wrote in problems "15" and "16" as your guide to convert the fraction "$\frac{3}{4}$" into an equivalent fraction such that the denominator equals "14".

D. We want you to use the "factor tree" triangular (Christmas Tree) format to write the "prime factors" for the following given numbers.

19. Write the prime factors for the composite number "12". Use "factor tree" notation.

A. First, write the solution as a multiplication problem involving all the prime factors.

B. Second, write the solution as a multiplication problem using exponents involving prime factors if applicable. Realize there are three ways to write the same composite number. We may write the composite number, "8" in the following three ways "$8, or\ 2 \times 2 \times 2, or\ 2^3$".

20. Write the prime factors for the composite number "20". Use "factor tree" notation.

A. First, write the solution as a multiplication problem involving all the prime factors.

B. Second, write the solution as a multiplication problem using exponents involving prime factors if applicable. Realize there are three ways to write the same composite number.

21. Write the prime factors for the composite number "100". Use "factor tree" notation to determine the solution. A. First, write the solution as a multiplication problem involving all the prime factors. B. Second, write the solution as a multiplication problem using exponents involving prime factors if applicable. Realize there are three ways to write the same composite number.

22. A. Write the prime factors for the composite number "7392". After you write the "factor tree" notation for the number "7392", test to see if any of the prime numbers will divide perfectly into the number 5629. B. Will any of the prime factors which

multiply to give the composite number 7392 divide into 5629? C. How can we illustrate/explain to students that the fraction "$\frac{5629}{7392}$" will not reduce? D. What is the GCF between the numerator "5629" and the denominator "7392"? This is the answer to a previous problem illustrated earlier in this chapter, and we said we would explain later why the fraction would not reduce. Incidentally, you may want to write the prime factors for the numerator, "5629". We guarantee the prime numbers "2, 3, 5, 7, and 11" will not divide perfectly into "5623" but there might be another prime number which will divide perfectly into "5623". E. Is the number "5623" a prime number or composite number?

EQUIVALENT FRACTION CONVERSION PROCEDURES ILLUSTRATED IN THIS CHAPTER

E. For the following problems, use the procedures illustrated in this chapter to convert the given fraction into an equal fraction with the correct denominator or numerator.

Example 1: $\frac{3}{4} = \frac{?}{16}$ $\qquad \frac{denominator\ of\ answer\ fraction}{denominator\ of\ given\ fraction} = \frac{16}{4} = 4 \ \therefore\ \frac{4}{4} = 1$

$$\frac{3}{4} = \frac{3}{4} \times 1 = \frac{3}{4} \times \frac{4}{4} = \frac{12}{16}$$

Example 2: $\frac{5}{8} = \frac{15}{?}$ $\qquad \frac{numerator\ of\ answer\ fraction}{numerator\ of\ given\ fraction} = \frac{15}{5} = 3 \ \therefore\ \frac{3}{3} = 1$

$$\frac{5}{8} = \frac{5}{8} \times 1 = \frac{5}{8} \times \frac{3}{3} = \frac{15}{24}$$

23. $\frac{7}{11} = \frac{?}{88}$ We know the trick to find the missing number. You need to illustrate why the trick works in your solutions as we did in examples "1." and "2.", just indicated.

24. $\frac{7}{15} = \frac{21}{?}$ 25. $\frac{47}{53} = \frac{?}{265}$ 26. $\frac{107}{319} = \frac{?}{1595}$

27. $\frac{3}{4} = \frac{?}{14}$ (You may write the numerator as a mixed number or a decimal.)

MIXED NUMBERS AND IMPROPER FRACTIONS

F. The mixed numbers and the improper fractions must be equal.

28. A. Convert the mixed number into an improper fraction: "$3\frac{1}{2} = \frac{?}{??}$. B. Write a short paragraph and explain how you converted the mixed number "$3\frac{1}{2}$" into an improper fraction. C. Also, write an additional paragraph explaining why your procedure works.

29. A. Convert the improper fraction into a mixed number: "$\frac{49}{8} = ?\frac{??}{???}$". B. Write a paragraph intended for fifth graders, which explains how we converted the improper fraction into the mixed number.

30. Convert the improper fraction into a mixed number: "$\frac{7360}{19} = ?\frac{??}{???}$". We expect you to use the procedures you wrote in the solution for problem 29.

31. Convert the given mixed number into an improper fraction: "$13\frac{7}{113} = \frac{?}{??}$". We assume you will use the procedures you wrote in the solution for problem 28.

GRAPH EACH NUMBER INDICATED ON A NUMBER LINE

G. A. First, graph all the numbers in each set of numbers on a horizontal Number Line. (Estimate where you believe each of the given numbers in each set of numbers should be placed on a number line and indicate which number is represented by each point.) The number zero (0) should be indicated at the far left of each of your number lines. The righthand end numbers are also given in these problems. B. Second, list the Numbers from Smallest to Largest using one of the following relationship symbols, "$<$ or $>$". C. Third, list the Numbers from Largest to Smallest using one of the following relationship symbols, "$\leq$ or $\geq$":

(There are three separate answers for questions 32-35 as indicated above.)

32. $\{\frac{3}{4}, \frac{7}{8}, \frac{1}{2}\}$ The righthand end number should be "2". Q.A. Q.B. Q.C.

33. $\{\frac{7}{8}, \frac{3}{4}, \frac{9}{10}, \frac{99}{100}\}$ The righthand end number should be "$1\frac{1}{2}$". Q.A. Q.B. Q.C.

34. $\{5\frac{7}{8}, 3\frac{3}{5}, 5\frac{7}{9}, 3\frac{5}{8}, 3\frac{7}{6}, 1\frac{99}{100}\}$ The righthand end number should be "8". Q.A. Q.B. Q.C.

35. $\{6\frac{8}{9}, 11\frac{5}{8}, 11\frac{9}{10}, 3\frac{11}{20}, 10\frac{3}{20}, 3\frac{7}{20}, 13\}$ The righthand end number should be "15". Q.A. Q.B. Q.C.

USING SETS OF MULTIPLICATION TABLES, FIND LCMS AND LCDS

THE INDICATED SETS ARE ACTUALLY SETS OF MULTIPLES OF THE GIVEN NUMBER

Example1. Illustrate using multiplication tables that the LCM is the number underlined in each set of multiples for the set of numbers - {4, 5, 6}. Here is the infinite set of multiples for the number "4" - {4, 8, 12, 16, 20, 24, 28, 32, 36, 40, 44, 48, 52, 56, 60, 64, 68, 72, ...}. Here is the infinite set of multiples for the number "5" - $\{5, 10, 15, 20, 25, 30, 35, 40, 45, 50, 55, \underline{60}, 65, 70, 75, 80, 85, 90, \ldots\}$. Here is the infinite set of multiples for the number "6" - $\{6, 12, 18, 24, 30, 36, 42, 48, 54, \underline{60}, 66, 72, 78, 84, 90, 96, \ldots\}$. The number "<u>60</u>" is the LCM for the three numbers 4, 5, 6. (Notice the notation at the end of each of the three sets of multiples, "..." listed above. The mathematics notation "..." written at the end of a set means the indicated set goes on to <u>infinity</u>, there is an unlimited list of terms or numbers which follow.) The notation "..." written in the middle of the set simply means something is missing which should be obvious.

Example2. Illustrate using multiplication tables that the LCD is the number written in **bold** print in each set of multiplies for each of the denominators in the fraction addition/subtraction problem: "$\frac{2}{3} + \frac{4}{8} - \frac{5}{6}$" - Here is the infinite set of multiples for the denominator "3" - {3, 6, 9, 12, 15, 18, 21, **24**, 27, 30, 33, 36, ...}. Here is the infinite set of multiples for the denominator "8" - $\{8, 16, \mathbf{24}, 32, 40, 48, \ldots\}$. Here is the infinite set of the multiples for the denominator "6" - $\{6, 12, 18, \mathbf{24}, 30, 36, 42, 48, \ldots\}$. The number "**24**" is the LCD for the three given denominators.

H. Use "set" notation and the multiples of the numbers involved to find the LCM or LCD for the given sets of numbers or fraction addition and subtraction problems. Indicate all answers in **bold** print.

36. $\{8, 10, 6\}$ Find the LCM.

37. $\{\frac{7}{8} + \frac{5}{24} - \frac{5}{6}\}$ Find the LCD.

38. $\{4, 6\}$ Find the LCM.

39. $\{\frac{3}{7} - \frac{5}{14}\}$ Find the LCD.

40. $\{6, 8, 12, 18\}$ Find the LCM.

41. $\{\frac{5}{8} - \frac{7}{12} + \frac{3}{4} + \frac{2}{3}\}$ Find the LCD.

42. $\{10, 15, 25, 30\}$ Find the LCM.

43. $\{\frac{7}{10} + \frac{2}{5} + \frac{7}{15} - \frac{2}{3}\}$ Find the LCD.

ADD AND SUBTRACT THE FOLLOWING FRACTION PROBLEMS

Some of the problems below will require you to find LCDs and convert some of the fractions into equivalent fractions with the correct LCD. In some of the problems, the LCD is evident. If you encounter a mixed number, you may change all the mixed numbers into improper fractions and add and subtract the fractions as improper fractions. Then, in the last step, if the answer is an improper fraction, you should convert the fraction into a mixed number. If you are going to teach students how to solve these problems, you need to know all the steps and always indicate how you determined special values of the number 1 to multiply fractions, with the intent to determine an equivalent fraction. You do not need to list all the steps to find the LCD at this time; we assume these problems are simple enough that you will use mental math to find the LCD for each problem. Even though you should be able to use mental math to find the LCD, we insist you write all the steps in your solution so everyone will understand how to convert a given fraction into an equivalent fraction. We also want you to write one big fraction, for all addition or subtraction fraction problems, prior to adding and subtracting the numerators. Some problems will require little work, such as problem "44", but even in this problem, we want you to write one big fraction indicating the addition of the two fractions prior to writing the final answer.

I. Write all your solutions using the horizontal (left to right) format, not the vertical (up and down) format.

44. $\frac{3}{11} + \frac{7}{11} = ?$

45. $\frac{2}{3} + \frac{1}{6} = ?$

46. $\frac{3}{8} - \frac{2}{8} = ?$

47. $\frac{3}{4} - \frac{1}{8} = ?$

48. $\frac{321}{1001} - \frac{292}{1001} + \frac{661}{1001} - \frac{595}{1001} = ?$

49. $\frac{5}{8} + \frac{5}{8} - \frac{5}{12} + \left| \frac{-3}{24} \right| = ?$

50. $\frac{5}{6} - \frac{1}{4} + \frac{1}{3} = ?$

51. $\frac{14}{15} - \frac{1}{15} - \left| \frac{+1}{3} \right| = ?$

52. $-\frac{7}{59} + \frac{0}{101} - \frac{1}{59} + \frac{51}{59} =?$

53. $\frac{5}{6} + \frac{5}{6} - \frac{1}{6} + \frac{3}{6} =?$

54. $3\frac{1}{5} + 5\frac{1}{3} = ?$ (Use improper fractions.)

55. $7\frac{1}{4} - 2\frac{1}{2} =?$ (Use improper fractions.)

ADD AND SUBTRACT THE FOLLOWING MIXED NUMBER PROBLEMS WITHOUT CONVERTING THE MIXED NUMBERS INTO IMPROPER FRACTIONS. WORK WITH THE FRACTIONS FIRST. SOME OF THE ADDITION PROBLEMS WILL REQUIRE YOU TO CONVERT THE FRACTION ANSWER INTO A MIXED NUMBER AND THEN CARRY A WHOLE NUMBER TO FIND THE FINAL ANSWER. SOME OF THE SUBTRACTION PROBLEMS WILL REQUIRE YOU TO BORROW IN ORDER TO ENSURE THE TOP FRACTION IN THE SUBTRACTION PROBLEM IS GREATER THAN THE BOTTOM FRACTION. (Refer back to example problem 12, "$7\frac{1}{4} - 2\frac{5}{8}$", in this Chapter, if you need to borrow to subtract fractions when the smaller fraction is on top (minuend) and the larger fraction is on the bottom (subtrahend).)

J. You should write down all the steps to solve the problem. We want you to illustrate that you understand all the procedures involved in the solutions at this time. We assume you know the tricks to solve the problems, but **we want you to illustrate why the mental tricks which you normally use are mathematically correct.** Write all your solutions using the horizontal format, not the vertical format.

56. $5\frac{3}{11} + 7\frac{3}{11} = ?$

57. $4\frac{3}{11} + 1\frac{6}{11} + 5\frac{2}{11} = ?$

58. $8\frac{3}{7} - 5\frac{2}{7} = ?$

59. $101\frac{89}{99} - 99\frac{5}{99} - 2\frac{84}{99} = ?$

60. $11\frac{7}{8} - 6\frac{3}{4} = ?$

61. $17\frac{1}{2} - \frac{1}{4} - 1\frac{1}{4} = ?$

62. $6\frac{3}{7} + 5\frac{3}{7} + 9\frac{3}{7} = ?$

63. $6\frac{5}{9} + 11\frac{7}{18} - 3\frac{1}{3} = ?$

64. $11\frac{1}{5} - 6\frac{4}{5} = ?$

65. $10\frac{1}{2} - 5\frac{2}{3} = ?$

66. $13\frac{1}{5} + 9\frac{4}{5} - \frac{3}{5} - 1\frac{3}{5} = ?$

67. $9\frac{1}{3} - 2\frac{1}{2} - 1\frac{3}{4} =?$

<u>FIND THE LCDs</u> FOR THE FOLLOWING PROBLEMS AND USE THE RULES/PROCEDURES INVOLVING FACTOR TREES AS ILLUSTRATED IN EXAMPLE PROBLEMS (4, 8, & 13) IN THIS CHAPTER

K. We want you to indicate all the steps involved to find the LCDs for the following problems using factor trees and prime numbers.

68. $\frac{5}{12} + \frac{7}{18}$ Find the LCD

69. $\frac{2}{15} + \frac{7}{20} - \frac{2}{25} = ?$ Find the LCD

70. $5\frac{7}{12} + 7\frac{5}{18} + 11\frac{1}{72} = ?$ Find the LCD

71. $-6\frac{7}{12} - 19\frac{5}{18} - 11\frac{1}{24} - 8\frac{7}{48} = ?$ Find the LCD

L. Review Your Notation:

72. Go back and look at every fraction problem you wrote in this section of problems/questions 1.-71. How many times in your notation did you write fractions with a slanted line?

M. Unit Fractions: (You may want to look up the definition of a unit fraction.)

73. If a pie is cut into 8 equal pieces, write the correct unit fraction.

74. If a rectangle is divided into 115 equal squares, write the proper unit fraction.

CHAPTER 4

CHALLENGING ADDITION AND SUBTRACTION FRACTION PROBLEMS: “WITHOUT RULES, THESE PROBLEMS WILL SEEM IMPOSSIBLE”

IF YOU UNDERSTAND THE RULES DISCUSSED IN THIS CHAPTER AND YOU CAN SIMPLIFY ALL THESE PROBLEMS, THEN YOU MIGHT BE PREPARED FOR ALGEBRA AND OTHER ADVANCED MATHEMATICS CLASSES IN HIGH SCHOOL.

Chapter 4

In Chapter 3, we focused on simple addition and subtraction fraction problems. When we explained how to find the least common denominators in problems 4, 8, and 13, the steps seemed cumbersome and unnecessary. Sometimes when a problem is simple, the rules seem difficult to understand and work with. People who are knowledgeable and know the rules and procedures to solve addition and subtraction fraction problems in arithmetic have developed their own set of steps to find LCDs, convert fractions into equivalent fractions, and then add and/or subtract the numerators of the fractions. These individuals do not need to think about the rules when they solve simple problems because the entire process is automatic for them. If you struggle when simplifying fraction addition and subtraction problems, doing all the necessary steps in your head to find equivalent fractions and then add/subtract the numerators of the equivalent fractions, you might find that the mental process is not that simple for all students (Lortie-Forgues et al., 2015). In the next example problem, the fractions involve the following four denominators: "12, 15, 20, and 30". Some people quickly realize the LCD is "60", but there are also many people who have little understanding of how to determine the LCD "60" for the four denominators.

You should be able to explain to your students how to determine the LCD for the following problem using four sets of multiplication tables and then use "Young's Conversion Theorem" to find the four equivalent fractions. Initially, we will refer to the four sets of multiplication tables for the four denominators and then use specific rules to find the LCD "60". Study the entire process used to find the solution to example 1 below, where we illustrate all the steps necessary to solve the most challenging fraction problems in arithmetic and rational expressions in algebra. Example 2 below is a difficult fraction arithmetic problem, and students will not be able to find the LCD without using the rules outlined in problem 1. If you understand the explanations, for example, problems 1-14 in Chapter 3 and example 1 below, you will be prepared to solve example 2 in this chapter. The procedures discussed to find the LCD for the next problem are the same procedures which were introduced in the previous chapter. One of the rules for teaching math well is to always introduce difficult concepts and procedures over an extended time frame. That is why we integrated the rules to find challenging LCDs and LCMs in the previous chapter, along with other problems where the rules were not required.

More Challenging Example Problems

You may want to introduce these types of problems late in the year in 5th grade or early in the year in 6th grade. When your students can simplify these types of fraction addition and subtraction problems with at least 80% accuracy, you can then feel confident your students are ready to enter an algebra class. If you never challenge your students to simplify these types of problems and learn the rules, you will be at least partially responsible for the problems some of your students may encounter when they are expected to simplify and solve rational expressions in Algebra 2.

1. Simplify: "$\frac{7}{12} - \frac{2}{15} + \frac{11}{20} - \frac{1}{30}$"

This is a problem which is simple enough that some of your best students might be able to compute the least common denominator in their heads by using their knowledge of the multiplication tables. The first rule everyone must know every time they add or subtract fractions in arithmetic is, "All the fractions must have identical denominators." This concept should have been illustrated over and over prior to getting to this point in arithmetic, and the students should have already been introduced to the mental procedures needed to find the least common denominators. That was the goal in Chapter 3 with problems 1-14. One should immediately notice when they look at the four fractions "$\frac{7}{12} - \frac{2}{15} + \frac{11}{20} - \frac{1}{30}$" there are four different denominators, and the problem involves both addition and subtraction. This problem is more difficult than the normal fifth-grade arithmetic textbook problems. Most fifth-grade teachers and some fifth-grade students will be able to look at this example problem and use their knowledge of the multiplication tables to quickly determine the least common denominator (LCD) for the four denominators "12, 15, 20, and 30" is "60".

The LCM for the four numbers 12, 15, 20, and 30 is also definitely "60". We are going to concentrate on the three words Least Common Multiple and explain why the number "60" is the LCM for the four numbers.

> Remember, before we begin to explain the rules to compute least common denominators (LCDs) or least common multiples (LCMs), it is important to understand the difference between these two similar, but slightly different expressions. A least common multiple is found for a list/group/set of different numbers, while a least common denominator is required when you are working with the denominators of fractions.

If you want to find the least common multiple for this problem, you must be familiar with the multiplication tables for all four numbers. Here are four short sets of multiples for each of the four numbers indicated:

- $\{12 \times 1 = 12, 12 \times 2 = 24, 12 \times 3 = 36, 12 \times 4 = 48, 12 \times 5 = \mathbf{60},$ and then $12 \times 6 = 72, etc.\};$
- $\{15 \times 1 = 15, 15 \times 2 = 30, 15 \times 3 = 45, 15 \times 4 = \mathbf{60},$ and then $15 \times 5 = 75,$ $etc.\};$
- $\{20 \times 1 = 20, 20 \times 2 = 40, 20 \times 3 = \mathbf{60},$ and then $20 \times 4 = 80,$ $etc.\};$
- $\{30 \times 1 = 30, 30 \times 2 = \mathbf{60},$ and then $30 \times 3 = 90, etc.\}.$

Notice the number "60" is a *multiple* of all four numbers. This means the number "60" is a *common multiple* for all four numbers. Finally, the number "60" is the smallest/least common multiple of all four numbers. If "60" is the LCM for the four numbers "12, 15, 20, and 30", then the number "60" is also the LCD for the four fractions "$\frac{7}{12}, \frac{2}{15}, \frac{11}{20}$, and $\frac{1}{30}$" with the denominators "12, 15, 20, and 30".

In Chapter 3, we introduced the rules required to find the most challenging LCDs for all types of fraction problems when we illustrated how to find the LCDs for problems 4, 8, and 13. The rules and procedures to find LCMs are frequently mentioned but not emphasized in elementary arithmetic textbooks because the textbook problems are so basic there is no need to learn the rules. If the students know the multiplication tables and remember a series of steps to convert a fraction into an equivalent fraction, they should be successful when they are required to add and subtract the simple fraction problems in the 5th, 6th, and 7th-grade textbooks. *(FRT 7: Is knowledge of multiplication and division facts the major indicator of success when solving fraction problems?)* Since the problems are so basic, the better students can do most of the math in their head without thinking about the rules. There is seldom a need to *emphasize* the rules to find LCDs and then go into detail on how to convert fractions into equal fractions in a 5th, 6th, or 7th-grade arithmetic class if you use the textbooks as your template for success. Many educators seem satisfied that less than 50% of the students in the 5th, 6th, 7th, and 8th grade can do the simple arithmetic addition and subtraction problems one or two months after fraction topics are discussed. A huge roadblock occurs when the students are required to solve fraction problems in algebra, referred to as rational expressions. When students are required to work with rational expressions (fractions in algebra), the students must remember the rules and procedures which were never taught in arithmetic, and the algebra teacher is then required to fix the problem. If over 50% of the students do not remember how to solve the simple problems illustrated in Chapter 3, this creates a difficult situation for the teachers and students when they work with rational expressions in algebra and advanced mathematics classes. Why would an educator be satisfied when less than 50% of the students are proficient when asked to solve certain types of problems, after the procedures to solve the problems are introduced in the early elementary grades and the students supposedly learned how to solve the problems using procedures starting in 4th or 5th grade (Siegler & Pyke et al., 2013)? If the students are never exposed to the rules and procedures to solve challenging arithmetic fraction problems, when they are asked to work with rational expressions in algebra, they are lost.

Remember, algebra rules are derived directly from arithmetic rules.

When a student becomes so frustrated and lost in any math class, it is a signal the student is turned-off with the present math class and probably future math classes. This is a major reason why so many students dislike math in general. It only takes one poor math teacher to ruin a student or a class full of students. Often the algebra teacher is referred to as the "poor math teacher," but often, the problem starts long before students enter the algebra teacher's classroom. When you are an inexperienced teacher, you depend on the textbook to help you plan your lessons and to decide what topics to teach in the classroom. You also depend on the textbook along with other workbooks written by the same publisher to determine the homework problems to assign for classwork and homework. Once you are an experienced teacher, you realize all the teachers are teaching the same way you are and, unfortunately, getting similar results. Teachers then ask, "Why do the students not 'remember' what they were supposed to have learned last year?" The real objective for any math teacher is not just to be a teacher but to make sure the students learn topics well and then remember what they learned. If you are a teacher and 90% of your students do not learn how to solve the problems in the textbook with 85%-90% accuracy, then you might consider modifying your teaching methods. If your students do not remember what you taught, then maybe the time you devoted to teaching a topic was not as productive as it could have been, and next year, the teacher will have to reteach the same topic.

The first step when you need to simplify the problem "$\frac{7}{12} - \frac{2}{15} + \frac{11}{20} - \frac{1}{30}$" is to find the LCD. The first step to find a least common denominator is to factor all the denominators of the fractions. Here are the four sets of factor trees for the four denominators, "12, 15, 20, and 30":

	12	15	20	30
	2×6	3×5	2×10	2×15
	$2 \times 2 \times 3$		$2 \times 2 \times 5$	$2 \times 3 \times 5$
or	$\{\mathbf{2^2 \times 3}\}$	$\{\mathbf{3 \times 5}\}$	$\{\mathbf{2^2 \times 5}\}$	$\{\mathbf{2 \times 3 \times 5}\}$

You now have all the information written down; you will need to find the LCD of the four fractions added and subtracted in this problem. To do so, write down a multiplication problem involving all the prime numbers/factors involved in the four sets of factor trees: "$2 \times 3 \times 5$". This is not the LCD for the four denominators, but it is close. The final step when finding the LCD is to refer to the factor tree multiplication problems just indicated with all the prime factors indicated. Look at the four sets of factor trees, above, and ask yourself the following question, "What is the greatest number of times each factor (prime number) occurred in one specific factor tree?" You will notice the prime factor "2" occurred twice in the set of prime factors for both "12 and 20" but only once in the set of prime factors for the number "30". According to the rule, the number "2" occurred twice in both the factor trees for "12 and 20", so the most the number "2" occurred in any one set of prime factors is twice. Therefore, when we find the LCD for the four denominators, the prime number "2" should be used twice when we multiply the prime factors. We could use either of the two notations: "2×2 or 2^2". The prime factor "3" occurred once in each of the groups of prime factors for the numbers "12, 15, and 30", so according to the rule, even though the number "3" was present in three of the sets of prime factors, the most the number "3" occurred in any one set of factors was once. This means when we find the LCD for the four denominators, we will only multiply by the prime number "3" once. The same is true for the prime number "5". The most the prime number "5" occurred in any one set of prime factors was again only once, even though it occurred in three different sets of factors. When you find the LCD for the four denominators, you should only multiply once by the prime number "5". Therefore, the LCD is computed using either of the following multiplication problems:

$$\text{“}2 \times 2 \times 3 \times 5 = 60 \quad \text{or} \quad 2^2 \times 3 \times 5 = 60\text{”.}$$

Why does the rule require you to use the largest exponent for each of the factors when finding the LCD/LCM? Let us respond to this question by using the two numbers "24" and "18". Many students may not be able to identify the LCM quickly without using a pencil and a piece of paper. The set of prime factors for the number "24" are $\{2 \cdot 2 \cdot 2 \cdot 3\}$, and the set of prime factors for the number "18" are $\{2 \cdot 3 \cdot 3\}$". The LCM is computed by multiplying the prime numbers "$2 \cdot 2 \cdot 2 \cdot 3 \cdot 3 = 72$". Since we are working with two numbers, we will focus on finding the LCM, which we know is a multiple of both "24" and "18". If we focus only on the number "2" and not on "$2 \cdot 2 \cdot 2$", which equals "8" or "2^3", then we would be focusing on numbers which are multiples of "2". The multiples of "2" are {2, 4, 6, 8, 10, etc.}, and there are a lot of numbers which are multiples of "2" and not multiples of "8". We could also consider the number "4", which is "$2 \cdot 2$" or "2^2" and look at the multiples of "4" which are {4, 8, 12, 16, 20, 24, 28, etc.}. Again, there are a lot of numbers which are multiples of the number "4" but not multiples of the number "8". Since the number "24" is divisible by the number "8" we know for a fact, the LCM must be divisible by the number "8" or "2^3" or "$2 \times 2 \times 2$". One may use the same reasoning with the number "3". The number "18" is a multiple of the number "9" which equals "$3 \cdot 3$" or "3^2". We must concentrate on numbers which are multiples of the number "9", not "3". Since we must find the LCM by concentrating on the two numbers "8" and "9", it is then logical why the LCM/LCD is "72.

The good news is, we are now ready to move on to step 2 in the process to find the answer to the problem "$\frac{7}{12} - \frac{2}{15} + \frac{11}{20} - \frac{1}{30}$". After we illustrate all the procedures required to solve this problem, we will illustrate how to find the LCD for the three fractions "$\frac{67}{88}$, $\frac{91}{96}$, and $\frac{103}{112}$" in example 2. This does not mean every 6th-grade student will be required to solve these types of problems daily, but the teacher should illustrate how to solve these problems when time permits. The goal in 5th grade is to introduce the rules necessary to simplify/solve all types of arithmetic fraction addition and subtraction problems. The goal in 6th grade is to emphasize the rules necessary to simplify/solve all types of arithmetic fraction addition and subtraction problems. The goal for all students before they enter an algebra class is, they master the entire process and can add and subtract all types of arithmetic addition and subtraction fraction problems. Even if all the students are not proficient when solving the most difficult addition and subtraction fraction problems, they will still be much more knowledgeable about the procedures and better prepared to enter an

Algebra 1 class. If the Algebra 1 teacher continues to review and teach the rules required to solve all types of addition and subtraction fraction problems, then even those students who may not have mastered the procedures when they entered the Algebra 1 class may reach a level of proficiency (level 8, 9, or 10 on my guesstimated 1-10 scale mentioned in Chapter 1) to be successful when they are required to work with rational expressions in Algebra 2.

Note we often use the word "simplify" when we talk about finding the answers for these fraction problems. We seldom use the word "solve" when we ask students to simply perform arithmetic operations. The word "solve" is used when we are solving an equation and an equation contains an equal relationship symbol (=). Every problem we have used as an example problem so far in this textbook has been a *simplification* problem, not an equation. Therefore, it is more proper for us to use the word "*simplify*" when we illustrate how to find the best way to write the answers to all the problems. The word "*simplify*" means to look at the given problem and write the answer in a more *simplified* form. Starting in pre-school, students are asked to find the answer to basic arithmetic problems such as "2 + 1", and teachers expect the students to respond with the answer "3". The answer "3" is a simplified form of the given problem "2 + 1". Here is the problem "2 + 1" written in the form of an equation, "2 + 1 =?" and in this case, you would find the value of the "?" which means you would solve the equation. Here is a similar equation where you need to solve for the question mark "?" involving the same three numbers, "1, 2, and 3". Find the value of the "?" given the equation: "2+? = 3". Do not get too concerned about the minor difference between the two words, "simplify" and "solve". Mathematicians often use the words interchangeably without thinking about the differences in arithmetic. Teaching Point: Problems contained in algebra textbooks are usually broken into four basic categories: "Simplify, Solve, Graph, and Word/Statement problems".

The first objective is to find the LCD for the four fractions indicated in the fraction addition and subtraction problem, "$\frac{7}{12} - \frac{2}{15} + \frac{11}{20} - \frac{1}{30}$". The second goal, after you find the LCD, is to find equivalent fractions with the LCD "60". When you are converting the four given fractions into equivalent fractions with the LCD "60" use "Young's Conversion Theorem". The process to convert the four fractions into equivalent fractions is the same process we repeatedly illustrated in Chapter 3 when we converted fractions into equivalent fractions with the required LCD. Some people might say writing the multiplication step indicating we are multiplying by the number $\underline{1}$ is cumbersome and not real helpful. The reason we insist students write the step focusing on multiplying by the number $\underline{1}$ is because in the future, when problems become more challenging, this step reinforces the process and the importance of "Young's Conversion Theorem".

Focus on each of the four fractions "$\frac{7}{12}, \frac{2}{15}, \frac{11}{20}$ and $\frac{1}{30}$" separately. When working with the fraction "$\frac{7}{12}$", concentrate on the denominator and divide the LCD "60" by the denominator "12". The answer to the division problem is "5". It is critical the answer after solving the division problem is a natural number because if there is a remainder after you solved the division problem, it means you do not have the least common denominator. The number "5" derived when solving the division problem "$\frac{60}{12} = 5$" is used to determine the form of the number $\underline{1}$, "$\frac{5}{5}$", to multiply the original fraction "$\frac{7}{12}$" by. The goal when working with the fraction "$\frac{7}{12}$" is to find the equal fraction with the LCD, "60". Here is the division problem required to determine the fraction which equals 1, "$\frac{\text{LCD}}{\text{Denominator First Fraction}} = \frac{60}{12}$".

The conversion process would look like this:

"$60 \div 12 = 5$ and $\frac{5}{5} = 1 \quad \therefore \quad \frac{7}{12} = \frac{7}{12} \times 1 = \frac{7}{12} \times \frac{5}{5} = \frac{7 \times 5}{12 \times 5} = \frac{35}{60}$".

The process of converting the other three fractions into equivalent fractions is illustrated in the following sentences. Notice, before we multiply each of the given fractions by the number 1, we first divide the LCD "60" by the respective denominator to determine the specific form of the number 1 to multiply each fraction. The conversion of the fraction "$\frac{2}{15}$" into an equivalent fraction with the denominator "60" looks like this: "$\frac{\text{LCD}}{\text{Denominator Second Fraction}} = 60 \div 15 = \frac{60}{15} = 4$ and $\frac{4}{4} = 1, \therefore \frac{2}{15} = \frac{2}{15} \times 1 = \frac{2}{15} \times \frac{4}{4} = \frac{2 \times 4}{15 \times 4} = \frac{8}{60}$". The conversion of the fraction "$\frac{11}{20}$" into the equivalent fraction with the denominator "60" will look like this: "$\frac{\text{LCD}}{\text{Denominator Third Fraction}} = 60 \div 20 = 3,\ and\ \frac{3}{3} = 1 \therefore \frac{11}{20} = \frac{11}{20} \times 1 = \frac{11}{20} \times \frac{3}{3} = \frac{11 \times 3}{20 \times 3} = \frac{33}{60}$". Finally, when you convert the fraction "$\frac{1}{30}$" into a fraction with the denominator "60", it will look like this: "$\frac{\text{LCD}}{\text{Denominator Fourth Fraction}} = \frac{60}{30} = 2,\ and\ \frac{2}{2} = 1 \therefore \frac{1}{30} = \frac{1}{30} \times 1 = \frac{1}{30} \times \frac{2}{2} = \frac{1 \times 2}{30 \times 2} = \frac{2}{60}$". (Notice, when we multiplied one of the given fractions by a fraction equal to 1, we used the one big fraction notation.)

Also, notice when we indicate we are dividing the LCD by a specific denominator, sometimes we write the division problem as a fraction, and sometimes we use the division symbol "÷" to indicate a division problem. When the LCD and the denominators are larger numbers, we may be forced to use a division box and solve a long division problem.

Make sure your students realize there are several ways to set up a division problem and they are proficient converting from one division notation into another division notation, automatically.

The basic procedures and notations taught in arithmetic will continually be used in advanced arithmetic and algebra solutions.

Go back and look at the conversion process for each of the four fractions involved in this addition and subtraction problem. In the first step, the goal was to find the LCD for the four denominators of the four fractions. The LCD was determined to be the number "60", and it was found by using mental math or **factor** trees and all the different **prime factors** involved in the **factor** trees. Each **prime factor** in the set of **factor** trees was used to find the LCD by multiplying all the **prime factors** with one caveat: For all **prime** numbers which occurred once and more than once in any set of **prime factors**, those **prime factors** were included in the multiplication process based on the most times the specific **factor** occurred in one set of the sets of **prime factors**. This does not mean if a **prime factor** occurred in several different **factor** tree sets, it would be used additional times in the multiplication process to find the LCD. A **prime factor** can only be used several times in the multiplication process to find the LCD if it occurs more than once in any one set of **prime factors** derived using **factor** trees.

LCMs and LCDs are computed using the same procedures.

We used bold print when we referred to the words "**prime**" and "**factors**" in the previous paragraph to emphasize the importance of both words when finding the LCD for several denominators. Everyone should already know what a **prime** number is. Not everyone knows the mathematical definition of the word "**factor(s)**. A "**factor**" is a number, term or expression which is one of the terms multiplied in a multiplication problem. If we write the multiplication problem "$2 \times 11 \times 15.2 \times 5\frac{3}{4} \times z \times (y + m)$", there are six **factors**. Note in the last sentence, "15.2" and "$5\frac{3}{4}$" each indicates a single number. The sixth factor is "$(y + m)$". Do not let these subtle teaching points go unnoticed by your students. (Refer to Chapter 2, where we emphasized a fraction indicates one point on a number line.)

In the second step, the goal is to find equivalent fractions for all the given fractions in the specific problem and make sure the equivalent fractions have the LCD determined in step 1. If the goal is to convert a particular fraction into an equivalent fraction, the best way to convert any number or expression is to multiply by a special form of the number 1. This is what "Young's Conversion Theorem" emphasizes. The rule used to determine the special form of the number 1, which you must multiply by when converting one fraction into an equivalent fraction, is, "Start with the LCD you have already determined and then divide the LCD by the denominator of the fraction you are going to convert into an equivalent fraction." The answer to the division problem (quotient) determines the form of the number 1; you will multiply the starting fraction by to find the equivalent fraction. If the quotient when you divide the LCD by the denominator of a specific fraction turns out to be "5", then the value of 1 you should multiply the starting fraction would be "$\frac{5}{5}$". Remember "$\frac{5}{5}$" is a special form of the number 1. In all four of the fractions involved in this problem, we divided the LCD "60" by the denominator of each fraction in the problem and then multiplied each fraction in the original problem by the special form of 1 determined in the division process. When you divide the LCD by any of the denominators in the given fractions, the quotient must be a natural number with no remainder. If there is a remainder when you do the division problem, then you either do not have the correct LCD, or you made a division mistake. We now have the following four equivalent fractions: "$\frac{7}{12} = \frac{35}{60}$, $\frac{2}{15} = \frac{8}{60}$, $\frac{11}{20} = \frac{33}{60}$, and $\frac{1}{30} = \frac{2}{60}$".

> Multiplying, adding, dividing, and subtracting a fraction equal to the number "1" in the form, "$\frac{n}{n}$", (examples of fractions in the form "$\frac{n}{n}$" are $\frac{6}{6}$, $\frac{77}{77}$, $\frac{105.2}{105.2}$, etc.), sounds like a simple procedure to understand, but is it?

Step three is the easiest step in the process. Simply substitute; go back to the original problem and replace each of the original fractions with the appropriate equivalent fraction with the LCD, and then just as in every other fraction addition and subtraction problem, add and subtract the numerators and keep the least common denominator.

Original Problem: $\frac{7}{12} - \frac{2}{15} + \frac{11}{20} - \frac{1}{30}$

Same Problem - All Denominators are "60: $\frac{35}{60} - \frac{8}{60} + \frac{33}{60} - \frac{2}{60}$

The problem may be written as one fraction: $\frac{35-8+33-2}{60}$

Do the arithmetic involving only the numerators: "$35 - 8 + 33 - 2 = 58$" The number "58" is the numerator in the answer with the denominator "60".

Here is the final answer - almost: $\frac{58}{60}$

Your students should realize the fraction "$\frac{58}{60}$" will reduce, and the final answer is "$\frac{29}{30}$".

Here is another vital teaching point: students who struggle with the multiplication tables might not recognize the numerator and the denominator in the fraction "$\frac{58}{60}$" will reduce by dividing both numbers in the fraction by "2". The number "2" in this situation is referred to as the GCF. This is a simple reducing problem, but the larger the numbers in the numerator and the denominator become, the more students will struggle to reduce fractions. When we wanted students to reduce large numbers in a fraction, we instructed them to set up factor trees for both the numerator and the denominator. Then rewrite the fraction and replace the numerator and the denominator with the prime numbers derived from the factor trees. Finally, continually emphasize to students any number, term, or expression divided by the identical number, term, or expression always cancels and becomes 1. The fraction

"$\frac{58}{60}$" written using factor trees looks like this: "$\frac{2\times29}{2\times2\times3\times5}$". Notice there is a single "2" in the numerator and two "2's" in the denominator. The "2" in the numerator will cancel with one of the "2's" in the denominator, and the fraction then becomes "$\frac{29}{2\times3\times5}$", which equals "$\frac{29}{30}$". Fittingly, this is the same method Algebra 1, and Algebra 2 instructors expect students to use when they simplify algebra fraction problems which involve reducing, multiplying, and dividing. This reducing procedure will be illustrated throughout this textbook with arithmetic problems and later in Chapter 8 with rational expressions.

Student Work	Factor Trees to the side
$\frac{7}{12}-\frac{2}{15}+\frac{11}{20}-\frac{1}{30}$	12 15 20 30
	$2\times2\times3$ 3×5 $2\times2\times5$ $2\times3\times5$
	The LCM is NOT: $2\times3\times5$ The LCM is $2\times2\times3\times5=60$
$\frac{60}{12}=5 \therefore \frac{7}{12}\times1=\frac{7}{12}\times\frac{5}{5}=\frac{35}{60}$	The alternate form of the LCM is $2^2\times3\times5=60$
$\frac{60}{15}=4 \therefore \frac{2}{15}\times1=\frac{2}{15}\times\frac{4}{4}=\frac{\mathbf{2\times4}}{\mathbf{15\times4}}=\frac{8}{60}$	Notice the additional big fraction "$\frac{\mathbf{2\times4}}{\mathbf{15\times4}}$"
$\frac{60}{20}=3 \therefore \frac{11}{20}\times1=\frac{11}{20}\times\frac{3}{3}=\frac{33}{60}$	
$\frac{60}{30}=2 \therefore \frac{1}{30}\times1=\frac{1}{30}\times\frac{2}{2}=\frac{\mathbf{1\times2}}{\mathbf{30\times2}}=\frac{2}{60}$	Notice the additional big fraction "$\frac{\mathbf{1\times2}}{\mathbf{30\times2}}$"

$$\frac{35}{60}-\frac{8}{60}+\frac{33}{60}-\frac{2}{60}=\frac{35-8+33-2}{60}=\frac{58}{60}=\frac{2\times29}{2\times2\times3\times5}=\frac{29}{30}$$

(In these examples, we started to illustrate how you may write <u>multiplication</u> problems involving fractions as <u>one big fraction</u>, just like the <u>one big fraction</u> idea when <u>adding</u> and <u>subtracting</u> fractions. When students begin to write the solutions to these problems using the one big fraction notation, they start to realize the difference between the denominator rule for adding and subtracting fractions and the denominator rule when multiplying fractions. The students will eventually learn the rule for dividing two fractions, but they will not have to learn an additional rule regarding how to work with the denominators after the fraction division problems are changed to fraction multiplication problems.) *(FRT 9: We believe if students solve addition, subtraction, multiplication, and division problems as one big fraction prior to the final computations, then much of the confusion with respect to different fraction rules will be eliminated.)*

Twice in the previous two pages we used the word cancel when we reduced a fraction. The word cancel is frequently used by teachers when reducing fractions. Technically the two numbers in the fraction are part of a division problem and the quotient equals **one (1).**

As a point of interest, when we divide the LCD by a denominator of a fraction we are working with, we suggest you use fractional notation rather than the division symbol "÷" or the division box. The fraction division notation is preferable because it is more practical when simplifying rational expressions (algebra fractions).

Students must be able to quickly convert from one division notation into another division notation.

One can hear the critics now. That is way too much work! Kids will never write that many steps. We would love to tell you all students will master the procedures to solve these types of problems with 90% accuracy, even low-achieving math students. But we cannot! We can say with confidence all students, even low achieving students, as a minimum will realize when they add and subtract fractions, they must find an LCD. Almost all students will learn how to multiply by the special form of the number 1. Students will understand when they add and subtract fraction problems, the procedures to multiply and divide fraction problems are significantly different. Students will realize when they have an addition or subtraction fraction problem with the same denominator, these are the easy problems, and they will quickly solve them with 80%-95% accuracy.

Since simplifying challenging arithmetic addition and subtraction fraction problems is probably the most difficult process to master in arithmetic, our goal for low-achieving 9th – 12th grade students must be to ensure they can simplify all types of fraction problems which they should have been able to simplify in 5th, 6th, 7th, and 8th-grade textbooks. Be satisfied if you accomplish this goal with 70% of these students by the end of the school year. The other reason we do not expect the low achieving 9th-12th grade students to master adding and subtracting challenging fraction problems is this might be the first year many of them learned how to add and subtract the simple addition and subtraction fraction problems. It will take an extra year or two of hard work from both the teachers and the students to ensure 75%-90% of these students reach level 8, 9, or 10 on the hypothetical, "1-10" scale discussed in Chapter 1. We frequently discuss the improvement low achieving students can experience throughout this textbook, but average and high achieving students do not argue when expected to write the indicated steps. In the end, they achieve at the "13-15" level mentioned in Chapter 1. With average and high achieving students, integrate some algebra fraction problems in the classroom discussions (example: $\frac{211}{x^2y^3} + \frac{367}{x^2y^3} - \frac{11.3}{x^2y^3} = \frac{566.7}{x^2y^3}$). Are you able to do the arithmetic addition and subtraction problem involving the numerators "211, 367, and 11.3" in your head without a calculator or without lining up the three numbers in the vertical addition format? We want you and your students to develop number sense applications and look for ways to group numbers so solutions can be computed in your head.

After you convert the four original fractions into equivalent fractions with the least common denominator "60", it is easy to arrange the fractions from smallest to largest or vice versa. The key when writing the given fractions from smallest to the largest is to simply work with the fractions with the LCD "60" and focus on the numerators. The following group of fractions is written in increasing order: "$\frac{2}{60}$, $\frac{8}{60}$, $\frac{33}{60}$, and $\frac{35}{60}$". This means the original group of fractions written from smallest to largest would be: "$\frac{1}{30}$, $\frac{2}{15}$, $\frac{11}{20}$, and $\frac{7}{12}$" or "$\frac{1}{30} \leq \frac{2}{15} \leq \frac{11}{20} \leq \frac{7}{12}$". You can also explain the difference between the two relationship symbols "$<$" and "$\leq$" when you write the fractions in increasing order. When we list the fractions in increasing order, we are not focused on the negative sign or subtraction operation symbol to the left of two of the fractions. We are only interested in the value of each individual fraction at this time. Every arithmetic teacher and mathematician should recognize a negative sign to the left of any number indicates the number is less than 0, and the positive numbers are greater than the negative numbers. In a sense, we are working with the *absolute value* of the fraction or the *magnitude* of the fraction. When adding and subtracting fractions, always check to ensure the fractions you start with are reduced, so the problem is less cumbersome and always check to ensure the final answer is reduced to the lowest terms.

Teach students to identify number patterns to mentally solve problems. Add and subtract these three numerators in your head, "211 + 367 – 11.3 from a previous problem. First subtract 211-11=200, then add 200+367=567 and finally subtract the decimal .3 yielding the numerator 566.7 in the final answer.

We hope you noticed how we interleave adding, subtracting, and multiplying fractions into one problem when writing the solution. We also interleave the concept of greater than and less than into our discussion involving many of our example problems (Patel et al., 2017; Richland et al., 2005).

Teaching Comment - In arithmetic and mathematics, there are two different signs which are placed to the left of any number or expression. The two signs are referred to as a positive (+) sign or a negative (−) sign. When we refer to a subtraction operation symbol

"−", or an addition operation symbol "+", we realize the notation for the operations and the notation for the signs look identical. Do not get too concerned about this minor difference, and do not let the students become confused about the difference between the sign notations and the operation notations. This is a topic which should be clarified by math teachers in middle school or high school.

In the example problem 1 above, we illustrated and explained how to find LCMs for a group of numbers and LCDs for a set of denominators involving fractions. We frequently illustrated how to use "Young's Conversion Theorem" to convert the original fractions into equivalent fractions with the least common denominator. There was a second theorem mentioned earlier in this textbook, but we have not yet illustrated extensively how to use "Young's Equation/Ratio Theorem". We applied "Young's Equation/Ratio Theorem" several times when illustrating how to simplify the previous example problems, but when solving basic arithmetic problems, it is not as obvious as it will be later when solving conversion problems.

> Here is the simplified version of "**Young's Equation/Ratio Theorem**". If you have an equation, which means the expression on the left side of the equation is equal to the expression on the right side of the equation, then you can form a fraction or ratio using both sides of the equation as either the numerator or denominator and the fraction or ratio will always equal 1. You need to be aware there is one exception to this statement.

Here are a few example arithmetic problems to illustrate the meaning of "Young's Equation/Ratio Theorem": "$8 + 1 = 9 \quad \therefore \frac{8+1}{9} = 1$ or $\frac{9}{8+1} = 1$", "$11 = 11 \quad \therefore \frac{11}{11} = 1$", "$10 \div 5 = 2 \quad \therefore \frac{10\div5}{2} = 1$ or $\frac{2}{10\div5} = 1$". All these equations are special equations referred to as identities. (Comment: We will explain the difference between an equation, an identity, and another special situation referred to as the Reflexive Property later in this textbook.)

There is a rule in arithmetic that states, "It is impossible to divide a number or expression by the number "0"." Here are two examples which are impossible to simplify based on this rule: "$0 = 2 - 2$ but $\frac{0}{2-2}$ and $\frac{2-2}{0}$" are impossible fractions to solve and "$6 + 5 - 11 = 6 \times 0$ but $\frac{6\times0}{6+5-11}$ and $\frac{6+5-11}{6\times0}$" are also impossible fractions to solve. The denominators in all four of the fractions indicated in this paragraph equal "0", and the correct mathematical answer for all four fractions is "The fractions are UNDEFINED".

Every time we divided the LCD by the denominator of a given fraction in previous problems already discussed in this book, we found a quotient. Once we found the quotient, we could write an identity and use "Young's Equation/Ratio Theorem" to help us find the special form of the number 1 to multiply the given fraction by and find the equivalent fraction with the LCD for the respective problem. In the problem just discussed "$\frac{7}{12} - \frac{2}{15} + \frac{11}{20} - \frac{1}{30}$", there were four fractions, and we had to divide the LCD "60" by each of the individual denominators. When we divided "60" by the denominator "12" above in the first fraction. "$\frac{7}{12}$", we found the quotient "5". We then visualized the equation "$5 = 5$", which is an *identity*, and applied "Young's Equation/Ratio Theorem" to determine the equation "$\frac{5}{5} = 1$". We already know the fraction "$\frac{5}{5} = 1$" based on our knowledge that a fraction is a special type of division problem. In the second fraction "$\frac{2}{15}$", we divided the LCD "60" by the denominator "15", and the quotient equaled "4". We realized "4 = 4" and used "Young's Equation/Ratio Theorem" to determine the fact "$\frac{4}{4} = 1$". We then used the same procedures to find the special values of the number 1 to multiply the fractions "$\frac{11}{20}$ and $\frac{1}{30}$".

We will continue to use "Young's Equation/Ratio Theorem" and "Young's Conversion Theorem" throughout this textbook when we illustrate how to solve more challenging arithmetic and algebra conversion problems. The more you read and study the illustrations contained in this textbook, the more comfortable you will become with the application of both theorems when simplifying a wide variety of math problems.

> Sometimes, a detailed solution seems so obvious when solving some problems, it might seem worthless. We want you to remember what we previously stated about simple problems. "When you use the correct rules to solve simple problems, the rules do not seem to be necessary, and it is easier to solve the problem without focusing on the rules."

2. Simplify: "$\frac{67}{88} + \frac{91}{96} - \frac{103}{112}$"

This problem is more challenging than previous examples, but our goals at this moment are to illustrate how to compute LCDs for all types of denominators, use "Young's Conversion Theorem" to find the three fractions equivalent to the original fractions, and then add and subtract the fractions to find the answer. Read the following explanation for adding and subtracting the three indicated fractions slowly. If you understand how we found the LCD "7,392", how we converted all three given fractions into equivalent fractions, and then how we added and subtracted the three fractions, you might/should understand how to simplify algebra addition and subtraction problems. If you understand the explanation to add and subtract the three indicated fractions in the next few paragraphs, this is the first step to "learning and remembering" how to work with these types of problems. The second step is the important step. If you are going to be successful in advanced mathematics classes, you must practice simplifying these types of problems until you have mastered the concepts and the procedures.

Step 1: Find the least common denominator for the three (3) denominators "88, 96, and 112" in the given fractions. We gave the least common multiple (LCM) for the three numbers at the end of Chapter 2. Remember, the least common denominator (LCD) for the denominators of the three indicated fractions must be the same as the LCM: "7,392". You will also be forced to use the rules discussed in the previous example problem to determine the LCD, just like you would have to do in an Algebra 2 class with rational expressions. We have attempted to explain the difference between an LCM and an LCD and how to find the LCM and LCD using factor trees (prime numbers) previously in this textbook. In this example problem, the number "7,392" is the smallest number which is a multiple of "88", "96", and "112". Therefore, "7392" is the LCM for the three numbers, and consequently "7392" is also the LCD. This also means when you multiply all three numbers by one of the natural numbers "2, or 3, or, 4, or 5, or 6, or 7, or 8, or 9, or 66, or 77, or 84" you will eventually find the product, the answer in a multiplication problem, will equal the number "7,392". The number "7,392" is the <u>smallest</u> number which is a multiple of each of the three numbers "88", "96", and "112" therefore all three numbers will divide evenly into "7,392". If you divide "7,392" by "88" the quotient is "84". If you divide "7,392 by 96 the answer is 77". If you divide "7,392 by 112 the quotient is 66". Since the last three sentences are mathematical division facts, this also means if you multiply "88 times 84 the product is 7,392" and "96 times 77 is 7,392" and "112 times 66 is "7,392".

We already illustrated how to use factor trees to compute the LCD/LCM for four previous problems. Three of the four problems were typical 5th or 6th grade arithmetic textbook problems in Chapter 3, and one of the four problems was example 1 just discussed, which is a little more challenging. If you are proficient with the multiplication tables, you could find the LCD/LCM for all four previous problems using mental math. When we find the LCD for the three fractions in this example problem "$\frac{67}{88}, \frac{91}{96}$, and $\frac{103}{112}$", we will use factor trees and explain the procedures to find the LCM "7,392" for the numbers "88, 96, and 112". Finding the sum and difference of the three fractions, "$\frac{67}{88}, \frac{91}{96}$, and $\frac{103}{112}$" is a challenging fraction arithmetic problem but expect all students who are going to enter an academic algebra class to be familiar with the entire process.

> Research indicates, almost all students recognize a fraction written as "$\frac{n}{n}, \frac{7}{7}, \frac{66}{66}, or\ \frac{10}{10}$", all equal "1". This makes sense, I hope.

Now, we will illustrate how to use "Young's Conversion Theorem" to simplify the problem "$\frac{67}{88} + \frac{91}{96} - \frac{103}{112}$". We did not yet go through the procedure using factor trees to find the LCD for this problem, but we will. The number "7,392" is the LCD for the three denominators "88, 96, and 112", so my next goal is to illustrate how to find the three fractions which are equal to the given fractions with the required LCD.

Step 2: In this step, the most important thing is to figure out the special form of the number $\underline{1}$ to multiply each of the three individual fractions by, to find equivalent fractions. Since we must determine this, use the procedure referred to as long division and divide the

LCD "7,392" by each of the individual denominators "88, 96, and 112". After doing the three (3) division problems, you end up with the following quotients: "84, 77, and 66" as previously indicated. Notice, the three quotients after dividing the LCD "7,392" by the three denominators "88, 96, and 112" are natural numbers with no remainders.

Your goal is <u>not</u> to find any common denominator for a group of fractions. Your goal must be to have your students find the least common denominator when they are adding and subtracting fractions in arithmetic. If you permit your students to simply multiply the denominators of the given fractions in an addition or subtraction problem to find a common denominator, you are creating additional work for your students in arithmetic and illustrating a method which will make many rational addition and subtraction problems nearly impossible to simplify/solve in Algebra 2.

When working with the first fraction "$\frac{67}{88}$", the following arithmetic procedures must be completed: "$\frac{\text{LCD}}{\text{Denominator First Fraction}} = 7{,}392 \div 88 = 84$" and then multiply the fraction by the number <u>1</u> written in the form "$\frac{84}{84} = 1$". The division problem when concentrating on the second fraction "$\frac{91}{96}$", becomes "$\frac{\text{LCD}}{\text{Denominator Second Fraction}} = 7{,}392 \div 96 = 77$" and multiply the second fraction by "$\frac{77}{77}$", which equals <u>1</u>. When working with the third fraction "$\frac{103}{112}$", solve the following division problem, "$\frac{\text{LCD}}{\text{Denominator Third Fraction}} = 7{,}392 \div 112 = 66$", and determine the special form of the number <u>1</u> used to find the equivalent fraction. The fraction "$\frac{66}{66}$" is the special fraction equal to <u>1</u> required to multiply the fraction "$\frac{103}{112}$" in this case.

$$88\overline{)7392}^{\,84} \qquad 96\overline{)7392}^{\,77} \qquad 112\overline{)7392}^{\,66}$$

Teachers may wonder if they should have the students do the long division process for all three division problems. Solving long division problems is so cumbersome, and the process involves so many different steps. Comment: "If you want your students to develop strong mental skills involving number sense, then the answer is simple: make sure they solve all or most of the division problems using pencil and paper." If you want your students not to develop a keen sense of numbers, then allow them to use calculators. There is research available for you to read which leads one to believe that learning the procedures and solving problems using the long division process is a strong indicator to determine if students will be successful in algebra (Siegler et al., 2012). Since you are the teacher, you must decide whether the students may use their calculators to find the quotients when they are dividing the LCD by the different denominators of the different fractions. The teacher must always decide whether to allow the students to use calculators or not use calculators to solve problems. The question should be, "Do you want to prepare your students to spontaneously focus on relationships between all types of numbers and be prepared for algebra? (McMullen, Hannula-Sormunen, & Lehtinen, 2017).

Once we find the three quotients "84", "77", and "66", the goal is to find the three equivalent fractions with the LCD "7,392". The three quotients computed are used to set up the following three identities and determine three fractions which all equal 1 and will be used to find the three equivalent fractions: "$84 = 84 \therefore \frac{84}{84} = 1$", "$77 = 77 \therefore \frac{77}{77} = 1$", and "$66 = 66 \therefore \frac{66}{66} = 1$". We set up the three *identities* and used "Young's Equation/Ratio Theorem" to set up the three specific fractions which all equal 1 and will be needed when we use "Young's Conversion Theorem" in step 3 below to convert the three given fractions into equivalent fractions.

> Research also indicates, students hesitate when solving the following example problems: "$\frac{11}{11} + 4\frac{1}{5} = 5\frac{1}{5}$", or "$11\frac{5}{8} - \frac{7}{7} = 10\frac{5}{8}$", "$\frac{12}{13} \times \frac{13}{13} = \frac{12}{13}$", or "$\frac{3}{4} \div \frac{9}{9} = \frac{3}{4}$". There are very few problems like these in standard U. S. arithmetic textbooks (Shiller, Fan, & Siegler, 2022).

"Very Important Teaching Point and a Detour from the Solution"

We are inserting a couple of paragraphs to help everyone understand the difference between an equation, an identity, and the Reflexive Property? Remember, an **equation** indicates two arithmetic or mathematics expressions are equal. (Examples - Single Equations and Double Equations: "$0 = 0$", "$2 + 5 = 7$", "$\frac{12}{3} = 4$", "$x = 5 + 2 \therefore x = 7$", "$y - 2 = 11 \therefore y = 13$", "$3^3 = \frac{81}{3}$".) Notice the left and right sides of the equations are equal, but not necessarily identical. An **identity** is a special type of equation. An **identity** is an equation where the left side of the equal symbol is *mathematically* **identical** to the right side of the equal symbol <u>if</u> the <u>arithmetic</u> and/or the <u>algebra</u> (advanced math) <u>computations</u> are <u>completed</u>. The following examples are all equations, and they are also mathematics **identities**: ("$2 + 5 = 7$", "$\frac{12}{3} = 4$", "$6 + 7 - 13 = 77 \times 0$", "$3^3 = \frac{81}{3}$", "$2(3 + x) = 6 + 2x$", "$3x + 5y - x + 2y = 2x + 7y$", "$7 = 7$", "$0 = 0$"). The next examples are all equations, and they are all **identities**, but they are a special type of **identity** which illustrates a property about numbers. The following equations/identities are all examples of the **Reflexive Property** which states the following fact, "Any term, number, or expression is equal to itself or **identical** to itself." (Examples: "$7 = 7$", "$0 = 0$", "$2 + 5 = 2 + 5$", "$\frac{12}{3} = \frac{12}{3}$", "$x = x$", "$x + 3^3 = x + 3^3$"). The **Reflexive Property** should remind you what happens when you stand in front of a mirror, you see your reflection. You need to recognize in an **equation** the expressions on the left side and right side of the equal relationship symbol, are always *mathematically* equal. An **identity** is a special equation such that when all mathematical operations are completed on both sides of the equation, you will recognize both sides are **identical**. The **Reflexive Property** is a special **identity** such that you recognize immediately the two sides are **identical**. No work is required to recognize the left and right sides of the equation are the same when you illustrate the **Reflexive Property.**

All the problems indicated in the previous paragraph were equations. Several were **identities,** and some of the **identities** were examples of the **Reflexive Property.** Often in mathematics, we are required to solve equations and determine a number or numbers which will make the equation an **identity**. In the first list of problems in the last paragraph, one example was: "$x = 5 + 2 \ \therefore \ x = 7$". This example involves two equations, and if you substitute the number "7" into the first equation for the variable "x" you have the **identity**, "$7 = 5 + 2$". The fourth example in the first list of equations was: "$y - 2 = 11 \ \therefore \ y = 13$". The previous example involves two equations, and if you substitute the number, "13" into the first equation for the variable "y" you have the **identity**, "$13 - 2 = 11$".

Here is a new example to illustrate when you solve an equation, there may be two (and sometimes more than two) solutions which may be substituted back into the original equation to form an **identity**: "$x^2 - 5x + 6 = 0$". The following two solutions both make the given equation an **identity**: "$x = 2 \ and \ x = 3$". When you substitute the number "2" into the equation, "$x^2 - 5x + 6 = 0$", the solution looks like this: "$2^2 - 5(2) + 6 = 4 - 10 + 6 = 0$". If you substitute the number "3" into the given equation, the solution looks like this: "$3^2 - 5(3) + 6 = 9 - 15 + 6 = 0$". When we substituted the two numbers "2" and "3" into the initial equation, the final equations in both cases turned out to be an **identity:** "$4 - 10 + 6 = 0$" or "$0 = 0$" and "$9 - 15 + 6 = 0$" or "$0 = 0$".

Since we have taken a detour to find the solution to the fraction problem, "$\frac{67}{88} + \frac{91}{96} - \frac{103}{112}$", this is an excellent time to illustrate another method to solve division problems if you know the answer must be an integer. This new method will work well when you divide the LCD "7,392" by each of the three denominators "88", "96", and "112" rather than using the long division process. Since we know the LCD for the three denominators "88", "96", and "112" is "7,392", we must realize all three of these denominators will divide into the LCD, with no remainder. We encourage you to illustrate the following division method to your students as an enrichment exercise late in the year in 5th grade and emphasize the procedure in 6th grade. We want all students to be proficient with this division procedure prior to entering Algebra 1. This procedure is not normally mentioned in arithmetic textbooks, but this procedure is the main method students will use when they work with rational expressions in Algebra 2. Expect students who have not mastered the multiplication and division facts to experience problems when working with this process, but we discovered if this process is presented over the course of 4-6 months and students practice working with this procedure frequently, students' mental math multiplication and division skills will significantly improve.

The method illustrated below will be emphasized in Chapter 8 when students are required to reduce, multiply, and divide fractions. The method involves the prime factors for all three denominators and the prime factors for the LCD. Look at the three following illustrations where we used prime factors to reduce the fractions and determine the three quotients: "84, 96, and 112". The method demonstrated below, is a method we want all teachers and students to understand when they finish reading and studying this textbook but not necessarily at this time. The method illustrated below is the most common way to divide/reduce fraction problems in algebra (rational expressions). Write the prime factors for the numerator, "7392". We already wrote the prime factors for the LCD "7392" near the end of Chapter 2, "2 × 2 × 2 × 2 × 2 × 3 × 7 × 11". Next, write the primes factors for the first denominator, "88" in the same faction "2 × 2 × 2 × 11".

$$\frac{7392}{88} = \frac{2\times2\times2\times2\times2\times3\times7\times11}{2\times2\times2\times11} = \frac{2\times2\times3\times7}{1} = 84 \qquad 84 = 84 \qquad \therefore \quad \frac{84}{84} = 1$$

We cancelled all the identical prime numbers in both the numerator and the denominator (actually, we divided the identical numbers) to find the fraction, "$\frac{2\times2\times3\times7}{1}$", and then we multiply the prime numbers to find the quotient "84". If you have the correct LCD and divide by one of the denominators you used to determine the LCD, after you cancel the identical numbers in the numerator and the denominator, the denominator will always be <u>1</u>. We will divide the LCD in factored form by the two other denominators "96" and "112", which are also in factored form, and we should end up with the answers "77" and "66". The prime factors for the composite number "96" are "2 × 2 × 2 × 2 × 2 × 3". The prime factors for the composite number "112" are "2 × 2 × 2 × 2 × 7".

$$\frac{7392}{96} = \frac{2\times2\times2\times2\times2\times3\times7\times11}{2\times2\times2\times2\times2\times3} = \frac{7\times11}{1} = 77 \qquad 77 = 77 \qquad \therefore \quad \frac{77}{77} = 1$$

$$\frac{7392}{112} = \frac{2\times2\times2\times2\times2\times3\times7\times11}{2\times2\times2\times2\times7} = \frac{2\times3\times11}{1} = 66 \qquad 66 = 66 \qquad \therefore \quad \frac{66}{66} = 1$$

This is a procedure which works well with large LCDs and large denominators. It is also the procedure students <u>will</u> use when they are simplifying rational expressions in a 2nd year Algebra class.

I used the word cancelled in a paragraph to describe what occurred when I divided a number by the same identical number and the quotient equaled "1". The two words cancel and cancelled are words which many people use, and many people think they understand, so I will continue to use both words. BUT the words cancel and cancelled are mathematics slang words which I wish I had a better <u>one-word</u> option to use. Just something to think about.

The detour is over; we are now getting back to solving the given problem, "$\frac{67}{88}+\frac{91}{96}-\frac{103}{112}$".

Step 3: In this step we use "Young's Conversion Theorem" and multiply each of three given fractions by the special forms of the number 1 found in step 2 and the previous paragraphs to find three equivalent fractions.

Fraction 1: "$\frac{67}{88}=\frac{67}{88}\times 1=\frac{67}{88}\times\frac{84}{84}=\frac{67\times 84}{88\times 84}=\frac{\mathbf{5628}}{\mathbf{7392}}$"- The denominator in the last fraction must equal "7,392". We also used one of the previous identities to determine a special fraction equal to 1 using "Young's Equation/Ratio Theorem": "$84=84 \quad \therefore \quad \frac{84}{84}=1$". Notice, how we write the multiplication problem, "$\frac{67\times 84}{88\times 84}$" in the conversion process as <u>one big multiplication</u> problem. We like this big multiplication fraction notation because it emphasizes why you need to multiply the numerators and the denominators separately.

Fraction 2: "$\frac{91}{96}=\frac{91}{96}\times 1=\frac{91}{96}\times\frac{77}{77}=\frac{91\times 77}{96\times 77}=\frac{\mathbf{7007}}{\mathbf{7392}}$"- In order to be correct, the denominator in the last fraction must equal "7,392". This is the second time we used an identity to determine a special fraction equal to 1 using "Young's Equation/Ratio Theorem": "$77=77 \quad \therefore \quad \frac{77}{77}=1$". We used the one big fraction multiplication notation in the solution.

Fraction 3: "$\frac{103}{112}=\frac{103}{112}\times 1=\frac{103}{112}\times\frac{66}{66}=\frac{103\times 66}{112\times 66}=\frac{\mathbf{6798}}{\mathbf{7392}}$"- Make sure the last fraction has the denominator "7,392". Again, we used one of the previous identities to determine a special fraction equal to 1 using "Young's Equation/Ratio Theorem": "$66=66 \quad \therefore \quad \frac{66}{66}=1$".

Step 4: Refer back to the given problem and then substitute the equivalent fractions which were computed in step 3 for the three original fractions.

> Get into the habit of writing fractions as one big fraction when adding/subtracting fractions and when reducing/multiplying/dividing fractions. This should be one of the steps right before you find the answer for the problem.

$$\frac{67}{88}+\frac{91}{96}-\frac{103}{112}$$

$$\frac{5628}{7392}+\frac{7007}{7392}-\frac{6798}{7392}$$

Step 5: If you know the rules for adding and subtracting fractions, you know once the fractions have the same denominator (refer to step 4), then you simply either add or subtract the numerators of all the fractions and keep the LCD. We suggest you rewrite the three fractions with the LCD, "7392" as one big fraction. Write the problem as one big addition and subtraction fraction problem and then add and subtract the numerators. Also, write fraction multiplication problems and division problems after they have been converted to multiplication problems as one big multiplication problem, and reduce the identical factors in the numerators and the denominators prior to multiplying the numerators and the denominators. Research indicates students frequently get confused with the rules to add and subtract fractions versus multiplying and dividing fractions (Siegler et al., 2017). Using the one big fraction notation for each situation is a great method to help students avoid the confusion between the different procedures to solve fraction problems. *(FRT 9: We believe if students solve addition, subtraction, multiplication, and division problems as one big fraction prior to the final computations, then much of the confusion with respect to different fraction rules will be eliminated.)*

"$\frac{5628}{7392} + \frac{7007}{7392} - \frac{6798}{7392}$" This expression may also be written as: "$\frac{5628+7007-6798}{7392}$"

Now, do the arithmetic addition and subtraction problem in the numerator - "5628+7007=12635 then 12635-6798=5837". We have the information to write the final answer: "$\frac{5837}{7392}$". You may want the students to check to determine if the final fraction will reduce, it will not. The best way to determine if the final fraction will reduce is to write both the numerator and denominator as the product of prime numbers using factor trees. Here is the numerator "5837" written after we use prime numbers to determine the factors of "5837": "$5837 = 13 \times 449$". We already know the denominator "7392" written in factored form looks like this: "$2^5 \times 3 \times 7 \times 11$". Remember, we shared the set of factors when we found the LCM for the numbers "88, 96, and 112". The final answer can be written with the numerator and the denominator factored, and you should be able to determine there are no identical factors in both the numerator and the denominator, which means the fraction will not reduce "$\frac{5837}{7392} = \frac{13 \times 449}{2^5 \times 3 \times 7 \times 11}$".

We still have not illustrated how we found the LCD "7392" for the three denominators "88, 96, and 112". We will use the same procedures using factor trees illustrated in example problem 1 in this chapter to find the LCD "60". These are the same procedures used in Chapter 3 to find the LCD, for example problems 4, 8, and 13. If you understand the explanation contained in the next several paragraphs to find the LCD "7392" for the three indicated numbers, you might be ready to work with rational expressions in Algebra 2.

When we gave you the LCD "7,392" for the three fractions indicated above, the goal at that time was to illustrate the Power of One (1) and the application of "Young's Conversion Theorem" to find equivalent fractions for the three given fractions with the LCD "7,392". We will illustrate how to use the same rules explained in elementary arithmetic textbooks to simplify (add/subtract) these five (5) algebra fraction problems (rational expressions) at the end of this textbook: "$\frac{5}{8x^3y^2z} + \frac{5}{12x^2y^4z}$"; "$\frac{x+2}{x^2-x-12} + \frac{x+2}{x^2+6x+9}$"; "$\frac{x}{x^2-6x+9} - \frac{x}{x^2-7x+12} - \frac{1}{x^2-8x+16}$"; "$\frac{3m}{m^2+3m+2} - \frac{5m}{m+1}$"; and "$\frac{\frac{s}{a+b}+\frac{x}{b}}{\frac{a}{s+x}}$". Just because we illustrate all the rules required to simplify these (5) rational expressions contained in Chapter 8, does not mean you are prepared to work with the indicated algebra problems, which will require more illustrations on our part and a great deal of practice on your part.

It is now time to find the LCD "7,392" for the three denominators "88, 96, and 112" using *factor trees.* As explained in example 1 above and in the three indicated problems in Chapter 3, the first step to find an LCD when you are working with any challenging fraction problem is to use factor trees. Here are the final sets of prime factors for each of the three original denominators: "$88 = 2 \times 44 = 2 \times 2 \times 22 = 2 \times 2 \times 2 \times 11$" or "$2^3 \times 11$"; "$96 = 2 \times 48 = 2 \times 2 \times 24 = 2 \times 2 \times 2 \times 12 = 2 \times 2 \times 2 \times 2 \times 6 = 2 \times 2 \times 2 \times 2 \times 2 \times 3$" or "$2^5 \times 3$"; and "$112 = 2 \times 56 = 2 \times 2 \times 28 = 2 \times 2 \times 2 \times 14 = 2 \times 2 \times 2 \times 2 \times 7$" or "$2^4 \times 7$". When we are finding the LCD, we initially set up the following multiplication problem "$2 \times 3 \times 7 \times 11$" involving the four prime numbers indicated in the three sets of prime factors. This is not the least common denominator. We must determine the most times the prime number "2" occurred in one of the three sets of factor trees. Next, determine the most times the factor "3" occurred in one of the sets of factors and the same thing for the factors "7" and "11". It is obvious that the factor "2" occurred several times in all three sets of factors. However, the number "2" occurred five (5) times in the factor tree for the denominator "96", only three (3) times in the set of factors for the denominator "88", and only four (4) times in the set of factors for the denominator "112". The prime factor "3" occurred once in the set of prime factors for 96, the prime factor "7" only occurred once in the set of prime factors for "112", and the factor "11" only occurred once in the set of prime factors for "88". Therefore, the prime factors "3, 7, and 11" were only used once when we multiplied to get the LCD, but the prime factor "2" was used "5" times when we multiplied the prime factors to get the LCD "7,392". With this analysis, you should realize we found the LCD "7,392" by multiplying the following prime numbers: "$2 \times 2 \times 2 \times 2 \times 2 \times 3 \times 7 \times 11$" or "$2^5 \times 3 \times 7 \times 11$" to get the LCD "7,392". We already illustrated how to convert the given fractions into equivalent fractions and then add and subtract the numerators to get the final answer.

Comment for all math and arithmetic teachers: Rational expressions (algebra fractions) are a great challenge for most students because algebra students must finally use the rules and procedures just explained to solve or simplify the most challenging arithmetic problems and algebra fraction problems. The simplified procedures using mental math skills, which less than 50% of high school students in the United States have mastered to solve basic addition and subtraction fraction problems, is inadequate for many of these same students when they are required to work with abstract algebra rational expressions (Kloosterman et al., 2010; Stigler et al., 2010). With this thought in mind, interleave/interweave fractions, and decimals into algebra equations (Patel et al., 2017; Richland et al., 2005).

In Pre-algebra and Algebra 1 illustrate how to solve the following types of equations by initially interleaving simple fractions into the equation: "$x - 3\frac{1}{3} = 8\frac{1}{3}$". Do not emphasize you simply add the number "$3\frac{1}{3}$" to both sides of the equation. Illustrate to the students they should add the identity (equation) "$3\frac{1}{3} = 3\frac{1}{3}$" to the given equation and concentrate on the addition problem on the left side of the equals relationship symbols "=" and then on the addition problem on the right side of the equals relationship symbols "=". Write the identity (equation) "$3\frac{1}{3} = 3\frac{1}{3}$" directly under the equation "$x - 3\frac{1}{3} = 8\frac{1}{3}$" and insist the equals "=" relationship symbols are lined up vertically. (Refer to the illustration below.) Do this because you want students to be prepared to solve simultaneous equations later this year or in a couple years and not be required to change their thinking process.

Here is another situation to further explain a special teaching principle, "Teach the topic today with the goal to prepare students to solve similar but more challenging problems next month, next year, or in two years." When secondary math teachers teach functions and functional notation, always emphasize how the students will encounter functional notation in math classes in two or three years and specifically emphasize the notation they will encounter when they work with the definition of a derivative. We mentioned function notation because this is a topic/notation which is introduced in Algebra 1 and emphasized in Algebra 2 prior to students entering higher-level math classes, but few students master all the little intricacies of functional notation. You need to illustrate how to solve the simple problems mentally using functional notation and then reference functional notation frequently, discuss rules and procedures on day 2 or day 4 or next week to help students master the meaning of functional notation, which is essential for students' success in future advanced mathematics classes.

Solve the equation "$x - 3\frac{1}{3} = 8\frac{1}{3}$" for the variable "$x$" and instead of simply focusing on the mixed number "$3\frac{1}{3}$" as a single number on the left side of the equation, focus on the identity, "$3\frac{1}{3} = 3\frac{1}{3}$" or "$+3\frac{1}{3} = +3\frac{1}{3}$".

Line up the identity, "$3\frac{1}{3} = 3\frac{1}{3}$", under the given equation.

Add the identity, "$3\frac{1}{3} = 3\frac{1}{3}$", to the original equation.

$$\begin{aligned} x - 3\tfrac{1}{3} &= +8\tfrac{1}{3} \\ +3\tfrac{1}{3} &= +3\tfrac{1}{3} \\ \hline x + 0 &= 11\tfrac{2}{3} \\ \therefore\ x &= 11\tfrac{2}{3} \end{aligned}$$

Emphasize the two numbers "$-3\frac{1}{3}$" and "$+3\frac{1}{3}$" on the left side of the first and second equations becomes "0" in the third equation. Emphasizing that "$-3\frac{1}{3} + 3\frac{1}{3} = 0$" may seem meaningless but consider it a major teaching point when balancing equations. Emphasize to your students how they should work with two equations and add the terms on the left side of the two equations to find the left-hand side of the third equation, and then add the terms on the right side of the two equations to determine the right-hand side of the third equation. This is the mathematically correct way to solve this problem, and it is the way students will be required to solve simultaneous equations later in their algebra careers.

Here is a similar algebra equation to the example problem, which was just discussed in the last section. The difference between the problem just illustrated, and the next problem is, "The next problem is much easier to understand how to find the solution." The difference between the two equations/illustrations is minor, but it proves one of the main points of this textbook, "Working with fractions intensifies the difficulty of very basic problems" (Van Doreen, Lehtinen, & Vershaffel, 2015). Interleaving fractions and decimals as often as possible into your regular classroom discussions, homework assignments, quizzes, and tests are an excellent teaching principle to help students learn (Patel et al., 2017; Richland et al., 2005). This textbook focuses on fractions, but decimals are still part of the discussion. Do you realize it is almost impossible to talk about fractions without discussing decimals?

Solve the equation "$x - 3 = 8$" for the variable "x" and instead of simply focusing on the single number "3", on the left side of the equation, focus on the identity, "$3 = 3$" or "$+3 = +3$".

$$x - 3 = 8$$

Line up the identity, "$3 = 3$", under the original equation.

$$\underline{+3 = +3}$$

Add the identity, "$3 = 3$", to the given equation.

$$\therefore x + 0 = 11$$

Emphasize the two numbers "-3" and "$+3$" on the left side

$$\therefore x = 11$$

of the first two equations combined to become "0" in the third equation. <u>We want to emphasize again that "$-3 + 3 = 0$" may seem meaningless but consider it a major teaching point when balancing equations.</u> Illustrate how students should work with two equations and add the terms on the left side of the two equations to find the left side of the third equation, and then add the terms on the right side of the two equations to determine the right side of the third equation. This is the mathematically correct way to solve this problem, and it is the way students will be required to solve simultaneous equations later in their algebra careers. Does this second illustration seem easier than the previous one?

The level of difficulty of the addition and subtraction fraction problem "$\frac{67}{88} + \frac{91}{96} - \frac{103}{112}$" is far beyond what students will encounter in their normal arithmetic textbook. We illustrate this type of example problem because we know in a couple of years, students will be asked to add/simplify the following types of fractions in their algebra class which were mentioned previously: "$\frac{5}{8x^3y^2z} + \frac{5}{12x^2y^4z}$ and $\frac{x+2}{x^2-x-12} + \frac{x+2}{x^2+6x+9}$".

Based on the way you teach addition and subtraction of fractions in 5th, 6th, 7th, and/or 8th grade prior to students entering an algebra class, how would you write the simplified form of the two rational expressions just indicated? Imagine you are the algebra teacher, and the students do not know anything about the rules for finding LCDs and converting fractions into equivalent fractions, and then adding and/or subtracting the numerators when they encounter a difficult arithmetic problem. The algebra teacher must spend several days (perhaps weeks) teaching arithmetic rules and then very quickly have the students apply the rules they never learned in arithmetic to an abstract algebra problem. No wonder students seem to do "okay" in the United States on international tests in fourth grade, and as the students get older, the United States students fall further behind. The students never learn the arithmetic rules in the primary grades, but when they are older, they must learn a completely new set of steps to work with fractions and immediately work with algebra rational expressions. This is asking a lot from your above average and average math students. Maybe the best students can handle the quick transition from arithmetic to algebra when working with fractions, but many students have great difficulty with this adjustment. United States students seem to do worse on international mathematics tests as they get older, maybe because their foundation with arithmetic rules is in many cases absent from their learning experiences. The students are rarely challenged in arithmetic to learn how to solve more difficult problems. If many of the students cannot solve simple fraction problems in their heads with little written work, should the challenging problems be taught in elementary school? Think about your answer, then think about the difficulty level of the problems students are asked to solve in your classroom. We will illustrate how to add (simplify) the two algebra addition problems at the end of this book, along with four other more challenging rational expressions. In Chapter 8, we have included a section illustrating the arithmetic rules discussed throughout this textbook and how the arithmetic rules are required when students enter higher-level math classes.

Two Teaching Comments:

When you initially explain how to solve a problem, make sure you illustrate the proper procedures which will work for all similar problems.

1. We believe: The first way students learn to solve a problem is usually the method which is embedded in their minds to solve future problems. If there is another method to solve a problem, the second method is often not the method initially used by most students when they encounter similar problems. *(FRT 2: The "First Learned Method" is the method students rely on most frequently.)*
2. We believe: Understanding and working with the rules and procedures for any difficult math concept requires time. The more you spread out the time to allow students to learn/master a math concept the better the students will "learn and remember" the procedures. *(FRT 5: If students are exposed to rules in mathematics for a longer time frame, then their long-term memory will improve.)*

   The following comments are two checklists for elementary teachers to focus on when they teach fraction addition and subtraction problems.

Checklist #1:

1. Make sure the students can find the least common denominators (LCDs) in their heads using their knowledge of the multiplication tables for <u>simple fraction problems</u>.
2. Apply "Young's Conversion Theorem" to find equivalent fractions for the original fractions given in the problem which do not have a denominator equal to the LCD.
3. Add and/or subtract the fractions to form a single fraction by concentrating on the numerators once the denominators are identical.

4. If necessary, reduce the fraction in the final step.

Checklist #2:

1. Illustrate and assign additional problems to ensure the students work with the rules (factor trees) to find the least common denominator (LCD) for addition and subtraction problems when the given denominators are larger and normally beyond the student's knowledge of their basic multiplication tables.

2. Determine specific fractions that equal 1, such as "$\frac{2}{2}$" and "$\frac{17}{17}$" which are necessary when converting fractions into equivalent fractions with the LCD determined in step 1.

3. Utilize "Young's Conversion Theorem" to find equivalent fractions for any fraction which does not have a denominator equal to the LCD.

4. Add and/or subtract the fractions by concentrating on the numerators.

5. If necessary, reduce the final fraction.

In step 2 in the second checklist above, the students must know how to use "Young's Equation/Ratio Theorem" to find specific fractions which equal the number 1 to multiply each of the given fractions. When converting fractions into equivalent fractions and multiplying by the following types of fractions "$\frac{12}{12}, \frac{88}{88}, \frac{5}{5}$", it must be obvious these fractions equal 1. Students must realize the three fractions just indicated were all derived from "Young's Equation/Ratio Theorem" and the three identities ($12 = 12$, $88 = 88$, and $5 = 5$). Do you remember how to determine the specific identity to use to convert any given fraction into an equivalent fraction with the necessary LCD? If not, please go back and review the example problems and explanations illustrated earlier in this chapter. Some teachers may think it is not important to emphasize these procedures at this time. The main reason we emphasize "$12 = 12$ and therefore $\frac{12}{12} = 1$" when solving these types of problems is to illustrate why the mental math skills used by good mathematicians work and to have all the students understand the steps required when they solve conversion problems in Chapter 6.

> Frequently, interleave these types of problems into your homework/classwork assignments: "$6\frac{3}{7} + \frac{12}{12} = 7\frac{3}{7}$", "$\frac{88}{88} \times \frac{33}{47} = \frac{33}{47}$".

using their knowledge of the multiplication tables. Students should also be able to quickly find the fraction equivalent to "$\frac{1}{2}$" since the LCD is "4" and determine the fraction "$\frac{1}{2}$" is equal to "$\frac{2}{4}$". Students must be able to solve simple addition and subtraction fraction problems like the problems in Chapter 2 and Chapter 3 quickly in their heads or with little written work, but they should also understand the rules to find the LCD and convert a fraction into an equivalent fraction by using "Young's Conversion Theorem". Wow, what a dream! Over 50% of the students entering seventh grade fail to solve simple fraction addition and subtraction problems with denominators of "2, 3, 4, 5, 6, 8, 9, 10, and 12", which was the first goal in the previous paragraph (McMullen et al., 2017, Lortie-Forgues et al., 2015, Heller et al., 1990).

> Another fraction problem to interleave into homework/classwork assignments to help develop number sense: Estimate the answer given "$\frac{6}{7} + \frac{13}{15} = ?$". Multiple choice: a. "1', b. "2", c. "3", or d. "$\frac{19}{22}$'. Ans. = "2".

Probably less than 50% of U.S. high school graduates can pull off the trick, which is to solve simple fraction addition and subtraction problems with denominators of "2, 3, 4, 5, 6, 8, 9, 10, and 12" (Stigler et al., 2010). If this is reality, then how can we continue to justify teaching arithmetic using the same procedures which have failed for decades? With this thought in mind, we believe it is important that 90% of all students can simplify all 5th, 6th, and 7th grade textbook fraction problems with 80%-90% accuracy.

Students must have a strong understanding of fractions if we want them to make accurate estimates with fraction arithmetic problems involving two fractions. Number sense with fractions is seldom emphasized at any grade level, and yet being able to estimate and mentally picture an answer is a key to mastering fractions. Since fraction knowledge is so crucial for success in algebra and high-level mathematics courses, fractions must be a major priority for all 4th, 5th, 6th, and 7th grade arithmetic teachers. The only way to ensure students get the opportunity to continually work with all types of fraction problems is to interleave/interweave a few fraction problems regularly into homework assignments, quizzes, and tests. If you begin to teach and emphasize challenging addition and subtraction fraction problems which are never mentioned in elementary textbooks or discussed in the classroom, the students will begin to understand how to solve the more difficult fraction problems, and in the process the students will become more proficient simplifying basic textbook fraction problems (Siegler et al., 2011; Torbeyns et al., 2015; Van Doreen et al., 2015). If this would happen, it would benefit all students and probably help them better understand arithmetic and consequently be better prepared for algebra.

Even though we are emphasizing procedures required to solve all types of fraction arithmetic problems, it is extremely important to illustrate how to solve the simple fraction problems with simple denominators of "2, 3, 4, 5, 6, 8, 10, and 12" using graphs, pictures, and computer illustrations.

> Understanding concepts first, leads to the development of procedures and rules, which leads to mastery in arithmetic and mathematics.

If all students learn are the concepts when working with any arithmetic topic, they will never be prepared for abstract problems in algebra. If students only learn procedures, they will never fully comprehend why the procedures work. Concepts and procedures work together to lead to full mastery of most mathematics topics, but students cannot be fully knowledgeable of most topics without understanding both concepts and procedures.

Below are the necessary steps for most students to write when they simplify example 2, "$\frac{67}{88}+\frac{91}{96}-\frac{103}{112}$". Many elementary teachers and many secondary mathematics teachers may not have realized why prime factors and the factor tree process were introduced in arithmetic. Who knew there was an important reason why the section on prime numbers and factor trees was mentioned in arithmetic textbooks? When working with factor trees and prime numbers, it is an excellent time to introduce the students to the "Fundamental Theorem of Arithmetic". If you do not know what I mean when I refer to the "Fundamental Theorem of Arithmetic", it may be something you should look up on the internet. If mathematicians bothered to coin such a statement, it might be important when teaching arithmetic. Rest assured, the theorem involves prime numbers, composite numbers, and factor trees.

Reminder: When we use the abbreviation *(FRT #: Comment)* we are suggesting "Future Research Topics" for math researcher to consider. A list of all the *Future Research Topics (FRTs)* suggested in this textbook are listed at the end of the textbook.

> When simplifying rational expressions in algebra, the first step when you intend to work with any rational expression will often require you to factor either the denominators of all the fractions or factor both the numerators and denominators of all the fractions. Of course, there are times when the problems are so basic, factoring might not be necessary. This same type of statement can be made regarding challenging arithmetic fraction problems, but instead of using the word "factor" in algebra, the phrases "factor trees" or "prime numbers" or "prime factors" should be used in arithmetic.

The following is a step-by-step illustration to solve the problem. You, the teacher, may decide which steps the students may skip when they write the solution.

$\frac{67}{88}+\frac{91}{96}-\frac{103}{112}$ Find the LCD off to the side using *prime factors.*

88	96	112
2×44	2×48	2×56
$2 \times 2 \times 22$	$2 \times 2 \times 24$	$2 \times 2 \times 28$
$2 \times 2 \times 2 \times 11$	$2 \times 2 \times 2 \times 12$	$2 \times 2 \times 2 \times 14$
	$2 \times 2 \times 2 \times 2 \times 6$	$2 \times 2 \times 2 \times 2 \times 7$
	$2 \times 2 \times 2 \times 2 \times 2 \times 3$	
$\{2^3 \times 11\}$	$\{2^5 \times 3\}$	$\{2^4 \times 7\}$

Not the LCD $2 \times 3 \times 7 \times 11$

$$LCD = \quad 2^5 \times 3 \times 7 \times 11 \ = 7{,}392$$

$7392 \div 88 = 84 \therefore \frac{84}{84} = 1 \therefore \frac{67}{88} \times 1 = \frac{67}{88} \times \frac{\mathbf{84}}{\mathbf{84}} = \frac{5628}{7392}$ These steps involve both "Young's

$\frac{7392}{96} = 77 \quad \therefore \frac{77}{77} = 1 \quad \therefore \frac{91}{96} \times 1 = \frac{91}{96} \times \frac{\mathbf{77}}{\mathbf{77}} = \frac{7007}{7392}$ Equation/Ratio Theorem" and

$\frac{7392}{112} = 66 \quad \therefore \frac{66}{66} = 1 \quad \therefore \frac{103}{112} \times 1 = \frac{103}{112} \times \frac{\mathbf{66}}{\mathbf{66}} = \frac{6798}{7320}$ "Young's Conversion Theorem".

$\frac{5628}{7392} + \frac{7007}{7392} - \frac{6798}{7392} = \frac{5628+7007-6798}{7392} = \frac{5837}{7392}$

Once we convert the three starting fractions into equivalent fractions with the LCD "7,392", it is easy to write the three fractions from smallest to largest. Even though the original fractions were somewhat challenging to convert into equivalent fractions with the same denominator, listing the fractions from smallest to largest is now simple. The numerators of the three new fractions are the key to writing the fractions from smallest to largest. Here are the three fractions written from smallest to largest: "$\frac{5628}{7392}, \frac{6798}{7392}, \frac{7007}{7392}$". It would be difficult to list the exact order of the three original fractions from smallest to largest without finding an LCD and then converting all the given fractions into equivalent fractions. The three original fractions listed from smallest to largest are "$\frac{67}{88}$, $\frac{103}{112}$, $\frac{91}{96}$".

If you know of a better way to determine how to list a set of fractions from the smallest to the largest and it works for two fractions, three fractions, four fractions, five fractions, we are ready to listen. Some of you should immediately realize you could convert all the given fractions into decimals and then, if you are proficient with decimals, list the fractions from smallest to largest. That would work, but this procedure also means you would have to perform three challenging long division problems to convert the fractions into decimals. Finding LCDs for several fractions is probably one of the most difficult procedures elementary students will ever be asked to master in any subject.

This might be a great teaching experiment and learning experience, "Ask students to write the three fractions from smallest to largest before you begin to simplify the original problem or ask them to graph the three fractions on a number line with 0 as the number on the left end of the number line and 1 as the number on the right end of the number line." Then ask the students why they thought some fractions are smaller or larger than others. It may be interesting to hear the comments from the students when they have not even been introduced to the procedures to find the solution (Siegler et al., 2011; Vukovic et al., 2014). You should be able to illustrate the solution by using computer graphics. Converting fractions into equivalent fractions using "Young's Conversion Theorem" might not be as difficult for students to master as you initially thought. The only way you will be able to get most of your students to master these procedures is to mention simplifying these types of fraction problems a couple times a month for two to three minutes or maybe five minutes each time. It will be a challenge, but this is the reason why you are an amazing teacher. This type of problem requires a lot of work, but if your students master the indicated procedures, they will "learn and remember" a wide variety of math concepts which are involved in the process. We do not expect teachers or students to solve these types of problems daily. Problems like examples 1, 3, and 4 in this section of the book should be mentioned once or twice a week, but a problem like example 2 (just discussed) or example problem 5 in this chapter, might be mentioned once a month or right before a holiday or on a day when some students are permitted to miss class because something special occurred in school (ex. field trip, assembly, snow delay, weather related problem, etc.).

The next two example problems are not extremely difficult arithmetic problems. The goal is to illustrate slightly more challenging arithmetic problems than most of the problems in arithmetic textbooks and to emphasize all the rules and steps necessary to solve the problems. We will also list only the steps we expect the students to write when they solve these problems. We expect teacher explanations to be more detailed than the basic steps the students should use when you illustrate how to solve these problems. We want the students to be able to solve the following two problems below without writing all the steps, but we also want the students to have a strong understanding of the required steps they may sometimes not write down. The goal is to have students do most of the work required to solve the following two problems in their head, but we still want students to know the rules required to back up the process. If you want the students to master the procedures to solve these types of problems, it cannot occur over 2 or 3 days or over 2 or 3 weeks. It will take constant short reviews and it might take all year or maybe two or three years for some students to "learn and remember" all the procedures involved. *(FRT 5: If students are exposed to rules in mathematics for a longer time frame, then their long-term memory will improve.)* We realize the procedures discussed in this textbook are probably not the way your teachers presented these topics when you were a student, and they are not the procedures illustrated in arithmetic textbooks today. The main difference between the way your teachers taught you how to simplify these fraction problems and the way this textbook illustrates these topics is not the procedure but the attention to detail on all the steps involved with the procedures and why the steps are important. The process is still the same process teachers used forty years ago, but we do not skip any steps as we illustrate why each step works. Teachers have consistently taught the steps to find LCDs and to convert fractions into equivalent fractions by teaching tricks which work, but they do not emphasize the mathematical procedures which are necessary to develop the tricks. The tricks sometimes require students to memorize certain procedures and to do the work in their head, without writing each step in the process. Teaching techniques may have changed over the years but the <u>rules</u> to add and subtract fractions in arithmetic and algebra have not changed.

Fraction number sense is seldom or never mentioned in textbooks or by teachers. Teaching fraction operation number sense is a topic which should be taught/mentioned frequently when time permits.

3. Simplify: "$\frac{5}{6} - \frac{1}{2} + 2\frac{3}{4}$" Convert the last fraction into an improper fraction.

"$\frac{5}{6} - \frac{1}{2} + \frac{11}{4}$"

The goals with respect to students solving example problems 3 and 4, which are a little more difficult than the typical problems students encounter in their 5th grade arithmetic textbooks, are for students to:

1. Identify the least common denominator in their heads.
2. Determine the special form of the number <u>1</u> to multiply each fraction.

3. Convert all three fractions into equivalent fractions by multiplying by the special form of the number 1 they just computed.
4. Write one big fraction with all the numerators from the converted fractions either added or subtracted in the numerator of the big fraction and the LCD in the denominator of the big fraction.
5. Compute the final answer.
6. Reduce if possible.

We avoid using the phrase "goes into" when we want students to determine the special form of the number 1 to multiply each fraction. Illustrate and emphasize to the students they need to divide the LCD by the denominator of the fraction they are trying to convert into an equivalent fraction and then use the quotient to determine the special form of the number 1. Write the division problem as a fraction when dividing the LCD by the denominator of the fraction you are working with. If the numbers are large, such as those in example problem number 2, illustrate how to use the long division procedures to find the quotient. There is nothing wrong if you use the phrase "goes into" when explaining the process, but if you only use the "goes into" phrase, some students never grasp the fact they are really supposed to do a division problem. For secondary math teachers, when students are learning the distributive property involving a term outside a quantity such as "$3(4x + 5)$", the teachers emphasize the simplified solution is derived by multiplying both terms inside the parentheses (quantity) by the number/term outside the quantity. Now, think about how you explain the procedure to factor the expression "$12x + 15$". Do you tell the students to determine the term or number which will *go into* both the terms and *factor out* the number "3" and write the answer as the product of two terms in the original form? The way we state our directions can have a great influence on how the students "learn and remember" the process. We prefer to frequently emphasize the word divide when we teach students to factor the expression "$12x + 15$". Therefore, we prefer to use the phrase *divide out* the number "3" from both terms and write the new expression as a multiplication problem.

Teacher Illustration

$$\frac{5}{6} - \frac{1}{2} + \frac{11}{4}$$

Find the LCD - Using "Factor Trees".

6	2	4
2×3	2	2×2

Step 1 to find LCD – "2×3" This is not the LCD, but it is the preliminary first step.

Step 2 to find LCD – "$2 \times 2 \times 3 = 12$" This is the LCD for the three denominators "6, 2, and 4.

Student Work

$$\frac{5}{6} - \frac{1}{2} + \frac{11}{4}$$

"12" is the LCD and the students should use their knowledge of the multiplication tables without any written work to determine the LCD. Students should write the steps indicating they are multiplying by the number 1.

$\frac{5}{6} \times 1 = \frac{5}{6} \times \frac{2}{2} = \mathbf{\frac{10}{12}}$ $\quad \frac{1}{2} \times 1 = \frac{1}{2} \times \frac{6}{6} = \mathbf{\frac{6}{12}}$

and $\frac{11}{4} \times 1 = \frac{11}{4} \times \frac{3}{3} = \mathbf{\frac{33}{12}}$

Convert all three fractions into equivalent fractions. The teacher should illustrate the division process using the LCD and the individual denominators of each fraction. The students should be able to do the mental division problem in their heads but still encourage the students to get into the habit of writing down the process of multiplying by 1 when they find an equivalent fraction.

$\frac{12}{6} = 2 \therefore \frac{2}{2} = 1 \quad \frac{12}{2} = 6 \therefore \frac{6}{6} = 1$

and $\frac{12}{4} = 3 \quad \therefore \frac{3}{3} = 1$

$\frac{5}{6} \times 1 = \frac{5}{6} \times \frac{2}{2} = \mathbf{\frac{10}{12}} \qquad \frac{1}{2} \times 1 = \frac{1}{2} \times \frac{6}{6} = \mathbf{\frac{6}{12}}$

and $\frac{11}{4} \times 1 = \frac{11}{4} \times \frac{3}{3} = \mathbf{\frac{33}{12}}$

$$\frac{10}{12} - \frac{6}{12} + \frac{33}{12} = \frac{10-6+33}{12}$$

$$\frac{10}{12} - \frac{6}{12} + \frac{33}{12} = \frac{10-6+33}{12}$$

All three fractions are now written with the least common denominator "12". Therefore, we can add and subtract the numerators "$10 - 6 + 33$", compute the answer, and keep the denominator "12". Encourage students to write one big fraction with all the numerators added and/or subtracted with the LCD prior to adding and/or subtracting the numerators:

$$\frac{37}{12} = 3\frac{1}{12}$$

$$\frac{37}{12} = 3\frac{1}{12}$$

Once the fractions are written with common denominators, you should be able to arrange the fractions from smallest to largest or largest to smallest by comparing the numerators. When you look at the three fractions with the common denominator "12", you can easily determine the fractions written from largest to smallest are "$\frac{33}{12}$, $\frac{10}{12}$, and $\frac{6}{12}$". This means if we write the three given fraction numbers from largest to smallest, the order of the three numbers would be "$2\frac{3}{4}, \frac{5}{6}$, and $\frac{1}{2}$" or "$2\frac{3}{4} > \frac{5}{6} > \frac{1}{2}$". Again, it might be interesting to ask the students to write the fractions from largest to smallest or graph the points on a number line prior to converting the fractions into equivalent fractions with the LCD. You might assume the students immediately recognize the mixed number "$2\frac{3}{4}$" is larger than the other two fractions, but you may be fooled.

4. Solve, we mean Simplify: $5\frac{2}{5} + \frac{11}{15} - 2\frac{2}{3}$

Teacher Illustration

$$5\frac{2}{5} + \frac{11}{15} - 2\frac{2}{3}$$

$$\frac{27}{5} + \frac{11}{15} - \frac{8}{3}$$

Use factor trees to find the LCD.

$5 = 5 \qquad 15 = 5 \times 3 \qquad 3 = 3$

Multiply the different prime factors.

This might be the LCD. "?" $\quad 3 \times 5 = 15$

The most times the factors "3" and "5" occurred in either set of factor trees is once. Therefore, the LCD is "$3 \times 5 = 15$".

Special forms of the number 1 are:

$$\frac{15}{5} = 3 \quad \frac{15}{15} = 1 \quad \frac{15}{3} = 5$$

$$3 = 3 \quad 1 = 1 \quad 5 = 5$$

$$\therefore \quad \frac{3}{3} = 1 \quad \frac{1}{1} = 1 \quad \frac{5}{5} = 1$$

Use "Young's Conversion Theorem" to find the three equivalent fractions.

$$\frac{27}{5} = \frac{27}{5} \times 1 = \frac{27}{5} \times \frac{3}{3} = \mathbf{\frac{81}{15}}$$

$$\frac{11}{15} = \frac{11}{15} \times 1 = \frac{11}{15} \times \frac{1}{1} = \mathbf{\frac{11}{15}}$$

$$\frac{8}{3} = \frac{8}{3} \times 1 = \frac{8}{3} \times \frac{5}{5} = \frac{8 \times 5}{3 \times 5} = \mathbf{\frac{40}{15}}$$

Student Work

$$5\frac{2}{5} + \frac{11}{15} - 2\frac{2}{3}$$

$$\frac{27}{5} + \frac{11}{15} - \frac{8}{3}$$

LCD is "15" using mental math.

Students should be able to complete the conversions with little work.

$$\frac{27}{5} \times 1 = \frac{27}{5} \times \frac{3}{3} = \mathbf{\frac{81}{15}} \qquad \frac{11}{15} \times 1 = \mathbf{\frac{11}{15}}$$

$$\frac{8}{3} \times 1 = \frac{8}{3} \times \frac{5}{5} = \mathbf{\frac{40}{15}}$$

Substitute the equivalent fractions for the original fractions.

$\frac{81}{15}+\frac{11}{15}-\frac{40}{15}=\frac{81+11-40}{15}$

$\frac{52}{15}=3\frac{7}{15}$

$\frac{81}{15}+\frac{11}{15}-\frac{40}{15}=\frac{81+11-40}{15}=$

$\frac{52}{15}=3\frac{7}{15}$

The next problem is the type of problem which should be discussed once a month or when the regular classroom schedule is modified.

5. Simplify: $52\frac{31}{125}-44\frac{79}{80}+27\frac{41}{50}-2\frac{6}{25}-17\frac{31}{40}$

Step 1: Convert all five numbers into improper fractions.

"$52\frac{31}{125}=\frac{6531}{125}$", "$44\frac{79}{80}=\frac{3599}{80}$", "$27\frac{41}{50}=\frac{1391}{50}$", "$2\frac{6}{25}=\frac{56}{25}$", "$17\frac{31}{40}=\frac{711}{40}$"

Step 2: Find the LCD by using factor trees with the five denominators: "125, 80, 50, 25, and 40."

> Teaching fraction number sense and especially teaching fraction operation number sense is a very difficult task. You will have to use illustrations frequently to help students understand why answers sometimes do not follow the same arithmetic logic which works with Natural Numbers. Example: Estimate the answer without solving the problem – "$\frac{3}{4}\times\frac{1}{2}$ =?" Multiple choice answers using decimals, "1.3", or "2.6", or ".75", or ".4". The best answer is ".4" because when you multiply two fractions each less than "1" and greater than "0", the product is smaller than either fraction. The exact answer is "0.375".

125	80	50	25	40
5×25	2×40	2×25	$\{5\times 5\}$	2×20
$\{5\times 5\times 5\}$	$2\times 2\times 20$	$\{2\times 5\times 5\}$		$2\times 2\times 10$
	$2\times 2\times 2\times 10$			$\{2\times 2\times 2\times 5\}$
	$\{2\times 2\times 2\times 2\times 5\}$			

The LCD might equal "2×5", when we set up the initial multiplication problem involving all the different prime factors indicated in the five sets of factors, but this is not the LCD. The LCD is "$2 \times 2 \times 2 \times 2 \times 5 \times 5 \times 5 = 2^4 \times 5^3 = 2000$".

> We assumed when you estimated the answer to the example problem above, you knew how to multiply/simplify the given problem – "$\frac{3}{4} \times \frac{1}{2} = ?$" using one big fraction "$\frac{3 \times 1}{4 \times 2} = \frac{3}{8} = 0.375$".

Step 3:

a. Divide the LCD "$2 \times 2 \times 2 \times 2 \times 5 \times 5 \times 5$" or "2000" by the denominators of the five fractions to determine the correct form of the number 1 by which to multiply each of the given fractions and thus determine equivalent fractions with the LCD "2000".

$$125\overline{)2000}^{\,16} \qquad 80\overline{)2000}^{\,25} \qquad 50\overline{)2000}^{\,40} \qquad 25\overline{)2000}^{\,80} \qquad 40\overline{)2000}^{\,50}$$

b. This is the second time we are going to illustrate how to use prime factors in both the numerator and the denominator to divide the LCD "$2 \times 2 \times 2 \times 2 \times 5 \times 5 \times 5$" or "2000" by the denominators of the five fractions to determine the correct form of the number 1 by which to multiply each of the given fractions and thus to determine an equivalent fraction with the LCD "2000". Remember this method is an excellent method to use when we know the quotient will be an integer with no remainder. We introduced this method when we took a detour to solve problem 2. earlier in this chapter.

$$\frac{4000}{125} = \frac{2\times2\times2\times2\times5\times5\times5}{5\times5\times5} = \frac{2\times2\times2\times2}{1} = 16 \qquad \frac{4000}{80} = \frac{2\times2\times2\times2\times5\times5\times5}{2\times2\times2\times2\times5} = \frac{5\times5}{1} = 25$$

$$\frac{2000}{50} = \frac{2\times2\times2\times2\times5\times5\times5}{2\times5\times5} = \frac{2\times2\times2\times5}{1} = 40 \qquad \frac{4000}{25} = \frac{2\times2\times2\times2\times5\times5\times5}{5\times5} = \frac{2\times2\times2\times2\times5}{1} = 80$$

$$\frac{2000}{40} = \frac{2\times2\times2\times2\times5\times5\times5}{2\times2\times2\times5} = \frac{2\times5\times5}{1} = 50$$

Step 4: Write the five identities based on the quotients in step 3 and then use "Young's Equation/Ratio Theorem" to determine the five special forms of the number 1 by which to multiply the five improper fractions determined in step 1.

"$16 = 16 \therefore \frac{16}{16} = 1$" "$25 = 25 \therefore \frac{25}{25} = 1$" "$40 = 40 \therefore \frac{40}{40} = 1$"

"$80 = 80 \therefore \frac{80}{80} = 1$" "$50 = 50 \therefore \frac{50}{50} = 1$"

Step 5: Multiply the five improper fractions in step 1 which were derived from the five given mixed numbers (rational numbers). Use the appropriate form of the number 1, determined in step 4 to multiply each of the improper fractions to find the five equivalent fractions to the improper fractions.

$$\frac{6531}{125} = \frac{6531}{125} \times 1 = \frac{6531}{125} \times \frac{\mathbf{16}}{\mathbf{16}} = \frac{104496}{2000} \qquad \frac{3599}{80} = \frac{3599}{80} \times 1 = \frac{3599}{80} \times \frac{\mathbf{25}}{\mathbf{25}} = \frac{89975}{2000}$$

$$\frac{1391}{50} = \frac{1391}{50} \times 1 = \frac{1391}{50} \times \frac{\mathbf{40}}{\mathbf{40}} = \frac{55640}{2000} \qquad \frac{56}{25} = \frac{56}{25} \times 1 = \frac{56}{25} \times \frac{\mathbf{80}}{\mathbf{80}} = \frac{4480}{2000}$$

$$\frac{711}{40} = \frac{711}{40} \times 1 = \frac{711}{40} \times \frac{\mathbf{50}}{\mathbf{50}} = \frac{\mathbf{711 \times 50}}{\mathbf{40 \times 50}} = \frac{35550}{2000}$$

Notice, the additional fraction indicated in bold print "$\frac{\mathbf{711 \times 50}}{\mathbf{40 \times 50}}$" to illustrate the difference between adding/subtracting fractions and multiplying fractions. We could have written one large fraction multiplication problem in all five problems listed above, but we only wrote the one large fraction in the fifth problem and then focused your attention on this notation. We like to use the one big fraction multiplication problem when we illustrate how to multiply fractions. *(FRT 9: We believe if students solve addition, subtraction, multiplication, and division problems as one big fraction prior to the final computations then much of the confusion with respect to different fraction rules will be eliminated.)*

Step 6: Refer to the original problem and substitute the fractions (improper fractions) determined in step 5 for the mixed numbers indicated in step 1.

$$52\frac{31}{125} - 44\frac{79}{80} + 27\frac{41}{50} - 2\frac{6}{25} - 17\frac{31}{40}$$

$$\frac{6531}{125} - \frac{3599}{80} + \frac{1391}{50} - \frac{56}{25} - \frac{711}{40}$$

$$\frac{104{,}496}{2000} - \frac{89{,}975}{2000} + \frac{55{,}640}{2000} - \frac{4{,}480}{2000} - \frac{35{,}550}{2000}$$

Step 7: Rewrite the five fractions which are added and subtracted in step 5 as one big fraction with the common denominator, 2000. Add and subtract the five numerators to determine an improper fraction with unusually large numbers.

$$\frac{104496}{2000} - \frac{89975}{2000} + \frac{55640}{2000} - \frac{4480}{2000} - \frac{35550}{2000} = \frac{104{,}496 - 89{,}975 + 55{,}640 - 4{,}480 - 35{,}550}{2000} = \frac{30{,}131}{2000}$$

Step 8: Convert the improper fraction in step 7 into a mixed number and then try and reduce the fraction.

$$2000\overline{)30131} \quad 15 \ r\ 131 \qquad = 15\frac{131}{2000} = 15.0655$$

We know the final fraction will not reduce because the only two prime numbers which will divide into the LCD, "2000" are "2" and "5", and neither the prime number "2" nor the prime number "5" will divide into the numerator "131". You could also illustrate why the number "131" is a prime number. You should notice when we solved/simplified the three previous arithmetic problems, they involved some numbers, which were mixed numbers. In every case, we converted the <u>mixed numbers</u> into <u>improper fractions</u> by multiplying the denominator times the whole number and then adding the numerator of the fraction to find the improper fraction with the starting denominator. This is one of the times in arithmetic and mathematics when using "Young's Conversion Theorem" is not the most efficient method to convert a number or math expression into an equivalent number or math expression. Here are three more types of problems when the use of "Young's Conversion

Theorem", is not the most efficient method to work with if you are converting numbers and expressions into equivalent numbers and expressions:

1. When you convert an improper fraction into a mixed number (division by the denominator is the best procedure). (Examples: Convert "$\frac{7}{3}$" into the mixed number, "$2\frac{1}{3}$" or convert "$\frac{30,131}{2000}$" into the mixed number, "$15\frac{131}{2000}$".)
2. When you convert a fraction into a decimal (basic division is the best procedure). (Examples: Convert the fraction (rational number) "$\frac{11}{20}$" into the terminating decimal (rational number), ".55". Convert the fraction (rational number) "$\frac{5}{6}$" into the repeating decimal (rational number), "0.8333...").
3. When you are converting a repeating decimal into a fraction (use algebra procedures with two equations). (Example: Convert "$.717171\ldots$" into the fraction, "$\frac{71}{99}$").

> As we previously indicated in this textbook, we suggest you convert mixed numbers into improper fractions in arithmetic to solve fraction addition and subtraction problems. We make this suggestion because students will never encounter a fraction in algebra written in the standard mixed number format, as indicated in these two examples: 1. "$2\frac{x}{y}$" or 2. "$x\frac{x+1}{x-1}$".

If you are teaching a class of high-achieving math students and some motivated average-achieving math students, to simplify the problem "$52\frac{31}{125} - 44\frac{79}{80} + 27\frac{41}{50} - 2\frac{6}{25} - 17\frac{31}{40}$", illustrate the five mixed numbers could be rewritten by grouping the positive mixed numbers first and then grouping the negative mixed numbers "$(+52\frac{31}{125} + 27\frac{41}{50} - 44\frac{79}{80} - 2\frac{6}{25} - 17\frac{31}{40})$". Also, illustrate how to work with the fractions first and then work with the whole numbers. There are two ways to approach this problem by focusing on the fractions and whole numbers separately. Before you demonstrate either of the two methods indicated below, illustrate how to simplify addition and subtraction mixed numbers that involve smaller numbers, prior to demonstrating how to simplify this problem. You must also make sure the students know how to add the positive and negative numbers separately.

In one method, you can concentrate on the positive mixed numbers, "$52\frac{31}{125} + 27\frac{41}{50} = 52\frac{496}{2000} + 27\frac{1640}{2000}$", and get the answer, "$+79\frac{2136}{2000} = 80\frac{136}{2000}$". Next, add the negative mixed numbers, "$-44\frac{79}{80} - 2\frac{6}{25} - 17\frac{31}{40} = -44\frac{1975}{2000} - 2\frac{480}{2000} - 17\frac{1550}{2000}$", and get the answer "$-63\frac{4005}{2000} = -65\frac{5}{2000}$". Complete the arithmetic problem "$+80\frac{136}{2000} - 65\frac{5}{2000} = 15\frac{131}{2000}$".

In the second option, you might illustrate to the students how they can work with the fractions first and then the whole numbers and not group the positive and negative mixed numbers. This would be an interesting discussion. This second option would require the students to work with the fractions in this order: "$\frac{31}{125} - \frac{79}{80} + \frac{41}{50} - \frac{6}{25} - \frac{31}{40} = \frac{496}{2000} - \frac{1975}{2000} + \frac{1640}{2000} - \frac{480}{2000} - \frac{1550}{2000} = \frac{496-1975+1640-480-1550}{2000} = \frac{-1869}{2000}$". If you add and subtract the whole numbers in the given problem, the solution is "$52 - 44 + 27 - 2 - 17 = +16$". If you want to determine the final answer, you must explain to the students how to simplify the problem "$+16 - \frac{1869}{2000}$" to derive the final answer "$15\frac{131}{2000}$". Notice in the illustration below the number 1 will pops up again when you illustrate how to subtract the number "+16" and the fraction "$\frac{1869}{2000}$".

$$+16 - \frac{1869}{2000} = 15 + 1 - \frac{1869}{2000} = 15 + \frac{2000}{2000} - \frac{1869}{2000} = 15\frac{131}{2000}$$

There is so much for students to learn in arithmetic prior to entering an algebra class, why would you want to rush students into an algebra class too early?

Remember, the rules required for success in algebra are learned in arithmetic.

The most dependent subject students will encounter in their education career is arithmetic and mathematics. There is a direct relationship between how knowledgeable and proficient a student is in arithmetic and how well the student will perform in higher level math courses (Torbeyns et al., 2015; Watts et al., 2014).

There is another type of conversion problem, such that the use of "Young's Conversion Theorem", might not be the best method to convert a number into an equivalent number—and we intentionally did not include this type of problem in the previous list. "The Power of the Number One (1)" is still very powerful when converting this fifth type of problem into an equivalent expression: when you reduce a fraction (Example: Reduce "$\frac{9}{12}$"). When you reduce fractions, you might be amazed how the number 1, along with factor trees and prime numbers, work together to convert fractions into simplified, reduced fractions. We will address this topic later in the book. Even though there are some conversion problems in arithmetic and mathematics such that the conversion process does not require you to use "Young's Equation/Ratio Theorem" and "Young's Conversion Theorem", you will still be surprised how often using these two theorems make conversion problems in arithmetic and high-level math courses much simpler and consistent. When you can emphasize one specific procedure to solve a wide variety of problems in arithmetic and advanced mathematics, it is beneficial to all students high achieving, average achieving, and low achieving, they do not have to learn a variety of tricks to solve similar problems. High-achieving math-oriented students must be aware of a wide variety of methods to solve problems. The more students know, the better prepared they will be to solve advanced mathematics problems. When students use "Young's Conversion Theorem", they will use the same procedures for a wide variety of "conversion" problems in mathematics as illustrated throughout the remainder of this textbook. The proclamation that it would be beneficial to all types of students to learn a single specific procedure to solve similar problems may not be a fact, but there is scant research to confirm or disprove the statement. *(FRT 10: We believe the more a single procedure can be used to solve a wide variety of math problems, it is beneficial to a wide range of students.)*

The process of adding and subtracting fractions is probably the single most difficult process for students in arithmetic to master, more difficult than learning how to simplify fraction multiplication and division problems. We added a special step to all fraction addition and subtraction problems when we encouraged you to emphasize "Young's Conversion Theorem". This step may seem petty, but it is a powerful step when students continue in their mathematics career. Since the process of multiplying and dividing fractions is less cumbersome than adding and subtracting fractions, it might be a good idea to simplify problems focused on reducing, multiplying, and dividing fractions first *when it is time to learn the rules.* When students are first learning the concepts of adding and subtracting fractions using charts, hands-on materials, and computer simulations, it is easier to illustrate solutions for addition and subtraction fraction problems than it is to illustrate graphically how to find the solutions to multiplication and division fraction problems. We want students to quickly solve basic addition and subtraction fraction problems which are the same types of problems modeled in Chapter 3, prior to trying to solve the more challenging problems illustrated in Chapter 4, where the rules and procedures required to solve the more difficult problems are emphasized. Another point of interest for teachers to stress when they teach fractions is to frequently discuss number sense as it relates to fractions. Teaching number sense with fractions is not a lost art; it is a topic many arithmetic and mathematics teachers ignore.

Number sense is not a chapter in any arithmetic textbook, but it is a concept which is important for student understanding for every arithmetic topic.

Many mathematics education researchers who analyze specific topics which indicate whether students will have success in advanced mathematics classes starting with algebra agree, the greatest indicator of success in advanced mathematics classes is a strong understanding of fractions (Torbeyns et al., 2015, Watts et al., 2014, Siegler et al., 2013, Siegler et. al., 2012). With this thought in mind, we list six of the best methods to use when teaching fractions and six of the least effective methods to use when teaching fractions in arithmetic starting in fourth grade. If your students become more successful solving all types of fraction problems, you will go home happy and feel great about being an arithmetic teacher. It is a fantastic feeling. This also means your students will have a greater chance to be successful in their math classes next year and future years. The list below indicates some *"Do's and Don'ts"* regarding teaching methods which you may want to think about if you want your students to master arithmetic fraction procedures and be successful in future math classes.

> Always point out the difference between the one big addition and subtraction fraction problem and the one big fraction multiplication problem. We are not aware of any other textbook which emphasizes the one big fraction notation, but we believe this is an important teaching point to emphasize. We therefore supply examples for students to reference, which will help them master the correct procedures for the two different types of problems.

1. **"Do"** teach fractions continually throughout the year, starting in August and ending in June. Talk about fractions as often as you can. You can always teach concepts involving fractions for 2-3 minutes a couple of times per week. If you could talk about fractions every day, that would be ideal but probably unrealistic. Students can begin to add and subtract fractions early in the year if the fractions have identical denominators, the

answers are less than 1, and they do not reduce. You can encourage students to graph points on a number line involving fractions. You can illustrate fractions are equivalent fractions even though the numbers in the numerators and the denominators of one fraction are larger compared to another fraction. You can illustrate that "$\frac{1}{2}$" of "$\frac{1}{2}$" is "$\frac{1}{4}$". There is always another concept or topic to discuss which will help students be more knowledgeable when working with fractions.

"Do Not" try to teach fractions as a separate topic for 3 weeks, 4 weeks, or 9 weeks and then teach another arithmetic topic and forget about fractions. You must realize when you teach your students to simplify fraction problems the rules involving fractions are different than the rules required when working with whole numbers.

2. **"Do"** continually give fraction questions as additional questions for homework. Interweave/interleave different arithmetic concepts into one problem. Students can add and subtract three or more fractions in the same problem. Students can work with fractions and natural numbers in the same problem.

   "Do Not" ignore facts about fractions which relate to other topics in arithmetic. When you are teaching any topic in mathematics, it is almost impossible to just concentrate on one topic and not include some aspect of another arithmetic concept. When you teach fractions, make sure students realize a fraction can be written as a decimal and vice versa. Make sure the students know a fraction can also be written as a percentage.

3. **"Do"** illustrate concepts involving fractions and then illustrate how procedures are derived from the concepts. Concepts must come first, when possible, and procedures should make sense based on concepts. As soon as the students understand a concept (picture graph, line segment, or computer simulation), introduce the new procedure.

Students should almost be able to explain the procedures to solve fraction problems based on the concepts which are illustrated.

"Do Not" simply begin to discuss the rules for reducing, multiplying, and dividing fractions without emphasizing the procedures and rules are different than the rules for adding and subtracting fractions. When you introduce a new procedure involving fractions, make sure you continually emphasize the rules for adding and subtracting fractions are significantly different than the rules for multiplying and dividing fractions. This is a fact which causes confusion for many students. Emphasize two sets of rules and procedures to simplify fraction problems. The two basic procedures are discussed later in this book. You need to continually indicate the different procedures involved for the different operations. Do not allow your students the chance to confuse the two different sets of rules. If you interleave operations into the same problem, you will discover many students will begin to understand the different procedures for the different operations and the confusion with respect to the different rules may never appear. Interleaving different operations when you begin to teach simplifying fractions will lead to over 90% of all students understanding the different rules to compare, add, and subtract fraction problems versus reducing, multiplying, and dividing fraction problems.

4. **"Do"** illustrate and emphasize rules which will be necessary for the students to solve more difficult problems this year, next year and in the future. When teaching fractions, emphasize how to use the rules involving factor trees. When simplifying challenging fraction problems in arithmetic and rational expressions in algebra, the first step when adding and subtracting fractions is to factor the denominators and determine the LCD.

The first step when you reduce, multiply, or divide challenging fractions in arithmetic and rational expressions in algebra is to factor all the numerators and denominators.

"Do Not" forget to emphasize the rules using factor trees. When teaching students how to solve/simplify fraction problems you will obviously teach the tricks you learned to find LCDs using your knowledge of multiplication and division facts. This is expected and is still an effective teaching procedure. Factor trees are not required when adding and subtracting simple arithmetic fraction problems, but they are the secret to simplifying and solving challenging fraction problems and rational expressions.

5. **"Do"** illustrate how to solve simple and challenging problems when you initially teach how to solve/simplify fraction problems. Mention some tricks but emphasize the rules necessary to solve all types of fraction problems. Before you assign problems involving fractions for the first time as homework, make sure you have taught the rules which work for simple and challenging fraction problems. If students have been exposed to the rules and procedures to solve the challenging fraction problems, they will look at the textbook problems and realize they are simple compared to the illustrations you presented. They will also learn the rules to solve the challenging problems as you continue to discuss the rules and procedures which lead to an understanding of the tricks. If you have used introduction sessions for 2-3 minutes over the past 1-2 months, the students will find the textbook problems are simple, and they will feel confident simplifying the additional homework problems.

   "Do Not" depend on the textbook problems as your guide to help the students "learn and remember" the different rules involving adding and subtracting fractions and then how to reduce, multiply and divide fractions. If you want your students to master all types of fraction simplification problems and you only use the textbook problems as your guide, your students will struggle to achieve the success you hope for. Do not depend on the simple fraction problems usually found in the textbooks as the only problems to assign for classwork, discussion, and homework.

6. **"Do"** review constantly if you want your students to remember how to simplify fraction problems 2-3 months after you teach the sections focused on fractions. You can review in a variety of ways: assign additional review homework problems; discuss review problems to introduce a class or to end a class; or interleave a concept already learned into one of your additional homework problems.

   "Do Not" believe students will remember all the rules involved with a topic 2 or 3 months after you taught the topic, without reviewing the topic frequently. Do not forget to review fraction problems on a regular basis, a minimum of twice per week.

(FRT 11: Six, "Do's and *"Do Not's" when teaching fractions. The previous section contains many topics to research and determine what works and does not work.)*

As you looked at the list of six teaching ideas above, perhaps you realized many but not all your arithmetic and mathematics teachers relied on some of the procedures indicated. If you were lucky, your teacher emphasized the positive things and shied away from less positive procedures. When you change your approach to teaching math beyond the textbook by adding a few new wrinkles, students will realize they are more successful solving difficult problems than their classmates in other math classes.

We already indicated the arithmetic topic which seems to be the number one indicator of students' success in algebra is a strong understanding of fraction topics. Another arithmetic skill which seems to be a strong indicator of students' success in advanced mathematics is the ability of students to solve long division problems (Siegler et al., 2012). Since we believe the research which indicates solving long division problems is a key indicator of success in algebra, that is why we want our students to complete the long division process when they divide the LCD "7,392" by the denominators "88, 96, and 112".

Since you have now finished studying this challenging section with respect to adding and subtracting fractions, we want you to think back to a suggestion made earlier: when teaching any topic in arithmetic or algebra, always focus your goals on how the students would solve more challenging problems in future math classes. If you finally understand how to solve these challenging arithmetic fraction addition and subtraction problems, you will be amazed how simple it is to simplify rational expressions in algebra. This is one of our main goals.

The Assignment Sections in this textbook are written with three goals in mind. The first goal is to make sure **you** are prepared to be an elementary arithmetic teacher or a secondary math teacher. The arithmetic problems are written to ensure **you** know all the rules and procedures which students need to "Learn and Remember" so they are prepared to be successful in Algebra and advanced math classes. We feel confident if **you** read, study, and take the time to answer all the questions contained in the assignment sections in Chapters 1-7, you will be prepared to teach elementary arithmetic. We assume when you answer all the assignment questions in Chapters 1-7 and you take the time to write out all the required steps to solve all the problems, you do this because you realize when you are the teacher you MUST illustrate and write every step involved to solve the problems. The second goal, which is a very important goal, is to make sure you are prepared to teach students using the teaching procedures which are mentioned and emphasized throughout this textbook. **The third goal which is the main goal must be to ensure that over 90% of your students "Learn and Remember" the concepts, rules, and procedures just like you have, once you complete all the problems contained in this textbook in Chapters 1-7. Secondary math teachers must be able to illustrate and solve every problem in this textbook including the arithmetic problems in Chapters 1-7 and the advanced math problems in Chapter 8.** It may surprise you if you plan on being a secondary math teacher, but sometime in your career and probably early in your career you will be working with students who struggle solving what we consider basic arithmetic problems. Secondary math teachers must be prepared to teach every level of math starting with 4th grade arithmetic up through calculus. **<u>YOU MUST READ THE COMMENTS IN THIS RECTANGLE.</u>**

If you are going to be an outstanding elementary arithmetic teacher or secondary math teacher, you must be dedicated. The word, LAZY, cannot be a word to describe your work ethic. The one word I use to describe the most amazing teachers I worked with is the word, "PASSION". If you have the "PASSION" to be the best you will be the best and the students, parents, other teachers, and the administration will immediately recognize your efforts to become the best. You need to demonstrate that "PASSION" now, as a student when you solve the problems in this textbook. Always do your best if you want to be the best.

Fourth Assignment

The problems given at the end of each chapter in this textbook ARE NOT written to ensure elementary students master all the procedures and concepts related to the topics discussed in each chapter. The problems at the end of each chapter ARE written so all elementary teachers, all students in college preparing to be an elementary teacher, all math teachers, and all students in college preparing to be a math teacher, understand the rules and procedures required to teach fraction problems and prepare students for advanced mathematics courses. Present education administrators and educators preparing to become an administrator need to study and solve the problems presented in this textbook, so they understand the challenges all elementary arithmetic teachers and secondary math teachers frequently encounter. The topics and concepts covered in Chapters 1-7 are all basic arithmetic concepts and involve rules and procedures necessary to solve more advanced math problems in the higher grades. This textbook is also written so parents who homeschool their children have a template to help them understand the concepts and in turn help their children master the concepts, rules, and procedures discussed and illustrated throughout this textbook.

FUNDAMENTAL THEOREM OF ARITHMETIC

A. Study the following two paragraphs. The Fundamental Theorem of Arithmetic might be something important since mathematicians decided to give it a special name. We find it hard to believe someone who teaches arithmetic cannot explain the Fundamental Theorem of Arithmetic and the importance of the Theorem when working with fractions. (Note: The following two concepts are directed to mathematics certified teachers or future mathematics certified teachers. These two topics are not concepts, which will benefit most arithmetic teachers, but elementary certified teachers need to understand, theorems which begin with the three words "The Fundamental Theorem" are considered powerful at all levels of mathematics. There is a theorem titled "The Fundamental Theorem of Algebra" which is important when solving polynomial equations starting in Algebra 1. There is also a theorem titled "The Fundamental Theorem of Calculus" which applies to derivatives, antiderivatives and integrals involving continuous functions.) The Fundamental Theorem of Arithmetic, The Fundamental Theorem of Algebra, and The Fundamental Theorem of Calculus, do not have to be memorized in arithmetic, algebra, or calculus to solve problems in either of these courses, BUT if you understand the meaning of each of these theorems with respect to the appropriate course, concepts discussed in the courses, and solutions to problems in the courses indicated by the names of the theorems will make more sense.

Our explanation of the "The Fundamental Theorem of Arithmetic" is: Every composite number has a unique (exactly one) set of prime factors for each composite number. When we use the two words "prime factors", we are indicating the prime numbers are multiplied based on our understanding of the word "factors". We suggest you look up the internet explanation of "The Fundamental Theorem of Arithmetic". Here are two examples to illustrate the meaning of the Fundamental Theorem of Arithmetic:

1. The only way to multiply a list or group of prime numbers such that the product of the prime numbers is "18", is "2 × 3 × 3". You may switch the order you multiply these three prime factors, and the product will still be "18", but this list of prime numbers multiplied is the only way (unique way) to multiply prime numbers and end up with the composite number "18".
2. The only way to multiply a list or group of prime numbers such that the product of the prime numbers is "100" is "2 × 2 × 5 × 5". You may switch the order of these four prime factors to end up with the product "100", but this list of prime numbers multiplied, is the only way (unique way) to multiply prime numbers and end up with the composite number "100".

   We strongly encourage everyone to write the two composite numbers mentioned in the examples above in three different forms.

1. Write a two or three paragraph explanation of "The Fundamental Theorem of Arithmetic".
2. Randomly select one, 3-digit composite number other than "100" and illustrate the meaning of the "Fundamental Theorem of Arithmetic".
3. Randomly select one, 4-digit composite number and illustrate the meaning of the "Fundamental Theorem of Arithmetic".
4. Randomly select one, 5-digit composite number and illustrate the meaning of the "Fundamental Theorem of Arithmetic".
5. We know the number 24 is a composite number. A. If we list the factors as "8 × 3" for the composite number "24", why are the factors "8 × 3" not an example of "The Fundamental

Theorem of Arithmetic"?" B. Are the factors "6 × 4" or "12 × 2" or "1 × 24" examples of the Fundamental Theorem of Arithmetic for the number "24"? Why or Why Not?

6. Why is the following list of factors, "1 × 3 × 5 × 5", not an example of "The Fundamental Theorem of Arithmetic" as it relates to the composite number "75"?

B. Write the factor trees (prime numbers) for the following composite numbers in a triangular format (Christmas tree format). Factor Tree Example for 12

2 × 6

2 × 2 × 3

7. 82 8. 144 9. 300 10. 400 11. 500 12. 150 13. 98 14. 361

The following numbers are almost all prime numbers written in set notation: {97, 113, 401, 619, 893, 1111}. There is a property which we have not stated up to this point in this textbook which allows us to determine a limit on the largest prime number <u>we need to test</u> when we want to determine if a prime number will divide into any of the numbers in the list. The following is a list of the prime numbers less than or equal to "43". There is a reason we selected the number "43" which we will explain as we determine why most of the numbers in the set of numbers {97, 113, 401, 619, 893, 1111} are prime numbers. Here are the prime numbers less than or equal to "43", {2, 3, 5, 7, 11, 13, 17, 19, 23, 29, 31, 37, 41, 43}. Start with the first number in the given list "97". We know based on the property which we are going to explain, the largest prime number we need to test to determine if the number, "97" is a prime number is "7". The largest prime number we need to consider when working with the number "113" is also "7". The largest prime number we need to test when evaluating the number "401" is "19". Here is the theorem which allows us to be confident the largest prime numbers indicated in the previous three examples, for the composite numbers, "97, 113, and 401" are the prime numbers "7, 7, and 19".

Theorem: "When you are trying to determine if a number is prime or composite, the largest prime number you need to test to determine if a prime number will divide perfectly into the given number will be less than the square root of the given number."

When focusing on the number "97" the square root of 97 is less than "10" because "$10^2 = 100$". If "97" is a composite number, then there will be a prime number less than "10" which will divide into "97". None of the prime numbers less than "10", (2, 3, 5, or 7) will divide perfectly into "97" therefore we are confident "97" is also a prime number.

When focusing on the number "113" we know the square root of "113" is less than "11" because "$11^2 = 121$" which is larger than "113". Since "$11^2 = 121$" which is greater than "113" the next smallest prime number is "7". Therefore, we only need to consider prime numbers less than "11" when determining if there is a prime number that will divide into "113" with no remainder. The largest prime number less than "11" is "7"; therefore, "7" is the largest prime number we need to test to determine if the number "113" is prime or composite.

When focusing on the number "401," we need to apply a little bit of number sense to determine what the largest prime number to focus on is, to determine if the number "401" is a prime number. Using our knowledge of numbers, we recognized immediately that "$20^2 = 400$". The number "401" is slightly larger than "20^2" so using our number sense, we realized "21^2" is going to be larger than "401". This means the largest prime number we need to consider when we test to determine if the number "401" is a prime or a composite number is the prime number "19". None of the prime numbers starting with the prime number "2" up through the prime number "19" will divide perfectly into the prime number "401". These are the set of prime numbers we would test to determine if the number "401" is a prime number: {2, 3, 5, 7, 11, 13, 17, & 19}.

When you work with the number "619", you should realize "$25^2 = 625$". If you are considered the expert in a 5th or 6th grade classroom, you need to have some basic number facts in your mental math memory. Therefore, the largest prime number we need to test to determine if the number "619" is a prime or composite number is "23". There is no prime number less than "25" which will divide perfectly into the number "619", therefore, the number "619 is also a prime number.

Do you realize "$30^2 = 900$"? If you have a strong sense of numbers, you should understand the largest prime number we need to consider is "29" if we are working with the number "893" and you understand how to apply the square root theorem which we are using. Oops, we just realized the prime number "19" divides into the number "893" perfectly and the quotient is "47". The number "893" is a composite number and the prime factors are "$19\ and\ 47$" because "$19 \times 47 = 893$". It is not an impossible problem, just a challenging problem. Again, you are the teacher so you will determine whether your students must use a pencil and a piece of paper when dividing the given number by the prime numbers to determine if a prime number will evenly divide into the given number or will you allow your students to use a calculator all the time or use a calculator only when the going gets tough. When the numbers are this large, the decision is your decision, there is no right or wrong answer. Initially, we would want the students to use their number sense and their long division skills, but once you know the students have mastered the long division procedures, a calculator is a nice tool to use sometimes.

We are now concentrating on the number "1111". Again, you may want to help your students develop some number sense and make a guess on how large a number greater than "30" it will take to find a number squared which is greater than "1111". We guessed "33" would be large enough to ensure we have a number squared which would be greater than "1111", but it would be fine to guess "$34^2 = 1156$" or "$35^2 = 1225$". If you test "33^2", the product is "1089" which we recognize is less than "1111", but since we have a basic understanding of numbers, we know "33", "34" and "35" are all composite numbers and without a doubt both "34^2" and "35^2" are greater than "1111". Even if you do not consider the numbers "33^2", "34^2", or "35^2" your mental number sense skills should tell you the largest prime number you need to consider is the prime number "31". The next prime number greater than "31" is "37", and your number sense should tell you "37^2" is relatively close to "40^2" which equals "1600". We will therefore only test prime numbers which are less than or equal to "31" to determine if the number "1111" is a prime or a composite number. **You must memorize some number facts, to develop mental number sense skills.**

FIND THE <u>LARGEST PRIME NUMBER</u> YOU NEED TO <u>TEST</u> WHEN YOU ARE DETERMINING IF THE GIVEN NUMBER IS A PRIME OR A COMPOSITE NUMBER.

C. Use the square root rule and your knowledge of the prime numbers to determine the largest prime number you need to consider. Your answer must be a prime number.

15. 51 16. 97 17. 67 18. 45 19. 105 20. 129

21. 171 22. 221 23. 297 24. 351 25. 419 26. 907

27. Which of the twelve numbers in problems 15-26 are prime numbers and which are composite numbers?

28. If a number(s) in the previous list of problems 15.-26. is a composite number, list the set of prime factors as a multiplication problem.

PRIME FACTORS AND FACTOR TREES

D. Using the "Factor Tree" method illustrated several times in this chapter, write the set of "Prime Factors" for the following composite numbers. Use exponential notation, in your final step if appropriate.

Example: Composite Number "60" – Factor Tree Notation

$$60$$
$$2 \times 30$$
$$2 \times 2 \times 15$$
$$2 \times 2 \times 3 \times 5$$

Exponential Notation: $2^2 \times 3 \times 5$

29. 45 30. 90 31. 200 32. 292 33. 2275 34. 1800 35. 1764 36. 10,000

E. Reduce the following fractions by using mental math. Mentally determine the GCFs and mentally reduce all these fractions. A. Write the GCF for the two numbers first, then copy the given fraction. B. Write the reduced fraction to the right using an equal relationship symbol. Do not use slanted lines. You should use a pencil and paper then write the answers quickly.

37. $\frac{5}{45}$ 38. $\frac{8}{28}$ 39. $\frac{33}{55}$ 40. $\frac{36}{54}$ 41. $\frac{24}{40}$ 42. $\frac{14}{16}$ 43. $\frac{9}{33}$ 44. $\frac{28}{35}$ 45. $\frac{18}{63}$

Here is a basic and important question you should ask yourself, "How important do you think it is to master the multiplication and division facts/tables in order to successfully simplify these problems?"

F. Reduce the following fractions when the numerators and the denominators are already in factored form.

46. $\frac{2\times2\times5\times5}{2\times2\times2\times5\times5}$ 47. $\frac{3\times7\times11\times11\times13}{11\times11\times13}$ 48. $\frac{2\times29\times31}{3\times29\times31}$ 49. $\frac{5\times z\times z\times a\times b}{7\times z\times z\times a\times b}$ 50. $\frac{2\times2\times b\times b\times d}{2\times2\times2\times b\times d}$

Reduce the following fractions by using "factor trees" in both the numerator and the denominator and then divide identical factors in both the numerator and the denominator.

Example: Reduce using "factor trees" - "$\frac{54}{72}$"

54	72
2×27	2×36
$2\times3\times9$	$2\times2\times18$
$2\times3\times3\times3$	$2\times2\times2\times9$
	$2\times2\times2\times3\times3$

Substitute the two sets of "Prime Factors" determined in the "Factor Trees" for the respective numerator and the denominator in the given fraction.

$\frac{54}{72}=\frac{2\times3\times3\times3}{2\times2\times2\times3\times3}=\frac{3}{2\times2}=\frac{3}{4}$ Do you realize the identical factors in the numerator and in the denominator, divide and become 1? The Most Powerful Number, One (1)!

G. Reduce the following fractions using the "factor tree" procedures just illustrated.

51. $\frac{45}{90}$ 52. $\frac{18}{39}$ 53. $\frac{25}{70}$ 54. $\frac{54}{81}$ 55. $\frac{125}{150}$ 56. $\frac{45}{80}$ 57. $\frac{93}{186}$ 58. $\frac{162}{189}$

LEAST COMMON DENOMINATORS (LCDs)

H. Use mental math and find the LCD for each problem.

59. $\frac{3}{8}+\frac{5}{12}$ 60. $\frac{55}{6}+\frac{77}{9}-\frac{33}{4}$ 61. $\frac{3}{4}+\frac{2}{5}-\frac{7}{10}-\frac{1}{5}$ 62. $\frac{701}{20}+\frac{550}{8}-\frac{112}{5}-\frac{12}{4}$ 63. $\frac{7}{8}-\frac{1}{5}$

64. $\frac{1}{6}+\frac{55}{8}$ 65. $\frac{7}{12}-\frac{7}{15}+\frac{7}{20}$ 66. $\frac{7}{10}-\frac{7}{15}-\frac{7}{20}+\frac{7}{30}$ 67. $-\frac{7}{8}-\frac{5}{8}-\frac{3}{8}$ 68. $\frac{7}{200}+\frac{7}{800}+\frac{7}{1600}$

Do you think mastery of the multiplication and division facts for the following numbers from "1, 2, 3, 4, 5, 6, 7, 8, 9, 10 and even 11, & 12" might be helpful when finding the LCDs for the given fractions? We assume you were able to determine the LCD for problem "68." using your basic knowledge of multiplication with the numbers indicated in the denominators along with an understanding of how to multiply by powers of "10".

FIND THE LCM FOR EACH SET OF PRIME NATURAL NUMBERS MULTIPLIED BELOW

(Comment: A Prime Number will always be a Natural Number.)

I. Given the following sets of "Prime Factors" which were derived using "Factor Trees", find the Least Common Multiple (LCM) since you will be working with sets of numbers and not working with fractions.

Example Problem: Here are three sets of Prime Factors for three different composite numbers – find the LCM. $300 = \{2 \times 2 \times 3 \times 5 \times 5\}$, $360 = \{2 \times 2 \times 2 \times 3 \times 3 \times 5\}$, and $210 = \{2 \times 3 \times 5 \times 7\}$ The LCM is NOT "$2 \times 3 \times 5 \times 7$". The LCM is

"$2 \times 2 \times 2 \times 3 \times 3 \times 5 \times 5 \times 7 = 12600$". Remember we used the prime number, "2" three times based on the fact the prime number, "2" occurred the most times in the second set of prime numbers for the number "360". The number "3" was used twice in the computation of the LCM because the prime number "3" occurred the most frequently in the second set of prime numbers where it occurred twice. The prime number "5" occurred twice in the first set of prime factors and the prime number "7" only occurred once in the third set of prime numbers.

69. Find the LCM given the two indicated composite numbers and the Sets of Prime Factors. $12 = \{2 \times 2 \times 3\},\ 490 = \{2, 5, 7, 7\}$.

70. Find the LCM given the three indicated composite numbers and the Sets of Prime Factors. $28 = \{2, 2, 7\},\quad 49 = \{7,7\},\quad 98 = \{2, 7, 7\}$

71. Find the LCM given the three indicated composite numbers and the Sets of Prime Factors. $75 = \{3, 5, 5\},\quad 250 = \{2, 5, 5, 5\}\quad 300 = \{2, 2, 3, 5, 5\}$

72. Find the LCM given the four indicated composite numbers and the Sets of Prime Factors. $80 = \{2, 2, 2, 2, 5\},\ 200 = \{2, 2, 2, 5, 5\},\ 30 = \{2, 3, 5\},\ 25 = \{5, 5\}$

FIND THE LCM FOR EACH SET OF VARIABLES AND TERMS MULTIPLIED BELOW

(Hint: The expressions written in the form $(a \pm b)$ are treated as single factors. Expressions in parentheses are treated the same way all the prime numbers were treated in the example and four problems "69.-72." above. Here are examples of quantities that should be treated as a single factor $\{\ (x + 2),\ (y - z),\ (x^2 + 7),\ (5 - z),\ etc.\}$. The following example contains two sets of factors (terms which are multiplied) involving numbers, variables (letters), and expressions. Find the LCM given the two sets of factors.

$8x^3yz(x+1) = 2 \cdot 2 \cdot 2 \cdot x \cdot x \cdot x \cdot y \cdot z \cdot (x+1)$

$12x^2y^2(x+1)^2(m-n) = 2 \cdot 2 \cdot 3 \cdot x \cdot x \cdot y \cdot y \cdot (x+1) \cdot (x+1) \cdot (m-n)$ The LCM could equal all the factors multiplied as indicated, $(2 \cdot 3 \cdot x \cdot y \cdot z \cdot (x+1) \cdot (m-n))$? We know this is not the LCM because some of the factors need to be used multiple times based on the procedures illustrated throughout this chapter. Therefore, the LCM written in expanded notation with all the factors indicated multiple times will be:

$LCM = 2 \cdot 2 \cdot 2 \cdot 3 \cdot x \cdot x \cdot x \cdot y \cdot y \cdot z \cdot (x+1) \cdot (x+1) \cdot (m-n)$. Here is the LCM written using the exponential notation: "$LCM = 2^3 \cdot 3 \cdot x^3 \cdot y^2 \cdot z \cdot (x+1)^2 \cdot (m-n)$". Here is the LCM written in condensed form: "$LCM = 24x^3y^2z(x+1)^2(m-n)$".

(Comment: the notation above "$(a \pm b)$" represents two slightly different notations – both "$(a+b)$ or $(a-b)$". Example: $(a \pm 3)$ indicates you must consider both "$(a+3)$" and "$(a-3)$".

J. Find the LCM written in expanded form, exponential form, and condensed form for all the factors indicated in the problems 73, 74, and 75, when the three forms are appropriate.

73. $\{x \cdot x \cdot y \cdot y \cdot z\}$, $\{x \cdot x \cdot x \cdot y \cdot z \cdot z \cdot z \cdot z\}$

74. $\{a \cdot b \cdot b \cdot (x+9)(8-y)\}$, $\{a \cdot a \cdot b \cdot b \cdot b \cdot (x+9)(x+9)\}$, $\{a \cdot b \cdot c \cdot (8-y)\}$

75. $\{3 \cdot 5 \cdot 5 \cdot m \cdot m \cdot m \cdot n \cdot (x+y)\}$, $\{2 \cdot 3 \cdot 3 \cdot 3 \cdot m \cdot n \cdot n \cdot n \cdot n \cdot (x+y) \cdot (x+y)\}$

K. Use "Factor Trees" and "Prime Numbers" and find the LCD for each problem.

76. $\frac{59}{64} - \frac{43}{48}$ 77. $\frac{7}{50} + \frac{9}{80} - \frac{9}{30} - \frac{7}{25}$ 78. $\frac{5}{6} - \frac{1}{2} + \frac{3}{14}$ 79. $\frac{7}{10} + \frac{13}{15} - \frac{11}{20} - \frac{7}{5} + \frac{3}{1}$

80. $\frac{7}{15} - \frac{5}{18}$ 81. $\frac{25}{99} - \frac{16}{121} + \frac{53}{66}$ 82. $\frac{7}{24} + \frac{5}{40} + \frac{7}{60} - \frac{5}{30} + 3$ 83. $\frac{7}{9} - \frac{5}{12}$

Add and subtract the fractions indicated in the next section. Find LCDs by using "Factor Trees" with "Prime Factors". Determine the special form of the number 1 required to convert each of the given fractions into equivalent fractions. Write the sum or difference of the fractions with the LCD as one big fraction. Complete the problem by adding and subtracting the numerators to find the final answer and reduce if appropriate.

Example: "$\frac{25}{28} + \frac{35}{36} + \frac{7}{12} - \frac{1}{1}$"

Factor Trees

28	36	12	1
2×14	2×18	2×6	*Not Necessary*
$2 \times 2 \times 7$	$2 \times 2 \times 9$	$2 \times 2 \times 3$	
	$2 \times 2 \times 3 \times 3$		
$2^2 \times 7$	$2^2 \times 3^2$	$2^2 \times 3$	

Not the LCD: "$2 \times 3 \times 7$

The LCD Equals: "$2 \times 2 \times 3 \times 3 \times 7 = 2^2 \times 3^2 \times 7 = 252$

$\frac{252}{28} = 9 \quad \therefore \quad 9 = 9 \quad \therefore \quad \frac{9}{9} = 1 \qquad \frac{25}{28} = \frac{25}{28} \times 1 = \frac{25}{28} \times \frac{9}{9} = \frac{25 \times 9}{28 \times 9} = \frac{225}{252}$

$\frac{252}{36} = 7 \quad \therefore \quad 7 = 7 \quad \therefore \quad \frac{7}{7} = 1 \qquad \frac{35}{36} = \frac{35}{36} \times 1 = \frac{35}{36} \times \frac{7}{7} = \frac{35 \times 7}{36 \times 7} = \frac{245}{252}$

$\frac{252}{12} = 21 \quad \therefore \quad 21 = 21 \quad \therefore \quad \frac{21}{21} = 1 \qquad \frac{7}{12} = \frac{7}{12} \times 1 = \frac{7}{12} \times \frac{21}{21} = \frac{7 \times 21}{12 \times 21} = \frac{147}{252}$

$\frac{252}{1} = 252 \quad \therefore \quad 252 = 252 \quad \therefore \quad \frac{252}{252} = 1 \qquad \frac{1}{1} = \frac{1}{1} \times 1 = \frac{1}{1} \times \frac{252}{252} = \frac{1 \times 252}{1 \times 252} = \frac{252}{252}$

$\frac{25}{28} + \frac{35}{36} + \frac{7}{12} - \frac{1}{1} = \frac{225}{252} + \frac{245}{252} + \frac{147}{252} - \frac{252}{252} = \frac{225+245+147-252}{252} = \frac{365}{252} = 1\frac{113}{252}$

L. When solving/simplifying the problems (84 – 89) use all the steps illustrated in the example problem just used as a model.

84. $\frac{3}{20} + \frac{3}{10} - \frac{7}{30}$ 85. $\frac{11}{54} - \frac{5}{36}$ 86. $\frac{5}{12} - \frac{7}{30} + \frac{7}{15} + \frac{7}{20}$

87. $\frac{7}{8} - \frac{7}{28} - \frac{7}{36} - \frac{1}{45} + \frac{1001}{1260}$ 88. $-\frac{1}{6} + \frac{7}{20} + 3$ 89. $2\frac{3}{14} + 3\frac{11}{21} - 1\frac{9}{28}$

SOLVE BASIC ALGEBRA 1 EQUATIONS BY LINING UP TWO EQUATIONS TO ADD AND SUBTRACT AND TO MULTIPLY AND DIVIDE THE GIVEN EQUATION BY THE SECOND EQUATION IN ORDER TO DETERMINE A THIRD EQUATION

Here is an example to illustrate how to line up two equations when you are solving a first-degree algebra equation with only one variable on either the left or right side of the equation and there is a number either added or subtracted to the variable. The goal is to get the variable by itself on one side of the equation and get the number away from the variable. Since the number on the same side of the equation in the first example is either added or subtracted to the variable, the goal is to figure out a way to add 0 to the variable, because we know if we add 0 to any term or number, we can ignore the 0 and simply write the number or term without the 0. (Examples to illustrate when you add or subtract 0 to a number or term you can forget about the 0 and simply write the number or term: "$5 + 0 = 5$, $0 + 7 = 7$, $11 - 0 = 11$, $a - 0 = a$, and $x = 0 + x$".) Our first objective when solving these types of problems is to locate the variable in the equation. In the example problem below the variable "y" is on the right side of the equation and then locate the number in the equation "9" also on the right side of the equation, which is subtracted from the variable "y". These are key observations because we now realize we want to add "9" in the second equation on the right side, to ensure the two "9's" combine and become 0. The rule is simple if you add a number to a variable in a first-degree algebra equation then you need to subtract that number, and if you are subtracting a number in the given equation, then you need to add the same number to achieve the goal of adding the number 0 to the variable. Remember, when we line up the two equations, if we add or subtract a number to one side of the equation, we need to use an identity and add or subtract the same number to the other side of the equation.

Example problem: Solve for the variable "y". $7 = y - 9$

Our goal is to get the "9" away from the variable "y".

To accomplish this goal, we will focus on the equation/identity. $+9 = \quad +9$

If we place the second equation directly under the first equation and line up the equal relationship symbols, we can find a third equation and the answer by doing the arithmetic on both sides of the first two equations.

Solution:

$$7 = y - 9$$

$$\underline{+9 = \quad +9}$$

$$16 = y + 0$$

$$\therefore 16 = y \text{ or } y = 16$$

Teaching principle number 5 is just as important as principle number 4, introduce new concepts frequently over an extended time frame, prior to assigning homework problems focused on a new concept. Principle number 5 encourages you to review constantly after you have taught a section/concept. Everyone will tend to forget how they solved problems if they do not continually reinforce the procedures which they learned last week or last month. If you do not review frequently, you will find the procedures/topics you taught well, will be forgotten by many students a month or two later.

One of the great things about solving algebra problems is, if you find the correct root/answer for the variable, when you refer-back to the original equation, "$7 = y - 9$" and replace the variable "y" with the answer you just determined, you form an identity. Here is an illustration to justify why the correct answer is "$y = 16$". If we are given the equation, "$7 = y - 9$", and we substitute the number "16" into the equation for the variable "y", then the new equation is written in this form "$7 = 16 - 9$". Once we complete the arithmetic problem on the right side of the equation, we end up with the identity, "$7 = 7$". This checking procedure justifies that the correct solution is indeed, "$y = 16$".

Comment, when we explain the difference between a variable and a label, it is important to realize a variable will normally represent a number. The variable "y" in the example problem, equaled "16".

Here is an example to illustrate how to line up two equations when you are solving a first-degree algebra equation with only one variable on either the left or right side of the equation, and the variable is either multiplied or divided by a number. In the next example below, "$28 = 7z$", the variable "z" is multiplied by the number "7". The goal to solve this type of problem is to change the multiplication problem between the number "7" and the variable "z" into the number 1 times the variable because everyone knows when they multiply a number or a term by the number 1, the number 1 may be dropped. (Examples to illustrate when you multiply or divide a number or term by 1 you can forget about the 1 and simply write the number or term: "$5 \times 1 = 5$, $1 \times 7 = 7$, $z \times 1 = z$, $11 \div 1 = 11$, $a \div 1 = a$, and $\frac{x}{1} = x$".) Since we want to accomplish this goal, we will divide the left side of the first equation by the left side of the second equation and then divide the right side of the first equation by the right side of the second equation. We must focus on the first equation and divide the first equation by the second equation/identity "$7 = 7$" to accomplish the desired results.

In the second example below, "$\frac{p}{3} = 11$" the variable "p", is divided by a number, "3" and we will create the second identity/equation, "$3 = 3$". In the solution to this example, we will multiply the left side of the given equation by the left side of the identity and at the same time, multiply the right side of the given equation by the right side of the identity.

Solution for the example problem: Solve for the variable "z". $28 = 7z$

Our goal is to get the "7" away from the variable "z".

To accomplish this goal, we will focus on the equation/identity. $7 = 7$

If we place the second equation directly under the first equation and line up the equals relationship symbols and divide we can find a third equation and the answer by doing the arithmetic on both sides of the two equations.

Solution: $28 = 7z$

Identity: $7 = 7$

We are going to divide the left side of the given equation by the left hand side of the identity and the right hand side of the given equation by the right hand side of the identity.

$$\frac{28 \;=\; 7z}{7 \;=\; 7}$$

We divide the given equation "$28 = 7z$" by the identity "$7 = 7$" to determine the last expression which is normally written in the more common form at the right.

$$\frac{28}{7} = \frac{7z}{7}$$

$$\therefore \quad \frac{28}{7} = 1z$$

$$\therefore \quad 4 = z \;\; or \;\; z = 4$$

When you refer to the equation, "$\frac{28}{7} = \frac{7z}{7}$" in the solution, this should remind you of the procedures most algebra teachers, probably around 99% of algebra teachers, emphasize when they solve the original problem, "$28 = 7z$". Most algebra teachers tell students to simply divide both sides by the number "7" *but there are times in advanced mathematics when it is beneficial to recognize you can divide a given equation by a second equation to get a third equation.* We do not mind if you want to emphasize you should divide both sides of the equation by the number "7", in fact, we encourage you to teach this method. We illustrated the two-equation division procedure to try and be consistent when we add and subtract two equations to determine a third equation, and therefore, we illustrate, it is permissible to divide a given equation by a second equation to determine a third equation. We want high-achieving and motivated math students to understand the common method illustrated by most textbooks and 99% of all algebra teachers, but we also want these students to understand the two-equation division procedure may be the only method to solve some advanced math problems. The two-equation division procedure is the reason why the simple procedure which 99% of teachers emphasize to students, works. It is also permissible to multiply a given equation by a second equation to determine a third equation which may be a helpful technique to use when solving some advanced mathematics problems. When teaching students to solve first-degree algebraic equations involving variables that are either multiplied or divided by a constant/number, we hope you illustrate both techniques and remind students even though it is much easier to simply work with the number when you are multiplying or dividing both sides of the equation to find the value of the variable, it is also a good idea to remember you can multiply or divide a given equation by a second equation to determine the third equation and determine the solution.

Again, we should check to ensure when we substitute the root/answer "4" for the variable "z" back into the given equation, "$28 = 7z$" we must end up with an identity. Here is the substitution illustration, "$28 = 7z$", then "$28 = 7(4)$", and finally we have the identity "$28 = 28$" once we complete the arithmetic problem on the right side of the equation.

In this example problem the variable "z" ended up equaling the number, "4". Variables in algebra are usually replaced with a number. This is a major difference between a variable and a label.

Solution for the example problem: Solve for the variable "p". $\frac{p}{3} = 11$

Our goal is to get the "3" away from the variable "p".

To accomplish this goal, we will focus on the equation/identity $3 = 3$

If we place the second equation directly under the first equation and line up the equals relationship symbols and multiply we can find a third equation and the answer by doing the arithmetic on both sides of the two equations.

Solution: $\frac{p}{3} = 11$

Identity: $3 = 3$

We are going to multiply the left side of the given equation by the left side of the identity and the right side of the given equation by the right side of the identity.

$$\frac{p}{3} = 11$$

We multiply the given equation "$\frac{p}{3} = 11$" by the identity "$3 = 3$"

$$\underline{\times 3 = \times 3}$$

to determine the last expression which is normally written in the more common form at the right.

$$\frac{p}{3} \times 3 = 11 \times 3$$

or

$$\frac{p \times 3}{3 \times 1} = 11 \times 3$$

In this example problem the variable, "p" ended up equaling the number "33".

$$\therefore \quad 1p = 33$$

$$\therefore \quad p = 33 \;\; or \;\; 33 = p$$

We should check to ensure when we substitute the root/answer "33" for the variable "p" back into the given equation, "$\frac{p}{3} = 11$" we end up with an identity in the final step. Here is the illustration where we substitute the number "33" for the variable "p", "$\frac{p}{3} = 11$", then "$\frac{33}{3} = 11$", and finally, we end with the identity, "$11 = 11$".

M. Here are some problems for you to solve. Indicate all the steps as illustrated above. We hope you can compute all the answers in your head without much work, but understanding the procedures is essential when the problems become more difficult than the simple problems indicated next, 90.-101. When solving the problems which involve multiplying and dividing the variable by a constant, we want you to illustrate the two-equation solution rather than the simple multiplying or dividing by a constant or a single number solution. It should now be obvious why the simple solution to only work with the constant, is based on sound mathematics principles and procedures. We expect students will use the basic simple notation solution when they solve problems in your class. Good students always check their answers to ensure that they've solved the problem correctly.

90.	$x + 3 = 6$	91.	$p + 101 = 201$
92.	$909 = z - 11$	93.	$5y = 55$
94.	$1020 = 510q$	95.	$\frac{a}{7} = 9$
96.	$a + 11.93 = 89.661$	97.	$\frac{r}{6.1} = 9.2$
98.	$3d = 67.2$	99.	$z - \frac{3}{8} = \frac{7}{24}$
100.	$\frac{7}{15} = t - \frac{2}{5}$	101.	$\frac{n}{.7} = \frac{3}{4}$

When we discussed the procedures to solve the problems in the section above, we referred to first-degree algebra equations with one variable, also referred to as linear equations. A first-degree algebra equation or linear equation with one variable simply means the equation contains one variable and the largest exponent of the variable is always **one (1)**. The variable may be written more than once in the equation, as in this example, "$2x + 6 - x = 9$", but in both cases involving the variable "x" the largest exponent for the variable "x" is 1. When the exponent of a variable is 1, the exponent 1, will not normally be written, but everyone is expected to realize the exponent is understood to be present. We refer to the number 1 in this type of situation as an invisible number. Here is the same equation written with the exponent 1 indicated with each of the "x" variables: "$2x^1 + 6 - x^1 = 9$". This is not the normal way to write this type of problem, but it is the correct way to interpret the meaning of the exponents.

If an equation contains a single variable with the largest exponent equal to 2, then the equation is referred to as a quadratic equation which means the degree of the equation is degree 2. Here is an example of a quadratic equation or 2nd-degree equation, "$x^2 + 3x = 4$". Notice, the variable "x" appears as both "x^2 and $3x$" but it is the same variable and the largest exponent for the variable "x" is 2 in the equation. Here is a second example of a 2nd-degree equation (quadratic equation): "$b = b^2$". If the largest variable exponent in an equation is 3, then the equation is referred to as a cubic equation or a 3rd-degree equation. Here are two examples of cubic equations, "$m^3 - 4m^2 + m + 6 = 0$" and "$r = r^3$". These are basic explanations of first, second, and third-degree equations.

The five examples just indicated, "$2x + 6 - x = 9$", "$x^2 + 3x = 4$", "$b = b^2$", "$m^3 - 4m^2 + m + 6 = 0$", and "$r = r^3$" can be used to give a simple explanation of The Fundamental Theorem of Algebra. The Fundamental Theorem of Algebra, written in its simplest form, is: "If you have an algebra equation with one variable indicated in the equation, then the largest exponent of the variable indicates the <u>maximum</u> number of solutions/roots for the equation." The first equation, "$2x + 6 - x = 9$" may have at most one solution. The only solution/root for the equation, "$2x + 6 - x = 9$", is "$x = 3$". In the 2nd-degree equations, "$x^2 + 3x = 4$" and "$b = b^2$" there may be at most two numbers which you may substitute into the equations and form an identity. The two roots/solutions for the 2nd-degree quadratic equation, "$x^2 + 3x = 4$", are "$x = -4$ & $x = 1$" and the roots of the equation "$b = b^2$", are "$b = 0$ & $b = 1$". In the third equation, "$m^3 - 4m^2 + m + 6 = 0$" the largest exponent for the variable "m" is 3, so there could be three roots for this equation, but not more than 3 roots and maybe less than 3 roots. The three roots for the 3rd-degree cubic equation, "$m^3 - 4m^2 + m + 6 = 0$", are "$m = -1$, $m = 2$, & $m = 3$" and the roots for the equation "$r = r^3$" are "$r = 0$, $r = -1$, and $r = +1$".

We will illustrate in the linear equation (1st-degree equation), "$2x + 6 - x = 9$" the solution/root is the number "3" by substituting the number "3" into the given equation and we will end with an identity. Here is the substitution and simplification of the problem to determine the identity: "$2x + 6 - x = 9$" then substitute "3" for each "x" as follows "$2(3) + 6 - 3 = 9$" do the arithemtic on the left side of the equation "$6 + 6 - 3 = 9$" and $\therefore$ "$9 = 9$".

When working with the quadratic equation, "$x^2 + 3x = 4$" we can illustrate the two indicated roots, "$x = -4$ & $x = 1$" are both correct solutions by substituting each root back into the given equation one at a time as indicated in the following illustrations. Substitute the root, "-4" into the given equation "$x^2 + 3x = 4$" as follows: "$(-4)^2 + 3(-4) = 4$". Do the arithmetic on the left side of the equation and get "$16 - 12 = 4$", then the identity "$4 = 4$" to confirm "-4" is truly a correct solution.

We must also substitute the second root "1" into the equation and do the arithmetic to end with an identity to ensure the number "1" is also a root as follows: "$x^2 + 3x = 4$" then, "$1^2 + 3(1) = 4$". Do the arithmetic on the left side of the equation and get "$1 + 3 = 4$" and conclude with the identity, "$4 = 4$" to confirm "1" is truly a correct solution.

When you are working with a cubic equation (degree 3), and you have three different roots (you may only have 1 or 2 roots, but in our two examples, there are 3 roots), you need to substitute each of the three roots independently into the given equation, and you must end up with three identities after substituting each root into the equation. Below is the illustration to substitute each of the three roots into the given equation,

"$m^3 - 4m^2 + m + 6 = 0$", then end with three identities.

$x = -1$ substitute $(-1)^3 - 4(-1)^2 + (-1) + 6 = 0$ then $-1 - 4 - 1 + 6 = 0$ $\therefore$ $0 = 0$

$x = 2$ substitute $(2)^3 - 4(2)^2 + (2) + 6 = 0$ then $8 - 16 + 2 + 6 = 0$ $\therefore$ $0 = 0$

$x = 3$ substitute $(3)^3 - 4(3)^2 + (3) + 6 = 0$ then $27 - 36 + 3 + 6 = 0$ $\therefore$ $0 = 0$

If a root or roots are correct answers/solutions, you will always end up with an identity when you complete the substitution process. You should be able to illustrate why the indicated roots for the 2nd-degree equation "$b = b^2$" are "$b = 0$ & 1" and why the roots for the 3rd-degree equation "$r = r^3$" are "$r = 0, 1, \& -1$". (Special Problem for secondary mathematics majors: How many solutions can you find to solve the following first-degree equation - "$2x + 9 = 8 + x + 1 + x$"? There are an infinite number of roots. Why? If you simplify both sides of the equation, the given equation is already an identity, and any number you substitute for the variable, "x" must also end as an identity.)

Another critical comment we did not make when referring to problems "90.-101." above is: "The inverse operation for addition is subtraction and vice-versa and the inverse operation for multiplication is division and vice-versa. It should be evident from the three examples and twelve problems, why we used the inverse operations to find the roots/solutions for all the first-degree equations.

GRAPH LINES USING A CARTESIAN COORDINATE SYSTEM WHICH IS FREQUENTLY REFERRED TO AS A RECTANGULAR COORDINATE SYSTEM

N. Graph the line given a Point and the Slope. Indicate a minimum of three points before you graph the line.

102. $(3,5)$ & $m = \frac{2}{3}$

103. $(2,1)$ & $m = \frac{1}{2}$

104. $(6,1)$ & $m = 1$

105. $(3,4)$ & $m = \frac{3}{2}$

We may only indicate two points in the graphical solution. Why are two points sufficient when graphing these problems? The answer is written in the solution section after the graph for problem 105.

O. Graph the line using the 3 or 4 given points.

106. $(2,2), (3,4), (4,6), and\ (5,8)$

107. $(7,8), (5,7), (3,6), and\ (1,5)$

108. $(5,1), (3,5),\ and\ (1,9)$

109. $(8,7), (7,4),\ and\ (6,1)$

LONG DIVISION WITH DECIMALS and REMAINDERS No calculators permitted.

P. When writing quotients as decimals either write the decimal as a repeating or terminating decimal. If the quotient is not a natural number, then always write your first solution as a natural number with a fraction (mixed number) indicated, then write the second solution as a decimal. We will tell you if the decimal is a terminating or repeating decimal.

110. $\frac{27}{9}$ =? The answer is a terminating decimal.

111. $\frac{27}{5}$ =? Write the answer in two forms. The answer is a terminating decimal.

112. $379050 \div 361 =?$ The answer is a terminating decimal.

113. $379050 \div 50 =?$ The answer is a terminating decimal.

114. $\frac{379050}{7}$ =? The answer is a terminating decimal.

115. $3793 \div 11 =?$ Write the answer in two forms. The quotient is a repeating decimal with a period of two numbers. (The period of a repeating decimal is the number of digits which repeat.)

116. $\frac{368.22}{.15}$ =? The answer may be written as a terminating decimal or a mixed number. Write the answer in both forms.

117. $1.0075 \div .25 =?$ Write the answer in two forms. The decimal is a terminating decimal.

118. $\frac{1\frac{4}{5}}{2\frac{7}{10}} = 1\frac{4}{5} \div 2\frac{7}{10} =?$ Write the answer as a fraction and as a repeating decimal.

THE INDICATED NUMBER IS NOT THE <u>LCM</u> FOR THE SET OF NUMBERS.

Q. Explain why the indicated LCM is NOT the LCM for the indicated set of numbers then use the rules illustrated in this textbook to find challenging LCMs and LCDs.

119. *Given set of numbers* $= \{36, 25, 18\}$, *Explain why the LCM is not* 2700.

120. *Given set of numbers* $= (15, 18, 24\}$, *Explain why the LCM is not* 1080.

CHAPTER 5

BEGIN TO LEARN HOW TO CONVERT THOUSANDS OF MATHEMATICS EXPRESSIONS INTO EQUIVALENT EXPRESSIONS

YOU WILL LEARN A LOT ABOUT THE NUMBER 1 IN THIS CHAPTER, WHICH MAY SOUND SIMPLE, BUT YOU PROBABLY NEVER THOUGHT ABOUT THE NUMBER 1 WRITTEN USING THE DIFFERENT NOTATIONS PRESENTED IN THIS CHAPTER.

Chapter 5

Important – Very Important!

Look at what "Young's Conversion Theorem" literally says. Young's Conversion Theorem" in its more advanced form, is stated like this: If you multiply any mathematical expression by a fraction, ratio, or term equal to 1, then the ending mathematical expression will be equivalent to the original mathematical expression even though they might not look identical. The only time the starting and ending mathematical expressions will be identical with respect to the Reflexive Property, is if you multiply by the number "1" or the fraction "$\frac{1}{1}$". "Young's Conversion Theorem" expands your knowledge of the number 1 and the Identity Property of One (1) for Multiplication

Remember: The Reflexive Property is a special type of identity. An identity is an equation such that the left and right sides of the equation are exactly-the-same, once all the arithmetic and advanced math procedures are completed on both sides of the equation. The Reflexive Property is a more specific type of equation. When you write an equation such that the Reflexive Property is evident, the two sides of the equation are identical without any additional math computations. These equations are examples of identities: "$7x = 7x$, $6.24 + 1 = 7.24$, $4x + 3x = 2x + 5x$, $6(3x + 2) = 18x + 12$, $9 + 1 = 10$". The following equations are also identities, but more specifically they are examples of the Reflexive Property: "$a = a, \frac{77}{93} = \frac{77}{93}, p + 1 = p + 1, 2y = 2y$". Imagine you see a reflection in a mirror.

The number 1 seems like such an easy number to understand, but there is a lot about the number 1 which needs to be clarified. Think about the following equations/identities and then the fractions which equal 1. If "8 = 6 + 2", what do the fractions "$\frac{6+2}{8}$" and "$\frac{8}{6+2}$" equal? Our belief is you agree "8 = 6+2", and you also believe the fractions "$\frac{6+2}{8} = 1$" and "$\frac{8}{6+2} = 1$". We can give you several examples, an infinite number of examples, where two arithmetic expressions are equal, and we form two fractions or ratios with the expressions and both fractions/ratios equal 1. There is only one exception to this rule: "$0 = 8 - 8$", but the ratios "$\frac{0}{8-8}$ and $\frac{8-8}{0}$", do not equal 1 because there is another powerful rule in mathematics which applies: "The denominator in a fraction CANNOT equal "0"." This means the two fractions "$\frac{0}{8-8}$" and "$\frac{8-8}{0}$" do not make sense. In fact, since the denominators in both fractions equal "0", every mathematician will say the fractions are undefined expressions. This also means you can never divide by the number "0".

Comment: We did not say it was impossible to solve a fraction problem if there is a "0" in the denominator. We said we cannot solve a fraction problem if the denominator equals "0". Here are two example problems which illustrate that it is possible to simplify a fraction with the number "0" in the denominator:

(Examples: "$\frac{8}{2+0+2} = \frac{8}{4} = 2$ and $\frac{8 \times 0}{(16+0)} = \frac{0}{16} = 0$").

Think about the following examples of equations/identities and then about the two ways to write fractions. Both fractions when written in the two different forms always equal one, 1.

1. "10 = 2 · 5". Therefore ("∴" is the mathematics notation for the word "therefore".)

"∴ $\frac{10}{2 \cdot 5} = 1$ and $\frac{2 \cdot 5}{10} = 1$".

Rather than write the two equations indicated in the last sentence and both equations equal the number "1", in this case mathematicians often write the two equations in the following condensed form: "$\frac{10}{2 \cdot 5} = 1 = \frac{2 \cdot 5}{10}$". We already discussed the facts involving the equation "$10 = 2 \cdot 5$", the number "10" and the multiplication problem "$2 \cdot 5$" are equal/equivalent and they represent an identity if written in equation format, but they do NOT represent an example of the Reflexive Property when written in the equation format.

An *identity* is a special *equation* where the left side is *identical* to the right side, after the arithmetic operations and the algebra (advanced math) operations are all completed.

2. "$4^2 = 16$": (This is an equation, and it is also an identity.)

∴ (*therefore*) "$\frac{4^2}{16} = 1 = \frac{16}{4^2}$"

The left and right sides of this equation are equivalent once the arithmetic procedure for the expression "4^2" is completed.

3. "$5^2 - 1 = 4^2 + 8$" ∴ "$\frac{5^2-1}{4^2+8} = 1 = \frac{4^2+8}{5^2-1}$".

You must realize, if you have two equivalent expressions, when you form a fraction or a ratio with both the left and right sides of the equation, the two fractions/ratios will always equal 1, except when the expressions equal "0". You cannot divide by "0", which also means the denominator in a fraction cannot equal "0".

4. "$701.125 - 700 = 1\frac{1}{8}$" $\therefore$ "$\frac{1\frac{1}{8}}{701.125-700} = 1 = \frac{701.125-700}{1\frac{1}{8}}$".

There must be a million ways to write the number 1. That is a compelling thought, but one must realize there are an infinite number of ways to write the number 1. The number 1 is so amazing because when you multiply or divide by the number 1 or a special form of the number 1, you will end with an equal number or expression. This special property about the number 1 illustrates The Power of the Number One (1) and the importance of the number 1 when working with basic arithmetic conversions and advanced mathematics topics.

We used the four example equations/identities listed above ($10 = 2 \cdot 5$ and $4^2 = 16$ and $5^2 - 1 = 4^2 + 8$ and $701.125 - 700 = 1\frac{1}{8}$) to illustrate the meaning of "Young's Equation/Ratio Theorem", which applies to both equations and identities. An equation means the left and right sides of the equals relationship symbol (=) are equal, and an identity is an equation where the left and right sides of the equals relationship symbol (=) are identical once all the arithmetic and mathematics procedures are completed. An identity is a special type of equation.

Wow, you probably never thought about writing the number 1 in the manner indicated in the four example problems listed above. Now hold on, we are going to expand your knowledge of the number 1, one more level after you understand some basic mathematics terminology. Based on the previous examples, you probably can make a conclusion about equal expressions. The conclusion is: if two expressions are equal, you can make two fractions or ratios which both, equal 1. Do not read over the previous statement quickly; think about it. *If two expressions are EQUAL, then you can make two fractions or ratios which both equal, one (1).* Consider writing this statement ten more times so the power of this statement begins to sink in. The statement in italicized print is so important we refer to it as "Young's Equation/Ratio Theorem". If two expressions are equal, then you can make two fractions or ratios which both, equal 1. Remember the only exception to this statement/theorem is the denominator in the fractions or ratios cannot equal "0".

Just because we gave you several examples to illustrate how to work with "Young's Equation/Ratio Theorem", writing several examples to illustrate the Theorem does not prove the Theorem is always true. Formal proofs of both "Young's Equation/Ratio Theorem" and "Young's Conversion Theorem" are given at the beginning of Chapter 8. In the next several paragraphs, we need to take a detour, and have you focus your thoughts on the difference between an equation an identity and a special identity referred to in math textbooks as the Reflexive Property, then how to use "Young's Equation/Ratio Theorem" in early elementary arithmetic classes. When teachers are explaining arithmetic and mathematics topics, there are often little concepts they feel are so obvious they do not completely explain the subtle differences between different terms. Let us explain the subtle differences between equations, identities, and the Reflexive Property. The following examples, "$6 = 6$" and "$3.2 = 3.2$", are both examples of the Reflexive Property because the left and right sides of the equal sign is like a reflection in a mirror. The two example problems also represent identities and equations. The following two examples, "$6 + 2 = 8$" and "$3(5 + 1) = 15 + 3$", are both identities and they are also equations, but they are not examples used to illustrate the Reflexive Property. The final two examples indicated in this paragraph are the equations, "$y = 2x + 1$" and "$x + y + 2z = 0$", but neither equation is an example of an identity or an example of the Reflexive Property.

You will form a fraction which equals 1 if you have an example which illustrates the Reflexive Property and then make a fraction out of the left and right sides of the equation as evidenced by the identities/equations which follow. The three examples in the next sentence are all equations, identities, and examples of the Reflexive Property. We used these types of examples involving identities earlier in Chapters 3 and 4: "$5 = 5 \therefore \frac{5}{5} = 1$", "$84 = 84 \therefore \frac{84}{84} = 1$", and "$66 = 66 \therefore \frac{66}{66} = 1$" when we explained how to add and subtract fractions. We then used "Young's Conversion Theorem" to convert the given fractions into equivalent fractions with a least common denominator. These three examples of the Reflexive Property could be introduced in 2nd, 3rd, or 4th grade. Here are two complicated identities which are also examples of the Reflexive Property, and you probably would not discuss these examples with 4th graders, but you may want to mention these examples with 5th graders:

(Examples: "$\frac{4}{5} = \frac{4}{5} \therefore \frac{\frac{4}{5}}{\frac{4}{5}} = 1$" and "$\frac{8.61}{77.1} = \frac{8.61}{77.1} \therefore \frac{\frac{8.61}{77.1}}{\frac{8.61}{77.1}} = 1$") This identity, "$0 = 0$", is the only exception to "Young's Equation/Ratio Theorem" because it is impossible to work with the following fraction, "$\frac{0}{0}$". Mathematicians consider this fraction to be *undefined* only because the denominator equals "0".

All the identities in this paragraph were written to illustrate how to use "Young's Equation/Ratio Theorem" and derive an expression equal to 1. We will use the word "identity" rather than the phrase Reflexive Property for most of these types of problems in the remainder of this textbook.

When we illustrated how to add and subtract all the fractions discussed in Chapters 3 and 4, ("$\frac{1}{2}+\frac{1}{4}$", "$\frac{7}{12}-\frac{2}{15}+\frac{11}{20}-\frac{1}{30}$", "$\frac{67}{88}+\frac{91}{96}-\frac{103}{112}$", "$\frac{5}{6}-\frac{1}{2}+2\frac{3}{4}$", "$5\frac{2}{5}+\frac{11}{15}-2\frac{2}{3}$", and several other examples) we had to convert all the fractions which did not have the correct LCD into equivalent fractions. When we converted these fractions into equivalent fractions, we divided the respective LCDs by the denominators of the given fractions. After we found the quotients for each of the division problems, we could have written identities for each of the quotients, such as the identity "$2=2$" or "$66=66$". Once we mentally thought about the identities involving the quotients, we wrote the fractions which equaled 1 such as "$\frac{2}{2}=1$" and "$\frac{66}{66}=1$", then multiplied the original fractions by the fractions we just determined.

In example 1 (Chapter 3), "$\frac{1}{2}+\frac{1}{4}$", when working with the fraction "$\frac{1}{2}$", we found the quotient "2" when we divided the LCD "4" by the denominator "2". We then multiplied the fraction "$\frac{1}{2}$" by the number 1 written using the fraction "$\frac{2}{2}$". We used the identity, "$2=2$" and applied "Young's Equation/Ratio Theorem" to determine the fraction "$\frac{2}{2}$", which equals "1". When we wrote the explanation to convert the fraction "$\frac{1}{2}$" into the equivalent fraction "$\frac{2}{4}$", you likely looked at the explanation and asked the question, "Why is he making such a simple conversion into something so difficult? You might have also thought about the following comment in your head: "This is what is wrong with mathematicians--they make things so difficult." Most people who are proficient with fractions quickly convert the fraction "$\frac{1}{2}$" into the equal fraction "$\frac{2}{4}$" in their head and do not even consider the actual reasons and the procedures they use. They mentally developed some basic tricks which work and just do the conversion in their head. The question is, "Do you really understand the rules you are using, and can you convert the more challenging problems in Chapter 4 in your head without thinking about the rules and procedures we emphasized in Chapters 3 and 4?

In Chapter 4, one of the example problems involved the fraction "$\frac{103}{112}$". We found the LCD "7,392" for all three fractions involved with the problem. We then found the quotient "66" when we divided the LCD 7,392" by the denominator "112". Next, we multiplied the fraction "$\frac{103}{112}$" by the number "1", written in the form "$\frac{66}{66}$". The fraction "$\frac{66}{66}$", which equals 1, was derived by using "Young's Equation/Ratio Theorem" with the identity "66=66".

We briefly mentioned the concept of identities earlier when we were converting fractions into equivalent fractions using "Young's Conversion Theorem" because it was obvious all the indicated fractions equaled 1: "$\frac{2}{2} = 1$" and "$\frac{88}{88} = 1$" and "$\frac{12}{12} = 1$". We did not write the identities "$2 = 2$ or $88 = 88$ or $12 = 12$" prior to writing the fractions "$\frac{2}{2}, \frac{88}{88}$, and $\frac{12}{12}$" derived from the identities. At the time, we did not want to emphasize an additional "obvious" concept when we were already trying to illustrate these two challenging math procedures: 1. How to find Least Common Denominators for all types of fraction problems; 2. How to convert given fractions into equivalent fractions using "Young's Conversion Theorem".

> To review, a mathematical *identity* is an equation in which the left side of the equation is identical to the right side of the equation after all the mathematical procedures have been completed.

Notice in the example problems listed above, the left and right sides of the equations were identical as indicated in the earlier section and the next section.

Here is "Young's Equation/Ratio Theorem" stated in the most practical form: "Fact: If you have an equation, you can form two fractions or ratios using the left side of the equation as the numerator and the right side of the equation as the denominator or vice-versa and both fractions and/or ratios will equal one. "Young's Equation/Ratio Theorem" can also be stated like this: "If two *mathematical expressions* are equal, then you can form two ratios using both the left and right sides of the equation, and both ratios equal 1." There is one important exception to this theorem: the denominator in any fraction or the divisor in any division problem cannot equal "0".

Note "Young's Equation/Ratio Theorem" applies to identities, equations, and examples of the Reflexive Property. It seems so obvious, "Young's Equation/Ratio Theorem" is a fact when you are working with identities and the Reflexive Property, you may initially write the fractions which equal 1 without specifically mentioning the theorem when students are converting simple fractions into equivalent fractions. "Young's Equation/Ratio Theorem" becomes more important when you convert different types of measurements into equivalent measurements later in this textbook.

It is now time to expand your knowledge of the number 1 to an even higher level. The following illustrations involve equations and strange-looking identities. Look at this example: "12 inches, equals 1 foot"; or "12 inches = 1 foot"; or "12 in. = 1 ft." Labels are extremely important when working with problems which measure a quantity involving magnitude. This means you can now start to discuss labels, or if you are thinking ahead, you have been emphasizing labels for the past two months, so labels are not new to your students. Since "12 in. = 1 ft.", this means we can form two equal ratios which both, equal <u>1</u>: "$\frac{12\ in.}{1\ ft.} = 1$ and $\frac{1\ ft.}{12\ in.} = 1$". All we did was use "Young's Equation/Ratio Theorem" to justify the ratios equal <u>1</u>. If two expressions are equal, then you can make two ratios that both, equal <u>1</u>. Hopefully, this all sinks in because it is the foundation for "Young's Conversion Theorem".

Here is an example of the one exception to "Young's Equation/Ratio Theorem", "$1 - 1 = 0$" $\therefore$ $\frac{1-1}{0} \neq 1 \neq \frac{0}{1-1}$". This example problem makes no sense to any mathematician, and this is one example of the only exception.

> If the denominator of a fraction equals <u>0</u>, it is mathematically impossible to work with the fraction. The fraction expression is considered UNDEFINED!

In "Chapter 6: Unit Conversions in Arithmetic", we illustrate how to use "Young's Equation/Ratio Theorem" and "Young's Conversion Theorem" in 5th grade when converting from one unit of measurement into a different unit of measurement and the magnitudes of the starting and ending expressions are equivalent. This is the way unit conversions are treated in chemistry, physics, engineering, and all related mathematics courses. The procedure to convert units in advanced math classes, engineering classes, physics classes, etc. is sometimes referred to as Dimensional Analysis. Our guess is: Few high school math or science teachers ever mention the phrase Dimensional Analysis in any of their classes. Since few people are familiar with the phrase Dimensional Analysis, we coined the names of the two Theorems which can be introduced in elementary school and illustrated throughout this textbook. "Young's Conversion Theorem" is also applicable for other conversion problems you teach in either 5th or 6th grade; it removes all the guesswork when converting decimals into percentages, percentages into decimals, or terminating decimals into fractions.

Before we illustrate how to convert from one unit of measurement into an equivalent unit of measurement, we must again take a short detour. This time we want to illustrate the importance of *labels* and the difference between *variables* and *labels* in arithmetic and advanced math courses. This is one of those simple topics which should be obvious, and teachers often assume the students will understand the concept with little explanation. In the following examples and throughout this book, you need to realize algebraically mathematicians treat labels and variables the same way. Labels and variables are not the same, and they are used in different ways in arithmetic and algebra, but when simplifying expressions or solving equations in arithmetic and algebra, the two different types of mathematical terms, "*labels*" and "*variables*", follow the same rules. What is the difference between a label and a variable? A label is simply a word used in an arithmetic or algebra problem <u>usually</u> to the right of a number but <u>sometimes</u> to the left of the number to indicate the type of objects the answer or the expression represents. A variable represents an unknown number <u>usually</u> in an equation, but it can also be in an expression. A variable represents a number, and a label tells you what type of object(s) you are working with. Think about the following simple example involving a label. You tell a child to go to the store and get 12 of something. This would be a poor way to tell someone what to buy because there is no label. This would make much more sense, "Go to the store and get 12 rolls." If you want to be more specific, you may make your label more exact by saying 12 hamburger rolls, but the label is important in either situation. The labels "rolls" or "hamburger rolls" will never represent a number. The labels simply state the directions in a more specific way, so the child knows exactly what to buy.

When a variable is written in an equation such as "$2x = 6$" the goal is to figure out what number replaces the variable "x" in the equation so the equation makes sense. When you substitute the number "3" into the equation for the variable "x", an amazing thing occurs. If the number "3" is the correct answer for the variable "x" in this equation, when you substitute the number "3", into the equation for the variable "x" and then multiply the two numbers, "2 and 3" on the left side of the equation, you will end up with the identity "$6 = 6$". Here is an amazing fact written in simplified form-- "Every time you find the value of a variable in an algebra equation, then substitute the number into the original equation and do the arithmetic on both the left and right sides of the equation, you end up with an identity if you found the correct value for the variable." Here are some simple examples to illustrate the important differences between the two words *label* and *variable* and the fact they are treated the same way when applying arithmetic and algebra rules.

$1.A.$ Labels when simplifying math expressions involving addition and subtraction –

"$2 \text{ roses} + 3 \text{ tulips} + 4 \text{ roses} - 1 \text{ tulip} = 6 \text{ roses and } 2 \text{ tulips} = 6 \text{ roses} + 2 \text{ tulips}$"

The labels "roses" and "tulips" mean what they indicate. There are 6 roses and 2 tulips, nothing more and nothing less. The labels simply tell you what type of objects (flowers) you are working with. It would be nonsensical to say you have "8 rosetulips". You can only add and subtract the two pairs of numbers "$2 + 4$" and "$3 - 1$" if the labels are identical. Some may say it would be correct to say you have 8 flowers, and we would not argue with you. Ha! Ha! (Notice the two labels did not change when we added and subtracted the numbers.)

$1.B.$ Here we work with variables when simplifying expressions involving addition and subtraction –

"2r + 3t + 4r – t or 2r + 3t + 4r – 1t = 6r + 2t"

You must treat the variables like labels when you add and subtract the different terms. You were only permitted to add and subtract the numbers in the previous example problem "1.A." above when you were working with roses in one situation and tulips in the second situation. The labels had to be identical to determine the correct answer, "6 roses and 2 tulips". The same is true when you are adding and subtracting expressions in algebra with variables. You may only add and subtract the numbers (coefficients) which are with the variables if you are working with terms which have the same variable. The rules for adding and subtracting terms with labels are the same when you are adding and subtracting terms with variables. (Notice the labels and variables do not change when we add and subtract the appropriate numbers. The numbers in these situations are referred to as *coefficients*.)

Important Teaching Point which is not emphasized by some teachers and consequently confuse some students - When a variable or a label does not have a number indicated to the left of the variable or label, it is understood the number 1 is located to the left of either the variable or label. We refer to the number 1 in this situation as an invisible number. Notice, the two expressions involving the variable "t" indicated in this example "2r + 3t + 4r – t or 2r + 3t + 4r – 1t". In the first algebraic expression the number 1 was not written to the left of the variable "t" but in the second expression the number 1 was written to the left of the variable "t".

Remember when you are working with a variable in algebra, the goal is usually to find a number to substitute for the variable when you are solving an equation. The example problem "2r + 3t + 4r – t" just discussed is an algebraic expression, not an equation, but the rules to combine the terms are the same rules you must use when you are working with expressions like the example problem, "2 roses + 3 tulips + 4 roses – 1 tulip" with labels. Terms in algebra which have identical variables are referred to as *like terms*. The terms "$2r$" and "$4r$" are like terms. The terms "$+3t$" and "$-1t$" are also like terms. Usually when you are given an algebra expression, the directions are to simplify the expression, not find the value of the variable or variables. If you are given an equation, you are usually asked to solve the equation, but you might be asked to graph the equation.

Since the problem "$2r + 3t + 4r - t$" is an expression, we do not know what number(s) should replace the variables "r" or "t" in the expression. If we tell you the variable "$r = 6$" and the variable "$t = 8$", then we can compute the number represented by the expression as follows: "$6r + 2t = 6 \cdot (6) + 2 \cdot (8) = 36 + 16 = 52$". The letters are referred to as variables because the numbers we decide to substitute for the variables "r" and "t" may change (vary) in a different example problem. Variables are also referred to as variables because the letters "r" and "t" seem to apply to the words, "roses" and "tulips" since this problem follows example problem "1.A." above. However, the letters "r and "t" may stand for something completely different. They may stand for red dots and turquoise dots on a piece of paper, or they may stand for the length of a radius in a circle and the length of a tangent touching a circle and a point outside the circle. The variables "r" and "t" can stand for an infinite number of things, and the things they represent do not have to begin with either the letter/variable "r" or "t". The variables "r" and "t" in this expression can be assigned any number the teacher wants you to work with when you are learning to work with variables.

Remember the word "simplify" means to rewrite a problem in a more condensed form.

Variables are called variables because the numbers which replace the variable will vary depending on the situation. There is no rule which states the variable "r" must equal the number "6" as indicated previously in the previous paragraph. The variable "r" in this example is determined by the teacher or the textbook directions. After you substitute the two numbers "6 and 8" for the two variables "r" and "t" and determine the answer is "52", the directions from the teacher or textbook may change the value of one or both variables and now say "$r = 11$" and "$t = \frac{1}{4}$". The solution to the expression would now become "$6r + 2t = 6 \cdot 11 + 2 \cdot \left(\frac{1}{4}\right) = 66 + \frac{1}{2} = 66\frac{1}{2}$".

> The meaning of a variable may change from one problem to another problem; sometimes the variable "r" may stand for the "rate" of a moving object, and another time the variable "r" may stand for the "radius" of a circle. The meaning of the variable "r" varies from situation to situation or equation to equation. This is one reason why variables are referred to as variables.

2.*A*. Simplifying terms which involve multiplication and labels –

> "3 $feet \times 4\, feet$ can be written as $3\, ft. \times 4\, ft. = 3 \cdot 4 \cdot ft. \cdot ft. = 12\, ft.^2$"

The reason we could write the final expression as "$12\, ft.^2$" is based on how you solve number expressions in arithmetic. Consider the following arithmetic equation/identity "$3 \times 3 = 3^2$". Fact: If you multiply two identical labels, variables, or terms, you can use the same type of exponential notation you use in arithmetic when you are working with numbers. (Examples - "$4 \times 4 = 4^2$", "$cm \times cm = cm^2$", "$5 \times 5 \times 5 = 5^3$", *and* "$in. \times in. \times in. = in.^3$"). The final answer "$12\, ft.^2$", when simplifying the multiplication expression "$3\, ft. \times 4\, ft.$", means we have a surface area which is equivalent to "12" squares and each of the squares has the following dimensions: "1 ft. by 1 ft." The way the problem is written seems to imply you have a shape (rectangle) with the dimensions "3 $ft.$ and 4 $ft.$" and the area of the shape is equivalent to "12 *squares*". The notation implies that each square has a length of "1 $ft.$" and a width of "1 $ft.$". If you encounter the expression "12 ft^2" in a separate problem, it does not mean you have "12 *squares*" placed side by side or "12 squares in a single picture". Some of the shapes might be equal to "2 $ft.^2$", and some of the shapes might represent "$\frac{1}{2}$ $ft.^2$". The answer "12 $ft.^2$" does mean if you place all the pieces together, the area of the final shape would equal "12 $ft.^2$" and the final shape may be a rectangle, a square, a trapezoid, or even a circle. The labels "$ft.$ *or* $ft.^2$" do not represent a number even though one may argue we know specific number facts about the labels "$ft.$ *and* $ft.^2$". In the given problem, and the final answer, you are never going to substitute a number in place of either the label "$ft.$" or the label "$ft.^2$" You may want to replace the labels "$ft.$" or "$ft.^2$" with different labels such as inches or miles, but if you are switching labels, then the numbers with the labels will also have to change appropriately. The labels in this problem mean exactly what we expect them to mean, and the meaning does not change from one problem to another problem.

2. *B*. Variables when simplifying terms involving multiplication –

"$3x \times 5x$ or $3x \cdot 5x = 3 \cdot 5 \cdot x \cdot x = 15\, x \cdot x$ or $15 \cdot x \cdot x = 15x^2$"

In the original expression "$3x \times 5x$", the variable "x" remains unknown. When you are working with <u>expressions</u> versus <u>equations</u> or <u>inequalities,</u> the objective is to rewrite the expression as a simpler expression which is easier to understand. One of the objectives in kindergarten when students are given two numbers and asked to rewrite two numbers with an operation symbol in a more condensed form is a simplification problem. What do you think the goal is in kindergarten when students are asked to write the answer to the following problem "$4+1$"? The assumed goal when students are asked to find the solution to the problem "$4+1$" is to get the students to rewrite the answer in the simpler/condensed form "5".

In algebra when you are asked to simplify an expression, you are asked to rewrite the problem in a more condensed form--not to solve for the variable. The teacher or the textbook may tell you what number or list of numbers to substitute for the variable if you are working with an expression. For instance, the teacher may ask you to find the answer for the simplified expression in this problem "$15x^2$" if the variable "x" equals the number "5". Later, the teacher might ask you to find the answer if the variable "x" equals "8". The answer for the initial problem "$3x \times 5x$" and the final simplified expression "$15x^2$" when "x" equals "5" is "375". When you substitute the number "5" into the initial expression "$3x \times 5x$", you would solve it this way: "$3x \times 5x = 3 \cdot 5 \quad \times \quad 5 \cdot 5 = 15 \times 25 = 375$". When you substitute the number "5" into the simplified expression "$15x^2$", the solution is written this way: "$15x^2 = 15 \times 5^2 = 15 \times 25{=}375$". If you substitute the number "8" into either the initial expression or the simplified expression the answer becomes "960. When substituting the number "8" into the initial expression, the problem looks like this: "$3x \times 5x = 3 \cdot 8 \quad \times \quad 5 \cdot 8 = 24 \times 40 = 960$", but if you substitute the number "8" for the variable "x" in the simplified expression, the solution looks like this: "$15x^2 = 15 \times 8^2 = 15 \times 64 = 960$". The simplified expression and the original expression are always equal, but the simplified expression is written in a more condensed format.

Teaching Point: After looking at examples "$2.A.$ and $2.B.$", we will write example "$2.A.$" which involves labels in a slightly different way, based on the way we wrote one of the steps in example "$2.B.$". In example "$2.B.$" in the one step, we wrote the problem as "$15 \cdot x \cdot x$", and this is an acceptable way to interpret the expression "$15x \cdot x$" because we should all agree there is an invisible multiplication operation symbol between the number "15" and the first variable "x". With this thought in mind and with the fact we treat labels in algebra the same way we treat variables in algebra, if we want to work with the expression "$12\,ft. \times ft.$", we will be allowed to algebraically write this expression as:

"$12 \times ft. \times ft. = 12\,ft.^2$". Realize it does not make much sense when using labels to write the multiplication operation symbol "×" between the number and the label/word, and it really does not make sense when verbalizing the expression to say the expression means "12 *times feet*" or "12 *of feet*". To properly work with the notation algebraically, the multiplication notation is implied but not written or emphasized.

$3.A.$ Labels when simplifying terms involving division -

$$\text{"}\frac{3\,yards^3}{2\,yards^2} = \frac{3\,yd.^3}{2\,yd.^2} = \frac{3\,yd. \cdot yd. \cdot yd.}{2\,yd. \cdot yd.} = \frac{3\,yd.}{2}\ or\ \frac{3}{2}\ yds.\,or\ 1\frac{1}{2}\ yds.\text{"}$$

The label "*yd.* or *yds.*" occurred three times in the numerator but only two times in the denominator. Therefore, two of these identical labels cancelled with each other and became 1, and the only remaining label in the final answer is the single label "*yd.*". This is the same rule you should have taught your students when they were reducing fractions using factor trees and numbers. Notice, we did change the final label from "*yd.*" to "*yds.*". The first label "*yd.*" is singular and the second label "*yds.*" is plural. There are only two times when a label may be changed and still be considered the same label. When the label is changed from a singular label to a plural label, or vice versa, we consider the labels to be the same label.

Labels are also considered to be the same if one label is an abbreviation for a word and another label is the complete word written out such as "lbs." and "pounds". When you are working with labels, we consider the singular form and the plural form of the label to be the same, and we consider the abbreviation and the entire word to be the same label. *When working with variables, if there is a minor difference when writing variable expressions, then mathematicians consider the variable expressions to be different (refer to the italicized exception below.)* This is the only difference between the algebraic rules to work with variables versus labels. The labels indicated next maybe written in slightly different forms, but the labels which are written as equations are equal labels: "$cm = centimeter\ or\ cm = centimeters$", "$quarts = qt.\,or\ quart = qt.$". The following variable expressions are not considered to be the same: "$x \neq x^2$", "$yz \neq yzs$", "$x^2y^5z \neq x^2y^4z$". *There is one exception to the sentence that is written above which is underlined and written using italicized letters.* Algebra expressions involving variables which are multiplied can be rearranged and if the order of the variables in one expression are rearranged so they match the variables in the other expression the expressions are considered like terms/expressions: "$xyz = yzx$", "$x^2y^5z = y^5zx^2$". The expressions on the left and right sides in both equations are written in different order but they are still considered to be like expressions. When you multiply several numbers in arithmetic, it is legal to rearrange the order of the factors: "$3 \times 4 \times 7 = 7 \times 4 \times 3$" and "$22.2 \times \frac{1}{4} \times 7.24 = 7.24 \times \frac{1}{4} \times 22.2$". We used a combination of two arithmetic properties which apply to these example problems, when we switched the order of the factors in the examples, the expressions are still equal. The laws are called "The Commutative Property for Multiplication" and "The Associative Property for Multiplication". We did not technically illustrate how to apply the Commutative or the Associative Property for Multiplication in either of the examples. The Commutative Property for Multiplication only involves two terms. The Associative Property for Multiplication involves three terms and parentheses (grouping) then switching the parentheses. If you want to learn more about the differences between the Commutative and Associative Properties for multiplication and switching the order of the factors when numbers or terms are multiplied, please investigate both properties on the internet or any Algebra 1 textbook. (You will need to understand the applications of these two theorems and their differences in future assignments.)

In the problem we just simplified, "$\frac{3\ yd.^3}{2\ yd.^2}$", we reduced the identical labels in the numerator and the denominator after we wrote the numerator and the denominator in expanded/factored form. In the next example problem below with variables, "$\frac{5x^3y^4}{2x^2y^2}$", we will rewrite the variables as multiplication problems in both the numerator and the denominator. We want to illustrate why it is appropriate to reduce/cancel the labels and variables, let us illustrate how to reduce an arithmetic fraction using factor trees and prime numbers first. You already simplified this type of problem in the previous assignment for Chapter 4.

Reduce: $\frac{12}{24}$	Factor Trees for both	12	and	24
		2 X 6		2 X 12
		2 X 2 X 3		2 X 2 X 6
				2 X 2 X 2 X 3

Reduce using Factor Trees: $\frac{12}{24} = \frac{2\times2\times3}{2\times2\times2\times3} = \frac{1}{2}$

We reduced/cancelled two "2's" in both the numerator and the denominator because they are identical factors. We also cancelled/reduced the "3" in the numerator with the "3" in the denominator. Remember, you can only reduce factors (factors are numbers or terms which are multiplied). We reduced/cancelled the label "yd." in the numerator and the denominator in the previous example problem the same way we cancelled the two "2's" and the "3" in the numerator and the denominator of the previous problem. We will cancel the "x" and "y" variables in the next problem using the same reasoning applied to cancel the two "2's" and the "3" in this example problem, "$\frac{12}{24} = \frac{2\times2\times3}{2\times2\times2\times3} = \frac{1}{2}$".

In the next example, we rewrite the numerator and the denominator as multiplication problems in the basic factored form. Therefore, we will be able to quickly identify the identical factors in both the numerator and the denominator.

$3.B.$ Using arithmetic rules when working with variables and simplifying math expressions involving division problems –

$$\text{"}\frac{5x^3y^4}{2x^2y^2} = \frac{5\cdot x\cdot x\cdot x\cdot y\cdot y\cdot y\cdot y}{2\cdot x\cdot x\cdot y\cdot y} = \frac{5\cdot x\cdot y\cdot y}{2} = \frac{5xy^2}{2}\text{"}$$

There are two "x" factors in the numerator and two "x" factors in the denominator. They both cancelled and became 1, with only one "x" remaining in the numerator. There are also two "$y's$" in the numerator and two "$y's$" in the denominator which are identical, and the two "y" variables both cancelled, and both became 1, which means there are exactly two "$y's$" remaining in the numerator. Later in this textbook, we will reduce, multiply and divide fractions using the same procedures we are illustrating when we simplify this problem and when we illustrated how to reduce the fraction "$\frac{12}{24}$" using factor trees. There are two major reasons why factor trees are presented in most 5th-grade arithmetic textbooks. The first reason is, to compute challenging LCDs or LCMs, you must use factor trees with prime numbers and use the rules which were explained when adding and subtracting fractions in Chapters 3 and 4. The second reason is when you are reducing, multiplying, and dividing difficult fraction problems the best method to use is the factor tree procedure. We used the factor tree method to simplify the previous two example problems. We frequently used the factor tree method in several example problems simplified in Chapters 3 and 4 and will continually emphasize the factor tree method throughout the remainder of this textbook. If you continually illustrate how to use factor trees when you are working with fractions, you will prepare your students to understand how to solve a wide range of problems in algebra.

The reason you may cancel a variable in the numerator with an identical variable in the denominator and they both become 1 is because of the following rule in arithmetic: "$\frac{a}{a} = 1$". Since "$\frac{a}{a} = 1$" is a basic arithmetic fact, all the following fractions equal 1: "$\frac{6}{6} = 1$, $\frac{11.2}{11.2} = 1$, $\frac{x}{x} = 1$, $\frac{2 \cdot 2}{2 \cdot 2} = 1$, $\frac{x \cdot y}{x \cdot y} = 1$, $\frac{x \cdot x \cdot y}{x \cdot x \cdot y} = 1$, $\frac{ft.}{ft.} = 1$, $\frac{min.}{min.} = 1, etc.$". We used the same principle when we worked with the identities "$2 = 2 \therefore \frac{2}{2} = 1$" and "$88 = 88 \therefore \frac{88}{88} = 1$" then we applied "Young's Equation/Ratio Theorem" to determine special forms of the number 1 to multiply the starting fractions, with the goal to compute equivalent fractions. The labels in example problem "3. A." cancelled in the same way the variables cancelled in example problem "3. B.". Labels and variables are not the same, but when solving algebraic problems and equations, the same rules apply to both labels and variables.

> The rules never change from arithmetic to algebra. Teachers must emphasize the rules required to solve challenging arithmetic problems if the goal is to prepare students for success in algebra and advanced math classes.

$4.A.$ Variables when working with equations – There are no labels involved in the next two examples involving equations.

$4.A.1.$ Find the value of the variable "y" in the equation "$ax + by = 10$" given the following information: the variable "$a = 4$", the variable "$x = 1$", and the variable "$b = 2$".

The equation becomes "$4 \cdot (1) + 2y = 10$". The next step becomes: "$4 + 2y = 10$" after you multiply the number "4" and the number "1". The following equation is derived by subtracting the number "4" from both sides of the equation to get the new equation: "$2y = 6$". Tell the students to line up the equation "$4 = 4$" underneath the equation "$4 + 2y = 10$", line up the equals "=" symbols, and subtract the terms on both sides of the equation. You might explain to students how to solve the equation "$4 + 2y = 10$" by asking them to "subtract the number "4" from both sides of the equation." We prefer you emphasize you are really subtracting the second equation "$4 = 4$" from the first equation. We already explained earlier in this textbook the reasons why we want the students to line up the two equations and determine a third equation. The value of the variable "y" when we solve the equation, "$2y = 6$" is "$y = 3$". The answer is found by dividing both the left and righthand sides of the equation by the number "2. You may also remind students they may work with the identity equation "$2 = 2$" and divide the equation, "$2y = 6$" by the identity "$2 = 2$" to find the solution "$y = 3$". Either way, if we solved the algebra equation correctly, we should be able to substitute all the numbers for the indicated variables back into the given equation, do the arithmetic on both sides of the equation, and the final equation will be the identity "$10 = 10$".

4.A.2. Find the value of the variable "b" in the equation "$A = \frac{1}{2}bh$" in which the variable "A" equals "15" and the value of the variable "h" equals "5".

Here is the equation (formula) after substituting the number values for the two variables, "A" and "h", "$15 = \frac{1}{2}b \cdot 5$". In the next step, we are going to rearrange the three factors in the multiplication problem on the right side of the equation. Rewrite the two numbers on the right side of the equation each as a fraction: "$15 = \frac{1}{2} \cdot 5 \cdot b$ then $15 = \frac{1}{2} \cdot \frac{5}{1} \cdot b$ and then $15 = \frac{5}{2} \times b$". There are several ways to complete the next step, but we are going to do the same thing we did in the previous example problem when we had a number times a variable on one side of the equation "$2y = 6\ or\ 6 = 2y$": we divided both sides of the equation by the number, "2" which is the coefficient with the variable. We found the answer "$y = 3$" after dividing both sides of the equation by the number "2". The equation we are solving in this paragraph is "$15 = \frac{5}{2} \times b$". The number (singular) we will concentrate is the number "$\frac{5}{2}$" which is the coefficient to the left of the variable "b". The fraction number/coefficient "$\frac{5}{2}$", may be treated in the same manner as the number/coefficient "2" in the previous problem. Therefore, in this problem we are going to divide both sides of the equation by the number "$\frac{5}{2}$" to find the number value for the variable "b". When dividing both sides of the equation by the fraction "$\frac{5}{2}$", we will have the opportunity to review the procedures required to divide by a fraction. We frequently illustrated how to <u>divide both sides of an equation by a fraction</u> when the fraction was a coefficient with a variable. This is an excellent time to interleave a fraction division problem when solving an equation.

When we divide both sides of the equation," $15 = \frac{5}{2} \times b$", by the number "$\frac{5}{2}$", the equation might be written like this: "$15 \div \frac{5}{2} = \frac{\frac{5}{2}}{\frac{5}{2}} \cdot b$". On the left side of the equation, we write the number "15" as a fraction by inserting the number 1 in the denominator; on the right side of the equation, we replace the complex fraction with the number 1 because the top part of the fraction (numerator) is identical to the bottom part of the fraction (denominator). In a fraction, when the numerator and the denominator are identical, they both cancel and become 1. Here is the equation now: "$\frac{15}{1} \div \frac{5}{2} = 1b$ or $\frac{15}{1} \div \frac{5}{2} = b$". The only remaining procedure to complete to find the number value of the variable "b" is to simplify the fraction division problem, on the left side of the equals (=) relationship symbol. Remember, when you are dividing two fractions, the rule is: "Invert the fraction to the right of the division operation symbol, (÷), and multiply the two fractions." Now, finish solving the problem: "$\frac{15}{1} \times \frac{2}{5} = b$, which becomes $\frac{3}{1} \times \frac{2}{1} = b \quad \therefore \; 6 = b$ or $b = 6$". Realize, we reduced the two fractions on the left side of the equals (=) relationship symbol before we multiplied them. If you do not understand how we derived the equation "$\frac{3}{1} \times \frac{2}{1} = b$" look at the numerator "15" in the first fraction and the denominator "5" in the second fraction and reduce these two numbers. We frequently write two or more fractions as one fraction when they are multiplied. We might also factor all the terms in both the numerator and denominator to determine the identical terms. Solve the arithmetic problem like this: "$\frac{15}{1} \times \frac{2}{5} = b \quad \frac{15 \times 2}{5} = b \quad \frac{3 \cdot 5 \times 2}{5} = b \quad \frac{3 \cdot 1 \times 2}{1} = b \quad \therefore 6 = b$". When solving algebra equations, frequently there are multiple ways to solve the same equation.

Additional Procedure to solve this problem: Since we are working with the <u>equation</u> "$15 = \frac{5}{2} \times b$" we also want students to understand it is permissible to multiply both sides of the <u>equation</u> by the denominator "2" and derive the equation "$30 = 5b$". This equation is much easier to solve since the fraction is removed, and the coefficient with the variable "b" is "5". If you are working with an equation involving fractions, and you identify the LCD for all the fractions involved in the equation, you may multiply both sides of the equation by the LCD to simplify (remove all the denominators in the equation) the given equation. We realized the number "2" in the equation "$15 = \frac{5}{2} \times b$" must be the LCD for all the terms in the equation. The equation, "$30 = 5b$" which is written without any fractions, was determined by multiplying both sides of the equation (every term on both sides of the equation, "$15 = \frac{5}{2} \times b$") by the LCD, "2". We encourage you to explain both procedures to all your students.

You can check to ensure the variable "b" equals "6" by substituting the number "6" back into the equation "$15 = \frac{1}{2}b \cdot 5$" for the variable "$b$". If "6" is the correct number to substitute for the variable "b" when you substitute (replace) the number "6" for the variable "b" in the equation, then solve the arithmetic problem on the right side of the equals symbol "="; you will end up with an identity. Here is the process to check to ensure the number "6" is the correct value for "b": "$15 = \frac{1}{2}b \cdot 5,\ 15 = \frac{1}{2} \cdot 6 \cdot 5,\ 15 = \frac{1}{2} \cdot 30,$ and finally, the identity $15 = 15$".

When solving this equation, we indicated we divided both sides of the equation by the fraction "$\frac{5}{2}$". In this situation, we concentrated on the number on the same side of the equation as the variable. When we encourage students to solve simple algebra equations involving a number on the same side of the equation added or subtracted to the variable, we encourage teachers to illustrate to the students, they should concentrate on adding or subtracting a second equation from the first equation—and to do so by concentrating on the left sides of the two equations then the right sides of the two equations to determine a third equation. The reason we encouraged this type of explanation was to better prepare students to solve simultaneous equations later in their algebra careers. If this written explanation seems too circuitous, please refer to the discussion regarding the example problem in Chapter 4, "$x - 3 = 8$" when we illustrated how to add the equation, "$+3 = +3$" to the equation, "$x - 3 = 8$" to derive the third equation, "$x + 0 = 11$" and then the final equation, "$x = 11$".

When multiplying and dividing a variable by a coefficient in an equation, such as the problem "$15 = \frac{5}{2} \times b$" above, we concentrated on the number, "$\frac{5}{2}$". Since we want to be consistent with our explanations, we should say divide the first equation, "$15 = \frac{5}{2} \times b$", by the second identity equation, "$\frac{5}{2} = \frac{5}{2}$", and then concentrate on the left sides of the two equations and then the right sides of both equations to determine the third equation, "$\frac{15}{1} \div \frac{5}{2} = b$". We think this would be proper and consistent with our beliefs that adding and subtracting two equations to determine a third equation is the best method to emphasize. The reason we do not emphasize multiplying and dividing two equations to determine a third equation is, there are few times when students will encounter a situation in advanced mathematics classes where the students will need to concentrate on dividing or multiplying a first equation by a second equation to determine a third equation, except when they are dividing by a single number when solving first degree equations in Algebra. Dividing and multiplying two equations to determine a third equation is still a valid technique and a procedure we would discuss with the high-achieving students and motivated average-achieving math students. (When students encounter proofs in geometry, there will be situations where it might be appropriate to illustrate the procedure of multiplying or dividing an original equation by a second equation to determine a third equation. If you want to prove the Pythagorean Theorem, you might encounter this type of situation.)

$4.B.$ How to use labels when working with equations - The reason we emphasized "variables" in example problems "$4.A.1.$ and $4.A.2.$" first and "labels" second in example problems "$4.B.1.$ and $4.B.2.$" below is because when you are required to work with equations which involve labels you will be required to find the value of the variable and thus work with both labels and variables at the same time in the same equation. In example problem "$4.A.2.$" above, "$A = \frac{1}{2}bh$", the problem is presented in a simple but generic form because every time you work with this type of problem in either algebra or geometry, the given information should have labels attached to all three variables as indicated in the next two example problems. We hope you recognized the equation/formula "$A = \frac{1}{2}bh$" is the standard equation to find the area of a triangle.

$4.B.1.$ Solve for the variable, "A" in the following equation, "$A = lw$".

We prefer to write the formula used to find the area of a rectangle in the following form: "$A_{rec.} = lw$". The notation used to represent the area of the rectangle "$A_{rec.}$" in the equation is referred to as *subscript notation,* and the purpose is to emphasize the goal when using this formula is to find the area of a rectangle and not the area of some other shape. The notation "$A_{rec.}$" is still considered a single variable, just like the single variable "l" which normally represents the longer side in a rectangle referred to as the length and the other single variable "w" which normally represents the shorter side in a rectangle referred to as the width. The words "length" and "width" in this formula are variables, but when we write the "length" and the "width" in the example problem in the next paragraph, the variables will have labels attached to the variables. We could have written the equation "$A = \frac{1}{2}bh$", as, "$A_{tri.} = \frac{1}{2}bh$" to emphasize we were finding the area of a triangle in the previous example problem "$4.A.2$". (Note: Subscript notation is often first introduced in algebra when students are required to work with the slope of a line: "$m = \frac{y_2 - y_1}{x_2 - x_1}$". When we use this formula to find the slope of a line, we know we are working with two distinct points. The points are referred to as Pt. 1 (x_1, y_1) and Pt. 2 (x_2, y_2).)

Here is the given information for this problem: the length of the rectangle is "$11\ cm$" and the width of the rectangle is "$7\ cm$". Here is the equation after substituting the numbers with labels into the formula: "$A_{rec.} = 11\ cm \ \cdot\ 7\ cm$". If you want to find the value of the variable "$A_{rec.}$", you must focus on the multiplication problem on the right side of the equation. The first thing we are going to do on the right side of the equation is change the order of the numbers and the labels, which is acceptable in a multiplication problem. The process of rearranging the order of the terms in a multiplication problem involves two properties: "The Commutative Property for Multiplication" and "The Associative Property for Multiplication". Here is the same problem with the terms on the right side rearranged: "$A_{rec.} = 11 \cdot 7 \cdot cm \ \cdot cm$". The final required step to determine the solution for the variable "$A_{rec.}$", looks like this: "$A_{rec.} = 77\ cm^2$". Notice, the final answer "$77\ cm^2$" not only involves the number "77", but also, because of the algebra rules involving the labels, the final answer also contains the proper label "cm^2". (Point of Interest: The Commutative Property and Associative Property also apply to addition.)

> $4.B.2.$ Solve for the variable "r" in the formula "$D = rt$" given the following facts: The distance from the starting point to the ending point is "370 $mi.$". This is the approximate distance from New York City, NY to Pittsburgh, PA. If we travel on a bicycle at an average speed (referred to as the rate, or variable "r") of "12 mph", how much time will the trip take? Do not consider any rest stops you will be forced to take which will increase the total time required for the trip.

If your goal is to determine the value for the variable "t", focus on the equation "$D = rt$" and the three variables "D", "r", and "t". The formula "$D = rt$" is the formula/equation used when a problem involves a moving object. The moving object may be a car, a jet, a rabbit, a snail, a rocket ship, a ray of light, etc. After substituting the specific values (including labels) into the formula for the two given variables, the new equation becomes "$370\ mi. = 12\ mph \cdot t$". If you want to solve this problem, you must know how to write the abbreviation "mph" algebraically. The algebraic notation for the abbreviation, "mph" is written as a ratio, "$\frac{mi.}{hr.}$". This means the best way to write the formula is now "$370\ mi. = 12\frac{mi.}{hr.} \cdot t$", which can also be written as "$370\ mi. = \frac{12}{1} \cdot \frac{mi.}{hr.} \cdot t$". Now, write the equation as "$370\ mi. = \frac{12\ mi.}{1\ hr.} \cdot t$". The goal is to find the value for the variable "t", which represents time. Notice, when the given formula/equation is written with the labels, not only will you find a number value for the variable "t", but you will have the correct label with the number in the final step.

To accomplish the desired goal, you must get the fraction "$\frac{12\ mi.}{1\ hr.}$" on the right side of the equation which is to the left of the variable "t" away from the variable. Since we are multiplying the variable "t" by the fraction, "$\frac{12\ mi.}{1\ hr.}$" we are going to divide both sides of the equation by the fraction "$\frac{12\ mi.}{1\ hr.}$". Here is the equation/formula written when both sides of the equation are divided by the indicated fraction: "$\frac{370\ mi.}{\frac{12\ mi.}{1\ hr.}} = \frac{\frac{12\ mi.}{1\ hr.}}{\frac{12\ mi.}{1\ hr.}} \cdot t$". On the right side of the equation, the fraction "$\frac{\frac{12\ mi.}{1\ hr.}}{\frac{12\ mi.}{1\ hr.}}$" becomes the number 1 because the fraction in the top is divided by the identical fraction in the bottom, which means when you do the division, the answer must be 1. On the left side of the equation/formula, we rewrite the fraction as a division problem using the division operation symbol (÷). Here is the equation written after making these mathematical changes: "$370\ mi. \div \frac{12\ mi.}{1hr.} = 1 \cdot t$". Wow, the solution to the problem is almost complete! You may want to emphasize on the left side of the equation, there are two fractions, we place the number 1 in the denominator for the expression "$370\ mi.$". This is the new equation: "$\frac{370\ mi.}{1} \div \frac{12\ mi.}{1\ hr.} = t$". We also dropped the number 1 to the left of the variable "t" on the right side of the equation. In the next equation, we focus on the left side of the last equation which involves a division problem with two fractions. On the left side of the equation, we invert and multiply by the fraction immediately to the right of the division "÷" operation symbol. Here is the equation written after inverting and multiplying the second fraction: "$\frac{370\ mi.}{1} \cdot \frac{1\ hr.}{12\ mi.} = t$". Prior to finishing the multiplication problem on the left side of the equation, we write the multiplication problem on the left side as one big fraction: "$\frac{370\ mi. \times 1\ hr.}{1 \times 12\ mi.} = t$". You should now recognize the left side of the equation becomes "$\frac{370\ hr.}{12}$" because the labels "$mi.$" in both the numerator and the denominator are identical and the only label remaining in the problem is "$hr.$" in the numerator. After you simplify the arithmetic problem (division problem, "$\frac{370}{12}$") on the left side of the equation, you get the number with a label for the variable:

"$30.8333\ldots\ hrs. = t$ or $30\frac{10}{12}\ hr. = t$ or $30\frac{5}{6}\ hr. = t$ or $t = 30\frac{5}{6}\ hr.$".

It is satisfying when you include labels in an equation with all the variables, you will solve the problems and apply the algebraic rules in the same way with the labels you apply algebra rules to variables to find the final answer. If you apply the algebra rules correctly, you will always have the correct label as part of the final answer. Labels are important to engineers, architects, chemists, and physicists--and this is the way they work with equations and formulas. After studying the previous examples involving labels and variables, we hope this clarifies the difference between the two words and clarifies in no way do they represent the same thing. Yet, both *labels* and *variables* are treated the same when working with algebraic expressions and equations.

The following paragraph emphasis a minor but important difference between the two notations used to write mathematical expressions when working with a variable versus working with a label.

When you write a mathematical expression involving a number and a variable, such as the following examples "$2x$ or $12.5y^3z$ or $\frac{3}{7}mr^5t^2$", there is NO space indicated between the number (coefficient) and the variable(s). When you write a mathematical expression involving a number and a label, such as the following examples "$2\ hour$ or $12.5\ pies$ or $\frac{3}{7}\ mi.$", there is always a space indicated between the number and the label (s). You should also notice, most of the time, when a label is abbreviated, there is a period indicated to the right of the abbreviation, such as:

"$inches = in.$ or $miles = mi.$ or $pounds = lbs.$" But some abbreviations are frequently written without the period to the write of the abbreviation such as:

"$mph = miles\ per\ hour$ or $meters = m$ or $cubic\ centimeters = cc$". If the abbreviation is a common abbreviation and there is a space between the number and the abbreviation, the period to the right of the abbreviation is sometimes not written or required. This minor difference in the two notations is important because without the space between the number and the label, there may be situations when a student may believe the abbreviation after the number is a variable and all the letters in the label abbreviation are supposed to be multiplied. We are always amazed how important it is to understand subtle differences when teaching different mathematics topics/concepts.

Two of the most important teaching principles which were mentioned early in this textbook involved using "2-3" minute introductions and reviews, 2-3 times per week. The introduction lessons should start a couple months before a topic or concept is formally presented in the textbook or classroom and then review the topic or concept for two or three months after the topic or concept is formally presented in class. This means in the beginning of the year you will focus on introducing topics you will present during the school year in September, October, and November but you must also review topics taught the year before. As the year continues you will find you introduce and review topics constantly.

Here are some additional classwork/homework problems which are NOT normally found in United States arithmetic textbooks involving the number "1": "$3\frac{15}{17} - \frac{7.2}{7.2} = 2\frac{15}{17}$", "$\frac{77}{79} \div \frac{101}{101} = \frac{77}{99}$", "$\frac{x}{y} \times \frac{2}{2} = \frac{x}{y}$", and "$379\frac{1}{13} + \frac{17}{17} = 380\frac{1}{13}$".

Fifth Assignment

LABELS AND VARIABLES - ADDING AND SUBTRACTING LIKE TERMS/EXPRESSIONS

A. Simplify the following expressions:

1. 1.5 feet + 3.75 ft.

2. $1\ rose + 219\ roses + 25\ tulips + 111\ turnips - 11\ tulips - 45\ roses$

3. $3\ apples + 5\ bananas - 2\ apples - 1\ apple$

4. $16\ cars + 25\ trucks - 3\ SUVs + 40\ trucks + 76\ SUVs - 1\ car + 5\ tractors$

5. $3ap - 1ap + 5ba - 2ap$

6. $5.5ax + 7.2ax + 2.2a^2 - 11.61ax - 1.17a^2$ (Hint: The expression "a^2" is different than "a". In fact, the expressions "a^2" and "a" are as different as the two numbers "25" and "5".)

7. $30\ Chevy\ cars + 60\ Ford\ trucks + 72\ Ford\ trucks + 111\ Dodge\ trucks - 6\ Chevy\ cars - 111\ Ford\ Trucks + 81\ Toyota\ cars - 21\ Ford\ trucks$

8. $37c + 10.7tf + 3.3tf - 2\frac{3}{4}tf - 35\frac{1}{2}c$ (Suggestion: Change both fractions to terminating decimals or change the terminating decimals to fractions or just solve it without changing anything. You decide which is easier.)

9. $33x^2y^3z + 37.5y^3zx^2 + 42.75z\,x^2y^3$ (These expressions are all like terms. They are like terms because of the Commutative and Associative Properties for Multiplication which will be explained later. The order in which numbers, terms, or expressions are multiplied does not change their value. You may also switch the order of numbers, terms, and expressions when you are adding numbers, terms, or expressions and the answer will not change. If we switch the order of two numbers, terms, or expressions when we are subtracting or dividing the final answer will

usually be significantly different. The only times you may switch the order of two given numbers in a subtraction or division problem is when the two given numbers are identical such as, "$6 - 6, \frac{6}{6}, 11.3 - 11.3, or\ \frac{11.3}{11.3}$".)

10. $7\frac{1}{2}xyz + 8\frac{3}{4}yzx - 1\frac{7}{8}zxy + 11.92x^2y^2z^2$ (Hint: The letter combination in the last term is not even close to matching the group of letters in the first three terms.)

11. $5\frac{3}{5}x^2y^2z + 5\frac{4}{5}x^2yz^2 - 4\frac{1}{5}x^2yz^2 - 2\frac{1}{5}x^2y^2z + 6\frac{3}{5}xy^2z^2 - 3\frac{1}{5}xy^2z^2$ (Hint: There are three matching pairs of like terms. Therefore, there will be three terms in the simplified answer.)

12. $5x^2 + 3x + 7 + 7x^2 + 9x - 2$ (Hint: There are also three pairs of like terms in the simplified form for this problem.)

13. $5x^3 + 4x^2 + 3x - 9 + 2x^3 - 2x^2 - x + 12$ (Hint: The term "$-x$" should be interpreted in your brain as "$-1x$". Again, the number "1" is understood to be present to the left of a variable or label when there is no number indicated. We refer to the number "1" in this type of situation as an invisible number.)

COMMUTATIVE PROPERTY AND ASSOCIATIVE PROPERTY

(BASIC ARITHMETIC FACTS)

The Commutative Property and Associative Property both involve only ONE equation and there is exactly ONE change from the left side of the given equation to derive the right side of the equation or vice-versa. The Commutative and Associative Properties address two unique and different changes on the left and right sides of an equation which seem so obvious, sometimes we overlook the importance of these two Properties.

The Commutative Property involves TWO numbers, variables, and/or expressions on the left side of the equation, and the right side of the equation switches the order of the TWO numbers, variables, and/or expressions. The normal way mathematicians write the Commutative Property is "$a + b = b + a \;\; or \;\; b + a = a + b$". This is the algebra notation usually used to illustrate the Commutative Property for <u>Addition</u>. The Commutative Property is a lot easier to understand when we use numbers instead of variables/letters, as you should realize in this example, "$7 + 2 = 2 + 7 \; or \; 2 + 7 = 7 + 2$". When you look at the equations with the two numbers "2 & 7" indicated, it is obvious the left and right sides of the equations are equal and switching the order of the addition problem is simple to understand. Here is an example of the Commutative Property using quantities/parentheses but still only two expressions:

"$(x + r) + (y - z) = (y - z) + (x + r) \; or \; (y - z) + (x + r) = (x + r) + (y - z)$".

Here is the important concept you must notice with respect to these examples, you must concentrate on the addition operation symbol "+" between the two quantities and switch the order of the quantities from the left side of the equation to get the right side of the equation. <u>Notice, the variables/letters inside the parentheses never switch in the order they are written.</u> When you look at this example, you must think of the *expression* "$(x + r)$", as a single number, term, and/or *expression* and "$(y - z)$" is the second number, term, and/or *expression*. This is a difficult concept for students to understand because they see four variables, but they should not concentrate on each variable; they must concentrate on the parentheses for each problem and think of the terms in the parentheses as <u>one</u>

term. Here is another example to illustrate the Commutative Property:

"$2 + (x - r) = (x - r) + 2 \quad or \quad (x - r) + 2 = 2 + (x - r)$". In this situation the number "2", is the first *number*, term, and/or *expression* and the *expression* "$(x - r)$" is the second number, term, and/or *expression*. All four examples just illustrated involve the "addition operation symbol" and the bottom line is, the Commutative Property tells you it does not matter which order you add two numbers, two terms, two expressions or a pair of numbers, terms, or expressions.

To be more exact the four examples just illustrated are examples of the **"Commutative Property for Addition".**

There is another arithmetic operation which allows you to switch the order of the numbers and still end up with the same answer. There are three basic arithmetic operations remaining to consider if we want to determine if the Commutative Property might apply. The other arithmetic operation, which permits you to switch the order of two numbers, and the answer will still be the same answer, is obviously multiplication. The following four examples involving multiplication use the same numbers, terms, and expressions we used to illustrate the Commutative Property for Addition but now we will illustrate the **Commutative Property for Multiplication**: "$ab = ba \quad or \quad ba = ab \quad or$ $a \cdot b = b \cdot a \quad or \quad b \cdot a = a \cdot b \quad or \quad a \times b = b \times a \quad or \quad b \times a = a \times b \quad or$ $(a)(b) = (b)(a) \quad or \quad (b)(a) = (a)(b)$". We find it interesting that there are several ways to indicate numbers, terms, or expressions are multiplied.

$$7 \times 2 = 2 \times 7 \qquad or \qquad 2 \times 7 = 7 \times 2$$

$$(x + r) \times (y - z) = (y - z) \times (x + r) \quad or \quad (y - z) \times (x + r) = (x + r) \times (y - z)$$

$2 \times (x-r) = (x-r) \times 2 \quad or \quad (x-r) \times 2 = 2 \times (x-r)$ Do NOT confuse this example problem with the Associative Property mentioned in the next paragraph. In this example problem the order of the number "2" and the quantity "$(x-r)$" *switched* from the left side of each equation to the right side of each equation. You must recognize the order of the variables/letters inside the pair of parentheses never switched around. When working with the Associative Property illustrated in the next paragraph the parentheses switch positions. A pair of parentheses which contains two or more terms or numbers is referred to as a quantity.

The Associative Property always involves three numbers, terms, and/or expressions but two of the three numbers, terms, and/or expressions are contained in a pair of parentheses referred to as a quantity. The Associative Property focuses on one change in the left and right sides of the equation. The change DOES NOT INVOLVE switching the order of the numbers, terms, or expressions. The single change from the left and right sides of the equation involves switching the placement of the parentheses. After we switch the placement of the parentheses in the following examples, study the change and notice the order of the numbers, variables, and expressions are in the same order on the left and right sides of the equations, but the parentheses switch from the second and third terms to the first and second terms or vice-versa.

The Associative Property can be illustrated for either addition or multiplication problems. In example "a." below, the first example illustrates the Associative Property for Addition and the second example in "a." below, illustrates the Associative Property for Multiplication.

a. $5 + (6 + 2) = (5 + 6) + 2 \quad The\ Answer = 13$

$5 \times (6 \times 2) = (5 \times 6) \times 2 \quad The\ Answer = 60$

b. $a\,(bc) = (ab)c \quad or \quad a \times (b \times c) = (a \times b) \times c$ This is the Algebra notation for the Associative Property for Multiplication.

This example is the normal Algebra notation used to illustrate the Associative Property for Addition. "$a + (b + c) = (a + b) + c$" or "$(a + b) + c = a + (b + c)$". When you refer to the first equation, the parentheses on the left side of the equation enclosed the second and third terms and on the right side of the same equation the parentheses enclosed the first and second terms, but <u>the order of the variables did not change</u>. In the second equation the left side enclosed the first and second terms and the right side enclosed the second and third terms, but again in the second equation <u>the order of the variables did not change</u>.

c. $(x + 2) + \{(x - 5) + (y - z)\} = \{(x + 2) + (x - 5)\} + (y - z)$ In this example there are three different *expressions.* Here are the three expressions/quantities: "$(x + 2)$", "$(x - 5)$", and "$(y - z)$". The three individual quantities are treated just like a number or a variable. In this example we used a pair of braces, "$\{\ and\ \}$", because the three expressions just indicated are enclosed in parentheses. In mathematics usually when we want to group variables, numbers, and/or terms we use parentheses. If we already grouped some terms together and used parentheses, we can also use a pair of brackets, "$[\ and\ ]$", or a pair of braces, "$\{\ and\ \}$", as indicated or a second set of parentheses. Notice, since we are illustrating the Associative Property for Addition in the example above, we enclosed the second and third quantities in the braces on the left side of the equation and then we switched the braces on the right side of the equation to enclose the first and second pair of quantities.

$$(x+2)\times\{(x-5)\times(y-z)\}=\{(x+2)\times(x-5)\}\times(y-z)$$

The Associative Property for Multiplication in the example above involves both quantities and braces. Notice, the three variables and the three numbers on the left side are in the same identical order on the right side of the equation. The braces, "{ *and* }", switched which quantities were enclosed inside the braces, not the order of the numbers or variables.

B. Identify if the property used to make the change in each equation below is the Commutative or Associative Property for Addition or the Commutative or Associative Property for Multiplication. This means there are four options when you select the appropriate property for the problems listed below.

14. $(a+11)+z=a+(11+z)$

15. $z\times 26.12=26.12\times z$

16. $(a+11)+z=(11+a)+z$ (Hint: The pair of parentheses on both sides of the equation enclosed the two terms "a" and "11". The variable "z" was not changed in any way from the left and right sides of the equation.)

17. $(a+m)\times\{3\times(y+7)\}=\{(a+m)\times 3\}\times(y+7)$ (Hint: Identify what changed from the left side of the equation to get the right side of the equation.)

18. $6+(ab)=(ab)+6$

19. $(ab\times cd)\times(mn)=ab\times(cd\times mn)$

Summary Teaching Point: Here are some general comments which may help when you want to recognize the Commutative and Associative Properties for both Addition and Multiplication. 1. Both the Commutative Property and the Associative Property involve one equation. 2. When identifying the Commutative Property and the Associative Property there is one change in the equation from the left side of the equation to determine the right side of the equation. 3. The one change from the left side of an equation to the right side of the equation when referring to the Commutative Property for both Addition and Multiplication is, there will be one pair of numbers, variables, and/or expressions with the order of the terms switched. 4. The one change from the left side of an equation to the right side of the equation when referring to the Associative Property for both Addition and Multiplication is the parentheses switch the grouping of the numbers, variables, and/or expressions but the order of the numbers, variables and expressions does not change.

> The Commutative and Associative Properties for both Addition and Multiplication are easy to understand when the problems involve numbers. This means when the Commutative and Associative Properties are applied in Algebra and advanced math courses the rules are derived from an understanding of arithmetic concepts, rules, and procedures first.

LABELS AND VARIABLES – MULTIPLYING AND DIVIDING EXPRESSIONS

C. Simplify the following expressions:

20. $3\,ft. \times 55\,ft. \times 7.5\,ft.$ Simplify the answer and write a statement/word problem where this might represent the solution to the problem.

21. $\frac{3 \cdot 3 \cdot 5 \cdot 71 \cdot a \cdot b \cdot b \cdot b \cdot (x+c) \cdot (x+c) \cdot (8+m)}{3 \cdot 71 \cdot a \cdot b \cdot (x+c) \cdot (x+c) \cdot (16+m)}$ (Hint: You may only cancel identical <u>factors</u>. You need to remember <u>factors</u> are numbers, terms, and/or expressions which are multiplied.) The expression "$(8+m)$" is a factor but the number "8" and the variable "m" are NOT factors.

22. $\frac{55\ yds.^3}{10\ yds.}$

23. $165\ miles \times \frac{1}{3\ hrs.}$ Simplify and write the answer in a form so 99% of adults will understand the form and verbally state the answer. We would hope you write the final answer using a three-letter abbreviation which is commonly used and not write the answer using fraction or ratio notation even though the answer is a ratio.

24. $16\ tablespoons \times \frac{1}{4\ days}$ Simplify and write the answer in a form so 99% of adults will understand the form, write a phrase to state the answer.

25. $16.2\ cm \times 12.1\ cm$ Write the simplified form of the given problem and then write a word/statement problem where the simplified solution might represent the answer to your statement problem. (Notice, the metric abbreviation "cm" does not have a period after the abbreviation. We think it is important to mention and why it is important to make sure there is a space between the number and the abbreviation, which is a label not a variable.)

26. $15\, d \cdot d \cdot d \cdot r \cdot r \cdot 10 \cdot d^2 \cdot r \cdot 2$ Write the answer in condensed form with a number and exponents for each variable.

27. $\frac{25 \cdot x^3 \cdot y^2 \cdot z \cdot 20 \cdot x^3 \cdot y}{10 \cdot x^4 \cdot y \cdot z \cdot 5 \cdot 2}$ Write the final answer in condensed form with exponents indicated. (Hint: If you have not learned and mastered the rules to work with exponents when terms are multiplied and/or divided, we suggest you write each term with and exponent, as a multiplication problem based on the exponent in each situation and then cancel the identical variables.)

(Comment: Remember when we use the word simplify in arithmetic and mathematics we mean, write the solution in a more condensed equivalent form.)

D. We will give you a formula/equation to solve the following problems. We will use subscript notation in some of our problems to help you understand what the formula/equation represents. Write the answer with the correct number and label indicated. In the solution make sure the labels are treated appropriately based on algebra rules to ensure the label in the solution is written correctly. Find the value of the variable on the left-hand side of the given equations.

28. $A_{tri.} = \frac{1}{2}bh \quad or \quad A_{tri.} = \frac{bh}{2}$ Given facts: $Base\ (b) = 10\ in.\ \ and\ Height\ (h) = 20\ in.$

29. $D = rt$ Given facts: $Rate\ of\ a\ moving\ object\ (r) = 400\ \frac{mi.}{hr.}\ \ and\ Time\ (t) =$ $5.5\ hrs.$

30. $C_{cir.} = 2\pi r$ Given fact: $Radius\ (r) = 1.5\ ft.$ The answer should not be written as a decimal. We want the final answer to be written so the number is exact (the number in the answer will indicate an infinite number of decimal places) therefore, the final answer should contain the number "π" in the answer and not the estimated decimal "3.14159". Make sure algebra rules are followed appropriately when referring to the labels to ensure the answer contains the correct label.

31. $V_{cube} = s^3$ Given fact: $Side\ (s) = 3.5\ cm$

32. $A_{cir.} = \pi r^2$ Given fact: $Radius\ (r) = 3\frac{1}{4}\ meters$ We want the final answer to be exact and contain the number "π" and either a mixed number or improper fraction along with the appropriate label.

33. $V_{sphere} = \frac{4}{3}\pi r^3$ Given fact: $Radius\ (r) = 6{,}371\ km.$ Again, the final answer should have the number "π" in the solution. You may leave a number in the denominator in the final answer and use the same type of notation which is used in the formula or write a decimal answer. What is the significance of this problem? (Look up the radius of the earth on the internet.) {This example problem might be a great problem to allow students to use a **calculator** to determine a rounded-off decimal answer.}

34. $A_{rec.} = lw$ Given facts: $length\ (l) = 3.123\ yds.\ and\ the\ width\ (w) = 2\ ft.$ (Hint: We suggest you convert one of the two given measurements into the same unit as the other measurement. The two types of linear measurement should be the same unit.)

FIND THE LCD FOR EACH SET OF FRACTIONS

E. Use "factor trees" for all the numbers in the denominators and if you are not an expert with the rules for multiplying and dividing exponents with variables, we suggest you write each variable with an exponent in expanded form to determine the exact number of times each variable is represented in the denominator. Remember, the different expressions (quantities in parentheses) are treated just like a single variable. Find the LCD for the following four problems.

35. $\frac{77}{85} + \frac{91}{105} - \frac{71}{90}$ (The answer is between 10,000 and 12, 000.)

36. $\frac{11}{x^2y} + \frac{13}{x^2y^3} + \frac{m}{x^2y^2z} - \frac{mn}{xy^3z^4}$

37. $\{\frac{777}{48z^2(x+9)}, \frac{777}{32z^3(x+9)^2}, \frac{777}{18z(x+9)^3}\}$

38. $\{\frac{9.1}{24x(y+x)^2}, \frac{8.1}{28x^3(y+x)(y+z)}, \frac{7.1}{32x^2(y+x)^2(y+z)}, \frac{6.1}{672x^3(y+x)^2(y+z)^2}\}$

FIND THE LCM FOR THE FOLLOWING SETS OF EXPRESSIONS

F. Remember the rules to find an LCM for a group/set of numbers, variables, and/or expressions are the same rules used to find the LCD in the previous problems. Find the LCM for the three problems below.

39. $\{88, 84, 92\}$ After you determine the LCM for the given numbers, check to make sure all three numbers divide into the LCM such that all the quotients are natural numbers.

40. $\{15, 20, 25, 50\}$ We want you to encourage your students to check their solutions to ensure the LCM is the correct LCM for all four numbers indicated. If you want to check to determine if the LCM is the correct LCM for all four numbers, you will have to set up four division problems.

41. $\{20x^3, 30x^4, 45xy, 90x^2y^2\}$ When you check to ensure your LCM is divisible by each of the given numbers and terms, we suggest you write four separate fractions. In the <u>numerator</u> write the "Prime Factors" for the LCM and write all the x & y" terms in expanded form without exponents. In the <u>denominator</u> of the first fraction focus on the first expression "$20x^3$" and completely factor this expression focusing on the number "20" using the prime factors "$2 \times 2 \times 5$" and the variable "x^3" written as "$x \cdot x \cdot x$". Repeat the same process by placing the other three expressions in the denominator and your LCM in the numerator. If you have found the LCM, when you simplify all four fractions the <u>denominator</u> must be <u>1</u> and the <u>quotient</u> will be the terms remaining in the <u>numerator</u>. (Repeat: When you reduce the four fractions the numerator will have terms remaining and the denominator will be <u>1</u> if you have done everything correctly.) The reason this will occur is because the numerator, LCD, will

contain every factor involved with the four terms in the denominators and the denominators will only contain the factors for one specific expression. (Notice, in the three previous problems you found LCMs, if these terms were denominators involving fractions you would use the same procedures to find the LCDs.)

FIND THE SOLUTIONS TO THE FOLLOWING PROBLEMS OR SIMPLIFY THESE PROBLEMS

G. The fractions added and subtracted include some problems which are basic problems. Some problems will require you to find the LCD and convert some or all the fractions into equivalent fractions with the LCD. In these situations, demonstrate using "factor trees" and "prime numbers" how you determined the LCD, indicate how you determine the special form of the number 1 to convert a fraction into an equivalent fraction, and then indicate how you multiply each of the given fractions by the special form of the number 1 which you just determined. If you identify any fractions with a denominator equal to 0, the correct answer/response for these fractions is simple, write "Undefined". We are never permitted to work with a faction when the denominator equals 0. Do you remember the "Hierarchy of operations for arithmetic?

42. $\frac{11}{12} + \frac{17}{18} - (\frac{2}{9} + \frac{5}{6})$ We assume you know how to write the answer as a mixed number and reduce the fraction if either or both situations occur.

43. $\frac{\{5^2 - (25 \div 2)\} + 7^3}{12 + 3^3 - (13 \times 3)}$

44. $\frac{7}{39} - \frac{65}{78} + \frac{25}{26}$ We assume you know how to reduce fractions.

45. $\frac{17}{18} - (\frac{4}{5} - \frac{2}{15})^2$ There are a couple of different ways to solve this problem, but one method will make the problem relatively simple compared to other methods. Make sure you reduce the answer completely.

46. $\frac{2x}{2x} + \frac{11+9}{2\,(10)} + \frac{33}{11}$ Remember, when there is no symbol or mathematics operation indicated between a number and a variable, the number and variable are multiplied. The multiplication symbols in the two expressions, "$2x$ *and* $2(10)$" are understood by all mathematicians as present and we consider the multiplication symbol in these two situations to be an invisible symbol. Why is it important to mention the variable "x" may never equal <u>0</u> in this problem?

47. $(\frac{8+11}{19(0)})(77.132)$ There are invisible multiplication symbols between the quantities, "$\left(\frac{8+11}{19(0)}\right)$ *and* (77.132)" and the two numbers "19 *and* (0)".

YOU MAY <u>NOT</u> REDUCE/CANCEL TERMS IN THE NUMERATOR AND THE DENOMINATOR WHICH ARE ADDED OR SUBTRACTED, YOU MAY ONLY REDUCE FACTORS

H. The following are examples to illustrate when you may reduce terms in the numerator and the denominator and when you may not reduce terms in the numerator and the denominator.

$a.$ $\frac{3\cdot r\cdot(g+7)\cdot d\cdot(d+r)}{3\cdot(g+7)\cdot(d-r)\cdot r} = \frac{d\cdot(d+r)}{(d-r)}$ Identify the identical factors in both the numerator and the denominator which will cancel. Remember a factor is a number, variable, or expression/quantity which is one of the terms in any multiplication problem. The number "3" in both the numerator and the denominator is multiplied by every term in both situations, therefore we may cancel the identical "$3's$". The variable "r" in both the numerator and the denominator is a factor in both situations, therefore we may cancel the identical "$r's$". The expression "$(g+7)$" in both the numerator and the denominator is multiplied by every term in both situations, therefore we may cancel the identical quantities "$(g+7)$" in both the numerator and the denominator. The remaining terms/factors in the numerator are "d & $(d+r)$" and the only remaining expression in the denominator is "$(d-r)$". None of these three quantities/factors are identical. Study the following situation when we substitute numbers into these expressions. Assume the variables "$d = 11$" and "$r = 2$" in the final simplified fraction, "$\frac{d \cdot (d+r)}{(d-r)}$". If we work with the fraction just indicated and substitute the two indicated numbers for the two variables, the substitution process looks like this: "$\frac{d \cdot (d+r)}{(d-r)} = \frac{11 \cdot (11+2)}{(11-2)}$" which equals "$\frac{11 \cdot 13}{9}$". There are no identical factors in both the numerator and the denominator in the final fraction just indicated, "$\frac{11 \cdot 13}{9}$" when we substituted the numbers "11 & 2" for the variables "d & r" respectively. This means there is no opportunity to reduce any numbers. The variable "$\boldsymbol{d}$" and the two expressions "$(\boldsymbol{d}+\boldsymbol{r})$" and "$(\boldsymbol{d}-\boldsymbol{r})$" are three factors, but all three factors are completely different. Just because there is a "d" in the numerator not inside a pair of parentheses, does not mean it will cancel with the "d" in the denominator. The "d" in the numerator is a factor all by itself, but the variable, "d" in the denominator is involved with the subtraction problem "$(d-r)$" therefore, the "d" in the denominator is not a factor and the expressions are different. The same is true about the two quantities "$(d+r)$" and "$(d-r)$", if you add the term "r"and then subtract the term "r" to a given term "d", the two final terms are obviously not identical terms. You may not reduce terms in the numerator and the denominator if they are involved in an addition or subtraction problem unless they are the same addition and subtraction expressions/quantities, which was the case with the expression "$(g + 7)$", contained in both the numerator and the denominator.

b. $\frac{11(x-11)^2(r+16)^2(x+8)d^3y}{22(x-11)^2(r+16)^3d^2y} = \frac{11(x-11)(x-11)(r+16)(r+16)(x+8)\cdot d\cdot d\cdot d\cdot y}{2\cdot 11(x-11)(x-11)(r+16)(r+16)(r+16)\cdot d\cdot d\cdot y} = \frac{d(x+8)}{2(r+16)}$

48. Simplify/Reduce $\frac{45\,x^3yz^2(x+4)^2(z-8)^2}{60x^3y^2z(x+4)^3(z-16)^2}$

49. Simplify/Reduce $\frac{x\,(2x-5)y^2(2x+15)}{x\,(3x-10)y(2x+15)^2}$

50. Simplify/Reduce $\frac{6x(3m^2+z^3+7)25y(6x+5)^3}{12y(6x+5)^2 5x^2(3m^2+z^3+7)}$

SOLVE THESE BASIC ALGEBRA EQUATIONS INVOLVING ADDITION AND SUBTRACTION WITH A VARIABLE ON ONE SIDE OF THE EQUATION

LINE UP TWO EQUATIONS AND EITHER ADD OR SUBTRACT BOTH THE LEFT AND RIGHT SIDES OF THE TWO EQUATIONS TO DETERMINE THE THIRD EQUATION

I. Since these are first degree addition and subtraction algebra problems the goal is to get the number zero (0) on the same side of the equation as the variable. Determine the special form of the identity required to solve the problem, then line up the two equations and solve for the variable. Lastly, go back and write the steps indicating you substituted the solution into the original equation and the answer is correct.

51. $x + 25 = 27$

52. $25.3 + m = 28.1$

53. $37\frac{3}{4} = z - 5\frac{5}{8}$

54. $\frac{7}{16} = \frac{7}{24} + r$

55. $\frac{3}{4} + c = \frac{17}{18}$

56. $y - 11.75 = 101.34$

57. $2001\frac{7}{12} = m - 3005\frac{7}{16}$

58. $3010\frac{7}{11} - 2999\frac{21}{22} = p$

First, notice the location of the equals relationship symbol, "=", compared to the two numbers and the variable.

SOLVE THESE BASIC ALGEBRA EQUATIONS INVOLVING MULTIPLICATION AND DIVISION WITH A VARIABLE ON ONE SIDE OF THE EQUATION

WRITE TWO EQUATIONS, THE GIVEN EQUATION AND AN IDENTITY EQUATION AND EITHER MULTIPLY OR DIVIDE THE LEFT SIDE OF THE FIRST EQUATION WITH THE LEFT SIDE OF THE IDENTITY EQUATION THEN MULTIPLY OR DIVIDE THE RIGHT SIDE OF THE FIRST EQUATION WITH THE RIGHT SIDE OF THE IDENTITY EQUATION

J. Since these are first degree multiplication and division problems the goal is to get the number one (1) with the variable and write the multiplication problem, with one (1), times the variable on one side of the equation. Determine the special form of the identity required to solve the problem, then line up the two equations and solve for the variable. Lastly, go back and write the steps indicating you substituted the solution into the original equation and the answer is correct. We realize you will probably encourage your students to simply multiply or divide both sides of the given equations by a particular number to solve the problems, but we still want you and the students to understand why the simple trick of multiplying or dividing both sides of an equation by a number works all the time. Additionally, the rule regarding multiplying and dividing the left sides of two equations and then the right sides of two equations to determine a third equation is a valid method to solve some special advanced mathematics problems.

59. $15q = 30$ 60. $\frac{g}{15} = 30$

61. $11.1 = \frac{t}{2.1}$ 62. $\frac{4}{5} = 4w$

63. $\frac{2}{5}k = 10$

64. $77.23j = 858.0253$ The answer is a terminating decimal.

65. $\left(\frac{3}{10}\right)\left(2\frac{6}{7}\right) = z$ (Notice the positioning of the two numbers.)

USE THE GIVEN FORMULAS WITH NO LABELS AND SOLVE FOR THE LEFT-HAND VARIABLE

K. The formulas you will need are indicated for each problem. Interesting question, "Does the number answer really make sense without a label indicated?"

66. $P_{rec.} = 2l + 2w \; or \; P_{rec.} = l + l + w + w$ Given facts: $Length\ (l) = 100 \; and \; Width\ (w) = 50$ Assume you are the owner of a farm, "How much fence should you buy to enclose your rectangular field since you do not have any labels?"

67. $A_{square} = s^2$ Given fact: $Side\ (s) = 25$ You are going to paint a wall in a building how much paint should you buy since you do not know the label?

68. $V_{rec.\ solid} = lwh$ Given facts $Length\ (l) = 75.5,\ Width\ (w) = 72.5, and\ Height\ (h) = 100$ If you are the designer for a toy company and your company will pack the Rectangular Solid with little cubes, "What size should the little cubes be in order to fit into the Rectangular Solid indicated in the problem? Could there be a

problem packing all the cubes into the rectangular solid because two of the measurements involve decimals? Since there are no labels, how are you going to determine how much material you will need to construct the Rectangular Solid and all the little cubes?

REFLEXIVE PROPERTY, SYMMETRIC PROPERTY, AND TRANSITIVE PROPERTY

(Additional Arithmetic Facts we consider important - and you should too)

Earlier we discussed in detail the specifics regarding the Commutative Property and the Associative Property for both Addition and Multiplication. Sometimes students get these two/four properties confused with some of the properties we are going to explain in the next few paragraphs. Just a reminder, both the Commutative Property for Addition and Multiplication involve **one** equation and the order of the two terms on one side of the equation switch their order on the other side of the equation. The Associative Property for both Addition and Multiplication also involves **one** equation but this time there are three terms and two of the terms are enclosed in one set of parentheses on one side of the equation. On the other side of the equation the parentheses are switched around but the order of the three terms does not change from the left side to the right side in the equation.

We already mentioned the Reflexive Property earlier in this textbook when we were talking about identities. The Reflexive Property involves **one** equation. One must realize the Reflexive Property is a very specialized form of an identity. The Reflexive Property simply means the left side of an equation is identical to the right side of the equation. The Reflexive Property should remind you of a mirror such that the reflection in the mirror is identical to the object in front of the mirror. The standard way mathematicians write the Reflexive

Property is "$a = a$". This algebra notation seems simple, but the implications are much more powerful than the simple application "$6 = 6 \; or \; 11.31 = 11.31$". The Reflexive Property may also be illustrated by referring to the following examples:

$\{3 + 4 = 3 + 4, \;\; m^2 - n = m^2 - n, \;\; 6(9)(11.1) = 6(9)(11.1), \;\; or \;\; 2xy = 2xy\}$.

The Symmetric Property always involves two different equations. The Symmetric Property focuses on the equal relationship symbol and when you start with the first equation such as "$x + 2 = 5$" you may flip the two sides of the equation and determine the second equation from the first equation but write "$5 = x + 2$". Notice the left and right sides of the equation flip sides. Students often confuse the Symmetric Property with the Commutative Property because something in both properties switches around BUT the difference is, the Commutative Property involves **one** equation, and the Symmetric Property involves **two** equations. The Commutative Property **switches the order of two terms** from one side of the equation to the other side of the equation and the Symmetric Property flips the left and right sides of the first equation to write the second equation. One property switches the order of two terms in one equation and the other property switches the sides of the equation, resulting in two equations. The first equation is the given equation, and the second equation is the flipped equation.

The Transitive Property always involves **three** equations. The first two equations involve two known facts which are assumed to be true, and we use the first two equations to determine the third equation. Here is an arithmetic interpretation of the Transitive Property "$6 + 2 = 8 \;\&\; 8 = 10 - 2$ which leads to the conclusion indicated in the third equation $6 + 2 = 10 - 2$". Notice, the right side of the first equation is identical to the left side of the second equation "8 & 8" and the first two equations are written so the two "$8's$" are next to each other and this fact is easy to identify. The third equation then becomes obvious since both the left side of the first equation and the right side of the second equation both equal "8", the two expressions must be equal.

Here is the algebra notation you will normally encounter in an arithmetic or math textbook to illustrate the Transitive Property "$a = b \;\&\; b = c \;\; \therefore a = c$". Here is a more complicated example of the Transitive Property for illustration:

"$a + b + c = 762 - r \;\;\&\;\; 762 - r = 369\,p \;\;\therefore\;\; a + b + c = 369p$".

Again, notice the position of the identical expressions "$762 - r$" and then how the third equation is written based on the left side of the first equation and the right side of the second equation.

When you work with both the Symmetric Property for equations and the Transitive property for equations, the individual terms on each side of the equations do not switch their order. If two of the terms on the left side of an equation flip around to write the right side of the equation, it must have something to do with the Commutative Property for either Addition or Multiplication. When using the Symmetric Property or the Transitive Property you will not change the order of terms on one side of the equation to determine another equation.

The Commutative and Associative Properties focus on two operations, addition and multiplication, and the ability to switch the order of the terms and get equivalent answers. The Reflexive, Symmetric, and Transitive Properties focus on the equal relationship symbol.

L. Identify whether we are using the Reflexive Property, the Symmetric Property, or the Transitive property for the first 6 problems (69-74) and then in the last 14 problems

(75-88) determine if we are using the Commutative Property for Addition, the Associative Property for Addition, the Commutative Property for Multiplication, the Associative Property for Multiplication, the Reflexive Property, the Symmetric Property, or the Transitive Property. These Properties all focus on rules which work for numbers in arithmetic first and then we replace the numbers with variables or expressions. If you do not understand the arithmetic rules and how they are going to be applied in other courses in two or three years, "Do you really feel confident instructing your students this year?"

69. $8 - 1 = 8 - 1$

70. $8 - z = p \quad \therefore p = 8 - z$

71. $(x - 8 + z)\left(9r + 10p - \frac{m}{n}\right) = (x - 8 + z)\left(9r + 10p - \frac{m}{n}\right)$

72. $(9 + ab) + 1 = 11.2^3 \ \& \ 11.2^3 = 77.912 + sz \quad \therefore \ (9 + ab) + 1 = 77.912 + sz$

73. $(ab + 2) = dm \ \& \ dm = 1001 \quad \therefore \quad (ab + 2) = 1001$

74. $(ab + 2) = 1001 \quad \therefore \quad 1001 = (ab + 2)$

75. $(9 + x) + 4 = 4 + (9 + x)$

76. $(9 + x) + 4 = 4 \quad \therefore \quad 4 = (9 + x) + 4$

77. $(9 + x) + 4 = 4 \ \& \ 4 = 9 - 5 \quad \therefore \quad (9 + x) + 4 = 9 - 5$

78. $16.21 - \left(x^2 + 3\frac{1}{2}\right) = 16.21 - \left(x^2 + 3\frac{1}{2}\right)$

79. $3(bc) = (3b)c$

80. $16.21 + \left(x^2 + 3\frac{1}{2}\right) = (16.21 + x^2) + 3\frac{1}{2}$

81. $(x + 1)(x + 2) = (x + 2)(x + 1)$

82. $(x + 1)(x + 2) = (x + 1)(x + 2)$

83. $(x + 1)(p - 11) = (x + 1)\,(x + 2)$ & $(x + 1)\,(x + 2) = p(z + 8)$

$\therefore \quad (x + 1)(p - 11) = p(z + 8)$

84. $(x + 1)(x + 2) = (x + 1)(2 + x)$ (Hint: Identify the change in the one quantity.)

85. $n^5 + 11.9 = \sqrt[3]{z} \quad \therefore \quad \sqrt[3]{z} = n^5 + 11.9$

86. $(6 \cdot x) + 11 = (x \cdot 6) + 11$ (Hint: Similar to problem "84" above.)

87. $(a + 6) + \{m + (c - 8)\} = \{(a + 6) + m\} + (c - 8)$

88. $(6 \cdot x) \cdot 11 = 6 \cdot (x \cdot 11)$

MATH DEFINITIONS (The foundation of Arithmetic and Mathematics):

A major objective of this textbook is to make sure all elementary teachers are knowledgeable about definitions of arithmetic/mathematics words, terms, and phrases. We realize some elementary teachers enjoy teaching reading more than they enjoy teaching arithmetic. Some other elementary teachers may enjoy teaching Social Studies and American History more than reading and arithmetic. Everyone is different, but when you are an elementary teacher, you must be an expert in all the subject areas you are teaching for your grade level and one or two grade levels in the future for your students. If your knowledge of math topics ends with what you teach this year, you need to expand your knowledge to ensure your students are prepared for the challenges they will encounter in future years. A problem which occurs in arithmetic which might not be a problem when teaching History, Science, or Art is, if you do not do an excellent job when presenting and illustrating how to solve arithmetic problems, your students will be behind next year in their arithmetic class or math class and maybe be behind for the rest of their high school career and beyond. You are the key to every child's success in arithmetic when they are sitting in your class. When a student struggles with reading, it also creates a problem in future years, but students who struggle with reading are continually required to read in other subjects such as health, social studies, science, etc. Reading is emphasized constantly throughout the school day, but arithmetic seems to be a standalone subject and only truly discussed during the arithmetic class. Even the arithmetic words and definitions are only mentioned in arithmetic or math class. We are concerned that many elementary teachers shy away from arithmetic and feel the one daily time slot scheduled for arithmetic is sufficient, so why should they consider mentioning arithmetic topics outside the normal time officially scheduled to teach arithmetic?

Since many elementary teachers enjoy teaching reading a little more than they enjoy teaching arithmetic, we believe these teachers would agree it is important to understand the definitions of words (all words, most of the words) in any book the students are required to read. Wow, we also think it is important that both teachers and students understand the meaning of words when they are reading a book or a paper, if we expect the teacher or student to comprehend the meaning of the passage they are required to read. What a powerful statement, "Student's need to know the definitions of the words contained in the materials they are required to read."

Mathematics teachers believe teachers and students must know the definitions of the words contained in arithmetic textbooks if they are going to be able to interpret what the directions are and how to interpret the explanations. No wonder arithmetic and mathematics are a challenge for many students. First, the students must understand how to solve all the problems using rules and procedures after they have memorized some basic facts. Second, the students must understand the definitions of the arithmetic and mathematics words mentioned in the textbooks if they are going to comprehend what they are supposed to do. Third, if students are going to "Learn and Remember" how to solve the problems in arithmetic and mathematics, students must understand the concepts and then practice the procedures required to solve the problems. If the students do not understand the concepts, they will have difficulty understanding how the procedures are developed. Without some practice to solve problems using the procedures and rules, there is little chance the students will remember the procedures which are illustrated by the teacher. Arithmetic and mathematics truly are courses which require a dedicated knowledgeable professional who has a desire to ensure all students master the concepts presented in the textbook.

M. Write the definitions of each word or phrase in your own words and then look up the internet/dictionary definition and determine if your definition matches the definition on the internet/dictionary. The following list contains words and phrases which were mentioned in this chapter and previously in this textbook. If you believe it is important to understand the meanings of words and phrases when you read, then we are confident you will want to fully comprehend the specifics of each word and phrase below.

89. Coefficient
90. Variable
91. Natural Numbers
92. Whole Numbers
93. Integers
94. Rational Numbers
95. Irrational Numbers
96. Horizontal Line
97. Vertical Line
98. Perpendicular Lines
99. Right Angle
100. Factor (s)

101. Composite Numbers
102. Prime Numbers
103. Prime Factors
104. Factor Trees
105. Infinity
106. Root of an Equation
107. Linear Equation (*First degree*)
108. Quadratic Equation (*Second degree*)
109. Cubic Equation (*Third degree*)
110. Like Terms in Algebra
111. Additive Identity Property of 0
112. Multiplicative Identity Property of 1
113. Magnitude of a point or number
114. Absolute Value
115. Fraction versus Ratio
116. Complex Fraction
117. Unit Fraction
118. Real Numbers
119. "Quantity" when used in a mathematical expression or problem.
120. "Invisible numbers and math terms". To our knowledge, no one has ever used the word "invisible" to describe these types of expressions, so you will have to use the information we supplied to write the definitions and then try to find other mathematics references for these types of expressions. There is also one label which we will mention later, which is not written in trigonometric expressions. We assume all secondary mathematics teachers quickly realize the invisible label is the label "Radians" when referring to an angle written in a trigonometric expression or function.

HIERARCHY OF OPERATIONS IN ARITHMETIC AND MATHEMATICS

N. You must know rules to work with problems involving a variety of mathematics procedures involving numbers, terms, and expressions to include addition, subtraction, multiplication, division, exponents, radicals (square roots, cube roots, etc.), and quantities (parentheses, brackets, and braces).

121. Write several paragraphs indicating how you would explain to your 6th grade students the rules and procedures to us the Hierarchy of Operation Rules in Arithmetic.

122. Write ten example problems with step-by-step solutions to illustrate how to apply the Hierarchy of Operation Rules to simplify arithmetic problems.

The objective of this textbook is to make sure all elementary teachers are knowledgeable about arithmetic rules, procedures, and facts. If the teacher does not understand all the rules, procedures, and facts involved with arithmetic problems why would you think they are prepared to instruct students to learn the rules, procedures, and facts? A second objective of this textbook is to ensure all certified mathematics teachers are knowledgeable about the arithmetic rules, procedures, and facts continually illustrated throughout this textbook. Part of this objective is to ensure all math teachers will know how to illustrate and explain how previously learned arithmetic rules and procedures are necessary to develop advanced mathematics concepts, rules, and procedures.

Remember, arithmetic definitions, rules, and procedures are the foundation for developing advanced mathematics rules and procedures.

Rules and procedures will not change as students continue their journey through their mathematics careers, but one thing we can guarantee, there will be many new definitions which will create opportunities to expand students' skills and knowledge. Understanding definitions is key to future mathematics growth.

CHAPTER 6

UNIT CONVERSIONS IN ARITHMETIC

DO NOT USE TRICKS TO TEACH UNIT CONVERSIONS IN ARITHMETIC.

USE THE TWO THEOREMS CONTINUALLY DISCUSSED THOUGHOUT THIS TEXTBOOK AND YOU WILL BE AMAZED WITH THE SUCCESS OVER 90% OF YOUR STUDENTS WILL ACHIEVE.

Chapter 6

"Young's Equation/Ratio Theorem" and "Young's Conversion Theorem" work together to convert arithmetic and mathematical expressions into equivalent arithmetic and mathematical expressions. The following example problems are given to illustrate how to apply both "Young's Equation/Ratio Theorem" and "Young's Conversion Theorem" when you are converting from one unit of measurement into an equivalent unit of measurement. Some of the example problems are simple conversions, and you should be able to complete the conversion process without thinking about the two new theorems. We want students to solve simple problems in their head without focusing on the rules. You must also realize rules will be advantageous to solve more challenging algebra problems. We want you to understand when completing conversion problems using the two theorems, "The number One (1) is the Most Powerful Number in the World of Arithmetic and Mathematics."

> We want you to think back to previous example problems when we made the statement, "When you are working with simple problems sometimes the rules seem to make things a little more difficult, but once you understand how to work with the rules, the rules really become the best way to solve a wide variety of problems."

Before you look at the example problems illustrated below, think back to the following problem mentioned earlier in Chapter 2. (Example problem: If a United States dollar is equal to 1.09 Canadian dollars, convert 25 Canadian dollars into United States dollars. The question many people ask themselves is, "Should I multiply or divide the number 25 by 1.09 to figure out the answer? The answer to this question is, "You should divide 25 by 1.09 to get the answer $22.936.") What was your first reaction when we asked you to convert 25 Canadian dollars into United States dollars? Did you hesitate for a moment and ask yourself the question, "Do I want to get a bigger number compared to the given number "25" or a smaller number compared to "25"? Even if you are an excellent mathematician, you had to think for a second to ensure you made the correct decision. Imagine you are a young student who struggles with arithmetic. Do you think this might be a problem which may confuse an average achieving 5th, 6th, or 7th grader? If you think these students might have difficulty determining whether they should multiply or divide by "1.09" to determine the correct answer, then you will be amazed by the power of the two theorems discussed throughout this textbook when solving the following conversion problems. Some 5th, 6th, and 7th grade arithmetic teachers might think this problem is not practical at this grade level, but we guarantee once you study the illustrations in this chapter you will find this problem is perfectly acceptable for 95% of these students. A step-by-step explanation to solve this problem will be given later in this chapter.

Here are some basic conversion example problems using labels:

1. Convert "48 oz. into lbs."

This is an easy problem, and hopefully you realize the answer is "3 *lbs.*". Now, study the solution and you should begin to understand how to use the two theorems, "Young's Equation/Ratio Theorem" and "Young's Conversion Theorem" when finding equivalent units of measure.

Fact: "16 oz. = 1 lb." $\therefore$ " $\frac{16 \text{ oz.}}{1 \text{ lb.}} = 1 = \frac{1 \text{ lb.}}{16 \text{ oz.}}$ " These two ratios which both equal the number 1 are derived by applying "Young's Equation/Ratio Theorem" to the given factual equation.

Conversion Procedure - Now, we will use "Young's Conversion Theorem":

"$48 \text{ oz.} = \frac{48 \text{ oz.}}{1} \times 1 = \frac{48 \text{ oz.}}{1} \times \frac{1 \text{ lb.}}{16 \text{ oz.}} = \frac{48 \text{ oz.} \cdot 1 \text{ lb.}}{1 \cdot 16 \text{ oz.}}$". We will use factor trees to simplify this problem in the next step as illustrated below, but your students should be able to reduce the last fraction indicated without using factor trees. We want students to solve simple reducing problems without using factor trees, but we also want them to realize using factor trees to reduce fractions is the best method to employ when the problems are challenging. When students are required to reduce, multiply and/or divide fraction problems involving large numbers in arithmetic, using factor trees for all the terms in the numerator and the denominator is the preferred procedure. If you are required to reduce, multiply, or divide a rational expression in algebra, the first step is to factor. (Factoring in algebra is the same process as employing factor trees in arithmetic.)

In the next step, we will reference the last fraction indicated and finish solving the problem:

We have repeated the following type of statement several times throughout this textbook. We feel the following statement is a powerful statement and every arithmetic/mathematics teacher should continually keep this statement in mind when they are teaching, "If students learn the correct procedures to solve challenging problems in arithmetic, then the procedures to solve algebra problems will seem much more natural."

$$\frac{48\,oz. \cdot 1\,lb.}{1 \cdot 16\,oz.} = \frac{2 \cdot 2 \cdot 2 \cdot 2 \cdot 3 \cdot oz \;\cdot 1 \cdot lb.}{1 \cdot 2 \cdot 2 \cdot 2 \cdot 2 \cdot oz.} = \frac{1 \cdot 1 \cdot 1 \cdot 1 \;\cdot\; 3 \cdot 1 \;\cdot\; 1 \cdot lb.}{1 \cdot \;1 \cdot 1 \cdot 1 \cdot 1 \;\cdot 1} = 3 \text{ lbs.}$$

Note, we must cancel all the identical terms in the numerator and denominator. Remember, "oz." in the numerator and "oz." in the denominator are identical mathematical terms/labels. In the last fraction expression before we wrote the answer "3 lbs." the first four "1's" in the numerator were derived when we reduced four "2's" in the numerator with four "2's" in the denominator. It is obvious the four "2's" in the numerator and the denominator cancelled and all the numbers became 1 in the process. What is important to understand is when we selected the ratio "$\frac{1\,lb.}{16\,oz.}$" to multiply the given measurement "48 *oz.*", the goal was to make sure we had the same label in the denominator "*oz.*" to cancel with the label "*oz.*" in the numerator. When we reduced/(divided out) the two labels, "*oz.*" we created the additional 1 in both the numerator and the denominator. When you cancel identical factors, they all become 1. When we say they cancel, we really mean each "2" in the denominator divides into a respective "2" in the numerator and they all become 1's. The same logic applies to the simple fraction, "$\frac{oz.}{oz.} = \frac{1}{1} = 1$".

Go back and look at the fraction "$\frac{2 \cdot 2 \cdot 2 \cdot 2 \cdot 3 \cdot oz. \ \cdot 1 \cdot lb.}{1 \cdot 2 \cdot 2 \cdot 2 \cdot 2 \cdot oz.}$" again and cancel the "2's" in the numerator and the denominator and use a pencil to make sure all four "2's" cancel along with the label "oz." in both the numerator and the denominator. If you use a pencil to cancel all the identical terms, you should understand where all the "1's" come from in the next fraction, "$\frac{1 \cdot 1 \cdot 1 \cdot 1 \cdot 3 \cdot 1 \ \cdot \ 1 \cdot \ lb.}{1 \ \cdot \ 1 \cdot 1 \cdot 1 \cdot 1 \cdot 1}$".

When you multiply by the number 1 in either the numerator or denominator, you may ignore all the 1's which are multiplied except the final 1 in the numerator if it is the only remaining number. When we demonstrated how to solve the problem, we made sure to write every step possible. The process of canceling all the identical numbers, terms, and labels may initially seem cumbersome for your students. Do not be concerned about what appears to be a cumbersome factoring procedure; illustrate both the factoring process and how to reduce the fraction "$\frac{48 \ oz. \ \ \cdot \ 1 \ lb.}{1 \ \cdot \ 16 \ oz.}$" without factoring the numbers "48" and "16". Many of your students should be able to get the correct answer "3 lbs." by dividing the number "48" by "16" and canceling the "*oz.*" labels.

> Teaching principle number 4 listed earlier in this textbook, suggested it is wise to introduce new concepts for 2-3 minutes 2-3 times per week a couple months before the concepts are presented in the textbook and before the first homework assignment in a new section. This teaching principle may appear to take instruction time away from the regular lessons and create a permanent loss in teaching time. The amazing thing which happens is, when the time comes to discuss the concepts and rules which have been introduced during the previous couple months the students already know how to solve the problems and the time saved when the new concept is presented, more than doubles the time lost over the previous months. We continually covered all the required concepts in all classes and often we had additional time to discuss more difficult problems. Many times, we introduced concepts at the end of the year that the students would encounter next year. All teachers knew we reviewed more frequently than other teachers, but they could never understand how we had time to cover more concepts without rushing at the end of the school year.

2. Convert $4\frac{3}{4}$ ft. into yards:

Are you able to compute the answer in your head? Maybe this will make you think about the rules to complete the conversion process?

Fact: 3 ft. = 1 yd. $\therefore \frac{3\,ft.}{1\,yd.} = 1 = \frac{1\,yd.}{3\,ft.}$ The two indicated ratios which both equal 1 are derived by using "Young's Equation/Ratio Theorem" and the given fact, "3 ft. = 1 yd."

Conversion Procedure using "Young's Conversion Theorem":

$$4\frac{3}{4}\text{ ft.} = \frac{19}{4}\text{ ft.} = \frac{19}{4} \cdot \frac{\text{ft.}}{1} \times 1 = \frac{19\text{ ft.}}{4} \times 1 = \frac{19\text{ ft.}}{4} \times \frac{1\text{ yd.}}{3\text{ ft.}} = \frac{19\text{ ft.} \cdot 1\text{ yd.}}{4 \cdot 3\text{ ft.}} = \frac{19\text{ yd.}}{12} = 1\frac{7}{12}\text{ yds.}$$

Wow! The final answer "$1\frac{7}{12}$ yds." would not have been our first guess. We used this problem as an example because it is more challenging, and few people can solve this problem in their head without showing any work. We also used this example problem to illustrate how to use both "Young's Equation/Ratio Theorem" and "Young's Conversion Theorem" in the same problem. When students are asked to convert a mathematical expression into an equivalent mathematical expression, if they understand and use both "Young's Equation/Ratio Theorem" and "Young's Conversion Theorem", the process will work well for simple conversion problems, but the same procedures will work for more challenging conversion problems encountered later in higher level mathematics courses.

Do not expect your students to write down the words "Young's Equation/Ratio Theorem" and/or "Young's Conversion Theorem" every time they solve a conversion problem. Emphasize the two theorems by name frequently and expect the students to understand how to use each theorem when they are converting expressions from one form into an equivalent form. The more you refer to the "theorems" by name and encourage your students to write the specific steps, we believe this will help your students remember the process. We named each of the theorems because naming them lends them greater importance. Consequently, everyone will be more likely to reference and use them.

The example problem just illustrated is a little more difficult than typical 5th grade arithmetic conversion problems because the given unit of measurement contains a mixed number. When you are introducing the procedures to convert different units of measurement into equivalent units of measurement, you should concentrate on examples which can easily be illustrated to be true by creating activities which require the students to physically measure different objects. Illustrate how to solve some challenging example problems when teaching students how to convert from one type of measurement into an equivalent measurement and interleave some other arithmetic topics. When the example problems are simple and some students can complete the conversions quickly in their head, the rules seem cumbersome. If you want your students to remember the steps required to convert more challenging conversion problems into equivalent expressions, you must insist the students write down the indicated steps, even when the initial problems seem simple. You should have known how to convert "$4\frac{3}{4}$ ft." into "$\frac{19}{4}$ ft.", by using the standard way to convert a mixed number into an improper fraction. The first thing we did was multiply the denominator of the fraction "4" times the whole number "4" and add the numerator "3" to get the numerator "19" of the improper fraction--and we kept the original denominator. Do your students understand why this conversion procedure works when converting mixed numbers into improper fractions? The number 1 plays an important part when explaining why this conversion procedure works.

$$4\frac{3}{4} = 1 + 1 + 1 + 1 + \frac{3}{4} = \frac{4}{4} + \frac{4}{4} + \frac{4}{4} + \frac{4}{4} + \frac{3}{4} = \frac{4+4+4+4+3}{4} = \frac{19}{4}$$

We already mentioned some types of arithmetic conversions which do not depend on "Young's Conversion Theorem" but many of the conversions in advanced math and science can easily be simplified using these theorems. Converting the mixed number "$4\frac{3}{4}$" into the fraction "$\frac{19}{4}$" did not require you to use "Young's Conversion Theorem". Just as a reminder, how would you convert the improper fraction, "$\frac{19}{4}$" back into a mixed number?

Teaching Point: You may ask, "Why would we give this second example as an illustration to convert from one unit into an equivalent unit?" The answer is simple; give at least one and often more than one illustration where the students are required to use the rules you are trying to emphasize. Otherwise, they might think if they find an easier method their method will always work, and it probably will not. Also, use more challenging types of problems, often involving fractions in "2-3" minute introduction sessions a month or two prior to assigning homework questions relating to a specific topic.

Another Teaching Point: Insist that students write the fact regarding the equivalence of the basic units involved in the problem as the first step, such as "16 oz. = 1 lb.". Then insist they write both ratios which equal the number 1, so they have the visual of the ratios on paper. This is the purpose of "Young's Equation/Ratio Theorem". Also, insist (especially when the students are learning the process) they write all the steps indicated in the conversion process because we want them to realize the way to convert many expressions from one form into an equivalent form is to multiply by the number 1. This is exactly what "Young's Conversion Theorem" states. It may seem unnecessary to indicate you are multiplying by the number 1 when you are setting up the conversion problem, but it is a powerful visual and it emphasizes the only number you can multiply by to get an equivalent answer is the number, 1.

3. Convert .225 mi. into ft. (semi-challenging problem)

Fact: 1 mi. = 5280 ft. $\therefore$ $\frac{1\text{ mi.}}{5280\text{ ft.}} = 1 = \frac{5280\text{ ft.}}{1\text{ mi.}}$ These two ratios are derived from "Young's Equation/Ratio Theorem".

Conversion procedure using "Young's Conversion Theorem": $.225\ mi. = \frac{.225\text{ mi.}}{1} =$

$$\frac{.225\text{ mi.}}{1} \times 1 = \frac{.225\text{ mi.}}{1} \times \frac{5280\text{ ft.}}{1\text{ mi.}} = \frac{.225\text{ mi.} \cdot 5280\text{ ft.}}{1 \cdot 1\text{ mi.}} = .225 \cdot 5280\text{ ft.} = 1188\text{ ft.}$$

We always use the ratio to replace the number 1 in the multiplication problem which contains the appropriate label in the denominator to cancel with the original label in the numerator. Then use the denominators and the numerators of the ratios to determine whether you should multiply or divide the numbers. Once the labels are set up correctly in the numerator and the denominator, it is easy to determine whether to multiply or divide the numbers. There is no guess work; just make sure the labels cancel appropriately. Students still need to know the correct facts regarding the numbers and the units to write the two ratios which both equal 1. Do you realize when you multiply by the number 1, you will either get the same answer you started with or you will get an answer equivalent to the answer you started with, even though it will look different than the starting expression? In this example problem, we wanted the students to practice multiplying by a decimal. Interleaving different math concepts with a present teaching topic is critical for long term learning (Patel et al., 2017; Richland et al., 2005).

4. Convert 42 inches into feet:

The solution to this problem should be easy to illustrate using a line segment, and some students might be able to solve this conversion problem in their head without using a pencil and a piece of paper. If we were teaching this problem, we would still emphasize the steps using the two "theorems", especially when students are first learning to convert expressions into equivalent expressions. Some students may quickly realize if they simply divide the number "42" by the number "12", they will get the correct number answer "3.5 or $3\frac{1}{2}$" for the problem, but if they simply divide by "12" using mental math they will not learn the procedures necessary to solve more challenging arithmetic conversion problems and they will not understand why the label "feet" appears in the converted answer. When learning how to convert from feet to inches or inches to feet in elementary school, many kids worry only about getting the correct number. Once they get the number, they just add the label to get the final answer because the teacher tells them to do it that way. If you follow the procedures illustrated to solve the problems in this section, you will automatically understand why the label is correct in the final answer.

Fact: 12 in. = 1 ft. $\therefore \ \frac{12\,in.}{1\,ft.} = 1 = \frac{1\text{ ft.}}{12\text{ in.}}$ Again, the two ratios which equal 1 were derived using "Young's Equation/Ratio Theorem".

Conversion Procedure using "Young's Conversion Theorem":

$42\text{ in.} = 42\text{ in.} \times 1 = \frac{42\text{ in.}}{1} \text{ X } \frac{1\text{ ft.}}{12\text{ in.}} = \frac{42\text{ in.} \cdot 1\text{ ft.}}{1 \cdot 12\text{ in.}} = \frac{42\text{ ft.}}{12} = \frac{2 \cdot 3 \cdot 7 \cdot \text{ft.}}{2 \cdot 2 \cdot 3} = \frac{7\text{ ft.}}{2} = 3\frac{1}{2}\text{ ft.} = 3.5\text{ ft.}$

If you simply divide the number "42" by "12", you will get the correct number "3.5", but can you really explain to your students using sound math reasoning why the units changed from inches to feet--or would you simply say, "This is the way to solve this problem"? The first important thing students must know is "12 in. = 1 ft.". If two expressions are equal, then you can form two ratios which equal 1. This is exactly what "Young's Equation/Ratio Theorem" states. After you write the fact "12 in. = 1 ft.", you can write the following two ratios which equal 1, "$\frac{12 \text{ in.}}{1 \text{ ft.}} = 1$ and $\frac{1 \text{ ft.}}{12 \text{ in.}} = 1$". You must then decide which one of the two ratios is the correct ratio to use to convert "42 in." into ft. This is relatively simple if you have demonstrated to your students over and over that a number or term or label divided by the same identical number or term or label will always equal 1. With this thought in mind, go back to the original given measurement "42 in." and write "42 in." with a denominator of 1. The given measurement "42 in." may now be written as "$\frac{42 \text{ in.}}{1}$". At this point, students must determine which of the two ratios we derived using "Young's Equation/Ratio Theorem" is the appropriate ratio to multiply by. Once our low-achieving 9th-grade students understood how to determine the correct ratio to multiply by, they considered these types of problems easy to solve. Once students learn how to multiply fractions, they should recognize how to reduce and multiply fractions involving simple numbers by using their mental multiplication and division facts. We found if students started to use factor trees to reduce large numbers, they demonstrated significant improvement with their mental multiplication and division facts and their accuracy improved significantly when solving all types of reducing and multiplying fraction problems. *(FRT 12: If students are required to frequently work with factor trees, will their multiplication and division mental skills improve? Notice, we used factor trees as a required process to solve fraction problems, not as an independent procedure.)*

You should have also taught your students the following fact, "$\frac{\text{in.}}{\text{in.}} = 1$". This means when your students decide which of the two ratios, they write in the beginning of the problem is the correct ratio to substitute for the number 1 they need to ensure the label in the numerator cancels with the label in the denominator. This is the reason we selected the ratio "$\frac{1 \text{ ft.}}{12 \text{ in}}$" as the ratio which equals 1, to use in the multiplication problem. We used the two words "multiplication problem" in the previous sentence because you need to emphasize when you are converting from one unit of measurement to another unit of measurement, you will always multiply by the number 1. Once you set up the multiplication problem involving the number 1 based on the set up of the fractions/ratios, you will either multiply or divide by the respective number involved in the conversion.

In one of the last steps, we frequently wrote the fractions which are multiplied as one fraction, cancelled the units and identical factors, and found the final solution. Isn't it amazing the unit "in." in the numerator of the fraction and the unit "in." in the denominator cancelled with each other and the only unit/label remaining in the numerator is the label "ft.", which is the label required for the answer after completing the conversion process?

5. Convert 500 United States dollars (USD) into Great Britain pounds (GBP).

If you want your students to convert from one unit of measurement into an equivalent currency amount, you must know the conversion rate for the day to properly complete the conversion. The conversion rates for different currencies change daily. Therefore, the exchange rate on Monday may be "1" (United States Dollar, USD) = "0.61" (Great Britain Pounds, GBP), and on Tuesday the conversion rate may change to "1" (USD) = "0.66" (GBP).

By the time students are in 5th grade in the United States, they know the symbol for the word "dollar" (USD) is "$". The symbol for "pound" in the United Kingdom (GBP) is "£". We will solve the first problem below using the abbreviations "USD" and "GBP" and then solve two other problems using the mathematical symbols "$" for dollars and "£" for pounds. You must realize the symbol "$" for dollar(s) and the symbol "£" for pound(s) are symbols which really represent a label, and these labels go to the left of the number rather than to the right of a number. When we first solve the conversion problem using the labels "USD" and "GBP", the labels are to the right of the given numbers, but when we use the symbols "$" and "£", they are to the left of the numbers. Still, the two different types of labels are algebraically treated in the same manner. If you go back to the section in Chapter 5, where we talked about the difference between a variable and a label, we made the comment labels are <u>usually</u> written to the right of the number with the label. These are two of the special situations where the label is written to the left of the number.

> Think about discussing this type of example problem to illustrate number sense, when you have 3-5 minutes to spare. Example number sense problem: Estimate the answer given the problem, "$2\frac{7}{8} \times 10\frac{1}{15} =$?" Multiple choice answers, pick the best answer, "20.5" or "5.9" or "29.76", or "$12\frac{8}{23}$". Ans.= "29.76

We are going to use the Monday conversion rate to convert "500 USD into GBP". If we know that "$1\ USD = 0.61\ GBP$", when you use "Young's Equation/Ratio Theorem", the two ratios indicated will both equal the number <u>1</u>: "$\frac{1\text{ USD}}{0.61\text{ GBP}} = 1 = \frac{0.61\text{ GBP}}{1\text{ USD}}$".

Here is the actual conversion process using "Young's Conversion Theorem": "$500\text{ USD} = \frac{500\text{ USD}}{1} = \frac{500\text{ USD}}{1} \times 1 = \frac{500\text{ USD}}{1} \times \frac{0.61\text{ GBP}}{1\text{ USD}} = \frac{500\text{ USD} \cdot 0.61\text{ GBP}}{1 \cdot 1\text{ USD}} = \frac{500 \cdot 0.61\text{ GBP}}{1} =$

$500 \times 0.61\text{ GBP} = 305\text{ GBP}$".

Notice, this is one of the times there is no period to the right of the abbreviations "USD" and "GBP". Usually, abbreviations for labels in mathematics will have a period to the right of the abbreviation. The reason most abbreviations have a period to the right of the abbreviation is to ensure the students realize the abbreviation is a label and not several variables which are multiplied. When we refer to the examples and indicate every step using both "Young's Equation/Ratio Theorem" and "Young's Conversion Theorem", it seems like a long process. Explain the entire process to students so they understand why the conversion process works. Do not insist they write every step in their homework or test conversion problems, but they should write enough steps to illustrate they understand the two-theorem process.

You must realize the dollar ($) symbol is like any other symbol or word. This means when we write a fraction using the dollar ($) symbol in the numerator and the dollar ($) symbol in the denominator, the symbols cancel. The pound symbol (£) is also treated like any other symbol or word. Just as the dollar ($) symbol in both the numerator and the denominator will cancel, if there is a pound (£) symbol in both the numerator and the denominator of a fraction, the pound (£) symbols will cancel.

In the next example we will use the "$" dollar symbol instead of the abbreviation "USD", and we will use the "£" pound symbol instead of the abbreviation "GBP". Here is what we would expect the students to write on homework or on a test if they are converting "$500" dollars to pounds using the conversion rate for Tuesday.

Step 1: $\$1.00 = £0.66 \quad \therefore \frac{\$1.00}{£0.66} = 1 = \frac{£0.66}{\$1.00}$

Step 2: $\$500 \times 1 = \frac{\$500}{1} \times \frac{£\,0.66}{\$1.00} = \frac{500 \times £\,.66}{1 \times 1} = £330$"

We expect the students will do the actual multiplication problem "500" times ".66" in the numerator of the fraction to the side of the main problem "500 × .66 = 330. We want the students to practice multiplying by the decimal, ".66". Based on our classroom experience working with low achieving students we believe there is a direct correlation between the number of occasions you get the students to use a pencil and a piece of paper to solve arithmetic problems and their improvement with arithmetic computation skills, math estimation skills, and number sense skills. *(FRT 6: The more students write the steps to solve problems, the better their long-term memory will be.)*

Now, try this conversion problem for Wednesday and assume the conversion rate on Wednesday is the same as Monday. Convert £330 in the problem we just computed using the Tuesday rate, back into U.S. Dollars using the Monday conversion rate.

Fact: "$\$1.00 = £0.61 \quad \therefore \quad \frac{\$1.00}{£0.61} = 1 = \frac{£0.61}{\$1.00}$ Use "Young's Equation/Ratio Theorem"

Conversion: $£330 = £330 \times 1 = £330 \times \frac{\$1.00}{£0.61} = \frac{£330}{1} \times \frac{\$1.00}{£0.61} = \frac{330 \times \$1.00}{1 \times 0.61} = \frac{\$330}{.61} = \$540.98$

Use "Young's Conversion Theorem".

Think about what happened when we used the Tuesday rate and started with $500, and then what happened when we used the Monday/Wednesday rate and started with £330. Did you think the difference in the daily rate of £0.05 per $1.00 would make this much difference in the value of the money?

6. Convert 32 oz. to lbs.

This should be an easy conversion problem, and you should be able to determine the answer in your head, but of course we will go through the process and quickly indicate all the steps. We hope many of your students can solve this problem using mental math, but we still want them to understand how to use the rules and procedures to solve the problem. Using "Young's

Equation/Ratio Theorem" you can derive the two following ratios which both equal the number 1. Fact: $16\text{ oz.} = 1\text{ lb.} \therefore \frac{16\text{ oz.}}{1\text{ lb.}} = 1 = \frac{1\text{ lb.}}{16\text{ oz.}}$

It is time to use "Young's Conversion Theorem" and multiply the expression "32 oz." by 1, but you must determine what special form of the number 1 to multiply by. We will write the expression "32 oz." as a fraction with a denominator of 1: "$32\text{ oz.} = \frac{32\text{ oz.}}{1}$". Once the expression, "32 oz.", is written as a fraction with the denominator equal to 1, you need to focus on the label "oz." in the numerator and determine the correct ratio is the ratio with the label "oz." in the denominator.

Here is the solution: $32\ oz. = \frac{32\ oz.}{1} = \frac{32\ oz.}{1} \cdot 1 = \frac{32\ oz.}{1} \cdot \frac{1\ lb.}{16\ oz.} = \frac{32\ oz. \cdot 1\ lb.}{1 \cdot 16\ oz.} = 2\ lbs.$

We assumed everyone would recognize the labels "*oz.*" in the numerator and the denominator cancelled/reduced and became 1 in the last step. We then divided the number "32" in the numerator by the number "16" in the denominator to find the solution "2 *lbs.*".

7. In the beginning of this textbook, we asked you to convert "$\frac{1}{24}$ *in.*" to "ft."

Here is how to solve this problem. Use "Young's Equation/Ratio Theorem" and write two ratios which equal 1: "$12\ in. = 1ft. \therefore \frac{12\ in.}{1\ ft.} = 1 = \frac{1\ ft.}{12\ in.}$". Set up the conversion problem using "Young's Conversion Theorem": "$\frac{1}{24}\text{in.} = \frac{1}{24} \times \frac{in.}{1} = \frac{1\text{ in.}}{24} \times 1 = \frac{1\text{ in.}}{24} \times \frac{1\text{ ft.}}{12\text{ in.}} = \frac{1\text{ in.} \cdot 1\text{ ft.}}{24 \cdot 12\text{ in.}} = \frac{1\text{ ft.}}{288} = \frac{1}{288}$ ft.". The label "in." in the initial problem was written to the right of the fraction. The label was then placed in the numerator to the right of the number "1", which is the correct rule. In the next-to-last fraction, the label "ft." was in the numerator to the right of the number "1", and in the final answer the label "*ft.*" was placed to the right of the fraction, which is also correct. The reason the label "*in.*" in the original problem, which was to the right of the fraction, must go in the numerator is because the problem could be written this way: "$\frac{1}{24} in. = \frac{1}{24} \times \frac{in.}{1} = \frac{1\, in.}{24}$". You must realize you are multiplying two fractions, "$\frac{1}{24}$" and "$\frac{in.}{1}$". When we arrived at this step in the solution, "$\frac{1 \text{ in.}}{24} \times \frac{1 \text{ ft.}}{12 \text{ in.}}$" we multiplied the numerator times the numerator and the denominator times the denominator to determine these two fractions, "$\frac{1 \text{ in.} \cdot 1 \text{ ft.}}{24 \cdot 12 \text{ in.}} = \frac{1 \text{ ft.}}{288}$". If your goal is to write the solution in the correct form, the opposite situation occurred with the last two fractions in the solution: "$\frac{1\, ft.}{288} = \frac{1}{288}\, ft.$". Remember, if there is no operation symbol between a number and a variable, then multiplication is implied. The same assumption is true when there is a label to the right of a number, and you are solving the problem as an algebra-type problem. To emphasize the expression "$\frac{1}{288}\, ft.$" represents a multiplication problem, we could refer to the expression as "$\frac{1}{288}$ *of a foot*" then we hope you realize when we use the simple word "*of* " in this situation, it means you should multiply the two terms, "$\frac{1}{288}$" and the label "*foot*".

Think about how we suggested you introduce new topics for 2-3 minutes on a regular basis for a couple weeks or months prior to requiring the students to solve problems on their own. Do you think your average student will be able to digest all the arithmetic concepts/procedures discussed in the previous paragraphs with respect to converting units, in four or five days? You are likely thinking you only teach the students to divide by 12 when they convert inches to feet, but you need to realize many students get confused when they must decide whether to multiply or divide by the different numbers whether the number is 12 when they are working with feet and inches, 5280 when they are working with feet and miles, or 100 when they are working with centimeters and meters. If you present these steps as we suggest, when your students are required to solve unit conversion problems, they will be prepared to solve more challenging conversion problems in the future. We suggest fourth grade teachers start introducing some of these concepts during the second semester.

Here is a major teaching point for understanding: When you illustrate solutions for problems to students, go overboard to explain the process. List all possible steps, even steps which seem obvious, so all students can understand the process in detail and why certain procedures work. This textbook also tries to do the same thing with written explanations. The author realizes some readers may still be confused when studying the solutions for the first couple problems in a set of examples.

One of the major problems with many mathematics textbooks and solution manuals is, the example problems and explanations in the solution manuals usually show most (but not all) of the mathematics steps. The solutions are presented using the steps an experienced mathematician would write to solve the problems, and there is seldom any type of written explanation to indicate how each step was derived. The assumption in many of these solutions is you should be able to figure out the reason for the steps and fill in the blanks for the steps skipped. Many great mathematics teachers have looked at solutions and asked: "How did they go from one step to the next step?"

You should understand we are trying to give you as much information as possible to explain these problems and at the same time, give you models to illustrate how you may want to explain these problems to your students. We do not expect the students to write every step we write in our solutions. Therefore, you must also give examples of the steps you want the students to write so you know they completely understand the steps involved in the process.

When students are writing the solution to a problem, do not require them to write excessive steps which might not be necessary once they have mastered the process but when you are illustrating the solutions, especially in the introductory lessons, we encourage you to write all the steps to help **all** students understand why the procedures are mathematically correct.

Teaching Point - To prove the stylistic point made frequently throughout this book about repeating explanations, we want to ask you two questions:

1. Can you explain the meaning of the phrase "Symmetric Property"?
2. What does the word "factor" mean?

We mentioned the phrase *Symmetric Property* earlier in this textbook, and we also indicated what the mathematical application of the phrase means. We also used the word *factor* earlier in this textbook. If you already knew what we meant when we used the phrase "Symmetric Property" and the word "factor", then it would not be necessary for us to repeat their meanings. How many people who did not know the meaning of the phrase and the word before they were introduced in this textbook, remember the meaning of the word and the phrase at this moment, without looking back? We also suggested you look up the explanation regarding the "Symmetric Property" on the internet if you were not familiar with the meaning of the phrase. We asked you to write the definitions/explanations of the phrase "Symmetric Property" and the word "factor" in a written assignment. We hope we introduced and reviewed enough so you can quickly explain the meaning of the phrase and word indicated in the last sentence, but if you cannot quickly explain the meanings of the phrase and word without looking back in this textbook, then you know we did not repeat the meanings of the phrase and word enough, so you feel confident explaining both the phrase and word. Repetition in arithmetic and mathematics is a necessary teaching tool at every grade level.

Since we do not expect the students to write every little step indicated in the illustrations, indicated below are shorter solutions for problems 1-4 from the list of example conversion problems just discussed.

1.	Convert 48 oz. to lbs.

16 oz. = 1 lb. $\therefore \frac{16\ oz.}{1\ lb.} = 1 = \frac{1\ lb.}{16\ oz.}$

48 oz. × 1 = $\frac{48\ oz.}{1} \times \frac{1\ lb.}{16\ oz.} = \frac{48\ oz. \times 1\ lb.}{1 \times 16\ oz.} = 3\ lb.$

Some students may still have to do some of the work on scratch paper or off to the side of the problem, such as dividing 48 by 16. If you refer to the illustration which indicates the steps which we encouraged the students to write with fewer steps indicated, the problem is more concise and easier to check and sometimes explain.

2.	Convert $4\frac{3}{4}\ ft.$ to yds.

3 ft. = 1 yd. $\therefore \frac{3\ ft.}{1\ yd.} = 1 = \frac{1\ yd.}{3\ ft.}$

$4\frac{3}{4} ft. = \frac{19\ ft.}{4} \times 1 = \frac{19\ ft.}{4} \times \frac{1\ yd.}{3\ ft.} = \frac{19\ ft. \cdot 1\ yd.}{4 \cdot 3\ ft.} = \frac{19}{12}\ yds. or\ 1\frac{7}{12}\ yds.$

3.	Convert .225 mi. to ft.

1 mi. = 5280 ft. $\therefore \frac{1\ mi.}{5280\ ft.} = 1 = \frac{5280\ ft.}{1\ mi.}$

.225 mi. × 1 = $\frac{.225\ mi.}{1} \times \frac{5280\ ft.}{1\ mi.} = 1{,}188\ ft.$

$$\begin{array}{r} 5280 \\ \times\ .225 \\ \hline 1188 \end{array}$$

Insist that the students write the two ratios which both equal 1 so they will have a visual to decide which ratio to use in the conversion problems--and also insist they indicate in the problem they are multiplying by the number 1. You may not think insisting students indicate they are multiplying by 1 is important, but it better prepares students to understand and solve more difficult problems in algebra and science. We also encouraged students to write the multiplication of two or more fractions as one fraction before they reduce and multiply the numerators and the denominators.

4.	Convert 42 in. to ft.

$$1\,ft. = 12\,in. \quad \therefore \quad \frac{12\,in.}{1\,ft.} = 1 = \frac{1\,ft.}{12\,in.}$$

$$\frac{42\,in.}{1} \times 1 = \frac{42\,in. \cdot 1\,ft.}{1 \cdot 12\,in.} = \frac{42}{12}\,ft. = 3.5\,ft.$$

You need to realize in all four of these problems, the first step indicated in the solution for the four problems involves "Young's Equation/Ratio Theorem". The students must know the required numbers (facts/factors) necessary to convert from one unit into another unit. The second part of each solution focuses on the application of "Young's Conversion Theorem".

We intentionally used detailed illustrations with each solution, not only indicating all the steps, but also writing explanations regarding the arithmetic procedures.

Some books refer to the fractions we derived using "Young's Equation/Ratio Theorem" which equal 1 as "unit multipliers". Some books will also refer to the numbers used to convert from one unit into another unit as "conversion factors": (Example: The number "12" is the conversion factor to multiply by when you are converting 5 feet into 60 inches.) We ask, "How many math and science teachers in middle school or high school use either of these two phrases, (unit multipliers, and conversion factors)?" We also ask, "How many elementary teachers are even familiar with the two phrases, (unit multipliers and conversion factors)?" The phrases "unit multipliers" and "conversion factors" are only used when converting between different units. Since the two phrases are seldom mentioned or used at all in either elementary school, middle school, or high school, that is the reason we decided to name our two Theorems and our two Theorems can be introduced and used for a wide variety of arithmetic and advanced mathematics problems starting with converting fractions into equivalent fractions in 4th grade.

In Chapter 2, we asked you to convert 25 Canadian dollars into United States dollars if the exchange rate is "1 United States Dollar equals 1.09 Canadian Dollars". We will use the abbreviation USD to indicate American dollars and CAD to indicate Canadian dollars. Both countries basically use the same symbol "$" to represent the dollar.

Convert 25 CAD to USD.

$1\ USD = 1.09\ CAD\ \therefore\ \frac{1\ USD}{1.09\ CAD} = 1 = \frac{1.09\ CAD}{1\ USD}$ The two ratios are derived by applying "Young's Equation/Ratio Theorem" to the conversion fact "$1\ USD = 1.09\ CAD$".

$$25\ CAD = 25\ CAD\ \times 1 = \frac{25\ CAD}{1} \times \frac{1\ USD}{1.09\ CAD} = \frac{25\ CAD\ \times\ 1\ USD}{1\ \times\ 1.09\ CAD} = \frac{25\ USD}{1.09} = 22.9357\ USD$$

When we set up the conversion process, we used "Young's Conversion Theorem", then it should be obvious why we needed to divide the number "25" by the number "1.09" based on the label in the given problem and the labels in the two ratios. This example problem requires the students to divide by the decimal "1.09". How many 5th graders remember how to do this division problem without a calculator? You can also review how to round-off the decimal answer, "22.9357 USD" to "22.94 USD". You may want to explain why a financial institution or business will usually round down and disregard the normal rounding-off rules and give you "$22.93" or maybe even slightly less.

The conversion rate of "1 $USD = 1.09$" maybe good on the first Monday in February this year but this conversion rate may not be appropriate again until some Friday next year. Money conversion rates change daily from country to country and seldom will all the conversion rates from all the countries in the world remain the same from one day till the next day. The conversion rates between two specific countries may remain the same for a few days but even the rates between two countries frequently change.

8. Here is a cute made-up word problem to illustrate once you understand the procedures and the application of the two theorems, even something you never heard about becomes an easy arithmetic conversion problem. In the land of "*GupaZupa*", the "*GuZu*" people measure the linear distance from a starting point to an ending point by using the new units of measurement, "*gogoes*" and "*dodoes*". A "*gogo*" is longer than a "*dodo*" and we know 5 "*gogoes*" equals 7 "*dodoes*". The question becomes, how many "*dodoes*" will you have, if you have 18 "*gogoes*"?

This seems like a nonsensical math problem, but it is also easy to solve, if you use "Young's Equation/Ratio Theorem" and "Young's Conversion Theorem" as indicated in previous problems.

Fact: "$5\ gogoes = 7\ dodoes$ $\therefore$ $\frac{5\ gogoes}{7\ dodoes} = 1 = \frac{7\ dodoes}{5\ gogoes}$ This is based on "Young's Equation/Ratio Theorem".

Conversion Process: Use "Young's Conversion Theorem" to complete the conversion procedure. $18\ gogoes = 18\ gogoes \times 1 = \frac{18\ gogoes}{1} \times \frac{7\ dodoes}{5\ gogoes} = \frac{18\ gogoes \times 7\ dodoes}{1 \times 5\ gogoes} =$ $\frac{18 \times 7\ dodoes}{5} = \frac{126\ dodoes}{5} = \frac{126}{5}\ dodoes = 25\frac{1}{5}\ dodoes\ or\ 25.2\ dodoes$

You could also solve these basic conversion problems by using two equal ratios and then solve using the cross-multiplication theorem. The reason we prefer to use "Young's Equation/Ratio Theorem" and "Young's Conversion Theorem" to solve these example conversion problems is fourfold.

1. It is easy to illustrate how to use the two theorems when students are converting fractions into equivalent fractions when they learn to add and subtract fractions.
2. If you use "Young's Equation/Ratio Theorem" and "Young's Conversion Theorem" to solve these basic conversion problems, your students will find the process not only works for basic conversions like the example problems, but it also works for a wide variety of other mathematics conversion problems.
3. By using the two theorems, you will be preparing students to work with a wide variety of science and engineering problems when several labels are involved.
4. When you solve the conversion problems in the next section, it is much simpler to use "Young's Equation/Ratio Theorem" and "Young's Conversion Theorem" than it is to use several ratios and set up a couple different cross-multiplication problems. Once you understand the Power of the Number One (1), "Young's Equation/Ratio Theorem", and "Young's Conversion Theorem", the seemingly impossible becomes possible.

> Again, the advanced form of "Young's Conversion Theorem" is: If you multiply any mathematical expression by a fraction, ratio, term, or expression equal to 1, then the ending mathematical expression will be equivalent to the original mathematical expression even though they might not look identical. The only time the starting and ending mathematical

expressions will look identical is if you multiply by the number "1" or the fraction "$\frac{1}{1}$".

Here are some more challenging Conversion Problems for 6th grade and beyond.

9.	Convert 50 $\frac{mi.}{hr.}$ (50 mph) into $\frac{ft.}{min.}$

If you want to begin working with this conversion problem, you must understand what the abbreviation "*mph*" means. Most people know the abbreviation "*mph*" represents the phrase "miles per hour". The important question is, "What does the work "per" mean in this expression?" The definition of the word "per" in arithmetic means three things: 1. Write as a ratio; 2. Divide; or 3. Write the numerator of the fraction using the variable/label of the first letter, and then the denominator of the fraction is the variable/label of the second letter. Therefore, we know the abbreviation "*mph*" is a ratio because of the word "per".

Teaching Point: When you are working with an expression with the word "per", you need to realize, often the label in the denominator after the word "per" contains an invisible number. The invisible number which is not written in this example problem but implied is the number 1 to the left of the label "hr." Therefore, you need to emphasize the expression "50 $\frac{\text{mi.}}{\text{hr.}}$" more specifically means "$\frac{\text{50 mi.}}{\text{1 hr.}}$". There are ratios involving the word "per" and the label in the denominator is a number other than 1 written with the label and we will illustrate a few of these types of situations.

Here are two example problems where the number in the denominator is not 1. If you are taking cough syrup the directions may say, "Take one tablespoon of syrup every 4 hours.

The problem could be stated in the following way, 1 tablespoon per 4 hours, mathematically written as: "$\frac{1\ tablespoon}{4\ hours}$". If you are in a store and the price is \$1.60 for (per) 3 cans of corn, the following ratio could be written "$\frac{\$1.60}{3\ cans}$".

Invisible numbers are often not written in arithmetic and mathematics expressions, especially the numbers 1 and 0. When these situations occur, it is the responsibility of the teacher to specifically point out to the students that the invisible numbers are present. The decimal point in an integer is an implied mathematical notation which is not always written along with the number "2" in a square root problem. A positive sign is always understood to be present to the left of any number or term when there is no sign indicated and a multiplication operation is understood to be present when two or more variables are written together in an expression. There are other situations in arithmetic and mathematics where numbers, signs, symbols, and labels are implied but not written. Can you think of any of these situations on your own? Prior to explaining the expression "$50\ mph = \frac{50\ mi.}{1\ hr.}$" we frequently inserted the number 1 in the denominator of several fractions when we illustrated our solutions. The number 1 written in the denominator of any number, term, or expression without a denominator indicated is always understood to be present if needed. We define numbers, signs, symbols, and labels as *invisible* numbers, signs, symbols, and labels when they are understood to be present when needed but not normally written.

To solve the indicated problem, there are two facts students must know: "$1\ mi. = 5280\ ft.$" and "$60\ min. = 1\ hr.$". The students can derive two sets of different ratios for each of the indicated facts using "Young's Equation/Ratio Theorem". Start with the fact "1 mi. = 5280 ft.". You can write the following two ratios, which equal 1, "$\frac{1\ \text{mi.}}{5280\ \text{ft.}} = 1$" and

"$\frac{5280\text{ ft.}}{1\text{ mi.}} = 1$". The second fact is "60 min. = 1 hr.". Using "Young's Equation /Ratio Theorem"

again, you can derive the following two ratios which equal 1, "$\frac{60\text{ min.}}{1\text{ hr.}} = 1 = \frac{1\text{ hr.}}{60\text{ min.}}$".

We are now going to use "Young's Conversion Theorem" to complete the conversion process, but in this problem since there are two different labels to convert. We are going to multiply by the number 1 twice.

$$50\frac{mi.}{hr.} = \frac{50}{1}\cdot\frac{mi.}{hr.} = \frac{50\cdot mi.}{1\cdot hr.} \times 1 \times 1 = \frac{50\cdot mi.}{1\cdot hr.} \times \frac{5280\cdot ft.}{1\cdot mi.} \times \frac{1\cdot hr.}{60\cdot min.} = \frac{50\cdot mi.\cdot 5280\cdot ft.\cdot 1\cdot hr.}{1\cdot hr.\cdot 1\cdot mi.\cdot 60\cdot min.} =$$

$$\frac{50\cdot 5280\,ft.}{60\cdot min.} = \frac{2\cdot 5\cdot 5\cdot 2\cdot 2\cdot 2\cdot 2\cdot 2\cdot 3\cdot 5\cdot 11\cdot ft.}{2\cdot 2\cdot 3\cdot 5\cdot min.} = \frac{4400\cdot ft.}{min.} = 4400\frac{ft.}{min.}\ or\ 4400\,ft.\ per\ min.$$

In the given problem, we wrote "$50\frac{mi.}{hr.}$". Understand there is no symbol indicated between the number "50" and the fraction "$\frac{mi.}{hr.}$". Therefore, this is algebraically interpreted to be a multiplication problem. You must realize you can rewrite the number "50" as a fraction, "$\frac{50}{1}$", so you are really multiplying the two fractions "$\frac{50}{1}\cdot\frac{mi.}{hr.}$", which illustrates why we write the ratio "$\frac{50\cdot mi.}{1\cdot hr.}$".

As indicated above, we multiplied by the number 1 twice because we had two different units (labels) to convert: miles to feet and hours to minutes. We substituted the two appropriate ratios for the number 1 when we multiplied to ensure the units cancelled in the numerator and denominator: "miles in the given numerator and miles in the denominator of the first ratio" and "hours in the given denominator and hours in the numerator of the second ratio". We formed one fraction and canceled the appropriate units. This is a confusing problem to convert if you use the cross-multiplication method.

Now take some time and re-study the indicated steps used to convert 50 miles per hour into feet per minute. When we wrote the fraction with the numbers and the units (feet and minutes), we decided to use "factor trees" to reduce. By the time students get this far in 5th grade arithmetic, they will probably be able to reduce the number 50 in the numerator and the number 60 in the denominator by simply dividing both numbers by 10 to get the fraction, "$\frac{50}{60} = \frac{5}{6}$". Therefore, at one point in the problem the fraction is, "$\frac{50 \cdot 5280\,ft.}{60 \cdot min.}$", and then the new fraction is "$\frac{5 \cdot 5280\,ft.}{6 \cdot min.}$". You will have to decide how often you want the students to use "factor trees" when they reduce, multiply, and divide fractions. We do not expect students to use *"factor trees"* 100% of the time when they reduce, multiply, and divide fractions, but we also do not want the students to forget that factoring is the first step when they are working with difficult fraction problems and when they are working with algebra fraction problems. You may then reduce the numbers 5280 in the numerator and the 6 in the denominator by dividing both numbers by 6. You then have 5 X 880, giving you the final number 4400 and the final units "$\frac{ft.}{min.}$".

There is one minor notation you may not have noticed when we wrote the abbreviation "*mph*" which represents the phrase/ratio "miles per hour". The notation we are going to mention may seem minor, but it is important when working with units. When we abbreviate labels, we <u>almost</u> always place a period to the right of the abbreviation. Not only is this proper notation, but when you are introducing algebra variables (letters), if there is no operation between the variables (letters), it means the variables are multiplied. In special situations when working with abbreviations we use often, we know the letters in the abbreviation are not multiplied because the abbreviations represent a word, label, unit, or phrase. If you do not write the period to the right of the abbreviation, someone may think the abbreviation represents several variables which are multiplied. That is why the period to the right of an abbreviation is important. The abbreviation "*mph*" is used so much in the United States it is assumed you know it represents the phrase "miles per hour".

> It seems so obvious when we say "$\frac{5}{5} = 1, \frac{77}{77} = 1, etc.$", one may say, we can cancel or reduce the "5's" and the "77's" in the fractions, but the real reason both fractions equal "1" is because these types of fractions represent division problems such as "$\frac{5}{5} = 5 \div 5 = 1$ and $\frac{77}{77} = 77 \div 77 = 1, etc.$" The application of the division process is why they both equal "1".

At the end of this textbook, Chapter 8, we use arithmetic rules and the two indicated theorems to simplify and solve some algebra, precalculus, and calculus problems. We will also further illustrate the Power of the Number One (1) when working with arithmetic, algebra, precalculus, and calculus problems.

> 10. Convert "2 $ft.^2$" into "$in.^2$":

In this example problem, the labels are written as "$ft.^2$" and "$in.^2$". In a geometry class many teachers prefer the notation: "square feet (sq. ft.)" and "square inches (sq. in.)". If you need to work with labels algebraically, you must write the labels using exponential notation: "$ft.^2$" and "$in.^2$".

Fact: 1 ft. = 12 in. $\therefore$ $\frac{1\,ft.}{12\,in.} = 1 = \frac{12\,in.}{1\,ft.}$ Of course, the two ratios were derived by using "Young's Equation/Ratio Theorem". Now, use "Young's Conversion Theorem" to complete the conversion process.

$$2\,ft.^2 = 2 \cdot ft. \cdot ft. = \frac{2 \cdot ft. \cdot ft.}{1} = \frac{2 \cdot ft. \cdot ft.}{1} \times 1 \times 1 = \frac{2 \cdot ft. \cdot ft.}{1} \times \frac{12\,in.}{1\,ft.} \times \frac{12\,in.}{1\,ft.} =$$

$$\frac{2 \cdot ft. \cdot ft. \cdot 12 \cdot in. \cdot 12 \cdot in.}{1 \cdot 1 \cdot ft. \cdot 1 \cdot ft.} = \frac{2 \cdot 12 \cdot in. \cdot 12 \cdot in.}{1} = 288 \cdot in. \cdot in. = 288\,in.^2$$

> When you encounter a fraction written in factored form such as, "$\frac{35}{55} = \frac{5 \times 7}{5 \times 11} = \frac{5}{5} \cdot \frac{7}{11}$", we say cancel or reduce, the number "5" in both the numerator and denominator. The reason this trick works is because we know the fraction "$\frac{5}{5} = 1$".

We multiplied by the number 1 twice when we illustrated how to solve the previous problem. When a number has an exponent of "2", it means you have the number times itself. If you understand this concept regarding numbers and exponents, you should then use the same logic to write "$ft.^2 = ft. \cdot ft.$". We needed to remove the label "$ft.$" twice because of the exponent, so this is the reason we multiplied by the number 1 twice when we completed the conversion problem. This is also the reason why the next to last step in the solution, "$288 \cdot in. \cdot in.$", became, "$288\ in.^2$".

Students could solve this problem by multiplying by the number 1 once if they know the following fact: "$1\ ft.^2 = 144\ in.^2 \therefore \frac{1\ ft.^2}{144\ in.^2} = 1 = \frac{144\ in.^2}{1\ ft.^2}$". We derived the two ratios by using "Young's Equation/Ration Theorem". The reason we did not initially use these two ratios is because very few students know "$1\ \text{ft.}^2 = 144\ \text{in.}^2$". This fact is seldom understood and remembered by the best math students, and it seems to be a conversion fact, average and low-level math students never remember. Once you have the two ratios you can easily use "Young's Conversion Theorem" to find the final answer by multiplying by the number 1 only one time as illustrated: "$2\ ft^2 = 2ft.^2 \times 1 = \frac{2\ ft.^2}{1} \times \frac{144\ in.^2}{1\ ft.^2} = 288\ in.^2$".

Teachers frequently assume the students realize certain things in math are obvious, but you should never assume the obvious is understood by all students. In fact, math topics/procedures we think are obvious are not obvious to many students.

You must explain the little things to all students, your goal should be to ensure over 90% of your students master the concepts which are necessary for the grade level you are teaching. This is the reason we mentioned the expression "*50 mph*" is really the number "50" times the ratio "$\frac{\text{mi.}}{\text{hr.}}$" in the first problem--and this is the reason we mentioned "ft.^2" really means "ft.× ft." in the second problem.

We explained the two words "fraction" and "ratio" are not perfect synonyms at the end of Chapter 2. We gave a detailed explanation regarding the subtle differences between fractions and ratios early in this textbook and then continually used the two words throughout the textbook. Are you able to explain the differences between the two words fraction and ratio? Please realize we only gave the explanation regarding the differences once. If you do not remember the differences between the two words, we strongly suggest you go back to Chapter 2 and refresh your memory since we use these two words frequently throughout this textbook. If the goal is to have you "learn and remember" the similarities and differences between the two words "fraction" and "ratio", maybe we need to reference the similarities and differences more frequently.

An amazing outcome occurred when we taught low achieving math students to work with prime numbers and factor trees when they simplified fraction problems. Their focus on the factor trees helped them memorize the multiplication tables and understand exponent notation, but most importantly, they improved significantly when they were required to reduce, multiply, and divide all types of fraction problems. This topic may prove to be a topic of interest for future math education researchers to investigate. We talked about "prime numbers" and "factor trees" as often as possible, at least twice a week, when we worked with students who were in grades, "9-12" and previously struggled with arithmetic throughout their education careers.

11. If a pipe is leaking water at the following rate, 144 cubic yards per day, "144 $\frac{yds.^3}{day}$", how many cubic feet is this per minute, "$\frac{ft.^3}{min.}$"?

Here is the same question written so the number in the denominator with the label is not the number 1, "$\frac{144\ ft.^2}{24\ hr.}$". If a pipe is leaking water at the rate of 144 cubic yards every 24 hours, how many cubic feet is this per minute? We only rewrote the problem in the second form to illustrate the number in the denominator with the label in this type of problem does not need to equal 1.

Facts: $3\,ft. = 1\,yd. \quad \therefore \quad \frac{3\,ft.}{1\,yd.} = 1 = \frac{1\,yd.}{3\,ft.}$ and $60\,min. = 1\,hr. \quad \therefore \quad \frac{60\,min.}{1\,hr.} = 1 = \frac{1\,hr.}{60\,min.}$

and $24\,hrs. = 1\,day \quad \therefore \quad \frac{24\,hrs.}{1\,day} = 1 = \frac{1\,day}{24\,hrs.}$

Conversion:

$$144\,\frac{yd.^3}{day} = \frac{144\,yd.^3}{day} = \frac{144 \cdot yd. \cdot yd. \cdot yd.}{day} = \frac{144 \cdot yd. \cdot yd. \cdot yd.}{day} \times 1 \times 1 \times 1 \times 1 \times 1 =$$

$$\frac{144 \cdot yd. \cdot yd. \cdot yd.}{1\,day} \times \frac{3\,ft.}{1\,yd.} \times \frac{3\,ft.}{1\,yd.} \times \frac{3\,ft.}{1\,yd.} \times \frac{1\,day}{24\,hr.} \times \frac{1\,hr.}{60\,min.} = \frac{144 \cdot 3 \cdot ft. \cdot 3 \cdot ft. \cdot 3 \cdot ft.}{24 \cdot 60\,min.} =$$

$$\frac{6 \cdot 3 \cdot ft. \cdot 3 \cdot ft. \cdot 3 \cdot ft.}{1 \cdot 60\,min.} = \frac{1 \cdot 3 \cdot ft. \cdot 3 \cdot ft. \cdot 3\ ft.}{10\,min.} = \frac{27 \cdot ft.\ ft.\ ft.}{10\,min.} = \frac{27\,ft.^3}{10\,min.} = 2.7\,\frac{ft.^3}{min.}$$

(Note: We multiplied by the number 1 five times. Three of the 1's indicated in the conversion problem are necessary to convert the label "$yd.^3$" which equals "$yd. \times yd. \times yd.$" to "$ft. \times ft. \times ft.$" which equals "$ft.^3$". We also needed to convert days to hours and then hours to minutes which required us to multiply by the number 1 two additional times. Thus, we need to multiply by 1 five times to complete the conversion process.)

When we reduced the fraction "$\frac{144 \cdot 3 \cdot ft. \cdot 3 \cdot ft. \cdot 3 \cdot ft.}{24 \cdot 60\,min}$", we realized the number "24" divided into the number "144" "6" times. That is why in the next fraction the number "6" is in the numerator and the number "24" became "1" in the denominator, "$\frac{6 \cdot 3 \cdot ft. \cdot 3 \cdot ft. \cdot 3 \cdot ft.}{1 \cdot 60\,min.}$". Next divide the number "6" in the numerator and the number "60" in the denominator by "6" to get the number "10" in the denominator, "$\frac{3 \cdot ft. \cdot 3 \cdot ft. \cdot 3 \cdot ft.}{10\,min.}$". The fraction then becomes, "$\frac{27 \cdot ft. \cdot ft. \cdot ft.}{10\,min}$". The rest of the steps to solve the problem should be evident.

You will find low achieving math students have great difficulty identifying a specific number to divide into two large numbers in the numerator and the denominator. When we encouraged students to rewrite the numbers using factor trees with prime numbers, we found all students showed improvement when they reduced fractions with large numbers, but the low achieving students illustrated the most improvement. *(FRT 13: If students frequently use "factor trees" when working with fractions, will their fraction arithmetic skills improve?)*

Back to the problem now: do you think this is a big pipe or a small pipe compared to the pipes in a typical house? Notice we multiplied by the number 1 five times. We could multiply by the number 1 twice if we used these two lesser known facts: "$27\ ft.^3 = 1\ yd.^3$ $\therefore$ $\frac{27\ ft.^3}{1\ yd.^3} = 1 = \frac{1\ yd.^3}{27\ ft.^3}$" and "$1440\ min. = 1\ day$ $\therefore$ $\frac{1440\ min.}{1\ day} = 1 = \frac{1\ day}{1440\ min.}$". The conversion process would look like this: "$\frac{144\ yd.^3}{1\ day} = \frac{144\ yd.^3}{1\ day} \times 1 \times 1 = \frac{144\ yd.^3}{1\ day} \times \frac{27\ ft.^3}{1\ yd.^3} \times \frac{1\ day}{1440\ min.}$". Notice, the first number in the numerator is "144" and the last number in the denominator is "1440". Did you realize the number "144" must divide into the number "1440" exactly "10" times? You would then have the following fraction after the labels are cancelled, "$\frac{27\ ft.^3}{10\ min.}$", and you should be able to derive the final answer as indicated above, "$\frac{27\ ft.^3}{10\ min.}$ *or* $2.7\ \frac{ft.^3}{min.}$ *or* $2.7\ ft.^3$ *per min.*

In the First Assignment, questions "14-23" pages 11-13, we asked you to convert several problems involving units of measurement into equivalent units of measurement. Then we asked you to explain why both the number changed and the units changed in each conversion problem. Most of you were probably comfortable explaining why the numbers changed, but we suspect many of you felt uncomfortable using mathematical logic to explain why the labels changed from feet to inches or hours to minutes. Hopefully, you now understand the arithmetic involved when converting both the numbers and the units when solving a wide variety of arithmetic conversion problems.

The process of focusing on unit conversions is important in engineering, architecture, chemistry, physics, and other advanced math and science professions, but it is also helpful with arithmetic conversion problems. The process is referred to as "Dimensional Analysis". The two-word phrase, "Dimensional Analysis" is not a phrase commonly mentioned in high school mathematics or science textbooks, but it is a phrase well known by college math and science professors.

Since the two-word phrase, "Dimensional Analysis", is not a common phrase to many people, one of the purposes of this textbook is to introduce the procedures of "Dimensional Analysis", to students starting in elementary school. "Dimensional Analysis" is the basis for the two theorems, "Young's Equation/Ratio Theorem" and "Young's Conversion Theorem".

12. In the imaginary land of "*GupaZupa*", we already know when the "*GuZu*" people measure the length of something, they use the two units of linear measurement referred to as "*dodoes*" and "*gogoes*". We know this important fact, "5 *gogoes* = 7 *dodoes*". Another amazing thing about the inhabitants of "*GupaZupa*" is they measure time using the following two types of units, "*zipps*" and "*dipps*". They told us 3 "*zipps*" is the same amount of time as 10 "*dipps*". Now, imagine you are flying along in your "*SpecialDecialHoverCraft*" at the following rate, "150 *gogoes per zipp*". We wonder what the rate would be if we use the ratio, "$\frac{dodoes}{dipp}$"?

Incidentally, you may ask the students which unit of time is the larger unit, "*zipps*" or "*dipps*"? Can you explain to your students why "*zipps*" must represent a larger unit of time than "*dipps*"?

Facts: $5\ gogoes = 7\ dodoes$ $\therefore$ $\frac{5\ gogoes}{7\ dodoes} = 1 = \frac{7\ dodoes}{5\ gogoes}$ and $3\ zipps = 10\ dipps$

$\therefore$ $\frac{3\ zipps}{10\ dipps} = 1 = \frac{10\ dipps}{3\ zipps}$

We used "Young's Equation/Ratio Theorem" to determine all four ratios.

Conversion: $150\ gogoes\ per\ zipp = 150\ \frac{gogoes}{zipp} = \frac{150}{1} \cdot \frac{gogoes}{zipp} = \frac{150\ gogoes}{1\ zipp} = \frac{150\ gogoes}{1\ zipp} \times$

$1 \times 1 = \frac{150\ gogoes}{1\ zipp} \times \frac{7\ dodoes}{5\ gogoes} \times \frac{3\ zipps}{10\ dipps} = \frac{150\ gogoes \cdot 7\ dodoes \cdot 3\ zipps}{1\ zipp \cdot 5\ gogoes \cdot 10\ dipps} = \frac{150 \cdot 7\ dodoes \cdot 3}{1 \cdot 5 \cdot 10\ dipps} =$

$\frac{150 \cdot 7 \cdot 3 \cdot dodoes}{1 \cdot 50 \cdot dipps} = \frac{3 \cdot 7 \cdot 3\ dodoes}{1\ dipp} = \frac{63\ dodoes}{dipp} = 63\ \frac{dodoes}{dipp} = \quad 63\ dodoes\ per\ dipp$

We could have used factor trees to reduce the numbers, but in this case the numbers reduced so easily, using factor trees was not necessary. Perhaps no one ever considered converting these types of measurements, but once you understand how to use both "Young's Equation/Ratio Theorem" and "Young's Conversion Theorem", you can sometimes do the unimaginable and make it seem simple. If we used factor trees to reduce the fraction, "$\frac{150\ gogoes\ \cdot\ 7\ dodoes\ \cdot\ 3\ zipps}{1\ zipp\ \cdot\ 5\ gogoes\ \cdot 10\ dipps}$", the fraction could be rewritten as:

"$\frac{150\ \cdot\ 7\ \cdot\ 3\ \cdot\ gogoes\ \cdot\ dodoes\ \cdot\ zipps}{1\ \cdot\ 5\ \cdot\ 10\ \cdot\ zipp\ \cdot\ gogoes\ \cdot\ dipps} = \frac{2\ \cdot\ 3\ \cdot\ 5\ \cdot\ 5\ \cdot\ 7\ \cdot\ 3\ \cdot\ gogoes\ \cdot\ dodoes\ \cdot\ zipps}{1\ \cdot\ 5\ \cdot\ 2\ \cdot\ 5\ \cdot\ zipp\ \cdot\ gogoes\ \cdot\ dipps} =$

$\frac{3\ \cdot\ 7\ \cdot\ 3\ \cdot\ dodoes}{1\ \cdot\ dipp} = \frac{63\ \cdot\ dodoes}{1\ \cdot\ dipp} = 63\ \frac{dodoes}{dipp}$".

The following problem is example problem number 5 from Chapter 3: "$\frac{5628}{7392} + \frac{7007}{7392} - \frac{6798}{7392}$". When we wrote the final answer "$\frac{5837}{7392}$", we made the statement this fraction will not reduce, and we would explain why later in this textbook. The first step when you want to reduce a challenging arithmetic fraction or an algebra rational expression is, "Factor both the numerator and the denominator." Here are the factor trees for both numbers:

5837	7392
13×449	2×3696
	$2 \times 2 \times 1848$
	$2 \times 2 \times 2 \times 924$
	$2 \times 2 \times 2 \times 2 \times 462$
	$2 \times 2 \times 2 \times 2 \times 2 \times 231$
	$2 \times 2 \times 2 \times 2 \times 2 \times 3 \times 77$
	$2 \times 2 \times 2 \times 2 \times 2 \times 3 \times 7 \times 11$

When we set up the fraction using the factor trees, it is immediately obvious there are no identical factors in both the numerator and the denominator, which is the only requirement when you determine whether a fraction will reduce.

$$\text{"}\frac{13 \cdot 449}{2 \cdot 2 \cdot 2 \cdot 2 \cdot 2 \cdot 3 \cdot 7 \cdot 11}\text{"}$$

When we illustrated the procedures to work with the conversion problems in this chapter, we continually illustrated how to use both "Young's Equation/Ratio Theorem" and "Young's Conversion Theorem" to complete the conversions. If you are in college and preparing to be an Engineer, Chemist, Physicist, etc., you may be required to purchase a book which contains the two words, "Dimensional Analysis" in the title. We doubt that many high school math teachers ever mention the phrase "Dimensional Analysis". If you understand how to use the two theorems repeatedly discussed and illustrated in this book, starting with finding equivalent fractions in 3rd or 4th grade, finding equivalent units of measurement in this chapter, and solving additional problems discussed later in this textbook - you have a basic understanding of what is meant by the two words, "Dimensional Analysis". "Young's Equation/Ratio Theorem" and "Young's Conversion Theorem" can be used in elementary school through high school and in high level college math and science courses which require students to convert challenging units of measurements into equivalent units of measurement. The expression "Dimensional Analysis" is generally only emphasized in professions where mathematics and labels are a necessity when solving problems which must be accurate and concise regarding the numbers and the units/labels in the final answer.

Interleaving previously learned concepts into additional problems included for homework, classwork, tests, and quizzes is a special way to review and not use classroom time. Seldom do textbooks interleave as frequently as we would like, but you can help students "learn and remember" topics for longer periods of time if you frequently interleave concepts into your classroom discussions, homework assignments, tests, and quizzes.

We have continually referred to three different notations to write a division problem. First, you may use fraction notation and the division sign is the horizontal line between the numerator and the denominator. Second, you may use the standard division symbol, "÷", between two terms. Third, you may use the division box with the divisor outside the box and the dividend inside the division box. If you are a secondary math teacher, can you think of a fourth basic notation which indicates division? Consider the following example: "$(16)(4^{-1})$". When you interpret this problem is it permissible to write the problem in one of the two following forms, "$16 \div 4 \; or \; \frac{16}{4}$"? When you introduce and teach negative exponents you might want to tell your students, negative exponents indicate division.

Two interesting number sense problems. Given the multiplication problem, "$\frac{3}{4} \times \frac{1}{2} =?$", is the product greater than "$\frac{3}{4}$" or less than "$\frac{3}{4}$"? Given the division problem, "$\frac{3}{4} \div \frac{1}{2} =?$", is the quotient greater than "$\frac{3}{4}$" or less than "$\frac{3}{4}$"? Many college graduates guess incorrectly when they are asked these two questions. In the multiplication problem the product, $\frac{3}{8}$", is less than "$\frac{3}{4}$" and in the division problem the quotient, "$\frac{6}{4} = \frac{3}{2} = 1\frac{1}{2}$" is greater than "$\frac{3}{4}$". Number sense when working with fractions, especially fractions greater than "0" and less than"1", creates unexpected results (Siegler, Lortie – Forgues et. al. 2015).

Sixth Assignment

COMPLETE THE FOLLOWING CONVERSION FACTS

A. Fill in the appropriate number for the value(s) of "x" in the following problems. The second fact in each question is probably a situation you never considered. We understand and just answer the question in each problem using your number sense memory and the given example. (Interesting comment: There is always a space between a number and a label. There is no space between a number and a variable.)

1. $1\ mi. = x\ ft.$ or $1\ ft. = \ x\ mi.$ (Answer: $1\ ft. = \frac{1}{5280}\ mi.$)
2. $1\ mi. = x\ yds.$ or $1\ yd. = x\ mi.$
3. $1\ gal. = x\ qts.$ or $1\ qt. = x\ gals.$
4. $1\ hr. = x\ min.$ or $1\ min. = x\ hrs.$
5. $1\ hr. = x\ sec.$ or $1\ sec. = x\ hrs.$
6. $1\ ton = x\ lbs.$ or $1\ lb. = x\ tons$
7. $1\ m. = x\ cm.$ or $1\ cm = x\ m$ (Interesting fact: Frequently in the metric system, the abbreviations do not end with a period to indicate the notation is an abbreviation. Meter is the U. S. spelling for the unit meters, but the Commonwealth spelling is "*Metre*".)
8. $1ft.^2 = 144\ in.^2$ or $1in.^2 = \ x\ ft.^2$
9. $1yd.^2 = 9\ ft.^2$ or $1\ ft.^2 = \ x\ yd.^2$
10. $1yd.^3 = 27\ ft.^3$ or $1ft.^3 = \ x\ yd.^3$

These are only a few conversion facts you may want to be familiar with. We could write several pages of conversion facts but in today's world of cell phones, if you do not know a conversion fact you can quickly look up the conversion fact for any common conversion you will ever encounter.

CREATE TWO FRACTIONS OR RATIOS WHICH BOTH EQUAL ONE (1)

B. Given the conversion fact, write two equal ratios which both equal one (1)

11. $1\ day = 24\ hrs.$

12. $1000\ ml = 1\ l$

13. $32\ U.S. fluid\ oz. = 1\ qt.$

14. $1\ U.S. cup = 48\ teaspoons$

15. $\$1 = 10$ dimes

16. $1000\ cm^3 = 1\ l$

The numbers "<u>24</u>", "<u>1000</u>", "<u>32</u>", "<u>48</u>", "<u>10</u>", and <u>1000</u>" in problems 11, 12, 13, 14, 15, and 16 are all considered "conversion factors". They are referred to as factors because when you convert from one unit into another equivalent unit you will frequently multiply by the appropriate number indicated, but sometimes divide.

WRITE ALL THE STEPS INDICATED IN THE EXAMPLE BELOW TO COMPLETE EACH CONVERSION PROBLEM IN THE NEXT THREE SECTIONS – PROBLEMS 17. – 37.

Example: Convert "108 in. into yards" - Fact: $1\ yd. = 36\ in.\ \therefore\ \frac{36\ in.}{1\ yd.} = 1 = \frac{1\ yd.}{36\ in.}$

Conversion: "$108\ in. = \frac{108\ in.}{1} = \frac{108\ in.}{1} \times 1 = \frac{108\ in.}{1} \times \frac{1\ yd.}{36\ in.} = \frac{108\ in. \times 1\ yd.}{1 \times 36\ in.} = \frac{108\ yds.}{36} = 3\ yds.$

C. Write all the steps illustrated in the example above to complete the following conversions. Once you become <u>experienced</u> solving these conversion problems by writing all the steps, then it might not be necessary to write every step indicated, but in the beginning, you need to understand why any trick which you may use in the future will work based on sound mathematics principals. Go back and look at your written explanations in the "First Assignment" when you were required to explain why a unit changed from one unit into another unit in different conversion problems.

17. $672\ in. = x\ ft.$

18. $500\ tons = x\ lbs.$

19. $7.5\ yds. = x\ ft.$

20. $775\ yds. = x\ mi.$

21. $82\frac{3}{4} ft. = x\ in.$

22. $82\frac{3}{4} ft. = x\ yds.$

23. $2\frac{1}{2}\ in. = x\ ft.$

24. $1000\ ft. = x\ mi.$

25. $1550\ lbs. = x\ tons$

UNCOMMON CONVERSION FACTS REQUIRED FOR SPECIAL SITUATIONS

D. If necessary, look up the conversion facts to complete the indicated conversions below. A calculator may be beneficial for some problems, but not all problems.

26. $7\frac{1}{3}\ fathoms = x\ feet$ Look up the conversion fact for feet and fathoms.

27. $5000\ in.^2 = x\ yds.^2$ Look up the conversion fact for square inches and square yards.

28. $8000\ ft. = x\ M$ Look up the conversion fact for feet in a nautical mile. The abbreviation "M" is used by the International Hydrographic Organization. The abbreviation "NM" is used by the International Civil Aviation Organization to represent a Nautical mile. At this time, you may ignore the 1.386 inches indicated in the conversion.

29. $67.29\ in. = x\ cm.$ Round the answer off to two decimal places.

30. $72\ cm^3 = x\ kg$ Assume all "$72\ cm^3$" are filled with water.

31. $0.6\ oz. = x\ grams$ Look up the conversion fact for grams and ounces.

SOLVE THE CONVERSIONS USING ONE, TWO, THREE OR MORE CONVERSION FACTS

E. You will need to know two or more conversion facts to complete the conversion problems which follow. Only use common conversion facts which most people should already know. You should not have to look up any conversion facts on your smartphone. A calculator may be beneficial for some problems.

32. $85\ cm^3 = x\ m^3$

33. $70\ \frac{km}{hr.} = x\ \frac{cm}{min.}$

34. $72 \frac{ft.^3}{day} = x\ \frac{yds.^3}{week}$

35. $73\ psi = x\ \frac{ozs.}{ft.^2}$ You need to recognize the abbreviation "psi" represents pounds of force per square inch inside an inflated object.

36. $85\ ft.^2 = x\ yds.^2$

37. $80\ mph = x\ \frac{in.}{sec.}$

ADD AND SUBTRACT THE FOLLOWING FRACTION PROBLEMS.

F. IF YOU DO NOT KNOW THE LCD BASED ON YOUR MULTIPLICATION AND DIVISION FACT KNOWLEDGE, THEN ILLUSTRATE HOW TO <u>FIND THE LCD</u> AND ILLUSTRATE ALL THE STEPS TO CONVERT THE FRACTIONS, WHEN NECESSARY, INTO EQUIVALENT FRACTIONS. You should be able to solve some of these problems by using mental math skills you have developed with many years of practice. If you can solve the problem using your mental math skills then just illustrate the basic steps, but always illustrate you multiply by the number 1 and then substitute a fraction or ratio equal to 1, so we know you understand the procedures. Reduce all solutions and write final answers as mixed numbers when appropriate.

38. $\left(\frac{7}{15}+\frac{23}{25}\right)-\left(\frac{7}{30}+\frac{3}{40}\right)$

39. $\left(\frac{7}{27}-\frac{1}{18}\right)+\left(\frac{43}{54}-\frac{7}{36}\right)$

40. $\left(5-\frac{11}{15}\right)-4$

41. $6\frac{7}{12}+5\frac{7}{30}-10\frac{3}{50}$

42. $\frac{3}{4}-\frac{7}{8}+\frac{11}{12}-\frac{1}{20}$

43. $301\frac{1}{2}+290\frac{1}{6}-370\frac{11}{12}$

44. $6\frac{5}{6}+11-\left(2\frac{2}{3}+4\frac{1}{15}-5\frac{3}{20}\right)$

COMMUTATIVE PROPERTY FOR ADDITION AND MULTIPLICATION, ASSOCIATIVE PROPERTY FOR ADDITION AND MULTIPLICATION, REFLEXIVE PROPERTY, SYMMETRIC PROPERTY, AND TRANSITIVE PROPERTY IN ARITHEMTIC AND ADVANCED MATH

G. Indicate which property is illustrated in the problems "45. – 51.". Remember the Commutative and Associative Properties apply to Addition and Multiplication Problems and the Reflexive, Symmetric, and Transitive Properties focus on equations. How can you consider yourself qualified to teach arithmetic when you do not understand these basic arithmetic properties? This question is an important but unfair question, and we are sure there are many excellent arithmetic teachers who have not mastered an understanding of these basic properties, but once you understand how these properties apply to basic arithmetic problems you will then understand why some of the concepts and procedures you teach work. We wonder how many certified mathematics teachers recognize the properties quickly, indicated in the 7 problems below.

45. $x + 1 = 1 + x$

46. $x + 1 = a$ & $a = 2x - 4$ $\quad\therefore\quad$ $x + 1 = 2x - 4$ Once you identify the property which applies in this situation, try to determine the value of the variables, "x & a".

47. $(x + 6) + y = x + (6 + y)$

48. $3\sqrt[3]{x} + \frac{4}{5}p^3 - 11.9 = 3\sqrt[3]{x} + \frac{4}{5}p^3 - 11.9$

49. $(x^2 \times y^3) \times z^5 = x^2 \times (y^3 \times z^5)$

50. $(x + 6) + 11 = 18$ $\quad\therefore\quad$ $18 = (x + 6) + 11$ We wonder if you can determine the value of the variable "x".

51. $(3 - x) \times p = p \times (3 - x)$

INVISIBLE NUMBERS, TERMS, LABELS, OPERATIONS AND MATHEMATICS SYMBOLS

H. We have never seen the word "*invisible*" applied the way we use the word to describe numbers, terms, operation symbols, parentheses, and a label, which are not written but understood to be present when mathematics expressions are written. We found when we emphasized these "*invisible*" symbols we helped many students understand what most people think is obvious. We have already mentioned some numbers and symbols which we refer to as *invisible numbers* or *symbols*. Here is our list of numbers, symbols, and even one label we refer to as *invisible* when writing arithmetic and mathematics expressions: {The number "<u>1</u>"; The number "<u>0</u>"; The number "<u>2</u>"; A decimal point "<u>.</u>"; A multiplication symbol "<u>×</u>"; The number "<u>10</u>"; Parentheses in the numerator and denominator of compound fractions involving quantities; The number "<u>*e*</u>"; The label "<u>*rads*</u>"}. The special label "*rads*" is used to indicate a specialized angle measurement in trigonometry which will be discussed in Chapter 8. The numbers "10" and "*e*" are special numbers and often invisible when working with logarithms, these numbers are beyond the scope of this book. (A <u>logarithm</u> is an <u>exponent</u> written in the form of an equation, both sides of the equation represent an exponent.) In the following problems/expressions, identify as many different invisible numbers and symbols as you can determine. If all the invisible symbols are written, the problems will look too cumbersome.

52. "5"
53. "37.1"
54. "$y = 3x + 2$"
55. "$2x$"
56. "$2x\sqrt{y}$"
57. "$3x + y = 10$"
58. "$(2x + \sqrt[3]{27})(9 - y)$"
59. "$3ab$"

DEFINITIONS

I. If students are going to comprehend what they are reading, we assume all reading teachers consider it important for students to fully understand definitions. How can anyone understand and be able to explain what they read, if there are several words in the reading passage, which they do not know the meaning? We have continually tried to explain in detail the definitions and meanings of many mathematics words which are contained in this textbook. Write what you believe is the correct definition for each word or phrase and then look the definition up on the internet/dictionary and compare the two definitions.

60. Rational Numbers
61. Terminating Decimals
62. Repeating Decimals
63. Fractions
64. Percent or Percents
65. Infinity
66. Perpendicular Lines
67. Slope of a Line
68. Our definition of *invisible numbers and symbols in arithmetic*

69. Least Common Multiple (LCM) - After you write the definition of the phrase Least Common Multiple, list three example problems where you illustrate what the LCM is for the numbers or expressions indicated in your examples.

70. Greatest Common Factor (GCF) - After you write the definition of the phrase Greatest Common Factor, list three example problems where you illustrate what the GCF is for the numbers or expressions indicated in your examples.

MULTIPLYING AND DIVIDING BY POWERS OF "10"

J. Do you teach your students tricks to multiply and divide by powers of "10"?

71. Write a one, two, or three paragraph explanation about the rules and procedures you tell students to use when they are required to multiply or divide by the following infinite set of numbers which are all powers of "10"

$\{10^1 = 10, \quad 10^2 = 100, \quad 10^3 = 1000, \quad 10^4 = 10{,}000, \quad 10^5 = 100{,}000, \ldots\}$.

COMMUTATIVE, ASSOCIATIVE, REFLEXIVE, SYMMETRIC, AND TRANSITIVE PROPERTIES

K. In your own works write a paragraph to help students understand the properties indicated below and indicate what you would tell students to help them identify the differences between each of the properties.

72. Commutative Property for Addition and Multiplication

73. Associative Property for Addition and Multiplication

74. Reflexive Property

75. Symmetric Property

76. Transitive Property

77. Identity Property for Multiplication - (Hint: Something to do with the number 1.)

78. Identity Property for Addition - (Hint: Something to do with the number 0.)

AREAS OF GEOMETRIC SHAPES AND CONVERSIONS USING UNFAMILIAR TYPES OF UNITS

L. You are given a standard formula to find the area of a geometric shape and the information to find the area of the shape indicated. After you find the area of the geometric planes, using the given information, you will be asked to convert the area you just determined into a less common type of area measurement. You will probably have to use your cell phone or computer to find the correct conversion factor, which will be required to complete the conversion.

79. $A_{rec.} = lw$ The given length is 710 feet, and the given width is 525 feet. Find the area of the rectangle, indicated and then convert the measurement into acres. Since you are required to determine the number of acres covered by the indicated rectangle you will need to know how many square feet are contained in an acre.

80. $A_{tri.} = \frac{1}{2}bh \; or \; A_{tri.} = \frac{bh}{2}$ Explain how to convert the first formula into the second formula. The given base for the triangle is 2020 km and the given height is 25 km. Find the area indicated in "km^2" and then convert the unit of measure into hectares. You will probably have to look up the number of square kilometers in a hectare.

81. Refer back to problems 12. and 16. in this section. Place problem 12. first, then use the symmetric property on problem 16. and write the equation as $1\,l = 1000\,cm^3$. Next, use the Transitive Property and create an additional conversion fact.

Important Comment: At the end of Chapter 6 we mentioned the two-word phrase "Dimensional Analysis". We believe it is important, and you should realize the problems presented and the solutions/illustrations in Chapter 6 used to complete the conversions should serve as an introduction to the topic referred to as "Dimensional Analysis". "Dimensional Analysis" is a topic of importance in professions which place great emphasis on the mathematics procedures involving labels when solving equations and formulas.

If you are preparing to be a secondary mathematics teacher or you already are a secondary mathematics teacher, we know some of you are wondering if we would ever mention the fact that the following expressions all equal 1: $10^0 = 1,\ 799^0 = 1, x^0 = 1,\ (22xy)^0 = 1,\ (x+1010)^0 = 1,\ (\frac{xy}{77})^0 = 1, etc.$ For someone who is not a secondary mathematics teacher or a math education major, the rule we are illustrating is: "Any number, term, or expression raised to the zero power always equals 1. The number 1 can be written using notations which are **not** normally mentioned in an elementary arithmetic class.

CHAPTER 7

OTHER ARITHMETIC CONVERSION PROCEDURES

THE ARITHMETIC CONVERSION PROBLEMS ILLUSTRATED IN THIS CHAPTER INVOLVE TERMINATING DECIMALS AND PERCENTAGES.

IT IS OUR BELIEF, IF TEACHERS USE THE TWO THEOREMS INTRODUCED AND ILLUSTRATED IN THIS TEXTBOOK, THE CONFUSION STUDENTS EXPERIENCE WHEN PERFORMING THE INDICATED CONVERSIONS IN THIS CHAPTER WILL BE GREATLY DEMINISHED.

Chapter 7

In this chapter, we will illustrate three more basic arithmetic conversions which students will encounter in 5th and 6th grade - convert *terminating decimals* into *fractions, percentages* into *decimals*, and *decimals* into *percentages.* All three of these conversion problems can easily be accomplished using "Young's Equation/Ratio Theorem" and "Young's Conversion Theorem". We specifically did not mention converting fractions into decimals because the best method to use when converting a fraction into a decimal is to understand a fraction is a type of division problem and the students should convert a fraction into a decimal by using the long division process. (Example: Convert the fraction. "$\frac{7}{8}$" into the terminating decimal "$.875$"). If you are going to convert repeating decimals into fractions, the process requires some basic knowledge of algebra which is beyond the scope of arithmetic, but we will explain how to convert repeating decimals into fractions at the end of Chapter 8. (Example: Convert the repeating decimal "0.9797…" into the fraction "$\frac{97}{99}$".)

Prior to explaining to your students how to convert a terminating decimal into a fraction, a percent into a decimal, or a decimal into a percent, the students must be proficient with the mental process of multiplying and dividing by powers of "10" using exponents which are greater than "0". We never want students to think when they multiply a natural number by "10" or "100" or "1000" they should add a zero, two zeros, or three zeros to the starting number. This is a poor way to explain how to multiply by powers of "10" because when you add a zero, two zeros, or three zeros to any number, you end up with the same number you started with.

Think about what you are saying when you give the following directions, "All you need to do when you multiply a natural number by "100" is add two zeros to the natural number." Here is the natural number, "32", and the goal is to have the students mentally multiply "32" by "100". If you tell your students to add two 0's to the number "32", you are telling them to perform the following arithmetic procedure: "$32 + 0 + 0$", which still equals, "32". Using the same logic, simplify the following problem by adding two 0's to the right of ".54": "$.54 \times 100$". If you tell the students to add two 0's to the right of the number "$.54$", they may write the answer, "$.5400$", which is incorrect. When you focus on these two examples, you should understand why using the phrase "add 0's" to the right of a number when you multiply by one of the numbers from the set of numbers, "{10, 100, 1000, 10000, etc.}" is really a poor way to explain how to mentally compute the correct answer. Does this also mean when you divide by a power of ten you tell students to take away (subtract) "0's"? Obviously, this is not going to work. In this section we only talk about the powers of "10" when the exponents are natural numbers. The set of natural numbers begins with the number 1 and is commonly referred to as the counting numbers. Students will later encounter problems such that the exponent may equal "0" or a negative integer or a fraction/decimal, but at this time the goal is to make sure the students can multiply and divide quickly in their head by the following numbers, "$\{10, 100, 1000, 10000, etc.\}$. By definition, a natural number is greater than "0". The set of natural numbers is written using the following notation - $N = \{1, 2, 3, 4, 5, \dots\}$. The set of whole numbers is slightly different, but the one little difference is a major difference to mathematicians. The set of whole numbers is written using the following notation: - $W = \{0, 1, 2, 3, 4, \dots\}$.

Your goal is to get the students to quickly be able to multiply and divide by powers of ten which are greater than or equal to "10" in their heads. It is much wiser to tell students, move the decimal to the left or right depending on the number of 0's in the power of ten they are multiplying or dividing by. You should also make sure the students recognize when they multiply by a power of ten using the numbers illustrated, the number gets larger--and they should move the decimal point to the right the same number of times the 0's appear in the power of ten. Just the opposite occurs when they divide by a power of ten using the numbers illustrated; the decimal point will move to the left based on the number of 0's involved in the power of ten they are dividing by.

Another key teaching point you need to emphasize is, if there is no decimal point in a number, then there is what we call an invisible decimal point to the right of every number which does not have a decimal point indicated. There are four examples to illustrate you move the decimal point to the right or to the left when you multiply or divide by a power of ten in the next couple pages. Before you tell your students about the rule to move the decimal point either to the left or to the right depending on whether you are dividing or multiplying by a power of ten, you must have the students solve these types of problems using a pencil and a piece of paper. If your students are really going to master the rules/tricks with respect to multiplying and dividing by powers of "10", your students must practice multiplying and dividing these types of example problems prior to using the tricks/rules. Once your students have successfully solved 10-20 of these types of problems using a pencil and a piece of paper, you might find the students quickly discover the rules on their own.

Teaching Point: We indicated when talking about multiplying and dividing by powers of ten, we wanted you to concentrate on numbers greater than or equal to ten. This means we are talking about the number "10" written with the following exponents: "$10^1 = 10$", "$10^2 = 100$", "$10^3 = 1000$", "$10^4 = 10000$", etc. At this time, we are not talking about the number "10" written using the following exponents: "$10^0 = 1$", "$10^{-1} = 0.1$", "$10^{-2} = 0.01$", "$10^{-3} = 0.001$", etc. or "$10^{\frac{3}{4}} = 5.623413$", "$10^{1.5} = 31.622777$ ", etc. The "0" exponent and negative exponents are not normally discussed in arithmetic until 6th, 7th, or 8th grade. We will not get into the discussion involving negative exponents at this time. The decimal and fraction exponents will normally not be discussed until students take Algebra 2. The answers for the last two examples with the exponents of "$\frac{3}{4}$ and 1.5" are not terminating decimals or repeating decimals; they are irrational numbers, which are beyond the scope of this textbook, and we used a calculator to compute the answers. Irrational decimals are decimals which never end and do not repeat.

Comment just to think about: The two solutions mentioned above, "$10^{\frac{3}{4}} = 5.623413$" and "$10^{1.5} = 31.622777$ ", can be computed without a calculator using procedures taught in calculus. Ironically, the calculus procedures to determine the solutions are arithmetic heavy and beyond the scope of this textbook, but calculators are programmed to solve these types of problems using arithmetic procedures. Since a calculator/computer can solve millions of one-step arithmetic problems per second, it seems instantaneous when we solve these types of problems with a calculator. One method some mathematicians will use to find these decimal solutions without a calculator is to use a rule derived in calculus referred to as Taylor's Formula/Theorem. Without a solid foundation of arithmetic, mathematicians would have never derived Taylor's Formula/Theorem, or other rules and procedures used in higher-level mathematics classes and science classes. If programmers did not completely understand the rules and procedures learned in arithmetic, our dependence on calculators and computers to solve these types of problems would be non-existent.

An *irrational number* is a decimal which does not terminate or repeat. Irrational numbers are the opposite of *rational numbers*. A rational number can always be written as a fraction using two integers. An irrational number can never be written as a fraction using two integers. Rational numbers can always be written as either a terminating or repeating decimal. There are an infinite number of rational numbers and there are an infinite number of irrational numbers. If you combine all the rational numbers and all the irrational numbers, you have the set of numbers referred to as the "Real Numbers". Sometime in 8th, 9th, or 10th grade arithmetic/math, teachers should discuss and illustrate the difference between the two number systems, rational and irrational numbers, and then discuss the set of real numbers.

When computing irrational decimals which go on forever and never repeat, I mentioned Taylor's Formula as one method to use. Newton's Method and Euler's Method are two other calculus methods which many mathematicians use to find the same solutions.

Did we mention the following fact, "$10^0 = 1$"? Once students learn to work with a negative exponent(s), it is easy to illustrate why any number, term, or expression with an exponent of "**0**", equals 1.

We will not repeat the comments discussed in the previous paragraph again in this textbook. We wonder how many people understand the comments mentioned in this paragraph and then we also wonder how many people will remember the comments mentioned in the previous paragraphs in two or three days.

Repeating specific topics in mathematics is a fundamental teaching rule for all mathematicians and explaining a concept using different terminology is also an essential teaching technique.

When you illustrate the rule to move the decimal point to the left or to the right when solving the next four example problems, go back and illustrate the assumed answer is the correct answer by physically solving these problems. A calculator is not an essential tool for students to use to solve these problems. In fact, if the students use the calculator when they are first simplifying these types of problems, you will probably find many of the students forget the rules/tricks two or three weeks after you discussed the indicated procedures. The students never mastered the rules/tricks because they never fully comprehended the concept of multiplying and dividing by powers of "10".

1. 345 × 100 Initially rewrite "345" as "345." or "345.0" or "345.00" and move the decimal point two places to the right to get the answer "34500." with the decimal point indicated or "34500" without the decimal point indicated. Students need to realize, not only is there an invisible decimal point to the right of the natural number "345", but there are also an infinite number of invisible 0's to the right of the decimal point. When you multiply by "100" the answer must get larger. Make sure the students realize the ending number "34500" is larger than the starting number "345". This may seem to be too easy, but it is a critical teaching point.
2. 3.45 × 1000 In this problem we simply want the students to understand they are permitted to move the decimal point three places to the right because they are multiplying by "1000" and the starting number "3.45" must get larger. Since there are three "0's" in the number "1000", this is the indicator to move the decimal point three places. Students must realize there is an invisible "0" to the right of the number/digit "5", and there are as many invisible 0's after the number "5", as you will ever need. The answer after moving the decimal point three places to the right is "3450. or 3450". The answer "3450" is much larger than the number you started with, "3.45". Always encourage your students to compare the magnitude of the answer to the starting number. This may seem like such a simple concept, but you would be amazed how many students struggle with decimal number comparison

problems. Placing numbers on a number line is always a great way to illustrate the magnitude of numbers.

3. $34.5 \div 10$ In this problem, you are dividing by the number, "10", and this will make the answer smaller. The trick/rule is simple: move the decimal point one place to the left to get the answer "3.45". Make sure the students realize the answer "3.45" is smaller than the given number "34.5". It is unbelievable how some concepts seem so simple to you and yet maybe 20%-30% of the students do not understand concepts you consider obvious, which is why we encourage you to question the students about the magnitudes of different decimals.

4. $.345 \div 10000$ When you solve the division problem "0.345 ÷ 10000", the answer should be much smaller than the given number ".345". Move the decimal point four places to the left, which means you will have to use four invisible 0's and realize ".345=0000.345" to get the solution ".0000345" or "0.0000345".

The following statement is a comment we frequently thought to be true, but we are baffled by the lack of understanding some students demonstrate with regards to the rules to multiply and divide a number by a power of ten. Statement: "We constantly found some/many (25%-40%) college bound students in 9th grade did not remember the basic rules regarding multiplying and dividing by powers of ten." Simply unbelievable! *(FRT 14: Mentally multiply and divide numbers by powers of ten. We wonder how many 6th, 7th, 8th, and 9th graders can mentally multiply and divide rational numbers by powers of ten? It might also be an interesting research question to ask* first year college students and high school seniors.*)*

The following simple examples illustrate how to convert a *terminating* decimal into a fraction using the two theorems introduced and discussed in this textbook. All four examples below are easy to convert into fractions if you know the process. The reasons we encourage you to use "Young's Equation/Ratio Theorem" and "Young's Conversion Theorem" to complete the conversions are for consistency and to reduce the number of rules/tricks required to solve more challenging problems. You may decide how you want to teach your students to convert these decimals into fractions. We usually want the final fraction to be a reduced fraction, and we frequently encourage students to use factor trees and cancel identical factors in both the numerator and the denominator.

Consider one more thought about using the two indicated theorems to convert *terminating* decimals into fractions: if students have been using "Young's Equation/Ratio Theorem" and "Young's Conversion Theorem" since 2nd, 3rd, 4th, or 5th grade, they may find using the two theorems with this type of conversion problem, is very natural. Since most of us never thought about converting *terminating* decimals into fractions using these two new theorems, it may seem awkward and cumbersome to us. Furthermore, we continually used italicized letters when we referred to *terminating* decimals in the previous paragraphs. The reason we used the italicized print is because we want you to realize we are only working with *terminating* decimal numbers in this section. There are two other types of decimal numbers used constantly in mathematics: repeating decimals (Examples: 0.666..., or .7878... etc.) and irrational decimals (non-terminating and non-repeating decimals) (Examples of irrational numbers: "$\pi = 3.1415926535\ldots$", or .012001200012000012... or "$\sqrt[2]{2} = 1.4142135623\ldots$"). Remember, both terminating and repeating decimals are referred to as rational numbers.

1. Convert "$.74\ into\ a\ fraction$"

Since students have mastered the concept of multiplying and dividing by powers of ten, greater than or equal to "10", it should be easy for the students to convert the decimal ".74" into a fraction using "Young's Equation/Ratio Theorem" and "Young's Conversion Theorem". First, the students must recognize there are two decimal places in the given number, ".74". This means the students must work with the identity "$100 = 100$". When they apply "Young's Equation/Ratio Theorem" with the identity "$100 = 100$", they derive the following *fraction* equation: "$\frac{100}{100} = 1$". Notice we used the word *fraction* in the last sentence and not the word *ratio.* Do you know why the word *fraction* is the proper word to use in this situation?

Now use "*Young's Conversion Theorem*" to convert the decimal "$.74$" into a fraction. Here is the conversion process: "$.74 = .74 \times 1 = \frac{.74}{1} \times \frac{100}{100} = \frac{.74 \times 100}{1 \times 100} = \frac{74}{100}$". Students should always check to ensure the final fraction is reduced. We encourage all students to use factor trees when they reduce, multiply, or divide fractions involving large numbers. The reason is simple: the first step when you simplify an algebra fraction (rational expression) is to factor and cancel the identical factors. Here is the process to reduce the fraction using factor trees "$\frac{74}{100} = \frac{2 \cdot 37}{2 \cdot 2 \cdot 5 \cdot 5} = \frac{37}{50}$".

The fraction "$\frac{74}{100}$" is not a difficult fraction to reduce, and we would be excited if over 60% of the students could accurately reduce this fraction without using factor trees.

> We want 100% of the students to realize, if the numbers or terms involved in a fraction are large numbers or algebraic terms, then the first step to reduce the fraction is to factor the numbers or terms in both the numerator and the denominator and cancel identical factors.

2. Convert "0.0175 into a fraction"

The students must recognize there are four decimal places involved with this terminating decimal and they must determine what special form of the number 1 to multiply this decimal, since the objective is to derive an equivalent fraction.

If you use "Young's Equation/Ratio Theorem" and the identity "$10000 = 10000$" then you can derive the following fraction equal to 1, "$\frac{10,000}{10,000} = 1$".

Some teachers tell students to use the following procedure to convert the terminating decimal "0.0175" into an equivalent fraction. Count the number of digits to the right of the decimal point, make the given decimal number "0.0175" into the natural number "175", place the new natural number "175" in the numerator of the fraction, and then divide by "10000" because the number "10000" has four 0's--and this is the number of digits to the right of the decimal point in the given decimal "0.0175". Think about how cumbersome this logic must seem to young students. It may not seem cumbersome to you because you have mastered the procedure and now it seems simple. Also, think about how the procedure we just discussed does not illustrate why the procedure works. We know you could also have the students think about the way they should pronounce or write the original number "0.0175". They should say or write the following: "$One\ hundred\ seventy-five\ ten-thousandths$" and use their knowledge of the final part of the expression "$ten-thousandths$" to determine what power of ten to divide the number "175" by. Do you think if a student has trouble working with the decimal, "0.0175" to begin with, do you expect these same students to have the knowledge to write the decimal number using the proper words? If you think this paragraph seems awkward to read and understand, then why do you think it is the best way to explain to students to convert a terminating decimal into a fraction?

Using "Young's Equation/Ratio Theorem" and "Young's Conversion Theorem" to convert the decimal ".0175" into a fraction not only works, but it also is based on sound mathematics principles. The other great thing about using the two theorems to convert a terminating decimal into a fraction is the students have been using the two theorems for a variety of other arithmetic conversion problems. If students are experienced solving conversion problems using both Young's Equation/Ratio Theorem and Young's Conversion Theorem, they will feel confident using the two theorems to convert numbers and expressions into equivalent numbers and expressions. It will be an automatic process for most of your students--maybe over 90% of them. The conversion process will look like this: "$.0175 = .0175 \times 1 = \frac{.0175}{1} \times \frac{10000}{10000} = \frac{175}{10000}$". Now use factor trees to reduce the fraction: "$\frac{5 \cdot 5 \cdot 7}{2 \cdot 2 \cdot 2 \cdot 2 \cdot 5 \cdot 5 \cdot 5 \cdot 5} = \frac{7}{2 \cdot 2 \cdot 2 \cdot 2 \cdot 5 \cdot 5} = \frac{7}{400}$".

Chapter 8 in this textbook, emphasizes the Power of the Number One (1), "Factor Trees", "Young's Equation/Ratio Theorem", and "Young's Conversion Theorem" and how understanding the rules discussed in arithmetic regarding these four topics applies to algebra problems.

The rules for arithmetic do not change when you decide to work with algebra problems and other advanced mathematics topics.

Did you ever wonder why "factor trees" were even mentioned in your arithmetic textbooks? You probably introduced the topic of "factor trees" along with "prime numbers" in arithmetic but never assigned problems which required your students to work with these two topics in arithmetic. In algebra, the "factor tree" process is simply referred to as factoring. In algebra, there is often an entire chapter focused on the topic of factoring, and then more advanced topics are discussed which require the students to understand the factoring process.

If students are used to reducing, multiplying, and dividing fractions by using factor trees, they will find it seamless to use the same procedures when working with rational expressions (algebraic fractions).

3. Convert ".8 into a fraction"

This simple decimal is one we expect 80% of adults to convert into a fraction quickly in their head and maybe 10%-20% of 5th graders to quickly come up with the fraction, "$\frac{4}{5}$". We used the percentages "80%" for adults and "10%-20% for 5th graders as wishful positive results. These two percentages mentioned are just guesstimates. Research might suggest these percentage estimates are too high as we are not aware of any research focusing on adults or 5th graders and their mental math skills when converting decimals into fractions. We want students to know basic facts about decimals and fractions, and we hope by the end of the school year in 6th grade over 50% of the 6th graders recognize the decimal "$.8 = \frac{4}{5}$" because of previous experiences. There will always be students who do not recognize simple decimal conversion and fraction facts. These students can always use the two theorems discussed throughout this textbook to convert the decimal ".8" into the equivalent fraction, "$\frac{4}{5}$". *(FRT 15: Mentally convert fractions into decimals, fractions into percentages, decimals into fractions, decimals into percentages, percentages into fractions, and percentages into decimals. You may ask these types of questions to first year college students, high school seniors, eighth graders, and sixth graders.)*

Use "Young's Equation/Ratio Theorem" with the identity "$10 = 10$" to determine the special from of the number 1, "$\frac{10}{10}$", to multiply ".8" by, to get the equivalent fraction.

Here is the process using "Young's Conversion Theorem" to convert the decimal ".8" into the fraction "$\frac{4}{5}$": "$.8 = .8 \times 1 = \frac{.8}{1} \times \frac{10}{10} = \frac{.8 \times 10}{10} = \frac{8}{10} = \frac{2 \cdot 2 \cdot 2}{2 \cdot 5} = \frac{4}{5}$". We would expect most students are able to reduce the fraction "$\frac{8}{10}$" into the fraction, "$\frac{4}{5}$" in their head, and they would not need to use factor trees.

4. Convert "0.012525 into a fraction"

Wow, this will require a little bit of thought. Note, there are six decimal places in the given decimal, and we must concentrate on the identity "1,000,000 = 1,000,000".

Using "Young's Equation/Ratio Theorem" with the identity just indicated, we know "$\frac{1{,}000{,}000}{1{,}000{,}000} = 1$".

Next use "Young's Conversion Theorem" along with the fact "$\frac{1{,}000{,}000}{1{,}000{,}000} = 1$" to find the fraction equivalent to the given decimal "0.012525". Set up the fraction multiplication problem "$\frac{.012525}{1} \times \frac{1{,}000{,}000}{1{,}000{,}000}$" to get the fraction "$\frac{12525}{1{,}000{,}000}$". Reduce the fraction using factor trees to find the reduced fraction equivalent to the given decimal "0.012525". Here is the illustration to convert the terminating decimal into the equivalent reduced fraction: "$.012525 = .012525 \times 1 = .012525 \times \frac{1{,}000{,}000}{1{,}000{,}000} = \frac{12525}{1{,}000{,}000} = \frac{3 \cdot 5 \cdot 5\ 167}{1000 \cdot 1000} =$

$\frac{3 \cdot 5 \cdot 5 \cdot 167}{2 \cdot 2 \cdot 2 \cdot 5 \cdot 5 \cdot 5 \cdot 2 \cdot 2 \cdot 2 \cdot 5 \cdot 5 \cdot 5} = \frac{3 \cdot 167}{2 \cdot 2 \cdot 2 \cdot 5\ \cdot\ 2 \cdot 2 \cdot 2 \cdot 5 \cdot 5 \cdot 5} = \frac{501}{40{,}000}$". We checked using a calculator to ensure the final reduced fraction, "$\frac{501}{40{,}000} = 0.012525$". Do not give this type of problem on a test, but it might be an interesting problem to discuss if you have a few extra minutes at the end of a class.

Keep in mind in the previous four example problems the fractions were written before the fractions were reduced ("$\frac{74}{100}$", "$\frac{175}{10000}$", "$\frac{8}{10}$", and "$\frac{12525}{1,000,000}$") and these fractions are written in the format you normally expect your students to use when rewriting the decimal in fraction form in the first step. By indicating the two theorems which are involved in the conversion process, it simply clarifies why the fraction is written with the appropriate denominator, and why the numerator which was derived from the decimal given to begin the problem now has the decimal point to the right of the last digit. Reread this paragraph carefully! The point we are trying to make is this: teachers tell their students when they convert a terminating decimal into a fraction to write the decimal number in the numerator without the decimal and then determine the denominator which must be a power of "10" based on the number of decimal places the students moved the decimal in the numerator. This is an example of one of the tricks we tell students to memorize to solve arithmetic and mathematics problems.

When reducing, multiplying, and dividing fractions, we encourage students to use factor trees for the numerators and the denominators with the intention to reduce the numerators and the denominators. We want the students to reduce simple problems by using their knowledge of multiplication and division facts. Sometimes students may use a combination of both procedures once they become proficient with both procedures and develop some number sense involving numbers.

5. Convert "9.072 into a mixed number and improper fraction"

In this problem we usually encourage the students to concentrate on the decimal ".072" and convert it into a fraction first. Then we write the number "9" to the left of the fraction to find the mixed number and determine the improper fraction. Concentrate on the decimal, ".072" and convert it into a fraction. Use "Young's Equation/Ratio Theorem" with the identity, "$1000 = 1000$", and derive the fraction equation, "$\frac{1000}{1000} = 1$".

Convert the decimal, "$.072$", into a fraction by utilizing "Young's Conversion Theorem". "$.072 = \frac{.072}{1} = \frac{.072}{1} \times \frac{1000}{1000} = \frac{.072 \times 1000}{1 \times 1000} = \frac{72}{1000} = \frac{36}{500} = \frac{18}{250} = \frac{9}{125}$"

The mixed number is "$9\frac{9}{125}$", and the improper fraction equals "$\frac{1134}{125}$".

If the original directions were to find the improper fraction, you could find the improper fraction more directly and not focus on the decimal and the number "9" separately. Remember, the number (rational number) "9.072" is a single number. It should be easy to explain this number is the sum of the natural number "9" plus the terminating decimal number (rational number) "$.072$" which is what we did in the previous illustration.

Convert the Rational Number, "9.072" into an improper fraction using "Young's Conversion Theorem". "$9.072 = \frac{9.072}{1} = \frac{9.072}{1} \times \frac{1000}{1000} = \frac{9072}{1000} = \frac{4536}{500} = \frac{2268}{250} = \frac{1134}{125}$"

In both conversion illustrations, we did <u>not</u> use factor trees to reduce the fractions. We divided both the numerators and the denominators repeatedly by the number "2". It obviously does not matter which method you decide to use to perform the conversion. The decision is up to you and up to your students. Students can prove the improper fraction "$\frac{1134}{125}$" is equal to the original number "9.072" by using long division. It might be an interesting class activity to determine how many 5th or 6th graders can divide the numerator "1134" by the denominator "125" to derive the quotient "9.072" without using a calculator.

Prior to discussing how to convert a terminating decimal into a fraction, we wanted to ensure teachers encouraged students to move the decimal point either to the left or to the right when they were multiplying or dividing by powers of ten and the exponent is a natural number. When the students are mentally proficient with the process of multiplying and dividing by powers of ten and they are also proficient with both "Young's Equation/Ratio Theorem" and "Young's Conversion Theorem", they will be able to convert any terminating decimal into a percent and any percent into a decimal. Sometime in 4th or 5th grade, teachers will begin to discuss problems involving percentages, but the real goal might be to have the 6th grade teachers emphasize percent problems of all types. Fifth grade teachers should introduce the conversion problems contained in the next section, and by the end of 6th grade the students need to master the process to convert a decimal into a percent and a percent into a decimal. When students start to work with percentages, whether in 5th or 6th grade, it is the appropriate time to emphasize how to convert back and forth between percentages and decimals.

> Think about the word "percent" and concentrate on the two syllables "per" and "cent". We already indicated that the word "per" means, divide. The word "cent" is "$\frac{1}{100}$" of a dollar. Interesting!

Here is a simple definition for the word or symbol "*Percent (%)*": The symbol "%" simply means - *divide by "100".* Remember, one of the definitions of the word "per" is to divide. Start with the definition of percent (divide by "100") and think about what happens when you are given the following percent: Rewrite the percent "100%" as a fraction. *When you encounter the percent symbol "%" to the right of a number or expression, it would be correct to tell the students to quickly write the given number in the numerator of a fraction and place the number "100" in the denominator to form the fraction.* This is a rule which will work when the given problem has a percent symbol "%" to the right of a number or expression, but if you only teach this one rule, then the students may not completely understand how to convert a number into a percent.

Using the stated italicized statement in the last paragraph, we can determine the following fact, "$100\% = \frac{100}{100}$". We hope you immediately recognize the fraction "$\frac{100}{100} = 1$". This seems so simple, but this also must mean "$100\% = 1$" based on the *transitive property*. This is a basic fact, derived from the definition of the word "percent" or the percent symbol, "%". We are now going to apply "Young's Equation/Ratio Theorem" to derive the following two fractions which both equal the number 1, "$\frac{100\%}{1} = 1 = \frac{1}{100\%}$". Keep in mind the percent symbol "%" could be considered a mathematics label, just like the labels: "in.", "ft.", "oz.", "min.", "etc." but it also could be treated like a number/fraction, "$\% = \frac{1}{100}$". When identical labels are written in a fraction in both the numerator and the denominator, the labels cancel and become 1. Also, when the same number appears in both the numerator and the denominator of a fraction, the numbers will cancel and become 1. Based on this comment, the following fractions all become 1: "$\frac{in.}{in.} = 1$", "$\frac{qt.}{qt.} = 1$", "$\frac{hr.}{hr.} = 1$", "$\frac{\$}{\$} = 1$", "$\frac{\%}{\%} = 1$, "$\frac{\frac{1}{100}}{\frac{1}{100}} = 1$", etc.

If you understand the previous paragraph, you are ready to convert percentages to decimals and decimals to percentages without guessing.

You could tell the students if the percent symbol "%" is written with a number, they need to divide by "100", but if they want to convert a number into a percent they need to multiply by "100". We assume they know how to multiply and divide by "100" by moving the decimal point either to the left or to the right using their mental math skills. Then reality sets in and we realize the students become confused with the two different tricks when they encounter several percent problems which vary in the degree of difficulty.

Teaching Point: Remember what the word "per" means in arithmetic. Then think about what the word "cent" means when working with money. You should understand why the word "percent" means - divide by "100" based on the definitions of the two syllables in the word "per - cent".

Here are four percent and decimal conversion problems. Two of the problems are relatively simple, and the other two create problems for some students who are good math students. We will convert all four problems into equivalent expressions using both "Young's Equation/Ratio Theorem" and "Young's Conversion Theorem". If you understand how to use these two theorems, the guesswork when converting a percent to a decimal and the decimal to a percent is removed. When students guess whether to move the decimal point two places to the left or two places to the right, even the best students sometimes make mistakes. Students must be able to mentally multiply and divide by the number "100" in all these conversion problems.

1. Convert the percent number, ".35%", into a decimal. The correct answer is .0035. Did you get it correct?

Step 1: Use "Young's Equation/Ratio Theorem" and derive two fractions which both equal 1. Fact: $100\% = 1$ $\quad\therefore \frac{1}{100\%} = 1 = \frac{100\%}{1}$

Step 2: Use "Young's Conversion Theorem" and multiply ".35%" by a special from of 1 based on one of the two ratios just derived. $.35\% = \frac{.35\%}{1} = \frac{.35\%}{1} \times 1 = \frac{.35\%}{1} \times \frac{1}{100\%} =$ $\frac{.35\% \times 1}{1 \times 100\%} = \frac{.35}{100} = .0035$ We hope you knew when we divided ".35" by "100" the decimal point needed to move two places to the left and the number got smaller. You need to be able to quickly do the mental math in your head when simplifying the division problem (fraction) "$\frac{.35}{100}$" to get the correct answer ".0035" or "0.0035".

We selected the fraction "$\frac{1}{100\%}$" to substitute for the number "1" in the problem because the given problem "$.35\%$" contained the percent symbol "%" in the numerator. The percent symbol "%" in the fraction "$\frac{1}{100\%}$" is in the denominator. The percent symbol "%" is a type of label; therefore, it can be treated as a label algebraically. The percent symbol "%" can also be thought of as the number "$\frac{1}{100}$".

The math symbol for the word percent, "%" is the only symbol we can think of which could stand for a number, "$\frac{1}{100}$" or a label.

We realize many teachers tell their students to change the percent "%" symbol when it is with a number into a fraction, and the percent "%" symbol in the numerator turns into the number "100" in the denominator. This trick works well when you want to convert "80%" into the fraction, "$\frac{80}{100}$". As we indicated earlier, students often use this trick to convert a percent into a decimal. This is an excellent trick--if the only problems the students will encounter are numbers with the percent symbol "%" to the right of the number. After students have mastered this trick, how do you explain to your students to convert a decimal into a percent? *Our guess is that you tell the students if you start with a decimal and want to convert the decimal into a percent, move the decimal point two places to the left and place the percent symbol "%" to the right of the new number.* Did we state the correct procedure in the last sentence to convert a decimal into a percent? No! *The correct way to convert a decimal into a percent would be to move the decimal point two places to the right and place the percent symbol to the right of the new number.*

If you did not immediately identify the incorrect statement in the previous paragraph, it proves our point, telling students to move the decimal point two places to the left and then two places to the right when working with percentages is a way to confuse even excellent math students. When students need to decide whether the correct way to solve the problem is to multiply or divide by "100" or move the decimal point to the left or to the right two places when they are switching back and forth between decimals and percentages and vice-versa, many students and adults get confused when their knowledge and understanding of a concept is based solely on tricks.

Our main purpose for writing this textbook is to get teachers and students to realize there is one method which works for many types of conversion problems students encounter in arithmetic and advanced math classes. We do not object to you presenting tricks which work to convert an expression into an equivalent expression, but if you can get everyone to work with one specific set of rules to convert expressions into equivalent expressions, the students will not only master the two "theorems" continually mentioned in this textbook, but in addition they might understand some of the reasons why some tricks work. Encourage students to do as much work in their head as possible, which means they must have a strong understanding of the procedures. Not only do we want the students to solve problems in their head, but we want them to understand why the tricks they use work mathematically. The tricks teachers usually illustrate to students to use when they want the students to quickly solve arithmetic and math problems are not tricks in the sense that, "out of the blue," there is a trick which works. Quite the opposite is true--the tricks are usually derived from a set of math procedures which are proven to work. Our concern is, if the students continue to only learn the tricks, they never understand why the tricks work and they never understand the math procedures used to validate the tricks. Most importantly, the students get confused when they need to use different tricks.

Refer to the phrase in the last paragraph, "but in addition they might understand some of the reasons why some tricks/rules work". With this thought in mind, think about the trick/procedure you tell your students to use when they solve a long division problem, and the divisor is a decimal. The divisor is the number outside the division box or the denominator in a fraction. The first step you probably tell your students is, move the decimal to the right in the divisor and make sure the divisor is now a natural number. At the same time, you move the decimal point in the divisor, you must move the decimal point in the dividend (the number inside the division box) the same number of places to the right as you needed to move the decimal in the divisor. We are not going to give a detailed explanation why this trick works, but we hope 90% of the people who read this textbook can now explain why this arithmetic rule works:

$.5\overline{).85}$ Changes to $\begin{array}{r} 1.7 \\ 5\overline{)8.5} \end{array}$

(Example Problem: Divide the decimal ".85" by the decimal ".5" using the long division box process. When you set up the division box, the divisor outside of the division box is ".5", and the dividend inside the division box is ".85". We are required to move the decimal point one place to the right for both numbers because the ".5" number outside the division box must be changed into the natural number "5"-- and at the same time the number inside the division box ".85" is changed to "8.5".) Can you explain why this trick works in arithmetic when you divide by a decimal? (Hint: First write the division problem as a fraction division problem "$\frac{.85}{.5}$" and use both "Young's Equation/Ratio Theorem" and "Young's Conversion Theorem" with the identity "$10 = 10$" and the equation "$\frac{10}{10} = 1$" to derive the new equivalent fraction "$\frac{8.5}{5}$". Now, rewrite the fraction using the long division box notation.)

2. Convert 72% into a decimal. (The correct answer is .72. We assume you got the correct answer quickly.)

Teachers and students usually get this conversion problem correct by simply understanding when they see the percent (%) symbol it means to divide by "100" and the answer is ".72". We realize good students and teachers can do this problem in their head, but just like any simple algebra problem students can do in their head (Example: $2 + x = 7 \therefore x = 5$), we encourage students to write every step. We especially want the students to write every step when they are learning the process for the first time. Therefore, the steps should be presented like this.

Step 1: Fact: $100\% = 1$ If you use "Young's Equation/Ratio Theorem", you get two fractions which both equal, 1. $\therefore$ "$\frac{100\%}{1} = 1 = \frac{1}{100\%}$".

Step 2: $72\% = \frac{72\%}{1} = \frac{72\%}{1} \times 1 = \frac{72\%}{1} \times \frac{1}{100\%} = \frac{72\% \times 1}{1 \times 100\%} = \frac{72}{100} = \frac{72.}{100} = .72$ Again, when we illustrated we are multiplying "72%" by "1", we wrote the ratio "$\frac{1}{100\%}$" to ensure the percent "%" symbols in both the numerator and the denominator cancelled.

3. Convert the decimal number, "72.76", into a percent. (Is the correct answer 7276% or .7272%? We believe even if you are a good math student, you probably must think for a couple seconds before you decide which answer is correct.)

This is a problem even good math students frequently find the *incorrect* answer ".7276%" when they convert the decimal "72.76" into a percent and they determine the solution using mental math.

Step 1: Derive two fractions which both equal, 1 using "Young's Equation/Ratio Theorem".

Fact: $100\% = 1$ $\quad\therefore\ \frac{1}{100\%} = 1 = \frac{100\%}{1}.$

Step 2: Use "Young's Conversion Theorem" and substitute one of the fractions indicated in step 1 for the number "1" when solving the conversion. $72.76 = 72.76 \times 1 = \frac{72.76}{1} \times \frac{100\%}{1} = \frac{72.76 \times 100\%}{1 \times 1} = \frac{7276\%}{1} = 7276\%$ Notice, we substituted the fraction "$\frac{100\%}{1}$" for the number 1 when we multiplied by the number 1. The reason we substituted the fraction "$\frac{100\%}{1}$" for the number 1 was because we wanted the final answer to have the percent symbol "%" in the numerator. We also assumed you were able to multiply by the number "100" in your head without using a pencil and a piece of paper or a calculator because you know how to solve this simple multiplication problem prior to working with percent problems.

4. Convert the decimal, "0.8", into a percent. (The correct answer is 80%. We hope you were able to solve this simple problem in your head. We already mentioned this basic problem earlier in this chapter written in another form.)

Step 1: Write the two appropriate fractions based on the fact, "100% = 1". Use "Young's Equation/Ratio Theorem" to derive the following two fractions, "$\frac{1}{100\%} = 1 = \frac{100\%}{1}$".

Step 2: Use "Young's Conversion Theorem" and substitute the fraction "$\frac{100\%}{1}$" for the number "1"; then multiply the number "0.8" by "1". The reason should be obvious: there is no percent symbol "%" in the given problem, and the goal is to end up with a percent symbol "%" in the numerator. $.8 = \frac{.8}{1} = \frac{.8}{1} \times 1 = \frac{.8}{1} \times \frac{100\%}{1} = \frac{.8 \times 100\%}{1 \times 1} = .8 \times 100\% = 80.\% = 80\%$

When we wrote the solutions to the previous four problems, we indicated all the steps involved in the conversion process. When you teach students to solve these problems, we expect you to demonstrate all the steps we indicated in the conversion process. We do not expect the students to write all the indicated steps when they solve the problems on a test or a quiz. Here are the steps the students should write.

1. Convert .35% into a decimal. $100\% = 1 \therefore \frac{1}{100\%} = 1 = \frac{100\%}{1}$

   $.35\% = .35\% \times 1 = \frac{.35\%}{1} \times \frac{1}{100\%} = \frac{.35\% \times 1}{1 \times 100\%} = \frac{.35}{100} = .0035$

2. Convert 72% into a decimal. $100\% = 1 \quad \therefore \frac{100\%}{1} = 1 = \frac{1}{100\%}$

   $72\% = \frac{72\%}{1} \times 1 = \frac{72\%}{1} \times \frac{1}{100\%} = \frac{72\% \times 1}{1 \times 100\%} = \frac{72.}{100} = .72$

3. Convert 72.76 into a percent. $100\% = 1 \quad \therefore \frac{1}{100\%} = 1 = \frac{100\%}{1}$

   $72.76 = 72.76 \times 1 = \frac{72.76}{1} \times \frac{100\%}{1} = \frac{72.76 \times 100\%}{1 \times 1} = 7276\%$

4. Convert .8 into a percent. $100\% = 1 \quad \therefore \frac{100\%}{1} = 1 = \frac{1}{100\%}$

   $.8 = \frac{.8}{1} \times 1 = \frac{.8}{1} \times \frac{100\%}{1} = .8 \times 100\% = 80\%$

Keep in mind "Young's Conversion Theorem" does not say you will get an answer which looks identical to the answer you started with (Reference the Reflexive Property). "Young's Conversion Theorem" does say you will get an equivalent answer/number/expression in the final step to the starting number/expression. Therefore, the following answers to the previous four problems are all equivalent not perfectly identical: "$.35\% = .0035$"; "$72\% = .72$"; "$72.76 = 7276\%$"; and "$.8 = 80\%$". Review: An identity is a mathematical equation such that when all the arithmetic and algebraic procedures are completed, the left and right sides of the equation are equivalent. This means all four equations are *identities.*

We realize there may be other ways to explain how to convert a percent into a decimal and a decimal into a percent. The reason we insist on teaching students the conversion procedures using "Young's Equation/Ratio Theorem" and "Young's Conversion Theorem" is to try to give students one standard process which works for many different types of conversion problems.

We previously mentioned there are a few problems in arithmetic which require students to use other conversion procedures. Here are a few arithmetic conversion problems, which do not involve the two indicated "theorems", when completing the conversion process.

1. Convert the fraction, "$\frac{4}{5}$" into a decimal. The best way to complete this problem is to divide the number, "4", by the number, "5", and get the decimal, "0.8 or .8".
2. Convert the mixed number, "$5\frac{3}{4}$", into an improper fraction. The standard procedure used to convert this mixed number into an improper fraction is to multiply the denominator, "4", and the whole number, "5", then add the numerator, "3", to get the new numerator "23", and keep the denominator, "4". The mixed number, "$5\frac{3}{4}$", then becomes "$\frac{23}{4}$".
3. Convert the improper fraction, "$\frac{49}{11}$", into the mixed number, "$4\frac{5}{11}$". You must divide the numerator, "49" by the denominator, "11", then write the remainder as a fraction or a decimal.
4. You may also want to reduce a fraction such as "$\frac{10}{15}$" and determine the equivalent fraction, "$\frac{2}{3}$", by dividing the numerator and the denominator by the greatest common factor (GCF), "5".

Convert the repeating decimal, ".333 …", into a fraction. If you are going to convert this repeating decimal into a fraction you must use algebra procedures to get the fraction, "$\frac{1}{3}$". The steps required to convert a repeating decimal into an equivalent fraction are illustrated later in this textbook in Chapter 8.

Even though there are a few types of conversion problems in arithmetic which do not require the use of the two main theorems discussed in this textbook in the conversion process, you should realize after studying this textbook many conversion problems discussed in arithmetic and many conversion problems in advanced mathematics can be transformed into equivalent numbers and expressions by using the two theorems. When you convert numbers and expressions into equivalent numbers and expressions, if you use the two theorems along with the procedures continually illustrated throughout this textbook to find expressions which are equivalent, you will not be forced to teach different tricks which work for different problems, but you can use mathematically based reasoning to find equivalent answers.

There are several more advanced conversions in chemistry and physics which go beyond the conversions which can be solved using "Young's Conversion Theorem". These conversions will require formulas and equations derived in advanced mathematics classes and science classes. Think about how you convert "$20° C$ into $68° F$". This conversion requires the equation/formula "$F = \frac{9}{5} C + 32°$", and you can substitute the given Centigrade/Celsius temperature "20°" into the formula for the variable "C" to compute the equivalent Fahrenheit temperature, "68°". If you are proficient with algebra rules, you can also use the same equation to compute the Celsius temperature if you are given the Fahrenheit temperature. We suggest you only emphasize this one equation when you want the students to convert between these two different types of temperature measurements because we do not want the students to have to memorize two formulas. Also, we want the students to be able to solve the equation for the variable "C" when the Fahrenheit temperature is given. You may give your students the following second formula: "$C=\frac{5}{9}(F - 32°)$", but that decision is up to you. This equation can easily be derived from the first equation if you are proficient with algebra rules and procedures. We should also explain to students in 7th, 8th, and/or 9th grade how to derive both equations based on the difference between the two temperature measurement scales.

Another science/physics formula which many people are familiar with is, "$E = mc^2$". We know how to apply the rules of algebra to this physics formula, what the two variables "E and m" stand for, and what the constant "c" represents. We have no knowledge of how to derive the actual formula. We will let the explanation up to the physics majors. The variable "E" represents energy, and the specific unit of measurement is referred to as "$joules,\ J$". The variable "m" stands for mass measured in "$Kilograms, kg$". The letter "c" stands for the speed of light measured in "$metres\ per\ second, ms^{-1}$". In this special formula, you are changing mass into energy, and obviously "Young's Conversion Theorem" is not the procedure used to complete the conversion. The letter "c" represents a constant (number/ratio) and not a variable: "$c = 299\ 792\ 458\ metres\ per\ second\ \ or\ c = \frac{299\ 792\ 458\ metres}{1\ second}$". We would not be surprised if Einstein used "Young's Equation/Ratio Theorem" and "Young's Conversion Theorem" in some form when he derived the theorem "$E = mc^2$", but again we will let the answer to this comment up to the physics majors.

> Question for Secondary Mathematics Teachers: Notice the negative exponent with the expression, "ms^{-1}". What does the negative exponent, "-1", represent?

There are other advanced conversions where mathematicians and scientists derived formulas to convert from one unit into another unit, but these formulas are far beyond the scope of this textbook. What is important to consider is, we believe many procedures used in science and engineering use "Young's Equation/Ratio Theorem" and/or "Young's Conversion Theorem", and just as importantly, many formulas and procedures used in science and engineering require students to work with labels using the same algebra procedures indicated earlier. Many of these advanced formulas involve different units of measurement, and the mathematicians and scientists make sure the algebra rules are followed with respect to the labels.

We realize some people use two equal ratios and cross-multiply to convert from one unit into an equivalent unit. We like the two-ratio cross-multiplication method in some situations, but it is cumbersome when converting more than one unit in a problem. The cross-multiplication method also has limitations when working with squares and cubes. It is not the way most conversion problems in science and advanced math problems are solved. We encourage you to mention the two-ratio cross-multiplication process to your students, but we hope you emphasize "Young's Equation/Ratio Theorem" and "Young's Conversion Theorem" when you are converting units and expressions in arithmetic and advanced mathematics into equivalent units and expressions. We do not emphasize the cross-multiplication process to the average and below average students when they work with conversion problems. We simply do not want the students to get confused when to use the cross-multiplication process and the two-theorem process. If you can get 90% of your students to correctly complete the indicated conversion problems using the two-theorem conversion process discussed in this textbook which emphasizes the number 1, why would you want to confuse some of your students with a method which works for a few special conversion situations? We did not say, "Never emphasize the cross-multiplication process." Quite the opposite, there are many great applications of the cross-multiplication process in arithmetic and algebra. For example, when you encounter a direct proportion problem and three of the four terms are given, it is an excellent time to use the cross-multiplication process to find the fourth term. When working with similar polygons we do not mention the two theorems discussed in this textbook, we emphasize the cross-multiplication process/theorem. We realize several of our example problems involve direct variations and thus the cross-multiplication method would be an appropriate procedure to use in some of our example problems. You may set up the simple conversion problems mentioned at the beginning of the Chapter 6 as cross-multiplication problems because they are examples of direct variation problems, but you will encounter problems when you solve the more difficult conversion problems previously mentioned in Chapter 6 and in this chapter.

Here is an observation we encountered frequently with many average college bound 9th graders. They frequently confused the cross-multiplication process with the rules for multiplying two fractions. Just something to think about when you are teaching students about the cross-multiplication process after they previously learned how to multiply **two** fractions earlier in their arithmetic career. Notice, we did not say the students confuse the cross-multiplication process when they multiply 3 or more fractions; they only get confused when they multiply two fractions. The reason students might get confused when they multiply two fractions and not 3 or more fractions is because most of the fraction multiplication questions contained in a typical 5th grade arithmetic textbook in the U.S. only involve two fractions.

If you have read every page so far in this textbook without studying the examples and solving the additional problems on your own, you still have a lot to learn. You can prove this statement correct by not writing down the solutions to any of the problems discussed in this textbook, not practicing the rules and procedures emphasized over and over in this textbook, and not completing the assignments at the end of each chapter. Then in a month or two after reading this textbook, try to explain how to convert "55 $\frac{in.^3}{hr.}$ into $\frac{ft.^3}{day}$" or convert "732.654 into a percent" or convert "$\frac{7}{1760}$ $mi.$ into $in.$". Our guess is, if you have not practiced and reviewed solving these types of problems for over six weeks, many of you will struggle to solve these conversions whether you use the rules emphasized in this textbook or you use the procedures you learned when you were in school and/or you have been teaching/illustrating in your arithmetic classes for years.

We often hear someone make the comment "drill and kill" when they are referring to students doing too much classwork and homework in arithmetic or math class. If you are one of the people who has made this comment in the past, do what we suggest in the last paragraph: do not practice or even think about the rules and procedures discussed in this textbook for several weeks and then go back and solve the types of problems we indicated. In retrospect, the wise person may coin mottos like this: "No Drill, then No Skill" or "Little Drill, Little Skill" or "More Drill, More Skill". If you really want students to "learn and remember" how to solve arithmetic and mathematics problems, we suspect there is a direct relationship between the amount of "drill" a student preforms and the amount of "skill" the student possesses two or three months later. We also believe there is a point in the number of problems students are required to solve where the improvement and their mastery to solve specific types of problems becomes flat (there is little to no improvement). This means the teacher must be a master teacher and determine how many problems are necessary for the students to solve if the goal is to have the students "learn and remember" the mathematics procedures for the topics he or she is teaching.

In the last paragraph, we implied there seems to be a direct correlation between students solving several arithmetic and advanced math problems, referred to as practice, and their ability to remember the procedures two weeks or two months later. We also stated there would be a leveling off in the students' learning based on the number of problems the students were required to solve and what the students would remember. With these two thoughts put together, it would be more appropriate to say the amount of practice students devote to solving arithmetic problems and remembering how to solve the problems a few weeks later is not a perfect direct relationship but more closely related to a logarithmic relationship/correlation. We also indicated over and over in this textbook you need to constantly review. If you taught an arithmetic or math topic well and you do not review the procedures and rules for two or three weeks or more, your students will quickly forget much of what they learned.

Unbelievable, But True

Important Comment: You may think using the "2-3" minute introductions frequently for two months before a specific topic is covered in the textbook and homework is assigned from the textbook, would create a situation where we would not be able to cover all the required topics for the course. Quite the opposite occurred. We always covered all the topics required in the curriculum and frequently covered additional concepts other teachers never had the time to cover. We simply are saying, we covered more topics and our students "learned and remembered" the concepts at a much higher rate than students in other classes.

How can this be true? The answer is simple, when it was time to discuss a topic in the classroom and assign problems for homework the students already knew how to solve most of the problems from the textbook. We saved significant time on the day or days we discussed the concepts to solve the problems and we saved time when we went over homework assignments. Since we also reviewed constantly, when new topics were presented in the textbook, we seldom had to go back and reteach previously learned materials and we did not have to review in preparation for special tests.

Interweave/Interleave several simple arithmetic problems which the students should be able to solve with a few challenging problems. Require the students to use rules to compute the solutions, which should give the students confidence with the number of problems they solved correctly and if they have difficulty solving the challenging problems, these will be the problems you illustrate how to solve in class the next day. Making sure students feel confident when they are given an assignment, quiz, or test is a goal all teachers should strive to accomplish.

WHY DO WE THINK IT IS IMPORTANT THAT ELEMENTARY TEACHERS, SECONDARY MATH TEACHERS, AND STUDENTS BECOME FAMILIAR WITH BOTH "YOUNG'S EQUATION/RATIO THEOREM" AND "YOUNG'S CONVERSION THEOREM?

If you want to determine an answer to the previous question, ask 10, 20, or 30 elementary teachers and then 10, 20, or 30 secondary math certified teachers to explain the following two-word phrases.

1. Given the two words "Dimensional Analysis": explain how these two words apply to the two main topics presented in this textbook: 1. Solving/simplifying all types of fraction problems and 2. Conversion problems.
2. Given the two words "Unit Multipliers": explain how these two words apply to the topics presented in this textbook.
3. Given the two words "Conversion Factors": explain how these two words apply to the topics presented in this textbook.

Our guess is if you ask 10, 20, or 30 secondary math certified teachers to explain all three of the phrases just mentioned you will find less than 50% of these teachers feel confident explaining the definitions of all three phrases, especially the two-word phrase "Dimensional Analysis". If you ask 10, 20, or 30 elementary teachers to explain the definitions of these three phrases you might be lucky to find 20% of the teachers have some understanding of all three phrases.

The three two-word phrases "Dimensional Analysis", "Unit Multipliers", and "Conversion Factors" are all related to both "Young's Equation/Ratio Theorem" and "Young's Conversion Theorem" and yet only an expert in mathematics can explain the meanings of the three indicated phrases.

We feel everyone who reads and studies this textbook will remember and be able to work with both "Young's Equation/Ratio Theorem" and "Young's Conversion Theorem", then understand the importance and applications of both theorems.

THIS IS WHY WE NAMED THE THEOREMS AND WROTE THIS TEXTBOOK. WE WANT TEACHERS TO USE THE THEOREMS AND REFER TO THEM BY NAME SO ALL STUDENTS UNDERSTAND THE IMPORTANCE OF THE TWO THEOREMS, ALL STUDENTS CAN APPROPRIATELY APPLY THE THEOREMS TO SOLVE A VARIETY OF ARITHEMTIC PROBLEMS, AND ALL STUDENTS ARE PREPARED TO SOLVE MANY ADVANCED MATHEMATICS PROBLEMS ENCOUNTERED IN ALGEBRA, TRIGONOMETRY, CALCULUS, CHEMISTRY, PHYSICS, ETC.

Additionally, we feel every teacher who reads, studies, and completes the assignments at the end of each chapter will be prepared to teach arithmetic in any elementary and middle school in the world. The arithmetic concepts and topics discussed, illustrated, and then assigned as additional work at the end of each chapter, cover a wide variety of arithmetic concepts from the basic to the more advanced. We also believe if every secondary math teacher reads, studies, and completes the assignments at the end of each chapter, they will understand how topics were presented/taught in arithmetic and use the same rules and procedures to teach topics in higher level mathematics courses.

Seventh Assignment

DEFINITIONS

In some problems you are requested to write your definition of a word or a phrase and then look up the definition on the internet or dictionary to determine if you understand the specifics about the definitions you should know. In other problems you will be asked to explain the differences between some words and some phrases, we think this is an important method to use to help you better explain the definitions of words and phrases.

A. Think about the difference between Natural Numbers and Whole Numbers.

1. Define the set of Natural Numbers in sentence form. Define Natural Numbers using set notation.
2. Define the set of Whole Numbers in sentence form. Define Whole Numbers using set notation.
3. What is the obvious difference between the set of Natural Numbers and the set of Whole Numbers?

   Think about the difference between Whole Numbers and Integers.

4. Define the set of Integers using a sentence. Define Integers using set notation.
5. Is every Natural Number an Integer? Justify your answer.
6. Is every Integer a Whole Number? Justify your answer.
7. How would you explain to your students the difference between the set of Whole Numbers, the set of Integers, and the set of Natural Numbers?

   Think about the differences between Rational Numbers and Integers.

8. a. How do you explain the definition of the set Rational Numbers to your students?

   b. Write five rational numbers using five slightly different forms. (Examples: Write a rational number with or without a decimal, as a mixed number, etc.)

9. Is every Integer a Rational Number? Justify your answer.

10. Is every Natural Number a Rational Number? Justify your answer.

11. NOT every Rational Number is an Integer. Give 3 examples of Rational Numbers which are not integers and 3 examples of Rational Numbers which are Integers. Write the 6 Rational Numbers using at least three different notations.

12. Give three examples of numbers which are Integers but not Whole Numbers.

13. How will you explain to your students the difference between the set of Natural Numbers, the set of Whole Numbers, the set of Integers, and the set of Rational Numbers?

B. Define the following words or phrases in your own words and then compare your definition with the internet or dictionary definition.

14. Fraction
15. Improper Fraction
16. Coefficient or Coefficients
17. Interleave (As it applies to mathematics)
18. Ratio
19. Prime Numbers
20. Per
21. Mixed Numbers
22. Percent
23. Absolute Values
24. Factors
25. Multiples
26. Terminating Decimal
27. Repeating Decimal
28. Define Irrational Numbers. Based on the definition, Irrational Numbers turn out to be Non-Terminating and Non-Repeating Decimals - (Examples: "0.10011000111...",

" $\sqrt{7} = 2.6457 \ldots$", "$\sqrt[3]{10} = 2.15443 \ldots$ ", "$\sqrt{5}$ ", "$\frac{4}{\sqrt[3]{20}}$ ", "7.232233222333... ", "$\sqrt{2}$ ")

We are looking for a two-word definition for Irrational Numbers. We indicated the definition with examples of the two words and several examples.

29. Explain what mathematicians are referring to when they mention "The Cartesian Coordinate System" and/or "The Rectangular Coordinate System".

PROPERTIES AND THEOREMS IN YOUR OWN WORDS

C. The following properties and theorems have been stated and illustrated frequently throughout this textbook. In your own words state the meaning of the properties and theorems and when appropriate use mathematics notation to illustrate the property or theorem.

30. Commutative Property for both Addition and Multiplication
31. Associative Property for both Addition and Multiplication
32. Reflexive Property
33. Symmetric Property
34. Transitive Property
35. Young's Equation/Ratio Theorem
36. Young's Conversion Theorem

TIMED AND ACCURACY

D. Solve the following sets of Multiplication and Division Problems as quickly and accurately as you can. Work with a friend or two and apply the same procedures you used to solve the problems for speed and accuracy at the end of Chapter 3 in the Third Assignment with one exception, write down your answers. All the problems involve Multiplying and Dividing by powers of "10". (Helpful Hints: Remember $10^0 = 1$, $10^1 = 10$, $10^2 = 100$, $10^3 = 1{,}000$, $10^4 = 10{,}000$, $10^5 = 100{,}000$, *etc.*).

37. Be fast and be accurate.

a. "34×10", "3.04×10^1", "0.034×1000", "$34 \div 10$", "$\frac{3004}{10^2}$", "$7.034 \div 100$", "$\frac{78.04}{10^0}$", "1000×0.301", "$.078 \div 10^2$", "$(3.001)(100)$", "$10^3 \times 0.5$", "$2\frac{1}{2} \times 1000$"

b. "$.021 \times 10^3$", "$\frac{32.104}{10^3}$", "$896.1 \div 10000$", "$.0931000 \times 10$", "6.71×10^0", "$\frac{.091}{10^0}$", "0.071×10^4", "$0.071 \div 10^3$", "$\frac{0.902}{10^3}$", "57×100", "$074.74 \div 100$", "$\frac{0.079}{10^2}$"

c. "$\frac{5.019}{100}$", "50.19×10^2", "$0.701 \div 10$", "$7.019 \div 10^3$", "3040×1000", "55.1×10^0", "$.099 \div 10^2$", "$100 \times .056$", "$\frac{7.1}{10^0}$", "$\frac{.071}{10^2}$", "8000×100", "12.601×10^3"

d. "$10^4 \times 11$", "$56 \div 10^4$", "$\frac{16.1}{1} \times \frac{1}{100}$", "$7\frac{1}{2} \times 10^1$", "$\frac{60}{1000}$", "$70.29 \div 10^4$", "$1000 \times 11.201$", "$10^4 \times .00007$", "$\frac{0.005}{10^2}$", "$0.15 \div 100$", "$0.3 \times 10^4$", "$\frac{7001}{100}$"

e. "$\frac{77.03}{1000}$", "10×88.9", "$8098 \div 10^4$", "$10^5 \times 0.071$", "9909×10^3", "$98.01 \div 100$", "50×1000", "$\frac{5}{1000}$", "$7002.3 \div 10^4$", "$10^5 \times 0.0998$", "$\frac{0.98}{1000}$", "0.987×10^4"

f. "0.9001×100", "$10 \times 2\frac{1}{2}$", "$3\frac{3}{4} \times 1000$", "$1\frac{1}{2} \div 10^2$", "$\frac{3\frac{1}{4}}{100}$", "5.2×1000", "$\frac{700.1}{10^3}$", "$10^5 \times 100$", "100×100", "$\frac{10^5}{100{,}000}$", "77.654×10^0", "$90087 \div 10^0$"

ILLUSTRATE HOW TO SOLVE THE FOLLOWING PROBLEMS USING BOTH "YOUNG'S EQUATION/RATIO THEOREM" AND "YOUNG'S CONVERSION THEOREM"

E. Write the solutions to solve the following problems illustrating how to use both "Young's Equation/Ratio Theorem" and "Young's Conversion Theorem" as demonstrated in this chapter.

Convert terminating decimals to fractions.

38. 0.78	39. 0.25	40. 0.355
41. 0.98	42. 0.9595	43. 0.31035

Convert a Percent into a Decimal.

44. 78%	45. 0.25%	46. 355%
47. 0.98%	48. 9.595%	49. 0.31035%

Convert the Number into a Percent.

50. 0.78	51. 25	52. 03.55
53. 0.98	54. 95.95	55. 0.31035

H. If you are given a decimal, convert it into both a fraction and a percent. If you are given a percent, convert it into both a decimal and a fraction. If you are given a fraction, convert it into both a decimal and a percent. In problems "44-49" and "50-55" above, once you determined the correct trick to convert between percentages and decimals and decimals and percentages it was easy to convert the other five problems in questions "45-49" and "51-55". Many people get the tricks confused when the problems are mixed up and they are required to convert between fractions, percentages, and decimals.

56. 0.78% 57. 0.25 58. $\frac{7}{8}$

59. $\frac{98}{100}$ 60. 95.95 61. 31035%

62. $1\frac{9}{20}$ 63. $7\frac{1}{2}\%$ 64. $7\frac{2}{5}$

COMMUTATIVE ($+$ *and* $\times$), ASSOCIATIVE ($+$ *and* $\times$), REFLEXIVE, SYMMETRIC, AND TRANSITIVE PROPERTIES

I. Identify which of the following basic arithmetic properties apply: (Commutative Property for Addition, Associative Property for Addition, Commutative Property for Multiplication, Associative Property for Multiplication, Reflexive Property, Symmetric Property, and Transitive Property).

65. $a + b = 6 \quad \therefore \quad 6 = a + b$

66. $m + n - 11 = m + n - 11$

67. $a \times (b \times c) = (a \times b) \times c$

68. $r = st \;\&\; st = m + n \quad \therefore \quad r = m + n$

69. $(5 + 6) \times 7 = 7 \times (5 + 6)$

70. $(5 + 6) \times 7 = (6 + 5) \times 7$

71. $(c + 9) + 11 = c + (9 + 11)$

There are two other powerful properties in arithmetic which everyone is familiar, but we did not ask you to identify these properties in any of the assignments at the end of the chapters. The first property which everyone will recognize is a property which applies to these example problems:

("$6 + 0 = 6$", "$7\frac{1}{4} = 7\frac{1}{4} + 0$", "$5 = 0 + 5$, *and* "$0 + 7.123 = 7.123$"). Everyone should recognize quickly in all these equations, a fact we all know, "When you add the number 0, to any number, you end with the same number with which you started." Mathematicians refer to this property as the Identity Property for Addition. The Identity Property for Addition simply states the ending number, term, or expression is identical to the starting number, term, or expression when you add the number zero. Since this is a fact in arithmetic and all mathematics problems, mathematicians refer to the number 0 as the identity element (number) for the operation of addition.

The second property which we frequently mentioned throughout this textbook is referred to as the Identity Property for Multiplication. The Identity Property for Multiplication simply states when you multiply by the number 1; the answer is identical to the number, term or, expression you started with. Since this is a fact in arithmetic and all mathematics, we refer to the number 1 as the identity element (number) for the operation of multiplication. "Young's Conversion Theorem" is an expansion of the Identity Property for Multiplication. Here are some examples to illustrate the Identity Property for Multiplication: ("$1 \times 6 = 6$", "$a \times 1 = a$", "$6.45 = 6.45 \times 1$", *and* "$7\frac{71}{99} = 1 \times 7\frac{71}{99}$").

J. Identify whether the equations represent the Identity Property for Multiplication or the Identity Property for Addition.

72. $9 + 0 = 9$

73. $16 \times 1 = 16$

74. $71.29 = 1 \times 71.29$

75. $0 + \frac{7}{8} = \frac{7}{8}$

76. $7\frac{1}{8} = 7\frac{1}{8} + 0$

77. $abc \times 1 = abc$

78. $(x + 7) + 0 = (x + 7)$

IDENTIFY WHETHER A NUMBER IS A NATURAL NUMBER, A WHOLE NUMBER, AN INTEGER, A RATIONAL NUMBER, OR AN IRRATIONAL NUMBER.

ALL THE NUMBERS LISTED BELOW ARE **REAL NUMBERS**

Frequently a number is a member of several sets of number systems. For instance, the number "5" is a **Natural** Number and a **Whole** Number. The Number "5" is also an **Integer** and a **Rational** Number because the number "5 may also be written as $\frac{5}{1}$". In this textbook, we did not emphasize the meaning of Real Numbers, but the number "5" is a Real Number. The opposite of a Real Number is an Imaginary Number. Imaginary numbers are normally taught in Algebra 2. We do mention Imaginary Numbers in Chapter 8, because Chapter 8 focuses on more advanced mathematics topics and procedures which utilize both "Young's Equation/Ratio Theorem" and "Young's Conversion Theorem". Write your answers as follows: <u>The number "5" is a Natural Number, a Whole Number, an Integer, a Rational Number, and a Real Number.</u> Every number you encounter prior to working with Imaginary Numbers in an advanced algebra class is probably a Real Number. The reason we did not emphasize Real Numbers is because if you want to have a strong understanding of Real Numbers you must also understand Imaginary Numbers, which are **not** normally considered part of an arithmetic curriculum.

K. Identify which set or sets of numbers the following numbers are members.

79. "-10" 80. "70.5" 81. "0" 82. "11.7171 ..." 83. "6"

84. "π" 85. "-6.5" 86. "2" 87. "$\sqrt{10}$" 88. "1"

IN A DIVISION PROBLEM, IF THE DIVISOR CONTAINS A DECIMAL THE RULE IS TO MOVE THE DECIMAL TO THE RIGHT AND DIVIDE BY A NATURAL NUMBER.

L. Illustrate why the decimal point in the dividend will move an equal number of times to the right as the decimal in the divisor for the following problems. Use "Young's Equation/Ratio Theorem" and "Young's Conversion Theorem" in all three illustrations. After you illustrate why the decimal point moves an equal number of times in both numbers to complete the division operation, solve the three problems using the long division box notation.

89. $3.75 \div .25$ 90. $\frac{716.23}{.002}$ 91. $2.656255 \div 101.5$

CONVERT THE FOLLOWING TEMPERATURES INTO FAHRENHEIT OR CELCIUS TEMPERATURES DEPENDING ON WHICH TYPE OF TEMPERATURE IS GIVEN.

M. When converting between Fahrenheit and Celsius temperatures only use the formula "$F = \frac{9}{5}C + 32$" and solve for the unknown variable. We prefer to emphasize one conversion equation rather than two conversion equations. We found students get confused when they are given both equations and then make a guess to determine which of the two equations they should use. If students are competent solving basic algebra equations, the second conversion equation is not necessary. We emphasize solving basic first-degree algebra equations so students do not have to memorize several equations for the same problem. When students are competent using the given equation "$F = \frac{9}{5}C + 32$" then we illustrate using algebra how to determine the second conversion equation.

92. $20°\ C$ 93. $80°\ F$ 94. $80°\ C$ 95. $200°\ F$

SOLVE BASIC ALGEBRA EQUATIONS

N. You should write all the solutions as if you are teaching students to solve the problems for the first time and you should not skip any steps when writing the solutions. In all your solutions use the two-theorem identity method which was illustrated frequently throughout the textbook.

96. $12x = 150$

97. $17.656 + p = 2011.7$

98. $101.1\,b = 370.9359$

99. $17\frac{3}{8} = c + 6\frac{11}{12}$

100. $5\frac{2}{5} = 5\frac{1}{5} + r$

101. $\frac{k}{2.1} = 3.7$

102. $\frac{w}{3\frac{1}{2}} = 3\frac{1}{2}$

103. $6.9 = 0.32m$ (Do not round off the answer.)

SOLVE BASIC ALGEBRA WORD PROBLEMS BASED ON KNOWN FORMULAS

O. We will write out the word problems as you would find them in an arithmetic book. You should know which formula to use based on the questions.

104. Find the area of a triangle given the length of the $Base = 7.5\ ft.$ and the length of the $Height = 3.25\ ft.$

105. Find the volume of a cube, given the length of one $Side = 2\frac{1}{2}\ in.$

106. Find the area of a circle given the length of the $Radius = \pi\ yds.$ Write the final solution as an exact answer involving the number "π".

107. Find the area of the rectangle given the $Lenght = 7\frac{3}{4}\ mi.$ and the $Width = 2.4\ mi.$

108. Find the volume of a rectangular solid given the $Length = .75\ yds.$, the $Width = 9\ in.$, and the $Height = 3\ ft.$ (Hint: Make sure all the units are the same unit of measurement before you begin to solve the problem.)

109. If the Circumference of a circle equals "$2\pi\ ft.$", what is the radius of the circle? The formula to find the Circumference of a circle is written in the following form: "$C = 2\pi r$".

110. How many acres are contained in a triangular field if the base of the triangle equals "75 $ft.$" and the height of the triangle equals "108.5 $ft.$"? If you want to use the field to raise animals, what type of animals would be the most appropriate to place in this field on a regular basis? "*Cows*" "*Horses*" "*Dogs*" "*Chickens*"

111. How many hectares are contained in a rectangular field if the length of the field is 1705 meters and the width is 900.75 meters? If you want to use the field to raise animals, what type of animals would be the most appropriate to place in this field?
"*Cows*" "*Horses*" "*Dogs*" "*Chickens*"

CHAPTER 8

WORK WITH MORE ADVANCED MATHEMATICS PROBLEMS USING "YOUNG'S EQUATION/RATIO THEOREM" AND "YOUNG'S CONVERSION THEOREM" – THE POWER OF ONE (1) IS AMAZING

WE HOPE YOU ARE AMAZED BY THE POWER OF THE NUMBER ONE BY NOW.

Chapter 8

Mathematicians often write using mathematics shorthand notation. Usually, when we write a theorem, we write the theorem using the proper mathematics notation and then let it up to the teacher to translate the math notation. We did the opposite in this textbook when we illustrated and discussed topics, and we did the opposite when we discussed the two new theorems: "Young's Equation/Ratio Theorem" and "Young's Conversion Theorem". We did this on purpose because we wanted everyone to understand the meaning of the theorems before we wrote the mathematics shorthand notation for the two theorems. The two proofs below are written using a basic proof format. There are other ways to write proofs, but many people are familiar with the proof format used below.

Here are the two theorems written using math notation:

Young's Equation/Ratio Theorem:

If "$a = b$" and "$a \neq 0$" and "$b \neq 0$", then "$\frac{a}{b} = 1$" and "$\frac{b}{a} = 1$".

Proof

1. $a = b, a \neq 0,\ b \neq 0$ — 1. Given
2. $\frac{a}{a} = 1$ — 2. Basic Math Assumption/Fact
3. $\therefore\ \frac{a}{b} = 1\ and\ \frac{b}{a} = 1$ — 3. Substitution

In "step 3." we actually focused on "step 2". We noticed in "step 2" the letter/variable "a" was in the denominator, and we also realized in "step 1" the letter/variable "b" is equal to the variable "a". This means we are permitted to substitute the letter "b" for the denominator "a" in "step 2" and write the equation "$\frac{a}{b} = 1$" in step 3. We did the same thing to derive the second equation in "step 3" except we substituted the letter "b" for the letter "a" in the numerator.

Young's Conversion Theorem: If "$a \times c = b$" and "$c = 1$", then "$a = b$".

Proof

1. $a \times c = b,\ c = 1$	1. Given
2. $a \times 1 = a$	2. Multiplication Identity Property for One (1)
3. $a \times c = a$	3. Substitution
4. $a = a \times c$	4. Symmetric Property
5. $a = b$	5. Transitive Property - (4th and 1st equation)

In "step 3" we need to reference "step 2" and rewrite the equation in "step 2" by replacing the number "1" in the "step 2" equation with the letter "c". The reason this is legitimate is because in "step 1" we knew the letter "c" is equal to the number "1", so in this problem the letter "c" and the number "1" are interchangeable. In "step 4" we switched the sides of the equation in "step 3", referred to as the *symmetric property* for equations. To derive the equation in "step 5", we mentally focused on the equation in "step 4" and then focused on the first equation in "step 1." If we write the equation in "step 4" first and then write the equation from "step 1" to the right of the "step 4" equation, the two equations will look like this: "$a = a \times c$" & "$a \times c = b$". The right side of the first equation is identical to the left-hand side of the second equation. This means the left side of the first equation is equal to the right side of the second equation, "$a = b$". We know this situation is referred to as the *transitive property* for equations.

Simplifying Rational Expressions Involving Reducing, Multiplying, and Dividing

Throughout the first part of this textbook, we continually used example arithmetic problems because we were trying to illustrate to elementary teachers how to use "Young's Equation/Ratio Theorem" and "Young's Conversion Theorem". Frequently, when we had to multiply fractions or reduce fractions, we used factor trees rather than the more common method taught by many elementary arithmetic teachers and secondary math teachers when they are teaching students to reduce, multiply, and/or divide fractions (after they invert and multiply the fraction to the right of the division operation symbol "÷"). The method we are referring to is to get students to use their knowledge of the multiplication tables to determine what number will divide into the numbers in the numerator and the denominator, and then do the division problem and make the numbers in both the numerator and denominator smaller. There is nothing wrong with trying to get students to recognize what numbers divide into numbers in both the numerator and the denominator. When the problems are simple, we strongly encourage students to reduce quickly in their head to find an equivalent fraction with smaller numbers in both the numerator and the denominator. Even when the fractions involve large numbers in either or both the numerator and/or the denominator, we want the students to be able to use their knowledge of the multiplication and division tables to reduce the fraction, but if they struggle reducing the fractions when the numbers are large, we encourage them to use factor trees. We want the students to understand if problems are challenging, the best way to solve the problem is to use factor trees. Here are a few quick examples to illustrate how we use factor trees to reduce, multiply, and divide fractions.

1. Reduce: "$\frac{25}{35}$".

We want the students to quickly recognize the number "5" will divide into each of the two numbers "25 and 35", and the simplified answer is "$\frac{5}{7}$". The number "5" is referred to as the Greatest Common Factor (GCF) for these two numbers.

We could also reduce the fraction "$\frac{25}{35}$" by rewriting both the numerator and the denominator in factored form using factor trees and prime numbers. Here are the steps to simplify this problem using factor trees and canceling identical factors in both the numerator and the denominator: "$\frac{25}{35} = \frac{5 \cdot 5}{5 \cdot 7} = \frac{5}{7}$". Refer to the middle fraction. The number/factor "5" in the denominator cancelled with one of the "5's" in the numerator. The only remaining number in the numerator is "5", and the only remaining number in the denominator is "7".

2. Multiply and find the reduced answer: "$\frac{5}{12} \times \frac{18}{25}$".

Students should quickly divide the number "5" by "5" and the number "25" by "5". We also expect students to quickly divide the number "12" by "6" and the number "18" by "6". The two new fractions after they are reduced become "$\frac{1}{2} \times \frac{3}{5}$", and you could write the two fractions as one fraction "$\frac{1 \times 3}{2 \times 5}$". The final reduced answer is "$\frac{3}{10}$".

You could tell the students to write the original problem as one fraction "$\frac{5 \times 18}{12 \times 25}$" and then multiply both numbers in the numerator and in the denominator to get the fraction "$\frac{90}{300}$", which makes the problem more difficult. You must now decide how you are going to illustrate the way to reduce this fraction. You could suggest that the numerator "90" and the denominator "300" are both divisible by the number "30". If the students do not recognize both numbers are divisible by "30", you can have them divide both numbers by the number "10" and then "3". It does not matter which of the indicated solutions you tell students to use to simplify the faction multiplication problem, "$\frac{5}{12} \times \frac{18}{25}$" to get the simplified form of the answer "$\frac{3}{10}$".

All three of the indicated solutions require the students to apply their knowledge of multiplication and division facts. If students did not recognize the numbers "30" and "10" divide evenly into both the numerator "90" and the denominator "300", they could begin by dividing each number by the number "2" or even "15". There are several ways to reduce the numbers when simplifying the problem, "$\frac{5}{12} \times \frac{18}{25}$".

We like the idea of writing the two original fractions as a single large fraction. There is nothing wrong with multiplying the numbers in the numerator and the numbers in the denominator first, but you should realize this problem became more difficult because instead of reducing first and working with smaller numbers, we multiplied first which required us to reduce larger numbers. **If you are required to reduce, multiply, or divide a rational expression in algebra, you would factor the numerators and denominators first.**

We continually encourage students to use factor trees when they are asked to simplify a fraction problem involving multiplication and/or reducing. Using factor trees will work when students are asked to simplify simple fraction multiplication and reducing problems, and factor trees will work when the students simplify the most difficult fraction multiplication and reducing problems.

> When reducing, multiplying, and dividing fractions in algebra, you would **never** multiply the numerators and the denominators first, and then try to reduce the fractions.

The following illustration which uses factor trees and prime numbers, is the way we frequently illustrated to students to simplify this fraction multiplication problem: "$\frac{5}{12} \times \frac{18}{25} = \frac{5 \times 18}{12 \times 25} = \frac{5 \times 2 \cdot 3 \cdot 3}{2 \cdot 2 \cdot 3 \times 5 \cdot 5} = \frac{1 \times 1 \cdot 1 \cdot 3}{1 \cdot 2 \cdot 1 \times 1 \cdot 5} = \frac{3}{10}$". The prime factors for the number "18" in the numerator are "2 · 3 · 3". The prime factors for "12" in the denominator are "2 · 2 · 3". Then the prime factors for the number "25" in the denominator are "5 · 5". You must recognize the identical factors "5, 2, and 3" will reduce/cancel in the numerator and in the denominator in-order-to determine the final answer "$\frac{3}{10}$". When the numbers/factors in both the numerator and denominator cancelled, we replaced each of the cancelled numbers with the number 1. This is a teaching point we feel is important to illustrate to the students but not important for the students to write every time.

3. Simplify the following problem: "$\frac{6}{7} \times \frac{14}{15} \div \frac{8}{5}$".

Teach reducing fractions, multiplying fractions, and dividing fractions as one topic, not as three separate topics. Obviously, the one major difference occurs when you divide by a fraction: you need to emphasize the fraction to the right of the division operation symbol "÷" must be inverted, and then the division problem becomes a multiplication problem. When we teach multiplying and dividing fractions involving simple numbers, we want the students to be able to quickly reduce the numerators and denominators once they have set up a multiplication problem by using their knowledge of the multiplication and division tables, but continually review and illustrate the factor tree and cancel process when simplifying fractions which involve multiplying, reducing, and dividing.

Teaching Point: The reason we continually emphasize the factor tree and cancel process is because the factor-and-cancel process is required to simplify similar rational expression problems in algebra.

We encourage students to set up a single fraction when they multiply and divide fractions. We want students to realize they should reduce first then multiply all the factors in the numerator and then multiply all the factors in the denominator. When simplifying the example problem "$\frac{6}{7} \times \frac{14}{15} \div \frac{8}{5}$", we want students in the first step to rewrite the problem as a multiplication problem with three fractions by inverting the fraction "$\frac{8}{5}$" into the fraction "$\frac{5}{8}$" and then to switch the division operation into a multiplication operation. The problem is now written as "$\frac{6}{7} \times \frac{14}{15} \times \frac{5}{8}$", and the problem can be rewritten as one large fraction "$\frac{6 \times 14 \times 5}{7 \times 15 \times 8}$". We can quickly reduce the numbers "6" and "15" by dividing them both by the number "3". We can also reduce both the numbers "7" and "14" by dividing them both by "7". After reducing these two sets of numbers, the fraction becomes "$\frac{2 \times 2 \times 5}{1 \times 5 \times 8}$". Now, reduce the "5" in the denominator with the "5" in the numerator, and both the "2s" in the numerator will reduce with the number "8" in the denominator. After canceling all the numbers, the only remaining number in the numerator is "1", and the only remaining number in the denominator is "2". The answer is "$\frac{1}{2}$".

> Teachers frequently use the word cancel when then are reducing fractions. Technically, we divide identical factors in the numerator and denominator and the quotient becomes "1". The word cancel is frequently used in this situation, but one must realize they solved a division problem.

If you encourage students to use factor trees with all the numbers in the numerator and all the numbers in the denominator, once the fraction is set up as one big fraction, we discovered the average and low achieving students were much more successful finding the answer. Amazingly, we found the low achieving students with practice began to recognize a number like "8" could be written as either "$2 \times 2 \times 2$ or 2^3". This is an example of what we meant when we commented earlier in this textbook about the joy teachers will feel--because the low achieving students' arithmetic skills will improve significantly by the end of the year. *(FRT 12: If students are required to frequently work with factor trees, will their multiplication and division mental skills improve? Notice, we used factor trees as a required process to solve fraction problems, not as an independent procedure.)* High achieving students usually recognize different numbers which divide into both the numerator and the denominator, but we still want the high achieving students to understand the importance of factor trees when they reduce, multiply, and divide fractions.

Here is how we suggest students write the big fraction using factor trees and then cancelling identical factors: "$\frac{6 \times 14 \times 5}{7 \times 15 \times 8} = \frac{2 \cdot 3 \times 2 \cdot 7 \times 5}{7 \times 3 \cdot 5 \times 2 \cdot 2 \cdot 2} = \frac{1}{2}$". Go back to the large fraction just written with all the factors indicated and cross out (cancel) two (2's) in both the numerator and the denominator, one (3) in both the numerator and the denominator, one (5) in both the numerator and the denominator, and one (7) in both the numerator and the denominator. When we cancelled identical factors/numbers in both the numerator and the denominator, we replaced the cancelled numbers with the number 1. You should understand why the final simplified answer is "$\frac{1}{2}$".

Teaching Comment: We assume most teachers use the following type of terminology to explain to their students how to divide a fraction by a fraction, "First, you must invert the fraction immediately to the right of the division operation symbol, "÷", and then change the division operation symbol into a multiplication operation symbol." There may be a few teachers who cannot explain why this procedure works when dividing fractions. If you understand "Young's Equation/Ratio Theorem" and "Young's Conversion Theorem", you can now illustrate to your class why the two changes applied to a division problem involving two fractions really works.

Try to follow the steps indicated below to explain how to solve the problem "$\frac{1}{2} \div \frac{3}{4}$". The following explanation will probably be too difficult for most of your 5th graders and many of your 6th graders, but your best students should be able to understand the steps indicated. More importantly, you should understand why you must invert and multiply the fraction to the right of the division operation symbol "÷" when you are dividing two fractions.

4. Simplify: $\frac{1}{2} \div \frac{3}{4}$

1. Step 1: Rewrite the division problem as a complex fraction, "$\frac{\frac{1}{2}}{\frac{3}{4}}$".

We used the following fact: There are three ways to write a division problem. We can write a division problem as a fraction, as a division problem using a division box, or as a division problem with the division symbol "÷". You must be able to rewrite division problems in either one of the three forms then switch from one form into another form. We switched from the division operation symbol "÷" format into the complex fraction format.

2. Step 2: Here is an identity fact: "$\frac{4}{3} = \frac{4}{3}$". Now, we will use "Young's Equation/Ratio Theorem" with the given identity and write the following identity, "$\frac{\frac{4}{3}}{\frac{4}{3}} = 1$".

3. Step 3: Using "Young's Conversion Theorem" convert the fraction "$\frac{\frac{1}{2}}{\frac{3}{4}}$" into a multiplication problem with two fractions. "$\frac{1}{2} \div \frac{3}{4} = \frac{\frac{1}{2}}{\frac{3}{4}} = \frac{\frac{1}{2}}{\frac{3}{4}} \times 1 = \frac{\frac{1}{2}}{\frac{3}{4}} \times \frac{\frac{4}{3}}{\frac{4}{3}} = \frac{\frac{1}{2}\times\frac{4}{3}}{\frac{3}{4}\times\frac{4}{3}} = \frac{\frac{1}{2}\times\frac{4}{3}}{\frac{3\times4}{4\times3}} = \frac{\frac{1}{2}\times\frac{4}{3}}{\frac{12}{12}} = \frac{\frac{1}{2}\times\frac{4}{3}}{1} = \mathbf{\frac{1}{2}} \times \mathbf{\frac{4}{3}} = \frac{1\times4}{2\times3} = \frac{4}{6} = \frac{2}{3}$". Focus on the fraction in bold: "$\mathbf{\frac{1}{2}} \times \mathbf{\frac{4}{3}}$" and notice the original

division fraction problem is now a fraction multiplication problem and the fraction which was to the right of the division operation symbol "÷" is now inverted. This is not a proof; it is only an illustration, and there are other ways to illustrate why you need to change the division "÷" problem into a multiplication "×" problem and invert the fraction to the right of the division symbol when you divide a fraction by a fraction. You must understand how to multiply two or more fractions prior to illustrating how to change the problem "$\frac{1}{2} \div \frac{3}{4} = \frac{1}{2} \times \frac{4}{3}$". When you are multiplying two or more fractions, concentrate on the multiplication problem in the numerator, and then concentrate on the multiplication problem in the denominator. As you reference the complex fraction in the illustration "$\frac{\frac{1}{2} \times \frac{4}{3}}{\frac{3}{4} \times \frac{4}{3}}$", the numerator "$\frac{1}{2} \times \frac{4}{3}$" becomes "$\frac{4}{6}$", and then focus on the denominator "$\frac{3}{4} \times \frac{4}{3}$" to get "$\frac{12}{12}$", which equals "1". This simplification process occurred in the middle of the solution above.

If you are proficient with algebra procedures you can **prove**, using variables instead of numbers the correct way to solve the problem "$\frac{a}{b} \div \frac{c}{d}$" is to invert and multiply by the fraction "$\frac{d}{c}$". To prove the division fraction problem "$\frac{a}{b} \div \frac{c}{d}$" will change to the fraction multiplication problem "$\frac{a}{b} \times \frac{d}{c}$", use the same procedures as illustrated using the two fractions "$\frac{1}{2}$ and $\frac{3}{4}$". If you use the same procedures, we used above with the two fractions "$\frac{1}{2}$" and "$\frac{3}{4}$", you will need to use the identity "$\frac{d}{c} = \frac{d}{c}$" and then apply "Young's Equation/Ratio Theorem" to get the equation "$\frac{\frac{d}{c}}{\frac{d}{c}} = 1$". You will also have to rewrite the original problem "$\frac{a}{b} \div \frac{c}{d}$" as a complex fraction "$\frac{\frac{a}{b}}{\frac{c}{d}}$" then apply "Young's Conversion Theorem" and multiply by the number

1 using the fraction "$\frac{\frac{d}{c}}{\frac{d}{c}}$".

Here is a way to **prove** the division problem "$\frac{a}{b} \div \frac{c}{d}$" will change into the problem "$\frac{a}{b} \times \frac{d}{c}$" and derive the correct solution "$\frac{ad}{bc}$".

Fact: "$\frac{d}{c} = \frac{d}{c} \quad \therefore \quad \frac{\frac{d}{c}}{\frac{d}{c}} = 1$" We used Young's Equation/Ratio Theorem.

Next: "$\frac{a}{b} \div \frac{c}{d} = \frac{\frac{a}{b}}{\frac{c}{d}} = \frac{\frac{a}{b}}{\frac{c}{d}} \times 1 = \frac{\frac{a}{b}}{\frac{c}{d}} \times \frac{\frac{d}{c}}{\frac{d}{c}} = \frac{\frac{a}{b} \times \frac{d}{c}}{\frac{c}{d} \times \frac{d}{c}} = \frac{\frac{a}{b} \times \frac{d}{c}}{\frac{cd}{dc}} = \frac{\frac{a}{b} \times \frac{d}{c}}{1} = \frac{\boldsymbol{a}}{\boldsymbol{b}} \times \frac{\boldsymbol{d}}{\boldsymbol{c}} = \frac{ad}{bc}$" We used Young's Conversion Theorem.

Before we illustrate how to simplify algebra expressions which involve reducing, multiplying, and dividing fractions, consider this personal story about factor trees. During my last seven years as a high school mathematics teacher, I asked the students the following questions in every academic class (college-bound students) every year.

"Did one of your elementary teachers every discuss using prime numbers and factor trees?" Almost 100% of the students indicated at least one elementary teacher discussed these two topics.

I then ask the following question, "Did any of your elementary teachers require you to use factor trees when you were comparing fractions, adding fractions, subtracting fractions, reducing fractions, multiplying fractions, or dividing fractions? "

During my last seven years as a high school math teacher, when I asked these two questions, it was probably the only time in my 38-year public education career that, 100% or close to 100% of the students gave the same answer. They were introduced to the concept of "factor trees" with "prime numbers", but none of the students recalled using factor trees and prime numbers to solve any arithmetic problems. As an elementary or secondary math teacher, did you ever think why students were introduced to factor trees in arithmetic? What were the reasons textbooks and teachers mentioned factor trees in arithmetic, and why were they usually mentioned when students were first learning the rules to work with fractions?

Here are the three example problems we just discussed prior to explaining why you need to invert and multiply when you solve a fraction division problem:

Reduce: "$\frac{25}{35}$"; Simplify: "$\frac{5}{12} \times \frac{18}{25}$"; and Simplify: "$\frac{6}{7} \times \frac{14}{25} \div \frac{8}{5}$".

We already illustrated all three example problems could be simplified by using factor trees, and we continually emphasize to the students in all classes, when we encounter a challenging fraction problem in arithmetic or advanced math classes, the first step is to use factor trees for arithmetic problems and factoring for advanced math problems.

Personal Comments:

1. It occurred to me when I was teaching algebra there was a total chapter dedicated to factoring in both the Algebra 1 textbook and the Algebra 2 textbook. I then realized when students were required to reduce, multiply, and divide rational expressions (algebra fractions), the first step was almost always to factor all the terms or expressions in both the numerators and the denominators of all the fractions and cancel the identical factors in both the numerator and the denominator. At the same time, I realized when students were asked to add and subtract rational expressions

(algebra fractions) the first step was to factor the denominators to find the LCD and convert the fractions into equivalent fractions with the LCD. Simply stated, when students work with *algebra fraction problems* which are added or subtracted, the first step is almost always "factor the denominators" if you wish to find the LCD. When students work with *algebra fraction problems* which involve reducing, multiplying, and dividing, the first step is almost always "factor all the numerators and all the denominators".

2. When I started to think about how important factoring is when simplifying rational expressions in algebra, I understood why mathematicians who write arithmetic textbooks usually introduce the concept of "factor trees" in arithmetic when the students first learn the procedures to work with fractions. Then the following question occurred to me: "Why do arithmetic teachers seldom emphasize prime numbers and factor trees when students are working with fractions in arithmetic?" The answer to this question is simple: Arithmetic teachers and most mathematics teachers depend on textbooks to help them determine what problems the students should solve and the level of difficulty for the textbook problems. Most arithmetic textbooks never require the students to solve challenging fraction problems, and the students should be able to solve all the textbook problems without using prime numbers and factor trees. Simply stated, **most arithmetic textbooks and even most pre-algebra textbooks always illustrate and assign basic fraction problems for homework and never challenge the students to solve more difficult fraction problems where they need to apply the rules using prime numbers and factor trees.** The authors who wrote the arithmetic textbooks briefly discussed prime

numbers and factor trees when they introduced the chapter focused on fractions, but they seldom or never assigned any problems which required the students to use prime numbers and factor trees to simplify the problems.

3. When I taught reducing, multiplying, and dividing fractions (rational expressions) in an algebra class, my first goal in all three cases (after the division problem was converted into a multiplication problem) was to factor all the numerators and denominators. I would then write the problem as one fraction (rational expression) and reduce by cancelling identical factors. Since the indicated procedures are the rules I emphasized, when I taught algebra fraction (rational expression) problems involving reducing, multiplying, and dividing fractions, I realized this might be the best way to teach students to reduce, multiply, and divide arithmetic fraction problems. However, instead of using the word factors, I used the two words "factor trees".

4. I taught fractions using <u>two</u> different sets of rules-- not 3, 4, 5, or 6 sets of procedures. This approach seemed to simplify the process for solving all six types of fraction problems.

1. Comparing fractions	2. Adding fractions
3. Subtracting fractions	4. Reducing fractions
5. Multiplying fractions	6. Dividing fractions

5. With this thought in mind, this is the reason why when I was teaching Algebra 1 or Algebra 2, I frequently used "2-3" minute reviews involving challenging arithmetic fraction problems and told the students the first step they will probably want to use when solving these problems is to use factor trees and concentrate on the prime numbers. I tried to teach one set of rules for comparing fractions, adding fractions,

and subtracting fractions. I then emphasized a second set of rules for reducing, multiplying, and dividing fractions.

6. Using the same factoring procedures, I frequently used in previous problems in earlier chapters and when I simplified the three simple example problems in this chapter, you should be able to quickly understand how to reduce, multiply, and divide rational algebraic expressions. Below are six rational expressions to simplify. The first three examples are easy rational expressions to factor and simplify and the second three examples are a little more challenging. When you study the following six example problems, write the problems on a piece of paper, take the time to cancel the identical factors (terms which are multiplied) using a pencil in both the numerators and denominators. Realize each pair of cancelled factors will become the number, 1.

We expect at least 95% of individuals who have studied this textbook will understand the procedures used to simplify these problems since we have continually introduced and illustrated the procedures frequently throughout this textbook. Now, we want you to work with these procedures.

The rules never change from arithmetic to advanced mathematics; the problems just become more exciting.

1. Reduce: $\frac{24x^3yz^2(x+7)^2}{60xy^2z^2(x+7)} = \frac{2\cdot2\cdot2\cdot3\cdot x\cdot x\cdot x\cdot y\cdot z\cdot z\cdot(x+7)\cdot(x+7)}{2\cdot2\cdot3\cdot5\cdot x\cdot y\cdot y\cdot z\cdot z\cdot(x+7)} = \frac{2\cdot x\cdot x\cdot(x+7)}{5\cdot y} = \frac{2x^2(x+7)}{5y}$

2. Simplify: $\frac{25ab^4(m-n)^3}{28mn^2} \times \frac{42m^3n}{45a^2b(m-n)^2} = \frac{25ab^4(m-n)^3 \times 42m^3n}{28mn^2 \times 45a^2b(m-n)^2} =$

$\frac{5\cdot5\cdot a\cdot b\cdot b\cdot b\cdot b\cdot(m-n)\cdot(m-n)\cdot(m-n) \times 2\cdot3\cdot7\cdot m\cdot m\cdot m\cdot n}{2\cdot2\cdot7\cdot m\cdot n\cdot n \quad \times 3\cdot3\cdot5\cdot a\cdot a\cdot b\cdot(m-n)\cdot(m-n)} = \frac{5\cdot b\cdot b\cdot b\cdot m\cdot m\cdot(m-n)}{2\cdot3\cdot na} = \frac{5b^3m^2(m-n)}{6an}$

3. Simplify: $\frac{26c(2c-1)}{9c^2} \div \frac{13(2c-1)^2}{12c} = \frac{26c(2c-1)}{9c^2} \times \frac{12c}{13(2c-1)^2} = \frac{26c(2c-1) \times 12c}{9c^2 \times 13(2c-1)^2} =$

$\frac{2\cdot13\cdot c\cdot(2c-1) \times 2\cdot2\cdot3\cdot c}{3\cdot3\cdot c\cdot c \times 13\cdot(2c-1)\cdot(2c-1)} = \frac{2 \times 2\cdot2}{3 \times (2c-1)} = \frac{8}{3(2c-1)}$

You need to understand some basic algebra factoring procedures to understand how to simplify the following three example problems. Even though the following problems are a little more challenging rational expression problems to simplify, the first step is to factor (factor trees in arithmetic) the numerators and the denominators.

4. Reduce/Simplify: $\frac{24\,x^2(4x^2-4x+1)}{12x^3(2x^2+5x-3)} = \frac{2\cdot2\cdot2\cdot3\cdot x\cdot x\cdot(2x-1)\cdot(2x-1)}{2\cdot2\cdot3\cdot x\cdot x\cdot x\cdot(2x-1)\cdot(x+3)} = \frac{2\cdot(2x-1)}{x\cdot(x+3)} = \frac{2(2x-1)}{x(x+3)}$

5. Simplify: $\frac{x^2-7x+6}{x^2-9} \times \frac{x^2-4}{x^2-8x+12} \div \frac{x+2}{x+3} = \frac{x^2-7x+6}{x^2-9} \times \frac{x^2-4}{x^2-8x+12} \times \frac{x+3}{x+2} = \frac{(x-6)(x-1)}{(x-3)(x+3)} \times$

$\frac{(x-2)(x+2)}{(x-6)(x-2)} \times \frac{x+3}{x+2} = \frac{(x-6)(x-1) \times (x-2)(x+2) \times (x+3)}{(x-3)(x+3) \times (x-6)(x-2) \times (x+2)} = \frac{(x-1)}{(x-3)}$ *or* $\frac{x-1}{x-3}$ (Parentheses can sometimes be invisible.)

6. Simplify: $\frac{x^2-6x+9}{x^2-4} \div \frac{x^2+5x+6}{x^2-5x+6} \times \frac{x^2+4x+4}{x-3} = \frac{x^2-6x+9}{x^2-4} \times \frac{x^2-5x+6}{x^2+5x+6} \times \frac{x^2+4x+4}{x-3} =$

$\frac{(x-3)(x-3)}{(x-2)(x+2)} \times \frac{(x-3)(x-2)}{(x+2)(x+3)} \times \frac{(x+2)(x+2)}{(x-3)} = \frac{(x-3)(x-3) \times (x-3)(x-2) \times (x+2)(x+2)}{(x-2)(x+2) \times (x+2)(x+3) \times (x-3)} =$

$\frac{(x-3)(x-3)}{(x+3)} = \frac{(x-3)^2}{(x+3)}$

Teaching Point: When we illustrated how to reduce, multiply, and divide fractions in arithmetic, we constantly emphasized the importance of factor trees. Look carefully at the six example problems listed above. The first thing we did was factor every numerator and every denominator to simplify the expressions. We do not know of any other method to simplify the problems listed above. Yes, we do know about adding and subtracting exponents when numbers and terms are multiplied and divided, but when we first introduce these rules, we use factors to derive the rules. Factor trees in arithmetic might be optional when simplifying basic reducing, multiplying, and dividing fraction problems, but factor trees are necessary when solving challenging arithmetic problems and factoring is the only procedure which works when you are required to simplify all types of rational expressions which involve reducing, multiplying, and dividing in algebra as illustrated above. If students understand how to use factor trees in arithmetic, then the students will know the rules to work with factors involving rational expressions.

The first three example problems listed above were problems we would give to low-achieving Pre-Algebra 9th-12th graders as quiz questions during the last marking period. Since these students worked with the factor tree and cancel procedures used for challenging arithmetic fraction reducing, multiplying, and dividing problems, they did not consider these three problems to be too difficult.

In the low-achieving Pre-Algebra classes, we emphasized fraction problems constantly, starting in September and ending in May. The rules required to reduce, multiply, and divide all types of arithmetic fraction problems, even the most challenging fraction problems, are easier than the rules for adding and subtracting challenging fraction problems. Therefore, we emphasized basic addition and subtraction fraction problems and avoided the challenging addition and subtraction fraction problems illustrated in Chapter 4 for the low-achieving high school math students. We were pleased with the progress these students experienced. Very few of these students planned to enter an (academic) Algebra 2 class in the future; therefore, it was not our goal for these students to master the types of problems illustrated in Chapter 4. In the end, these students improved significantly with all types of fraction problems, conversion problems, decimal problems, and other basic arithmetic problems. By the end of the year, over 90% of these students were proficient adding and subtracting fractions with a common denominator, and about 50% of the students were able to add and subtract simple addition and subtraction problems which did not have a common denominator. Also, 75%-90% of the low-achieving students used the rules indicated when they reduced, multiplied, and divided all types of fraction problems--and they were very proficient when they were required to add and subtract basic fraction problems. Over 90% of these students knew the procedures for adding and subtracting fractions were significantly different than the procedures necessary to reduce, multiply, and divide fractions. These students knew the two basic sets of procedures to solve the different types of fraction problems mentioned above. Also remember what was said earlier in this textbook, "Learning how to solve all types of fraction problems will take years for some students to master." Since the low-achieving math students who entered the Pre-Algebra course in September were not knowledgeable with basic arithmetic facts and procedures, their fraction arithmetic skills were weak. The goal was to have these students "learn and remember" the rules to compare, add, subtract, reduce, multiply, and divide the basic textbook fraction problems and in some cases slightly more challenging fraction problems. That is why the goal was not to have these students master how to solve challenging arithmetic addition and subtraction problems by the end of the school year. These types of problems can only be discussed once the students have mastered the simple problems emphasized in Chapter 3.

The main reason we used the types of examples listed above was to illustrate to all teachers and students the importance of factoring in algebra and factor trees in arithmetic. We realize these example problems might be a little more challenging than the normal example problems you will find in your algebra textbooks, but we consider the first three example problems to be basic Algebra 1 problems. We considered problems 4, 5, and 6 to be relatively simple problems to reduce, multiply, and divide for students in any Algebra 2 class. We should only illustrate how to simplify these types of algebra rational expression problems to students after we illustrate how to use factor trees to reduce challenging arithmetic problems and after we discuss some basic algebra factoring procedures.

When we gave these types of problems as additional homework problems, we did not expect the students to write every little step which we continually illustrated, but the students needed to understand the importance of using factors and factor trees when they reduced, multiplied, and divided fractions after these types of problems were discussed. It is amazing how easy the textbook problems will be for most of your students after they understand how to solve these example problems. We did not teach, so students could solve the questions on a standardized test; we taught so students understood the problems which were beyond the textbook and the normal standardized test questions. If you teach so your students only understand the basic test questions, if there is a slight variation with a few of the test problems, the students will often feel overwhelmed and lost.

The second reason we illustrated how to simplify these rational expressions is to point out the Power of the Number One (1). You may look at all these examples and not realize what we mean when we mention the phrase, "The Most Powerful Number: One (1)". Every time we cancelled a number or term in the numerator with an identical number or term in the denominator, the terms which cancelled technically all became 1. When you multiply by the number 1 or divide by the number 1, the other numbers or terms do not change. The only time the number 1 should appear in the final answer after multiplying or dividing several numbers or terms is when the only number or term remaining in the numerator is the number 1. All the other 1's which appear after you either reduce, cancel, or divide the identical numbers will not normally be written in the final answer. The number 1 is a very amazing number and sometimes a very amazing invisible number.

Many students also started to understand the basic rules about adding and subtracting exponents when they were multiplying and dividing rational expressions without telling them the rules. Go back to all our examples in this section and previously discussed earlier in this textbook. Focus strictly on one of the variables or one of the numbers in each problem. The same rules that apply to numbers apply to variables. Look at this next example problem. Initially, focus on the number "3", and another time focus on the variable "x". Then focus on the number "2" and on the variable "y". Notice when they are written in factored form you can discuss the rules for adding exponents when you multiply identical numbers. You can also discuss the rules for subtracting the exponents when you divide identical numbers and terms. Simplify: "$\frac{27\,x^5 \cdot 24\,y^2 \cdot x^2y^3}{16\,x^3 \cdot 18\,y^6}$". This is a typical example problem we would use to illustrate the rules for adding and subtracting exponents when the numbers or terms are either multiplied or divided. We would use this type of problem as an example in several of our "2-3" minute introductions 2-3 months before the students are required to learn the rules. Start the discussion by first focusing on the numbers "2 and 3", and then focus on the variables "x and y".

Since we have been emphasizing both prime numbers and factor trees, first write the given problem in factored form: "$\frac{3\cdot3\cdot3\cdot x\cdot x\cdot x\cdot x\cdot x \cdot 2\cdot2\cdot2\cdot3\cdot y\cdot y \cdot x\cdot x\cdot y\cdot y\cdot y}{2\cdot2\cdot2\cdot2\cdot x\cdot x\cdot x \cdot 2\cdot3\cdot3\cdot y\cdot y\cdot y\cdot y\cdot y\cdot y}$". At this point in the problem, you may want to cancel the identical numbers and variables in both the numerator and the denominator and get the final simplified answer: "$\frac{3^2x^4}{2^2y^1} = \frac{9x^4}{4y}$". There are so many math concepts to discuss with the students regarding how to simplify this problem, we are going to allow you to think about how you would simplify this problem and have the students focus on the exponents of the two numbers "2" and "3" and the two variables "x" and "y" once the numerator and the denominator are written in this form: "$\frac{3^3x^5 \cdot 2^3 3^1 y^2 \cdot x^2 y^3}{2^4 x^3 \cdot 2^1 3^2 y^6}$". We will not tell you what to say to the students but there are many simple but important arithmetic/algebra rules involved in this problem, it might be a great discussion problem for the students to help them determine the rules for multiplying and dividing numbers and the terms involving exponents. Have fun with this type of problem! The students should already know how to find the final answer using factors, but now you want them to discover the rules to help them solve this type of problem quickly without writing every step. After discussing this problem with the students, it is easy to go to the example problems in the textbook and have the students use the rules they discovered.

We know it is hard to believe, but the rules in algebra are derived from the rules in arithmetic. If you teach the rules in arithmetic well, it is an easy transition to use the same rules in algebra.

Simplifying Rational Expressions Involving Addition and Subtraction

We already illustrated how to simplify basic arithmetic addition and subtraction fraction problems involving relatively simple LCDs in Chapter 3. We explained how to find LCDs when the numbers were a little more challenging than the typical textbook problems in Chapter 4. We illustrated how to use "Young's Equation/Ratio Theorem" and "Young's Conversion Theorem" to find equivalent fractions with the LCD in both Chapters 3 and 4. In the next two rational expression problems, we will illustrate how to use the identical procedures to find the LCD, to convert the given algebra fractions into equivalent fractions, and then to add the numerators, keep the LCD, and find the final answer. If the first two example problems below seem confusing, then go back to Chapters 3 and 4 and study the rules required to solve challenging arithmetic addition and subtraction fraction problems.

If you forgot the rules and procedures which were illustrated in Chapters 3 and 4 to solve challenging addition and subtraction fraction problems, we want to thank you for helping us prove our previous point about "drill and kill". If you need to refer to Chapters 3 and 4, then it is obvious you need more drill to master the skill. Remember, two of my additional comments were, "No Drill, then No Skill" and "More Drill, then More Skill". If you feel it is necessary to look back to Chapters 3 and 4 to reinforce your knowledge, then obviously you need more drill, if you want to acquire more skill. Do not feel guilty if you believe you need to refer to the previous chapters to reinforce your understanding of the rules; you might be a member of the majority.

When students are asked to simplify an algebra addition problem or subtraction problem with unlike denominators, the first three steps should be.

1. Write the factors for the denominators.
2. Find the LCD using the factors.
3. Convert the fractions into equivalent fractions.

Once we realized students need to focus on the three steps indicated to begin to simplify addition and subtraction rational expressions, we started to teach challenging arithmetic fraction problems involving comparing, adding, and subtracting fractions using the same rules and procedures. You should realize, we use the same basic procedures and terminology when solving algebra fraction problems which we use when we simplify arithmetic fraction problems. The one exception is, instead of using the phrase "factor trees" for arithmetic problems, we use the word "factors" for algebra problems. An additional step we often include in the explanations when students are adding and/or subtracting two or more fractions, after we determine the LCD, is to write the entire problem as one big fraction problem with the LCD written one time in the denominator. We also usually write multiplication and division fraction problems as one big fraction after we change the division operation "÷" symbol to a multiplication problem and invert the fraction to the right of the division operation symbol prior to reducing and completing the multiplication process.

(FRT 9: We believe if students solve addition, subtraction, multiplication, and division problems as one big fraction prior to the final computations then much of the confusion with respect to different fraction rules will be eliminated.)

If you did not use the 2-3 minutes introductions for 2-3 months prior to assigning homework problems, then you may continue to use the 5 minutes at the end of a class to allow students to start their homework assignments. You will simply continue to lose limited classroom teaching time.

1. Add (simplify) the following 2 fractions: $\frac{5}{8x^3y^2z} + \frac{5}{12x^2y^4z}$

This is a relatively simple Algebra 2 problem, but if you never learned the rules in arithmetic to find LCDs and how to convert fractions into equivalent fractions using "Young's Conversion Theorem", you might be lost. This is the type of problem which illustrates why we recommend teaching addition and subtraction of difficult arithmetic problems starting late in the year in Algebra 1 and early in the year in Algebra 2 since most of the students entering your class have not been exposed to the types of problems illustrated throughout this textbook. When students enter an Algebra 1 or Algebra 2 class, well over 90% of the students have no idea how to add and subtract fraction problems illustrated in Chapter 4. We also know the sooner we go back and teach arithmetic skills which were never taught regarding fractions, the chances students will be successful in future math classes are greatly increased. We continually use "2-3" minute introductory sessions and review sessions at the beginning of a class or the end of the class. In lesson plans, we always indicate a topic to introduce or review if we finished the class five minutes early. There are too many concepts in arithmetic and math which many students have not mastered. Every minute is an opportunity for 1 or 2 more students to finally understand a concept they might not have mastered. If we can only explain the concept one more time in a slightly different way.

We do not recommend students be allowed to start their homework at the end of the period. This is an excellent time to either introduce or review topics. Why give the students 5 or 6 minutes to begin their homework and answer questions at the end of the period whenever we have already talked about the topic intermittently and assigned similar problems for additional homework problems for 4 to 6 weeks? The students already know how to solve most of the problems.

In the first step, we found the LCD for the two denominators and wrote the factors for the denominators in both fractions. Here is the first denominator written in factored form: "$2 \cdot 2 \cdot 2 \cdot x \cdot x \cdot x \cdot y \cdot y \cdot z$". The second denominator, when factored will look like this: "$2 \cdot 2 \cdot 3 \cdot x \cdot x \cdot y \cdot y \cdot y \cdot y \cdot z$". We will use the same rules to determine the LCD for the two denominators, "$8x^3y^2z$ and $12x^2y^4z$" which we used to find the LCD "60" for the four denominators "12, 15, 20, and 30" in Chapter 4, example 1.

We will write a multiplication problem involving all the different factors from both the denominators "$8x^3y^2z$ and $12x^2y^4z$". Write a multiplication problem using the five different factors from the two sets of factors "$2 \cdot 3 \cdot x \cdot y \cdot z$". This is not the LCD for the two denominators yet. To find the LCD, we must decide the most times each individual factor appears in any one set of factors. The number "2" occurred "3" times in one set of factors and "2" times in the second set of factors; therefore, when computing the LCD, the factor "2" must occur "3" times. The number "3" only occurred once in the one set of factors; therefore, the factor "3" will only occur once in the final LCD. Using the same logic for the variables "x, y, and z", this means the variable, "x", must occur "3" times in the LCD, the factor, "y", must occur "4" times in the LCD, and the factor, "z", must occur only once in the LCD. Now, we are ready to write the LCD for the two given denominators in this problem:

"$2 \cdot 2 \cdot 2 \cdot 3 \cdot x \cdot x \cdot x \cdot y \cdot y \cdot y \cdot y \cdot z$ or $2^3 \cdot 3 \cdot x^3y^4z$ or $24x^3y^4z$".

> Important Reminder: You may only cancel or reduce identical factors in the numerator and denominator of a fraction.

Remember, a factor is a number, term, or expression which is multiplied in a multiplication problem. When you cancel/reduce a fraction you may only reduce factors. Never reduce a term which is added or subtracted or part of a factor. Here is a rational expression which will not reduce: "$\frac{x+2}{2}$". The number "2" in the numerator is added to the variable "x". This means the number "2" in the numerator may not reduce in this situation. Here is an example where you may reduce: "$\frac{(x+2)}{x(x+2)} = \frac{1}{x}$". The factors "$(x+2)$" in both the numerator and the denominator "$\frac{(x+2)}{(x+2)}$" are identical. Therefore, they cancel/reduce. You may ask, "In the numerator, how can we say the expression "$(x+2)$" is a factor?" The answer is simple. We could rewrite the numerator of the fraction this way: "$\frac{1 \cdot (x+2)}{x \cdot (x+2)}$", and now you should realize the two factor expressions are identical, and they cancel/reduce and become <u>1</u>. Once you cancel the factor "$(x+2)$" in both the numerator and the denominator, the fraction can be written like this: "$\frac{1 \cdot 1}{x \cdot 1}$". This is a situation where the only number/term remaining in the numerator of the fraction is the number <u>1</u>. Therefore, the final simplified answer is "$\frac{1}{x}$".

In the second step to simplify the problem "$\frac{5}{8x^3y^2z} + \frac{5}{12x^2y^4z}$", we determine what two special forms of the number 1 to multiply each of the two algebraic fractions (rational expressions) by to get two equivalent fractions with the least common denominator "$2^3 \cdot 3x^3y^4z$". Since we need to find the special form of the number 1 to multiply each fraction by, we must divide the LCD "$2^3 \cdot 3x^3y^4z$" by both denominators in the given fractions. When we are working with the first fraction "$\frac{5}{8x^3y^2z}$", we divide the LCD by the denominator of the first fraction, and the solution to the problem would look like this: "$(2^3 \cdot 3x^3y^4z) \div (8x^3y^2z)$"--but this problem is much easier to solve if you write the division problem as a fraction. Therefore, we rewrite the division problem as a fraction in vertical (up and down) form and then write both the numerator and the denominator in factored form to reduce the two expressions. Remember, if a factor in the numerator is identical to a factor in the denominator, then the individual factors will both cancel and both will become 1 in the numerator and the denominator. Here is the solution to the first division problem involving the LCD and the denominator of the first fraction:

"$\frac{\text{LCD}}{\text{Denominator First Fraction}} = \frac{24x^3y^4z}{8x^3y^2z} = \frac{2\cdot2\cdot2\cdot3\cdot x\cdot x\cdot x\cdot y\cdot y\cdot y\cdot y\cdot z}{2\cdot2\cdot2\cdot x\cdot x\cdot x\cdot y\cdot y\cdot z} = 3 \cdot y \cdot y = 3y^2$".

We encourage the students to write fractions using a horizontal line (vinculum) and not use a slanted line. Think how much more complicated this solution looks using slanted lines when working with the fractions: "LCD/Denominator First Fraction $= 24x^3y^4z/8x^3y^2z = 2\cdot2\cdot2\cdot3\cdot x\cdot x\cdot x\cdot y\cdot y\cdot y\cdot y\cdot z/2\cdot2\cdot2\cdot x\cdot x\cdot x\cdot y\cdot y\cdot z = 3y\cdot y = 3y^2$".

If you are having difficulty figuring out how we determined the solution is "$3 \cdot y \cdot y$ or $3y^2$" for the fraction division problem, please refer to the previous section where we reduced basic algebra rational expressions. Based on the division problem, we now use the identity, "$3y^2 = 3y^2 \quad \therefore \quad \frac{3y^2}{3y^2} = 1$". (The second equation, "$\frac{3y^2}{3y^2} = 1$" was derived by applying "Young's Equation/Ratio Theorem" with the identity "$3y^2 = 3y^2$".) In the next step, we will multiply the first fraction by the following form of the number 1: "$\frac{3yy}{3yy} = 1$ or $\frac{3y^2}{3y^2} = 1$". When you do the division problem with the LCD and the denominator of one of the fractions in the addition or subtraction problem, the quotient (in this situation "$3 \cdot y \cdot y$ or $3y^2$") will not have any terms in the denominator. All the numbers/terms in the denominator cancelled and became 1. This is a key point in the solution, which indicates you probably did everything correct so far.

Here is the fraction division problem with the LCD and the dominator of the second fraction: "$\frac{\text{LCD}}{\text{Denominator Second Fraction}} = \frac{24x^3y^4z}{12x^2y^4z} = \frac{2 \cdot 2 \cdot 2 \cdot 3 \cdot x \cdot x \cdot x \cdot y \cdot y \cdot y \cdot y \cdot z}{2 \cdot 2 \cdot 3 \cdot x \cdot x \cdot y \cdot y \cdot y \cdot y \cdot z} = 2x$". We used the same reducing process we used previously to cancel identical terms in the numerator and the denominator, and after canceling the identical factors the only two terms remaining were "2 and x". This means in the next step we must determine the special form of the number 1 needed to multiply the second fraction. Using "Young's Equation/Ratio Theorem", we know "$2x = 2x \quad \therefore \quad \frac{2x}{2x} = 1$". This means we should multiply the second fraction by "$\frac{2x}{2x}$" since the goal is to determine a fraction equal to the second fraction, "$\frac{5}{12x^2y^4z}$". Again, notice when we divided the LCD "$24x^3y^4z$", by the denominator of the second fraction "$12x^2y^4z$", the denominator of the answer (quotient, "$\frac{2x}{1} = 2x$") equaled 1.

In this step, we use "Young's Conversion Theorem" to find two equivalent fractions to the given fractions with the LCD "$24x^3y^4z$". The process for converting the fraction, "$\frac{5}{8x^3y^2z}$", into an equal fraction with the correct LCD looks like this: "$\frac{5}{8x^3y^2z} = \frac{5}{8x^3y^2z} \times 1 =$

$\frac{5}{8x^3y^2z} \times \frac{3y^2}{3y^2} = \frac{5 \cdot 3 \cdot y \cdot y}{8 \cdot x \cdot x \cdot x \cdot y \cdot y \cdot z \cdot 3 \cdot y \cdot y}$. In the next equation, we rearranged the factors in the denominator, so the numbers are together, and the identical variables are together. The equivalent fraction for the first fraction with the LCD is "$\frac{5 \cdot 3 \cdot y \cdot y}{8 \cdot 3 \cdot x \cdot x \cdot x \cdot y \cdot y \cdot y \cdot y \cdot z} = \frac{15y^2}{24x^3y^4z}$". This means the two fractions which follow are equal and the second fraction has the common denominator which is required if we want to add the two fractions in the original problem: "$\frac{5}{8x^3y^2z} = \frac{15y^2}{24x^3y^4z}$".

Here are the steps required to find the equivalent fraction with the LCD "$24x^3y^4z$" for the second fraction "$\frac{5}{12x^2y^4z}$". We already determined the special form of the number 1 to multiply the second fraction, two paragraphs back when we divided the LCD by the denominator of the second fraction and found the quotient, "2x". We now apply "Young's Conversion Theorem" to the second fraction and multiply the second fraction "$\frac{5}{12x^2y^4z}$" by the fraction "$\frac{2x}{2x}$", which equals 1. Here is the solution when we multiply the two fractions: "$\frac{5}{12x^2y^4z} \times 1 = \frac{5}{12x^2y^4z} \times \frac{2x}{2x} = \frac{5 \cdot 2 \cdot x}{12 \cdot x \cdot x \cdot y \cdot y \cdot y \cdot y \cdot z \cdot 2 \cdot x} = \frac{10x}{12 \cdot 2 \cdot x \cdot x \cdot x \cdot y \cdot y \cdot y \cdot y \cdot z} = \frac{10x}{24x^3y^4z}$". The last fraction has the required LCD, and the second fraction in the addition problem is equivalent to the new fraction: "$\frac{5}{12x^2y^4z} = \frac{10x}{24x^3y^4z}$".

Two original fractions: $\frac{5}{8x^3y^2z} + \frac{5}{12x^2y^4z}$

Substitute the two equivalent fractions: $\frac{15y^2}{24x^3y^4z} + \frac{10x}{24x^3y^4z}$

Write the two fractions as one fraction $\frac{15y^2+10x}{24x^3y^4z}$ with the LCD and then focus on adding and/or subtracting the numerators. $\frac{5(3y^2+2x)}{24x^3y^4z}$.

The final step when adding the two fractions is by far the simplest. First, write the original problem, and underneath the original problem, substitute the two equivalent fractions. The answer will appear in the final step. Notice in the original problem the numerators were identical--that was not a priority when we solved the problem. When adding and subtracting fractions normally there is nothing special when you have equal numerators. Your complete mindset must be focused on getting equal denominators. When you multiply and divide fractions, there is nothing special when numerators are equal, which means you almost never worry about concentrating on equal numerators when adding, subtracting, multiplying, or dividing fractions. Equal numerators might have some significance when comparing fractions, but this is a special situation.

All we did to find the final answer was write the numerators as an addition problem and made sure we kept the LCD as the final denominator. The reason we wrote the two numerators as an addition problem in the next to last fraction below and did not combine them was the same reason discussed earlier in this textbook when we added the expression "$2\,roses + 3\,tulips$" and the answer was "$2\,roses + 3\,tulips$". There is no way we can add these two terms and keep the labels "roses and tulips". In algebra, you may only add terms which have identical labels or identical variables and exponents. The two terms in the numerator "$15y^2$ and $10x$" are as different as a radish is to a horse, they are not even close to being identical variable expressions. We were able to factor out the number "5" to obtain the final numerator. Ironically, when we use the expression "factor out", what we really mean is "divide out" a common term—therefore, we wrote a multiplication problem after we divided each of the two terms by the number "5".

Wow, are Algebra 2 students really expected to add these types of fractions? The answer is definitely, "Yes".

> Arithmetic definitions, rules, and facts are the basis for algebra rules and procedures.

Do not expect the students to write every step we indicated, but they must be familiar with all the arithmetic rules and procedures if they are going to add the two fractions.

Teaching Point: When we have students add and subtract fractions, usually one of the last steps we want the students to write is a single fraction with the numerators either added or subtracted and the denominator equal to the LCD. The reason we want the students to get into the habit of writing the addition and subtraction problem as one fraction prior to adding and subtracting the numerators is to help them focus on adding and subtracting the numerators and understand how to write the answer with the LCD. It would be great to have every elementary teacher understand what type of problems the students will encounter when they enter an algebra class or an advanced math class. This is not practical under the current teacher certification requirements in the United States, but it is a dream. Always try to introduce and teach topics in your classes with the belief you are teaching the techniques and procedures the students will be required to use in the higher-level math classes beyond what you are presently teaching. Why would you want to teach the students some tricks which work for simple problems in a lower-level math course but will confuse them at the next level in mathematics?

After we discuss the next example problem, we will write the solutions for both problems indicating the steps we would encourage the students to write when they are learning how to simplify these problems. We realize if you are already proficient with simplifying these types of algebra rational expressions, you do not specifically think about all the little steps we indicated. If you are already proficient with the procedures to simplify this type of problem, you already have developed a process in your mind which works. When students begin to solve these types of problems, we want them to develop the skills to do a lot of the work in their heads without writing each individual step, but as teachers we need to illustrate all the steps, so the students develop the right mental steps in their minds. Mental skills (tricks) are only great if they are the correct skills which will work for all types of problems.

2. Add/Simplify the following two fractions (combine the two fractions and form one fraction). $\frac{x+2}{x^2-x-12}+\frac{x+2}{x^2+6x+9}$

We immediately notice the two denominators are not equal. Therefore, it is impossible to add the two fractions and get one fraction without finding the least common denominator. The numerators are equal, but this means absolutely nothing to us--our focus is on the denominators because we are adding two fractions. The first step when finding an LCD given two or more fractions which do not have identical denominators is to factor the denominators of all the fractions. If you want to understand the solution to this problem, you will have to be familiar with some basic algebra procedures.

Here is the first denominator, written in factored form: "$x^2 - x - 12 = (x - 4)(x + 3)$". Here is the second denominator, written in factored form: "$x^2 + 6x + 9 = (x + 3)(x + 3)$ which could also be written using the following exponential notation: "$(x + 3)^2$". (In arithmetic and algebra when we refer to a problem written in "factored form" we mean the problem is written as a multiplication problem.)

In the second step when finding an LCD, we need to go back and form a multiplication problem using all the different factors. There are only two factors involved when writing these two denominators in factored form. The two factors multiplied are:

"$(x-4)$ times $(x+3) = (x-4)(x+3)$". The LCD is not "$(x-4)(x+3)$" because just as with every other example problem illustrated when we found an LCD, we need to determine the most times any one of the factors appears in the set of factored denominators. You must notice the factor "$(x-4)$" appeared once in the first factored denominator, and the factor "$(x+3)$" also only occurs once in the first set of factors. More importantly, the factor "$(x+3)$" appeared two times in the second denominator when it was written in factored form. Therefore, the LCD for the two denominators is "$(x-4)(x+3)(x+3) = (x-4)(x+3)^2$". In this problem, neither of the two factors used to determine the LCD is a number or a variable. Both factors used to find the LCD are expressions/quantities.

> You must recognize the word "factor" represents a number, term, or expression which is part of a multiplication problem.

In the third step, we must determine what special form of the number 1 to multiply each of the two fractions (rational expressions) by to make sure they have the same LCD "$(x-4)(x+3)(x+3)$". Since you must determine the special form of the number 1 to multiply each of the two given fractions, we will divide the LCD by the denominator of the first fraction and then divide the LCD by the denominator of the second fraction as illustrated below.

First fraction: $\frac{\text{LCD}}{\text{Denominator Fraction 1}} = \frac{(x-4)(x+3)^2}{x^2-x-12} = \frac{(x-4)(x+3)(x+3)}{(x-4)(x+3)} = (x+3)$ Notice the two identical factors/expressions "$(x-4)$ and $(x+3)$" in the numerator and the denominator canceled, and the only remaining factor was "$(x+3)$" in the numerator. This will help us determine the special form of the number 1 to multiply the first fraction, since we want to find an equivalent fraction.

Second fraction: $\frac{\text{LCD}}{\text{Denominator Fraction 2}} = \frac{(x-4)(x+3)^2}{x^2+6x+9} = \frac{(x-4)(x+3)(x+3)}{(x+3)(x+3)} = (x-4)$ Notice again the two identical factors/expressions "$(x+3)$ and $(x+3)$" which appear in both the numerator and denominator canceled. Therefore, the remaining factor is "$(x-4)$". The answer "$(x-4)$" will help us determine the special form of the number 1 to multiply the second fraction by to find an equivalent fraction.

Reference the two division (fractions) problems just solved; the quotient in the first problem was "$(x+3)$" and the quotient in the second problem was "$(x-4)$". This means in the next step when you apply "Young's Conversion Theorem", the two special forms of the number 1 to be used to convert the two respective fractions in this problem into equivalent fractions are "$\frac{(x+3)}{(x+3)}$" and "$\frac{(x-4)}{(x-4)}$". Do you realize these two fractions which both equal the number 1, came from the identities "$x+3=x+3$ and $x-4=x-4$"? After we determined the two identities we needed to use, we knew we were going to use "Young's Equation/Ratio Theorem" to determine the fractions equal to 1 required to multiply each of the two given fractions.

In the next step, we convert the two given fractions in this problem into equivalent fractions by multiplying by the two special forms of the number 1. The process to convert each of the two fractions into equivalent fractions with the indicated least common denominator "$(x-4)(x+3)(x+3)$" is illustrated below using "Young's Conversion Theorem":

The first fraction: "$\frac{x+2}{x^2-x-12} = \frac{x+2}{x^2-x-12} \times 1 = \frac{(x+2)}{(x-4)(x+3)} \times \frac{(x+3)}{(x+3)} = \frac{(x+2)(x+3)}{(x-4)(x+3)(x+3)} = \frac{x^2+3x+2x+6}{(x-4)(x+3)(x+3)} = \frac{x^2+5x+6}{(x-4)(x+3)(x+3)}$" is now converted into an equivalent fraction with the required LCD. Notice, the denominator is written in what is called factored form, the terms in the numerator were multiplied and like terms were added. This is the normal format for adding and subtracting rational expressions (fractions) in algebra.

The second fraction: "$\frac{x+2}{x^2+6x+9} = \frac{x+2}{x^2+6x+9} \times 1 = \frac{(x+2)}{(x+3)(x+3)} \times \frac{(x-4)}{(x-4)} = \frac{(x+2)(x-4)}{(x+3)(x+3)(x-4)} =$ $\frac{x^2-4x+2x-8}{(x+3)(x+3)(x-4} = \frac{x^2-2x-8}{(x+3)(x+3)(x-4)}$" is now converted by using "Young's Conversion Theorem" into an equivalent fraction with the required LCD. Again, notice the denominator remained in factored form, the terms in the numerator were multiplied in the final format and the like terms were subtracted.

In the final steps below, we rewrite the given problem and then substitute the two equivalent fractions with the required LCD underneath each of the two original fractions. We then write the two fractions as one fraction. At this point we will either add or subtract the two numerators and keep the LCD in the final answer, just as in any arithmetic addition problem.

$$\frac{x+2}{x^2-x-12} + \frac{x+2}{x^2+6x+9}$$

$$\frac{x^2+5x+6}{(x-4)(x+3)(x+3)} + \frac{x^2-2x-8}{(x-4)(x+3)(x+3)}$$

Since the two fractions have the same denominator, it is acceptable to write the two fractions as one big fraction and add the numerators and keep the LCD.

$$\frac{(x^2+5x+6)+(x^2-2x-8)}{(x-4)(x+3)(x+3)} = \frac{x^2+5x+6+x^2-2x-8}{(x-4)(x+3)(x+3)}$$

All we did with the first fraction above to get the second fraction was remove the parentheses from both expressions in the numerator. In the next step, we will add the terms in the numerator and keep the LCD in the denominator.

$$\frac{2x^2+3x-2}{(x-4)(x+3)(x+3)}$$

The last fraction is the final answer, but just like every arithmetic problem involving addition or subtraction, the last thing which must be considered is, "Will the last fraction/answer reduce"? In arithmetic, the best way to teach students to reduce is to factor both the numerator and the denominator and then cancel any identical factors. The denominator is already in factored form, but we must try and factor the numerator to determine whether the rational expression (algebra fraction) will reduce. If there are any identical factors in the numerator and the denominator, we will cancel them. There are no identical factors in both the numerator and the denominator. Normally, the final answer is written in factored form so everyone can tell with a glance, the fraction is completely reduced.

$$\frac{2x^2+3x-2}{(x-4)(x+3)(x+3)} = \frac{(2x-1)(x+2)}{(x-4)(x+3)^2}$$

If you are an arithmetic teacher and you do not teach your students the following steps to simplify all types of fraction addition and subtraction problems, you have placed many of your students in a difficult situation when they enter an Algebra 2 class. The steps necessary to solve every arithmetic addition and subtraction problem are listed below.

1. Use the rules to find the least common denominators (LCDs) for all types of arithmetic problems using factor trees.

2. Determine the special form of the number 1 to multiply the fractions which do not have a denominator equal to the LCD using "Young's Equation/Ratio Theorem".

3. Convert fractions into equivalent fractions using "Young's Conversion Theorem" or simply by multiplying by the special form of the number 1 previously determined.

4. Only add and subtract the numerators of fractions with identical denominators; preferably have the students write a single fraction with the LCD prior to adding and/or subtracting the numerators.

5. Finally, use factor trees to reduce the final fraction.

Somehow, all teachers who teach arithmetic and/or mathematics must learn to focus on the rules necessary to solve all types of fraction problems, (not just easy problems), and help each other become successful at all levels of mathematics. If the students do not know the rules required in arithmetic to solve slightly more difficult fraction problems, then it is imperative the algebra teacher take extra time to go back and teach the more difficult arithmetic problems. If extra time is taken away from the algebra teacher to teach the arithmetic curriculum, then the algebra teacher might not have time in his/her class to really have the students "learn and remember" all the required topics necessary in the algebra class. This means the students will be behind when they enter an advanced math class. For students to be successful next year in math class and beyond, it is imperative the students master the topics from your class this year.

We know this is a high expectation, but the goal for every math teacher must be that 90% of the students master the concepts this year with the goal to be prepared for the math classes/topics next year. The other major drawback about having the algebra teacher go back and teach the students how to solve challenging arithmetic fraction problems is the students must learn a completely new set of procedures which they never learned in arithmetic to solve difficult problems. Further, when students must learn the procedures in a couple days or weeks, they never have a chance to really master the rules.

Remember, the previous two algebra problems were for illustration only, for arithmetic teachers. If you are an algebra teacher, you need to be familiar with all the rules for all the steps required to solve all the problems. In many cases you are forced to teach tricks to help students try and solve these problems in your Algebra 2 class, but can you really say the average second-year algebra student is highly proficient solving these types of algebra problems? The more embarrassing question is: "Can your Algebra 2 students really solve a difficult arithmetic problem involving challenging fractions without a calculator?" Simplifying these types of algebra fractions used to be a requirement in all Algebra 2 classes. We are aware some Algebra 2 teachers are not able to discuss these types of rational expressions during the school year. Maybe it is because there is not enough time in the school year or maybe because the students entering the class in the fall have not mastered the required topics in arithmetic and Algebra 1 required to proceed in an academic Algebra 2 class. Schools still refer to the class as an Algebra 2 class but not all the topics which were covered in Algebra 2 classes in the 1990's are covered in present Algebra 2 classes. Topics covered years ago in Algebra 2 classes are now not taught until the students take a more advanced algebra class the next year in school.

Teaching Point: We believe the more you challenge students to solve difficult problems, the more they will focus on the different rules for different types of problems. Even if 90% of your students have not mastered solving the challenging problems, you will be amazed how they are able to distinguish the different rules required to add, subtract, reduce, multiply, and divide fractions. If you continually challenge all your students, your best students will reach level "13-15" indicated earlier in this textbook on the imaginary scale of "1-10". Your average students will achieve at the "10-12" level, and almost all the remaining students will achieve at the "8-10" level. You may find a few of your students do not reach level "8", but even most of the low achieving students will usually illustrate significant improvement. Dare to have all your students reach level "9" on the imaginary scale, but realistically, know if you are successful with 90% or more of your students reaching level "9", you have come close to achieving the goal.

Here are the necessary steps most students should indicate when they simplify the first example problem above.

1.	$\frac{5}{8x^3y^2z} + \frac{5}{12x^2y^4z}$

Find the LCM Factor both denominators $8x^3y^2z = 2 \cdot 2 \cdot 2 \cdot x \cdot x \cdot x \cdot y \cdot y \cdot z$

$$12x^2y^4z = 2 \cdot 2 \cdot 3 \cdot x \cdot x \cdot y \cdot y \cdot y \cdot y \cdot z$$

Not the LCD $2 \cdot 3 \cdot x \cdot y \cdot z$

This is the LCD $2 \cdot 2 \cdot 2 \cdot 3 \cdot x \cdot x \cdot x \cdot y \cdot y \cdot y \cdot y \cdot z = 2^3 \cdot 3x^3y^4z = 24x^3y^4z$

Divide the LCD by the first denominator $\frac{24x^3y^4z}{8x^3y^2z} = 3y^2 \therefore \frac{3y^2}{3y^2} = 1$ Important Procedure!

Divide the LCD by the second denominator $\frac{24x^3y^4z}{12x^2y^4z} = 2x \therefore \frac{2x}{2x} = 1$ Important Procedure!

Find Equivalent fractions with the LCD $\frac{5}{8x^3y^2z} \times 1 = \frac{5}{8x^3y^2z} \times \frac{3y^2}{3y^2} = \frac{15y^2}{24x^3y^4z}$

$$\frac{5}{12x^2y^4z} \times 1 = \frac{5}{12x^2y^4z} \times \frac{2x}{2x} = \frac{10x}{24x^3y^4z}$$

Original Fractions $\frac{5}{8x^3y^2z} + \frac{5}{12x^2y^4z}$

Substitute Equivalent Fractions and $\frac{15y^2}{24x^3y^4z} + \frac{10x}{24x^3y^4z} = \frac{15y^2+10x}{24x^3y^4z} = \frac{5(3y^2+2x)}{24x^3y^4z}$

simplify the solution.

Here are the necessary steps most students should indicate when they simplify the second example problem above.

2. $\frac{x+2}{x^2-x-12}+\frac{x+2}{x^2+6x+9}$

Find the LCM Factor both denominators $x^2-x-12=(x-4)(x+3)$

$$x^2+6x+9=(x+3)(x+3)=(x+3)^2$$

Not the LCD $(x-4)(x+3)$

This is the LCD $(x-4)(x+3)(x+3)$ or $(x-4)(x+3)^2$

Divide the LCD by the first denominator $\frac{(x-4)(x+3)(x+3)}{(x-4)(x+3)}=(x+3)\ \therefore\ \frac{(x+3)}{(x+3)}=1$

Divide the LCD by the second denominator $\frac{(x-4)(x+3)(x+3)}{(x+3)(x+3)}=(x-4)\ \therefore\ \frac{(x-4)}{(x-4)}=1$

Find Equivalent Fractions with the $\frac{x+2}{x^2-x-12}\times 1=\frac{x+2}{x^2-x-12}\times\frac{(x+3)}{(x+3)}=\frac{(x+2)\cdot(x+3)}{(x-4)(x+3)\cdot(x+3)}$

LCD $\frac{x+2}{x^2+6x+9}\times 1=\frac{x+2}{x^2+6x+9}\times\frac{(x-4)}{(x-4)}=\frac{(x+2)\cdot(x-4)}{(x+3)(x+3)\cdot(x-4)}$

Original Fractions $\frac{x+2}{x^2-x-12}+\frac{x+2}{x^2+6x+9}$

Substitute Equivalent Fractions and $\frac{(x+2)\cdot(x+3)}{(x-4)(x+3)\cdot(x+3)}+\frac{(x+2)\cdot(x-4)}{(x+3)(x+3)\cdot(x-4)}=$

simplify the solution. $\frac{(x+2)(x+3)+(x+2)(x-4)}{(x-4)(x+3)(x+3)}=\frac{(x^2+5x+6)+(x^2-2x-8)}{(x-4)(x+3)^2}=$

Remove the parentheses in the $\frac{x^2+5x+6+x^2-2x-8}{(x-4)(x+3)^2}=\frac{2x^2+3x-2}{(x-4)(x+3)^2}=\frac{(2x-1)(x+2)}{(x-4)(x+3)^2}$

numerator and combine like terms. Factor the numerator in the last step.

The two illustrations just indicated are probably more detailed explanations than you would find in an algebra answer textbook for the example problems.

Example problems 3, 4, and 5 are also for illustration for arithmetic teachers, but they are the types of problems students in Algebra 2 should master. In example 3, we will go into a detailed explanation. We will indicate all the mathematics steps we would illustrate to the students when explaining the problem and then list the steps the students should indicate to simplify the problem.

3. Simplify: "$\frac{x}{x^2-6x+9} - \frac{x}{x^2-7x+12} - \frac{1}{x^2-8x+16}$" Study each solution below separately. First study the teacher illustration and then look at the student work illustration.

Teacher Illustration

Factor All Denominators to find the LCD.

$$\frac{x}{x^2-6x+9} - \frac{x}{x^2-7x+12} - \frac{1}{x^2-8x+16}$$

$x^2 - 6x + 9 = (x-3)(x-3) = (x-3)^2$

$x^2 - 7x - 12 = (x-3)(x-4)$

$x^2 - 8x + 16 = (x-4)(x-4) = (x-4)^2$

Not the LCD $(x-3)(x-4)$

LCD $= (x-3)^2(x-4)^2$ or

LCD $= (x-3)(x-3)(x-4)(x-4)$

Divide the LCD by the three denominators.

$$\frac{(x-3)(x-3)(x-4)(x-4)}{(x-3)(x-3)} = (x-4)(x-4)$$

$\therefore \frac{(x-4)(x-4)}{(x-4)(x-4)} = 1$ Fraction 1

Student Work

$$\frac{x}{x^2-6x+9} - \frac{x}{x^2-7x+12} - \frac{1}{x^2-8x+16}$$

$$\frac{x}{(x-3)(x-3)} - \frac{x}{(x-3)(x-4)} - \frac{1}{(x-4)(x-4)}$$

LCD $= (x-3)(x-3)(x-4)(x-4)$

$$\frac{x}{x^2-6x+9} \times 1 = \frac{x}{x^2-6x+9} \times \frac{(x-4)(x-4)}{(x-4)(x-4)}$$

$$\frac{x}{x^2-7x+12} \times 1 = \frac{x}{x^2-7x+12} \times \frac{(x-3)(x-4)}{(x-3)(x-4)}$$

$$\frac{1}{x^2-8x+16} \times 1 = \frac{1}{x^2-8x+16} \times \frac{(x-3)(x-3)}{(x-3)(x-3)}$$

Substitute the three equivalent fractions.

$$\frac{x(x-4)(x-4)}{(x-3)^2(x-4)^2} - \frac{x(x-3)(x-4)}{(x-3)^2(x-4)^2} - \frac{1(x-3)(x-3)}{(x-3)^2(x-4)^2}$$

Begin to multiply the numerators.

$$\frac{x(x^2-8x+16)}{(x-3)^2(x-4)^2} - \frac{x(x^2-7x+12)}{(x-3)^2(x-4)^2} - \frac{1(x^2-6x+9)}{(x-3)^2(x-4)^2}$$

$\frac{(x-3)(x-3)(x-4)(x-4)}{(x-3)(x-4)} = (x-3)(x-4)$

$\therefore \frac{(x-3)(x-4)}{(x-3)(x-4)} = 1$ Fraction 2

$\frac{(x-3)(x-3)(x-4)(x-4)}{(x-4)(x-4)} = (x-3)(x-3)$

$\therefore \frac{(x-3)(x-3)}{(x-3)(x-3)} = 1$ Fraction 3

Multiply the original fractions by <u>1</u>

$\frac{x}{x^2-6x+9} \times 1 = \frac{x}{x^2-6x+9} \times \frac{(x-4)(x-4)}{(x-4)(x-4)}$

$\frac{x}{x^2-7x+12} \times 1 = \frac{x}{x^2-7x+12} \times \frac{(x-3)(x-4)}{(x-3)(x-4)}$

$\frac{1}{x^2-8x+16} \times 1 = \frac{1}{x^2-8x+16} \times \frac{(x-3)(x-3)}{(x-3)(x-3)}$

Rewrite each of the three multiplication fraction problems indicated above as one fraction multiplication problems for all three situations, indicated below.

$\frac{x}{x^2-6x+9} \times \frac{(x-4)(x-4)}{(x-4)(x-4)} = \frac{x(x-4)(x-4)}{(x-3)(x-3)(x-4)(x-4)}$

$\frac{x}{x^2-7x+12} \times \frac{(x-3)(x-4)}{(x-3)(x-4)} = \frac{x(x-3)(x-4)}{(x-3)(x-4)(x-3)(x-4)}$

$\frac{1}{x^2-8x+16} \times \frac{(x-3)(x-3)}{(x-3)(x-3)} = \frac{1\,((x-3)(x-3)}{(x-4)(x-4)(x-3)(x-3)}$

Finish multiplying the numerators.

$\frac{x^3-8x^2+16x}{(x-3)^2(x-4)^2} - \frac{x^3-7x^2+12x}{(x-3)^2(x-4)^2} - \frac{x^2-6x+9}{(x-3)^2(x-4)^2}$

Write one fraction with the LCD.

$\frac{(x^3-8x^2+16x)-(x^3-7x^2+12x)-(x^2-6x+9)}{(x-3)(x-3)(x-4)(x-4)}$

Remove the parentheses in the numerator.

$\frac{x^3-8x^2+16x-x^3+7x^2-12x-x^2+6x-9}{(x-3)(x-3)(x-4)(x-4)}$

Combine like terms in the numerator.

$\frac{-2x^2+10x-9}{(x-3)(x-3)(x-4)(x-4)}$ or $\frac{-(2x^2-10x+9)}{(x-3)^2(x-4)^2}$

Neither of the final expressions has any identical factors in both the numerator and denominator; therefore, no terms will reduce.

Replace the three original fractions with the

three equivalent fractions.

$$\frac{x}{x^2-6x+9}-\frac{x}{x^2-7x+12}-\frac{1}{x^2-8x+16}$$

$$\frac{x(x-4)(x-4)}{(x-3)^2(x-4)^2}-\frac{x(x-3)(x-4)}{(x-3)^2(x-4)^2}-\frac{1(x-3)(x-3)}{(x-3)^2(x-4)^2}$$

Begin to multiply the numerators.

$$\frac{x(x^2-8x+16)}{(x-3)^2(x-4)^2}-\frac{x(x^2-7x+12)}{(x-3)^2(x-4)^2}-\frac{1(x^2-6x+9)}{(x-3)^2(x-4)^2}$$

Finish multiplying the numerators.

$$\frac{x^3-8x^2+16x}{(x-3)^2(x-4)^2}-\frac{x^3-7x^2+12x}{(x-3)^2(x-4)^2}-\frac{x^2-6x+9}{(x-3)^2(x-4)^2}$$

Write one fraction with the LCD.

$$\frac{(x^3-8x^2+16x)-(x^3-7x^2+12x)-(x^2-6x+9)}{(x-3)(x-3)(x-4)(x-4)}$$

Important fact to remember: In arithmetic, the denominator of a fraction determines if a fraction will be a terminating decimal or a repeating decimal. The fraction will **only convert** into a **terminating decimal** if the "Prime Factors" of the **denominator of a reduced** fraction, **only** contains the two prime factors contained in the following set {2, 5}. (Examples: $\frac{1}{2}=.5$, $\frac{1}{5}=.2$, $\frac{4}{5}=.8$, $\frac{7}{10}=.7$, $\frac{17}{20}=.85$, $\frac{7}{250}=.028$, $\frac{9}{80}=.1125$). Write the prime factors of the 7 denominators contained in our example problems, and you will find the only prime factors are "2" and "5".

Follow-up fact: If the "Prime Factors" of a denominator of a **reduced** fraction contains a prime number other than "2" or "5", the fraction will always be a repeating decimal when converted. (Ex.: $\frac{8}{12}=\frac{2}{3}=0.666\ldots$, $\frac{40}{45}=\frac{8}{9}=0.888\ldots$, $\frac{2}{14}=\frac{1}{7}=0.142857142857\ldots$, $\frac{15}{36}=\frac{5}{12}=0.41666\ldots$, $\frac{1}{24}=.041666\ldots$, $\frac{7}{15}=.4666\ldots$, $\frac{10}{12}=\frac{5}{6}=0.833\ldots$.

Write the prime factors of the 7 denominators contained in our example problems focusing on the reduced fractions, and you will find the prime factors consisted of at least one factor which is not a "2" or "5".

Remove the parentheses, pay attention to the negatives

to the left of the terms written inside the parentheses.

$$\frac{x^3-8x^2+16x-x^3+7x^2-12x-x^2+6x-9}{(x-3)(x-3)(x-4)(x-4)}$$

Combine like terms in the numerator.

$$\frac{-2x^2+10x-9}{(x-3)(x-3)(x-4)(x-4)} \text{ or } \frac{-(2x^2-10x+9)}{(x-3)^2(x-4)^2}$$

You cannot factor the numerator.

Therefore, there are no common factors to reduce.

You may want to explain to your algebra students how we converted the next to last fraction "$\frac{-2x^2+10x-9}{(x-3)(x-3)(x-4)(x-4)}$" into the equivalent fraction "$\frac{-(2x^2-10x+9)}{(x-3)^2(x-4)^2}$". Please do not say "take a negative out of all the terms in the numerator" to write the final rational expression.

The correct way to tell the students to convert the next to last fraction into the final fraction is to tell them to "factor out (divide out) a negative one (-1) from each of the terms in the numerator." When we used the words *"factor out"* to explain how we rewrote the expression with the negative sign to the left of the parentheses, we discovered several students became confused. When we used the phrase *"factor out"*, it did not indicate to the students a specific type of mathematics operation. It was more beneficial to students and more proper to say, (divide each of the terms by '-1') and then write the answer as the product of two factors. Sometimes just a minor change in your words will help some students better understand the directions. We factored out (divided out) a negative <u>one</u> in the numerator in the next to last fraction "$\frac{-2x^2+10x-9}{(x-3)(x-3)(x-4)(x-4)}$" to get the last fraction "$\frac{-(2x^2-10x+9)}{(x-3)^2(x-4)^2}$".

We prefer to say "divided out" the <u>negative one</u> from each of the terms in the numerator rather than the phrases *factor out* or *take out* because of the way teachers explain the *distributive property.* If the following problem is given and the directions are to write the solution without parentheses, how do you explain to the students to solve the problem "$-2(2x^2-5x+7)$"? We assume you tell the students to multiply each term inside the quantity by the "-2" to the left of the set of parentheses to derive the solution "$-4x^2+10x-14$". If you tell students to multiply each term by the number or term outside the set of parentheses when you describe the *distributive property*, then when you perform the opposite type of procedure, why would you not use the word *divide* when you want the students to write the problem as a product of terms? Some teachers illustrate how they multiply each term in the parentheses by the number "-2", as indicated in the illustration of the *distributive property* below. We know the number outside the parentheses can be on either the left or right side of the parentheses, and the same can be said when you divide out (*factor out*) a GCF.

$$-2(2x^2 - 5x + 7) = (\mathbf{-2})(\mathbf{2x^2}) - (\mathbf{-2})(\mathbf{5x}) + (\mathbf{-2})(\mathbf{7}) = -4x^2 + 10x - 14$$

Using the same type of illustration, we would illustrate to students when asked to factor out a term or number, it is more proper to say *divide out* the term or number as indicated in the example below. Students must first understand the first word in the phrase "*factor out*" is the word *factor.* This is significant because the word *factor* indicates you are going to write a multiplication problem, but if you need to write the multiplication problem you must divide each term by the factor you are focusing on. Here is an arithmetic example problem where we want you to factor the given number "493". We will give you a hint, the smallest prime number which is a factor of "493" is "17". If you are going to find a second factor, the smartest thing to do is divide "493" by "17". "$493 \div 17 = \frac{493}{17}$", but in this problem using the long division process is probably the best method.

$$17\overline{)493}\quad 29$$

When factoring large numbers, usually the best way to find a second factor is to divide the given number by a factor which works. The word "*factoring*" means to write the given problem as a multiplication problem. If you are going to determine a second factor once you know the first factor, you should divide the original number by the known factor. The number "493" written in factored form is "17×29".

Explain to students when they are asked to *factor out* a term or number it is more proper to say *divide out* the term or number, as indicated in my example below. Using the word *factor* is correct, but the procedure requires division.

Given the expression "$-4x^2 + 10x - 14$", you need to determine the number, "2" or "-2" will divide into all the indicated terms. Off to the side of the given problem, simplify the following division problems: "$\frac{-4x^2}{-2} + \frac{10x}{-2} - \frac{14}{-2} = 2x^2 - 5x + 7$". Write the two factors as a multiplication problem "$-2(2x^2 - 5x + 7)$". In this problem, the number "2" or "-2" is referred to as the GCF, Greatest Common Factor. A GCF is the largest number, term, or expression which will divide into a group of numbers, terms, or expressions.

When you factored the expression "$-4x^2 + 10x - 14$", you may use the two-theorem procedure illustrated throughout this textbook involving "Young's Equation Ratio Theorem" and "Young's Conversion Theorem". Use the identity "$-2 = -2 \quad \therefore \quad \frac{-2}{-2} = 1$" and derive the indicated fraction which equals 1. Next, use "Young's Conversion Theorem", and multiply the given expression by the special fraction equal to 1.

$$-4x^2 + 10x - 14 = (-4x^2 + 10x - 14) = 1(-4x^2 + 10x - 14) = \frac{-2}{-2}(-4x^2 + 10x - 14) =$$

$$\frac{-2}{-2} \times \frac{(-4x^2+10x-14)}{1} = \frac{-2(-4x^2+10x-14)}{(1) \quad (-2)} = \frac{-2}{1}\left(\frac{-4x^2}{-2} + \frac{10x}{-2} - \frac{14}{-2}\right) = -2(2x^2 - 5x + 7).$$

Do not expect the students to factor the original expression this way, but this illustration demonstrates why the factoring out trick or dividing out trick works.

Expect 90%-95% of advanced algebra students to be able to simplify rational expressions like Example 3: "$\frac{x}{x^2-6x+9} - \frac{x}{x^2-7x+12} - \frac{1}{x^2-8x+16}$". They may skip a few steps listed under the column labeled "student work", but in some form or another they should normally indicate most of the required steps. If you want your students to be successful in precalculus and calculus, they need to be able to work with these types of fraction problems.

If you are a mathematics-oriented student who is (or was) successful in advanced mathematics courses, you probably do not mentally think about all the steps indicated. You developed your own set of tricks/steps which worked, but when you need to explain the rules which work for all types of fraction problems and rational expressions to a student with average math skills, it is probably best to emphasize the rules which work for both challenging arithmetic problems and for extremely difficult algebra and calculus problems. Once you know the rules/procedures and you have practiced simplifying these types of problems, you will then determine which steps you can skip when you write the solutions. We hope the procedures become automatic and less burdensome to you once you practice solving these problems. Do you think a little drill may help improve your skills?

The sooner students learn the rules in arithmetic, the better chance students will have to be successful in algebra.

Mathematics educators and mathematics education researchers generally agree the most important topic in arithmetic which predicts success in algebra and advanced math courses is a strong understanding of fraction concepts and fraction procedures (Bailey et al., 2012; Booth et al., 2012; Siegler et al., 2012; Watts et al., 2014). Now, we will make another emphatic statement: "A strong knowledge of all the concepts involving rational expressions in algebra is a great indicator of success for students in precalculus and calculus." If students can simplify and solve rational expressions in algebra, it may also predict success in other math focused subjects such as chemistry, physics, and engineering. *(FRT 16: We suggest that there is a direct correlation between students' abilities to work with rational expressions in algebra and their success in Trigonometry, Calculus, Engineering, Physics, Chemistry and other advanced mathematics and science courses.)*

4. Simplify: "$\frac{3m}{m^2+3m+2} - \frac{5m}{m+1}$" This problem is easier than example 3.

a. If your objective is to find the LCD, factor the first denominator "$m^2 + 3m + 2 = (m + 2)(m + 1)$", then you need to realize the only factor of the second denominator is "$(m + 1)$". In the next step, multiply the factors which are different to begin to determine the

LCD "$(m+1)(m+2)$". This might be the LCD, or it might not be the LCD. We must look at the factors in both denominators and ask the question, "Did either of these two factors occur more than once in either of the two given denominators? The answer is simple: each factor "$(m+1)$ and $(m+2)$" only occurred a maximum of one time in each of the two factored denominators; therefore, the "$LCD = (m+1)(m+2)$".

b. Determine the specific value of the number 1 to multiply each fraction, if you want to convert each fraction into an equivalent fraction with the correct LCD. Divide the LCD by each of the given denominators. Fraction 1: "$\frac{\text{LCD}}{\text{Denominator first fraction}} = \frac{(m+1)(m+2)}{(m+1)(m+2)} = 1$". This fraction already has the correct LCD, which is a great situation. Fraction 2: "$\frac{\text{LCD}}{\text{Denominator second fraction}} = \frac{(m+1)(m+2)}{m+1} = (m+2)$". This means we should set up the identity "$(m+2) = (m+2)$". Use "Young's Equation/Ration Theorem" and determine the correct form of the number 1 to multiply the second fraction, "$\frac{(m+2)}{(m+2)} = 1$".

c. The first fraction already has the correct LCD, so there is no need to multiply the first fraction, "$\frac{3m}{m^2+3m+2}$", by any special fraction equal to 1. Find the equivalent fraction with the correct LCD for the second fraction, "$\frac{5m}{m+1}$" and multiply by the special form of the number 1 found in the previous paragraph: "$\frac{(m+2)}{(m+2)} = 1$". The second fraction when converted into an equivalent fraction looks like this: "$\frac{5m}{m+1} \times 1 = \frac{5m}{m+1} \times \frac{m+2}{m+2} = \frac{5m \cdot (m+2)}{(m+1)(m+2)} = \frac{5m(m+2)}{(m+1)(m+2)}$".

d. Look at the two given fractions and substitute the two equivalent fractions with the LCD for the two original fractions. The first fraction is the same fraction because the first fraction already has the correct LCD, and the denominator is now written in factored form. Here is the problem now: "$\frac{3m}{(m+1)(m+2)} - \frac{5m(m+2)}{(m+1)(m+2)}$".

e. We want the students to write the two fractions which are added or subtracted as one fraction prior to adding or subtracting the numerators. Here is the problem written as one fraction: "$\frac{3m\ -\ \{5m(m+2)\}}{(m+10(m+2)}$". We could have multiplied the terms in the numerator of the second fraction prior to forming one fraction. This is your choice. We are going to multiply the terms in the second numerator in the next step. Always pay careful attention to the numerators of fractions when the fractions are subtracted. If a fraction is subtracted, write the numerator as a quantity (enclosed in parentheses or brackets or braces) to emphasize all the terms in the quantity are affected by the subtraction operation symbol.

Teaching Point: It is a good idea when the students write addition and subtraction rational expressions as one big fraction to include all the numerators in parentheses to avoid confusion. It is strongly encouraged when the numerators are subtracted to place the subtracted numerator in parentheses, but it is not necessary to place the numerators in parentheses when the numerators are added.

f. Now concentrate on simplifying the numerator. Multiply "$5m$" and the quantity "$(m+2)$", "$5m(m+2) = 5m^2 + 10m$". The fraction with the new numerator now looks like this: "$\frac{3m-\{5m^2+10m\}}{(m+1)(m+2)}$". Simplify the numerator to find the final answer:

"$\frac{3m-5m^2-10m}{(m+1)(m+2)} = \frac{-5m^2-7m}{(m+1)(m+2)} = \frac{-m(5m+7)}{(m+1)(m+2)}$".

Once we factored the numerator in the last step, we knew immediately there were no identical factors in both the numerator and the denominator. Therefore, the fraction will not reduce. We divided out (factored out) the GCF "$-m$" from the numerator, "$-5m^2 - 7m$".

5. Simplify: "$\frac{\frac{s}{a+b}+\frac{x}{b}}{\frac{a}{s+x}}$"

a. You must recognize this is a complex fraction, so one of the first things we focus on is rewriting the fraction as a horizontal division problem "$(\frac{s}{a+b} + \frac{x}{b}) \div (\frac{a}{s+x})$". Notice, when we wrote the numerator and denominator in horizontal form, we enclosed both the numerator and the denominator in a pair of parentheses. This is an important teaching point which will help students avoid basic mistakes when they are working with complex fractions. In this problem, it is not necessary to enclose the denominator, "$(\frac{a}{s+x})$" in a pair of parentheses, but we did for consistency. Note a complex fraction is a fraction with at least one fraction in either the numerator or the denominator or both.

b. In this step, we can either focus on the division operation symbol "÷" between the first and second quantities or focus on the two fractions in the first quantity which are added. The first thing we will do is rewrite the division problem as a multiplication problem "$(\frac{s}{a+b} + \frac{x}{b}) \times (\frac{s+x}{a})$". We inverted the fraction to the right of the division operation symbol "÷" and changed the fraction division problem into a fraction multiplication problem.

c. Now focus on adding the two fractions contained inside the first set of parentheses. When working with the first quantity "$(\frac{s}{a+b} + \frac{x}{b})$", the LCD for the two fractions is "$b(a+b)$". When we divide the LCD by the denominator of the first fraction "$\frac{b\,(a+b)}{(a+b)}$", the quotient is simply "b". We now know to multiply the first fraction by the following fraction which equals <u>1</u>, "$\frac{b}{b} = 1$". When we divide the LCD by the denominator of the second fraction "$\frac{b(a+b)}{b}$", the quotient is "$(a+b)$". We will multiply the second fraction by the fraction "$\frac{(a+b)}{(a+b)}$", which equals <u>1</u>. Were you able to determine that the LCD for the two denominators was "$b(a+b)$", without an explanation? The first denominator "$(a + b)$" will not factor any further, so the only factor of the first denominator is "$(a + b)$". The only factor in the second denominator is "b". The first step to find the LCD is to multiply the factors of all the denominators. Since there is only one factor in each denominator, the first thought is the LCD might be "$b(a + b)$". We ask the question, "Did either of the factors occur more than once in either denominator?" Obviously, the answer to this question is "No." Therefore, the LCD is "$b(a + b)$". We wonder how many people were able to determine in their head that the LCD at the beginning of this paragraph was "$b(a + b)$"?

Convert the two fractions inside the first set of parentheses into equivalent fractions with the LCD "$b(a + b)$". Since we want to find the equivalent fraction for the first fraction, we need to multiply the first fraction by 1. We will multiply the first fraction by "$\frac{b}{b}$": "$\frac{s}{(a+b)} \times 1 = \frac{s}{(a+b)} \times \frac{b}{b} = \frac{\boldsymbol{bs}}{\boldsymbol{b(a+b)}}$". We will multiply the second fraction, "$\frac{x}{b}$" by the fraction "$\frac{(a+b)}{(a+b)}$", which equals 1: "$\frac{x}{b} \times 1 = \frac{x}{b} \times \frac{(a+b)}{(a+b)} = \frac{\boldsymbol{x(a+b)}}{\boldsymbol{b(a+b)}}$".

In this step we substitute the two equivalent fractions into the first quantity "$(\frac{s}{a+b} + \frac{x}{b})$" and obviously we will add the two converted fractions for the two original fractions: "$(\frac{\boldsymbol{bs}}{\boldsymbol{b(a+b)}} + \frac{\boldsymbol{x(a+b)}}{\boldsymbol{b(a+b)}})$". Refer to the two fractions in the previous sentence and write the two fractions indicted in bold print as one fraction addition problem: "$(\frac{bs + x(a+b)}{b(a+b)})$". Focus on the numerator inside the parentheses to simplify the entire fraction: "$(\frac{bs + ax + bx}{b(a+b)})$". We used the distributive property to multiply the variable "x" and the quantity "$(a + b)$".

d. Write the entire problem again but use the new fraction inside the first quantity to complete the problem: "$\left(\frac{bs + ax + bx}{b(a+b)}\right) \times (\frac{s+x}{a}) = \frac{(bs + ax + bx)(s + x)}{ab(a+b)}$". Write the two fractions which were multiplied as one big fraction and keep both the numerator and the denominator in factored form, so we immediately know there are no common factors to cancel. You could also multiply the two factors in the numerator and the solution would look like this: "$\frac{(bs+ax+bx)(s+x)}{ab(a+b)} = \frac{bs^2+bsx+axs+ax^2+bxs+bx^2}{ab(a+b)} = \frac{bs^2+2bsx+asx+ax^2+bx^2}{ab(a+b)}$", but it is up to you if you consider this a necessary step. We would not consider it so--because if the problem is going to reduce, it needs to be in factored form, which is this version of the answer, "$\frac{(bs+ax+bx)(s+x)}{ab(a+b)}$".

These are the types of problems students must be able to simplify to prove in trigonometry that two expressions are identities. These are also the types of problems students must be able to simplify to find derivatives in calculus. Understanding fractions in arithmetic is the key to understanding rational expressions in algebra and being able to work with rational expressions is the key to understanding challenging problems in precalculus and calculus.

> Solving advanced mathematics problems is only possible if you know all the rules in arithmetic. Without arithmetic rules, there are no advanced mathematics rules.

There is a direct correlation between how well students really know their arithmetic facts and procedures, especially with respect to simplifying and solving a wide variety of fraction problems, and how well they will perform in algebra and higher-level mathematics courses (Bailey et al., 2015; Jordan et al., 2013). This means as soon as possible, all arithmetic teachers must begin to emphasize the rules to solve all types of fraction problems. Without a solid foundation in arithmetic, most students are doomed when they enter higher level math courses. So why would you insist a student take algebra when they really need an extra year or two solving challenging arithmetic problems without using a calculator? If all students have a solid understanding of how to solve all types of arithmetic problems and Algebra 1 problems, they will have a greater chance to be successful in life. Too few students trying to earn a bachelor's degree are proficient solving all types of arithmetic problems and Algebra 1 problems (Schneider et al., 2010; Stigler et al., 2010).

Teaching Point: When we illustrated how to use factor trees in arithmetic to determine LCDs for challenging addition and subtraction problems, it may have seemed like a nuisance. If you go back and look at the five example rational expressions which are added and subtracted above, you should notice the first thing we did with all the denominators involved was to factor the denominators to determine the LCD. Even in example problem 5, we had to concentrate on the two denominators which did not factor and treat each denominator as a single factor. We applied the same rules for the algebra problems used to find LCDs as we used to find LCDs for the challenging arithmetic problems earlier in this textbook. When working with algebra rational expressions which are added or subtracted, the only method which will work is to factor (factor trees) all the denominators to determine the LCDs. Indeed, if your students know the rules to work with all types of fraction arithmetic problems, they will not have to learn a new set of rules to work with rational expressions involving adding, subtracting, reducing, multiplying, and dividing in algebra.

Teaching Point: Tell your students in Algebra 2 and Precalculus the first step when working with rational expressions (all rational expressions) is almost always to factor. If they are adding and/or subtracting rational expressions, then the first step normally is to factor the denominators. If they are reducing, multiplying, and/or dividing rational expressions, then the first step normally is to factor all the numerators and all the denominators. Being able to factor rational expressions is critical when simplifying rational expressions. Being able to use factor trees is critical when working with challenging arithmetic fraction problems. Generally, the only time students will not use factor trees in arithmetic or factors in algebra to simplify fractions is when the numbers or expressions are simple and involve little or no written work to solve. Understanding how to use factor trees and the rules involving factor trees in arithmetic to work with fractions is essential if students are going to master simplifying rational expressions in algebra.

The next example problem is a challenging rational expression involving a complex fraction with multiplication, division, addition, and subtraction of rational expressions. If you can simplify this rational expression on your own, you are ready for an Honors Precalculus class. If you think you understand all the steps when they are written, you are ready to practice simplifying these types of problems and you will soon be ready to enter an Honors Precalculus Class. As you study the following illustration, concentrate on how many times we had to factor (factor trees in arithmetic) to find the correct solutions. As you concentrate on how many times, we had to factor to simplify the left side of the problem you should finally understand why we constantly emphasize factor trees and the rules to use factor trees when we teach students how to multiply and divide fractions in arithmetic.

If your students are taught the rules to find LCDs when they learn how to add, subtract, and compare fractions using "factor trees", they will be prepared to add and subtract rational expressions in algebra. If your students are taught the rules to reduce, multiply, and divide fractions using "factor trees" they will be confident when they reduce, multiply, and divide rational expressions in algebra.

In the next example problem, the directions are to **simplify** the left side of the given equation; you will know you did all the work correctly when you end up with the identity "$\frac{12x}{x-2} = \frac{12x}{x-2}$". This identity is an example of the special situation referred to as the Reflexive Property.

6.	$\dfrac{\frac{6x^2}{x^2-5x+6}}{\frac{x}{x^2-x-6}} - \dfrac{\frac{(x-1)}{x^2-4x+4}}{\frac{x^2-2x+1}{x^2-7x+10}} \div \dfrac{\frac{1}{x-1}}{\frac{6x^2}{x-5}} = \dfrac{12x}{x-2}$

If we want to simplify the left side of the equation, we must work with each of the three complex fractions independently. Before we begin to simplify each of the three complex fractions, we want to focus on the following setup of the three fractions: "$\frac{?}{?} - \frac{?}{?} \div \frac{?}{?}$". We want to decide early in the solution process the order we should work with the three fractions prior to subtracting and dividing the fractions. Should we initially group the first two fractions together and subtract the two fractions after they are simplified--and then divide by the third fraction? Or should we group the last two fractions and do the division problem first—and then subtract the answer from the first fraction? The correct way to group the three fractions would be "$\frac{?}{?} - \left(\frac{?}{?} \div \frac{?}{?}\right)$ or $\frac{?}{?} + \left(-\frac{?}{?} \div \frac{?}{?}\right)$". The rules for the order of operations taught in arithmetic state that numbers which are multiplied and/or divided should be completed first (from left to right), and numbers which are added and/or subtracted should be completed in the final step. Here is an example to help you understand how to simplify the given problem: "$6 - 4 \div 2 = 6 + (-4 \div 2) = 6 + (-2) = 4$ or $6 - (4 \div 2) = 6 - 2 = 4$". The subtraction operation symbol is a little tricky in this example problem because it does not matter which way you work with the subtraction symbol. In some problems involving a subtraction operation symbol you need to be careful how you work with the symbol when it is to the left of a quantity (parentheses).

Be careful when you explain why it does not make a difference whether the subtraction operation symbol is inside the quantity or outside the quantity. (Hint: You could rewrite the problem in this form: "$6 - 4 \div 2 = 6 + \{-1 \times (4 \div 2)\}$". It would not be correct to move the subtraction operation symbol outside the quantity the same way if the given problem is written in the following form, "$6 - 4 + 2 \neq 6 - (4 + 2)$". Why? The problem could be written as "$6 - 4 + 2 = 6 + (-4 + 2)$". The only change from the original problem to this example problem is, we switched the division operation symbol "÷" to an addition operation symbol "+" to the left of the number "2".

The problem can now be written as: $\dfrac{\frac{6x^2}{x^2-5x+6}}{\frac{x}{x^2-x-6}} - \left(\dfrac{\frac{(x-1)}{x^2-4x+4}}{\frac{x^2-2x+1}{x^2-7x+10}} \div \dfrac{\frac{1}{x-1}}{\frac{6x^2}{x-5}}\right) = \dfrac{12x}{x-2}$

We are now going to simplify the first complex fraction: $\dfrac{\frac{6x^2}{x^2-5x+6}}{\frac{x}{x^2-x-6}}$

1. Rewrite the complex fraction as a division problem using the division operation symbol "÷".

$$\frac{6x^2}{x^2-5x+6} \div \frac{x}{x^2-x-6}$$

2. Since we know this is a fraction division problem, we invert and multiply the fraction to the right of the division operation symbol.

$$\frac{6x^2}{x^2-5x+6} \times \frac{x^2-x-6}{x}$$

3. The reason we continually use factor trees to reduce fractions when simplifying arithmetic multiplication problems is because in this step, the only way to reduce the rational expression in step 2. is to factor all the numerators and denominators when possible. Here is the same problem written in factored form.

$$\frac{6 \cdot x \cdot x}{(x-2)(x-3)} \times \frac{(x-3)(x+2)}{x}$$

4. We could have written the last step as one big fraction, but we decided to write the problem as one big fraction in this step.

$$\frac{6 \cdot x \cdot x \cdot (x-3)(x+2)}{(x-2)(x-3) \cdot x}$$

5. Since this is one big multiplication/division problem, we may cancel identical factors. The identical factors in both the numerator and the denominator are "x and $(x-3)$". Therefore, the new fraction should be written in the following simplified form:

$$\frac{6x(x+2)}{(x-2)}$$

Nothing will reduce. The number "2" in the numerator and in the denominator are not factors; they are both part of a factor. The expressions "$(x+2)$ and $(x-2)$" are as different as "9" and "13". These expressions are not equal, and they are not identical. Therefore, they cannot cancel. Later in this explanation, we will substitute the fraction "$\frac{6x(x+2)}{(x-2)}$" for the first original fraction because we know the following fact: $\dfrac{\frac{6x^2}{x^2-5x+6}}{\frac{x}{x^2-x-6}} = \dfrac{6x(x+2)}{(x-2)}$

It is now time to simplify the second complex fraction.

$$\frac{\frac{(x-1)}{x^2-4x+4}}{\frac{x^2-2x+1}{x^2-7x+10}}$$

We follow the same steps used to simplify the first complex fraction.

1. Rewrite the division problem $\qquad \frac{(x-1)}{x^2-4x+4} \div \frac{x^2-2x+1}{x^2-7x+10}$

2. Invert and multiply $\qquad \frac{(x-1)}{x^2-4x+4} \times \frac{x^2-7x+10}{x^2-2x+1}$

3. Factor $\qquad \frac{(x-1)}{(x-2)(x-2)} \times \frac{(x-2)(x-5)}{(x-1)(x-1)}$

4. One Big Fraction $\dfrac{(x-1) \times (x-2)(x-5)}{(x-2)(x-2) \times (x-1)(x-1)}$

5. Cancel Identical Factors $\dfrac{(x-5)}{(x-2)(x-1)}$

Later in this illustration we will substitute the simplified fraction "$\dfrac{(x-5)}{(x-2)(x-1)}$" for the second fraction because we know the following fact: $\dfrac{\frac{(x-1)}{x^2-4x+4}}{\frac{x^2-2x+1}{x^2-7x+10}} = \dfrac{(x-5)}{(x-2)(x-1)}$

Now simplify the third complex fraction. $\dfrac{\frac{1}{x-1}}{\frac{6x^2}{x-5}}$

Follow the same basic steps as indicated for the previous two complex fractions to simplify this fraction.

1. Rewrite the division problem $\dfrac{1}{x-1} \div \dfrac{6x^2}{x-5}$
2. Invert and multiply $\dfrac{1}{x-1} \times \dfrac{x-5}{6x^2}$
3. Factor if possible $\dfrac{1}{x-1} \times \dfrac{x-5}{6 \cdot x \cdot x}$
4. One big fraction $\dfrac{1 \times (x-5)}{(x-1) \times 6 \cdot x \cdot x}$
5. Reduce if possible or simplify $\dfrac{(x-5)}{6xx(x-1)}$

We will substitute this fraction "$\dfrac{(x-5)}{6xx(x-1)}$" for the third fraction "$\dfrac{\frac{1}{x-1}}{\frac{6x^2}{x-5}}$" in the next segment of the solution because the two fractions are equal.

$$\frac{\frac{1}{x-1}}{\frac{6x^2}{x-5}} = \frac{(x-5)}{6xx(x-1)}$$

Go back to the original problem and substitute the three simplified fractions for the three complex fractions.

$$\frac{\frac{6x^2}{x^2-5x+6}}{\frac{x}{x^2-x-6}} - \left(\frac{\frac{(x-1)}{x^2-4x+4}}{\frac{x^2-2x+1}{x^2-7x+10}} \div \frac{\frac{1}{x-1}}{\frac{6x^2}{x-5}}\right) = \frac{12x}{x-2}$$

$$\frac{6x(x+2)}{(x-2)} - \left(\frac{(x-5)}{(x-2)(x-1)} \div \frac{(x-5)}{6xx(x-1)}\right) = \frac{12x}{x-2}$$

The previous two equations are excellent examples to illustrate why mathematicians use the word *simplify* when working with arithmetic problems and algebra problems. When you look at the first group of fractions on the left side of the equation and then look at the second group of fractions on the left side of the equation, the left side of the second equation is a simplified form of the left side of the first equation. There is still a lot of work to perform on the left side of the second equation to complete the process.

Remember, the directions were to simplify the left side of the equation and end up with the identity, "$\frac{12x}{x-2} = \frac{12x}{x-2}$". We will concentrate our efforts on the division problem in the parentheses (quantity). $\frac{(x-5)}{(x-2)(x-1)} \div \frac{(x-5)}{6xx(x-1)}$

1. Invert and multiply $\frac{(x-5)}{(x-2)(x-1)} \times \frac{6xx(x-1)}{(x-5)}$

2. One big fraction $\frac{(x-5) \times 6xx(x-1)}{(x-2)(x-1) \times (x-5)}$

3. Reduce $\frac{6xx}{(x-2)}$

We now know the following fact: $\left(\frac{(x-5)}{(x-2)(x-1)} \div \frac{(x-5)}{6xx(x-1)}\right) = \frac{\mathbf{6xx}}{\mathbf{(x-2)}}$, which means we will replace the big quantity with the fraction" $\frac{6xx}{(x-2)}$" soon.

Original problem $$\frac{\frac{6x^2}{x^2-5x+6}}{\frac{x}{x^2-x-6}} - \left(\frac{\frac{(x-1)}{x^2-4x+4}}{\frac{x^2-2x+1}{x^2-7x+10}} \div \frac{\frac{1}{x-1}}{\frac{6x^2}{x-5}}\right) = \frac{12x}{x-2}$$

Substitute three simplified fractions into the original problem.

$$\frac{6x(x+2)}{(x-2)} - \left(\frac{(x-5)}{(x-2)(x-1)} \div \frac{(x-5)}{6xx(x-1)}\right) = \frac{12x}{x-2}$$

Substitute the new simplified fraction for the division problem inside the parentheses.

$$\frac{6x(x+2)}{(x-2)} - \left(\frac{6xx}{(x-2)}\right) = \frac{12x}{x-2}$$

This is still not quite an identity in terms of the Reflexive Property. Rewrite the left side of the equation as one big fraction with the same LCD. This is simple because both fractions on the left side of the equation have the same denominator "$(x-2)$".

$$\frac{6x(x+2) - 6xx}{x-2} = \frac{12x}{x-2}$$

The left side is still not identical to the right side, so we must do some more work on the left side of the equation. Multiply "$6x(x+2)$" *(the distributive property)* to get the product "$6x^2 + 12x$". The fraction on the left side of the equation may now be written as "$\frac{6x^2+12x - 6x^2}{x-2}$".

We know have the following equation. $\frac{6x^2+12x - 6x^2}{x-2} = \frac{+12x}{x-2}$

Combine the like terms "$+6x^2$" and "$-6x^2$" in the numerator.

The equation could be written as $\frac{0+12x}{x-2} = \frac{12x}{x-2}$

Write the identity to finish the problem $\frac{12x}{x-2} = \frac{12x}{x-2}$

Mission accomplished. At last, the left side of the final equation *(identity)* is written in a simplified form compared to the given problem—agreed? The final equation "$\frac{12x}{x-2} = \frac{12x}{x-2}$" indicates we accomplished our final goal. This identity is written in the desired format referred to as the Reflexive Property.

You must understand all the rules involving adding, subtracting, multiplying, dividing, and reducing fractions in arithmetic along with how to use factor trees in arithmetic and factors in algebra to be successful in algebra and higher-level math and science classes. We believe, there is a direct correlation between student knowledge of arithmetic concepts and procedures, when compared with their success in algebra and advanced mathematics classes.

When simplifying and solving arithmetic and math problems, there are almost always many ways to find the solutions, but students must always follow arithmetic rules which they should have already learned. When we illustrated how to simplify the left hand side of the problem "$\frac{\frac{6x^2}{x^2-5x+6}}{\frac{x}{x^2-x-6}} - \left(\frac{\frac{(x-1)}{x^2-4x+4}}{\frac{x^2-2x+1}{x^2-7x+10}} \div \frac{\frac{1}{x-1}}{\frac{6x^2}{x-5}}\right) = \frac{-12x}{x-2}$", there was not one exact procedure to simplify the expressions on the left hand side of the equation. The steps we used to simplify the left side of the equation may vary in the order we illustrated, but all the steps must follow procedures which can be verified by using arithmetic rules.

If you are an elementary arithmetic teacher, you may look at the previous example problem and say, "I do not need to be able to work with that type of problem because my students will never encounter these types of problems." We understand your perspective. We did not illustrate how to simplify the previous problem for you to master solving this problem. We illustrated how to simplify the previous problem so you would understand how important it is to begin to teach the rules to solve all arithmetic fraction problems using the procedures necessary to solve the most challenging fraction problems when your students are finished with their arithmetic classes, and they enter an algebra, calculus, or physics class in 4 to 6 years. The following statement is a dream many algebra teachers express when students enter their algebra class: "I hope the students this year can actually solve fraction arithmetic problems." If you are an elementary arithmetic teacher, you can make this dream come true and help students in your class be successful for many years in mathematics.

When do you think arithmetic students can simplify the following three addition and subtraction rational expression problems? Simple answer and more advanced answers.

1. $\frac{362}{7x^2y} - \frac{176}{7x^2y} + \frac{981.5}{7x^2y} = \frac{362-176+981.5}{7x^2y} = \frac{1167.5}{7x^2y}$ or $\frac{1167\frac{1}{2}}{7x^2y} = \frac{\frac{2335}{2}}{7x^2y} = \frac{2335}{2} \div \frac{7x^2y}{1} = \frac{2335}{2} \times \frac{1}{7x^2y} = \frac{2335}{14x^2y}$

These are three problems with three simple answers for 5th and 6th graders. Two special solutions for problems 1 and 3, for older students and all teachers to think about.

2. $\frac{6\frac{1}{2}}{x(x-10)} + \frac{2\frac{1}{4}}{x(x-10)} - \frac{0}{x(x-10)} + \frac{1\frac{1}{4}}{x(x-10)} = \frac{6\frac{1}{2}+2\frac{1}{4}-0+1\frac{1}{4}}{x(x-10)} = \frac{10}{x(x-10)}$

3. $\frac{908.9}{(x+2)(x-1)} - \left(\frac{49.77}{(x+2)(x-1)} - \frac{22}{(x+2)(x-1)}\right) + \frac{.989}{(x+2)(x-1)} = \frac{908.9}{(x+2)(x-1)} - \left(\frac{27.77}{(x+2)(x-1)}\right) +$

$\frac{.989}{(x+2)(x-1)} = \frac{882.119}{(x+2)(x-1)}$ "*simple answer − more advanced answer*" $\frac{882.119}{(x+2)(x-1)} \times \frac{1000}{1000} =$

$\frac{882119}{1000(x+2)(x-1)}$

We think at least 50% of 5th graders should be able to simplify these problems and 90% of 6th graders should be able to simplify these problems. What percent of your 5th and 6th grade students do you think can simplify these problems? Notice, all three problems were addition and subtraction problems and the denominators in all three examples were identical.

Understanding the procedures illustrated in the previous section involving rational expressions is one of the major requirements for any student who plans on being successful in a Precalculus (Trigonometry) Course and any Calculus 1, 2, and 3 Course, but understanding the procedures is not enough, you must practice working with these types of problems until all the indicated steps are automatic for you. There are many other concepts and procedures you must master in order to be confident when you enter one of the advanced math courses just indicated to include topics such as: functional notation, writing the slope of a line using functional notation, graphing polynomial functions, graphing exponential and logarithmic functions, graphing rational expression functions, recognizing the general shape of a graph when given a function, how to multiply by the number 1 in ways not specifically indicated in this book, etc. Of course, when you enter a Precalculus (Trigonometry) class you must memorize the six definitions of the Trig Functions and then how to work with inverse

Trig Functions. These are just some of the additional math topics you must master before you take advanced mathematics courses but as indicated in the first sentence of this paragraph you must be a master when working with rational expressions in algebra and fractions in arithmetic.

The prime factors in the numerator in the problem above are: $882119 = 7 \cdot 23 \cdot 5479$, interesting.

You will only be able to navigate the road ahead in Precalculus and Calculus after you master simplifying and solving all the problems indicated in this textbook including the remainder of Chapter 8. If you never mastered working with fractions in arithmetic and rational expressions in algebra, the road ahead may prove to be a roadblock. If you are confident with your skills involving fractions and rational expressions, you are prepared to attack all the new math challenges you will encounter.

Simplifying Algebra Fractions with Square Roots in the Denominator

1. Simplify: $\frac{7}{\sqrt{13}}$

Fact: Use "Young's Equation/Ratio Theorem" with the identity "$\sqrt[2]{13} = \sqrt[2]{13}$" and the special form of the number 1 to multiply the given fraction by "$\frac{\sqrt[2]{13}}{\sqrt[2]{13}} = 1$".

Use "Young's Conversion Theorem" to simplify the fraction. "$\frac{7}{\sqrt[2]{13}} = \frac{7}{\sqrt[2]{13}} \times 1 = \frac{7}{\sqrt[2]{13}} \times \frac{\sqrt[2]{13}}{\sqrt[2]{13}} = \frac{7 \times \sqrt[2]{13}}{\sqrt[2]{13} \times \sqrt[2]{13}} = \frac{7\sqrt[2]{13}}{\sqrt[2]{169}} = \frac{7\sqrt[2]{13}}{13} = \frac{7\sqrt{13}}{13}$". The exponent "2" indicated in some of the square root radicals is not necessary. This is the only type of math problem in which the number "2" is usually not written, but every mathematician understands the number "2" is present. We refer to the number "2" in the square root notation as an *invisible number*.

We know you will not insist the students write all the indicated steps. We also want you to realize if the students have been exposed to "Young's Equation/Ratio Theorem" and "Young's Conversion Theorem" repeatedly over the past 1, 2, 3, or 8 years, they will automatically understand the steps and you will only have to discuss why we focused on the identity "$\sqrt{13} = \sqrt{13}$" to simplify the given fraction expression. When a fraction in algebra contains a square root or any type of root (radical expression) in the denominator, mathematicians consider this to be a poor form in which to write the answer. Therefore, you need to simplify a fraction with a root in the denominator, and the simplified fraction will only have the expression containing a root (radical expression, "$\sqrt{\ }$") in the numerator. Mathematicians refer to this process as rationalizing the denominator.

2. Simplify: $\frac{11}{6+\sqrt{8}}$

Fact: Use "Young's Equation/Ratio Theorem" with the identity "$6 - \sqrt[2]{8} = 6 - \sqrt[2]{8}$" and determine the correct form of the number 1 to multiply the given fraction. Obviously, you will have to explain why we used the identity "$6 - \sqrt[2]{8} = 6 - \sqrt[2]{8}$" to determine the special form of the number 1, "$\frac{6-\sqrt{8}}{6-\sqrt{8}} = 1$".

Using "Young's Conversion Theorem" along with some algebra rules the students must know prior to simplifying this fraction, the conversion looks like this: $\frac{11}{6+\sqrt[2]{8}} = \frac{11}{6+\sqrt[2]{8}} \times 1 =$ $\frac{11}{6+\sqrt[2]{8}} \times \frac{6-\sqrt[2]{8}}{6-\sqrt[2]{8}} = \frac{11 \times (6-\sqrt[2]{8})}{(6+\sqrt[2]{8})(6-\sqrt[2]{8})} = \frac{11(6-\sqrt[2]{8})}{36-6\sqrt[2]{8}+6\sqrt[2]{8}-\sqrt[2]{64}} = \frac{11(6-\sqrt[2]{8})}{36-\sqrt[2]{64}} = \frac{11(6-\sqrt[2]{8})}{36-8} = \frac{11(6-\sqrt[2]{8})}{28}$. If you are a math teacher, you realize this problem is not written in simplified form yet. Here is the final solution in simplified form when we focus on the numerator. We realize we can simplify the "$\sqrt{8}$" and write it as "$\sqrt{4 \cdot 2} = \sqrt{4} \cdot \sqrt{2} = 2\sqrt{2}$". We then factored out (divided out) the number "2" in the numerator and reduced the fraction:

$$\frac{11(6-\sqrt{8})}{28} = \frac{11(6-\sqrt{4 \cdot 2})}{28} = \frac{11(6-2\sqrt{2})}{28} = \frac{11 \cdot 2\,(3-\sqrt{2})}{2\times 14} = \frac{11(3-\sqrt{2})}{14}.$$

We could have simplified the denominator in the original problem and written the problem like this: "$\frac{11}{6+\sqrt[2]{8}} = \frac{11}{6+2\sqrt{2}}$". Then we would have multiplied the fraction "$\frac{11}{6+2\sqrt{2}}$" by the following form of the number 1 "$\frac{6-2\sqrt{2}}{6-2\sqrt{2}}$". In arithmetic and higher-level math courses, frequently there are several ways to compute the final solution. This is the reason why your better math students should be exposed to different methods to solve the same problem.

The following types of expressions used in algebra and other advanced math courses are referred to as conjugates: (Examples: "$6 + \sqrt[2]{8}$ & $6 - \sqrt[2]{8}$" and "$6 + 2\sqrt{2}$ & $6 - 2\sqrt{2}$"). Notice the only change between the two expressions is the switching of the positive and negative signs. When you multiply conjugates, something special occurs, in these examples the radicals disappear. There are other forms of conjugates which we will be illustrating later in this chapter when we determine special forms of 1 to multiply expressions, with the goal to eliminate a certain term in the expression.

Simplifying Algebra Fractions with Other Roots in the Denominator

1. Simplify: $\frac{5}{\sqrt[3]{9}}$

Fact: We are going to use the identity "$\sqrt[3]{3} = \sqrt[3]{3}$" and then use "Young's Equation/Ratio Theorem" to derive the following form of the number 1, "$\frac{\sqrt[3]{3}}{\sqrt[3]{3}} = 1$".

Multiply the given fraction by the special form of the number 1 to simplify the fraction: "$\frac{5}{\sqrt[3]{9}} = \frac{5}{\sqrt[3]{9}} \times 1 = \frac{5}{\sqrt[3]{9}} \times \frac{\sqrt[3]{3}}{\sqrt[3]{3}} = \frac{5 \times \sqrt[3]{3}}{\sqrt[3]{9} \times \sqrt[3]{3}} = \frac{5\sqrt[3]{3}}{\sqrt[3]{27}} = \frac{5\sqrt[3]{3}}{3}$". You make the decision regarding how you are going to explain why we selected the identity, "$\sqrt[3]{3} = \sqrt[3]{3}$" to determine the form of the number 1 indicated to multiply the given fraction when we used "Young's Conversion

Theorem". The goal is to make the denominator the cubed root of a perfect cube, "27". If we would like to make this problem a little more challenging, we may want to change the number "5" into the number "6" or "9" in the numerator. If we replace the number "5" with the number "6", the final answer will look like this, "$\frac{6\sqrt[3]{3}}{3}$" and the reduced fraction would become "$2\sqrt[3]{3}$". If the number "5" in the numerator was a "9" the problem would look like this, "$\frac{9\sqrt[3]{3}}{3}$" and the final reduced answer would be "$3\sqrt[3]{3}$".

2. Simplify: $\frac{x-1}{\sqrt[5]{x^3}}$

Fact: "$\sqrt[5]{x^2} = \sqrt[5]{x^2}$" $\therefore$ "$\frac{\sqrt[5]{x^2}}{\sqrt[5]{x^2}} = 1$". We used Young's Equation/Ratio Theorem and indicated the identity involving the number <u>1</u>.

Conversion: $\frac{x-1}{\sqrt[5]{x^3}} = \frac{x-1}{\sqrt[5]{x^3}} \times 1 = \frac{x-1}{\sqrt[5]{x^3}} \times \frac{\sqrt[5]{x^2}}{\sqrt[5]{x^2}} = \frac{(x-1) \times \sqrt[5]{x^2}}{\sqrt[5]{x^3} \times \sqrt[5]{x^2}} = \frac{(x-1)\sqrt[5]{x^2}}{\sqrt[5]{x^3 \cdot x^2}} = \frac{\sqrt[5]{x^2}(x-1)}{\sqrt[5]{x^5}} = \frac{\sqrt[5]{x^2}(x-1)}{x}$

We used "Young's Conversion Theorem" along with some algebra rules.

Point out to your students the variable "x" in the denominator will not cancel with either of the "$x's$" in the numerator. You still must explain to your students why we used the fact: "$\sqrt[5]{x^2} = \sqrt[5]{x^2}$". Our goal is to make the denominator the fifth root of a term to the fifth power.

Simplifying Fractions with Imaginary Numbers in the Denominator

If you want to simplify problems with an imaginary number in the denominator, you must know the **definition** of the **<u>number</u>** "i". The exact definition of the <u>number</u> "i" is: "$i = \sqrt{-1}$". After you understand the definition of the number "i" and you explain the definition of imaginary numbers and complex numbers to your students, you can explain how to use previously learned arithmetic and algebra concepts to derive the additional facts/theorems with respect to the following imaginary number expressions: "$i^2 = i \cdot i = \sqrt{-1} \cdot \sqrt{-1} = (-1)^{\frac{1}{2}} \cdot (-1)^{\frac{1}{2}} = (-1)^1 = -1$", "$i^3 = i^2 \cdot i = (-1) \cdot i = -i$", "$i^4 = i^2 \cdot i^2 = (-1) \cdot (-1) = 1$", "$i^5 = i^4 i^1 = 1 \cdot i = i$", "$i^6 = i^4 i^2 = 1 \cdot (-1) = -1$", "$i^7 = i^4 i^3 = 1 \cdot -i = -i$", "$i^8 = i^4 \cdot i^4 = 1 \times 1 = 1$", "$i^9 = i$", etc.". Students should recognize a pattern after you illustrate several examples with the number "i" and an exponent greater than "4".

Fact, the basic rules for exponents come from a solid understanding of arithmetic, then the rules to work with both fraction and decimal exponents are taught in algebra.

1. Simplify: $\frac{4}{i}$

Fact: "$i = i$" $\therefore$ $\frac{i}{i} = 1$ Young's Equation/Ratio Theorem with identity

Conversion: $\frac{4}{i} = \frac{4}{i} \times 1 = \frac{4}{i} \times \frac{i}{i} = \frac{4 \cdot i}{i \cdot i} = \frac{4i}{i^2} = \frac{4i}{-1} = -4i$ Young's Conversion Theorem

2. Simplify: $\frac{2+i}{3-i}$

Fact: "$3 + i = 3 + i$" $\therefore$ $\frac{3+i}{3+i} = 1$ Young's Equation/Ratio Theorem with identity

Conversion: $\frac{2+i}{3-i} = \frac{2+i}{3-i} \times 1 = \frac{2+i}{3-i} \times \frac{3+i}{3+i} = \frac{(2+i)(3+i)}{(3-i)(3+i)} = \frac{6+2i+3i+i^2}{9+3i-3i-i^2} = \frac{6+5i+(i^2)}{9-(i^2)} = \frac{6+5i+(-1)}{9-(-1)} =$

$\frac{5+5i}{9+1} = \frac{5(1+i)}{10} = \frac{(1+i)}{2}$ Young's Conversion Theorem

We used the identity "$3 + i = 3 + i$" in this problem because we knew from experience when we multiply the denominator "$3 - i$" which is in the given denominator by "$3 + i$", all the expressions containing the number "i" or some form of the number "i" would cancel.

Notice, we used a different type of conjugate to determine the special identity fact.

3. Simplify: $\frac{7}{i^3}$

Fact: "$i = i$" $\therefore$ $\frac{i}{i} = 1$

Conversion: $\frac{7}{i^3} = \frac{7}{i^3} \times 1 = \frac{7}{i^3} \times \frac{i}{i} = \frac{7i}{i^4} = \frac{7i}{+1} = 7i$

The goal to simplify these three problems is to make sure the **number**, "i" does not appear in the denominator.

Setting Up Ratios When Working with Dilations in Geometry

1. If triangle "ΔABC" and triangle "ΔDEF" are similar, and ΔABC is dilated by a factor of 1.25 to form the larger ΔDEF, what is the ratio between the larger triangle and the smaller triangle?

We set up several ratios based on the given information.

$$\frac{\text{Larger }\Delta}{\text{Smaller }\Delta} = \frac{\Delta\text{DEF}}{\Delta\text{ABC}} = \frac{1.25}{1}$$

Most students would prefer not to work with the ratio "$\frac{1.25}{1}$" because it contains a decimal. Convert the decimal fraction into a fraction with a natural number in the numerator and a natural number in the denominator.

Fact: "$100 = 100$" $\therefore$ $\frac{100}{100} = 1$ Young's Equation/Ratio Theorem with identity

Conversion: $\frac{1.25}{1} = \frac{1.25}{1} \times 1 = \frac{1.25}{1} \times \frac{100}{100} = \frac{1.25 \times 100}{1 \times 100} = \frac{125}{100} = \frac{5 \cdot 5 \cdot 5}{2 \cdot 2 \cdot 5 \cdot 5} = \frac{5}{2 \cdot 2} = \frac{5}{4}$

We used "Young's Conversion Theorem" along with factor trees to get the final ratio, "$\frac{5}{4}$".

We hope you immediately realize the decimal number "1.25" equals the mixed number "$1\frac{1}{4}$", which can then be written as the improper fraction "$\frac{5}{4}$".

This problem is a little more challenging if the original goal is to find the ratio between the smaller and larger triangle. Refer to the next example problem to understand the slight difference in difficulty based on the way the ratios are written.

2. If ΔGHI and ΔJKL are similar triangles and ΔGHI is dilated by a factor of 2.875 to form ΔJKL, what is the ratio between the smaller triangle and the larger triangle?

We set up several ratios based on the given information.

$$\frac{\text{Smaller } \Delta}{\text{Larger } \Delta} = \frac{\Delta\text{GHI}}{\Delta\text{JKL}} = \frac{1}{2.875}$$

Again, most students would prefer not to work with the ratio "$\frac{1}{2.875}$" because the denominator of the ratio involves a decimal. Convert the decimal ratio into a ratio so both the numerator and the denominator are natural numbers.

Fact: "$1000 = 1000$" $\therefore$ $\frac{1000}{1000} = 1$ Young's Equation/Ratio Theorem with identity

Conversion: $\frac{1}{2.875} = \frac{1}{2.875} \times 1 = \frac{1}{2.875} \times \frac{1000}{1000} = \frac{1 \times 1000}{2.875 \times 1000} = \frac{1000}{2875} = \frac{25 \cdot 40}{25 \cdot 115} = \frac{40}{115} = \frac{8}{23}$

We used "Young's Conversion Theorem" along with our mental knowledge regarding the factor "25" when we wrote the numerator as "25 × 40" and then the denominator as "25 × 115". We then used our multiplication knowledge regarding the number "5" when we reduced the fraction "$\frac{40}{115}$". If you do not follow the logic, maybe we should have used factor trees to simplify the fraction "$\frac{1000}{2875}$".

If you recognize the decimal ".875", and the fraction "$\frac{7}{8}$" are equal, you may have simplified the fraction "$\frac{1}{2.875}$" differently. You could have written the ratio in the following form, "$\frac{1}{2\frac{7}{8}}$" and then simplify the ratio in the following manner:

"$\frac{1}{2\frac{7}{8}} = \frac{1}{\frac{23}{8}} = 1 \div \frac{23}{8} = 1 \times \frac{8}{23} = \frac{8}{23}$".

Some people think the word, "dilate", simply means to make something bigger. In geometry the word, "dilation", means to make a geometric shape smaller or larger, but the shapes are always similar.

In this section we continually used the word ratio rather than the word fraction on purpose. Remember a ratio will either have two labels (one in the numerator and one in the denominator) or no labels indicated (if the labels are identical then they will cancel). When referring to the lengths of the sides of a triangle, all the lengths would have a linear label written with each of the measurements. In the examples indicated, the labels were not mentioned, but if they were listed, the labels would normally be identical and cancel. A ratio is a special type of fraction, so it would have also been acceptable to use the word *fraction* when working with these two example problems.

When working with similar shapes, the best method to use when you know three out of four corresponding facts regarding the lengths of the sides of similar shapes is to emphasize the cross-multiplication process. For example, if triangle "ΔABC" and triangle "ΔXYZ" are similar, triangle "ΔABC" is the larger triangle, and the ratio of similarity between the two triangles is "$\frac{7}{5}$", what would be the length of the corresponding side in the smaller triangle if the side in the larger triangle is "6 *in.*"?

Cross-multiplication set up: $\frac{\text{Larger triangle}}{\text{Smaller triangle}}$ $\qquad \frac{7}{5} = \frac{6\ in.}{x}$

Cross-multiply using the two ratios: $\qquad 7x = 30\ in.$

Divide both sides by the number "7": $\qquad \frac{7x}{7} = \frac{30\ in.}{7}$

Answer: $\qquad 1x = \frac{30}{7}\ in. \qquad \therefore\ x = 4\frac{2}{7}\ in.$

Notice, the correct label automatically appears in the final answer.

It would have been also correct to refer to the ratio of triangles as "$\frac{Smaller\ triangle}{Larger\ triangle}$" and use the ratio "$\frac{5}{7}$" then use the proportion "$\frac{5}{7} = \frac{x}{6\ in.}$". We illustrated how to use both ratios involving the smaller and larger triangles because we wanted to indicate how we encouraged students to set up an <u>initial</u> ratio involving the larger and smaller triangle as a template for the proportion and it does not matter which set up the students decide to focus their efforts, but they must make sure they are consistent when solving the problem.

(Refer back to these examples: "$\frac{\text{Larger triangle}}{\text{Smaller triangle}}$" and "$\frac{\textit{Smaller triangle}}{\textit{Larger triangle}}$".)

> Suggestion: When introducing dilations in Geometry, we suggest you reference what occurs when you look through a pair of binoculars. If you look through the binoculars one way everything appears to be larger, but if you reverse the binoculars everything looks smaller.

Converting Radians to Degrees and Degrees to Radians

1. Convert: $\frac{3}{4}\pi\ rads\ into\ degrees$

Fact: "$\pi\ rads = 180°\ \ \therefore\ \ \frac{\pi\ rads}{180°} = 1 = \frac{180°}{\pi\ rads}$" Using "Young's Equation /Ratio Theorem", it is easy to get the two ratios which both equal the number <u>1</u>.

Use "Young's Conversion Theorem" to convert the radian measurement into a degree measurement. $\frac{3}{4}\pi\ rads = \frac{3}{4}\pi\ rads \times 1 = \frac{3}{4} \cdot \frac{\pi\ rads}{1} \times 1 = \frac{3\ \pi\ rads}{4} \times \frac{180°}{\pi\ rads} = \frac{3\ \pi\ rads\ \times\ 180°}{4\ \times\ \pi\ rads} = \frac{3 \times 180°}{4} = 135°$

When teaching this topic, insist the students write down the basic fact: "$\pi\ rads = 180°$" and the two ratios which both equal <u>1</u>: "$\frac{\pi\ rads}{180°} = 1 = \frac{180°}{\pi\ rads}$". When the students are doing the actual conversion problem, insist they indicate how to multiply by a special form of the number <u>1</u>, at least initially, and write these steps: "$\frac{3\ \pi}{4}\ rads\ \times 1 = \frac{3\pi\ rads}{4} \times \frac{180°}{\pi\ rads} = \frac{3 \times 180°}{4} = 135°$ ".

Typically, when students are working with the six trigonometric expressions [$\sin\theta$, $\cos\theta$, $\tan\theta$, $\csc\theta$, $\sec\theta$, and $\cot\theta$] or the six trigonometric functions

$[f(\theta) = \sin\theta, f(\theta) = \cos\theta, f(\theta) = \tan\theta, f(\theta) = \csc\theta, f(\theta) = \sec\theta,$ and $f(\theta) = \cot\theta]$, there must be some type of angle measurement indicated to the right of the trig abbreviations where the Greek letter theta "θ" appears. Usually, the expression to the right of the trig abbreviation is either a degree or a radian. If there is no label with the expression to the right of the trig abbreviation, mathematicians automatically know the label with the expression must be radian(s). The label radian (rad.) is an invisible label when writing trig functions when you are referring to the angle. If there is a degree symbol, " ° " written with the number or term to the right of the trig abbreviation, you know for a fact you are working with degrees. There are other types of angle measurements you could discuss, but in high school trigonometry or precalculus, these are the two main angle measurement systems students will work with. In calculus, most (all) of the problems will require the students to work with radians.

2. Convert: $485°$ *to radians*

Fact: $180° = \pi\ rads\ \therefore\ \frac{180°}{\pi\ rads} = 1 = \frac{\pi\ rads}{180°}$ Applied: Young's Equation/Ratio Theorem

Conversion: $485° = 485° \times 1 = \frac{485°}{1} \times \frac{\pi \text{ rads}}{180°} = \frac{485° \times \pi \text{ rads}}{1 \times 180°} = \frac{485 \times \pi \text{ rads}}{180} = \frac{97\ \pi \text{ rads}}{36} =$

$\frac{97}{36}\pi \text{ rads} = \frac{97\ \pi}{36} \text{ rads}$ Applied: Young's Conversion Theorem

Here is a trig equation using both the angle "$485°$" and the equivalent angle "$\frac{97}{36}\pi\ rads$", "$\tan 485° = \tan\frac{97\pi}{36}$". Notice, the degree symbol is indicated in the notation on the left side of the equation, but on the right side of the equation the radian notation is understood to be present. You should also recognize when we converted "485°" to "$\frac{97\pi}{36}\ rads$". We treated the degree symbol, " ° " with the given angle measurement "485°" in the numerator of the first fraction above as a label and the degree symbol, " ° " with the angle "180°" in the denominator as a label. We then cancelled the degree symbols in the numerator and in the denominator.

3. Solve: $\sin 60° = y$

This is a basic trigonometric equation, and early in the course, students should realize the answer for the "y" variable is either "$\frac{\sqrt[2]{3}}{2}$" or (*approximately*) ".8660" based on the definition of the sine function involving a "30°, 60°, 90°" triangle. This means the answer should be written as "$\sin 60° = \frac{\sqrt[2]{3}}{2}$ or .8660". The same problem could be written as $\sin\frac{\pi}{3} = y$, and the answer would be written as "$\sin\frac{\pi}{3} = \frac{\sqrt[2]{3}}{2}$ or .8660". We can also write the equation/identity "$\sin 60° = \sin\frac{\pi}{3}$". The fraction with the radical in the numerator, "$\frac{\sqrt[2]{3}}{2}$", is an irrational number. This is important to know since it means the decimal, ".8660" is also irrational and the decimal, ".8660…" never repeats and never terminates (ends). There are procedures derived in calculus which can be used to compute the decimal answer for the fraction (irrational number), "$\frac{\sqrt[2]{3}}{2}$" without using a calculator. The method we prefer to use is referred to as Taylor's Formula (Series), but this topic is beyond the scope of this textbook.

Converting 60° to $\frac{\pi}{3}$ radians is a common conversion, and this is a conversion fact most students memorize early in trigonometry. The conversion procedure looks like this:

Fact: $180° = \pi\, rads \;\therefore\; \frac{180°}{\pi\, rads} = 1 = \frac{\pi\, rads}{180°}$

Conversion: $\frac{60°}{1} \times \frac{\pi\, rads}{180°} = \frac{60° \times \pi\, rads}{1 \times 180°} = \frac{\pi}{3} rads$

When we write an angle measurement using radians separate from a trigonometric abbreviation, "$\frac{\pi}{3}$ *rads*", we must write the label with the angle measurement. The invisible label "*rads*" is only understood to be present when the radian angle is written to the right of a trig abbreviation.

Notice the degree notation symbol, " ° " is indicated with the angle "60" to the right of the abbreviation "sin". It is **improper** to write just the abbreviation "sin" or any of the other five trig functions without having an angle indicated to the right of the trig abbreviation. When writing any of the six trigonometric abbreviations, there is always some sort of angle written to the right of the abbreviation. Never simply write "sin" without an angle indicated to the right of the abbreviation. The only time the abbreviation for radians (rad) is not written but understood to be present is when radians are the angle measurement for a specific trigonometric expression or function.

4. Solve: $\sin\frac{7\pi}{3} = y$

Believe it or not, this is basically the same problem as example problem number 3. The angle is understood to be written in radians, and one way to have the students solve this problem is to convert the radians to degrees. When students are first learning to work with radians, do not mind if they convert the radian angle measurement to degrees, but eventually you want the students to be as comfortable working with radians as they are working with degrees. If we convert the angle measurement into degrees, the conversion process will follow the normal procedures as discussed throughout this textbook.

1. Fact: The problem, "$\sin\frac{7\pi}{3} = y$" is written with the angle "$\frac{7\pi}{3}$". The given angle to the right of the trig abbreviation "sin" does not have a degree symbol indicated. Therefore, the angle measurement must be radians.

2. Fact: $180° = \pi\ rads$ $\quad\therefore\quad$ $\frac{180°}{\pi\ rads} = 1 = \frac{\pi\ rads}{180°}$ Using Young's Equation/Ratio Theorem.

3. Rewrite the given problem with the invisible label "$\sin\frac{7\,\pi}{3} = \sin\frac{7\pi}{3}\ rads = \sin\frac{7\,\pi\ rads}{3}$".

Now, the objective is to convert the angle "$\frac{7\,\pi\ rads}{3}$" which is written in radians to degrees.

Conversion: Use "Young's Conversion Theorem" and the identity derived in the previous paragraph. "$\frac{7\,\pi\ rads}{3} = \frac{7\,\pi\ rads}{3} \times 1 = \frac{7\,\pi\ rads}{3} \times \frac{180°}{\pi\ rads} = \frac{7\,\pi\ rads \times 180°}{3 \times \pi\ rads} = \frac{7 \times 180°}{3} = \frac{7 \times 60°}{1} = 7 \times 60° = 420°$". We encourage students to write the label *radians* when they are converting radians to degrees or vice versa. This way, they can focus on the label and not try to remember the labels in their heads. The original problem is now written so the angle is written as "$\sin 420° = y$".

> We really want the students to be comfortable working with both radians and degrees, but in the beginning many students feel more comfortable working with degrees.

When students are taught to work with **angles involving trig functions**, they are supposed to think about the angle going around a circle. If you start at a point on a circle where the radius intersects the circle and then go around the circle back to the starting point, you should realize one revolution around the circle equals "360°". Once you make one complete revolution around the circle and you are back at the starting point, <u>when working with trig functions</u>, the angle restarts at zero, and you can basically ignore the first "360°" and concentrate on the remaining angle. Mathematically, this means every time you work with an angle greater than "360°", you should subtract "360°" from the starting angle and only work with the difference after you subtract the two angles. Perhaps you can tell the students to divide the original angle by "360° " and focus on the remainder.

When this circle-type conversion is taught in precalculus textbooks, the circle is usually placed on an (x, y) axis. The center of the circle is the origin. The normal starting point to begin going around the circle is the point where the circle intersects the positive "x" axis. Then start tracing the circle in a counterclockwise rotation.

Most students in high school realize, one complete revolution in a circle is equal to "360° ".

Once we concentrate on radians, the students must understand one revolution equals "$2\pi\ rads.$". We already know $180° = \pi\ rads$, so if each side of the equation is doubled, we derive the following fact/equation: "$360° = 2\pi\ rads$". In this problem, you need to realize $2\pi\ rads. = \frac{6}{3}\pi\ rads$. Example problem 4 was originally written as "$\sin\frac{7\pi}{3} = y$". The angle in the given problem is "$\frac{7\ \pi\ rads}{3}$". We know one revolution is "$360° = 2\pi\ rads = \frac{6}{3}\pi\ rads$". If we are permitted to ignore the first ($360°\ or\ \frac{6}{3}\pi\ rads$), then we can concentrate on the remaining angle after we subtract either "360° or "$2\pi\ rads$" which equals "$\frac{6}{3}\pi\ rads$. Therefore, we concentrate on either, "60° or $\frac{\pi\ rads}{3}$". We found the angle "60° " by solving the following subtraction problem: "$420° - 360° = 60°$ ". We found the angle "$\frac{\pi\ rads}{3}$" by solving the following subtraction problem: "$\frac{7\ \pi\ rads}{3} - \frac{6\ \pi\ rads}{3} = \frac{7\pi\ rads - 6\ \pi\ rads}{3} = \frac{\pi\ rads}{3}$".

The problem can now be written as "$\sin 60° = \frac{\sqrt[2]{3}}{2}$", which is the same as the previous example problem. We want the students to recognize as soon as possible the original problem can be rewritten as "$\sin\frac{7\pi}{3} = \sin\frac{7\ \pi\ rads}{3} = \sin\frac{\pi\ rads}{3} = \frac{\sqrt[2]{3}}{2}$" and <u>concentrate exclusively on</u>

radians, but it usually takes about a month or more for students to feel confident working directly with radians and not focus on degrees.

Teaching Point: When a trig problem involves angles greater than "2π *rads* or 4π *rads* or 6π *rads etc.* or $360°$ or $720°$ or $1080°$ *etc.*", students need to work with an angle less than or equal to "2π *rads* or $360°$". There are two ways to explain to the students how to determine the smaller angle measurement. The students can either divide by "2π *rads* or $360°$" and then concentrate on the remainder, or they can subtract "2π *rads* or $360°$" several times until they get an angle smaller than "2π *rads* or $360°$". As the math teacher, you can decide how you want your students to find the angle measurement less than "2π *rads* or $360°$". Also, remember there is an additional situation to consider when working with the two trig functions "$\tan\theta = f(\theta)$ and $\cot\theta = f(\theta)$".

Did you realize we performed a special type of conversion in this example problem, and we did not use either "Young's Equation/Ratio Theorem" or "Young's Conversion Theorem"? Switching the angle from $420°$ into $60°$ is usually only required when working with trig functions/expressions. We never said "$420° = 60°$", but when working with any of the six trig functions which are based on a circle, this type of conversion will work. This is a special situation. You may use this type of logic involving angles and circles with all six of the trigonometric functions. Therefore, the other five pairs of trigonometric expressions are also equal: "$\cos\frac{7\pi}{3} = \cos\frac{\pi}{3}$, $\tan\frac{7\pi}{3} = \tan\frac{\pi}{3}$, $\csc\frac{7\pi}{3} = \csc\frac{\pi}{3}$, $\sec\frac{7\pi}{3} = \sec\frac{\pi}{3}$, $\cot\frac{7\pi}{3} = \cot\frac{\pi}{3}$" or "$\cos 420° = \cos 60°$, $\tan 420° = \tan 60°$, $\csc 420° = \csc 60°$, $\sec 420° = \sec 60°$, $\cot 420° = \cot 60°$".

5. Convert $2\frac{3}{8}$ *revolutions into degrees*

Facts: "$1\ rev. = 360°$ $180° = \pi\ rads$ $360° = 2\pi\ rads$ $1\ rev. = 2\pi\ rads$

Since the problem requires you to convert from revolutions to degrees, we will focus on the first equation (fact) and derive the following two ratios which equal 1, "$\frac{1\ rev.}{360°} = 1 = \frac{360°}{1\ rev.}$" after using "Young's Equation/Ratio Theorem".

Conversion: Use "Young's Conversion Theorem", "$2\frac{3}{8}\ rev. = \frac{19}{8} rev. = \frac{19}{8} \times \frac{1\ rev.}{1} = \frac{19\ rev.}{8} =$

$\frac{19\ rev.}{8} \times 1 = \frac{19\ rev.}{8} \times \frac{360°}{1\ rev.} = \frac{19\ rev. \times 360°}{8 \times 1\ rev.} = \frac{19 \times 360°}{8} = \frac{19 \times 45°}{1} = 855°$".

6. Convert: $\frac{7}{15}\ rev.\ into\ radians$

Fact: We use the fourth fact listed in the previous example: "$1\ rev. = 2\pi\ rads$ $\therefore$

$\frac{1\ rev.}{2\ \pi\ rads} = 1 = \frac{2\ \pi\ rads}{1\ rev.}$", after using "Young's Equation/Ratio Theorem".

Conversion: Use "Young's Conversion Theorem" "$\frac{7}{15} revs. = \frac{7\ revs.}{15} \times 1 = \frac{7\ revs.}{15} \times \frac{2\pi\ rads}{1\ rev.} =$

$\frac{7 \times 2\pi\ rads}{15} = \frac{14\pi\ rads}{15}\ or\ \frac{14\pi}{15}\ rads$".

Notice, in the previous example problem it is important to use the label "*rads*".

7. Solve: $\sin 1 = y$

This example creates problems for many Precalculus students. Several students fail to understand how to solve this problem because they have not paid attention to a fact we repeatedly stated in this section. There is always some type of angle measurement immediately to the right of the trig expression "sin θ " and if the angle is written in terms of degrees, the degree symbol is placed at the top right of the angle. If there is NO degree symbol or angle measurement symbol indicated, then the angle is understood to be written in radians. This problem could be rewritten as "sin 1 $rad = y$". You will never see this type of notation written in a Precalculus textbook, "**sin 1** $\boldsymbol{rad = y}$", it will always be written as "sin 1 $= y$" with no radian measurement symbol indicated.

Convert the 1 radian into degrees: Fact: $\pi\ rads = 180°$ $\therefore \frac{\pi\ rads}{180°} = 1 = \frac{180°}{\pi\ rads}$ We used "Young's Equation/Ratio Theorem".

Now use "Young's Conversion Theorem" to figure out the approximate degree indicated by "1 rad". Conversion: $1\ rad = \frac{1\ rad}{1} = \frac{1\ rad}{1} \times 1 = \frac{1\ rad}{1} \times \frac{180°}{\pi\ rads} = \frac{180°}{\pi} \approx 180° \div 3.14159 \approx 57.2958°$ If we want to find the approximate answer to the given problem "sin 1 $= y$" you may use a calculator, just make sure the setting is on "radians". Students in Precalculus are usually permitted to use a calculator to compute the approximate decimal answer. A good approximation is "sin 1 ≈ 0.8415".

> The label "*rads*" is only invisible when it is the label for an angle when you are writing one of the six trig functions or expressions.

Two Simple Calculus Problems and Solutions Using Both Theorems

We will start by explaining a basic calculus theorem involving limits with infinity and rational expressions. Find the limit of the following rational expressions "$\frac{1}{x}, \frac{1}{x^2}, \frac{2}{x^3}, \frac{5}{x^4}, \frac{101.6}{x^{12}}$" as the value of "$x$" approaches infinity. To a trained mathematician, he/she realizes the number in the numerator is irrelevant and the "x" variables in the denominators are significant. If we just analyze the first fraction "$\frac{1}{x}$" and assume the numbers in the denominator expressed by the variable "x" get larger and larger; we have the following types of examples to consider: "$\frac{1}{1}, \frac{1}{10}, \frac{1}{1000}, \frac{1}{1{,}000{,}000}, \frac{1}{9{,}999{,}999}, \frac{1}{\infty}$". You must realize the larger the denominator becomes the smaller the value of the fraction becomes. We say if the value of the denominator in the fraction "$\frac{1}{x}$" gets larger, the value of the fraction approaches <u>zero</u> (0). The mathematics/calculus notation is written using the following notation: "$\lim_{x\to\infty} \frac{1}{x} = 0$". This also means all the other examples also approach <u>0</u>: "$\lim_{x\to\infty} \frac{1}{x^2} = 0$", "$\lim_{x\to\infty} \frac{2}{x^3} = 0$", "$\lim_{x\to\infty} \frac{5}{x^4} = 0$" and "$\lim_{x\to\infty} \frac{101.6}{x^{12}} = 0$". Another limit fact you must be familiar with in order to simplify the first problem below is, the limit of any number written by itself and referring to the variable "x" as "x approaches infinity" is the actual number: (Examples: "$\lim_{x\to\infty} 6 = 6$"; "$\lim_{x\to\infty} 7.8 = 7.8$"; "$\lim_{x\to\infty} \frac{7}{10} = \frac{7}{10}$"; and "$\lim_{x\to\infty} \pi = \pi$"). There is obviously no "x" variable in any of these examples, therefore the value of "x" is insignificant.

Using the information just given regarding simple limits involving infinity, "∞", find the limits of the following two basic calculus problems.

1. $\lim_{x\to\infty} \frac{4x^3-x-2}{7x^3+4x+1}$

When we find the limit to this rational expression we need to focus on the denominator and the variable "x" with the largest exponent. This means we need to concentrate on the expression "$7x^3$" but more specifically concentrate on "x^3".

Step 1: Multiply the rational expression by <u>1</u>, but what form of <u>1</u>? We set up an identity based on the denominator and apply "Young's Equation/Ratio Theorem", "$\frac{1}{x^3} = \frac{1}{x^3} \quad \therefore \quad \frac{\frac{1}{x^3}}{\frac{1}{x^3}} = 1$".

Step 2: Multiply the limit rational expression by the form of 1 just determined in the previous step. We will use "Young's Conversion Theorem" to write the expression in a different form.

$$\text{“}\lim_{x\to\infty}\frac{4x^3-x-2}{7x^3+4x+1} = \lim_{x\to\infty}\left(\frac{4x^3-x-2}{7x^3+4x+1}\times 1\right) = \mathbf{\lim_{x\to\infty}\left(\frac{4x^3-x-2}{7x^3+4x+1}\times\frac{\frac{1}{x^3}}{\frac{1}{x^3}}\right)} =$$

$$\lim_{x\to\infty}\frac{(4x^3-x-2)\cdot\frac{1}{x^3}}{(7x^3+4x+1)\cdot\frac{1}{x^3}} = \lim_{x\to\infty}\frac{\frac{(4x^3-x-2)}{1}\cdot\frac{1}{x^3}}{\frac{(7x^3+4x+1)}{1}\cdot\frac{1}{x^3}} = \lim_{x\to\infty}\frac{\frac{(4x^3-x-2)\cdot 1}{1\cdot x^3}}{\frac{(7x^3+4x+1)\cdot 1}{1\cdot x^3}} =$$

$$\lim_{x\to\infty}\frac{\frac{(4x^3-x-2)}{x^3}}{\frac{(7x^3+4x+1)}{x^3}} =$$

$$\lim_{x\to\infty}\frac{\frac{4x^3}{x^3}-\frac{x}{x^3}-\frac{2}{x^3}}{\frac{7x^3}{x^3}+\frac{4x}{x^3}+\frac{1}{x^3}} = \lim_{x\to\infty}\frac{\frac{4}{1}-\frac{1}{x^2}-\frac{2}{x^3}}{\frac{7}{1}+\frac{4}{x^2}+\frac{1}{x^3}} = \lim_{x\to\infty}\frac{4-\frac{1}{x^2}-\frac{2}{x^3}}{7+\frac{4}{x^2}+\frac{1}{x^3}} =$$

$$\frac{\lim_{x\to\infty}4-\lim_{x\to\infty}\frac{1}{x^2}-\lim_{x\to\infty}\frac{2}{x^3}}{\lim_{x\to\infty}7+\lim_{x\to\infty}\frac{4}{x^2}-\lim_{x\to\infty}\frac{1}{x^3}} = \frac{4-0-0}{7+0-0} = \frac{4}{7}\text{“}.$$

If you are a Calculus 1 student, you quickly realize how to mentally find the limits of these simple problems after you solved 3, 5, or 10 example problems. When students first solve these types of problems, we believe it is important to write all the steps to simplify the problems prior to using mental math skills.

We wrote the step which illustrates "Young's Conversion Theorem" in bold in the solution. Most calculus textbooks will not write the solution with this amount of detail.

We wrote the solution so every student who has studied all the problems illustrated throughout this textbook should understand every step, but we do not expect every elementary teacher to solve this type of problem on their own. We assume every math certified teacher not only understands every step which was written but they can solve this type of problem on their own without indicating any work, but we encourage all students to write most of the steps indicated to illustrate they understand the procedures.

2. $\lim_{x \to \infty} \left(\sqrt{x^2+3} - x\right)$

If we wish to find the limit to this algebraic expression containing a variable inside the radical and the addition or subtraction of an additional term with the same variable outside the radical, we need to focus on the entire expression and determine how we can clean-up the radical expression in the numerator and maybe concentrate our efforts on the denominator. This sounds like we want to make a major change to the given problem, which is exactly what we are going to do. The key to finding the limit for this problem is the denominator of the problem and not the numerator. That seems strange because in the problem there does not appear to be a denominator because there is no fraction involved.

Step 1: In order to find the limit of the indicated problem, " $\lim_{x \to \infty} (\sqrt{x^2+3} - x)$" the first thing we need to do is figure out how to find an equivalent form of the given algebraic expression. We mentioned a concept earlier in this chapter when we referred to conjugates. We wrote some examples of conjugates, and we asked you to notice the difference between the two conjugate expressions, "The sign between the first and second terms will either change from a positive sign to a negative sign or vice versa." Using the conjugate concept, we believe the best identity to use to find a special value of the number 1 is "$(\sqrt{x^2+3}+x) = (\sqrt{x^2+3}+x)$ $\therefore$ $\frac{\sqrt{x^2+3}+x}{\sqrt{x^2+3}+x} = 1$" "Young's Equation/Ratio Theorem" comes to the rescue again.

Step 2: We now need to multiply the given limit problem, " $\lim_{x \to \infty} (\sqrt{x^2+3} - x)$ ", by the number 1 derived in the previous step. We will apply "Young's Conversion Theorem" again, but you will have to follow along as we illustrate all the arithmetic, algebra, and calculus limit rules in the solution.

$$"\lim_{x\to\infty}(\sqrt{x^2+3}-x) = \lim_{x\to\infty}(\sqrt{x^2+3}-x)\times 1 = \lim_{x\to\infty}(\sqrt{x^2+3}-x)\times\frac{\sqrt{x^2+3}+x}{\sqrt{x^2+3}+x} =$$

$$\lim_{x\to\infty}\frac{(\sqrt{x^2+3}\ -x)}{1}\cdot\frac{(\sqrt{x^2+3}\ +x)}{(\sqrt{x^2+3}\ +x)} = \lim_{x\to\infty}\frac{(\sqrt{x^2+3}\ -x)\cdot(\sqrt{x^2+3}\ +x)}{1\ \cdot\ \sqrt{x^2+3}\ +x} =$$

$$\lim_{x\to\infty}\frac{(\sqrt{x^2+3}\ -x)\ (\sqrt{x^2+3}\ +x)}{1\ \cdot\ (\sqrt{x^2+3}\ +x)} = \lim_{x\to\infty}\frac{(\sqrt{x^2+3})^2+x\sqrt{x^2+3}\ -x\sqrt{x^2+3}-x^2}{(\sqrt{x^2+3}\ +x)} =$$

$$\lim_{x\to\infty}\frac{((x^2+3)+0-x^2)}{\sqrt{x^2+3}\ +x} = \lim_{x\to\infty}\frac{((x^2+3)-x^2)}{\sqrt{x^2+3}\ +x} = \lim_{x\to\infty}\frac{(x^2+\ 3-x^2)}{\sqrt{x^2+3}\ +x} = \lim_{x\to\infty}\frac{+\ 3}{\sqrt{x^2+3}\ +x} =$$

We are not finished in fact we will use "Young's Equation/Ratio Theorem" and "Young's Conversion Theorem" again in the next two steps.

If you focus on the third line in the solution above to change from the first limit expression into the second equivalent limit expression, we used an Algebra procedure many people refer to as "First – Outer – Inner – Last" (FOIL). Below is the line to which we refer.

$$"\lim_{x\to\infty}\frac{(\sqrt{x^2+3}\ -x)\ (\sqrt{x^2+3}\ +x)}{1\ \times\ (\sqrt{x^2+3}\ +x)} = \lim_{x\to\infty}\frac{(\sqrt{x^2+3})^2+x\sqrt{x^2+3}\ -x\sqrt{x^2+3}-x^2}{(\sqrt{x^2+3}\ +x)} ="$$

In order to get the next limit expression in the fourth line (first expression) we recognized the two middle expressions in this limit: "$\lim_{x\to\infty}\frac{(\sqrt{x^2+3})^2+x\sqrt{x^2+3}\ -x\sqrt{x^2+3}-x^2}{(\sqrt{x^2+3}\ +x)}$" are identical and one is positive and the other is negative which means they cancel each other and we get the number zero (0) in the first limit expression in the fourth line: "$\lim_{x\to\infty}\frac{((x^2+3)+0-x^2)}{\sqrt{x^2+3}\ +x}$". In the same two limits just indicated we also, got rid of the square root expression in the first term of the numerator, "$(\sqrt{x^2+3})^2$" and wrote "(x^2+3)". We can do this based on our understanding of arithmetic and square roots. Study the following examples involving square roots and the exponent "2": (Examples: "$\sqrt{4}=\sqrt{2^2}\ or\ \sqrt{2}^2=2$" and "$\sqrt{25}=\sqrt{5^2}\ or\ \sqrt{5}^2=5$" and "$\sqrt{121}=\sqrt{11^2}\ or\ \sqrt{11}^2=11$" and "$\sqrt{x^2}\ or\ \sqrt{x}^2=x$" and "$(\sqrt{x^2+3})^2=x^2+3$". You must recognize when you have a square root with a term <u>squared</u> inside the square root, the solution becomes the term inside the square root. (We can make additional comments about this type of problem, but it is not necessary at this time. We are assuming all the values inside the square root are positive, "$x > 0$" in our examples. This is a fact: One should know that the term "x^2", must be positive therefore $x^2 \geq 0$ which is more relative than just knowing "$x > 0$".)

Step 3: We are still not able to quickly find the limit of the last limit in the 4th line from above: "$\lim\limits_{x\to\infty} \frac{+\,3}{\sqrt{x^2+3}\,+x}$". We are going to use another identity and "Young's Equation/Ratio Theorem" for a second time to complete this problem.

Identity: "$\frac{1}{x} = \frac{1}{x} \quad \therefore \quad \frac{\frac{1}{x}}{\frac{1}{x}} = 1$" We used "Young's Equation/Ratio Theorem".

It is amazing how important arithmetic rules are when we solve more advanced problems in higher level math courses.

On the previous page we indicated that we cancelled the two expressions, "$+\ x\sqrt{x^2+3}$" and "$-\ x\sqrt{x^2+3}$". Technically, we subtracted the two terms, and the difference is zero (0).

Step 4: Use "Young's Conversion Theorem" again and multiply the last limit expression "$\lim\limits_{x\to\infty} \frac{+\,3}{\sqrt{x^2+3}\,+x}$" by the special form of 1, "$\frac{\frac{1}{x}}{\frac{1}{x}}$" just determined in Step 3.

$$\text{"}\lim_{x\to\infty} \frac{+\,3}{\sqrt{x^2+3}\,+x} = \lim_{x\to\infty} \frac{3}{\sqrt{x^2+3}\,+x} \times 1 = \lim_{x\to\infty} \frac{3}{\sqrt{x^2+3}\,+x} \times \frac{\frac{1}{x}}{\frac{1}{x}} = \lim_{x\to\infty} \frac{3\cdot\frac{1}{x}}{(\sqrt{x^2+3}+x)\cdot\frac{1}{x}} =$$

$$\lim_{x\to\infty} \frac{\frac{3}{1}\cdot\frac{1}{x}}{\frac{(\sqrt{x^2+3}\,+x)}{1}\cdot\frac{1}{x}} = \lim_{x\to\infty} \frac{\frac{3}{1}\cdot\frac{1}{x}}{\frac{(\sqrt{x^2+3}\,+x)\cdot 1}{1\cdot x}} = \lim_{x\to\infty} \frac{\frac{3}{x}}{\frac{(\sqrt{x^2+3}\,+x)}{x}} = \lim_{x\to\infty} \frac{\frac{3}{x}}{\frac{\sqrt{x^2+3}}{x}+\frac{x}{x}}\text{"}$$

Some people might be asking themselves, "How did we change the denominator in this expression, "$\frac{(\sqrt{x^2+3}\,+x)}{x}$", into the denominator "$\frac{\sqrt{x^2+3}}{x} + \frac{x}{x}$" in the last two limit expressions?"

Again, we will look at some arithmetic examples to illustrate what we did:

"$\frac{3}{7}+\frac{2}{7}=\frac{3+2}{7}=\frac{5}{7}$ *or* $\frac{5}{7}=\frac{3+2}{7}=\frac{3}{7}+\frac{2}{7}$" and "$\frac{15}{17}-\frac{4}{17}=\frac{15-4}{17}=\frac{11}{17}$ *or* $\frac{11}{17}=\frac{15-4}{17}=\frac{15}{17}-\frac{4}{17}$"

and "$\frac{7}{17}+\frac{2}{17}-\frac{3}{17}-\frac{4}{17}=\frac{7+2-3-4}{17}=\frac{2}{17}$ or $\frac{2}{17}=\frac{7+2-3-4}{17}=\frac{7}{17}+\frac{2}{17}-\frac{3}{17}-\frac{4}{17}$" and "$\frac{x}{2rt}+\frac{6}{2rt}=\frac{x+6}{2rt}$ or $\frac{x+6}{2rt}=\frac{x}{2rt}+\frac{6}{2rt}$" and "$\frac{\sqrt{7}+1}{4}=\frac{\sqrt{7}}{4}+\frac{1}{4}$" and (focus on the right hand side of the examples just indicated) "$\frac{(\sqrt{x^2+3}+x)}{x}=\frac{\sqrt{x^2+3}}{x}+\frac{x}{x}$". If you are adding or subtracting two or more terms in the numerator and there is a single denominator (a denominator with a single term or the product of terms) then you can separate the numerators and create 2 or 3 or more fractions based on the addition and subtraction terms in the numerator and the given denominator.

Step 5: In this step we will also use an arithmetic concept with algebra to write the limit in a form so we can finally find the limit. Study these examples again regarding square roots: (Examples: "$\sqrt{2}^2=\sqrt{2^2}=2$", "$\sqrt{100}^2=\sqrt{100^2}=100$", and "$\sqrt{x^2}=x$ or $x=\sqrt{x^2}$"). The last limit expression we wrote above, may be written as two separate limits and then three separate limits which involve division and addition as indicated below.

$$\lim_{x\to\infty}\frac{\frac{3}{x}}{\frac{\sqrt{x^2+3}}{x}+\frac{x}{x}}=\frac{\lim\limits_{x\to\infty}\frac{3}{x}}{\lim\limits_{x\to\infty}\left(\frac{\sqrt{x^2+3}}{x}+\frac{x}{x}\right)}=\frac{\lim\limits_{x\to\infty}\frac{3}{x}}{\lim\limits_{x\to\infty}\frac{\sqrt{x^2+3}}{x}+\lim\limits_{x\to\infty}\frac{x}{x}}=\frac{\lim\limits_{x\to\infty}\frac{3}{x}}{\boldsymbol{\lim\limits_{x\to\infty}\frac{\sqrt{x^2+3}}{x}}+\lim\limits_{x\to\infty}\frac{x}{x}}=$$

$$\frac{\lim\limits_{x\to\infty}\frac{3}{x}}{\lim\limits_{x\to\infty}\frac{\sqrt{x^2+3}}{\sqrt{x^2}}+\lim\limits_{x\to\infty}\frac{x}{x}}=\frac{\lim\limits_{x\to\infty}\frac{3}{x}}{\lim\limits_{x\to\infty}\sqrt{\frac{x^2+3}{x^2}}+\lim\limits_{x\to\infty}\frac{x}{x}}=\frac{\lim\limits_{x\to\infty}\frac{3}{x}}{\lim\limits_{x\to\infty}\sqrt{\frac{x^2}{x^2}+\frac{3}{x^2}}+\lim\limits_{x\to\infty}\frac{x}{x}}=$$

In the last three limits on the line just written above, in all three limit problems we need to focus on the denominator, especially with the limit, "$\lim\limits_{x\to\infty}\frac{\sqrt{x^2+3}}{x}$", written in bold print in the illustration. We substituted "$\sqrt{x^2}$ for x" in the denominator of the first limit on the far left second line. In the second limit on the second line, we wrote the entire expression as a big square root with a fraction inside the square root, "$\sqrt{\frac{x^2+3}{x^2}}$". In the third limit we wrote the big fraction inside the square root as two little fractions in the square root which we already illustrated arithmetically is a legal process. We will now continue finding the solution.

$$\text{"}\frac{\lim\limits_{x\to\infty}\frac{3}{x}}{\lim\limits_{x\to\infty}\sqrt{\frac{x^2}{x^2}+\frac{3}{x^2}}+\lim\limits_{x\to\infty}\frac{x}{x}} = \frac{\lim\limits_{x\to\infty}\frac{3}{x}}{\lim\limits_{x\to\infty}\sqrt{1+\frac{3}{x^2}}+\lim\limits_{x\to\infty}\frac{x}{x}} = \frac{\lim\limits_{x\to\infty}\frac{3}{x}}{\lim\limits_{x\to\infty}\sqrt{1+\frac{3}{x^2}}+\lim\limits_{x\to\infty}\frac{x}{x}} =$$

$$\lim_{x\to\infty}\frac{\frac{3}{x}}{\sqrt{1+\frac{3}{x^2}}+1} = \frac{0}{\sqrt{1+0}+1} = \frac{0}{\sqrt{1}+1} = \frac{0}{1+1} = \frac{0}{2} = 0\text{"}$$

In the last line in the solution of his problem, we used the Limit rules discussed with the first calculus example problem such as: "$\lim\limits_{x\to\infty}\frac{1}{x} = 0$" and "$\lim\limits_{x\to\infty}\frac{1}{x^2} = 0$" and "$\lim\limits_{x\to\infty} 6 = 6$".

The final answer is zero (0), do you know why, based on your understanding of arithmetic?

Some people might think as soon as we realized the numerator would equal zero (0) we could conclude the final answer was going to equal 0. This is a good observation, but we wanted to find out what the limit of the denominator was going to equal. If the limit of the denominator also equaled 0, then we would encounter an answer which is not really an answer, because the answer would be undefined. We would have been forced to use L'Hopital's Rule (Bernoulli's Rule) if both the numerator and denominator both equaled "0" or "$\pm\infty$" which is beyond the scope of this textbook.

We have written a detailed explanation with illustrations to find the limits of the two indicated calculus limit questions in this section. For students who have mastered arithmetic and algebra, the previous pages contain a "2 or 3" day lecture/explanation to explain how to find the limits for the two indicated problems. With practice and experience almost all calculus students will be able to identify the two limits using mental math as "$\frac{7}{4}$" and "0". Even after a calculus student has solved several of these problems and understands all the rules and procedures, we still want inexperienced calculus students to write out the procedures/steps on a test, but we do not expect them to go into the detail we illustrated in our explanation. Here are the two solutions we would expect beginning calculus students to write on a first test to demonstrate their understanding of the procedures.

1. $\lim\limits_{x\to\infty}\frac{4x^3-x-2}{7x^3+4x+1}=\lim\limits_{x\to\infty}\frac{4x^3-x-2}{7x^3+4x+1}\times\frac{\frac{1}{x^3}}{\frac{1}{x^3}}=\lim\limits_{x\to\infty}\frac{\frac{(4x^3-x-2)}{1}\times\frac{1}{x^3}}{\frac{(7x^3+4x+1)}{1}\times\frac{1}{x^3}}=$

$\lim\limits_{x\to\infty}\frac{\frac{(4x^3-x-2)}{x^3}}{\frac{(7x^3+4x+1)}{x^3}}=\lim\limits_{x\to\infty}\frac{\frac{4x^3}{x^3}-\frac{x}{x^3}-\frac{2}{x^3}}{\frac{7x^3}{x^3}+\frac{4x}{x^3}+\frac{1}{x^3}}=\lim\limits_{x\to\infty}\frac{\frac{4}{1}-\frac{1}{x^2}-\frac{2}{x^3}}{\frac{7}{1}+\frac{4}{x^2}+\frac{1}{x^3}}=\lim\limits_{x\to\infty}\frac{4-\frac{1}{x^2}-\frac{2}{x^3}}{7+\frac{4}{x^2}+\frac{1}{x^3}}=$

$\frac{4-0-0}{7+0-0}=\frac{4}{7}$"

In the second expression, we still want the students to indicate they are multiplying by a special form of the number 1, but at this level we expect all students to be familiar with both "Young's Equation/Ratio Theorem" and "Young's Conversion Theorem". If a student indicates they are multiplying the first expression by "$\frac{\frac{1}{x^3}}{\frac{1}{x^3}}$", this will indicate to the instructor that the student knows and understands the correct rules and procedures to solve the problem. In the second line in the solution, the instructor can determine if the student has mastered all the arithmetic concepts involving fractions and how to rewrite a fraction with a denominator as several fractions with the same denominator when the terms in the numerator are added and subtracted. When the limit notation is removed and the arithmetic problem appears in the solution, "$\frac{4-0-0}{7+0-0}=\frac{4}{7}$", the instructor will understand that the student understood how to apply the new limit theorems which are used in this section. Before someone begins to solve this limit problem, the person must be an expert with arithmetic fraction rules and then apply the rules in arithmetic to algebra rational expressions and lastly, complete the easy part of the problem, which is to find the limit.

> The simplest procedure in this solution is the Calculus step at the end of the problem. Understanding arithmetic rules and procedures and then applying algebra rules and procedures which are derived from the arithmetic concepts are the challenging steps in the solution. Students must master arithmetic rules and procedures, if they expect to master the algebra rules and procedures and then apply the rules and procedures from both arithmetic and algebra to find the solution. What an exciting problem.

2. $\lim\limits_{x\to\infty}(\sqrt{x^2+3}-x) = \lim\limits_{x\to\infty}[(\sqrt{x^2+3}-x) \times \frac{\sqrt{x^2+3}+x}{\sqrt{x^2+3}+x}] =$

$$\lim_{x\to\infty}\frac{(\sqrt{x^2+3}-x)(\sqrt{x^2+3}+x)}{1 \quad \times \quad (\sqrt{x^2+3}+x)} = \lim_{x\to\infty}\frac{(\sqrt{x^2+3})^2 + x\sqrt{x^2+3} - x\sqrt{x^2+3} - x^2}{(\sqrt{x^2+3}+x)} =$$

$$\lim_{x\to\infty}\frac{((x^2+3)-x^2)}{\sqrt{x^2+3}+x} = \lim_{x\to\infty}\frac{(x^2+3-x^2)}{\sqrt{x^2+3}+x} = \lim_{x\to\infty}\frac{3}{\sqrt{x^2+3}+x} \times 1 = \lim_{x\to\infty}\frac{3}{\sqrt{x^2+3}+x} \times \frac{\frac{1}{x}}{\frac{1}{x}} =$$

$$\lim_{x\to\infty}\frac{\frac{3}{x}}{\frac{(\sqrt{x^2+3}+x)}{x}} = \lim_{x\to\infty}\frac{\frac{3}{x}}{\frac{\sqrt{x^2+3}}{x}+\frac{x}{x}} = \lim_{x\to\infty}\frac{\frac{3}{x}}{\frac{\sqrt{x^2+3}}{\sqrt{x^2}}+\frac{x}{x}} = \lim_{x\to\infty}\frac{\frac{3}{x}}{\sqrt{\frac{x^2+3}{x^2}}+\frac{x}{x}} =$$

$$\lim_{x\to\infty}\frac{\frac{3}{x}}{\sqrt{\frac{x^2}{x^2}+\frac{3}{x^2}}+\frac{x}{x}} = \lim_{x\to\infty}\frac{\frac{3}{x}}{\sqrt{1+\frac{3}{x^2}}+\frac{x}{x}} = \lim_{x\to\infty}\frac{\frac{3}{x}}{\sqrt{1+\frac{3}{x^2}}+1} = \frac{0}{\sqrt{1+0}+1} = \frac{0}{1+1} = \frac{0}{2} = 0$$

There are two times in this condensed illustration when we multiplied an expression by a special form of the number 1. In both situations when we multiplied by a fraction equal to 1, we bolded the expressions. We expect students who are taking calculus to be familiar with both "Young's Equation/Ratio Theorem" and "Young's Conversion Theorem", but at this level we would not expect them to continually refer to the theorems. We still hope they indicate they are multiplying by the number 1, so others can follow their logic.

A secondary math certified teacher should easily follow these shortened solutions.

We do not expect every elementary teacher to solve these types of problems, but we hope all elementary teachers can follow the steps in the illustrations and recognize the importance of arithmetic as it relates to advanced mathematics procedures.

Arithmetic rules and procedures are the key components in all advanced mathematics solutions. Arithmetic teachers are the master foundation contractors to build the mathematics skyscraper.

Convert Repeating Decimals into Fractions

We are only illustrating how to find the fractions equivalent to the given *repeating* decimals because this is one of the times using "Young's Equation/Ratio Theorem" and/or "Young's Conversion Theorem" is not the procedure to use when completing the conversion. To find the three fractions for the three given *repeating* decimal example problems illustrated below, you will have to have some basic knowledge of algebra concepts involving equations. One of the key rules you must know is you may multiply both sides of an equation by the same number. The other key rule is you must know how to line up two equations with the goal to subtract both sides of the two equations to determine a third equation. This is one of the reasons we want students to solve the problem "$x - 3 = 8$" mentioned in the middle of Chapter 4 by writing the equation "$3 = 3$" below the given equation "$x - 3 = 8$" and add the equation "$+3 = +3$" from the first equation to derive the third equation "$x = 11$". Notice, the problems in this section are *repeating* decimals, and you are not using either of the two theorems continually mentioned throughout this textbook. Earlier, we explained how to use both "Young's Equation/Ratio Theorem" and "Young's Conversion Theorem" to convert *terminating* decimals into fractions, not *repeating* decimals into fractions.

1. Convert: .6565... into a fraction.

Set the decimal equal to the variable "x".	$.6565\ldots = x$
Identity equation to multiply both sides of the equation.	$100 = 100$
Multiply both sides by "100".	$100\,(.6565\ldots) = 100 \cdot x$
We use "100" because there are 2 repeating numbers.	$65.6565\ldots = 100x$
Line up the fourth and first equations.	$.6565\ldots = \quad x$

The number of repeating decimals is referred to as the period of the repeating decimal.

Now, subtract the first equation from the fourth equation.	$65.6565\ldots = 100x$
Notice, we put a subtraction operation sign with both sides.	$\underline{-.6565\ldots = -1x}$
Get the new equation and solve for "x".	$65.0000\ldots = 99x$
Next, use the indicated	$65 = 99x$
identity equation to divide both sides of the equation.	$99 = 99$
Divide both sides by "99", and "x" will equal the fraction.	$\frac{65}{99} = \frac{99x}{99}$
The rational number, which was a repeating decimal is now	$\frac{65}{99} = x$

the fraction, "$\frac{65}{99}$".

Originally the variable "x" in the first equation equaled the repeating decimal, "$.6565\ldots$". In the last equation the variable "x", equaled the fraction "$\frac{65}{99}$". If we use the *transitive property,* the repeating decimal equals the fraction "$.6565\ldots = \frac{65}{99}$".

This is a simple repeating decimal to convert into a fraction because the repeating decimal begins immediately after the decimal point.

2. Convert: .333... into a fraction. You should know immediately the repeating decimal ".333 ..." is equal to the fraction "$\frac{1}{3}$".

The variable "x" will equal the fraction in the last step.	$x = .333\ldots$
Identity equation to multiply both sides of the equation.	$10 = 10$
Multiply both sides by "10".	$10 \cdot x = 10(.333\ldots)$
We multiply by "10" because there is one repeating number.	$10x = 3.333\ldots$
Place the first equation under the fourth equation.	$x = 0.333\ldots$
Now, subtract the first equation from the third equation.	$10x = \quad 3.333\ldots$
We put a subtraction symbol on both sides of the equation.	$\underline{-1x = -0.333\ldots}$
Get a new equation after subtracting the two equations.	$9x = \quad 3.000$
Next, use the indicated	$9x = \quad 3$
identity equation to divide both sides of the equation.	$9 = 9$
Divide both sides by the number "9".	$\frac{9x}{9} = \frac{3}{9}$
The variable "x" originally equaled the repeating decimal (.333 ...).	$x = \frac{1}{3}$

Now, the variable "x" equals the fraction $(\frac{1}{3})$.

The two example problems are simple repeating decimals to convert into fractions because the repeating decimal begins immediately after the decimal point. Compare the first two repeating decimal example illustrations to the solution in the next example problem. Notice, when we subtracted the first equation from the fourth equation in both example problems, we placed a negative one (-1) with the single variable "x" on the right side of the first example and on the left side of the second example. Students sometimes forget there is an invisible 1 to the left of a variable which does not have a coefficient indicated in the given problem.

3. Convert .617888... into a fraction.

This problem is different than the first two examples because the numbers to the right of the decimal point do not start to repeat immediately after the decimal point as they did in the first two example problems. Therefore, the first goal is to multiply the given repeating decimal by "1000" to get the decimal point to the left of the repeating number (digit) "8". Refer to the fourth equation below. After we multiply the original equation by the number "1000", the decimal point will be between the "7" and the first "8". We need to refer to the first equation again—and this time we multiply the first equation by "10,000" to get the decimal point immediately after the first repeating number or numbers. The fifth equation below was determined by multiplying the first equation by "10,000". In the first two example problems above, we only had to multiply the first equation once to get the decimal point in the third equation immediately to the right of the first group of repeating numbers. In this example problem, we must multiply the first equation twice and then subtract the two new equations determined after we multiply by "10,000" one time and "1,000" another time.

The variable "x" will equal a fraction in the final step. $x = .617888\ldots$

Multiply both sides of the equation by "1000". $1000x = 1000(.617888\ldots)$

Multiply both sides of the first equation by "10,000". $10000x = 10000(.617888\ldots)$

Here is the second equation after multiplying by 1000. $1000x = 617.888\ldots$

Here is the third equation after multiplying by 10000. $10000x = 6178.888\ldots$

Use the fifth equation and $10000x = 6178.888\ldots$

the fourth equation. $1000x = 617.888\ldots$

Now subtract the 4th equation from the 5th equation.

$$\begin{aligned} 10000x &= 6178.888\ldots \\ \underline{-1000x} &\underline{= -617.888\ldots} \end{aligned}$$

Solve for the variable "x" in this equation. $9000x = 5561.$

Divide both sides of the equation by the number "9000. $\frac{9000x}{9000} = \frac{5561}{9000}$

In this equation the variable "x" equals the fraction. $x = \frac{5561}{9000}$

In the beginning, the variable (x) equaled the repeating decimal (0.617888...). In the last equation, the variable (x) equals the fraction $(\frac{5561}{9000})$. Using the first and last equation in this illustration and the *transitive property*, the following is a fact: " $x = 0.617888\ldots = \frac{5561}{9000}$ ". Does this fraction reduce? The best way to determine if the fraction will reduce is to write both the numerator and the denominator in factored form: "$\frac{67 \times 83}{9 \times 1000} = \frac{67 \times 83}{3\times3\times2\times2\times2\times5\times5\times5}$". Do you notice any identical factors, in both the numerator and the denominator? The fraction $\frac{5561}{9000}$ will not reduce. When students are determining the prime factors "67 and 83" for the numerator "5561" we expect the students will use a calculator to help them factor "5561".

The last three problems in this section turned out to be equations which needed to be solved. Many of the other example problems in this textbook were simplification problems where the goal was to take the original expression and rewrite the original expression in an equivalent form. The great thing about solving algebra equations is once you determine the value of the variable, you can always check to ensure the answer is correct. In the last three repeating decimal problems you can easily check to determine if the fraction determined to be the answer for the variable "x" represents the original repeating decimal given in the problem. The checking process is simple. Divide the numerator by the denominator, and the answer after solving the long division problem must be the repeating decimal you started with--or somewhere you made a mistake. Put another way, one of the greatest things about solving algebra equations is you can substitute the solution into the original equation, and you will end up with an *identity*.

Throughout this textbook when we reduced, multiplied, and divided fractions (after the fraction to the right of the division operation symbol (÷) was changed to a multiplication operation "×" and the fraction was inverted), we emphasized if the numbers in the numerators and the denominators were large, the procedure which would always work is to rewrite all the numbers in the numerator and the denominator using factor trees. This is the best way to illustrate to students how to simplify these types of problems in arithmetic, and it is the only way to simplify these types of problems when working with rational expressions in algebra. When you use the factor tree and cancel/reduce method to simplify reducing, multiplying, and dividing fractions, the Power of the Number One (1) is illustrated over and over. If you do not understand what we mean, refer to many previous examples illustrated earlier in this textbook. You will notice when we reduced or cancelled identical terms, the terms became 1. This may seem obvious, but it is a powerful fact regarding the number 1.

We could use both "Young's Equation/Ratio Theorem" and "Young's Conversion Theorem" to reduce, multiply, and divide fractions, but it is not the most practical method to use on a regular basis. Here is a simple illustration to reduce the fraction "$\frac{12}{20}$" by using the two theorems emphasized in this textbook, "Young's Equation/Ratio Theorem" and "Young's Conversion Theorem":

Fact: $\frac{1}{4} = \frac{1}{4}$ $\therefore$ $\frac{\frac{1}{4}}{\frac{1}{4}} = 1$ We used "Young's Equation/Ratio Theorem" with the identity to find the equation equal to 1.

Now use "Young's Conversion Theorem" to reduce the fraction, "$\frac{12}{20}$".

$$\frac{12}{20} = \frac{12}{20} \times 1 = \frac{12}{20} \times \frac{\frac{1}{4}}{\frac{1}{4}} = \frac{12 \times \frac{1}{4}}{20 \times \frac{1}{4}} = \frac{\frac{12}{1} \times \frac{1}{4}}{\frac{20}{1} \times \frac{1}{4}} = \frac{\frac{12 \times 1}{1 \times 4}}{\frac{20 \times 1}{1 \times 4}} = \frac{\frac{12}{4}}{\frac{20}{4}} = \frac{\frac{3}{1}}{\frac{5}{1}} = \frac{3}{5}$$

It is not practical to use the two-theorem process on a regular basis to reduce fractions, but it is a procedure high achieving and motivated math students should be familiar with. We applied the same logic to reduce the fraction "$\frac{12}{20}$" that we used to convert a fraction division problem into a fraction multiplication problem earlier in this textbook.

Indeed, the most powerful number is the Number, One (1). Not only do "Young's Equation/Ratio Theorem" and "Young's Conversion Theorem" depend on a strong understanding of the number 1, but every time you reduce a fraction by cancelling identical numbers or terms, when you cancel the numbers or terms in the numerator and the denominator, the numbers and terms all become 1's. When you multiply by the number 1, the number 1 disappears, unless it is the only term left in the numerator. Did you ever think about the number of times the number 1 is understood to be present in a problem but not written, but when you write the number 1 it sometimes makes the problem easier to understand. Zero is probably the second most powerful number, and it is also frequently an invisible number. When it is written, it often makes problems much simpler as well.

Here are three simple problems you may want to ask education administrators at all levels: elementary principals, secondary principals, assistant superintendents, and superintendents. Administrators who were either science or math majors prior to becoming an administrator should find these problems to be relatively simple. Do not ask the administrators these questions to embarrass them. Ask these questions so the administrators might understand a few of the problems arithmetic and mathematics teachers frequently encounter. You want the administrators to realize if students only understand basic arithmetic concepts, it is not good enough. There is much more involved when solving challenging arithmetic problems than just understanding some basic rules. Being able to solve a wide variety of arithmetic and math problems involves memorizing facts and then applying a variety of math procedures (tricks based on sound mathematics principles). When solving arithmetic and mathematics problems, students must know basic arithmetic facts and then be able to apply rules derived in arithmetic to solve a wide variety of problems. Just knowing the facts is not enough without knowing the rules, but if the students do not know the facts, then their chance of success in arithmetic and mathematics is almost zero.

Problem #1: Combine or add the following two fractions and form one fraction.

$$\frac{3}{4} + \frac{1}{x}$$

Problem #2: Find the answer to the following arithmetic problem.

$$0.1^3 - 8 \text{ or } (0.1)^3 - 8$$

Problem #3: If the Area of a circle is "π", what is the radius? The formula to find the area of a circle is "$A = \pi r^2$ or $A_{cir.} = \pi r^2$".

I asked over forty education administrators (not math or science majors), these three questions. My non-scientific results were poor. I never had one of the administrators give the correct answer to the first problem "$\frac{3x+4}{4x}$". I had a couple education administrators correctly solve the second problem, "-7.999". I also had a few administrators get the correct answer to the third problem: "$r = 1$". My goal when I asked these questions was to get the administrators to understand that simply knowing facts is not enough when it comes to simplifying and solving math problems. Teaching arithmetic and mathematics requires a special type of teacher with special talents. As an arithmetic teacher or math teacher, you can make a difference.

We leave you with two thoughts.

1. It only takes one *poor* arithmetic teacher or math teacher to ruin the math career of a student.
2. It takes several *special* arithmetic and mathematics teachers to ensure the success of all students.

The two topics which I tried to focus on throughout this textbook were:

1. Solving/Simplifying all types of fraction problems.
2. Converting units of measurement into *equivalent* units of measurement and converting arithmetic/math expressions into *equivalent* arithmetic/math expressions.

Previously in this textbook (Fourth Assignment pages 212-215 and pages 232-235) we mentioned the Fundamental Theorem of Arithmetic, the Fundamental Theorem of Algebra, and the Fundamental Theorem of Calculus. We hope you understand the importance of the Fundamental Theorem of Arithmetic which is an important topic as it relates to the topics presented in this textbook. We wrote comments about the Fundamental Theorem of Algebra and explained the basics regarding this theorem. We did not say much about the Fundamental Theorem of Calculus because it involves concepts which are beyond the scope of this textbook. We want to go back and mention some special situations which were not mentioned when we explained the importance of the Fundamental Theorem of Algebra.

The basic concept involving the Fundamental Theorem of Algebra is: "If you have a polynomial equation involving one variable, the largest exponent of the variable involved in the equation indicates the maximum number of roots/answers which can be found to substitute into the equation for the variable which will make the expression an identity. (A polynomial equation basically means there are no variables in the denominator of a fraction.) We used examples to indicate if the largest exponent in the equation is "1" then there is a maximum of 1 solution for this type of equation referred to as a linear equation. We indicated if the largest exponent in the equation is "2" then there are a maximum of 2 solutions for this type of equation referred to as a quadratic equation. We also indicated if the largest exponent in the equation is "3" then there is a maximum of 3 correct solutions for this type of equation referred to as a cubic equation. When we were illustrating how the exponent dictated the maximum number of roots to look for when solving these equations, we indicated the answers and then substituted each answer back into the equations and always ended with an identity which proved that the answers we had found were correct answers. The same logic may be applied to a polynomial equation with one variable such as this example: "$x^5 + 5x^4 + 6x^3 - x^2 - 5x - 6 = 0$". There are a maximum of 5 numbers which will make this equation an identity when the numbers are substituted for the variable "x". Three of the 5 solutions are, $x = 1, -2, and - 3$. The other 2 solutions are imaginary numbers and beyond the scope of this textbook, but every math major should be able to find the other two solutions.

There is a point of interest which we never indicated regarding these types of Algebra equations. It is possible there may not be any solutions and it is also possible there are an infinite number of solutions. The first example below is an example where there are an INFINITE number of Solutions. The second example below is an example where there are NO Solutions.

Ex. 1. We start with a fact which we know is always true such as "$8 - 3 = 5$". Now change the arithmetic expression into an algebra equation, "$x + 8 - 3 = x + 5$". The first goal is to do the arithmetic on both sides of the equation, and we get the identity, "$x + 5 = x + 5$" which we immediately recognize is an example of the Reflexive Property and it is always true. Pick any number, substitute your number into the given equation, "$x + 8 - 3 = x + 5$". You will find that every number you substitute into this basic algebra 1 first degree equation will make the ending equation true.

Ex. 2. We start with an expression which is never true such as "$8 - 3 = 12$". Now change the arithmetic expression into an algebra equation, "$8 - 3 + x = 12 + x$". Do the arithmetic on both sides and you end up with an arithmetic expression which is never true, "$5 + x = 12 + x$". Since we started with an untrue arithmetic fact you will never find a number to substitute for the variable "x" which will make the statement true. There are no solutions to this problem.

Eighth Assignment

CHANGE FRACTION DIVISION PROBLEMS INTO FRACTION MULTLIPLICATION PROBLEMS

A. Change the following problems from fraction division problems into fraction multiplication problems by illustrating all the steps as indicated in this chapter or some other method you can justify. Write your procedures in the form of a proof, but you do not have to give a reason for each step.

1. $\frac{3}{4} \div \frac{3}{4}$ 2. $\frac{7}{8} \div \frac{3}{4}$ 3. $\frac{7}{11} \div \frac{6}{7}$ 4. $1\frac{2}{5} \div 2\frac{1}{5}$ 5. $\frac{a}{d} \div \frac{x}{z}$ $(d, x, z \neq 0)$

REWRITE EACH OF THE GIVEN DIVISION PROBLEMS USING THE TWO OTHER NOTATIONS TO INDICATE DIVISION AND THEN FIND THE QUOTIENTS

B. In arithmetic there are three ways to write a division problem. Take the given division problems and rewrite the given division problems using the two other common division notations. Find the quotients for the given problems. You only need to find the quotient for each problem once. (Question for Secondary Math majors: Can you think of a fourth or fifth math notation which indicates division?)

6. $\frac{243.14}{42.9}$ (Round off the final answer to the nearest thousandths.)

7. $210 \div 2100$ 8. $2\frac{1}{4} \div \frac{9}{10}$ 9. $\frac{\frac{17}{8}}{2}$

10. $17 \div 35$ (The quotient should be a repeating decimal.)

11. $2.260524 \div 0.3166$ (The quotient should be a terminating decimal.)

BASIC ALGEBRA PROBLEMS INVOLVING REDUCING, MULTIPLYING AND DIVIDING FRACTIONS SIMPLIFY THE FOLLOWING PROBLEMS

C. Prior to reducing and finding the final answer, write the entire problem as one big fraction.

12. $\frac{d^2}{m^3 d} \div \frac{d}{(x+1)} \times \frac{m}{(x+1)}$

13. $\frac{5t^4yz^3(x+6)(z+8)^2}{8t^4yz^2(x+6)(z+8)}$ (Make sure the numerator and the denominator are written in factored form in the final answer. The reason we want both the numerator and the denominator written in factored form is because it is easy to determine if there are any additional factors which will cancel/reduce.)

14. $\frac{24x^2}{(x+7)^3} \times \frac{x^2}{30yz} \times \frac{5yz(x+7)^2}{x^3(x+3)}$

15. $5\frac{2}{11} \times 11\frac{5}{6} \times 12\frac{1}{2} \div 4047$

16. $\frac{a^3\,(x-z)^4}{p^5} \div \frac{z^2(r-1)^2}{p^4} \times \left(\frac{z\,(r-1)}{p} \div \frac{(x-z)^3}{a^2(r-1)^2}\right)$

EASY ALGEBRA PROBLEMS INVOLVING ADDING AND SUBTRACTING FRACTIONS

SIMPLIFY THE FOLLOWING PROBLEMS

D. We want you to write each problem as one or two big fractions when appropriate prior to adding and subtracting these fractions. Keep the solutions simple.

17. $\frac{24}{(x+4)} + \frac{16}{(x+ym^3)} - \frac{8}{(x+4)} - \frac{16}{(x+ym^3)}$

18. $\frac{2.5}{x^2y^2z} + \frac{5.08xy}{5} - \frac{5.08xy}{5} + \frac{2.5}{x^2y^2z}$

19. $\frac{x}{8} + \frac{y}{9} - \left(\frac{y}{9} + \frac{x}{8}\right) + \frac{37.891}{37.891}$

20. $\frac{(x+4)}{(p-z)^4} + \frac{(2x+8)}{(p-z)^4} - \frac{(3x+11)}{(p-z)^4}$

21. $\frac{77.91}{(x+11)^4} - \frac{66.987}{(x+11)^4} + \frac{111.2}{(x+11)^4}$

SIMPLIFY ALGEBRA PROBLEMS INVOLVING REDUCING, MULTIPLYING, AND DIVIDING FRACTIONS WHICH ARE MORE CHALLENGING (Rational Expressions)

E. Prior to reducing the multiplication and division problems, write the problems as one big fraction, then reduce and find the simplified answers. It is normal to write the final simplified answers in factored form which makes it easy to determine if any remaining factors will reduce/cancel. Illustrate/write all the steps you would use to teach young students to simplify these problems for the first time.

22. $\frac{x^3 + 8x^2 + 15x}{x^4 - 25x^2}$

23. $\frac{4x^2 - 4x - 48}{5x^2 + 40x + 75} \times \frac{3dm - 5}{3dm - 5} \times \frac{15x^2 - 135}{12x^2 - 96x + 192}$

24. $\frac{x^4 - 7x^3 + 12x^2}{y^3 - 7y^2 + 12y} \div \frac{3x^4 - 18x^3 + 24x^2}{y^4 - 9y^3 + 20y^2} \times \frac{44.81x}{44.81x}$

25. $\frac{p^2 + 12p + 36}{p^2 - p - 20} \div \frac{p^2 - 3p - 28}{p^2 - 12p + 35} \times \frac{p^2 - 5p - 36}{p^3 - 3p^2 - 54p}$

26. $\frac{x^3 - x^2 - 2x}{x^2 + 2x - 63} \times \frac{x^2 - 15x + 56}{x^5 - 11x^4 + 30x^3} \times \frac{x^3 + 3x^2 - 54x}{x^2y - 7xy - 8y} \div \frac{16xy^2}{16xy^2}$

27. $\frac{m^4 - 2m^3 + m^2}{m^2 - 2m - 35} \div \frac{m^2 + 8m - 9}{m^3 + 2m^2 - 63m} \div \frac{m^5 - 5m^4 + 4m^3}{m^2 + 8m - 9}$

SIMPLIFY ALGEBRA PROBLEMS INVOLVING ADDING AND SUBTRACTING FRACTIONS WHICH ARE MORE CHALLENGING (Rational Expressions)

F. Prior to adding and subtracting the numerators write the expressions as one big fraction with the Least Common Denominator indicated once in the denominator. Illustrate/write all the steps you would use to teach young students to simplify these problems for the first time.

28. $\frac{30}{x^2 + 8x + 12} + \frac{4x+5}{x+2}$

29. $\frac{5}{x^2 - 9} - \frac{2}{x^2 + x - 6} - \frac{3}{x^2 + 6x + 9}$

30. $\frac{5x}{(x+5)(x-5)} + \frac{3(x+1)}{x^2 - 2x - 15} - \frac{5}{x+3}$

31. $\frac{-(5x - 2)}{x - 5} - \frac{5x}{5 - x}$

32. $\frac{a-1}{a^2 - 9} - \frac{1-a}{9 - a^2} + 30\frac{7}{13} + \frac{2ax}{2ax}$

33. $\frac{7}{p^2 + 4p + 4} - \frac{7}{p^2 + 7p + 10}$

34. $\frac{x + 5}{x^2 - 7x + 12} - \frac{x - 5}{x^2 - 5x + 4}$

SIMPLIFY THE FOLLOWING RATIONAL EXPRESSIONS

G. Remember this textbook is written to help you prepare to be a mathematics teacher. When solving the problems in this section indicate most of the steps as illustrated in this textbook and this chapter. The major difference between the illustrations in this textbook and your work when solving these problems is, when you are teaching you will verbalize your explanations for each step instead of writing explanations for each step.

35. $p^2 + \frac{z}{z + \frac{1}{pz}}$

36. $\left(\frac{x}{x^2 - 1} - \frac{2}{x^2 - 2x + 1}\right) \times \frac{x^2 - 2x + 1}{2}$

37. $\frac{x}{x^2 - 1} + \frac{1}{x^2 - 2x + 1} \times \frac{1 - x^2}{2}$

38. $\frac{r^2 - 14r + 49}{-2r + r^2 - 35} \cdot \frac{-4r^2 - 12r + r^3}{r^3 + 42r - 13r^2}$

ARE THESE EQUATIONS SIMPLY EQUATIONS OR ARE THEY ALSO EXAMPLES OF IDENTITIES AND FINALLY ARE THEY SPECIAL IDENTITIES WHICH WE REFER TO AS THE REFLEXIVE PROPERTY? IDENTIFY THE MOST SPECIFIC REFERENCE TO THE FOLLOWING EQUATIONS.

H. We want you to recognize the subtle differences between the three expressions: Equations, Identities, and the Reflexive Property.

39. $2x + 6 = 8$

40. $6 + 8 + 0 = 16 - 0 - 2$

41. $z^{16} + \frac{7.7}{11} = z^{16} + \frac{7.7}{11}$

42. $6x + 7 = 6x + 5 + 2$

43. $11.2x^2 + \frac{3}{11.2}x = 11.2x^2 + \frac{3}{11.2}x$

44. $t^2 - 1 = 0$

COMPARE ARITHMETIC FRACTIONS WITH EQUAL DENOMINATORS OR EQUAL NUMERATORS AND ARRANGE THE FRACTIONS IN ORDER FROM MINIMUM TO MAXIMUM BASED ON THEIR MAGNITUDE

I. We expect you to use mental math and number sense to arrange the fractions in increasing order.

45. $\frac{7}{13}, \frac{7}{10}, \frac{7}{11}$

46. $\frac{88}{10.1}, \frac{79.89}{10.1}, \frac{1.8989}{10.1}, \frac{18.989}{10.1}$

47. $\frac{\sqrt[3]{37}}{\sqrt{27}}, \frac{\sqrt[3]{37}}{\sqrt{73}}, \frac{\sqrt[3]{37}}{\sqrt{10}}, \frac{\sqrt[3]{37}}{\sqrt{41}}$

48. $\frac{\sqrt{7}}{\sqrt[4]{71}}, \frac{\sqrt{3}}{\sqrt[4]{71}}, \frac{\sqrt{19}}{\sqrt[4]{71}}, \frac{\sqrt{17}}{\sqrt[4]{71}}$

RADICALS IN DENOMINATORS

J. Rationalize the denominators and indicate when you use both "Young's Equation/Ratio Theorem" and "Young's Conversion Theorem". Illustrate the conversion process as if you are explaining the procedures for the first time to young students. Write the answers as one fraction in simplified form.

49. $\frac{7}{\sqrt{3}} + \frac{3}{\sqrt{5}}$

50. $\frac{5+\sqrt{7}}{2\sqrt{7}} - \frac{5-\sqrt{3}}{5\sqrt{3}}$

51. $\frac{7}{6-\sqrt{3}} + \frac{7}{6-\sqrt{3}}$

52. $\frac{5}{2\sqrt[3]{5}} - \frac{2}{3\sqrt[3]{5}}$

53. $\frac{x}{5+\sqrt{x}}$

IMAGINARY NUMBERS

K. Convert the fractions below with the goal to <u>not</u> have any <u>Imaginary numbers</u> in the denominator. Assume you are explaining these conversion problems for the first time to a classroom of young students and write all the steps you would expect the students to write to illustrate they completely understand the process.

54. $\frac{10}{i^3+\sqrt{7}}$ 55. $\frac{3i-6}{1-2i}$ 56. $\frac{25}{2-11i}$ 57. $\frac{5i}{7-i^3}-\frac{5}{7-i^3}$ 58. $\frac{11}{7i^9}+\frac{10}{7\sqrt{-1}}$

RADIANS, DEGREES, AND REVOLUTIONS

L. Complete the following conversion problems and illustrate how to use both "Young's Equation/Ratio Theorems" and "Young's Conversion Theorem" to perform the conversions between radians, degrees, and revolutions.

59. Convert $\frac{3}{10}$ rads to degrees (The number, "π" may appear in the denominator.)

60. Convert $3\frac{7}{8}$ revs. to radians (The number, "π" may appear in the numerator.)

61. Convert .8 radians to degrees (The number, "π" may be in the denominator.)

62. Convert 144° to rads.

63. Convert 3.5 rads to revolutions (The number, "π" should appear in the denominator and the faction should be written using integers.)

64. Convert $6\frac{3}{4}$ rev. to rads, then convert the answer into rads less than 2π rads.

65. Convert 840° into a radian angle measurement less than 2π rads.

REPEATING DECIMALS TO FRACTIONS

M. Find the fraction equivalent to the given decimal. If the decimal is a repeating decimal, use either two or three equations to complete the process. Make sure to use the procedures illustrated in this chapter to complete all the conversions. Indicate all the steps to prove your fraction solution is indeed the correct fraction equivalent to the given decimal.

66. Convert the repeating decimal into a fraction "0.891891 ... "
67. Convert the repeating decimal into a mixed number 707.01888 ... "
68. Convert the repeating decimal "0.999 ... "into a fraction. Once you have determined the fraction answer is an Integer (which can also be written as a fraction), explain why this event occurred.
69. Convert the decimal 0.7272 into a fraction.
70. Convert the decimal 0.30121212 ... into a fraction.
71. Convert the number 87.1982982982 ... into a mixed number.

CELSIUS AND FAHRENHEIT TEMPERATURES

N. Convert the given temperatures by using this formula, "$F = \frac{9}{5}C + 32°$". At this moment, we do not want you to use the conversion equation, ""$C = \frac{5}{9}(F - 32°)$".

72. Find the Fahrenheit temperature equivalent to 40° C
73. Find the Celsius temperature equivalent to 136° F
74. Find the Celsius temperature equivalent to 92° F
75. Find the Fahrenheit temperature equivalent to 5° C

76. Write "2 or 3" paragraphs to explain how the conversion equation "$F = \frac{9}{5}C + 32°$" is derived based on the two temperature scales referred to as Fahrenheit and Celsius. You may have to look up the explanation on the internet and then write your interpretation. We wonder why the fraction "$\frac{9}{5}$" and the number "32" appears in the formula?

77. Start with the equation "$F = \frac{9}{5}C + 32°$", then algebraically determine the equation "$C = \frac{5}{9}(F - 32°)$". Illustrate every step as if you are explaining the equation transformation for the first time to a classroom of Pre-Algebra students.

THEOREMS AND PROPERTIES

0. Throughout this textbook we have explained and used several theorems and properties which apply to arithmetic and mathematics. In the next set of questions write 1 or 2 paragraphs to illustrate how you will explain these theorems and properties to your students in 7th, 8th, 9th grade and beyond.

78. Reflexive Property

79. Associative Property of Multiplication

80. Transitive Property

81. Commutative Property of Multiplication

82. Distributive Property

83. Young's Equation/Ratio Theorem

84. Symmetric Property

85. Commutative Property of Addition

86. A. Identity Property of Multiplication

B. What is the Identity Element for Multiplication? Why?

87. Associative Property of Addition

88. Young's Conversion Theorem

89. A. Identity Property of Addition

B. What is the Identity Element for Addition? Why?

90. The Fundamental Theorem of Arithmetic

Properties, Theorems, and Definitions are important when developing rules and procedures in arithmetic and mathematics. Ironically, once students master the rules and procedures, they frequently forget the exact meaning of the Properties, Theorems, and Definitions. Good mathematicians will still remember the basic meanings of the Properties, Theorems, and Definitions but they will frequently not remember the specific names of the Properties and Theorems and the subtle differences between the Properties and Theorems. Good mathematicians will remember definitions of many arithmetic and mathematics words frequently mentioned throughout this textbook, but again they may not remember subtle facts about the definitions. There is one Theorem almost everyone remembers because it was discussed and illustrated so much in mathematics, therefore the Theorem is difficult to forget. We are thinking about the Pythagorean Theorem. Maybe in the future, students will remember both "Young's Equation/Ratio Theorem" and "Young's Conversion Theorem" by name, but it really is not important to remember them by name, but we feel it is important to know how to apply these two Theorems to solve a wide variety of arithmetic and mathematics problems.

CHAPTER 9

IMPORTANT – THREE PHRASES YOU WILL ENCOUNTER IN OTHER TEXTBOOKS

THE PHRASES MENTIONED IN THIS CHAPTER ARE SELDOM MENTIONED IN ELEMENTARY OR SECONDARY MATH TEXTBOOKS AND WHEN AUTHORS ILLUSTRATE HOW TO USE THESE PHRASES TO SOLVE PROBLEMS, THEY DO NOT GO INTO THE DETAIL THIS TEXTBOOK DEMONSTRATES TO DETERMINE THE SOLUTIONS FOR A WIDE VARIETY OF ARITHMETIC AND MATH PROBLEMS.

Chapter 9

Throughout this entire textbook, we concentrated on the two theorems "Young's Equation/Ratio Theorem" and "Young's Conversion Theorem" to emphasize the only number or expression you may multiply to determine an equivalent number or expression is the number 1. This is a fact confirmed by the Multiplication Identity Property of One (1), which is a standard arithmetic fact/property taught by every elementary and secondary math teacher starting early in elementary school.

This entire textbook was written based on my experiences as a secondary principal and math teacher for slightly less than 38 years and an invited guest of a math research team at Carnegie Mellon University for 6 years. Below is a list of three math terms (phrases) with definitions, which are mentioned by not emphasized in this textbook, but are closely related to the two theorems and the goals of this textbook. You can ask goggle about the three phrases and other implied words and phrases, and you will find they all work together to help teachers and students further understand the two theorems.

We named the two theorems in this textbook, because naming them will have a greater impact on people remembering them and how to work with them to convert numbers and expressions into equivalent numbers and expressions. The terms/phrases listed in this chapter when combined are the basis for both Young's Equation/Ratio Theorem" and "Young's Conversion Theorem". If we already have terms and phrases which cover the two Theorems discussed throughout this textbook, then why is it important to name the two theorems? *The answer to this question is simple but powerful,* "**Ask 20 arithmetic teachers the following three questions: 1. "What are the definitions of the terms/phrases listed below?" 2. When did you discuss the terms and phrases mentioned below with your students?" 3. "When did you illustrate how to use the terms and phrases indicated below, to solve problems in your classroom?" Next, ask the same three questions to 20 high school mathematics teachers.** Without even asking the questions to 20 elementary and 20 secondary math teachers, you probably would guess, few if any of the teachers are familiar with these terms and expressions and even less teachers illustrate how to use these terms and expressions to solve problems. **This is the reason we named the two theorems mentioned in this textbook and this is also why we illustrated how to use the two theorems to solve arithmetic problems and advanced math problems for a variety of problems.**

If you research all the literature regarding the terms listed below you will find the procedures indicated by the terms utilize the procedures illustrated in this textbook using the two theorems with three important exceptions. The **first exception** is the illustrations written in this textbook using the two theorems are written so every small detail is illustrated and there is little deviation when using the theorems from one example to another example. The **second exception** is the terms listed below assume the reasoning behind the definitions/explanations is understood without any proof or little explanation because the authors think the explanations are obvious. The **third exception** is, the two theorems illustrated throughout the textbook apply to arithmetic fraction problems, arithmetic unit conversion problems, percentages to decimals and vice-versa, algebra rational expression problems, fractions with imaginary numbers in the denominator, fractions with radicals in the denominator, radians – degrees - revolution problems, and many more problems in advanced math, science, engineering, and medicine. Here are the terms (phrases) other authors use when they discuss some of the conversion problems mentioned in this textbook.

Definitions with references –

1. Conversion Factor(s): 1. www.vocabulary.com/dictionary/conversion A factor by which a quantity that is expressed in one set of units must be multiplied to convert it into another set of units. 2. www.nwcg.gov.gov/course 2.1 Unit Conversion and Conversion Factors - A unit conversion expresses the same property as a different unit of measurement. For instance, time can be expressed in minutes instead of hours etc. 3. www.thoughtco.com/definition-of-conversion-factor Anne Marie Helmenstine, Ph.D. December 3, 2018 – A conversion factor is defined as a numerical ratio or fraction used to express a measurement given in one unit as another unit. A conversion factor is always equal to 1. Examples: 1 minute/60 seconds and 1000 grams/ 1 kilogram. 4. www.mathhelp.com Measurement Customary Unit Conversions Video
2. Unit Multiplier(s): 1. Marta Hidegkuti– teaching – conversion Unit multipliers Part 1 # Sample Problems Marta Hidegkuti – A unit multiplier (or conversion factor) is a fraction with value 1 that we use to convert quantities. Because the value of the unit multiplier is 1, we can multiply any quantity by them without changing their value. 2. You Tube - Donna Young – math – unit multipliers. How can we write 1 as a fraction? Many ways, 1/1, 2/2, 84/84. 3. You Tube – larryschmidt, August 19, 2011, Unit Multipliers and Conversion
3. Dimensional Analysis: 1. https://www.chem.tamu.edu/class/fyp/mayhrev/mr-da.html Dimensional Analysis (also called Factor-Label Method or the Unit Factor Method) is a problem-solving method which uses the fact that any number or expression can be multiplied by one without changing its value 2. Khan Academy April 20, 2017, Intro to dimensional analysis (video) 3. The AudiopediaYouTube – Oct 22, 2016. What is dimensional analysis? What does dimensional analysis mean? - Used in Engineering and Science to focus on units when converting units. 4. www.study.com Video Unit Conversion and Dimensional Analysis (Also mentions Conversion Factors). There are college level books which focus on Dimensional Analysis. You may find it interesting to google books which focus on dimensional analysis.

An excellent teacher in any subject is a blessing for the community, for the school, and for the students.

An excellent arithmetic or mathematics teacher is a “dream come true” for everyone who has had the opportunity, to learn from such a person. If you are an arithmetic or mathematics teacher, strive to be the best and focus on becoming better.

Ninth Assignment

Practice Final Test Assignments for Elementary Education Majors and Secondary Mathematics Majors

The final test for Elementary Education Majors consists of two parts, Part A questions 1-110 and Part B questions 1-20. The first 110 questions in Part A are **1**-point questions. The 20 questions in Part B are **2**-point questions. There are 130 questions for a total of 150 points in the final test for Elementary Education Teachers. To achieve at the 90% level if you are an elementary education major you must get a score of 135 or better. We expect a student who is in college ready to enter the classroom for the first time as an elementary "student teacher" would correctly solve at least 90% of the questions accurately. If a person is presently an elementary teacher, we would hope because of their experience they would be embarrassed if they did not achieve at the 90% level after they read and study this textbook. The questions in Part A, 1-110 (**1**-point questions), Part B, 1-20 (**2**-point questions), Part C, 1-10 (**1**-point questions), and Part D, 1-20 (**2**-point questions) consist of a total of 200 points and comprise the final test for Secondary Math Education Majors. We expect if a student is mathematics major in college ready to enter the classroom for the first time as a "student teacher" they would correctly solve at least 95% of the questions accurately, which means they would earn a minimum grade of 190 out of 200 points. If a person is an experienced secondary mathematics teacher, we would hope because of their experience they would be embarrassed if they did not achieve a minimum score of 95% after they read and study this textbook. If a person is preparing to be an Education Administrator, they should be able to achieve at the 90% level for all 160 questions with a total of 200 points after they read and study this textbook. If a person is already an Education Administrator, we would hope they would read and study this textbook for their own personal professional development and again they would score a minimum of 90% (180 points out of 200 possible points) after they read and study this textbook.

The **1**-point questions will be graded for accuracy but there must be evidence the person taking the test illustrates all the steps continually illustrated throughout this textbook. Since you are required to indicate the steps to illustrate how to solve a problem using the rules emphasized in this textbook if you emphasize most of the steps (example 4 out of 5 steps) you will be given full credit but if you only indicate 3 out of 5 steps which we consider necessary you will receive no credit even if you have the correct mathematical answer. Our advice to everyone who takes the final test is, try not to skip any steps when you are illustrating how to solve a problem and several steps need to be written. When we grade the definitions, our emphasis will focus on whether you hit all the necessary requirements to correctly define a math word or phrase. Do not be too wordy but make sure you hit the basic facts regarding every definition. You may think our requirements are high, but we believe every student who sits in your classroom deserves a teacher who is prepared to illustrate/explain every math challenge the students may encounter in your arithmetic/mathematics classroom.

We expect elementary teachers will require between 3 hours and 4 hours to achieve at the 90% level. We expect secondary mathematics teachers will require between 4.5 hours and 6 hours to complete the secondary math teacher test to achieve at the 95% level. We therefore recommend 4 hours for elementary teachers and 6 hours for secondary math teachers. There is a lot of written work required which will lengthen the time needed to complete both tests versus simply solving the problems. We suggest that the test be given in two sessions for elementary teachers and three sections for secondary math teachers, to avoid writer's fatigue. Section 1 would consist of Part A. Section 2 would consist of Parts B & C. Section 3 would consist of Part D. Once a student starts to solve the problems for a section of the test, they must complete that section before attempting another section of the test.

Students preparing to be an elementary teacher, or already an elementary teacher, or preparing to be a school administrator, or already a school administrator may earn additional credit by correctly solving some of the questions in the additional sections which are designed for secondary math students and educators.

FINAL TEST

PART A QUESTIONS 1-110 ARE ALL WORTH **1** POINT

PART A IS FOR BOTH ELEMENTARY AND SECONDARY MATH TEACHERS

(The use of a Calculator, Cell Phone or Computer of any type is **NOT** permitted.)

1. Write a "1, 2, or 3" paragraph summary about the rules and procedures you would emphasize to students, so they can solve future fraction addition and/or subtraction problems with identical denominators similar, to this example problem: $\frac{7}{12} + \frac{1}{12} - \frac{3}{12}$. (This problem does not require students to reduce the final answer. Therefore, do not worry about explaining how to reduce fractions in your response.)

Simplify the following problems. (No requirement to show any work.)

2. $\frac{7}{53} + \frac{4}{53} + \frac{1}{53} - \frac{5}{53} - \frac{2}{53} =$

3. $\frac{2}{x} + \frac{3}{x} - \frac{1}{x} =$

4. $\frac{5}{301} - \frac{2}{301} + \frac{11}{301} + \frac{9}{301} =$

5. $\frac{15}{xyz} + \frac{2}{xyz} + \frac{10}{xyz} + \frac{1}{xyz} - \frac{3}{xyz} =$

6. $\frac{11}{10.79} - \frac{5}{10.79} - \frac{4}{10.79} - \frac{2}{10.79} + \frac{0}{10.79} =$ (The denominator in the answer may be "10.79".)

7. Write a "1, 2, or 3" paragraph summary, about the rules and procedures you would emphasize to students so they can solve all unit conversion problems which only involve changing from one unit of measurement to another unit of measurement. If the students are supposed to convert feet into inches, or miles into feet, or tons into pounds, or quarts into gallons, etc., they will have to know the required facts

(conversion factors) related to the specific units they are asked to convert. Therefore, do not go into detail about the different units and the equivalent units with the appropriate numbers involved. Your explanation should concentrate on the general procedures students need to use to convert from one unit of measurement into an equivalent unit of measurement, once they know the number involved with the conversion of the two units. Your explanation should indicate how to find the correct number and label in the conversion process.

Copy the problem and place one of the following relationship symbols $\{<, =, or\ >\}$ between the two given numbers to make a truthful mathematics statement.

8. $7\frac{7}{99}$? $7\frac{7}{9}$ 9. $0.1609999\ldots$? $0.161616\ldots$ 10. $\frac{3}{13}$? $\frac{30}{130}$

Find the LCM and GCF for the following "set" of numbers. You must get the correct answer for both the LCM and GCF to get credit for this problem. Indicate which number is the LCM and which number is the GCF. (No work required.)

11. $\{8, 12, 16, 24\}$ (Use mental math to find both the LCM and GCF.)

Illustrate why we know the number "7,488" is the LCM for the given set of numbers below and why we know the number "22,464" is not the LCM. You need to write two explanations to receive credit for problem "12.", reference the two numbers. There are several ways to write your explanations to convince us you can explain why one number is the LCM and the other number is not the LCM.

12. $LCM = 7{,}488$ $\{72, 64, 78\}$ Why is the number "22,464" NOT the LCM?

This section involves long division problems. Write all the steps. If the quotient involves a remainder, write the remainder as a decimal rounded off to two decimal places (the nearest hundredth). (Show all your work.)

13. $\frac{64193}{23}$

14. $22523000 \div 1010$

15. $\frac{73}{151}$ *or* $73 \div 151$

16. $\frac{66}{8}$

Graph the line indicated in the next section in a "Cartesian Coordinate System" also known as a "Rectangular Coordinate System". If you use graph paper, it should make these problems a little easier and probably more accurate. If you do not use graph paper, you will have to estimate the position of all the points indicated based on the given information. If you are given a point and a slope, indicate a minimum of three points before you graph the line. If you are given three or four points just use the points indicated to graph the line. Make sure you indicate the lines extend in both directions to infinity.

17. Point = (4, 1), $m = \frac{5}{2}$

18. Point 1= (4, 1) and Point 2= (5, 2) and Point 3= (6, 3)

19. Point = (2, 1), $m = 3$

20. Point 1= (6, 4) and Point 2= (5, 3) and Point 3= (4, 2) and Point 4= (3, 1)

Write the factor trees (prime numbers) for the following composite numbers in a triangular format (Christmas tree format). Do not use exponential notation in your final answer.

21. 432

22. 2000

Write the explanation of the following theorems and properties. Initially use sentences to write the meaning of each of the theorems and properties and then write an example to illustrate the theorem or property.

23. The Fundamental Theorem of Arithmetic
24. Young's Equation/Ratio Theorem
25. Young's Conversion Theorem
26. The Reflexive Property
27. The Commutative Property of Multiplication
28. The Symmetric Property
29. The Associative Property of Addition
30. The Transitive Property

We expect you to reduce the following fractions by using mental math.

31. $\frac{77}{121}$ 32. $\frac{49}{98}$

Reduce the following fractions when the numerators and the denominators are written in factored form. Write the answer as a fraction with an integer in both the numerator and the denominator. If the denominator equals 1 then the numerator is the simplified answer.

33. $\frac{3 \times 7 \times 11 \times 11 \times 13}{11 \times 11 \times 13}$ 34. $\frac{5 \cdot z \cdot z \cdot a \cdot b \cdot b}{7 \cdot z \cdot z \cdot a \cdot b}$ *(Illustrate canceling procedure)*

Reduce the following fractions using the "factor tree" and "prime number" procedure.

35. $\frac{93}{186}$ *(Must show work)* 36. $\frac{162}{189}$ *(Must show all work)*

Find the LCM for the three indicated composite numbers and the three Sets of Prime Factors which are already indicated. The answer is a natural number. (*Show all work*)

37. $28 = \{2, 2, 7\}$, $49 = \{7,7\}$, $98 = \{2, 7, 7\}$

Find the <u>LCM</u> written in "expanded form", "exponential form", and "condensed form" (if appropriate) for all the factors indicated. The factors are already indicated for the given expressions. There are two or three answers for each question.

38. $x^2y^2z = \{x \cdot x \cdot y \cdot y \cdot z\}$, $x^3yz^4 = \{x \cdot x \cdot x \cdot y \cdot z \cdot z \cdot z \cdot z\}$

39. $75m^3n(x + y) = \{3 \cdot 5 \cdot 5 \cdot m \cdot m \cdot m \cdot n \cdot (x + y)\}$

$54mn^4(x + y)^2 = \{2 \cdot 3 \cdot 3 \cdot 3 \cdot m \cdot n \cdot n \cdot n \cdot n \cdot (x + y) \cdot (x + y)\}$

Use "Factor Trees" and "Prime Numbers" and find the LCD for each problem.

40. $\frac{59}{36} - \frac{43}{48}$

41. $\frac{25}{99} - \frac{16}{121} + \frac{53}{66}$ (*Show all work*)

When solving the next three problems use <u>all the steps illustrated in this textbook</u> to find LCDs, change fractions into equivalent fractions with the LCD, and use one large fraction before you find the answer.

42. $\frac{5}{36} - \frac{5}{54}$

43. $\frac{7}{8} - \frac{7}{28} - \frac{7}{36} - \frac{1}{45} + \frac{1001}{1260}$ (The answer must be a reduced mixed number.)

44. $2\frac{3}{14} + 3\frac{11}{21} - 1\frac{9}{28}$ (The answer must be a reduced mixed number.)

Solve the following eight (45.-52.) first degree algebra problems. We hope you can compute all the answers in your head without much work for the first four problems, but understanding the procedures is essential when the problems become more difficult. Problems (49.-52.) are a little more challenging and you might not be able to compute the answer in your head without indicating any work. Therefore, in this section for all eight problems use the given equation and a second equation which you determine, line up the equations and illustrate how to derive the answer for the given equation as frequently illustrated throughout this textbook. Emphasize in your solutions why the numbers zero and/or one are important numbers when solving these problems.

45. $909 = z - 11$

46. $p + 101 = 201$

47. $0.03d = 67.2$

48. $\frac{a}{7} = 9$

49. $z - \frac{3}{8} = \frac{7}{24}$ (Reduce the answer if practical.)

50. $\frac{n}{.7} = \frac{3}{4}$ (Write the final answer as a terminating decimal or a reduced fraction.)

51. $3.3d = 67.2$ (Round the repeating decimal of to the nearest thousandth.)

52. $a + 11.93 = 89.661$ (Write the final answer as a terminating decimal.)

Solve the following division problems. Show all the work to solve both problems.

53. $1.0075 \div .25 =?$ Write the answer as a terminating decimal and as a mixed number with an integer in both the numerator and the denominator.

54. $\frac{1\frac{4}{5}}{2\frac{7}{10}} = 1\frac{4}{5} \div 2\frac{7}{10} =?$ Write the answer as a fraction and as a repeating decimal.

Explain why the indicated LCM is NOT the LCM for the given set of numbers. Use the rules continually illustrated throughout this textbook to prove your conclusions.

55. Given the set of numbers $= \{36, 25, 18\}$, Why is the LCM not 2700?

56. Given set of numbers $= \{15, 18, 24\}$, Why is the LCM not 1440?

Simplify the following expressions.

57. $16\ cars + 25\ trucks - 3\ SUVs + 40\ trucks + 76\ SUVs - 1\ car + 5\ tractors$

58. 1.5 feet + 3.75 ft.

59. $3ap - 1ap + 5ba - 2ap$

60. $33\, x^2y^3z + 37.5\, y^3zx^2 + 42.75\, z\, x^2y^3$

61. $7\frac{1}{2}\, xyz + 8\frac{3}{4}\, yzx\ - 1\frac{7}{8}\, zxy + 11.92\, x^2y^2z^2$

62. $5x^3 + 4x^2 + 3x - 9 + 2x^3 - 2x^2 - x + 12$

Simplify the following expressions.

63. $3\, ft. \times 55\, ft. \times 7.5\, ft.$

64. $\frac{3 \cdot 3 \cdot 5 \cdot 71 \cdot a \cdot b \cdot b \cdot b \cdot (x+c) \cdot (x+c) \cdot (8+m)}{3 \cdot 71 \cdot a \cdot b \cdot (x+c) \cdot (x+c) \cdot (16+m)}$

65. $\frac{55\, yds.^3}{10\, yds.}$

66. $\frac{25 \cdot x^3 \cdot y^2 \cdot z \cdot 20 \cdot x^3 \cdot y}{10 \cdot x^4 \cdot y \cdot z \cdot 5 \cdot 2}$

We will give you a formula/equation and some information. Use the given information and find the exact answer for the missing term. (Show all work)

67. $D = rt$ Given facts: $Rate\ of\ a\ moving\ object\ (r) = 400\ \frac{mi.}{hr.}\ and\ Time\ (t) =$ $5.5\ hrs.$

68. $A_{cir.} = \pi r^2$ Given fact: $Radius\ (r) = 1\ ft.$ The answer should not be written as a decimal. The answer should be written as an irrational number accurate to over 1,000,000 decimal places. This means the answer must contain the number, "π".

69. $V_{cube} = s^3$ Given fact: $Side\ (s) = 3.5\ cm$

Find the LCD for the given problems. Write all the steps required to find the LCD.

70. $\frac{77}{85} + \frac{91}{105} - \frac{71}{90}$

71. $\frac{11}{x^2y} + \frac{13}{x^2y^3} + \frac{m}{x^2y^2z} - \frac{mn}{xy^3z^4}$

Find the LCM for the following sets of numbers. Write all the steps required to find the LCM.

72. $\{88, 84, 92\}$

73. $\{20x^3, 30x^4, 45xy, 90x^2y^2\}$

Simplify the following problems. If necessary, write the final answer as a mixed number and reduce the final answer if it contains a fraction.

74. $\frac{\{5^2 - (25 \div 2)\} + 7^3}{12 + 3^3 - (13 \times 3)}$

75. $\frac{7}{39} - \frac{65}{78} + \frac{25}{26}$

76. $\frac{17}{18} - (\frac{4}{5} - \frac{2}{15})^2$

Identify the Arithmetic/Mathematics Property illustrated in each of the following problems. If the Property applies to either addition or multiplication, indicate this in your answer with the appropriate property. Use sentences to explain what changed in each problem to lead you to your conclusions regarding the properties you selected.

77. $(9 + x) + 4 = 4 + (9 + x)$

78. $8 - z = p \;\therefore p = 8 - z$

79. $(ab + 2) = dm$ & $dm = 1001$ $\therefore$ $(ab + 2) = 1001$

80. $(x + 1)(x + 2) = (x + 1)(x + 2)$

81. $3(bc) = (3b)c$

82. $16.21 + \left(x^2 + 3\frac{1}{2}\right) = (16.21 + x^2) + 3\frac{1}{2}$

83. $(x + 1)(x + 2) = (x + 2)(x + 1)$

Indicate all the factors before you reduce the following fraction.

84. Simplify/Reduce: $\frac{45\,x^3yz^2(m+4)^2(z-8)^2}{60x^3y^2z(m+4)^3(z-16)^2}$

Write the definition of the word or phrase. After you write your explanation to define the word or phrase, use mathematics notation to illustrate the meaning of the word or phrase if there is an appropriate mathematics notation for the definition.

85. Coefficient (Hint: There is no mathematical notation required.)
86. Variable (No special math notation required.)
87. Natural Numbers (Hint: There is a special mathematical notation required.)
88. Whole Numbers (Special mathematics notation is required.)
89. Integers (Special mathematics notation is required.)
90. Rational Numbers (Elementary teachers do not have to include the mathematics notation to indicate the set of Rational Numbers, but Secondary mathematics teachers must include the mathematics notation after the written explanation.)
91. Prime Number (Special mathematical notation required.)
92. Composite Number (Special mathematical notation required.)

93. Factor or Factors (No special mathematics notation required.)

94. Fraction (There is a notation you could write, but not required for this answer.)

95. Interleave as it refers to arithmetic and mathematics problems.

96. Multiples (Multiple) (No special mathematics notation required.)

Create two fractions or ratios which both equal, 1, based on the given information.

97. $1000\,ml = 1\,L$ 98. $1\,yd.^2 = 9\,ft.^2$

Complete the conversion problems using both "Young's Ratio/Equation Theorem" and "Young's Conversion Theorem". Show all the steps even if you can solve the problem quickly in your head.

99. $0.76\,mi.\ \ to\ \ ft.$

100. $500\,in.\ to\ yds.$ (Write the exact simplified answer in any form you believe appropriate.)

101. $7\frac{1}{2}\ km\ \ to\ m$ (Preferred notation) or $7\frac{1}{2}\ km.\ \ to\ m.$

102. $100\,oz.\ \ to\ lbs.$ (Write the exact simplified answer in any form you believe is appropriate.)

Solve the following multiplication and division problems. If you can solve the problems in your head just write the answers. Indicating work is not required but acceptable.

103. $\frac{3004}{10^2}$ 104. 0.3×10^4

Complete the following conversion problems. Illustrate all the steps required when using both "Young's Equation/Ratio Theorem" and "Young's Conversion Theorem".

105. 0.78% Convert the percent into a decimal and a reduced fraction.

106. 95.95 Convert the decimal into a reduced mixed number and a percent.

107. $\frac{7}{8}$ Convert the fraction into a decimal and a percent.

108. 31035% Convert the percent into a decimal and a mixed number with a reduced fraction.

109. $3\frac{3}{4}$ Convert the mixed number into a decimal number and a percent.

110. 0.0015 Convert the decimal into a percent and a reduced fraction.

PART B ELEMENTARY TEACHER ARITHMETIC FINAL

PART B IS FOR BOTH ELEMENTARY AND SECONDARY MATH TEACHERS

The Next 20 Problems are all Worth 2-Points.

(**1** Point for the correct answer and **1** point for the work illustrated. Do not skip any necessary steps. We will decide what is necessary so it would be wise to indicate all the steps you remember.)

Simplify the arithmetic fraction problems in this section. Always illustrate how to use the "Fundamental Theorem of Arithmetic" in each problem to find LCDs and reduce the fractions in the final answer. Always indicated how to use both "Young's Equation/Ratio Theorem" and "Young's Conversion Theorem", when appropriate, but you do not need to reference the theorems by name. Always indicate the one big fraction concept when solving these problems.

Simplify the following problems. All final answers must be written as a reduced fraction or a mixed number with a reduced fraction.

1. $\frac{7}{16}+\frac{7}{10}-\frac{7}{15}=?$

2. $\frac{5}{6}-\frac{5}{8}+\frac{7}{30}=?$

3. $\frac{15}{32}\times\frac{8}{25}\div\frac{3}{4}=?$

4. $1\frac{7}{8}\div\left(\frac{5}{2}\right)^2\times\frac{5}{6}=?$

5. $4\frac{7}{8}+7\frac{3}{20}-6\frac{7}{24}=?$

6. $\left(\frac{7}{15}+\frac{7}{24}\right)\div 6\frac{1}{8}=?$

7. $\left(\frac{2}{5}\right)^2\div 4+\frac{7}{30}=?$

8. $\frac{7}{24}+\frac{13}{30}-\frac{1}{9}+\frac{13}{18}=?$

9. $\frac{7}{200}\times\frac{0}{2000}\times\frac{11}{13}\div\frac{5}{6}=?$

10. $\frac{39.75}{2001}+\frac{41.15}{2001}-\frac{0}{5}+\frac{52.1}{2001}=?$

Complete all the conversions indicated below. Indicate all the steps illustrated in this textbook to receive full credit.

11. 7.75 $yds.\ \ into\ \ in.$

12. 10,540 $cm\ \ into\ \ km$

13. 36,000,000 $sec.\ \ into\ \ hrs.$

14. 19,800 $ft.\ \ into\ \ mi.$

15. 3.75 $gal.\ \ into\ \ qts.$

16. 189 $in.\ \ into\ \ ft.$ (You may write the final answer using a fraction or a decimal.)

17. 3.5 $yds.^2\ \ into\ \ in.^2$

18. 30,000 $cm.^3\ \ into\ \ m.^3$ $\quad or \quad$ $normally\ written\ as$ 30,000 $cm^3\ \ into\ \ m^3$

19. 48 $mph\ \ into\ \ \frac{ft.}{min.}$

20. In the city of "*Luppa*" they measure liquid containers using the measurements referred to as "*k&ks*" and "*l&ns*". The following is a known fact in the city of "*Luppa*", "3 $k\&ks = 7\ l\&ns$". Convert "25 $l\&ns\ \ into\ \ k\&ks$". Write the final answer as a mixed number with a label.

Elementary Education Majors are finished. We hope you did well. Parts A and B concentrate on arithmetic concepts and procedures. All Elementary Teachers and all Secondary Mathematics Teachers must be experts regarding how to illustrate, solve, and teach the problems in the two previous sections. If you are presently an elementary teacher or planning to become an elementary teacher, you may want to try to earn bonus points and attempt the problems in Parts "C & D", below. You may earn a maximum of 10 bonus points if you are an elementary education major or teacher.

PARTS C AND D ARE BOTH REQUIRED PARTS OF THE FINAL TEST FOR STUDENTS PREPARING TO BE A SECONDARY MATHEMATICS TEACHER OR THEY ARE ALREADY A SECONDARY MATHEMATICS TEACHER. PRESENT ELEMENTARY TEACHERS AND STUDENTS PREPARING TO BE AN ELEMENTARY TEACHER ARE ENCOURAGED TO TAKE PARTS C AND D FOR THE OPPORTUNITY TO POSSIBLY EARN EXTRA CREDIT.

PART C

The 10 questions in Part C are **1**-point questions. We hope you can solve these problems without indicating much work, but we want you to illustrate all the steps as if you are teaching students to solve these problems for the first time. This means you should illustrate when you use "Young's Equation/Ration Theorem" and Young's Conversion Theorem. You do not need to reference the theorems by name when you use the theorems.

1. Convert "$54\frac{3}{4}$ ft." into yds. (Write the answer as a mixed number.)
2. Convert " 787.78" into a percent
3. Convert "7992 $in.^2$ into $ft.^2$ 4. Convert "120 mph into $\frac{ft.}{sec.}$
5. Convert "$\frac{50\ in.^3}{min.}$ into $\frac{ft.^3}{day}$ (Write the answer as a reduced mixed number.)
6. Convert 15,000 l." into ml. or frequently written as " 15,000 l into ml"
7. Convert "3 mm" into dekameters 8. Convert "$\frac{7}{8}$ %" into a reduced fraction
9. Convert "1.78 mi. into yds.
10. Convert "3.75 meters into inches – use the following fact: 1 in = 2.54 cm.

Roundoff the answer to the nearest thousandth.

PART D

You are expected to illustrate all the steps you feel are necessary to receive full credit for each problem. Each problem is worth **2** points, **1** point for the correct answer and **1** point for the work illustrated. We expect you to illustrate the "Fundamental Theorem of Arithmetic", "Young's Equation/Ratio Theorem", and Young's Conversion Theorem" frequently and properly when solving these problems. We do not expect you to refer to the three indicated theorems by name when you use the theorems. Do not take a chance and skip too many steps, remember you are supposed to be prepared to be a secondary mathematics teacher and illustrate how to solve these problems to a wide variety of students. There are 20 problems in this section. We assume the students who are working with these problems know the rule to convert a fraction division problem into a fraction multiplication problem. Use the one big fraction concept when appropriate.

1. $\dfrac{14r^2 + 9r^3 + r^4}{r^3 - r^2 - 6r} \div \dfrac{r^4 + 12r^3 + 35r^2}{r^3 + 10r^2 + 25r}$

2. $1 - \dfrac{5}{f^2 - 5f + 6} + \dfrac{2f}{f^2 - 9}$

3. $\dfrac{(m^3 + 8m^2 + 15m)(2m + m^2 - 8)}{(12m + m^3 + 7m^2)(4 - 4m + m^2)}$

4. $\dfrac{-\frac{t}{y} + t^2y}{ty - \frac{4t}{y}}$ (Write the solution in factored form.)

5. $\dfrac{7}{c^2 - 7c + 10} - \dfrac{2c}{c^2 - 10c + 25} - \dfrac{5c}{c^2 - 4c + 4}$ (Write the solution in factored form.)

6. $\dfrac{4x^2 + 4x - 3}{3x^2 - 4x + 1} \cdot \dfrac{x^2 - 1}{6x^2 + 7x - 5} \div \dfrac{4x^2 - 9}{9x^2 + 12x - 5}$

7. $\dfrac{v}{v^2 - 4} + \dfrac{v}{v^2 + v - 2} - \dfrac{v}{1 - v^2}$ (Write the solution in factored form.)

8. $\left(\frac{x^2+5x+6}{x^2-5x+6} \div \frac{x^2+4x+4}{x^2-4}\right) - \frac{6}{x-3}$ (Write the solution in factored form if appropriate.)

9. $\frac{(3y^2-11y-4)(15y^2-26y+8)}{(9y^2-24y+16)(25y^2-20y+4)}$

10. $\frac{2d-15+d^2}{d^3+11d^2+28d} \div \frac{d^2+7d+10}{9d^2+d^3+14d}$

11. $\frac{w+1}{w^2-1} - \frac{w+1}{1-w}$ (Write the solution in factored form.)

12. $(\frac{7}{x+5})^2 - \frac{7}{x+5}$ (Write the solution in factored form.)

13. $\frac{21}{84} + \frac{21}{92} - \frac{21}{96} + \frac{21}{100}$ (We wonder if the answer will reduce. Hint: Try the following prime numbers, "7 and 23", when you might want to reduce the fraction. At least one of them will work.)

14. $\frac{3}{c^2+7c+12} + \frac{5}{c^2-9} + \frac{7}{c^2+c-12}$ (Write the denominator in factored form.)

15. $\frac{3x+7}{x^2-4} + \frac{7}{-2-x} - \frac{1-x}{4-x^2}$ (Write the denominator in factored form.)

16. $\frac{125x^3y-25x^2y}{25x^2y-y}$

17. $\frac{rs}{r-\frac{sr}{s-\frac{r}{s^2}}}$

18. $\left(\frac{x-5}{x^2-25} + x\right)\left(\frac{x^2+2x-15}{x-3}\right)$

19. $77\frac{17}{24} - 101\frac{29}{30} - 87\frac{59}{80}$ (Write the final answer as a mixed number.)

20. We know a mixed number such as "$6\frac{3}{4}$" can be converted into the improper fraction "$\frac{27}{4}$". Now, assume the following two expressions, "$x\frac{1}{x}$" and "$x\frac{2}{x^2}$", both represent a mixed number. Solve the following mixed number subtraction problem, "$x\frac{1}{x} - x\frac{2}{x^2}$".

DONE/COMPLETED/FINISHED

References

Bailey, D. H., Hoard, M. K., Nugent, L., & Geary, D. C. (2012). Competence with fractions predicts gains in mathematics achievement. *Journal of Experimental Child Psychology,* 113, 447-455. doi: 10.1016/j.jecp.2012.06.004

Bailey, D. H., Siegler, R. S., & Geary, D. C., (2014). Early predictors of middle school fraction knowledge. *Developmental Science.* 17. 775-785. doi:10.1111/desc.12155

Bailey, D. H., Zhou, X., Zhang, Y., Cui, J., Fuchs, L. S., Jordon, N. C., Gersten, R., & Siegler, R. S. (2015). Development of fraction concepts and procedures in U. S. and Chinese children. *Journal of Experimental Child Psychology.* 129. 68-83. doi: 10.1016/j.jecp.2014.08.006

Booth, J. L., & Newton, K. J., (2012). Fractions: Could they be the gatekeeper's doorman? *Contemporary Educational Psychology.* 37. 247-253. doi: 10.1016/j.cedppsych.2012.07.001

Booth, J. L., Newton, K. J., & Twiss-Garrity, L. K., (2014). The impact of fraction magnitude knowledge on algebra performance and learning. *Journal of Experimental Child Psychology.* 118. 110-118. doi: 10.1016/j.jecp.2013.09.001

Booth, J. L., & Siegler, R. S., (2008). Numerical magnitude representations influence arithmetic learning. *Child Development* 79. 1016-1031.

Braithwaite, D. W., Pyke, A. A., & Siegler, R. S., (2017). A computational model of fraction arithmetic. *Psychological Review.* 124 (5). 603-605. doi:10.1037/rev0000072

Braithwaite, D. W., & Siegler, R. S., (2018). Students learn spurious associations in their math textbooks: Examples from fraction arithmetic. *Journal of Experimental Psychology: Learning, Memory, and Cognition.* doi:10.1037/xlm0000546

Braithwaite, D. W., Tian, J., & Siegler, R. S. (2018). Do children understand fraction addition? *Developmental Science.* Early bird on line publication, September 12, 2017. doi: 10.1111. desc. 12601

Fazio, L. K., Dewolf, M., & Siegler, R. S., (2016). Strategy use and strategy choice in fraction magnitude compartison. *Journal of Experimental Psychology: Learning, Memory, and Cognition.* 42. 1-16 doi: 10.1037/xlm0000153

Fazio, L. K., Kennedy, C., & Siegler, R. S., (2016). Improving children's knowledge fraction magnitudes. *PLOS ONE* doi: 10.1371/journal/one.0165243

Heller, P. M., Post, T. R., Behr, M., & Losh, R. (1990). Qualitative and numerical reasoning about fractions and rates by seventh and eighth grade students. *Journal for Research in Mathematics Education.* 21(5), 388-402.

Jordan, N. C., Hansen, N., Fuchs, L. S., Siegler, R. S., Gersten, R., & Micklos, D., (2013). Developmental predictors of fraction concepts and procedures. *Journal of Experimental Child Psychology.* 116. 45-58.

Kloosterman, P., (2010). Mathematics skills of 17-year-olds in the United States: 1978 to 2004. *Journal for Research in Mathematics Education, 41, 20-51.*

Lortie – Forgues, H., Tian, J., & Siegler, R. S. (2015). Why is learning fraction and decimal arithmetic so difficult? *Developmental Review.* 38, 201-221.

McMullen, J., Hannula-Sormunen, M., & Lehtinen, E., (2017). Spontaneous focusing on quantitative relations as a predictor of rational number and algebra knowledge. *Contemporary Educational Psychology,* 51.

Ni, Y., & Zhou, Y. D. (2005). Teaching and learning fraction and rational numbers: The origins and implications of whole number bias. *Educational Psychologist.* 40(1), 27-52.

Niederberger, M. (2012). Learning fractions and division early will help America's students as they tackle tougher problems ahead, a research study finds Formula written for math success. *Pittsburgh Post-Gazette,* (Vol. 85 NO. 324, pp.1,3.)

Patel, R., Liu, R., & Koedinger, K. (2017). When to block versus interleave practice? Evidence against teaching fraction addition before fraction multiplication. *In Proceedings of the 38th Annual Meeting of the Cognitive Science Society, Philadelphia, PA,* (Vol. 1. No. 3.2, pp. 2-3.)

Richland, L. E., Bjork, R. A., Finley, J. R., & Linn, M. C. (2005). Linking cognitive science to education: Generation and interleaving effects. In B. G. Bara, L. Barsalou & M. Bucciarelli (Eds.), Proceedings of the *Twenty-Seventh Conference of the Cognitive Science Society.* (pp. 1850-1855) Mahwah, NJ: Lawrence Erlbaum.

Schneider, M. & Siegler, R. S. (2010), Representations of the magnitudes of fractions, *Journal of Experimental Psychology: Human Perception and Performance,* 36(5), 1227-1238.

Shiller, L. K., Fan, A., & Siegler, R. S. (2022). The Power of One The Importance of Flexible Understanding of an Identity Element. *Journal of Numerical Cognition,* Vol. 8(3), 430-442. https://doi.org/10.5964/jnc.7593

Siegler, R. S., Duncan, G. J., Davis-Kean, P. E., Duckworth, K., Claessens, A., Engel, M., Susperreguy, M. I., & Chen, M. (2012). Early predicators of high school mathematics achievement. *Psychological Science,* 23(7), 691-697.

Siegler, R. S., Fazio, L. K., Bailey, D. H., & Zhou, X. (2013). Fractions: The new frontier for theories of numerical development. *Trends in Cognitive Science,* 17, 13-19.

Siegler, R. S., & Lortie – Forgues, H., (2015). Conceptual knowledge of fraction arithmetic. *Journal of Educational Psychology.* 107. 909-918. doi: 10.1037/edu0000025

Siegler, R. S., & Lortie – Forgues, H., (2017). Hard lessons: Why rational number arithmetic is so difficult for so many people. *Current Directions in Psychological Science.* 26(4). 346-351 doi:10.1177/0963721417700129. NOTE: This article can be accessed at the journal's. sagepub. com/doi/full/101177/0963721417700129

Siegler, R. S., & Pyke, A. A. (2013). Development and individual differences in understanding of fractions. *Development Psychology*, 49, 1994-2004.

Siegler, R. S., Thompson, C. A., & Schneider, M. (2011). An integrated theory of whole number and fractions development. *Cognitive Psychology*, 62, 273-296.

Stigler, J. W., Givvin, K. B., & Thompson, B. (2010). What community college developmental mathematics students understand about mathematics. *The MathAMATYC Educator*, 10, 4-16.

Torbeyns, J., Schneider, M., Xin, Z., & Siegler, R. S. (2015). Bridging the gap: Fraction understanding is central to mathematics achievement in students from three different continents. *Learning and Instruction*, 37, 5-13.

Van Doreen, W., Lehtinen, E., & Verschaffel, L. (2015). Unraveling the gap between natural and rational numbers. *Learning and Instruction,* 37, 1-4.

Vukovic, R. K., Fuchs, L. S., Geary, D. C., Jordon, N. C., Gersten, R., & Siegler, R. S. (2014). Sources of individual differences in children's understanding of fractions. *Child Development*, 85, 1461-1476. doi: 10.117/cdev.12218.

Watts, T. W., Duncan, G. J., Siegler, R. S., & Davis-Kean, P. E. (2014). What's past is prologue: Relations between early mathematics knowledge and high school achievement. *Educational Research*, 43, 352-360. doi: 10.3102/001318X14553660

https://www.education.pa.gov & https://siegler.tc.columbia.edu

Here are the five teaching principles I mentioned in Chapter 1, page 3, which I focused on when I was a math teacher and I continually referred to throughout this textbook.

1. Illustrate and emphasize how to use the rules to solve challenging problems related to specific topics.
2. Emphasize minor concepts teachers often assume the students understand but they really do not.
3. Show students how to use the present topic to solve future mathematics problems.
4. Introduce new topics in short "2-4" minute segments starting one or two months before assigning homework problems from the textbook involving the new topic.
5. Review previously learned topics in short "2-4" minute segments for one or two months after the topic was presented in the textbook.

As you finish reading/studying this textbook, we hope you realize there is one type of arithmetic/mathematics problems which we did not emphasize, and many students struggle to solve. All arithmetic and mathematics teachers must find time to teach these types of problems and not completely depend on the arithmetic or math textbook. The type of problems I am trying to make you think about are word problems or story problems which make all students and teachers think about applications of mathematics as it relates to real world situations.

Just a suggestion to help you teach word problems, but I realize time is always a problem, which is why arithmetic and mathematics teachers cannot waste class time. Once you lose time you never get it back. During the summer, select 12-14 different types of word problems which you want your students to master, "Learn and Remember, by the end of the school. Next, narrow the list down to 6-9 types of problems which might be more manageable. Use Teaching Principles, 4 and 5 mentioned above, introduce one or two of the word problems starting in September, then continue to introduce a new type of word problem monthly or bi-monthly for the rest of the school year. Review the word problems already discussed in previous months by Interleaving the word problems into your homework assignments, quizzes, and tests.

If every arithmetic and math teacher emphasized and then reviewed 8 different types of word problems per school year and continued to review word problems taught the previous two years, maybe word problems would not be the most feared problems in arithmetic and mathematics.

These teaching suggestions will work well for most students until the students enter an Algebra 2 class. At this juncture in the mathematics curriculum, word problems become more challenging, and teachers need to probably focus on 10-12 different types of word problems. One of the greatest things about teaching mathematics is, higher level mathematics courses will always become more challenging for both the students and teachers.

Suggested Future Mathematics Education Research Topics

Future Research Topics (FRT)

1. a. If teachers use these "Five Teaching Principles", we believe students will demonstrate improvement in all their arithmetic skills. Page 3

   b. These are our nonscientific findings which we observed after using the "Five Teaching Principles" previously mentioned. Page 6
2. The "First Learned Method" is the method students rely on most frequently. Pages 32, 37, & 185
3. Compare the difference between students' performance if they use horizontal line fraction notation versus slanted line notation. Page 46
4. Teach to a level beyond the textbook expectations. Page 66
5. If students are exposed to rules in mathematics over a longer time frame, then their long-term memory will improve. Page 68, 83, 83, 185, & 192
6. The more students write the steps to solve problems the better their long-term memory will be. Page 70, 120, & 312
7. Is knowledge of multiplication and division facts the major indicator of success when solving fraction problems? Page 92, 95, 110, & 150
8. We believe writing fraction problems using the horizontal format versus the vertical format will lessen the confusion of the rules for adding, subtracting, multiplying, and dividing fractions. We also believe the horizontal fraction format will better prepare students to solve rational expression problems in algebra. Page 98
9. We believe if students solve addition, subtraction, multiplication, and division problems as one big fraction prior to the final computations, then much of the

confusion with respect to different fraction rules will be eliminated. Page 116, 162, 177, 200, & 411

10. We believe the more a single procedure can be used to solve a wide variety of math problems, it is beneficial to a wide range of students. Page 205
11. Six, "Do's" and "Do Not's" when teaching fractions. The previous section contains many topics to research and determine what works and does not work. Page 210
12. If students are required to frequently work with factor trees, will their multiplication and division mental skills improve? Notice, we used factor trees as a required process to solve fraction problems, not as an independent procedure. Page 308, 328 (Pink Box Comment), & 396
13. If students frequently use "factor trees" when working with fractions, will their fraction arithmetic skills improve? Page 330
14. Mentally multiply and divide numbers by powers of ten. We wonder how many 6th, 7th, 8th, and 9th graders can mentally multiply and divide rational numbers by powers of ten? It might also be an interesting research question to ask first year college students and high school seniors. Page 351
15. Mentally convert fractions into decimals, fractions into percentages, decimals into fractions, decimals into percentages, percentages into fractions, and percentages into decimals. You may ask these types of questions to first year college students, high school seniors, eighth graders, and sixth graders. Page 356
16. We suggest there is a correlation between students' abilities to work with rational expressions in algebra and their success in Trigonometry, Calculus, Engineering, Physics, Chemistry and other advanced mathematics and science courses. Page 434

TWO TOPICS FOR SECONDARY MATHEMATICS TEACHERS TO THINK ABOUT

1. When you teach algebra there are basically four types of problems which students are asked to work with in their assignments. A. The directions can be written using one word, **"Simplify"**. We discussed simplifying problems throughout this textbook. Students are required to rewrite the given problems in a more condensed form. The given expressions do NOT contain an equals relationship symbol. B. Again, the directions can be written using one word, **"Solve"**. We illustrated how to solve several algebra problems and the goal is to determine the solutions which could be substituted back into the given equation for the variable to make the given equation an "Identity". These problems always involve at least one equals relationship symbol. Sometimes there is only one answer required and sometimes there maybe more than one solution for the given equation. It is possible to have two or more equations and two or more variables in one problem and the goal is to determine solutions for all the variables which make all the given equations "Identities". C. The one word in the directions this time is the word, **"Graph"**. The problem may contain one or more variables and one or more equations, but the goal is to determine several points to place on a graph to form an algebraic shape. In Algebra 1 the given equation or equations involve the two variables "x *and* y" and the graphs can be placed In a Cartesian Coordinate System. In Algebra 2 and higher-level mathematics classes, the graphs will become more challenging. D. The fourth type of problems given in an Algebra course are the famous problems we all love, **Word/Statement** problems. These problems are always the most difficult to teach and for most students the most difficult to solve. Students must be able to **read** and **interpret** all the words contained in the statement problem. A strong math vocabulary is essential. It is necessary to interpret all the words in the statement problem and then change the words into an equation or two, written using algebraic symbols. You may need to know basic formulas to solve some word problems if they involve perimeter, area, volume, etc. After you write the equation or equations, then you must use your knowledge to solve the equations which you wrote when you interpreted the words into an algebra equation or equations.

WOW WOW WOW WOW

2. When students enter a Calculus class, the Calculus teacher often assumes the students have mastered the notation referred to as functional notation. This might be a poor assumption, my guess is over 50% of the students who enter a Calculus class are familiar with functional notation, but they have not mastered some important implied information hidden in the notation. It is important to discuss functional notation in Algebra 2 starting in September and ending in April or May. In Calculus we use functional notation early in the course when we present the definition of a derivative. On day one in your Calculus class, ask the students to explain what the following notation means, "$f(m-2) = ?$". If your Calculus students had an excellent Algebra 2 and/or Precalculus teacher, they will recognize the functional notation represents a POINT which usually indicates an "x and y" value in an ordered pair. The "x" value in the notation is the expression, "$m-2$" and the "y" value in the point is either the question mark, "?" or the notation "$f(m-2)$". The ordered pair (point) may be written using either of the following forms to represent the point(x, y): $(m-2, ?)$ *or* $(m-2, f(m-2))$. Here is a simple example problem representing two points: *point* 1 *is* $f(6) = 7$ *and point* 2 *is* $f(5) = 10$. The two points are $(6, 7)$ *and* $(5, 10)$. Finally, ask your Calculus students to interpret the following notation involving two points and the slope formula, "$\frac{y_2-y_1}{x_2-x_1}$": "$\frac{f(x)-f(x-h)}{h}$". If you are an Algebra 2 or Precalculus teacher, do you think 90% of your students can identify the two points, in the last rational expression and write both points as ordered pairs? Also, will they recognize the expression is the slope formula written using functional notation? Important questions, which every calculus student must be able to explain.

Solutions to Assignment Questions

First Assignment:

1. Significant comments - Identify the LCD, the fractions must have identical denominators, then add and subtract the numerators of all fractions with the LCD, the numerator in the answer is the sum/difference of the numerators with identical denominators, keep the LCD, then check to reduce. (Explaining how to reduce is not required in this answer.)

2. $\frac{5}{9} - \frac{1}{9} = \frac{4}{9}$ **3.** $\frac{4}{7} + \frac{2}{7} = \frac{6}{7}$ **4.** $\frac{7}{12}$ **5.** $\frac{5}{53}$ **6.** $\frac{4}{x}$ **7.** $\frac{23}{301}$ **8.** $\frac{25}{xyz}$ **9.** $\frac{8}{k^3m}$ **10.** 0 **11.** $\frac{25}{(x+y)}$

12. $7/12 + 5/6 - 7/24$ & $7/12 \times 24/35 \div 2/5$ & *more* **13.** In algebra 99% of the problems are written using the horizontal format. **14.** This answer is addressed in Chapter 5 **15.** 24 inches **16.** 3 miles **17.** 5 tons **18.** 10800 seconds **19.** 120 hours **20.** 1.5 meters **21.** 60 *ninos* **22.** & **23.** The answers are addressed in Chapter 5.

Second Assignment:

Problems **1, 2, 3,** and **4** - Write your definition, then refer to the internet for an exact definition. **1.** Ex: $\frac{1}{5}$ & $\frac{76}{101}$ The numbers "1" and "76" are both numerators. **2.** Refer to the example in problem 1. the numbers "5" and "101" are denominators. **3.** The divisor is the number outside the division box, usually on the left side. **4.** The dividend is the number inside the division box. **5.** The numerator in a fraction and the dividend in a long division problem. The denominator in a fraction and the divisor in a long division problem. **6.** Quotient 7. 8. 9. 10. Write your definition, then refer to the internet for an exact definition. **7.** The parts – numerator, line, and denominator - The numerator is the number of given parts used from the whole, the line indicates division, and the denominator represents the total parts in the whole. **8.** Ex: Multiples of $9 = \{9, 18, 27, \ldots\}$ Ex: Multiples of $8 = \{8, 16, 24, 32, \ldots\}$ **9.** Ex: Factors of $36 = \{1, 2, 3, 4, 6, 9, 12, 18, 36\}$ because $36 = 1 \times 36, 36 = 2 \times 18,\ 36 = 3 \times 12,\ 36 = 4 \times 9, \& \ 36 = 6 \times 6\}$ Ex: Factors of $45 = \{1, 3, 5, 9, 15, 45\}$ **10.** Ex: 1. Set of even Natural Numbers starting with $10 - \{10, 12, 14, 16, 18, 20, 22, 24, 26, \ldots\}$ 2. Set of the last six small letters of the alphabet $\{u, v, w, x, y, z\}$ **11.** 12, 13, 14. Write your definition, then refer to the internet for an exact definition. 11. Notation - $N = \{1, 2, 3, 4, \ldots\}$ **12.** Notation - $W = \{0, 1, 2, 3, 4, \ldots\}$ **13.** Notation - $I = \{\ldots - 4, -3, -2, -1, 0, 1, 2, 3, 4, \ldots\}$ **14.** Check in this Chapter for the mathematical notation. **15.** Natural Numbers are often referred to as the counting numbers and they are the numbers parents initially teach their children, when they are learning to count. The Whole Numbers refer to objects when you have complete objects such as two whole pizza pies. If you eat one slice from one pie, you have 1 whole pie remaining plus a part of a pie. Once one pie is completely gone you have 1 whole pie remaining. If 1 slice is removed from the last pie, then you have zero (0) whole pies remaining. **16.** Reference the first 5 letters in the word Rational. A Rational number is a fraction, and a ratio is a special type of fraction. **17.** Place a 6 - inch line on a piece of paper, place "0" at the far left of the line segment and 1 at the far right of the line segment. Make sure there are 4 equally spaced hash marks between the numbers "0" and "1" which means you have 5 short line segments between "0" and "1". Place a mark/point on the third hash mark to represent the magnitude from zero, "$\frac{3}{5}$". **18.** Place a 6 - inch line on a piece of paper, place "0" at the far left of the line segment and indicate the numbers 1, 2, and 3 on the line segment. Between the numbers 2 and 3 place 4 equally spaced hash marks in the same manner you placed hash marks in problem 17. between 0 and 1. Place a mark/point on the third hash mark between the numbers 2 and 3. **19.** Line segment with 0, at the left and 1 at the right. Use 10 hash marks and place a mark on the 7th hash mark. **20.** Line segment with 0, at the left and 8 at the right. Indicate the numbers on the number line from 0 to 8, then place 10 equally spaced hash marks between 7 and 8 and place a mark on the 7th hash mark between 7 and 8. **21.** Refer to problems 17 & 19. **22.** Solution 1: Place a 6 - inch line on a piece of paper, place "0" at the far left of the line segment. At the far right place the number 800. We know the given number is close to 700 so place 7 equally spaced hash marks between 0 and 800. Place your mark just slightly or almost on top of the number 700 and ignore the fraction, "$\frac{3}{11}$" and realize your point is just slightly beyond the hash mark representing the number 700 because your given problem is 702. Solution 2: Place a 6 - inch line on a piece of paper, place 700 close to the far left of the line segment but not at the very end of the line segment and the number 710 at the far right of the segment. Place 9 equally placed hash marks between 700 and 710, therefore you will have 10 small line segments between 700 and 710. Place a mark slightly past the 2nd hash mark which represents 702 and make sure your hash mark is less than half-way between 702 and 703. **23.** The solution is much like the solutions for problems 17, 19, and 21. **24.** The solution is much like the solution for problem 23. We suggest you use the 2nd solution and place the number 1990 close to the far left of the segment but not at the very end of the segment and the number 2000 at the far right of the segment. **25.** Convert the improper fraction to "5 1/8" and refer to the solution for problem 20. **26.** Refer to problems 17, 18, 21, and 23. Think of the fraction "$\frac{51}{100}$" as just slightly past the midpoint of the line segment.

17.

18.

19.

20.

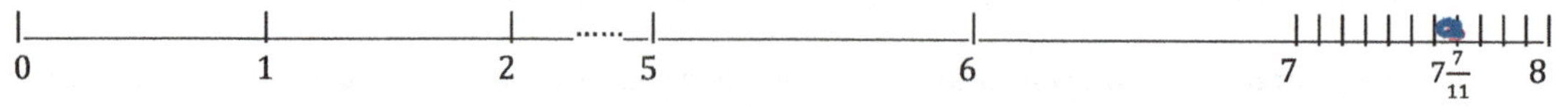

21.

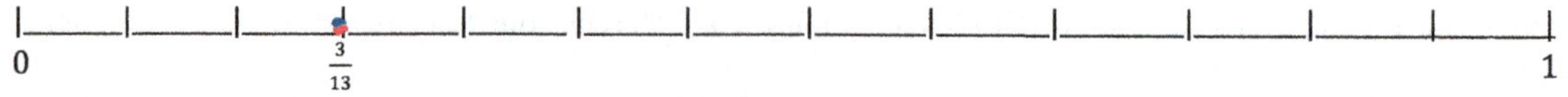

22a.

It is difficult to indicate the fine difference between 700 and $702\frac{3}{11}$ in the last graph. We prefer the next type of graph in this situation. We will use a graph like the graph in number 20 and indicate some numbers are missing.

22b.

We tried to magnify the numbers between 700 and 710 and estimated where the fraction $\frac{3}{11}$ would occur between 702 and 703.

23.

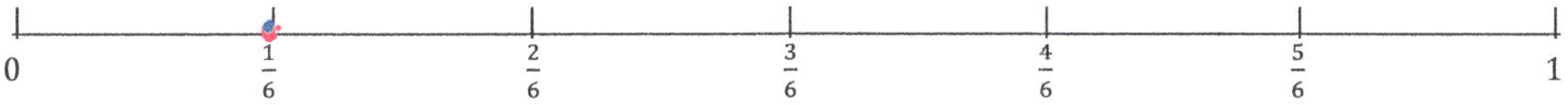

24a.

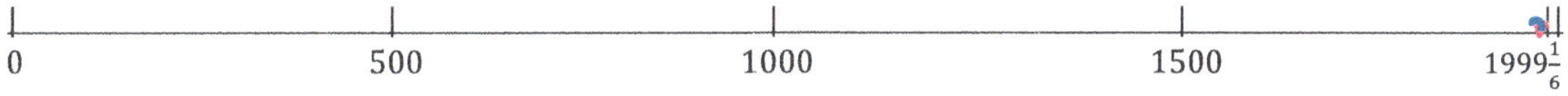

This solution to this example is like the solution to problem 22 therefore, we are going to give a second example of the graph.

24b.

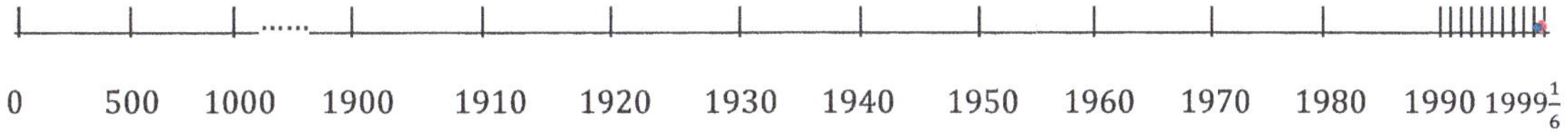

25.

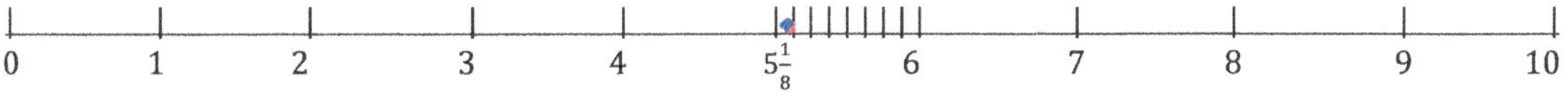

26.

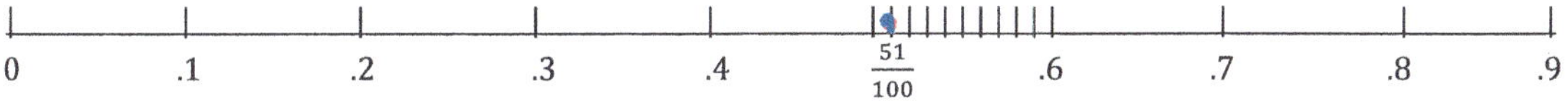

27. You should draw a 6 – inch line vertically and recognize the decimals each represent one point on the number line. You must recognize the decimal 0.6 represents the fraction $\frac{6}{10}$ and use the same logic to plot the point as you did for problems 17, 19, 21, & 23 except place the 0 at the bottom of the line and the number 1 at the top of the line. **28.** Refer to problem 27. to draw the vertical line but then refer to the solution for problem 18. to determine the position of the point. **29.** Think of the decimal as 0.64 and then $\frac{64}{100}$. Reference problem 26. to estimate the placement of the point. **30.** Place the number 0 at the bottom of the vertical line and the number 10 at the top of the vertical line. To determine the solution to the problem, refer to problems 28 and 29 combined. **31.** Refer to problems 27 and 29 to help you determine where to place the point. **32.** Refer to the solution for problem 22. **33.** Refer to the solution for problem 23. **34.** Refer to the solution for problem 24. **35.** Refer to the solution for problem 26. **36.** Fact: the decimal equals 0.51 and then refer to the solution for problem 26. (The fractions in problems 17-26 are equal or almost equal to the decimals in problems 27-36, use vertical lines rather than horizontal lines.) **37.** 3 **38.** 5 **39.** $2\frac{4}{7}$ **40.** $2\frac{1}{5}$ **41.** $2\frac{2}{25}$ **42.** 7,361 **43.** There are 5 answers to compute. Write the solutions in the following form to illustrate you multiply by 1 and use "Young's Conversion Theorem".

$\frac{3}{4} = \frac{3}{4} \times 1 = \frac{3}{4} \times \frac{2}{2} = \frac{3 \times 2}{4 \times 2} = \frac{6}{8}$ $\frac{3}{4} = \frac{3}{4} \times 1 = \frac{3}{4} \times \frac{3}{3} = \frac{3 \times 3}{4 \times 3} = \frac{9}{12}$ $\frac{3}{4} = \frac{3}{4} \times 1 = \frac{3}{4} \times \frac{7}{7} = \frac{3 \times 7}{4 \times 7} = \frac{21}{28}$

$$\frac{3}{4} = \frac{3}{4} \times 1 = \frac{3}{4} \times \frac{12}{12} = \frac{3 \times 12}{4 \times 12} = \frac{36}{48} \qquad \frac{3}{4} = \frac{3}{4} \times 1 = \frac{3}{4} \times \frac{27}{27} = \frac{3 \times 27}{4 \times 27} = \frac{81}{108}$$

44. The same 5 steps as indicated in problem 43. Answers $\frac{10}{12}, \frac{15}{18}, \frac{35}{42}, \frac{60}{72}, \frac{135}{162}$ **45.** The same 5 steps as the previous problems. Answers $\frac{18}{20}, \frac{27}{30}, \frac{63}{70}, \frac{108}{120}, \frac{243}{270}$ **46.** The same 5 steps as the previous problems. Answers $\frac{26}{20}, \frac{39}{30}, \frac{91}{70}, \frac{156}{120}, \frac{351}{270}$ **47.** The same 5 steps as the previous problems. Answers $\frac{26}{32}, \frac{39}{48}, \frac{91}{112}, \frac{156}{192}, \frac{351}{432}$ **48.** The same 5 steps as the previous problems. Answers $\frac{82}{86}, \frac{123}{129}, \frac{287}{301}, \frac{492}{516}, \frac{1107}{1161}$

49. Both numbers use the same two digits. Both numbers can be written as a fraction - $\frac{38}{1}$ and $\frac{3}{8}$ which means they are both Rational Numbers. Both numbers are derived by using arithmetic operations. (38 can be written in expanded form using both multiplication and addition - $\frac{3}{8}$ is a division problem.) Both numbers represent one point on a number line referred to as the magnitude. **50.** & **51.** The same four facts, which were stated for the two numbers in problem 49. are relevant for the two numbers in problems 50. and 51. In problem 49., there are two multiplication problems required when writing the number 38 in expanded form. Example $38 = 3 \times 10 + 8 \times 1$ To write the expanded form of the number 216 it requires 3 multiplication problems and then the sum. Example using exponents with the powers of 10 $2 \times 10^2 + 1 \times 10^1 + 6 \times 10^0$ Here is the expanded form of the number 3101 written using both notations $3 \times 1000 + 1 \times 100 + 0 \times 10 + 1 \times 1 = 3 \times 10^3 + 1 \times 10^2 + 0 \times 10^1 + 1 \times 10^0$ **52.** < **53.** > **54.** > **55.** < **56.** > **57.** < **58.** = **59.** = **60.** = **61.** > **62.** Explain why the word "Least" is appropriate when working with an LCM. Explain why the word "Common" is appropriate when working with an LCM. Explain why the word "Multiple" is appropriate when finding an LCM. The LCM for the 3 numbers (3, 6, and 9) is 18. Study the three sets of multiplication tables for the 3 given numbers: Here is the set of multiplication tables for the number 3 - {3, 6, 9, 12, 15, **18**, 21, ... }. Here is the set of multiplication tables for the number 6 – {6, 12, **18**, 24, ...}. Here is the set of multiplication tables for the number 9 – {9, **18**, 27, ...}. Use the multiplication tables as a guide to explain why the Least Common Multiple for the given numbers is 18. **63.** Use the same basic explanation and example for this problem as you used for problem 62. The difference is the **LCD** is the LCM for **the denominators** of **several fractions**. **64.** The procedures/rules to determine LCMs and LCDs are identical but an LCM may apply to any group of numbers or the denominators of fractions, the LCD only applies when you are working with the denominators of two or more fractions. **65.** Your Explanation **66.** Explain why the word "Greatest" is appropriate when working with a GCF. Explain why the word "Common" is appropriate when working with a GCF. Explain why the word "Factor" is appropriate when working with a GCF. The GCF for the 3 numbers (3, 6, and 9) is 3. Study the three sets of factors (numbers which will divide into the given numbers without a remainder, thus creating the opportunity to write a multiplication problem) for the 3 given numbers. Here is the set of factors for the number 3 - {1, **3**}. Here is the set of factors for the number 6 – {1, 2, **3**, 6}. Here is the set of factors for the number 9 – {1, **3**, 9}. Using the three sets of factors just listed as a guide, explain why the Greatest Common Factor for the given numbers is 3. **67.** Example Problems: Reduce the fraction, $\frac{27}{36}$, the GCF is 9. Reduce the fractions before you multiply the fractions, $\frac{7}{10} \times \frac{14}{21}$, The GCF for the two numbers, 7 and 21 is 7 and the GCF for the two numbers, 10 and 14 is 2. If you are asked to factor the expression $(6x + 12)$, the GCF is 6. In Problems 68-72 you are required to explain why you know you have the correct LCM and GCF for each set of given numbers. You may either write your explanation in sentence/paragraph form or you may use example problems using sets of multiplication tables or sets of factors to illustrate why your solutions are correct. **Problem 70 below, is an excellent example solution. 68.** LCM=12 The set of multiplication tables for 6 - {6, **12**, 18, ...} and the set of multiplication tables for 4 – {4, 8, **12**, 16...} GCF=2 The set of factors for 6 – {1, **2**, 3, 6} and the set of factors for 4 – {1, **2**, 4} **69.** LCM=30 and GCF=2 **70.** LCM=60 and GCF=2 Three sets of multiplication tables for the set of numbers {6. 10, 4}. The set of multiples for the number 6 = {6, 12, 18, 24, 30, 36, 42, 48, 54, **60**, 66, ...}. The set of multiples for the number 10 = {10, 20, 30, 40, 50, **60**, 70, ...}. The set of multiples for the number 4 = {4, 8, 12, 16, 20, 24, 28, 32, 36, 40, 44, 48, 52, 56, **60**, 64, ...} The **bold** number "**60**" in each set is the "**LCM**" for the numbers 6, 10, & 4. The set of factors for the number 6 = {6, 3, **2**, 1}. The set of factors for the number 10 = {1, **2**, 5, 10}. The set of factors for the number 4 = {1, **2**, 4}. The bold number "**2**" is the "**GCF**" for the three numbers 6, 10, & 4. **71.** LCM=48 and GCF=4 **72.** LCM=36 and GCF=3 **73.** LCM=45 and GCF=1 **74.** Four sets of multiplication tables: 15 - {15, 30, 45, 60, 75, **90**, 105, ...} 30 – {30, 60, **90**, 120, ...} 5 – {5, 10, 15, 20, 25, 30, 35, 40, 45, ..., 75, 80, 85, **90**, 95, ...} 45 – {45, **90**, 135, ...} **75.** Three sets of multiplication tables: 72 – {72, 144, 216, ..., 7344, 7416, **7488**, 7560, ...} 64 – {64, 128, 192, ..., 7360, 7424, **7488**, 7552, ...} 78 – {78, 156, 234, ..., 7332, 7410, **7488**, 7566, ...} We are sure you wish one of your teachers had taught you a better way to find the LCM 7488 in this problem. **There is,** and we will illustrate how to use "factor trees" and the Fundamental Theorem of Arithmetic to find LCMs and GCFs for all arithmetic problems and rational expressions in algebra. **76.** Three sets of multiplication tables for the numbers 15, 75, and 25. **77.** Three sets of multiplication tables for the three numbers 70, 98, and 42 or you can learn the rules which will be emphasized throughout this book and are required if you are going to work with rational expressions in algebra. 78.- 81. To identify a GCF for two or more numbers without using rules the best way to illustrate a number is the GCF is to list all the factors of the numbers you are working with. **78.** List the sets of factors for the three indicated numbers: 24 – {1, 2, 3, 4, 6, 8, **12**, 24} 12 – {1, 2, 3, 4, 6, **12**} 48 – {1, 2, 3, 4, 6, 8, **12**, 16, 24, 48} **79.** Three sets of factors: 60 – {1,2, 3, 4, 5, 6, 10, **12**, 15, 20, 30, 60} 48 – {1, 2, 3, 4, 6, 8, **12**, 16, 24, 48} 36 – {1, 2, 3, 4, 6, 9, **12**, 18, 36} **80.** Six sets of factors: 90 – {1, 2, 3, 5, **6**. 9, 10, 15, 18, 30, 45, 90} 24 – {1, 2, 3, 4, **6**, 8, 12, 24} 12 – {1, 2, 3, 4, **6**, 12} 60 - {1,2, 3, 4, 5, **6**, 10, 12, 15, 20, 30, 60} 48 – {1, 2, 3, 4, **6**, 8, 12, 16, 24, 48} 36 – {1, 2, 3, 4, **6**, 9, 12, 18, 36} **81.** Three sets of factors: 51 – {1, 3, **17**, 51} 85 – {1, 5, **17**, 85} 34 – {1, 2, **17**, 34} **82.** $64193 \div 23 = 2791$ **83.** $22523000 \div 1010 = 22300$ **84.** $73 \div 151 \approx 0.48344 \approx 0.48$ **85.** $7 \div 691 \approx 0.01013 \approx 0.01$

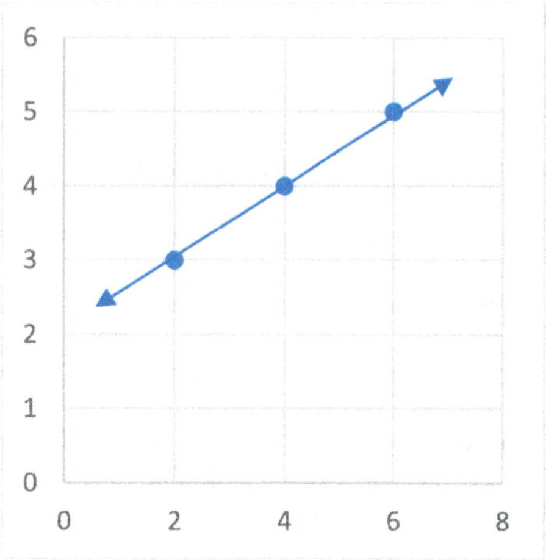

86.

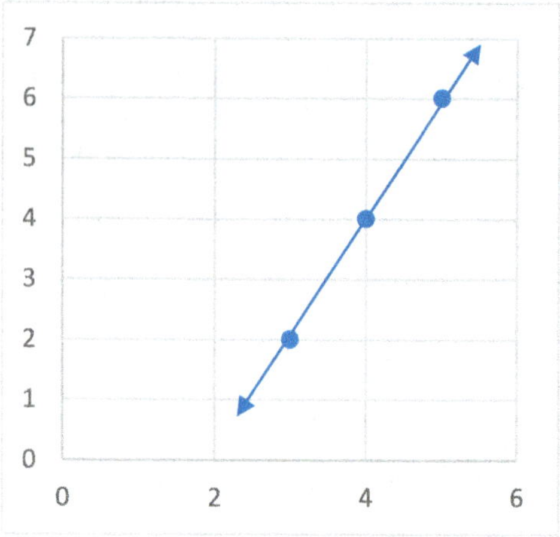

87.

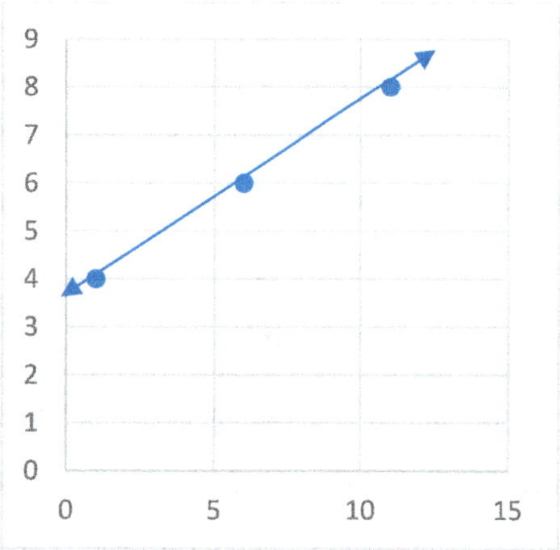

88.

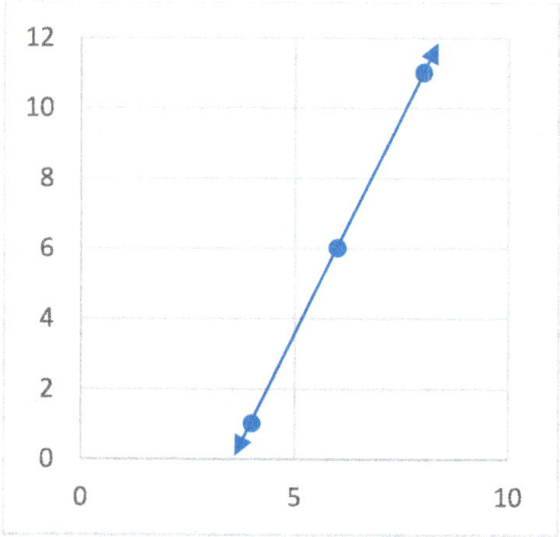

89.

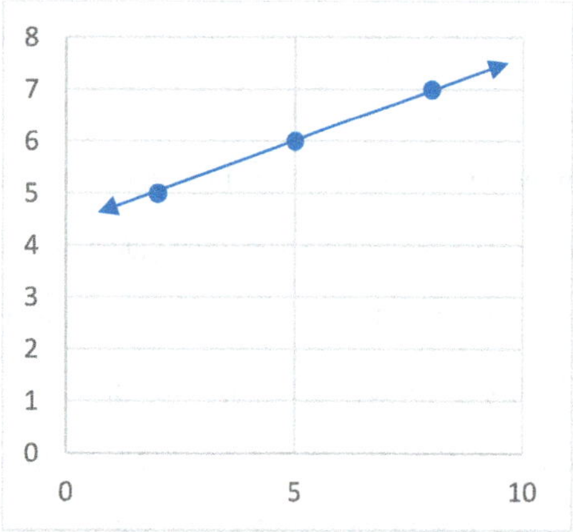

90.

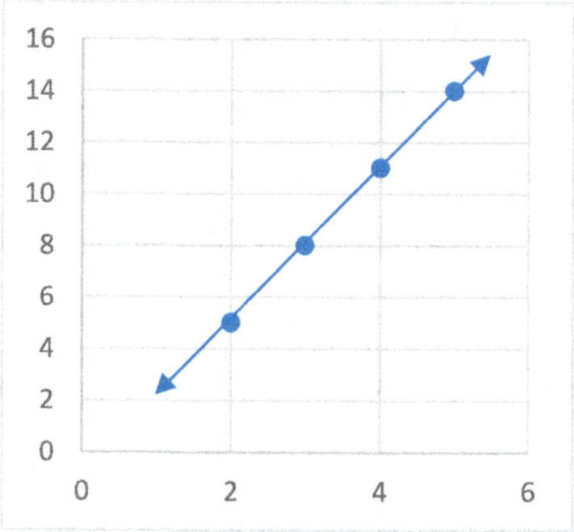

91.

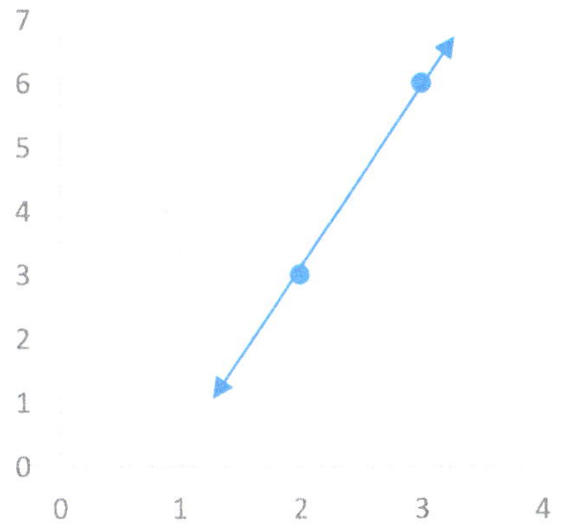

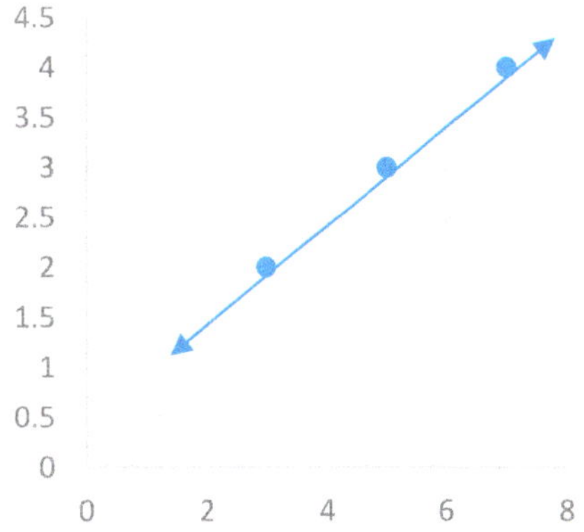

92.

93.

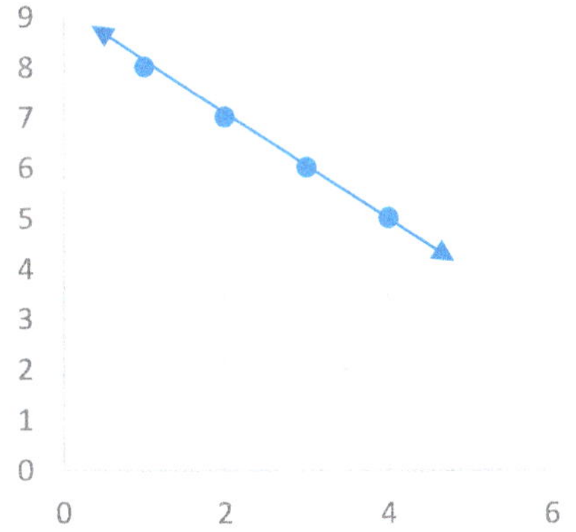

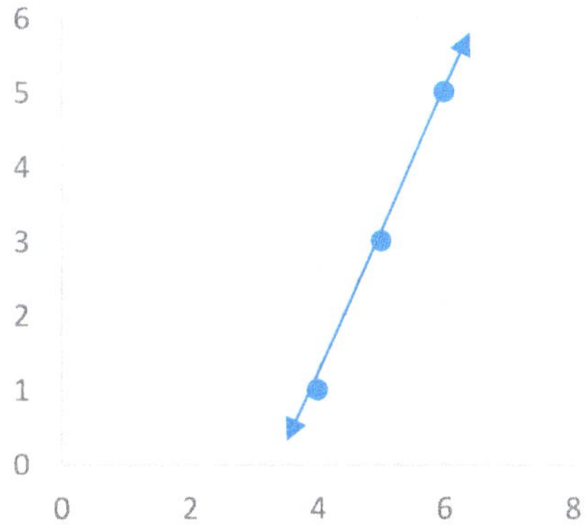

94.

95.

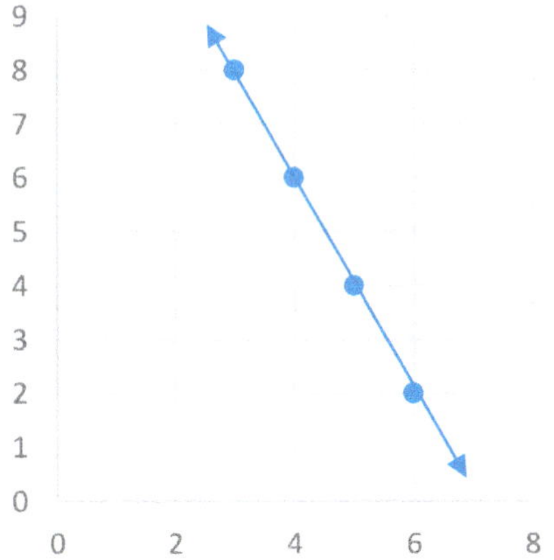

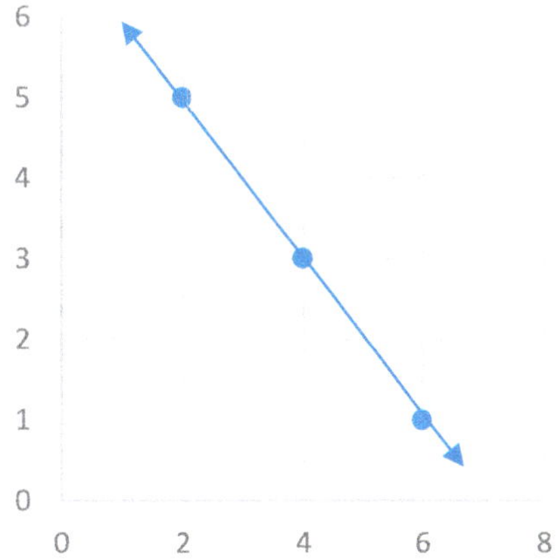

96.

97.

(Comment: The graphs in problems 86.-91. all move in an upward direction as the graphs go from left to right. The reason this occurs in all six graphs is because all the graphs have a positive slope. Notice in problems 92.-97. three of the lines go downward as the lines go from left to right. These lines have a negative slope.)

98. $m = \frac{rise}{run} = \frac{y_2-y_1}{x_2-x_1} = \frac{6-3}{3-2} = \frac{3}{1} = 3$ *or* $m = \frac{rise}{run} = \frac{y_2-y_1}{x_2-x_1} = \frac{3-6}{2-3} = \frac{-3}{-1} = 3$ The order of the "y" numbers in the numerator and the "x" values in the denominator is not important BUT it is important that matching "y" and "x" values are used in the same order in both the numerator and the denominator. **99.** It does not matter which two points are selected. We decided to select the following two points, (5, 3) and (7, 4). $m = \frac{rise}{run} = \frac{y_2-y_1}{x_2-x_1} = \frac{4-3}{7-5} = \frac{1}{2}$ or we could select the points, (3, 2) and (5, 3) $m = \frac{y_2-y_1}{x_2-x_1} = \frac{3-2}{5-3} = \frac{1}{2}$ or we could select the points, (3, 2) and (7, 4) $m = \frac{y_2-y_1}{x_2-x_1} = \frac{4-2}{7-3} = \frac{2}{4} = \frac{1}{2}$

Third Assignment:

1. A. Rational Number - Write your definition, then refer to the internet for an exact definition. Include in your explanation terms/words like the word fraction, how to form a fraction, a fraction is a number, etc. B. Examples of Rational Numbers - $\frac{3}{10}, \frac{-11}{101}, \frac{777}{-1}, etc.$ Examples of Irrational Numbers – $\sqrt{7}, \pi, \frac{\sqrt[3]{7}}{5}, etc.$ **2. A.** LCM - Write your definition, then refer to the internet for an exact definition. B. Basic explanation - Least means smallest, Common means a member of all sets of multiplies, Multiple means multiplication tables. C. Find the LCM for the two numbers "6 & 9". Set of Multiples of 6 – {6, 12, **18**, 24, ...} Set of multiples of 9 – {9, **18**, 27, ...} 18 is the LCM for the numbers "6 & 9". **3. A.** LCD - Write your definition, then refer to the internet for an exact definition. B. Basic explanation - Least means smallest, Common means a member of all sets of multiplies for the denominators of the given fractions, Denominator means focus on the multiplication tables for the denominator of the given fractions. C. Find the LCD for the two fractions "$\frac{5}{6}$ & $\frac{8}{9}$". Set of Multiples of the denominator 6 – {6, 12, **18**, 24, ...} Set of multiples of the denominator, 9 – {9, **18**, 27, ...} 18 is the LCD for the two denominators "6 & 9". **4. A.** GCF - Write your definition, then refer to the internet for an exact definition. B. Basic Explanation – Greatest means the largest, Common means a member of all the sets of factors for all the numbers involved, Factor means to write all the numbers which will divide into the given number and realize they are factors because if a number will divide perfectly into a number, then the number can be written using a multiplication problem involving two or more factors. C. Find the LCD for two or more numbers. Find LCD the numbers, "10, 15, 20". Set of Factors of 10 – {1, 2, **5**, 10}, Set of Factors of 15 – {1, 3, **5**, 15}, Set of Factors of 20 – {1, 2, 4, **5**, 10, 20}. The number "5" is the GCF. Find the LCD for the numerator and the denominator of the fraction, $\frac{10}{20}$. Write the set of factors of 10 – {1, 2, 5, **10**} and the set of factors of 20 – {1, 2, 4, 5, **10**, 20}. The number 10 is the GCF. **5. A.** Interleave - Write your definition, refer to the comments in this textbook, then refer to the internet for an exact definition. B. Examples: Simplify this fraction problem - $\frac{101}{207} + \frac{7}{207} - \frac{3}{207}$ (remember to reduce), Simplify this fraction problem - $\frac{5^2}{7} - \frac{3^2}{7}$ (remember to write the answer as a mixed number). **6. A.** Prime Numbers - Write your definition, then refer to the internet for an exact definition. B. Prime Numbers – {2, 3, 5, 7, 11, 13, 17, 19, ...}. Note: We do not consider negative Integers to be members of the set of Prime Numbers. **7. A.** Composite Numbers - Write your definition, then refer to the internet for an exact definition. B. Composite Numbers – {4, 6, 8, 9, 10, 12, 14, 15, 16, 18, 20, ...}. Note: We do not consider negative Integers to be members of the set of Composite Numbers although you may find some authors mention negative Integers when discussing Composite Numbers. (Refer to the Internet). **8.** A Prime Number has exactly two factors, the given number and 1. A Composite Number has at least three factors, the given number, the number 1, and at least one other factor. **9.** Mixed Number - Write your definition, then refer to the internet for an exact definition. Note: A mixed number can be either positive or negative. The Whole Number and the fraction represent an addition problem. If there is no sign to the left of the Whole Number, the entire expression is considered positive. If there is a negative sign to the left of the Whole Number, mathematicians consider both the whole number and the fraction to be negative numbers and you should add the two numbers and the answer is negative. The mixed number in both situations represents a single point on a number line. **10.** Improper Fraction - Write your definition, then refer to the internet for an exact definition. Note: An Improper Fraction can always be converted into a Mixed Number or Integer. The numerator of the fraction is always greater than or equal to the denominator, but make sure the denominator does NOT EQUAL 0. **11. A.** Absolute Value - Write your definition, then refer to the internet for an exact definition. Note: The number or expression inside the absolute value notation is always positive when the absolute value notation lines are removed. If there is a negative sign to the left of the absolute value notation lines (outside the absolute value expression) then the expression inside the absolute value notation initially becomes positive BUT the negative sign to the left of the absolute value notation makes the number or expression negative. B. What is the distance traveled in this situation if you start at point A, travel to point B and then return to point A? If city A is located on a number line at point 0, each space on the number line represents 1 mile, and city B is located at point 13, what is the total distance for the entire trip? Students should start at point 0, move to the right, and count the spaces until they reach the point at 13. Now move to the left, which is considered a negative direction back to the starting point 0. What is the total distance covered when you arrive back at the starting point, 0? Answer – 26 miles. Point of interest, you moved in a positive direction 13 miles and a negative direction of 13 miles, but the total distance was 26 miles and you ended up where you started, so when you finished your trip, you went nowhere.

12. a. $\frac{5}{7}, \frac{15}{79}, \frac{20}{35}, \frac{5}{13}, \frac{4}{5}, 0, \frac{32}{40}, \frac{5}{8}, \frac{8}{101}, \frac{10}{14}, \frac{10}{49}, 1, 8, 12, 2, 20$ b. $\frac{6}{7}, \frac{6}{79}, \frac{24}{42}, \frac{2}{13}, \frac{4}{9}, 0, \frac{35}{42}, \frac{3}{7}, \frac{11}{203}, \frac{15}{18}, \frac{12}{25}, 1, 12, 8, 5, 12$

c. $\frac{6}{7}, \frac{13}{79}, \frac{16}{28}, \frac{4}{13}, \frac{2}{9}, 0, \frac{12}{21}, \frac{7}{9}, \frac{15}{97}, \frac{20}{32}, \frac{9}{16}, 1, 18, 12, 2, 24$ d. $\frac{4}{7}, \frac{13}{79}, \frac{25}{30}, \frac{6}{17}, \frac{6}{11}, \frac{1}{8}, \frac{18}{48}, \frac{4}{9}, 10\frac{9}{55}, \frac{28}{4}, \frac{4}{25}, 1, 20, 30, 3, 20$

e. $\frac{4}{5}, \frac{1}{17}, \frac{42}{49}, \frac{12}{13}, \frac{5}{9}, \frac{1}{14}, \frac{30}{70}, 1, \frac{13}{1001}, \frac{16}{18}, \frac{12}{25}, \frac{6}{13}, 24, 12, 5, 30$ f. $\frac{5}{8}, \frac{7}{83}, \frac{20}{55}, \frac{11}{13}, 0, \frac{3}{10}, \frac{30}{48}, \frac{7}{11}, \frac{14}{53}, \frac{21}{27}, \frac{49}{81}, 0, 36, 24, 3, 24$

g. $\frac{8}{11}, \frac{7}{83}, \frac{45}{63}, \frac{5}{19}, \frac{2}{17}, \frac{2}{11}, \frac{90}{100}, \frac{3}{17}, 1, \frac{15}{25}, \frac{20}{49}, \frac{12}{13}, 36, 9, 24, 5$ h. $\frac{13}{14}, \frac{15}{101}, \frac{12}{33}, \frac{5}{17}, \frac{5}{13}, \frac{1}{10}, \frac{48}{54}, \frac{5}{23}, \frac{11}{47}, \frac{22}{99}, \frac{8}{121}, \frac{15}{17}, 36, 9, 30, 9$

i. $\frac{7}{10}, \frac{13}{80}, \frac{10}{15}, \frac{10}{13}, \frac{4}{25}, 0, \frac{12}{22}, \frac{4}{17}, \frac{17}{42}, \frac{15}{18}, \frac{15}{56}, \frac{10}{19}, 30, 8, 36, 12$ j. $\frac{7}{10}, \frac{13}{180}, \frac{63}{72}, \frac{12}{17}, \frac{7}{23}, 0, \frac{14}{26}, \frac{10}{29}, \frac{17}{42}, \frac{50}{60}, \frac{25}{56}, \frac{10}{17}, 60, 12, 72, 11$

k. $\frac{9}{11}, \frac{11}{60}, \frac{25}{45}, \frac{13}{19}, \frac{8}{25}, 1, \frac{21}{33}, 0, \frac{23}{42}, \frac{33}{36}, \frac{21}{64}, \frac{17}{19}, 18, 8, 30, 9$ l. $\frac{7}{50}, \frac{19}{89}, \frac{49}{63}, \frac{9}{11}, \frac{4}{25}, \frac{9}{10}, \frac{16}{26}, \frac{3}{13}, \frac{27}{52}, \frac{150}{180}, \frac{15}{88}, \frac{15}{23}, 20, 72, 4, 11$

13. A. 5 ft. B. Write how you would explain to students how to convert the number and the label. **14. A.** 10,080 min. B. Write how you would explain to students how to convert the number and the label. **15. A.** $\frac{5}{8} \times 1 = \frac{5}{8} \times \frac{9}{9} = \frac{45}{72}$ B. Explain why we multiply by 1 and why we multiplied by the fraction "$\frac{9}{9}$". **16. A.** $\frac{8}{9} \times 1 = \frac{8}{9} \times \frac{8}{8} = \frac{64}{72}$ B. Explain why we multiply by 1 and why we multiplied by the fraction "$\frac{8}{8}$" **17.** 55 mph $= \frac{55\ mi.}{1\ hr.} = \frac{4840\ ft.}{1\ min.}$ **18.** $\frac{3}{4} \times 1 = \frac{3}{4} \times \frac{3.5}{3.5} = \frac{10.5}{14}$ *or* $\frac{10\frac{1}{2}}{14}$ **19.** Prime Factors: $12 = 2 \times 2 \times 3$ or $12 = 2^2 \times 3$ **20.** Prime Factors: 20 - $20 = 2 \times 2 \times 5$ or $20 = 2^2 \times 5$ **21.** $100 = 2 \times 2 \times 5 \times 5$ or $100 = 2^2 \times 5^2$

22. 7392

2×3696

$2 \times 2 \times 1848$

$2 \times 2 \times 2 \times 924$ Factors for 5629 – 13×433

$2 \times 2 \times 2 \times 2 \times 462$ Fraction - $\frac{5629}{7392} = \frac{13 \times 433}{2^5 \times 3 \times 7 \times 11}$

$2 \times 2 \times 2 \times 2 \times 2 \times 231$ No identical factors in the two numbers.

$2 \times 2 \times 2 \times 2 \times 2 \times 3 \times 77$

$2 \times 2 \times 2 \times 2 \times 2 \times 3 \times 7 \times 11$ or $2^5 \times 3 \times 7 \times 11$

23. $\frac{7}{11} = \frac{x}{88}$ *because* $\frac{88}{11} = 8$ $\therefore$ $\frac{8}{8} = \mathbf{1}$

$\frac{7}{11} = \frac{7}{11} \times \mathbf{1} = \frac{7}{11} \times \frac{\mathbf{8}}{\mathbf{8}} = \frac{56}{88}$

24. $\frac{7}{15} = \frac{21}{x}$ $\frac{21}{7} = 3$ $\therefore$ $\frac{3}{3} = \mathbf{1}$

$\frac{7}{15} = \frac{7}{15} \times \mathbf{1} = \frac{7}{15} \times \frac{3}{3} = \frac{21}{45}$

25. $\frac{47}{53} = \frac{47}{53} \times 1 = \frac{47}{53} \times \frac{5}{5} = \frac{235}{265}$

26. $\frac{107}{319} = \frac{107}{319} \times \mathbf{1} = \frac{107}{319} \times \frac{5}{5} = \frac{535}{1595}$

27. $\frac{3}{4} = \frac{?}{14}$ $\frac{14}{4} = 3\frac{2}{4} = 3\frac{1}{2}$ *or* 3.5

$\frac{3}{4} = \frac{3}{4} \times \mathbf{1} = \frac{3}{4} \times \frac{3.5}{3.5} = \frac{10.5}{14}$

28. A. $3\frac{1}{2} = \frac{7}{2}$ B. Most people will say multiply the denominator "2" times the whole number "3" and add the numerator "1" to get the new numerator "7". C. Explain how the number "$3\frac{1}{2} = 1 + 1 + 1 + \frac{1}{2} = \frac{2}{2} + \frac{2}{2} + \frac{2}{2} + \frac{1}{2} = \frac{7}{2}$". **29. A.** $\frac{49}{8} = 6\frac{1}{8}$ B. Divide the numerator "49" by the denominator "8" to determine the whole number "6" and the remainder is "1", therefore the fraction in the solution is "$\frac{1}{8}$". We would expect you to discuss the illustration in problem 28. C. to illustrate why the division remainder procedure works. **30.** $\frac{7360}{19} = 387\frac{7}{19}$ 31. $13\frac{7}{113} = \frac{1476}{113}$

32. A.

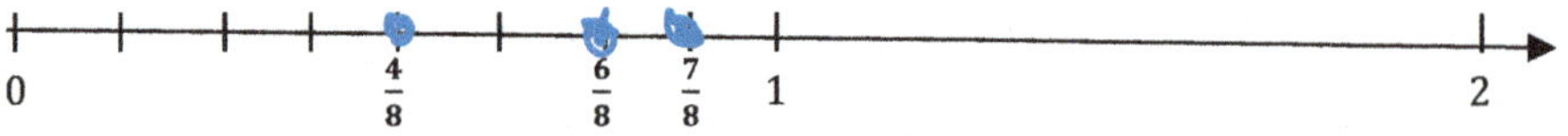

32. A. You must know that "$\frac{1}{2} = \frac{4}{8}$ *and* $\frac{3}{4} = \frac{6}{8}$ B. $\frac{1}{2} < \frac{3}{4} < \frac{7}{8}$ C. $\frac{7}{8} \geq \frac{3}{4} > \geq \frac{1}{2}$ **33. A.** Graph on a horizontal number line reference the directions. B. $\frac{3}{4} < \frac{7}{8} < \frac{9}{10} < \frac{99}{100}$ C. $\frac{99}{100} \geq \frac{9}{10} \geq \frac{7}{8} \geq \frac{3}{4}$ **34. A.** Graph on a horizontal number line reference the directions. B. $1\frac{99}{100} < 3\frac{3}{5} < 3\frac{5}{8} < 3\frac{7}{8} < 5\frac{7}{9} < 5\frac{7}{8}$ C. $5\frac{7}{8} \geq 5\frac{7}{9} \geq 3\frac{7}{8} \geq 3\frac{5}{8} \geq 3\frac{3}{5} \geq 1\frac{99}{100}$

35. A. 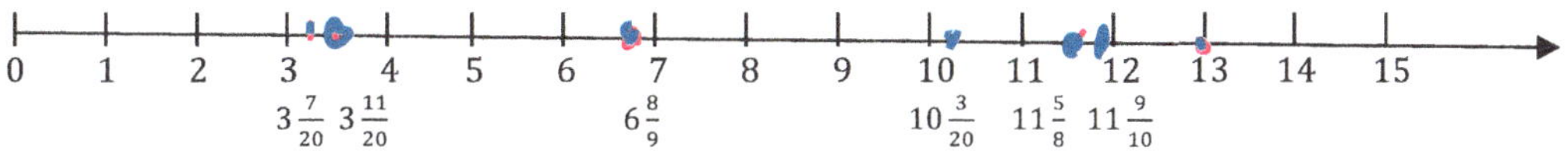

35. A. Graph on a horizontal number line reference the directions. B. $3\frac{7}{20} < 3\frac{11}{20} < 6\frac{8}{9} < 10\frac{3}{20} < 11\frac{5}{8} < 11\frac{9}{10} < 13$ C. $13 \geq 11\frac{9}{10} \geq 11\frac{5}{8} \geq 10\frac{3}{20} \geq 6\frac{8}{9} \geq 3\frac{11}{20} \geq 3\frac{7}{20}$ **36.** Multiples of 8, 10, & 6: 8 – {8, 16, 24, 32, 40, 48, 56, 64, 72, 80, 88, 96, 104, 112, **120**, 128, ...}; 10 – {10, 20, 30, 40, 50, 60, 70, 80, 90, 100, 110, **120**, 130, ...}; 6 – {6, 12, 18, 24, 30, 36, 42, 48, 54, 60, 66, 72, 78, 84, 90, 96, 102, 108, 114, **120**, 126, ...} $\therefore$ $LCM = 120$. **37.** 8 – {8, 16, **24**, 32, ...}; 24 – {**24**, 48, 72, ...}; 6 – {6, 12, 18, **24**, 30, ...} $\therefore$ $LCD = 24$. **38.** 4 – (4, 8, **12**, 16, ...}; 6 – {6, **12**, 18, ...} $\therefore$ $LCM = 12$. **39.** 7 – (7, **14**, 21, ...}; 14 – {**14**, 28, 42, ...} $\therefore$ $LCD = 14$. **40.** $LCM = 72$. **41.** 8 – {8, 16, **24**, 32, ...}; 12 – {12, **24**, 36, ...}; 4 – {4, 8, 12, 16, 20, **24**, 28, ...}; 3 – {3, 6, 9, 12, 15, 18, 21, **24**, 27, ...}; $\therefore$ $LCD = 24$. **42.** LCM = 150. **43.** 10 – {10, 20, **30**, 50, ...}; 5 – {5, 10, 15, 20, 25, **30**, 35, ...}; 15 – {15, **30**, 45, ...}; 3 – {3, 6, 9, 12, 15, 18, 24, 27, **30**, 33, ...}; $\therefore$ $30 = LCD$. (Problems 44-67 write all the steps as we indicated in several of the solutions even though we skipped a few steps in some problems.) **44.** $\frac{3}{11} + \frac{7}{11} = \frac{3+7}{11} = \frac{10}{11}$ **45.** $LCD = 6$ $\frac{2}{3} + \frac{1}{6} = \frac{4}{6} + \frac{1}{6} = \frac{4+1}{6} = \frac{5}{6}$ **46.** $\frac{3}{8} - \frac{2}{8} = \frac{3-2}{8} = \frac{1}{8}$ **47.** $LCD = 8$ $\frac{3}{4} - \frac{1}{8} = \frac{6}{8} - \frac{1}{8} = \frac{6-1}{8} = \frac{5}{8}$ **48.** $\frac{321-292+661-595}{1001} = \frac{95}{1001}$ **49.** $LCD = 24$ $\frac{5}{8} + \frac{5}{8} - \frac{5}{12} + |\frac{-3}{24}| = \frac{5}{8} + \frac{5}{8} - \frac{5}{12} + \frac{3}{24} = \frac{15}{24} + \frac{15}{24} - \frac{10}{24} + \frac{3}{24} = \frac{15+15-10+3}{24} = \frac{23}{24}$ **50.** $LCD = 12$ $\frac{10}{12} - \frac{3}{12} + \frac{4}{12} = \frac{10-3+4}{12} = \frac{11}{12}$ **51.** $\frac{8}{15}$ **52.** $\frac{43}{59}$ **53.** $\frac{12}{6} = 2$ **54.** $LCD = 15$ $3\frac{1}{5} + 5\frac{1}{3} = \frac{16}{5} + \frac{16}{3} = \frac{48}{15} + \frac{80}{15} = \frac{48+80}{15} = \frac{128}{15} = 8\frac{8}{15}$ **55.** $LCD = 4$ $7\frac{1}{4} - 2\frac{1}{2} = \frac{29}{4} - \frac{5}{2} = \frac{29}{4} - \frac{10}{4} = \frac{20-10}{4} = \frac{19}{4} = 4\frac{3}{4}$ **56.** $5\frac{3}{11} + 7\frac{3}{11} = \frac{3}{11} + \frac{3}{11} + 5 + 7 = \frac{3+3}{11} + 5 + 7 = \frac{6}{11} + 12 = 12\frac{6}{11}$ **57.** $4\frac{3}{11} + 1\frac{6}{11} + 5\frac{2}{11} = \frac{3}{11} + \frac{6}{11} + \frac{2}{11} + 4 + 1 + 5 = \frac{3+6+2}{11} + 4 + 1 + 5 = \frac{11}{11} + 4 + 1 + 5 = 1 + 4 + 1 + 5 = 11$ **58.** $8\frac{3}{7} - 5\frac{2}{7} = \frac{3}{7} - \frac{2}{7} + 8 - 5 = \frac{3-2}{7} + 8 - 5 = \frac{1}{7} + 8 - 5 = 3\frac{1}{7}$ **59.** 0 **60.** $5\frac{1}{8}$ **61.** 16 **62.** $20\frac{9}{7} = 20 + \frac{9}{7} = 20 + 1\frac{2}{7} = 21\frac{2}{7}$ **63.** $LCD = 18$ $6\frac{5}{9} + 11\frac{7}{18} - 3\frac{1}{3} = \frac{5}{9} + \frac{7}{18} - \frac{1}{3} + 6 + 11 - 3 = \frac{10}{18} + \frac{7}{18} - \frac{6}{18} + 6 + 11 - 3 = \frac{10+7-6}{18} + 6 + 11 - 3 = \frac{11}{18} + 14 = 14\frac{11}{18}$ **64.** $11\frac{1}{5} - 6\frac{4}{5} = 10 + 1\frac{1}{5} - 6\frac{4}{5} = 10 + 1 + \frac{1}{5} - 6\frac{4}{5} = 10 + \frac{5}{5} + \frac{1}{5} - 6 - \frac{4}{5} = \frac{5+1-4}{5} + 10 - 6 = \frac{2}{5} + 4 = 4\frac{2}{5}$ **65.** $LCD = 6$ $10\frac{1}{2} - 5\frac{2}{3} = 10\frac{3}{6} - 5\frac{4}{6} = 9 + 1 + \frac{3}{6} - 5 - \frac{4}{6} = 9 + \frac{6}{6} + \frac{3}{6} - 5 - \frac{4}{6} = \frac{6+3-4}{6} + 9 - 5 = \frac{5}{6} + 4 = 4\frac{5}{6}$ **66.** $\frac{1}{5} + \frac{4}{5} - \frac{3}{5} - \frac{3}{5} + 13 + 9 - 0 - 1 = \frac{5}{5} - \frac{6}{5} + 21 = 1 - \frac{6}{5} + 21 = 1 + 21 - 1\frac{1}{5} = 1 + 21 - 1 - \frac{1}{5} = 1 + (21 - 1) - \frac{1}{5} = 1 + 20 - \frac{1}{5} = \frac{5}{5} - \frac{1}{5} + 20 = 20\frac{4}{5}$ (The great thing about arithmetic and math is there is frequently more than one way to simplify/solve a problem. This is only a suggestion of a solution.) **67.** $5\frac{1}{12}$

Problems **68.- 71.** Focus on the denominators of the fractions.

68. 12	18		**69.** 15	20	25	
2×6	2×9	Not the LCD - 2×3		2×10		Not the LCD - $2 \times 3 \times 5$
$2 \times 2 \times 3$	$2 \times 3 \times 3$	$LCD = 2^2 \times 3^2 = 36$	3×5	$2 \times 2 \times 5$	5×5	$LCD = 2^2 \times 3 \times 5^2 = 300$

70. 12 18 72

2×36

$2 \times 2 \times 18$

$2 \times 2 \times 2 \times 9$

$2 \times 2 \times 2 \times 3 \times 3$

$2^2 \times 3$ 2×3^2 $2^3 \times 3^2$

Not the LCD - 2×3 $LCD = 2^3 \times 3^2 = 72$

71. 12 18 24 48

2×24

$2 \times 2 \times 12$

$2 \times 2 \times 2 \times 6$

$2 \times 2 \times 2 \times 2 \times 3$

$2^2 \times 3$ 2×3^2 $2^3 \times 3$ $2^4 \times 3$

Not the LCD - 2×3 $LCD = 2^4 \times 3^2 = 144$

72. We hope we never used slanted lines unless we are illustrating why we think slanted lines make fraction problems more difficult. **73.** $\frac{1}{8}$ **74.** $\frac{1}{115}$

Fourth Assignment:

1. Rewrite what was just explained, then use the internet to further understand the *Fundamental Theorem of Arithmetic.*

2. 105

3×35

$3 \times 5 \times 7$

3. 4040

2×2020

$2 \times 2 \times 1010$

$2 \times 2 \times 2 \times 505$

$2 \times 2 \times 2 \times 5 \times 101$

4. 10250

2×5125

$2 \times 5 \times 1025$

$2 \times 5 \times 5 \times 205$

$2 \times 5 \times 5 \times 5 \times 41$

5. A. The number "8" is not a prime number. B. No: The numbers "6 & 4" are not prime numbers. No: The number "12" is not a prime number. No: The numbers "1 & 24" are not prime numbers.

1. The number "1" is not a prime number.

7. 82

2×41

8. 144

2×72

$2 \times 2 \times 36$

$2 \times 2 \times 2 \times 18$

$2 \times 2 \times 2 \times 2 \times 9$

$2 \times 2 \times 2 \times 2 \times 3 \times 3$

9. 300

2×150

$2 \times 2 \times 75$

$2 \times 2 \times 3 \times 25$

$2 \times 2 \times 3 \times 5 \times 5$

10. 400

2×200

$2 \times 2 \times 100$

$2 \times 2 \times 2 \times 50$

$2 \times 2 \times 2 \times 2 \times 25$

$2 \times 2 \times 2 \times 2 \times 5 \times 5$

11. 500

2×250

$2 \times 2 \times 125$

$2 \times 2 \times 5 \times 25$

$2 \times 2 \times 5 \times 5 \times 5$

12. 150

2×75

$2 \times 3 \times 25$

$2 \times 3 \times 5 \times 5$

13. 98

2×49

$2 \times 7 \times 7$

14. 361

19×19

15. 7 **16.** 7 **17.** 7 **18.** 5 **19.** 7 **20.** 11 **21.** 13 **22.** 13 **23.** 17 **24.** 17 **25.** 19 **26.** 29

27. Prime – 97, 67, 419, 907 Composite – 51, 45, 105, 129, 171, 221, 297, 351

28. $51 = 3 \times 17$ $45 = 3 \times 3 \times 5$ $105 = 3 \times 5 \times 7$ $129 = 3 \times 43$ $171 = 3 \times 3 \times 19$ $221 = 13 \times 17$ $297 = 3 \times 3 \times 3 \times 11$ $351 = 3 \times 3 \times 3 \times 13$

29. $45=3^2\times 5$ **30.** $90=2\times 3^2\times 5$ **31.** $200=2^3\times 5^2$ **32.** $292=2^2\times 73$ **33.** $2275=5^2\times 91$

34. $1800=2^3\times 3^2\times 5^2$ **35.** $1764=2^2\times 3^2\times 7^2$ **36.** $10000=2^4\times 5^4$ **37. A.** GCF=5

B. $\frac{5}{45}=\frac{1}{9}$ **38. A.** GCF=4 B. $\frac{8}{28}=\frac{2}{7}$ **39. A.** GCF=11 B. $\frac{33}{55}=\frac{3}{5}$ **40. A.** GCF=18 B. $\frac{36}{54}=\frac{2}{3}$ **41. A.** GCF=8 B. $\frac{24}{40}=\frac{3}{5}$

42. A. GCF=2 B. $\frac{14}{16}=\frac{7}{8}$ **43. A.** GCF=3 B. $\frac{9}{33}=\frac{3}{11}$ **44. A.** GCF=7 B. $\frac{28}{35}=\frac{4}{5}$ **45. A.** GCF=9 B. $\frac{18}{63}=\frac{2}{7}$ **46.** $\frac{1}{2}$

47. 21 **48.** $\frac{2}{3}$ **49.** $\frac{5}{7}$ **50.** $\frac{b}{2}$ **51.** 45 90 **52.** 18 39 **53.** 25 70 **54.** $\frac{54}{81}=\frac{2\times3\times3\times3}{3\times3\times3\times3}=\frac{2}{3}$

59. 24 **60.** 36 **61.** 20 5×9 2×45 2×9 3×13 5×5 2×35 **55.** $\frac{125}{150}=\frac{5\times5\times5}{2\times3\times5\times5}=\frac{5}{6}$

62. 40 **63.** 40 $5\times 3\times 3$ $2\times 5\times 9$ $2\times 3\times 3$ $2\times 5\times 7$ **56.** $\frac{45}{80}=\frac{3\times3\times5}{2\times2\times2\times2\times5}=\frac{9}{16}$

64. 24 **65.** 60 **66.** 60 $2\times 5\times 3\times 3$ **57.** $\frac{93}{186}=\frac{3\times31}{2\times3\times31}=\frac{1}{2}$

67. 8 **68.** 1600 $\frac{45}{90}=\frac{5\times3\times3}{2\times5\times3\times3}=\frac{1}{2}$ $\frac{18}{39}=\frac{2\times3\times3}{3\times13}=\frac{6}{13}$ $\frac{25}{70}=\frac{5\times5}{2\times5\times7}=\frac{5}{14}$ **58.** $\frac{162}{189}=\frac{2\times3^4}{3^3\times7}=\frac{6}{7}$

69. $2^2\times 3\times 5\times 7^2=2940$ **70.** $2^2\times 7^2=196$ **71.** $2^2\times 3\times 5^3=1500$ **72.** $2^4\times 3\times 5^2=1200$

73. $xxx\cdot yy\cdot zzzz=x^3y^2z^4$ **74.** $aabbbc(x+9)(x+9)(8-y)=a^2b^3c(x+9)^2(8-y)$

75. $2\cdot3\cdot3\cdot3\cdot5\cdot5\cdot m\cdot m\cdot m\cdot n\cdot n\cdot n\cdot n\cdot(x+y)\cdot(x+y)=2\cdot3^3\cdot5^2\cdot m^3n^4(x+y)^2=1350m^3n^4(x+y)^2$

Problems 76-83 only focus on the denominators. **76.** 64 48

77. 50 80 30 25 **78.** 6 <u>2</u> 14 **79.** 10 15 20 <u>5</u> <u>1</u> 2×32 2×24

2×25 2×40 2×15 <u>5×5</u> <u>2×3</u> <u>2×7</u> <u>2×5</u> <u>3×5</u> 2×10 $2\times 2\times 16$ $2\times 2\times 12$

<u>$2\times 5\times 5$</u> $2\times 2\times 20$ <u>$2\times 3\times 5$</u> <u>$2\times 2\times 5$</u> $2\cdot2\cdot2\cdot8$ $2\cdot2\cdot2\cdot6$

$2\cdot2\cdot2\cdot10$ $LCD\ 6,2,14=2\cdot3\cdot7=42$ $2\cdot2\cdot2\cdot2\cdot4$ $2\cdot2\cdot2\cdot2\cdot3$

<u>$2\cdot2\cdot2\cdot2\cdot5$</u> $LCD\ 10,15,20,5,1=2^2\cdot3\cdot5=60$ <u>$2\cdot2\cdot2\cdot2\cdot2\cdot2$</u>

$LCD\ 50,80,30,25=2^4\cdot3\cdot5^2=1200$ $LCD\ 64,48=2^6\cdot3=192$

80. 15 18 **81.** 99 121 66 **82.** 24 40 60 30 1 **83.** 9 12

$LCD\ 15,18=2\cdot3\cdot3\cdot5=90$ $LCD\ 24,40,60,30,1=2^3\cdot3\cdot5=120$

$LCD\ 99,121,66=2\times3^2\times11^2=2178$ $LCD\ 9,12=2^2\times3^2=36$

84. $\frac{3}{20}+\frac{3}{10}-\frac{7}{30}$ $20=2\cdot10=2\cdot2\cdot5$ $10=2\cdot5$ $30=2\cdot3\cdot5$ $\therefore$ $LCD\ 20,10,30=2^2\cdot3\cdot5=60$

Determine 3 values of <u>1</u> to multiply each fraction. $\frac{60}{20}=3\ \therefore\ \frac{3}{3}=1$ $\frac{60}{10}=6\ \therefore\ \frac{6}{6}=1$ $\frac{60}{30}=2\ \therefore\ \frac{2}{2}=1$

Multiply each fraction by <u>1</u> to find 3 equivalent fractions for the 3 given fractions.

$\frac{3}{20}=\frac{3}{20}\times1=\frac{3}{20}\times\frac{3}{3}=\frac{9}{60}$ $\frac{3}{10}=\frac{3}{10}\times1=\frac{3}{10}\times\frac{6}{6}=\frac{18}{60}$ $\frac{7}{30}=\frac{7}{30}\times1=\frac{7}{30}\times\frac{2}{2}=\frac{14}{60}$

$\therefore\ \frac{3}{20}=\frac{9}{60}$ $\therefore\ \frac{3}{10}=\frac{18}{60}$ $\therefore\ \frac{7}{30}=\frac{14}{60}$

$\frac{3}{20}+\frac{3}{10}-\frac{7}{30}=\frac{9}{60}+\frac{18}{60}-\frac{14}{60}=\frac{9+18-14}{60}=\frac{13}{60}$

85. $\frac{11}{54}-\frac{5}{36}$ $54 = 2\times 27 = 2\times 3\times 9 = 2\times 3\times 3\times 3$ $36 = 2\times 18 = 2\times 2\times 9 = 2\times 2\times 3\times 3$

$\therefore$ $LCD\ 54, 36 = 2^2\cdot 3^3 = 108$ Determine 2 values of 1 to multiply each fraction.

$\frac{108}{54} = 2$ $\therefore$ $\frac{2}{2} = 1$ $\frac{108}{36} = 3$ $\therefore$ $\frac{3}{3} = 1$ Multiply both fractions by 1 to find 2 equivalent fractions.

$\frac{11}{54} = \frac{11}{54}\times 1 = \frac{11}{54}\times\frac{2}{2} = \frac{11\times 2}{54\times 2} = \frac{22}{108}$ $\therefore$ $\frac{5}{54} = \frac{22}{108}$ $\frac{5}{36} = \frac{5}{36}\times 1 = \frac{5}{36}\times\frac{3}{3} = \frac{5\times 3}{36\times 3} = \frac{15}{108}$ $\therefore$ $\frac{5}{36} = \frac{15}{108}$

$\frac{11}{54}-\frac{5}{36} = \frac{22}{108}-\frac{15}{108} = \frac{22-15}{108} = \frac{7}{108}$ (The fraction, $\frac{7}{108}$ has no common factors to reduce. $\frac{7}{108} = \frac{7}{2\cdot 2\times 3\cdot 3\cdot 3}$)

86. All steps indicated with no short cuts. The previous two example solutions were condensed solutions.

$\frac{5}{12}-\frac{7}{30}+\frac{7}{15}+\frac{7}{20}$ Factor Trees 12 30 15 20 *This is the preferred notation to*

2×6 2×15 3×5 2×10 *write when illustrating to students*

$2\times 2\times 3$ $2\times 3\times 5$ 3×5 $2\times 2\times 5$ *how to solve these problems.*

$LCD\ 12, 30, 15, 20 = 2\times 2\times 3\times 5 = 2^2\times 3\times 5 = 60$

Since the LCD = 60, determine the 4 specific values of 1 to multiply each of the given fractions, then multiply each fraction by the fraction which equals 1 for each situation.

$\frac{60}{12} = 5$ $\therefore$ $5 = 5$ & $\frac{5}{5} = 1$ $\frac{60}{30} = 2$ $\therefore$ $2 = 2$ & $\frac{2}{2} = 1$

$\frac{5}{12} = \frac{5}{12}\times 1 = \frac{5}{12}\times\frac{5}{5} = \frac{5\times 5}{12\times 5} = \frac{25}{60}$ $\therefore$ $\frac{\mathbf{5}}{\mathbf{12}} = \frac{\mathbf{25}}{\mathbf{60}}$ $\frac{7}{30} = \frac{7}{30}\times 1 = \frac{7}{30}\times\frac{2}{2} = \frac{7\times 2}{30\times 2} = \frac{14}{60}$ $\therefore$ $\frac{\mathbf{7}}{\mathbf{30}} = \frac{\mathbf{14}}{\mathbf{60}}$

$\frac{60}{15} = 4$ $\therefore$ $4 = 4$ & $\frac{4}{4} = 1$ $\frac{60}{20} = 3$ $\therefore$ $3 = 3$ & $\frac{3}{3} = 1$

$\frac{7}{15} = \frac{7}{15}\times 1 = \frac{7}{15}\times\frac{4}{4} = \frac{7\times 4}{15\times 4} = \frac{28}{60}$ $\therefore$ $\frac{\mathbf{7}}{\mathbf{15}} = \frac{\mathbf{28}}{\mathbf{60}}$ $\frac{7}{20} = \frac{7}{20}\times 1 = \frac{7}{20}\times\frac{3}{3} = \frac{7\times 3}{20\times 3} = \frac{21}{60}$ $\therefore$ $\frac{\mathbf{7}}{\mathbf{20}} = \frac{\mathbf{21}}{\mathbf{60}}$

$\frac{5}{12}-\frac{7}{30}+\frac{7}{15}+\frac{7}{20} = \frac{25}{60}-\frac{14}{60}+\frac{28}{60}+\frac{21}{60} = \frac{25-14+28+21}{60} = \frac{60}{60} = 1$

87. $\frac{7}{8}-\frac{7}{28}-\frac{7}{36}-\frac{1}{45}+\frac{1001}{1260}$ Factors for the denominators 8, 28, 36, 45, 1260. $8 = 2\cdot 2\cdot 2 = 2^3$

$28 = 2\cdot 2\cdot 7 = 2^2\times 7$ $36 = 2\times 2\times 3\times 3 = 2^2\times 3^2$

$45 = 3\cdot 3\cdot 5 = 3^2\cdot 5$ $1260 = 2\times 2\times 3\times 3\times 5\times 7 = 2^2\times 3^2\times 5\times 7$

$LCD\ 8, 28, 36, 45, 1260 = 2\times 2\times 2\times 3\times 3\times 5\times 7 = 2520$

$\frac{2520}{8} = 315$ $\therefore$ $315 = 315$ & $\frac{315}{315} = 1$ $\frac{2520}{28} = 90$ $\therefore$ $90 = 90$ & $\frac{90}{90} = 1$ $\frac{2520}{36} = 70$ $\therefore$ $70 = 70$ & $\frac{70}{70} = 1$

$\frac{2520}{45} = 56$ $\therefore$ $56 = 56$ & $\frac{56}{56} = 1$ $\frac{2520}{1260} = 2$ $\therefore$ $2 = 2$ & $\frac{2}{2} = 1$

$\frac{7}{8} = \frac{7}{8}\times 1 = \frac{7}{8}\times\frac{315}{315} = \frac{7\times 315}{8\times 315} = \frac{2205}{2520}$ $\frac{7}{28} = \frac{7}{28}\times 1 = \frac{7}{28}\times\frac{90}{90} = \frac{7\times 90}{28\times 90} = \frac{630}{2520}$

$\frac{7}{36} = \frac{7}{36}\times 1 = \frac{7}{36}\times\frac{70}{70} = \frac{7\times 70}{36\times 70} = \frac{490}{2520}$ $\frac{1}{45} = \frac{1}{45}\times 1 = \frac{1}{45}\times\frac{56}{56} = \frac{1\times 56}{45\times 56} = \frac{56}{2520}$

$\frac{1001}{1260} = \frac{1001}{1260}\times 1 = \frac{1001}{1260}\times\frac{2}{2} = \frac{1001\times 2}{1260\times 2} = \frac{2002}{2520}$

$\frac{7}{8}-\frac{7}{28}-\frac{7}{36}-\frac{1}{45}+\frac{1001}{1260} = \frac{2205}{2520}-\frac{630}{2520}-\frac{490}{2520}-\frac{56}{2520}+\frac{2002}{2520} = \frac{2205-630-490-56+2002}{2520} = \frac{3031}{2520} = \frac{7\times 433}{7\times 360} = \frac{433}{360} = 1\frac{73}{360}$

88. $-\frac{1}{6}+\frac{7}{20}+3=-\frac{1}{6}+\frac{7}{20}+\frac{3}{1}$ Factors for the denominators 6, 20, 1. $6=2\times3$ $20=2\times2\times5$

$\mathbf{1}$ *is not a Prime Number or a Composite Number, therefore there are no Prime Factors for* $\mathbf{1}$.

$$LCD\ 6,20,1=2\times2\times3\times5=2^2\times3\times5=60$$

$$\frac{60}{6}=10 \therefore 10=10\ \&\ \frac{10}{10}=1 \quad \frac{60}{20}=3 \therefore 3=3\ \&\ \frac{3}{3}=1 \quad \frac{60}{1}=60 \therefore 60=60\ \&\ \frac{60}{60}=1$$

$$\frac{1}{6}=\frac{1}{6}\times1=\frac{1}{6}\times\frac{10}{10}=\frac{1\times10}{6\times10}=\frac{10}{60} \therefore \frac{1}{6}=\frac{10}{60} \quad \frac{7}{20}=\frac{7}{20}\times1=\frac{7}{20}\times\frac{3}{3}=\frac{7\times3}{20\times3}=\frac{21}{60} \therefore \frac{7}{20}=\frac{21}{60}$$

$$3=\frac{3}{1}=\frac{3}{1}\times1=\frac{3}{1}\times\frac{60}{60}=\frac{3\times60}{60}=\frac{180}{60} \quad \therefore\ 3=\frac{180}{60}$$

$-\frac{1}{6}+\frac{7}{20}+3=-\frac{1}{6}+\frac{7}{20}+\frac{3}{1}=-\frac{10}{60}+\frac{21}{60}+\frac{180}{60}=\frac{-10+21+180}{60}=\frac{191}{60}=3\frac{11}{60}$ We encourage you to illustrate how to simplify this problem without converting the whole number 3 into the improper fraction, $\frac{180}{60}$.

89. $2\frac{3}{14}+3\frac{11}{21}-1\frac{9}{28}=\frac{31}{14}+\frac{74}{21}-\frac{37}{28}$ Factors for the denominators 14, 21, 28. $14=2\times7$ $21=3\times7$

$$28=2\times14=2\times2\times7 \qquad LCD\ 14,21,28=2\times2\times3\times7=84$$

$$\frac{84}{14}=6 \therefore 6=6\ \&\ \frac{6}{6}=1 \quad \frac{84}{21}=4 \therefore 4=4\ \&\ \frac{4}{4}=1 \quad \frac{84}{28}=3 \therefore 3=3\ \&\ \frac{3}{3}=1$$

$$2\frac{3}{14}=\frac{31}{14}=\frac{31}{14}\times1=\frac{31}{14}\times\frac{6}{6}=\frac{31\times6}{14\times6}=\frac{186}{84} \qquad 3\frac{11}{21}=\frac{74}{21}=\frac{74}{21}\times1=\frac{74}{21}\times\frac{4}{4}=\frac{74\times4}{21\times4}=\frac{296}{84}$$

$$1\frac{9}{28}=\frac{37}{28}=\frac{37}{28}\times1=\frac{37}{28}\times\frac{3}{3}=\frac{37\times3}{28\times3}=\frac{111}{84}$$

$$2\frac{3}{14}+3\frac{11}{21}-1\frac{9}{28}=\frac{31}{14}+\frac{74}{21}-\frac{37}{28}=\frac{186}{84}+\frac{296}{84}-\frac{111}{84}=\frac{186+296-111}{84}=\frac{371}{84}=4\frac{35}{84}=4\frac{5\times7}{7\times12}=4\frac{5}{12}$$

We encourage you to illustrate how to solve this problem using mixed numbers and not converting the given mixed numbers into improper fractions at the beginning of the solution.

90.	**91.**	**92.**	**93.**
$x+3=\ 6$	$p+101=\ 201$	$909=z-11$	$5y=55$
$\underline{-3=-3}$	$\underline{-101=-101}$	$\underline{+11=\ +11}$	$5\ =5$
$x+0=\ 3$	$p+\ 0=\ 100$	$920=z+\ 0$	$5y\ \div5=55\ \div\ 5$ *or* $\frac{5y}{5}=\frac{55}{5}$
$\boldsymbol{x}\ =\ \mathbf{3}$	$\boldsymbol{p}\ =\ \mathbf{100}$	$\mathbf{920}=\boldsymbol{z}$	$1y=11 \quad \therefore\ \boldsymbol{y}=\mathbf{11}$
Ck. $3+3=\ 6$	$100+101=201$	$909=920-11$	$5\times11=55$
Identities $6=6$	$201=201$	$909=909$	$55=55$

We illustrated how to check the solutions to these four example problems by substituting the four bold colored answers back into the original equations and ending with identities. When you are teaching, we hope you illustrate to your students how to check their answers to ensure the answers are correct.

94. $1020 = 510q$

$510 = 510$

$1020 \div 510 = 510q \div 510$

$\frac{1020}{510} = \frac{510}{510}q$

$2 = 1 \times q$

$\mathbf{2 = q}$

95. $\frac{a}{7} = 9$

$7 = 7$

$\frac{a}{7} \times \frac{7}{1} = 9 \times 7$

$\frac{a \times 7}{7 \times 1} = 9 \times 7$

$1 \times a = 63$

$\mathbf{a = 63}$

96. $a + 11.93 = 89.661$

$\underline{-11.93 = -11.93}$

$a + 0 = 77.731$

$\mathbf{a = 77.731}$

97. $\frac{r}{6.1} = 9.2$

$6.1 = 6.1$

$\frac{r}{6.1} \times \frac{6.1}{1} = 9.2 \times 6.1$

$\frac{r \times 6.1}{6.1 \times 1} = 9.2 \times 6.1$

$1 \times r = 56.12$

$\mathbf{r = 56.12}$

We consider it a great teaching tool to frequently encourage students to check their answers to determine if the solutions are correct.

98. $3d = 67.2$

$3 = 3$

$3d \div 3 = 67.2 \div 3$

$\frac{3d}{3} = \frac{67.2}{3}$

$1 \times d = 22.4$

$\mathbf{d = 22.4}$

99. $z - \frac{3}{8} = \frac{7}{24}$

$\underline{+\frac{3}{8} = +\frac{3}{8}}$

$z + 0 = \frac{7}{24} + \frac{3}{8}$

$z = \frac{7}{24} + \frac{9}{24}$

$z = \frac{7+9}{24}$

$z = \frac{16}{24} = \frac{2 \times 8}{3 \times 8}$

$\mathbf{z = \frac{2}{3}}$

100. $\frac{7}{15} = t - \frac{2}{5}$

$\underline{\frac{2}{5} = +\frac{2}{5}}$

$\frac{7}{15} + \frac{2}{5} = t + 0$

$\frac{7}{15} + \frac{6}{15} = t$

$\frac{7+6}{15} = t$

$\mathbf{\frac{13}{15} = t}$

101. $\frac{n}{.7} = \frac{3}{4}$

$.7 = .7$

$\frac{n}{.7} \times .7 = \frac{3}{4} \times .7$

$\frac{n}{.7} \times \frac{.7}{1} = \frac{3}{4} \times .7$

$\frac{n \times .7}{.7 \times 1} = .75 \times .7$

$\frac{n \times 1}{1} = .525$

$\mathbf{n = 0.525}$

You may want to check some of these answers.

If one is going to solve all types of algebra problems, knowing basic facts about fractions and decimals along with being able to convert fractions into equivalent fractions using mental math skills is a great benefit when solving problems.

The great thing about solving algebra problems and many other advanced mathematics problems is, frequently, there is more than one way to solve the problem. Several of the equations in problems 90-101 can be solved using different steps/procedures than the way we illustrated how to solve the problems. We encourage teachers and students to find alternative ways to solve problems.

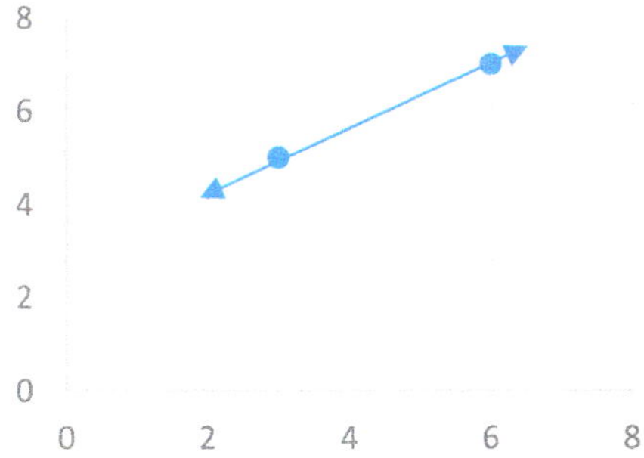

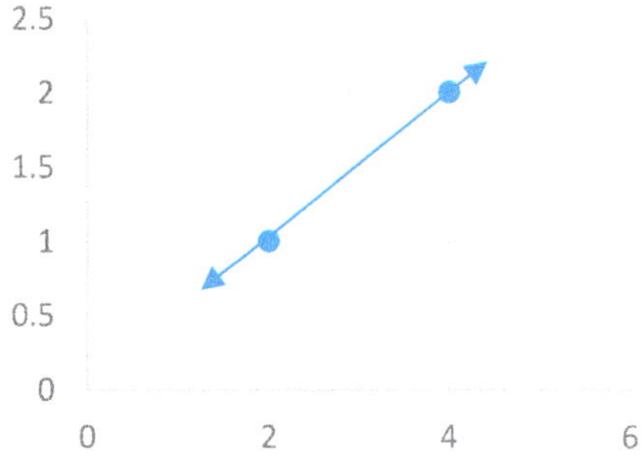

102.

103.

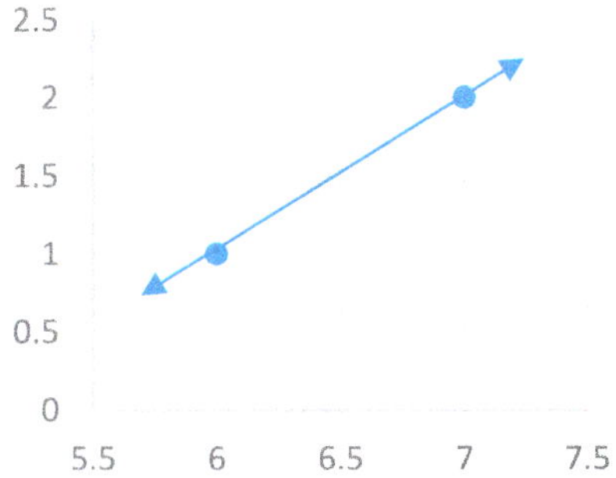

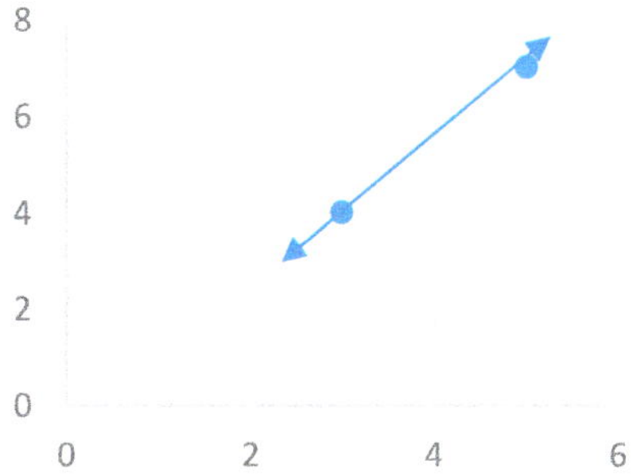

104.

105.

In geometry you will learn, TWO points is all which are required to find the equation of a line and therefore, TWO points are all which are required to graph a line.

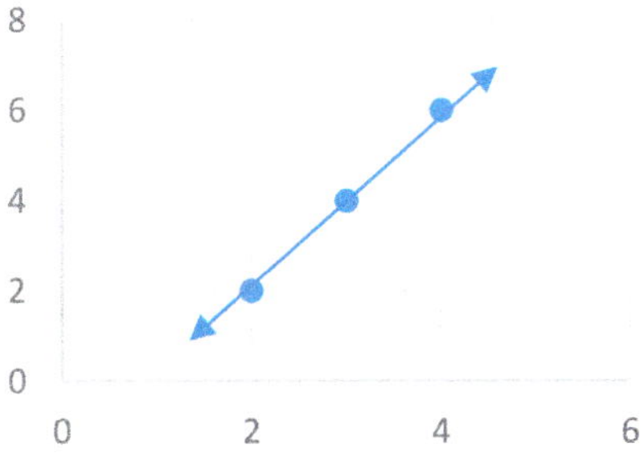

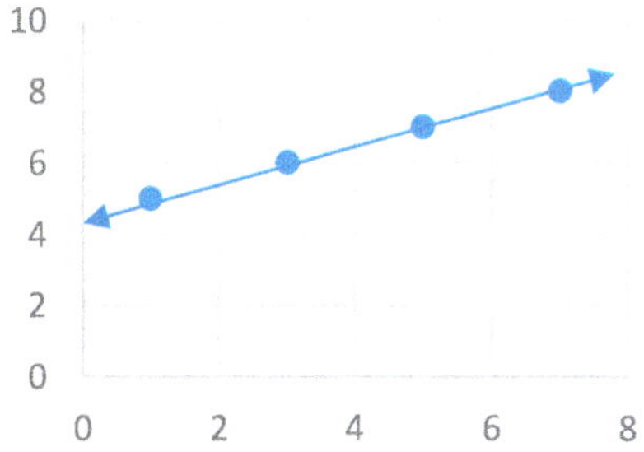

106.

107.

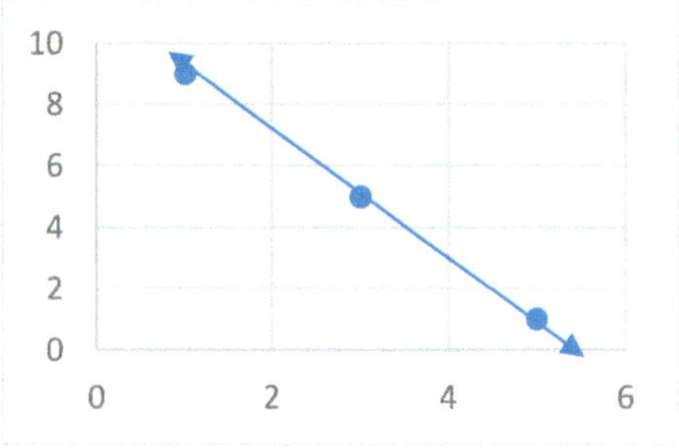

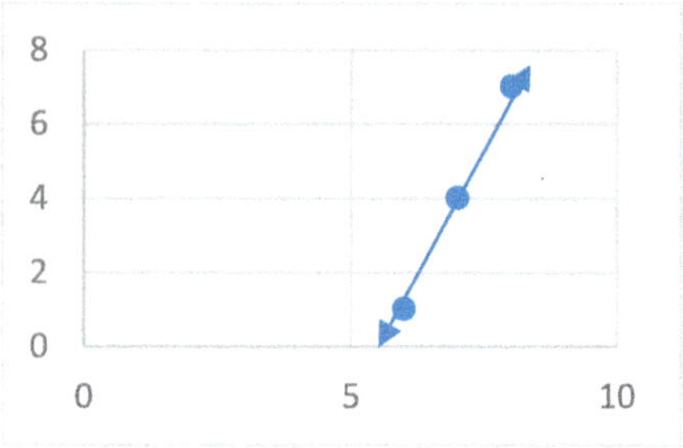

108. **109.**

Notice the x axis on one of the graphs does not start at 0. Some of the axes are not numbered (1, 2, 3, ...).

110. 3 **111.** $5\frac{2}{5}$ *or* 5.4 **112.** 1050 **113.** 7581 **114.** 54150 **115.** $344\frac{9}{11}$ *or* 344.8181 ...

116. $2454\frac{4}{5}$ *or* 2454.8 **117.** $4\frac{3}{100}$ *or* 4.03 **118.** $1\frac{4}{5}\div 2\frac{7}{10}=\frac{9}{5}\div\frac{27}{10}=\frac{9}{5}\times\frac{10}{27}=\frac{9\times10}{5\times27}=\frac{3\cdot3\times2\cdot5}{5\times3\cdot3\cdot3}=\frac{2}{3}=0.66\ldots$

119. Prime Factors of $36=2\times2\times3\times3$ $25=5\times5$ $18=2\times3\times3$

LCD $36, 25, 18=2\times2\times3\times3\times5\times5=900$ The number "2700" is a common denominator but not the Least Common Denominator.

120. Prime Factors of $15=3\times5$ $18=2\times3\times3$ $24=2\times2\times2\times3$

LCD $15, 18, 24=2\times2\times2\times3\times3\times5=360$ The number "1080" is a common denominator but not the Least Common Denominator.

Fifth Assignment:

1. 5.25 ft. **2.** 175 roses + 111 turnips +14 tulips another option 111 turnips + 175 roses +14 tulips

3. 5 *bananas* **4.** 15 cars + 65 trucks + 73 SUVs + 5 tractors *"The order of the terms may be rearranged by using both the Associative and Commutative Properties."* **5.** 5 *ba* *or* 5 *ab*

6. $1.03a^2+1.09ax$ **7.** 24 *Chevy cars* + 111 *Dodge trucks* + 81 *Toyota cars* **8.** $1.5c+11.25tf$ *or* $1\frac{1}{2}c+11\frac{1}{4}tf$ **9.** $113.25x^2y^3z$ **10.** $14\frac{3}{8}xyz+11.92x^2y^2z^2$ **11.** $3\frac{2}{5}x^2y^2z+1\frac{3}{5}x^2yz^2+3\frac{2}{5}xy^2z^2$

12. $12x^2+12x+5$ **13.** $7x^3+2x^2+2x+3$ **14.** Associative Addition (parentheses switched)

15. Commutative Multiplication (order of two terms are switched) **16.** Commutative Addition (order of two terms in parentheses switched) **17.** Associative Multiplication (braces switched) **18.** Communitive Addition (order of two terms switched) **19.** Associative Multiplication (parentheses switched *grouping*) **20.** 1237.5 $ft.^3$ (Find the volume of a rectangular solid.) **21.** $\frac{15b^2(8+m)}{(16+m)}$ **22.** 5.5 $yds.^2$

23. $55\ \frac{miles}{hour} = 55\ mph$ **24.** $4\ \frac{tablespoons}{day} = 4\frac{tbsp.}{day} = 4\ tablespoons\ per\ day$ **25.** $196.02\ cm^2$ Find the area of *the* rectangle, given the length of the base is, 16.2 cm and the height is, 12.1 cm. **26.** $300d^5r^3$ **27.** $5x^2y^2$

28. $A_{tri.} = \frac{1}{2} \times 10\ in. \times 20\ in. = 100\ in.^2 \therefore A_{tri.} = 100\ in.^2$

29. $D = \frac{400\ mi.}{1\ hr.} \times \frac{5.5\ hrs.}{1} = \frac{2200 \times mi. \times hrs.}{hr.} = 2200\ mi.$ **30.** $C = 2\pi \times 1.5\ ft. = 3\pi\ ft.$

31. $V_{cube}\ (3.5\ cm)^3 = 3.5\ cm \times 3.5\ cm \times 3.5\ cm = 42.875\ cm^3$ **32.** $A_{cir.} = \pi \times \frac{13}{4}\ m \times \frac{13}{4}\ m = \frac{169}{16}\pi\ m^2$

33. $V_{sphere} = \frac{4}{3}\pi\ (6371\ km)^3 = \frac{\pi \times 4 \times 6371 \times 6371 \times 6371 \times km \times km \times km}{3} = 344{,}795{,}470{,}414.67\ \pi\ km^3$

34. $A_{rec.} = 3.123\ yds. \times \frac{2}{3}\ yds. = 2.082\ yds.^2\ \ or\ \ A_{rec.} = 9.369\ ft. \times 2\ ft. = 18.738\ ft.^2$

35. 85 105 90

$\underline{5 \times 17}$ 3×35 2×45

$\underline{3 \times 5 \times 7}$ $\underline{2 \times 3 \times 3 \times 5}$

Not LCD $2 \times 3 \times 5 \times 7 \times 17$

$LCD = 2 \times 3 \times 3 \times 5 \times 7 \times 17 = 10710$

36. x^2y x^2y^3 xy^3z^4

$x \cdot x \cdot y$ $x \cdot x \cdot y \cdot y \cdot y$ $x \cdot y \cdot y \cdot y \cdot z \cdot z \cdot z \cdot z$

$LCD = x \cdot x \cdot y \cdot y \cdot y \cdot z \cdot z \cdot z \cdot z = x^2y^3z^4$

37. $48z^2(x+9)$ $32z^3(x+9)^2$ $18z(x+9)^3$

$2^4 \cdot 3 \cdot z^2 \cdot (x+9)$ $2^5 \cdot z^3 \cdot (x+9)^2$ $2 \times 3^2 \cdot z \cdot (x+9)^3$

$LCD = 2^5 \cdot 3^2 \cdot z^3(x+9)^3 = 288z^3(x+9)^3$

38. $24x(y+x)^2$ $28x^3(y+x)(y+z)$ $32x^2(y+x)^2(y+z)$ $672x^3(y+x)^2(y+x)^2$

$2^3 \cdot 3 \cdot x \cdot (y+x)^2$ $2^2 \cdot 7 \cdot x^3(y+x)(y+z)$ $2^5 \cdot x^2(y+x)^2(y+z)$ $2^5 \cdot 3 \cdot 7 \cdot x^3(y+x)^2(y+z)^2$

$LCD = 2^5 \cdot 3 \cdot 7 \cdot x^3(y+x)^2(y+z)^2 = 672 \cdot x \cdot x \cdot x \cdot (y+x)(y+x)(y+z)(y+z) =$

$LCD = 672x^3(y+x)^2(y+z)^2$

39. $88 = 2 \cdot 2 \cdot 2 \cdot 11 = 2^3 \cdot 11$ $84 = 2 \cdot 2 \cdot 3 \cdot 7 = 2^2 \cdot 3 \cdot 7$ $92 = 2 \cdot 2 \cdot 23$

$LCD = 2 \cdot 2 \cdot 2 \cdot 3 \cdot 7 \cdot 11 \cdot 23 = 42504$ Check $\frac{42504}{88} = 483$ $\frac{42504}{84} = 506$ $\frac{42504}{92} = 462$ Checks are Good

40. $15 = 3 \times 5$ $20 = 2 \times 2 \times 5$ $25 = 5 \times 5$ $50 = 2 \times 5 \times 5$ $LCD = 2^2 \cdot 3 \cdot 5^2 = 300$

Check $\frac{300}{15} = 20$ $\frac{300}{20} = 15$ $\frac{300}{25} = 12$ $\frac{300}{50} = 6$ Checks for all four denominators work.

41. $20x^3 = 2^2 \cdot 5 \cdot x^3$ $30x^4 = 2 \cdot 3 \cdot 5 \cdot x^4$ $45xy = 3^2 \cdot 5 \cdot x \cdot y$ $90x^2y^2 = 2 \cdot 3^2 \cdot 5 \cdot x^2 \cdot y^2$

$LCD = 2^2 \cdot 3^2 \cdot 5 \cdot x^4y^2 = 180x^4y^2$ Check $\frac{180x^4y^2}{20x^3} = \frac{9xy^2}{1}$ $\frac{180x^4y^2}{30x^4} = \frac{6y^2}{1}$ $\frac{180x^4y^2}{45xy} = \frac{4x^3y}{1}$ $\frac{180x^4y^2}{90x^2y^2} = \frac{2x^2}{1}$

Checks to ensure the LCD is divisible by the four denominators. **42.** $\frac{11}{12} + \frac{17}{18} - \left(\frac{2}{9} + \frac{5}{6}\right) = \frac{33}{36} + \frac{34}{36} - \left(\frac{8}{36} + \frac{30}{36}\right) = \frac{67}{36} - \frac{38}{36} = \frac{29}{36}$ **43.** $\frac{\{5^2 - (25 \div 2)\} + 7^3}{12 + 3^3 - (13 \times 3)} = \frac{\{25 - 12.5\} + 343}{12 + 27 - 39} = \frac{355.5}{0} = undefined$ It is impossible to solve a fraction problem when the denominator equals **"0"**. **44.** $\frac{7}{39} - \frac{65}{78} + \frac{25}{26}$ Find the LCD. $39 = 3 \times 13$ $78 = 2 \times 3 \times 13$ $26 = 2 \times 13$ $LCD = 2 \times 3 \times 13 = 78$ Convert fractions into equivalent fractions with the LCD. $\frac{78}{39}=2 \therefore 2=2\ and\ \frac{2}{2}=1,\quad \frac{78}{78}=1 \therefore 1=1\ \&\ \frac{1}{1}=1,\quad \frac{78}{26}=3 \therefore 3=3\ \&\ \frac{3}{3}=1$

Now, multiply each of the given fractions by 1 to find three equivalent fractions with the LCD, 78. $\frac{7}{39}=\frac{7}{39}\times 1=\frac{7}{39}\times\frac{2}{2}=\frac{14}{78}$, $\frac{65}{78}=\frac{65}{78}\times 1=\frac{65}{78}\times\frac{1}{1}=\frac{65}{78}$, $\frac{25}{26}=\frac{25}{26}\times 1=\frac{25}{26}\times\frac{3}{3}=\frac{25\times 3}{26\times 3}=\frac{75}{78}$ Solve the problem now. $\frac{7}{39}-\frac{65}{78}+\frac{25}{26}=\frac{14}{78}-\frac{65}{78}+\frac{75}{78}=\frac{14-65+75}{78}=\frac{24}{78}=\frac{2\times2\times2\times3}{2\times3\times13}=\frac{2\times2}{13}=\frac{4}{13}$ **45.** $\frac{17}{18}-(\frac{4}{5}-\frac{2}{15})^2=$

$\frac{17}{18}-\left(\frac{12}{15}-\frac{2}{15}\right)^2=\frac{17}{18}-\left(\frac{10}{15}\right)^2=\frac{17}{18}-\left(\frac{2}{3}\right)^2=\frac{17}{18}-\frac{4}{9}=\frac{17}{18}-\frac{8}{18}=\frac{9}{18}=\frac{3\times3}{2\times3\times3}=\frac{1}{2}$ **46.** $\frac{2x}{2x}+\frac{11+9}{2\,(10)}+\frac{33}{11}=$

$1+\frac{20}{20}+3=1+1+3=5$ (If the variable "x" equals "0" then the first fraction is undefined.) **47.**

$\left(\frac{8+11}{19(0)}\right)(77.132)=\frac{19}{0}(77.132)=undefined$ It is impossible to work with a fraction if the denominator equals **"0"**. **48.** $\frac{45x^3yz^2(x+4)^2(z-8)^2}{60x^3y^2z(x+4)^3(z-16)^2}=\frac{3\cdot3\cdot5\cdot x\cdot x\cdot x\cdot y\cdot z\cdot z\cdot(x+4)(x+4)(z-8)(z-8)}{2\cdot2\cdot3\cdot5\cdot x\cdot x\cdot x\cdot y\cdot y\cdot z\cdot(x+4)(x+4)(x+4)(z-16)(z-16)}=\frac{3\cdot z\cdot(z-8)(z-8)}{2\cdot2\cdot y\cdot(x+4)(z-16)(z-16)}=$

$\frac{3z(z-8)^2}{4y(x+4)(z-16)^2}$ **49.** $\frac{x\,(2x-5)y^2(2x+15)}{x\,(3x-10)y(2x+15)^2}=\frac{x\cdot(2x-5)\cdot y\cdot y\cdot(2x+15)}{x\cdot(3x-10)\cdot y\cdot(2x+15)(2x+15)}=\frac{y(2x-5)}{(3x-10)(2x+15)}$

50. $\frac{6x(3m^2+z^3+7)25y(6x+5)^3}{12y(6x+5)^2 5x^2(3m^2+z^3+7)}=\frac{5(6x+5)}{2x}$

51.	**52.**	**53.**	**54.**
$x+25=27$	$25.3+m=28.1$	$37\frac{3}{4}=z-5\frac{5}{8}$	$\frac{7}{16}=\frac{7}{24}+r$
$-25=-25$	$-25.3=-25.3$	$+5\frac{5}{8}=+5\frac{5}{8}$	$-\frac{7}{24}=-\frac{7}{24}$
$x+0=2$	$0+m=2.8$		
$\therefore x=2$	$\therefore m=2.8$	$37\frac{6}{8}=z-5\frac{5}{8}$	$\frac{21}{48}=\frac{14}{48}+r$
Check Solutions Below		$+5\frac{5}{8}=+5\frac{5}{8}$	$-\frac{14}{48}=-\frac{14}{48}$
$2+25=27$	$25.3+2.8=28.1$	$42\frac{11}{8}=z+0$	$\frac{7}{48}=0+r$
Good $27=27$	*Good* $28.1=28.1$	$\therefore 43\frac{3}{8}=z$	$\therefore \frac{7}{48}=r$
		Check $37\frac{3}{4}=43\frac{3}{8}-5\frac{5}{8}$	$\frac{7}{16}=\frac{7}{24}+\frac{7}{48}$
		Good $37\frac{3}{4}=37\frac{3}{4}$	*Good* $\frac{21}{48}=\frac{21}{48}$

55. $c = \frac{7}{36}$ **56.** $y = 113.09$ **57.** $m = 5006\frac{49}{48} = 5007\frac{1}{48}$ **58.** $10\frac{15}{22} = p$ **59.** $15q = 30$ **60.** $\frac{g}{15} = 30$

61. $11.1 = \frac{t}{2.1}$ **62.** $\frac{4}{5} = 4w$ **63.** $k = 25$ **64.** $j = 11.11$ $\div 15 = \div 15$ $\times 15 = \times 15$

$\times 2.1 = \times 2.1$ $\div 4 = \div 4$ **65.** $\frac{6}{7} = z$ $\frac{15}{15}q = \frac{30}{15}$ $15 \times \frac{g}{15} = 15 \times 30$

$2.1 \times 11.1 = 2.1 \times \frac{t}{2.1}$ $\frac{4}{5} \div 4 = \frac{4w}{4}$ **66.** $P_{rec.} = 2l + 2w$ $1q = 2$ $1g = 450$

$23.31 = 1t$ $\frac{4}{5} \times \frac{1}{4} = 1w$ $P_{rec.} = 2 \cdot 100 + 2 \cdot 50$ $q = 2$ $g = 450$

$23.31 = t$ $\frac{4 \times 1}{5 \times 4} = w$ $P_{rec.} = 200 + 100 = 300$ *Check the answers below.*

Check the answers below. $\frac{1}{5} = w$ $P_{rec.} = 300$ *SOMETHING* $15q = 30$ $\frac{g}{15} = 30$

$11.1 = \frac{t}{2.1}$ $\frac{4}{5} = 4w$ $15 \times 2 = 30$ $\frac{450}{15} = 30$

$11.1 = \frac{23.31}{2.1}$ $\frac{4}{5} = \frac{4}{1} \times \frac{1}{5}$ **67.** $A_{sq.} = s^2$ $A_{sq.} = 25^2$ *Great* $30 = 30$ & $30 = 30$

Good $11.1 = 11.1$ & $\frac{4}{5} = \frac{4}{5}$ $A_{sq.} = 625$ *SOMETHING squared*

68. $V_{rec.\ solid} = lwh$ $V_{rec.\ solid} = 75.5 \times 72.5 \times 100 = 547{,}375$ *SOMETHING cubed* **69.** Reflexive Property – No change from the left side to the right side – one equation. **70.** Symmetric Property - Left and right sides switched – two equations. **71.** Reflexive Property – Left and right sides are identical no changes from the left and right sides – one equation. **72.** Transitive Property – Left side of the first equation equals the right side of the second equation to get the third equation, three equations. **73.** Transitive Property **74.** Symmetric Property **75.** Commutative Property Addition – switched the order of the quantity term and the number "4", left side and right side – one equation. **76.** Symmetric Property - switched the order of the two terms on the left and right sides – two equations. **77.** Transitive Property

78. Reflexive Property **79.** Associative Property Multiplication – three terms switched the grouping of the parentheses – one equation. **80.** Associative Property Addition – three terms switched the grouping of the parentheses – one equation. **81.** Commutative Property Multiplication – Switched the order of the two groups (parentheses) – one equation. **82.** Reflexive Property – left and right sides of the equation are the same – one equation. **83.** Transitive Property – Left side of the first equation equals the right side of the second equation to form the third equation – three equations. **84.** Commutative Property Addition– Switched the order of the terms in the quantity (x+2) – one equation. **85.** Symmetric Property – Flipped the sides in the equation to form a second equation. **86.** Commutative Property Multiplication – Switched the order of the two terms in the quantity, $(6 \cdot x)$ – one equation. **87.** Associative Property Addition - Switched the grouping of the braces – one equation. **88.** Associative Property Multiplication – Switched the grouping of the parentheses – one equation. **Problems 89-117** involve definitions of mathematical words or phrases. The definitions of most of these words and phrases as they relate to arithmetic and mathematics can be looked up on the internet or and old fashion dictionary. We have made some comments about a few of the phrases and words. **91.** Use the internet definition but here is the mathematics notation commonly used: $N = \{1, 2, 3, 4, \ldots\}$ **92.** Use the internet definition but here is the mathematics notation commonly used: $W = \{0, 1, 2, 3, 4, \ldots\}$ **93.** Use the internet definition but here is the mathematics notation commonly used: $I = \{\ldots, -3, -2, -1, 0, 1, 2, 3, \ldots\}$ **94.** Use the internet definition but here is the mathematics notation commonly used: $Q = \{\frac{x}{y} : \forall x \in I \text{ and } \forall y \in I, y \neq 0\}$ **95.** Not Rational

(Look up the definitions on the internet to find the definitions for problems 96.-100., 103.-114., and 116.-118.)

101. *Composite Numbers* $= \{4, 6, 8, 9, 10, 12, 14, 15, \ldots\}$ **102.** *Prime Numbers* $= \{2, 3, 5, 7, 11, 13, 17, \ldots\}$

115. Refer to the explanation at the end of Chapter 1. **119.** Quantity – A Quantity in mathematics refers to the terms contained in a set of parentheses, brackets, or braces. The "Quantity" is represented by the terms inside a set of parentheses, brackets, and/or braces. **120.** Invisible numbers and math symbols: You will NOT find the definition of this type of expression in a dictionary or on the internet. We refer to this type of situation in the textbook when we reference the number 1 which is not specifically written in a problem because mathematicians know the number 1 is understood to be present in an expression even though it is not written. Consider the situation when the exponent of a term is 1 or when the denominator of a term is not written or when the coefficient of a term is not written. The following numbers, terms, label, operation notations, etc. may also be present but not written in specific circumstances: {0, 2, e, 10, *rads*, the multiplication operation symbol and more}. Here is the simple definition of invisible numbers *and* math symbols: *Anytime mathematicians know that a number, term, label, operation, or symbol is present but not written.* **121.** Think about how you would explain the order of operations which is often referred to as PEMDAS. The letter "P" is a basic reference to the word "parentheses". The letter "E" refers to all types of "exponents". The letters "M", "D", "A", and "S" refer to the arithmetic operations, "multiplication", "division", "addition", and "subtraction". **122.** Here is one example to explain the Hierarchy of Operations. $\frac{2^3+\frac{3}{4}(6+2)^2-6}{\sqrt{16+9}+(4+1)}$ Step 1 Focus on the 3 sets of "parentheses". You may only see two sets of parentheses but the numbers, 16 and 9, in the square root involve invisible parentheses. $\frac{2^3+\frac{3}{4}(8)^2-6}{\sqrt{25}+5}$ Step 2 Focus on the exponents but you must realize the square root is a special type of exponent. $\frac{8+\frac{3}{4}(64)-6}{5+5}$ Step 3 Focus on the multiplication problem. $\frac{8+\frac{192}{4}-6}{5+5}$ Step 4 Focus on the division problem, fraction, in the numerator even though the big fraction is a division problem. We cannot complete the big fraction division problem until after we complete all the other problems in both the numerator and the denominator. $\frac{8+48-6}{5+5}$ Step 5 We are going to focus on the addition and subtraction problems in the numerator and denominator. We need to mention even though we do not see any parentheses in the numerator or the denominator, all three numbers in the numerator are enclosed in a set of invisible parentheses. The answer is "5". We hope you recognized there were invisible parentheses in the denominator with the expression "5 + 5" which equals "10". The mnemonic/acronym "PEMDAS" means, "Please Excuse My Dear Aunt Sally".

I seldom mentioned tricks or special phrases to help students learn certain procedures. I never <u>emphasized</u> the acronym "FOIL" "First, Outer, Inner, and Last" when multiplying two binomials, but I did mention it because many other teachers emphasize the word "FOIL". I feel a little different about the acronym "PEMDAS", and I did frequently use the acronym with my low-achieving students, and it seemed to help them focus. The point I am trying to make is, "Mentioning mathematics tricks and acronyms **sometimes** may help some students, but if you use too many tricks and acronyms the students will get confused and not remember the rules and procedures which must be "Learned and Remembered". Sometimes a trick or an acronym may help some students but too many tricks and acronyms will compound the confusion some students experience.

Sixth Assignment:

1. $1\ mi. = 5280\ ft. or\ 1\ ft. = \frac{1}{5280}\ mi.$ **2.** $1\ mi. = 1760\ yds. or\ 1\ yd. = \frac{1}{1760}\ mi.$ **3.** $1\ gal. = 4\ qts. or\ 1\ qt. = \frac{1}{4}\ gal.$

4. 1 hr.=60 min. or 1 min.=$\frac{1}{60}$ $hr.$ **5.** $1\ hr. = 3600\ sec. or\ 1\ sec. = \frac{1}{3600}\ hr.$ **6.** $1\ ton = 2000\ lbs. or\ 1\ lbs. = \frac{1}{2000}\ ton$

7. $1\ m = 100\ cm\ \ or\ 1\ cm = \frac{1}{100}\ m$ **8.** $1\ in.^2 = \frac{1}{144}\ ft.^2$ **9.** $1\ ft.^2 = \frac{1}{9}\ yd.^2$ **10.** $1\ ft.^3 = \frac{1}{27}\ yd.^3$

11. $\frac{1\,day}{24\,hrs.} = 1 = \frac{24\,hrs.}{1\,day}$ **12.** $\frac{1000\,ml}{1\,l} = 1 = \frac{1\,l}{1000\,ml}$ **13.** $\frac{32\,U.S.\ Fluid\ Oz.}{1\,qt.} = 1 = \frac{1\,qt.}{32\,U.S.\ Fluid\ Oz.}$ **14.** $\frac{1\,U.S.\ cup}{48\,tsp.} = 1 = \frac{48\,tsp.}{1\,U.S.\ cup}$

15. $\frac{\$1}{10\,dimes} = 1 = \frac{10\,dimes}{\$1}$ **16.** $\frac{1000\,cm^3}{1\,l} = 1 = \frac{1\,l}{1000\,cm^3}$ **17.** $672\,in. = x\,ft.$ $Fact$: $12\,in. = 1\,ft.$ $\therefore \frac{12\,in.}{1\,ft.} = 1 = \frac{1\,ft.}{12\,in.}$

$672\,in. = 672\,in. \times 1 = \frac{672\,in.}{1} \times \frac{1\,ft.}{12\,in.} = \frac{672\,in. \times 1\,ft.}{1 \times 12\,in.} = \frac{672\,ft.}{12} = 56\,ft.$

18. 500 tons = x lbs. *Fact:* 2000 lbs.= 1 ton

$\therefore \frac{2000\,lbs.}{1\,ton} = 1 = \frac{1\,ton}{2000\,lbs.}$

$500\,tons = 500\,tons \times 1 = \frac{500\,tons}{1} \times \frac{2000\,lbs.}{1\,ton}$

$\frac{500\,tons \times 2000\,lbs.}{1 \times 1\,ton} = 1{,}000{,}000\,lbs.$

19. $7.5\,yds = x\,ft.$ $Fact$: $3\,ft. = 1\,yd.$ $\therefore \frac{3\,ft..}{1\,yd.} = 1 = \frac{1\,yd.}{3\,ft.}$

$7.5\,yds = 7.5\,yds. \times 1 = \frac{7.5\,yds.}{1} \times \frac{3\,ft.}{1\,yd.} = \frac{7.5\,yds \times 3\,ft.}{1 \times 1\,yd.} =$

$\frac{7.5 \times 3\,ft.}{1} = 7.5 \times 3\,ft. = 22.5\,ft.$

20. $775\,yds. = x\,mi.$ $Fact$: $1760\,yds. = 1\,mi.$

$\therefore \frac{1760\,yds.}{1\,mi.} = 1 = \frac{1\,mi.}{1760\,yds.}$

$775\,yds. = 775\,yds. \times 1 = \frac{775\,yds.}{1} \times \frac{1\,mi.}{1760\,yds.} =$

$\frac{775\,yds. \times 1\,mi.}{1 \times 1760\,yds.} = \frac{775\,mi.}{1760} = \frac{5 \times 5 \times 31\,mi.}{2 \times 2 \times 2 \times 2 \times 2 \times 5 \times 11} = \frac{155}{352}\,mi.$

21. $82\frac{3}{4}\,ft. = x\,in.$ $Fact$: $12\,in. = 1\,ft.$ $\therefore \frac{12\,in.}{1\,ft.} = 1 = \frac{1\,ft.}{12\,in.}$

$82\frac{3}{4}\,ft. = 82\frac{3}{4}\,ft. \times 1 = \frac{331\,ft.}{4} \times \frac{12\,in.}{1\,ft.} = \frac{331\,ft. \times 12\,in.}{4 \times 1\,ft.} =$

$\frac{331 \times 3\,in.}{1 \times 1} = 993\,in.$

22. $82\frac{3}{4}\,ft. = x\,yds.$ $Fact$: $1\,yd. = 3\,ft.$

$\therefore \frac{1\,yd.}{3\,ft.} = 1 = \frac{3\,ft.}{1\,yd.}$

$82\frac{3}{4}\,ft. = 82\frac{3}{4}\,ft. \times 1 = \frac{331\,ft.}{4} \times \frac{1\,yd.}{3\,ft.}$

$\frac{331\,ft. \times 1\,yd.}{4 \times 3\,ft.} = \frac{331\,yd.}{12} = 27\frac{7}{12}\,yds.\ or\ \approx 27.583\,yds.$

23. $2\frac{1}{2}\,in. = x\,ft.$ $Fact$: $1\,ft. = 12\,in.$

$\therefore \frac{1\,ft.}{12\,in.} = 1 = \frac{12\,in.}{1\,ft.}$

$2\frac{1}{2}\,in. = 2\frac{1}{2}\,in. \times 1 = \frac{5\,in.}{2} \times \frac{1\,ft.}{12\,in.} =$

$\frac{5\,in. \times 1\,ft.}{2 \times 12\,in.} = \frac{5\,ft.}{24} = \frac{5}{24}\,ft.\ or\ 0.208333\ldots ft.\ or\ \approx 0.21\,ft.$

24. $1000\,ft. = x\,mi.$ $Fact$: $1\,mi. = 5280\,ft.$

$\therefore \frac{1\,mi.}{5280\,ft.} = 1 = \frac{5280\,ft.}{1\,mi.}$

$1000\,ft. = 1000\,ft. \times 1 = \frac{1000\,ft.}{1} \times \frac{1\,mi.}{5280\,ft.}$

$\frac{1000\,ft. \times 1\,mi.}{1 \times 5280\,ft.} = \frac{1000\,mi.}{5280} = \frac{1000}{5280}\,mi. = \frac{25}{132}\,mi.$

25. $1550\,lbs. = x\,tons$ $Fact$: $1\,ton. = 2000\,lbs.$

$\therefore \frac{1\,ton}{2000\,lbs.} = 1 = \frac{2000\,lbs.}{1\,ton}$

$1550\,lbs. = 1550\,lbs. \times 1 = \frac{1550\,lbs.}{1} \times \frac{1\,ton}{2000\,lbs.} =$

$\frac{1550 \times 1\,ton}{1 \times 2000} = \frac{1550\,ton}{2000} = \frac{31}{40}\,ton\ or\ 0.775\,ton$

26. $7\frac{1}{3}\,fathoms = x\,ft.$ $Fact$: $1\,fath. = 6\,ft.$

$\therefore \frac{1\,fath.}{6\,ft.} = 1 = \frac{6\,ft.}{1\,fath.}$

$7\frac{1}{3}\,fath. = \frac{22}{3}\,fath. \times 1 = \frac{22\,fath.}{3} \times \frac{6\,ft.}{1\,fath.}$

$\frac{22\,fath. \times 6\,ft.}{3 \times 1\,fath.} = \frac{22 \times 2\,ft.}{1} = 44\,fath.$

27. $5000\,in.^2 = x\,yd.^2$ $Fact$: $1\,yd.^2 = 1296\,in.^2$

$\therefore \frac{1\,yd.^2}{1296\,in.^2} = 1 = \frac{1296\,in.^2}{1\,yd.^2}$

$5000\,in.^2 = 5000\,in.^2 \times 1 = \frac{5000\,in.^2}{1} \times \frac{1\,yd.^2}{1296\,in.^2} =$

$\frac{5000\,in.^2 \times 1\,yd.^2}{1 \times 1296\,in.^2} = \frac{5000\,yd.^2}{1296} = 3\frac{1112}{1296}\,yd.^2 = 3\frac{139}{162}\,yd.^2$

28. $8000\,ft. = x\,NM$ $Fact$: $1\,NM = 6076.1155\,ft.$

Used Calculator $\therefore \frac{1\,NM}{6076\,ft.} = 1 = \frac{6076\,ft.}{1\,NM}$

29. $67.29\,in. = x\,cm$ $Fact$: $1\,in. = 2.54\,cm$

$\therefore \frac{1\,in.}{2.54\,cm} = 1 = \frac{2.54\,cm}{1\,in.}$

$8000\,ft. = 8000\,ft.\ \times 1 = \frac{8000\,ft.}{1} \times \frac{1\,NM}{6076\,ft.}$

$\frac{8000\,ft.\times 1\,NM}{1\times 6076\,ft.} = \frac{8000\,NM}{6076} = 1\frac{481}{1519}\,NM \approx 1.3167\,NM$

$67.29\,in. = 67.29\,in.\ \times 1 = \frac{67.29\,in.}{1}\times\frac{2.54\,cm}{1\,in.} =$

$\frac{67.29\,in.\times 2.54\,cm}{1\times 1\,in.} = \frac{67.29\times 2.54\,cm}{1\times 1} = 170.92\,cm$

30. $72\,cm^3 = x\,kg$ $\quad Fact\text{: } 1000\,cm^3 = 1\,kg$

Water fact only $\therefore \frac{1000\,cm^3}{1\,kg} = 1 = \frac{1\,kg}{1000\,cm^3}$

$72\,cm^3 = 72\,cm^3\ \times 1 = \frac{72\,cm^3}{1}\times\frac{1\,kg}{1000\,cm^3}$

$\frac{72\,cm^3\times 1\,kg}{1\times 1000\,cm^3} = \frac{72\,kg}{1000} = 0.072\,kg$

31. $0.6\,oz. = x\,grams \quad Fact\text{: } 1\,oz. = 28.35\,gm$

$\therefore \frac{1\,oz.}{28.35\,gm} = 1 = \frac{28.35\,gm}{1\,oz.}$

$0.6\,oz. = 0.6\,oz.\ \times 1 = \frac{0.6\,oz.}{1}\times\frac{28.35\,gm}{1\,oz.} =$

$\frac{0.6\,oz.\times 28.35\,gm}{1\times 1\,oz.} = \frac{0.6\ \times 28.35\,gm}{1\times 1} = 17.01\,gm$

32. $85\,cm^3 = x\,m^3 \quad Fact\text{: } 1\,m = 100\,cm$

$\therefore \frac{1\,m}{100\,cm} = 1 = \frac{100\,cm}{1m}$

$85\,cm^3 = 85\,cm^3 \times 1\times 1\times 1 =$

$85\,cm^3 \times \frac{1\,m}{100\,cm}\times\frac{1\,m}{100\,cm}\times\frac{1\,m}{100\,cm} =$

$\frac{85\,cm^3}{1}\times\frac{1\,m}{100\,cm}\times\frac{1\,m}{100\,cm}\times\frac{1\,m}{100\,cm} =$

$\frac{85\times cm\times cm\times cm\times 1\times m\times 1\times m\times 1\times m}{1\times 100\,cm\times 100\,cm\ \times 100\,cm} =$

$\frac{85\times m\times m\times m}{100\times 100\times 100} = \frac{80\,m^3}{1000000} = 0.000085\,m^3$

33. $70\,\frac{km}{hr} = x\,\frac{cm}{min.} \quad Facts\text{: } 1\,km = 1000\,m\ \&\ 1m = 100\,cm\ \&$ $1\,hr. = 60\,min.$ $\quad \therefore \frac{1\,km}{1000\,m} = 1 = \frac{1000\,m}{1\,km}\ \&$

$\frac{1\,m}{100\,cm} = 1 = \frac{100\,cm}{1\,m} \quad \& \quad \frac{1\,hr.}{60\,min.} = 1 = \frac{60\,min.}{1\,hr.}$

$70\,\frac{km}{hr.} = 70\,\frac{km}{hr.}\times 1\times 1\times 1 =$

$\frac{70\,km}{1\ hr.}\times\frac{1000\,m}{1\,km}\times\frac{100\,cm}{1\,m}\times\frac{1\,hr.}{60\,min.} =$

$\frac{70\times km\times 1000\times m\times 100\times cm\times 1\times hr.}{1\times hr.\times 1\times km\times 1\times m\times 60\times min.} =$

$\frac{70\times 1000\times 100\times cm}{60\times min.} = \frac{7\times 100000\times cm}{6\times min.} = \frac{350{,}000}{3}\,\frac{cm}{min.}$

34. $72\,\frac{ft.^3}{day} = x\,\frac{yd.^3}{wk.} \quad Fact\text{: } 3\,ft. = 1\,yd.\ \&\ 1\,wk. = 7\,days$

$\therefore \frac{1\,wk.}{7\,days} = 1 = \frac{7\,days.}{1\,wk.}\ \&\ \frac{3\,ft.}{1\,yd.} = 1 = \frac{1\,yd.}{3\,ft.}$

$72\,\frac{ft.^3}{day} = 72\,\frac{ft.^3}{day}\times 1\times 1\times 1\times\ 1 =$

$\frac{72}{1}\times\frac{ft.^3}{day}\times\frac{1\,yd.}{3\,ft.}\times\frac{1\,yd.}{3\,ft.}\times\frac{1\,yd.}{3\,ft.}\times\frac{7\,days.}{1\,wk.} =$

$\frac{72\times ft.\times ft.\times ft.\times 1\times yd.\times 1\times yd.\times 1\times yd.\times 7\,days}{1\times day\ \times 3\times ft.\ \times 3\times ft.\times 3\times\ ft.\times\ 1\times\ wk.} =$

$\frac{72\times yd.\times yd.\times yd.\times 7}{3\times 3\times 3\times wk.} = \frac{56\,yd.^3}{3\,wk.} = 18\frac{2}{3}\,\frac{yds.^3}{wk.}$

35. $73\,\frac{lbs.}{in.^2} = x\,\frac{oz.}{ft.^2} \quad Facts\text{: } 1\,lb. = 16oz.\ \&\ 1\,ft. = 12\,in.$

$\therefore \frac{1\,ft.}{12\,in.} = 1 = \frac{12in.}{1\,ft.}\ \&\ \frac{1\,lb.}{16\,oz.} = 1 = \frac{16\,oz.}{1\,lb.}$

$73\,\frac{lbs.}{in.^2} = 73\,\frac{lbs.}{in.^2}\times 1\ \times 1\ \times 1$

$\frac{73\,lbs.}{1\ in.^2}\times\frac{16\,oz.}{1\,lb.}\times\frac{12\,in.}{1\,ft.}\times\frac{12\,in.}{1\,ft.} =$

$\frac{73\times\ lbs.\times 16\times oz.\times 12\times in.\ \times 12\times in.}{1\times\ in.\times\ in.\ \times 1\times\ lb.\ \times 1\times ft.\ \times 1\times\ ft.} =$

$\frac{73\times 16\ \times 12\ \times 12\ \times oz.}{1\times\ ft.\times\ ft.} = 168192\,\frac{oz.}{ft.^2}$

36. $85\,ft.^2 = x\,yds.^2 \quad Fact\text{: } 1\,yd. = 3\,ft.$

$\therefore \frac{1\,yd.}{3\,ft.} = 1 = \frac{3\,ft.}{1\,yd.}$

$85\,ft.^2 = 85\,ft.^2\times 1\times 1 =$

$\frac{85\,ft.^2}{1}\times\frac{1\,yd.}{3\,ft.}\times\frac{1\,yd.}{3\,ft.}$

$\frac{85\,ft.\times ft.\times yd.\times yd.}{9\,ft.\times ft.} = \frac{85\,yd.^2}{9} = 9\frac{4}{9}\,yd.^2$

37. $80\,\frac{mi.}{hr.} = x\,\frac{in.}{sec.} \quad Facts\text{: } 5280\,ft. = 1\,mi.\ \&\ 12\,in. = 1\,ft.\ \&$ $60\,min. = 1\,hr.\ \&\ 60\,secs. = 1\,min.\ \therefore \frac{5280\,ft.}{1\,mi.} = 1 = \frac{1\,mi.}{5280\,ft.}\ \&$

$\frac{12\,in.}{1\,ft.} = 1 = \frac{1\,ft.}{12\,in.}\ \&\ \frac{60\,min.}{1\,hr.} = 1 = \frac{1\,hr.}{60\,min.}\ \&\ \frac{1\,min.}{60\,sec.} = 1 = \frac{60\,sec.}{1\,min.}$

$80\,\frac{mi.}{hr.}\times 1\ \times 1\ \times 1\ \times 1 = \frac{80\,mi.}{hr.}\times\frac{5280\,ft.}{1\,mi.}\times\frac{12\,in.}{1\,ft.}\times\frac{1\,hr.}{60\,mins.}\times\frac{1\,min.}{60\,secs.}$

$\frac{80\times 5280\times 12\times in.}{60\times 60\times secs.} = \frac{8}{6}\times\frac{5280}{60}\times\frac{12\,in.}{secs} = \frac{4\times 88\times 12\,in.}{3\,secs.} = 1408\,\frac{in.}{sec.}$

38. $\left(\frac{7}{15}+\frac{23}{25}\right)-\left(\frac{7}{30}+\frac{3}{40}\right)=\left(\frac{280}{600}+\frac{552}{600}\right)-\left(\frac{140}{600}+\frac{45}{600}\right)=\frac{832}{600}-\frac{185}{600}=\frac{647}{600}=1\frac{47}{600}$ $LCD = 2\times2\times2\times3\times5\times5=600$

39. $\left(\frac{7}{27}-\frac{1}{18}\right)+\left(\frac{43}{54}-\frac{7}{36}\right)=\left(\frac{28}{108}-\frac{6}{108}\right)+\left(\frac{86}{108}-\frac{21}{108}\right)=\frac{22}{108}+\frac{65}{108}=\frac{29}{36}$ $LCD = 2\times2\times3\times3\times3=2^2\cdot3^3=108$

40. $\left(5-\frac{11}{15}\right)-4=4\frac{4}{15}-4=\frac{4}{15}$ **41.** $6\frac{7}{12}+5\frac{7}{30}-10\frac{3}{50}=6+5-10+\frac{7}{12}+\frac{7}{30}-\frac{3}{50}=1+\frac{175}{300}+\frac{70}{300}-\frac{18}{300}=1\frac{227}{300}$

42. $\frac{3}{4}-\frac{7}{8}+\frac{11}{12}-\frac{1}{20}=\frac{90}{120}-\frac{105}{120}+\frac{110}{120}-\frac{6}{120}=\frac{90+110-105-6}{120}=\frac{89}{120}$ $LCD=2\times2\times2\times3\times5=2^3\times3\times5=120$

43. $301\frac{1}{2}+290\frac{1}{6}-370\frac{11}{12}=301+290-370+\frac{1}{2}+\frac{1}{6}-\frac{11}{12}=221+\frac{6}{12}+\frac{2}{12}-\frac{11}{12}=220+\frac{12}{12}+\frac{8}{12}-\frac{11}{12}=220\frac{3}{4}$

44. $6\frac{5}{6}+11-\left(2\frac{2}{3}+4\frac{1}{15}-5\frac{3}{20}\right)=\frac{41}{6}+\frac{11}{1}-\left(\frac{8}{3}+\frac{61}{15}-\frac{103}{20}\right)=\frac{410}{60}+\frac{660}{60}-\left(\frac{160}{60}+\frac{244}{60}-\frac{309}{60}\right)=\frac{1070}{60}-\frac{95}{60}=\frac{975}{60}=16\frac{1}{4}$

45. Commutative Property Addition – Switched the order of the terms – one equation. **46.** Transitive Property – Left side of the first equation equals the right side of the second equation to determine the third equation – three equations - the right side of the first equation is identical to the left side of the second equation. To solve for the two variables focus on the third equation and determine that "$x = 5$ *then* $a = 6$. **47.** Associative Property for *Addition* – Switched the parentheses grouping – one equation. **48.** Reflexive Property – No changes from the left and right sides of the equation – one equation. **49.** Associative Property Multiplication – Switched the parentheses grouping – one equation. **50.** Symmetric Property – Switched the order of the left and right sides of the equation – two equations. $x = 1$ **51.** Commutative Property Multiplication – Switched the order of the quantity and the variable, from the left side to the right side – one equation. **52.** Invisible ones and invisible decimal point and maybe more " $\frac{5.0^1}{1}$ ". **53.** Invisible ones and zeros and maybe more " $\frac{0037.100^1}{1}$ ". **54.** Invisible ones, decimal point, multiplication operation symbol, and maybe more " $\frac{y^1}{1}=3\times x^1+\frac{2.00}{1}$ ". **55.** Invisible ones, invisible decimal point, invisible zeros, invisible multiplication symbol and maybe more "$\frac{2.00^1}{1}\times\frac{x^{1.0}}{1.00}$ ". **56.** Many invisible ones, invisible decimal points, an invisible two and maybe more " $\frac{(2.0)^1\times 1x^{1.0}\times\sqrt[2]{y^1}}{1}$ ". **57.** Many invisible ones, invisible decimal points, an invisible multiplication operation symbol, and maybe more. Did anyone think about invisible positive signs? " $+\frac{3}{1}\cdot x+1y^1=+10.00$ ". **58.** Many invisible ones, decimal points, zeros, positive signs, and many more "$\left(+2\cdot x+\frac{\sqrt[3]{27}}{1}\right)\times\left(+9^1-\frac{1y}{1}\right)$ ". **59.** Invisible ones, decimal point, zeros, multiplication operation symbols, and maybe more " $03.00\times a^1\times b^1$ ". You decide. Problems **60. - 67.** are definitions which you can use the internet, but you should have most of the definitions memorized at this point *in* the textbook. **68.** You will not find the definition of this phrase on the internet, but the explanation is contained in this textbook and you just worked with 8 problems which focused on invisible numbers, terms, operations, and symbols. **69. & 70.** Look up the definitions of the two phrases on the internet if you still do not know the definitions. Here is one example of a Least Common Multiple and a Greatest Common Factor between the three terms "$8x^3y, 12\ xyz.\ and\ 16xyz^2$". The LCM equals " $48x^3yz^2$ ". The GCF equals " 4xy ". **71.** There is a lot you can say about multiplying and dividing by multiples and powers of 10, but if you mention moving the decimal point to the left or right in your explanation, make sure you mention that this is a trick and you want the students to understand why the trick works. The focus in your explanation should concentrate on why the trick works, not on the trick. Problems **72. - 78.** are mathematical phrases/expressions which you can look up on the internet.

79. $A_{rec.} = lw = 710\,ft. \times 525\,ft. =$

$372{,}750\,ft.^2\ \ Now\ Convert\ into\ acres - \ Fact{:}\ 1\ acre = 43{,}560\,ft.^2 \ \therefore\ \frac{1\ acre}{43{,}560\,ft.^2} = 1 = \frac{43{,}560\,ft.^2}{1\ acre}$

$$372{,}750\,ft.^2 = 372{,}750\,ft.^2 \times 1 = \frac{372{,}750\,ft.^2}{1} \times \frac{1\ acre}{43{,}560\,ft.^2} = \frac{372{,}750\ acres}{43{,}560} = 8\frac{24{,}270}{43560}\ acres = 8\frac{809}{1452}\ acres \approx 8.56\ ac$$

80. $A_{tri.} = \frac{1}{2}bh = \frac{1 \times 2020\ km \times 25\ km}{2} = \frac{1010\ \times 25\ km^2}{1} = 25250\ km^2\ \ Now\ Convert\ into\ hectares - Fact{:}$

$$100\ hectares = 1\ km^2 \ \therefore\ \frac{100\ ha}{1\ km^2} = 1 = \frac{1\ km^2}{100\ ha}\quad 25250\ km^2 = 25250\ km^2 \times 1 = \frac{25250\ km^2}{1} \times \frac{100\ ha}{1\ km^2} = 2{,}525{,}000\ ha$$

81. $1000\ ml = 1000\ cm^3 \ \therefore\ 1\ ml = 1\ cm^3$

Seventh Assignment:

1. Natural Numbers – are defined as the counting numbers. Numbers which are normally the first numbers, adults encourage a child to use when they learn to count. How do you tell a young child to count using their fingers? The Natural Numbers start with "1" and increase by "1" to infinity. Notation - $N = \{1, 2, 3, \ldots\}$.

2. Whole Numbers – are defined as the numbers used for counting objects which are **not** missing any pieces or parts. Whole Numbers begin with the number zero and increase by "1" to infinity. Here is an example to explain Whole Numbers - If you have three candy bars still in the unopened wrappers you have three whole candy bars. If you give two candy bars to your friends which are still in the wrappers, you then have one whole candy bar. If you open the wrapper and take a bite from the remaining whole candy bar you now have zero whole candy bars remaining. You only have part of a candy bar but not a whole candy bar. Notation - $W = \{0, 1, 2, 3, \ldots\}$.

3. The difference is Natural Numbers do not include the number <u>0</u>, but whole numbers do include the number <u>0</u>. Whole numbers start with the number <u>0</u> and increase by one forever, which means all the Natural numbers are Whole numbers. **4.** Integers – are all the Natural Numbers which can be either positive or negative from negative infinity to positive infinity including <u>0</u>. Notation - $\{\ldots, -3, -2, -1, 0, 1, 2, 3, \ldots\}$. **5.** Yes - Refer to the Notation for an Integer in problem 4. **6.** No – Integers include negative Natural numbers, and the set of Whole numbers does not include any negative numbers. **7.** Refer to the definitions listed above and the set notation for the three sets of numbers. **8.** a. Rational Numbers – are numbers which can be written as a fraction using two integers and the denominator of the fraction cannot equal zero. The fractions can include negative integers or positive integers or zero in the numerator, but the denominator may only include a negative or positive integer. Notation - $Q = \{\frac{x}{y}: \forall x \varepsilon \text{I and } \forall y \varepsilon \text{I}, y \neq 0\}$. b. Examples of Rational Numbers: $(\frac{-3}{5}, \frac{4}{-9}, 5\ or\ \frac{5}{1}, \frac{-8}{-2}, \frac{7}{1000}, 7.5, -88.75, 3\frac{7}{8})$.

8. Yes - Every Integer can be written with a denominator of 1. **10.** Yes – Every Natural Number can be written with a denominator of 1. **11.** Examples: Such that a Rational Number is NOT an Integer $(3.75, \frac{7}{8}, 87.5\%)$. Examples such that a Rational Number is an Integer $(-100 = \frac{100}{-1}, 2000 = \frac{-4000}{-2}, 13 = \frac{13}{1})$ **12.** Numbers which are Integers but not Whole Numbers – (-8, -15, -10). **13.** Refer back to the previous 12 problems and summarize the definitions to answer the question. Problems **14.-27.** Refer to the internet for definitions. **28.** The definition of an Irrational Number is *Not Rational*. **29.** Both expressions represent a way to graph points on a two-dimensional surface (plane), using a horizontal axis and a vertical axis. Problems **30.-34.** Refer to the internet for definitions and previous examples in the textbook. **35. & 36.** Refer to the definitions explained in this textbook.

37. *a.* 340, 30.4, 34, 3.4, 30.04, .07034, 78.04, 301, .00078, 300.1, 500, 2500

b. 21, .032104, .08961, .931, 6.71, .091, 710, .000071, .000902, 5700, .7474, .00079

c. .05019, 5019, .0701, .007019, 3040000, 55.1, .00099, 5.6, 7.1, .00071, 800000, 12601

d. 110000, .0056, .161, 75, .06, .007029, 11201, .7, .00005, .0015, 3000, 70.01

e. .07703, 889, .8098, 7100, 9909000, .9801, 50000, .005, .70023, 9980, .00098, 9870

f. 90.01, 25, 3750, .015, .0325, 5200, .7001, 10000000, 10000, 1, 77.654, 90087

38. $\frac{100}{100} = 1 \therefore 0.78 \times 1 = \frac{.78}{1} \times \frac{100}{100} = \frac{.78 \times 100}{100} = \frac{78}{100} = \frac{39}{50}$ **39.** $\frac{100}{100} = 1 \therefore .25 \times 1 = \frac{.25}{1} \times \frac{100}{100} = \frac{.25 \times 100}{100} = \frac{25}{100} = \frac{1}{4}$

40. $\frac{1000}{1000} = 1 \therefore .355 \times 1 = \frac{.355}{1} \times \frac{1000}{1000} = \frac{.355 \times 1000}{1000} = \frac{355}{1000} = \frac{71}{200}$ **41.** $\frac{100}{100} = 1 \therefore .98 \times 1 = \frac{.98}{1} \times \frac{100}{100} = \frac{98}{100} = \frac{49}{50}$

42. $\frac{10000}{10000} = 1 \therefore .9595 \times 1 = \frac{.9595}{1} \times \frac{10000}{10000} = \frac{9595}{10000} = \frac{1919}{2000}$ **43.** $\frac{100000}{100000} = 1 \therefore .31035 \times 1 = \frac{31035}{100000} = \frac{6207}{20000}$

When solving problems 44.-55. we will use the following fact in every conversion: $100\% = 1 \therefore \frac{100\%}{1} = 1 = \frac{1}{100\%}$

We skipped a few steps in some of these solutions.

44. $\frac{1}{100\%} = 1 \therefore 78\% \times 1 = \frac{78\%}{1} \times \frac{1}{100\%} = \frac{78\% \times 1}{1 \times 100\%^\wedge} = \frac{78}{100} = .78$ **45.** $\frac{1}{100\%} = 1 \therefore \frac{.25\%}{1} \times \frac{1}{100\%} = \frac{.25}{100} = .0025$

46. $\frac{1}{100\%} = 1 \therefore 355\% \times 1 = \frac{355\%}{1} \times \frac{1}{100\%} = \frac{355\% \times 1}{1 \times 100\%} = \frac{355}{100} = 3.55$ **47.** $\frac{1}{100\%} = 1 \therefore 0.98\% \times 1 = \frac{.98\% \times 1}{100\%} = .0098$

48. $9.595\% \times 1 = \frac{9.595\%}{1} \times \frac{1}{100\%} = \frac{9.595\% \times 1}{1 \times 100\%} = \frac{9.595}{100} = .09595$ **49.** $\frac{1}{100\%} = 1 \therefore \frac{0.31035\%}{1} \times \frac{1}{100\%} = \frac{0.31035}{100} = .0031035$

50. $\frac{100\%}{1} = 1 \therefore 0.78 \times 1 = \frac{0.78}{1} \times \frac{100\%}{1} = 0.78 \times 100\% = 78\%$ **51.** $25 \times 1 = \frac{25}{1} \times \frac{100\%}{1} = 25 \times 100\% = 2500\%$

52. $\frac{100\%}{1} = 1 \therefore 3.55 \times 1 = \frac{3.55}{1} \times \frac{100\%}{1} = 3.55 \times 100\% = 355\%$ **53.** $0.98 \times 1 = \frac{.98}{1} \times \frac{100\%}{1} = .98 \times 100\% = 98\%$

54. $\frac{100\%}{1} = 1 \therefore 95.95 \times 1 = \frac{95.95}{1} \times \frac{100\%}{1} = 95.95 \times 100\% = 9595\%$ **55.** $\frac{100\%}{1} = 1 \therefore \frac{0.31035}{1} \times \frac{100\%}{1} = 31.035\%$

When solving problems **56.-64.** we will multiply by all the forms of the number <u>**1**</u> indicated to solve problems 38.-55.

We skipped a few steps in some of these solutions.

56. $\frac{1}{100\%} = 1,\ .78\% \times 1 = \frac{.78\%}{1} \times \frac{1}{100\%} = \frac{.78\%}{100\%} = \frac{.78}{100} = .0078 \quad \frac{10000}{10000} = 1,\ .0078 \times 1 = .0078 \times \frac{10000}{10000} = \frac{78}{10000} = \frac{39}{5000}$

57. $\frac{100}{100} = 1, .25 \times 1 = \frac{.25}{1} \times \frac{100}{100} = \frac{.25 \times 100}{1 \times 100} = \frac{25}{100} = \frac{1}{4} \quad \frac{100\%}{1} = 1, .25 \times 1 = \frac{.25}{1} \times \frac{100\%}{1} = \frac{.25 \times 100}{1 \times 1} = .25 \times 100\% = 25\%$

58. Long division - $\frac{7}{8} = 0.875 \quad 100\% = 1 \therefore \frac{100\%}{1} = 1\ \&\ 0.875 = .875 \times 1 = \frac{.875}{1} \times \frac{100\%}{1} = \frac{.875 \times 100\%}{1 \times 11} = 87.5\%$

59. $\textit{Mentally divide by } 100\ \frac{98}{100} = .98\ \textit{reduce}\ \frac{98}{100} = \frac{49}{50} \quad 100\% = 1 \therefore \frac{100\%}{1} = 1\ \&\ .98 \times 1 = \frac{.98}{1} \times \frac{100\%}{1} = 98\%$

60. $\frac{100}{100} = 1\ \&\ 95.95 = 95 + .95 \therefore \frac{.95}{1} \times \frac{100}{100} = \frac{95}{100} = \frac{19}{20} \therefore 95.95 = 95\frac{19}{20}\ \&\ 95.95 \times 1 = \frac{95.95}{1} \times \frac{100\%}{1} = 9595\%$

61. $\frac{1}{100\%} = 1 \therefore \frac{31035\%}{1} \times 1 = \frac{31035\%}{1} \times \frac{1}{100\%} = \frac{31035\%}{100\%} = \frac{31035}{100} = 310.35\ \&\ 310.35 = 310 + \frac{35}{100} = 310\frac{7}{20}$

62. $\textit{Long division } 1\frac{9}{20} = 1.45\ \&\ 100\% = 1 \therefore \frac{100\%}{1} = 1\ \&\ 1.45 \times 1 = \frac{1.45}{1} \times \frac{100\%}{1} = \frac{1.45 \times 100\%}{1 \times 1} = 145\%$

63. $\textit{Mental math } 7\frac{1}{2}\% = 7.5\% \therefore 7.5\% \times 1 = \frac{7.5\%}{1} \times \frac{1}{100\%} = \frac{7.5}{100} = .075\ \&\ .075 \times 1 = \frac{.075}{1} \times \frac{1000}{1000} = \frac{75}{1000} = \frac{3}{40}$

64. $\textit{Division or mental math } 7\frac{2}{5} = 7.4\ \&\ 100\% = 1 \therefore \frac{100\%}{1} = 1\ \&\ 7.4 \times 1 = \frac{7.4}{1} \times \frac{100\%}{1} = 7.4 \times 100\% = 740\ \%$

65. Symmetric Property – flipped expressions in the two equations. **66.** Reflexive Property - One equation - one side is the reflection of the other side. **67.** Associative Property Multiplication – One equation – switched the parentheses - grouping of terms. **68.** Transitive Property – Left side of the first equation is the left side of the third equation, the right side of the second equation is the right side of the third equation and the middle expressions of the first two equations are identical – three equations. **69.** Commutative Property Multiplication – Switched the order of the quantity and the number – one equation. **70.** Commutative Property Addition – Switched the order of the two numbers in the quantity - one equation. **71.** Associative Property Addition – Switched the grouping of terms in the quantities, but notice, the individual terms did not switch in their order, one equation. **72.** Identity Property for Addition – When you add <u>zero</u> you get the same answer – one equation.

73. Identity Property for Multiplication – When you multiply by <u>one</u> you get the same answer - one equation. **74.** Identity Property for Multiplication **75.** Identity Property for Addition **76.** Identity Property for Addition **77.** Identity Property for Multiplication **78.** Identity Property for Addition **79.** "-10" is Integer, Rational, Real **80.** 70.5 is Rational, Real **81.** "0" is Whole, Integer, Rational, Real

82. "11.7171..." is Rational, Real - Terminating and Repeating Decimals can always be converted into fractions with integer numbers. **83.** "6" is Natural, Whole, Integer, Rational, Real **84.** "π" is Irrational, *Real* this is a non- terminating and a non-repeating decimal **85.** "-6.5" is Rational, Real **86.** "2 " is Natural, Whole, Integer, Rational, Real **87.** "$\sqrt{10}$ " Irrational, Real **88.** "1" is Natural, Whole, Integer, Rational, Real **89.** $100 = 100 \therefore \frac{100}{100} = 1\ \&\ 3.75 \div .25 = \frac{3.75}{.25} \times 1 = \frac{3.75}{.25} \times \frac{100}{100} =$

$\frac{3.75 \times 100}{.25 \times 100} = \frac{375}{25} = 375 \div 25 = 15$ **90.** $1000 = 1000 \therefore \frac{1000}{1000} = 1\ \&\ \frac{716.23}{.002} = \frac{716.23}{.002} \times \frac{1000}{1000} = \frac{716.23 \times 1000}{.002 \times 1000} = \frac{716230}{2} =$

$716230 \div 2 = 358115$ **91.** $10 = 10 \therefore \frac{10}{10} = 1$ & $2.656255 \div 101.5 = \frac{2.656255}{101.5} = \frac{2.656255}{101.5} \times 1 = \frac{2.656255}{101.5} \times \frac{10}{10} =$

$\frac{2.656255 \times 10}{101.5 \times 10} = \frac{26.56255}{1015} = 26.56255 \div 1015 = 0.02617$

92. $F = \frac{9}{5} C + 32°$

$F = \frac{9}{5} \times \frac{20°}{1} + 32°$

$F = \frac{9 \times 20°}{5 \times 1} + 32°$

$F = \frac{180°}{5} + 32°$

$F = 36° + 32°$

$F = 68°$

93. $F = \frac{9}{5} C + 32°$

$80° = \frac{9}{5} \times C + 32°$

$\underline{-32° = \quad -32°}$

$48° = \frac{9}{5} \times C + 0$

$48° = \frac{9C}{5}$

$\frac{9}{5} = \frac{9}{5}$

$48° \div \frac{9}{5} = \frac{9C}{5} \div \frac{9}{5}$

$\frac{48°}{1} \times \frac{5}{9} = \frac{9C}{5} \times \frac{5}{9}$

$\frac{48° \times 5}{1 \times 9} = \frac{9 \cdot C \cdot 5}{5 \cdot 9}$

$\frac{240°}{9} = 1C$

$26\frac{2}{3}° = C$

94. $F = \frac{9}{5} C + 32°$

$F = \frac{9}{5} \times \frac{80°}{1} + 32°$

$F = \frac{9 \times 80°}{5 \times 1} + 32°$

$F = \frac{720°}{5} + 32°$

$F = 144° + 32°$

$F = 176°$

You might believe it would be easier to solve problems 93. and 95., if you used the other form of the conversion theorem. I agree.

So, what is the other conversion theorem?

95. $F = \frac{9}{5} C + 32°$

$200° = \frac{9}{5} \times C + 32°$

$\underline{-32° = \quad -32°}$

$168° = \frac{9}{5} \times C + 0$

$168° = \frac{9C}{5}$

$\frac{9}{5} = \frac{9}{5}$

$168° \div \frac{9}{5} = \frac{9C}{5} \div \frac{9}{5}$

$\frac{168°}{1} \times \frac{5}{9} = \frac{9C}{5} \times \frac{5}{9}$

$\frac{168° \times 5}{1 \times 9} = \frac{9 \cdot C \cdot 5}{5 \cdot 9}$

$\frac{840°}{9} = 1C$

$93\frac{1}{3}° = C$

If you cannot answer the question above, then we argue, it is probably wiser to memorize one theorem and use it in both situations.

96. $12x = 150$

$12 = 12$

$\frac{12x}{12} = \frac{150}{12}$

$1x = 12.5 = 12\frac{1}{2}$

$x = 12.5 = 12\frac{1}{2}$

97. $17.656 + p = 2011.7$

$\underline{-17.656 \quad = -17.656}$

$0 + p = 1994.044$

$p = 1994.044$

98. $101.1b = 370.9359$

$101.1 = 101.1$

$\frac{101.1b}{101.1} = \frac{370.9359}{101.1}$

$1b = \frac{3709.359}{1011}$

$b = 3.669$

99. $17\frac{3}{8} = c + 6\frac{11}{12}$

$-6\frac{11}{12} = \quad -6\frac{11}{12}$

$17\frac{3}{8} = 17\frac{9}{24} = 16 + 1 + \frac{9}{24} =$

$16 + \frac{24}{24} + \frac{9}{24} = 16\frac{33}{24}$ & $\frac{11}{12} = \frac{22}{24}$

$16\frac{33}{24} - 6\frac{22}{24} = c + 6\frac{22}{24} - 6\frac{22}{24}$

$10\frac{11}{24} = c + 0$

$10\frac{11}{24} = c$ *or*

$c = 10\frac{11}{24}$

We are going to check the solutions for problems 96, 97, and 98 (below).

Checks	$12x = 150$	$17.656 + p = 2011.7$	$101.1b = 370.9359$
	$12 \cdot 12.5 = 150$	$17.656 + 1994.044 = 2011.7$	$101.1 \cdot 3.669 = 370.9359$
Identities	$150 = 150$ *Good*	$2011.7 = 2011.7$ *Good*	$370.6953 = 370.6953$ *Good*

100. $5\frac{2}{5} = 5\frac{1}{5} + r$

$5.4 = 5.2 + r$

$\underline{-5.2 = -5.2}$

$0.2 = 0 + r$

$0.2 = \quad r \ or$

$r = 0.2$

101. $\frac{k}{2.1} = 3.7$

$\times 2.1 = \times 2.1$

$\frac{k}{2.1} \times \frac{2.1}{1} = 3.7 \ \times 2.1$

$\frac{k \cdot 2.1}{2.1 \cdot 1} = 7.77$

$k \ \times 1 = 7.77$

$k = \ 7.77$

102. $\frac{w}{3\frac{1}{2}} = 3\frac{1}{2}$

$\frac{w}{3.5} = 3.5$

$\times 3.5 = \times 3.5$

$\frac{w}{3.5} \times \frac{3.5}{1} = 3.5 \times 3.5$

$w \times 1 = 12.25$

$w = 12.25$

103. $6.9 = 0.32\, m$

$\div 0.32 = \div 0.32$

$\frac{6.9}{.32} = \frac{.32}{.32} m$

$21.5625 = 1m$

$21.5625 = m \ or$

$m = 21.5625$

Notice, we did not use one set pattern to solve all the different problems. We did this to illustrate that there are frequently more than one set of steps to solve equations but certain principles must always be followed.

104. $A_{tri.} = \frac{1}{2} bh$

$A_{tri.} = \frac{1}{2} \times 7.5\, ft. \times 3.25\, ft.$

$A_{tri.} = \frac{1}{2} \cdot \frac{7.5\, ft.}{1} \cdot \frac{3.25\, ft.}{1}$

$A_{tri.} = \frac{1 \cdot 7.5\, ft. \cdot 3.25\, ft.}{2 \cdot 1 \cdot 1}$

$A_{tri.} = \frac{24.375\, ft.^2}{2} = 12.1875\, ft.^2$

105. $V_{cube} = s^3$

$V_{cube} = (2\frac{1}{2}\ in.)^3$

$V_{cube} = (2.5\ in.)^3$

$V_{cube} = 2.5\ in. \cdot 2.5\ in. \cdot 2.5\ in$

$V_{cube} = 15.625\ in.^3$

106. $A_{cir.} = \pi r^2$

$A_{cir.} = \pi \cdot (\pi\ yds.)^2$

$A_{cir.} = \pi \cdot \pi\ yd. \cdot \pi\ yd.$

$A_{cir.} = \pi^3 yd.^2$

107. $A_{rec.} = lw$

$A_{rec.} = 7\frac{3}{4}\ mi. \cdot 2.4\ mi.$

$A_{rec.} = 7.75\ mi. \cdot 2.4\ mi.$

$A_{rec.} = 18.6\ mi.^2$

108. $V_{rec.\ solid} = lwh$

$V_{rec.\ solid} = .75\ yd. \cdot 9\ in. \cdot 3\ ft.$

$V_{rec.\ solid} = .75\ yd. \cdot .25\ yd. \cdot 1\ yd.$

$V_{rec.} = 0.1875\ yd^3$

$Facts:\ 1\ yd.^3 = 27\ ft.^3$ &

$1\ yd.^3 = 46{,}656\ in.^3$

$\frac{1\ yd.^3}{27\ ft.^3} = 1 = \frac{27\ ft.^3}{1\ yd.^3}$ &

$V_{rec.solid} = 0.1875\ yd^3 \cdot 1 =$

$0.1875\ yd^3 \cdot \frac{27\ ft.^3}{1\ yd.^3} =$

$V_{rec.\ solid} = 5.0625\ ft.^3$

$\frac{1\ yd^3}{46{,}656\ in.^3} = 1 = \frac{46{,}656\ in.^3}{1\ yd.^3}$

$V_{rec.solid} = 0.1875\ yd^3 \times 1 =$

109. $C = 2\pi r$

$2\pi\ ft. = 2\pi r$

$\div 2\pi = \div 2\pi$

$\frac{2\pi\ ft.}{2\pi} = \frac{2\pi \cdot r}{2\pi}$

$1 \cdot ft = 1 \cdot r$

We need to focus on the variable "r" and the number "2π" which is the coefficient of "r".

$\therefore\ 1 = r\ or\ r = 1$

110. $A_{tri.} = \frac{bh}{2}$

$A_{tri.} = \frac{75\ ft. \cdot 108.5\ ft.}{2}$

$A_{tri.} = \frac{8137.5\ ft. \cdot ft.}{2}$

$A_{tri.} = 4068.75\ ft.^2$

$Fact:\ 1\ acre = 43560\ ft.^2\ \therefore$

$\frac{1\ acre}{43560\ ft.^2} = 1 = \frac{43560\ ft.^2}{1\ acre}$

$A_{tri.} = 4068.75\ ft.^2 \cdot 1 =$

$4068.75\ ft.^2 \cdot \frac{1\ acre}{43560\ ft.^2} =$

$\frac{4068.75\ acre}{43560} =$

$A_{tri.} \approx 0.093\ acre$

Probably a "dog"

Maybe a few "chickens"

111. $A_{rec.} = lw$

$A_{rec.} = 1705\ m \cdot 900.75\ m$

$A_{rec.} = 1535778.7\ m^2$

$Fact:\ 1\ ha = 10{,}000\ m^2\ \therefore$

$\frac{1\ hectare}{10{,}000\ m^2} = 1 = \frac{10{,}000\ m^2}{1\ ha}$

$A_{rec.} = 1535778.7\ m^2 \times 1 =$

$1535778.7\ m^2 \cdot \frac{1\ hectare}{10{,}000\ m^2} =$

$\frac{1535778.7\ hectare}{10{,}000} =$

$A_{rec.} = 153.57787\ ha$

Probably "*Cows & Horses*"

$0.1875\ yd^3 \cdot \frac{46{,}656\ in.^3}{1\ yd.^3} =$ In problem 108. we converted $yd.^3$ into $ft.^3$ and into $in.^3$.

$V_{rec.solid} = 8748\ in.^3$ All three solutions are acceptable and equivalent.

Eighth Assignment:

1. Fact: $\frac{4}{3} = \frac{4}{3}$ $\therefore$ $\frac{\frac{4}{3}}{\frac{4}{3}} = 1$ We know the answer to the given problem is <u>1</u> but the directions are to illustrate why the fraction division problem turns into a fraction multiplication problem. $\frac{3}{4} \div \frac{3}{4} = \frac{\frac{3}{4}}{\frac{3}{4}} = \frac{\frac{3}{4}}{\frac{3}{4}} \times 1 = \frac{\frac{3}{4}}{\frac{3}{4}} \times \frac{\frac{4}{3}}{\frac{4}{3}} = \frac{\frac{3}{4}\times\frac{4}{3}}{\frac{3}{4}\times\frac{4}{3}} = \frac{\frac{3}{4}\times\frac{4}{3}}{\frac{3\times4}{4\times3}} = \frac{\frac{3}{4}\times\frac{4}{3}}{1} = \frac{3}{4} \times \frac{4}{3}$ Mission accomplished the last step is now a multiplication problem with the right fraction inverted. Sometimes the simplest problems are the most difficult to use to illustrate why a new procedure will work.

2. Fact: $\frac{4}{3} = \frac{4}{3}$ $\therefore$ $\frac{\frac{4}{3}}{\frac{4}{3}} = 1$ Concentrate on the fraction to the right of the division operation symbol, "÷".

$\frac{7}{8} \div \frac{3}{4} = \frac{\frac{7}{8}}{\frac{3}{4}} = \frac{\frac{7}{8}}{\frac{3}{4}} \times 1 = \frac{\frac{7}{8}}{\frac{3}{4}} \times \frac{\frac{4}{3}}{\frac{4}{3}} = \frac{\frac{7}{8}\times\frac{4}{3}}{\frac{3}{4}\times\frac{4}{3}} = \frac{\frac{7}{8}\times\frac{4}{3}}{\frac{3\times4}{4\times3}} = \frac{\frac{7}{8}\times\frac{4}{3}}{1} = \frac{7}{8} \times \frac{4}{3}$ *Mission Accomplished*

3. Fact: $\frac{7}{6} = \frac{7}{6}$ $\therefore$ $\frac{\frac{7}{6}}{\frac{7}{6}} = 1$ $\frac{7}{11} \div \frac{6}{7} = \frac{\frac{7}{11}}{\frac{6}{7}} = \frac{\frac{7}{11}}{\frac{6}{7}} \times 1 = \frac{\frac{7}{11}}{\frac{6}{7}} \times \frac{\frac{7}{6}}{\frac{7}{6}} = \frac{\frac{7}{11}\times\frac{7}{6}}{\frac{6}{7}\times\frac{7}{6}} = \frac{\frac{7}{11}\times\frac{7}{6}}{\frac{6\times7}{7\times6}} = \frac{\frac{7}{11}\times\frac{7}{6}}{1} = \frac{7}{11} \times \frac{7}{6}$ *Done*

4. Fact: $\frac{5}{11} = \frac{5}{11}$ $\therefore$ $\frac{\frac{5}{11}}{\frac{5}{11}} = 1$ $1\frac{2}{5} \div 2\frac{1}{5} = \frac{7}{5} \div \frac{11}{5} = \frac{\frac{7}{5}}{\frac{11}{5}} = \frac{\frac{7}{5}}{\frac{11}{5}} \times 1 = \frac{\frac{7}{5}}{\frac{11}{5}} \times \frac{\frac{5}{11}}{\frac{5}{11}} = \frac{\frac{7}{5}\times\frac{5}{11}}{\frac{11}{5}\times\frac{5}{11}} = \frac{\frac{7}{5}\times\frac{5}{11}}{\frac{11\times5}{5\times11}} = \frac{\frac{7}{5}\times\frac{5}{11}}{1} = \frac{7}{5} \times \frac{5}{11}$ *Done*

5. Fact: $\frac{z}{x} = \frac{z}{x}$ $\therefore$ $\frac{\frac{z}{x}}{\frac{z}{x}} = 1$ $\frac{a}{d} \div \frac{x}{z} = \frac{\frac{a}{d}}{\frac{x}{z}} = \frac{\frac{a}{d}}{\frac{x}{z}} \times 1 = \frac{\frac{a}{d}}{\frac{x}{z}} \times \frac{\frac{z}{x}}{\frac{z}{x}} = \frac{\frac{a}{d}\times\frac{z}{x}}{\frac{x}{z}\times\frac{z}{x}} = \frac{\frac{a}{d}\times\frac{z}{x}}{\frac{x\times z}{z\times x}} = \frac{\frac{a}{d}\times\frac{z}{x}}{1} = \frac{a}{d} \times \frac{z}{x}$ *Proof Completed*
(Why did we indicate that the variables "d, x, and z≠ 0?) Answer: A denominator may never equal zero "0".

6. $243.14 \div 42.9 = 5.668$ $42.9\overline{)243.14}$ **7.** $\frac{210}{2100} = 0.1$ $2100\overline{)210}$ **8.** $\frac{\frac{9}{4}}{\frac{9}{10}} = 2\frac{1}{2}$ $0.9\overline{)2.25}$

9. $\frac{17}{8} \div \frac{2}{1} = \frac{17}{16} = 1\frac{1}{16}$ $2\overline{)2.125}$ **10.** $\frac{17}{35} = 0.4857142857142 \ldots$ $35\overline{)17}$ **11.** $\frac{2.260524}{0{,}3166} = 7.14$ $0.3166\overline{)2.260524}$

12. $\frac{d{\cdot}d \times (x+1) \times m}{m{\cdot}m{\cdot}m{\cdot}d \times d \times (x+1)} = \frac{1}{m^2}$ **13.** $\frac{5z(z+8)}{8}$ **14.** $\frac{2{\cdot}2{\cdot}2{\cdot}3{\cdot}x{\cdot}x \times x{\cdot}x \times 5{\cdot}y{\cdot}z{\cdot}(x+7)(x+7)}{(x+7)(x+7)(x+7) \times 2{\cdot}3{\cdot}5{\cdot}y{\cdot}z \times x{\cdot}x{\cdot}x{\cdot}(x+3)} = \frac{4x}{(x+7)(x+3)}$

15. $\frac{57}{11} \times \frac{71}{6} \times \frac{25}{2} \times \frac{1}{4047} = \frac{25}{132}$ **16.** $\frac{a^3(x-z)^4 \times p^4}{p^5 \times z^2(r-1)^2} \times \left[\frac{z(r-1) \times a^2(r-1)^2}{p \times (x-z)^3}\right] = \frac{a^3(x-z)^4}{p \times z^2(r-1)^2} \times \frac{z(r-1) \times a^2(r-1)^2}{p \times (x-z)^3} =$

$\frac{a^5(x-z)(r-1)}{p^2 z}$ **17.** $\frac{24-8}{(x+4)} + \frac{16-16}{(x+ym^3)} = \frac{8}{(x+4)} + \frac{0}{(x+ym^3)} = \frac{16}{x+4}$ **18.** $\frac{2.5+2{,}5}{x^2y^2z} + \frac{5.08xy-5.08xy}{5} = \frac{5}{x^2y^2z} + \frac{0}{5} = \frac{5}{x^2y^2z}$

19. $\frac{x}{8} - \frac{x}{8} + \frac{y}{9} - \frac{y}{9} + 1 = 0 + 1 = 1$ **20.** $\frac{(x+4)+(2x+8)-(3x+11)}{(p-z)^4} = \frac{x+4+2x+8-3x-11}{(p-z)^4} = \frac{1}{(p-z)^4}$ **21.** $\frac{77.91-66.987+111.2}{(x+11)^4} =$

$\frac{122.123}{(x+11)^4}$ **22.** $\frac{x(x+5)(x+3)}{x^2(x-5)(x+5)} = \frac{(x+3)}{x(x-5)} = \frac{x+3}{x(x-5)}$ **23.** $\frac{4(x-4)(x+3)}{5(x+5)(x+3)} \times \frac{3dm-5}{3dm-5} \times \frac{15(x+3)(x-3)}{12(x-4)(x-4)} =$

$\frac{4(x-4)(x+3)}{5(x+5)(x+3)} \times 1 \times \frac{15(x+3)(x-3)}{12(x-4)(x-4)} = \frac{4(x-4)(x+3) \times 15(x+3)(x-3)}{5(x+5)(x+3) \times 12(x-4)(x-4)} = \frac{(x-3)(x+3)}{(x+5)(x-4)}$ **24.** $\frac{x^2(x-3)(x-4)}{y(y-3)(y-4)} \times \frac{y^2(y-5)(y-4)}{3x^2(x-2)(x-4)} \times 1 =$

$\frac{x^2(x-3)(x-4) \times y^2(y-5)(y-4) \times 1}{y(y-3)(y-4) \times 3x^2(x-2)(x-4) \times 1} = \frac{y(x-3)(y-5)}{3(y-3)(x-2)}$ **25.** $\frac{(p+6)(p+6) \times (p-5)(p-7) \times (p-9)(p+4)}{(p-5)(p+4) \times (p-7)(p+4) \times p(p-9)(p+6)} = \frac{(p+6)}{p(p+4)}$

26. $\frac{x(x-2)(x+1) \times (x-7)(x-8) \times x(x+9)(x-6)}{(x+9)(x-7) \times x^3(x-5)(x-6) \times y(x-8)(x+1)} \div 1 = \frac{x(x-2)(x+1) \times (x-7)(x-8) \times x(x+9)(x-6)}{(x+9)(x-7) \times x^3(x-5)(x-6) \times y(x-8)(x+1)} = \frac{(x+2)}{xy(x-5)}$

27. $\frac{m^2(m-1)(m-1) \times m(m+9)(m-7) \times (m+9)(m-1)}{(m-7)(m+5) \times (m+9)(m-1) \times m^3((m-4)(m-1)} = \frac{(m-1)(m+9)}{(m+5)(m-4)}$ **28.** $LCD = (x+6)(x+2)$

Determine fractions which equal 1 in order to find equivalent fractions with the LCD. $\frac{LCD}{1st\ denominator}$

$\frac{(x+6)(x+2)}{(x+6)(x+2)} = 1$ ∴ *Multiply the first fraction by the fraction,* $\frac{1}{1}$. $\frac{LCD}{2nd\ denominator}$ $\frac{(x+6)(x+2)}{(x+2)} = x+6$

We know $(x+6) = (x+6)$ ∴ $\frac{(x+6)}{(x+6)} = 1$ $\frac{30}{x^2+8x+12} \times 1 + \frac{4x+5}{x+2} \times 1 = \frac{30}{x^2+8x+12} \times \frac{1}{1} + \frac{4x+5}{x+2} \times \frac{(x+6)}{(x+6)} =$

Write the multiplication problems as one − big − fraction. $\frac{30 \times 1}{(x+6)(x+2) \times 1} + \frac{(4x+5) \times (x+6)}{(x+2) \times (x+6)} =$ *Keep the denominators in factored form and multiply the numerators.* $\frac{30}{(x+6)(x+2)} + \frac{(4x+5)(x+6)}{(x+6)(x+2)} =$

$\frac{30}{(x+6)(x+2)} + \frac{4x^2+29x+30}{(x+6)(x+2)}$ *Write the addition problem as one − big − fraction.* $\frac{30 + 4x^2+29x+30}{(x+6)(x+2)} =$

$\frac{4x^2+29x+60}{(x+6)(x+2)}$ *We included a few comments to make it easier to understand specific steps. You do not have to include any comments in your solutions. We also skipped a few steps in our solutions which you many want to illustrate when you are explaining the solutions to your students.*

In problems 29.-34., we will illustrate the basic steps only. You need to illustrate all the steps you would use when you solve these problems in class for your students.

29. $LCD = (x+3)(x+3)(x-3)(x-2)$ $\frac{5}{(x+3)(x-3)} \times \frac{(x+3)(x-2)}{(x+3)(x-2)} - \frac{2}{(x+3)(x-2)} \times \frac{(x+3)(x-3)}{(x+3)(x-3)} -$

$\frac{3}{(x+3)(x+3)} \times \frac{(x-3)(x-2)}{(x-3)(x-2)} = \frac{5(x^2+x-6)}{(x+3)(x+3)(x-3)(x-2)} - \frac{2(x^2-9)}{(x+3)(x+3)(x-3)(x-2)} - \frac{3(x^2-5x+6)}{(x+3)(x+3)(x-3)(x-2)} =$

$\frac{5x^2+5x-30 - (2x^2-18) - (3x^2-15x+18)}{(x+3)(x+3)(x-3)(x-2)} = \frac{20x-30}{(x+3)(x+3)(x-3)(x-2)} = \frac{10(2x-3)}{(x+3)(x+3)(x-3)(x-2)}$

30. $LCD = (x-5)(x+5)(x+3)$ $\frac{5x}{(x-5)(x+5)} \times \frac{(x+3)}{(x+3)} + \frac{3(x+1)}{(x-5)(x+3)} \times \frac{(x+5)}{(x+5)} - \frac{5}{x+3} \times \frac{(x+5)(x-5)}{(x+5)(x-5)} =$

$\frac{5x^2+15x}{(x-5)(x+5)(x+3)} + \frac{3x^2+18x+15}{(x-5)(x+5)(x+3)} - \frac{5x^2-125}{(x-5)(x+5)(x+3)} = \frac{5x^2+15x + 3x^2+18x+15 - 5x^2+125}{(x-5)(x+5)(x+3)} = \frac{3x^2+33x+140}{(x-5)(x+5)(x+3)}$

31. $LCD = x-5$ $\frac{-5x+2}{x-5} - \frac{5x}{-(x-5)} = \frac{-5x+2}{x-5} + \frac{5x}{x-5} = \frac{2}{x-5}$ **32.** *Initially only work with the first two* fractions.

$LCD = a^2 - 9 = (a-3)(a+3)$ $\frac{a-1}{a^2-9} - \frac{1-a}{-(a^2-9)} + 30\frac{7}{13} + \frac{26x}{26x} = \frac{a-1}{a^2-9} + \frac{1-a}{(a^2-9)} + 30\frac{7}{13} + 1 = \frac{a-1+1-a}{(a^2-9)} +$

$31\frac{7}{13} = \frac{0}{(a-3)(a+3)} + 31\frac{7}{13} = 31\frac{7}{13}$ **33.** $LCD = (p+2)(p+2)(p+5)$ $\frac{7}{(p+2)(p+2)} \times \frac{p+5}{p+5} - \frac{7}{(p+5)(p+2)} \times \frac{P+2}{p+2} =$

$\frac{7p+35}{(p+2)(p+2)(p+5)} - \frac{7p+14}{(p+2)(p+2)(p+5)} = \frac{21}{(p+2)(p+2)(p+5)}$ **34.** $LCD = (x-3)(x-4)(x-1)$ $\frac{x+5}{(x-3)(x-4)} \times \frac{(x-1)}{(x-1)} -$

$\frac{x-5}{(x-4)(x-1)} \times \frac{x-3}{x-3} = \frac{(x+5)(x-1)}{(x-3)(x-4)(x-1)} - \frac{(x-5)(x-3)}{(x-3)(x-4)(x-1)} = \frac{x^2+4x-5\ -\ (x^2-8x+15)}{(x-3)(x-4)(x-1)} = \frac{x^2+4x-5-x^2+8x-15}{(x-3)(x-4)(x-1)} =$

$\frac{12x-20}{(x-3)(x-4)(x-1)} = \frac{4(3x-5)}{(x-3)(x-4)(x-1)}$ **35.** $p^2 + \frac{\frac{z}{z^2p+1}}{pz} = p^2 + \left\{\frac{z}{1} \div \frac{z^2p+1}{pz}\right\} = p^2 + \left\{\frac{z}{1} \times \frac{pz}{z^2p+1}\right\} = \frac{p^2}{1} + \frac{z^2p}{z^2p+1}$ *Now,*

we use the LCD $= z^2p + 1$ $\quad \frac{p^2}{1} \times \frac{z^2p+1}{z^2p+1} + \frac{z^2p}{z^2p+1} \times \frac{1}{1} = \frac{z^2p^3+p^2+z^2p}{z^2p+1} = \frac{p(z^2p^2+p+z^2)}{z^2p+1}$

36. *LCD for the quantity* $= (x-1)(x-1)(x+1)$ $\left(\frac{x}{(x-1)(x+1)} \times \frac{(x-1)}{(x-1)} - \frac{2}{(x-1)(x-1)} \times \frac{x+1}{x+1}\right) \times \frac{x^2-2x+1}{2} =$

$\left(\frac{x^2-x}{(x-1)(x-1)(x+1)} - \frac{2x+2}{(x-1)(x-1)(x+1)}\right) \times \frac{(x-1)(x-1)}{2} = \frac{x^2-3x-2}{(x-1)(x-1)(x+1)} \times \frac{(x-1)(x-1)}{2} = \frac{x^2-3x-2}{2(x+1)}$ **37.** *Multiplication*

First $\frac{x}{(x-1)(x+1)} + \left[\frac{1}{(x-1)(x-1)} \times \frac{-(x-1)(x+1)}{2}\right] = \frac{x}{(x-1)(x+1)} + \left[\frac{-(x+1)}{2(x-1)}\right] = \frac{x}{(x-1)(x+1)} - \frac{(x+1)}{2(x-1)}$ *LCD for the*

subtraction problem $= 2(x+1)(x-1)$ $\frac{2x}{2(x-1)(x+1)} - \frac{(x+1)(x+1)}{2(x-1)(x+1)} = \frac{2x - (x+1)(x+1)}{2(x-1)(x+1)} = \frac{-x^2-1}{2(x-1)(x+1)}$

38. $\frac{(r-7)(r-7)}{(r-7)(r+5)} \times \frac{r(r-6)(r+2)}{r(r-6)(r-7)} = \frac{(r+2)}{(r+5)}$ *or* $\frac{r+2}{r+5}$ **39.** <u>Equation</u> only **40.** Equation but more specifically an <u>Identity</u>

41. It is an equation, and it is an identity, but it is a special type of identity referred to as the <u>Reflexive Property</u>.

42. <u>Equation but more specifically an Identity</u>. **43.** It is an equation, and it is an identity, but is a special type of identity referred to as the <u>Reflexive Property</u>. **44.** <u>Equation</u> only **45.** $\frac{7}{13}, \frac{7}{11}, \frac{7}{10}$ **46.** $\frac{1.8989}{10.1}, \frac{18.989}{10.1}, \frac{79.89}{10.1}, \frac{88}{10.1}$

47. $\frac{\sqrt[3]{37}}{\sqrt{73}}, \frac{\sqrt[3]{37}}{\sqrt{41}}, \frac{\sqrt[3]{37}}{\sqrt{27}}, \frac{\sqrt[3]{37}}{\sqrt{10}}$ **48.** $\frac{\sqrt[2]{3}}{\sqrt[4]{71}}, \frac{\sqrt[2]{7}}{\sqrt[4]{71}}, \frac{\sqrt[2]{17}}{\sqrt[4]{71}}, \frac{\sqrt[2]{19}}{\sqrt[4]{71}}$ **49.** $\frac{7}{\sqrt{3}} \times \frac{\sqrt{3}}{\sqrt{3}} + \frac{3}{\sqrt{5}} \times \frac{\sqrt{5}}{\sqrt{5}} = \frac{7\sqrt{3}}{\sqrt{9}} + \frac{3\sqrt{5}}{\sqrt{25}} = \frac{7\sqrt{3}}{3} + \frac{3\sqrt{5}}{5} =$

$LCD = 15$ $\frac{7\sqrt{3}}{3} \times \frac{5}{5} + \frac{3\sqrt{5}}{5} \times \frac{3}{3} = \frac{35\sqrt{3}}{15} + \frac{9\sqrt{5}}{15} = \frac{35\sqrt{3}+9\sqrt{5}}{15}$ **50.** $\frac{5+\sqrt{7}}{2\sqrt{7}} \times 1 - \frac{5-\sqrt{3}}{5\sqrt{3}} \times \mathbf{1} = \frac{5+\sqrt{7}}{2\sqrt{7}} \times \frac{\sqrt{7}}{\sqrt{7}} - \frac{5-\sqrt{3}}{5\sqrt{3}} \times \frac{\sqrt{3}}{\sqrt{3}} =$

$\frac{5\sqrt{7}+7}{2\times 7} - \frac{5\sqrt{3}-3}{5\times 3}$ *The LCD for the two fractions equals* "$2 \times 3 \times 5 \times 7 = 210$ $\frac{5\sqrt{7}+7}{2\times 7} \times 1 - \frac{5\sqrt{3}-3}{5\times 3} \times 1$

$\left\{\frac{5\sqrt{7}+7}{2\times 7} \times \frac{5\times 3}{5\times 3} - \frac{5\sqrt{3}-3}{5\times 3} \times \frac{2\times 7}{2\times 7}\right\} = \frac{75\sqrt{7}+105}{2\times3\times5\times7} - \frac{70\sqrt{3}-42}{2\times3\times5\times7} = \frac{75\sqrt{7}-70\sqrt{3}+147}{210}$ **51.** *Fact:* $6+\sqrt{3} = 6+\sqrt{3}$

$\therefore \frac{6+\sqrt{3}}{6+\sqrt{3}} = 1$ *Notice the Identical denominators* $\frac{14}{6-\sqrt{3}} \times 1 = \frac{14}{6-\sqrt{3}} \times \frac{6+\sqrt{3}}{6+\sqrt{3}} = \frac{84+14\sqrt{3}}{36+6\sqrt{3}-6\sqrt{3}-3} = \frac{14(6+\sqrt{3})}{33}$

52. *Fact:* $\sqrt[3]{25} = \sqrt[3]{25}$ $\therefore \frac{\sqrt[3]{25}}{\sqrt[3]{25}} = 1$ $\frac{5}{2\sqrt[3]{5}} \times \frac{\sqrt[3]{25}}{\sqrt[3]{25}} - \frac{2}{3\sqrt[3]{5}} \times \frac{\sqrt[3]{25}}{\sqrt[3]{25}} = \frac{5\sqrt[3]{25}}{2\sqrt[3]{125}} - \frac{2\sqrt[3]{25}}{3\sqrt[3]{125}} = \frac{5\sqrt[3]{25}}{2\times5} - \frac{2\sqrt[3]{25}}{3\times5}$ $LCD = 2\times3\times5$

$\frac{5\sqrt[3]{25}}{2\times5} \times 1 - \frac{2\sqrt[3]{25}}{3\times5} \times 1 = \frac{5\sqrt[3]{25}}{2\times5} \times \frac{3}{3} - \frac{2\sqrt[3]{25}}{3\times5} \times \frac{2}{2} = \frac{3\times5\sqrt[3]{25}}{3\times2\times5} - \frac{(2\times2\sqrt[3]{25})}{2\times3\times5} = \frac{11\sqrt[3]{25}}{30}$

53. *Fact:* $5-\sqrt{x} = 5-\sqrt{x}$ $\therefore \frac{5-\sqrt{x}}{5-\sqrt{x}} = 1$ $\frac{x}{5+\sqrt{x}} \times 1 = \frac{x}{5+\sqrt{x}} \times \frac{5-\sqrt{x}}{5-\sqrt{x}} = \frac{x\ (5-\sqrt{x})}{(5+\sqrt{x})\ (5-\sqrt{x})} = \frac{5x-x\sqrt{x}}{25-x}$ *or* $\frac{x(5-\sqrt{x})}{25-x}$

54. *Facts:* $i^3 = -i$ & $(i+\sqrt{7}) = (i+\sqrt{7})$ $\therefore \frac{i+\sqrt{7}}{i+\sqrt{7}} = \frac{\sqrt{7}+i}{\sqrt{7}+i} = 1$ $\frac{10}{-i+\sqrt{7}} = \frac{10}{\sqrt{7}-i} = \frac{10}{\sqrt{7}-i} \times 1 = \frac{10}{\sqrt{7}-i} \times \frac{\sqrt{7}+i}{\sqrt{7}+i} =$

$\frac{10(\sqrt{7}+i)}{(\sqrt{7}-i)(\sqrt{7}+i)} = \frac{10(\sqrt{7}+i)}{7-i^2} = \frac{10(\sqrt{7}+i)}{8} = \frac{5(\sqrt{7}+i)}{4}$ **55.** *Fact:* $\frac{1+2i}{1+2i} = 1$ $\frac{3i-6}{1-2i} \times \frac{1+2i}{1+2i} = \frac{6i^2+3i-12i-6}{1-4i^2} = \frac{-6-9i-6}{1+4} =$

$\frac{-3(3i+4)}{5}$ **56.** $2+11i = 2+11i$ $\therefore \frac{2+11i}{2+11i} = 1$ $\frac{25}{2-11i} \times \frac{2+11i}{2+11i} = \frac{25(2+11i)}{4-121i^2} = \frac{25(2+11i)}{4+121} = \frac{25(2+11i)}{125} = \frac{2+11i}{5}$

57. *Fact* $i^3 = -i$ $\frac{5i}{7+i} - \frac{5}{7+i} = \frac{5i-5}{7+i} = \frac{5(i-1)}{7+i} \times \frac{7-i}{7-i} = \frac{5(-i^2+8i-7)}{49-i^2} = \frac{5(8i-6)}{50} = \frac{10(4i-3)}{50} = \frac{(4i-3)}{5}$

58. $\frac{11}{7i}+\frac{10}{7i}=\frac{21}{7i}\times\frac{i}{i}=\frac{21i}{7i^2}=\frac{21i}{-7}=-3i$ **59.** *Fact*: $\pi\ rads = 180° \therefore \frac{\pi\ rads}{180°}=1=\frac{180°}{\pi\ rads}$ $\frac{3\ rads}{10}\times 1=$

$\frac{3\ rads}{10}\times\frac{180°}{\pi\ rads}=\left(\frac{54}{\pi}\right)°$ *approimate answers not required* 17.89° **60.** *Fact*: $2\pi\ rads = 360°$ &

$360° = 1\ rev. \therefore 2\pi\ rads = 1\ rev$ & $\frac{2\pi\ rads}{1\ rev.}=1=\frac{1\ rev.}{2\pi\ rads}$ $\frac{31}{8}\ revs.=\frac{31\ revs.}{8}\times\frac{2\pi\ rads}{1\ rev.}=\frac{31\pi\ rads}{4}=$

$7\frac{3}{4}\ \pi\ rads$ **61.** $\frac{0.8\ rads}{1}\times 1=\frac{0.8\ rads}{1}\times\frac{180°}{\pi\ rads}=\frac{0.8\ rads\ \times\ 180°}{1\ \times\ \pi\ rads}=(\frac{144}{\pi})°$ **62.** $\frac{144°}{1}\times\frac{\pi\ rads}{180°}=\frac{4}{5}\pi\ rads$

63. $\frac{3.5\ rads}{1}\times\frac{1\ rev.}{2\pi\ rads}=\frac{1.75}{\pi}\ revs.=\frac{7}{4\pi}\ revs.$ **64.** $\frac{27\ revs.}{4}\times\frac{2\pi\ rads}{1\ rev.}=\frac{27\pi\ rads}{2}=13\frac{1}{2}\pi\ rads-12\pi\ rads=$

$1\frac{1}{2}\pi\ rads=\frac{3}{2}\pi\ rads$ **65.** $\frac{840°}{1}\times\frac{\pi\ rads}{180°}=\frac{14}{3}\pi\ rads=4\frac{2}{3}\pi\ rads$ *Now, if 2π radians equals* 1

revolution then 4π radians equal two complete revolutions. Therefore, subtract $4\frac{2}{3}\pi$ rads and

4π rads. $4\frac{2}{3}\pi\ rads-4\pi\ rads=\frac{2}{3}\pi\ rads$ **66.** $1000x = 891.891891 \ldots$ **67.** $1000x = 18.88 \ldots$

$\underline{-\ x = \ -.891891\ldots}$

$999x = 891$

$x=\frac{891}{999}=\frac{33}{37}$

67. (continued)

$\underline{-100x = -1.88\ldots}$

$900x = 17$

$x=\frac{17}{900}$

Given problem was $707.01888\ldots \therefore$

$707.01888\ldots = 707\frac{17}{900}$

Check: $707\frac{17}{900}=707.01888.$

68. $10x = 9.99\ldots$

$\underline{-1x = -.99\ldots}$

$9x = 9$

$x=\frac{9}{9}=1$

$0.999.. = 1$ *because there are no numbers between* $1\ \&\ 0.999\ldots$

69. $100x = 72.7272\ldots$

$\underline{-x = -\ .7272\ldots}$

$99x = 72$

$x=\frac{72}{99}=\frac{8}{11}$

Checks: $\frac{8}{11}=0.7272\ldots$ $\frac{33}{37}=0.891891\ldots$

70. $10{,}000x = 3012.1212\ldots$

$\underline{-100x = -30.1212\ldots}$

$9{,}900x = 2982.$

$x=\frac{2982}{9900}=\frac{2\cdot 3\cdot 7\cdot 71}{2^2\cdot 3^2\cdot 5^2\cdot 11}=\frac{7\cdot 71}{2\cdot 3\cdot 25\cdot 11}=\frac{497}{1650}$

71. $10{,}000x = 1982.982982\ldots$

$\underline{-10x = -1.982982\ldots}$

$9{,}990x = 1981.$

$x=\frac{1981}{9990}$ *but the answer to the original problem is* $87\frac{1981}{9990}$

72. $F=\frac{9}{5}\times 40°+32°$

$F = 72° + 32°$

$F = 104°$

Check the fraction answers to problems **70.** *and* **71.** *by doing long division.* $\frac{497}{1650}=0.301212\ldots$ &

$87\frac{1981}{9990}=87.1982982\ldots$ *All six repeating decimals, problems 66. −71., were converted into fractions therefore, these six repeating decimals are rational numbers.*

73. $136° = 1.8\,C + 32°$

$104° = 1.8C$

$\frac{104°}{1.8}=C$

$57.77\ldots° = C = 57\frac{7}{9}°$

74. $92° = 1.8\,C + 32°$

$60° = 1.8C$

$60° \div 1.8 = C$

$33.33\ldots° = C = 33\frac{1}{3}°$

75. $F = 1.8 \times 5° + 32°$ (We know "$1.8=\frac{9}{5}$".)

$F = 9° + 32°$

$F = 41°$

76. Key points to mention in your paragraph: A. When you use a Fahrenheit thermometer the freezing temperature for water is 32° and the boiling temperature for water is 212°. The difference between the two temperature is 180°. B. When you use a Celsius thermometer the freezing temperature for water is 0° and the boiling temperature for water is 100°. The difference between the two temperatures is 100°. C. When you make ratios out of the two differences between freezing and boiling water involving the two types of temperature measurements, the ratios could be written in two forms: either $\frac{180°}{100°}$ which is equivalent to the ratio/fraction, $\frac{9}{5}$ or $\frac{100°}{180°}$ which is equivalent to the ratio/fraction, $\frac{5}{9}$. D. Compare the freezing temperatures, between the two types of temperature measurements (0° and 32°). It is easy to determine when water is in two identical tubes and one tube is set up using the Celsius measurements 0° to 100° and the other tube is set up using the Fahrenheit measurements 32° to 212°, if the temperature in the room is freezing, the water in each tube will be at the same height in the tubes. As the temperature in the room rises the water will rise at the same rate in each tube. E. If one tube starts at +32°and the other tube starts at 0° you should be able to determine why you add 32° in the formula. You must also realize the fluids will rise at the same rate but the numbers in the Fahrenheit thermometer are closer together and the Fahrenheit numbers will go up quicker than the Celsius numbers which is why the ratio, $\frac{9}{5}$ is relevant.

77. $F = \frac{9}{5}C + 32°$ Subtract 32° *from both sides of the equation.*

$$F = \frac{9}{5}C + 32°$$

$$\underline{-32° = \quad -32°}$$

$$F - 32° = \frac{9}{5}C + 0°$$

$F - 32° = \frac{9}{5}C$ Divide both sides of the equation by the fraction, $\frac{9}{5}$.

$$\div\frac{9}{5} = \div\frac{9}{5}$$

$$(F - 32°) \div \frac{9}{5} = \frac{\frac{9}{5}C}{\frac{9}{5}}$$

$(F - 32°) \times \frac{5}{9} = 1C$ Now the equation may be written as $\frac{5}{9}(F - 32°) = C$ *or* $C = \frac{5}{9}(F - 32°)$

Problems **78. –90.** Refer to the Internet and previous references in this textbook for the exact explanations and examples of theorems and properties.

Ninth Assignment:

PRACTICE FINAL TEST Part A:

In a few problems, little to no work will be required, maybe just answers.

The objective of this final test for both elementary majors and secondary math majors is to have you, a future arithmetic teacher or mathematics teacher, demonstrate you understand every step required to solve the problems then explain the steps to your students when you are in the classroom and the students look to you as the expert. **If you expect to receive credit for your answers to the questions on this test which specifically asks you to write all the steps to solve a problem, you must write all the steps continually emphasized in the example problems throughout this textbook.**

We do not expect your students to write every step which you must write to solve similar types of problems when you are the teacher. We do expect you will write many of the steps you indicate on this final test when you explain and/or illustrate solutions to your students, but it is unrealistic to expect all your students to write every step you write in your initial explanations.

You will be the expert in your classroom so you must decide which steps are the required steps for your students to write when they solve your problems.

Teaching arithmetic and mathematics is an "art" you need to make sure your students make the write strokes at the right time.

1. Key Points – A. Must have the same Least Common Denominator for all the fractions which are added or subtracted. B. Write one big fraction with all the numerators of the fractions added and subtracted in the numerator of the big fractions. C. Only write the LCD once in the big fraction. D. Form one fraction after adding and subtracting the numbers in the numerator to find the numerator of the new fraction and keep the denominator which you have been using. D. Check to see if the new simplified fraction will reduce. E. The LCD may be a number, one or more variables multiplied, and/or one or more quantities multiplied.

2. $\frac{5}{53}$ **3.** $\frac{4}{x}$ **4.** $\frac{23}{301}$ **5.** $\frac{25}{xyz}$ **6.** 0 **7.** Key Points – A. The first piece of information which must be used to convert from any unit of measurement into an equivalent unit measurement with a different label is to write the equation (identity) involving the unit of measurement given on one side of the identity and on the other side of the identity the unit of measurement required after the conversion is completed. It is important that one of the units indicated in the identity contains the conversion factor number for the two units indicated. B. Set up two different ratios which equal one. C. Multiply the given unit of measurement by the number 1. D. Multiply the given unit measurement by the appropriate ratio equal to 1 and continue the conversion process. E. Make sure the label with the given measurement cancels appropriately with the ratio which equals 1. F. Set up one big fraction multiplication problem and complete the multiplication and/or division process to complete the unit conversion process.

8. $7\frac{7}{99} < 7\frac{7}{9}$ **9.** $0.160999\ldots < 0.161616\ldots$ **10.** $\frac{3}{13} = \frac{30}{130}$ **11.** $LCM = 48$ & $GCF = 4$

12. $72 = 2 \times 2 \times 2 \times 3 \times 3$ $64 = 2 \times 2 \times 2 \times 2 \times 2 \times 2$ $78 = 2 \times 3 \times 13$ $\therefore$ $LCD = 2^6 \times 3^2 \times 13 = 7{,}488$

$22{,}464$ *is a Common Denominator but it is not the LCD becasue it is 3 times bigger than necessary.*

13. 2791 **14.** 22,300 **15.** 0.48 **16.** $8.25 = 8\frac{1}{4}$

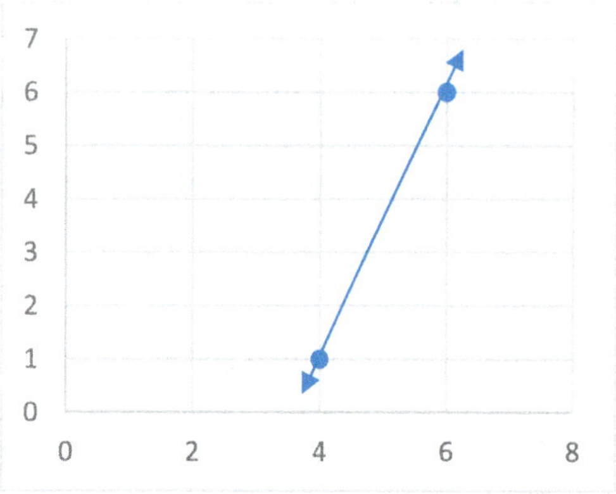

17.

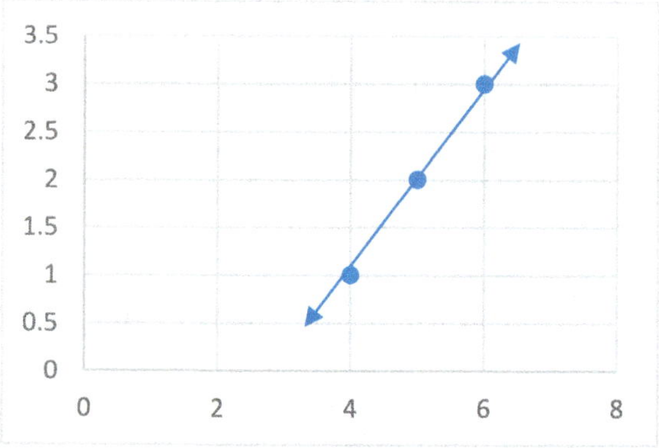

18.

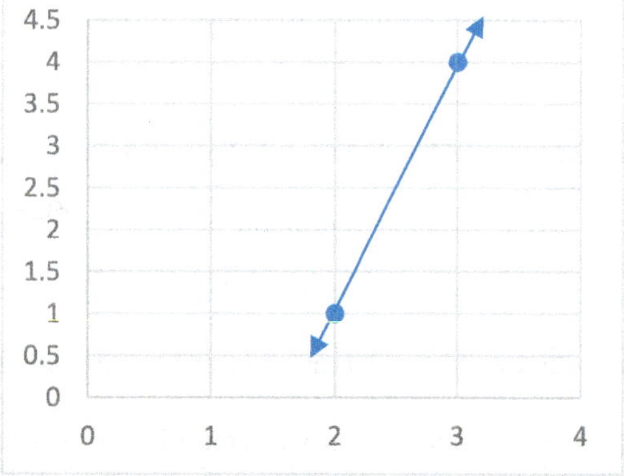

19.

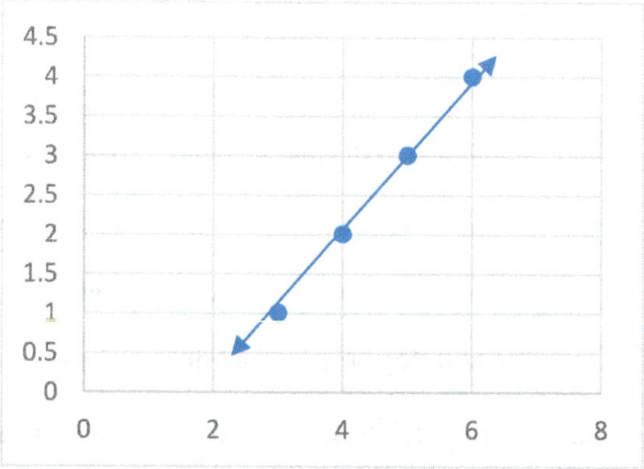

20.

21. 432

2×216

$2 \times 2 \times 108$

$2 \times 2 \times 2 \times 54$

$2 \times 2 \times 2 \times 2 \times 27$

$2 \times 2 \times 2 \times 2 \times 3 \times 9$

$2 \times 2 \times 2 \times 2 \times 3 \times 3 \times 3$

22. 2000

2×1000

$2 \times 2 \times 500$

$2 \times 2 \times 2 \times 250$

$2 \times 2 \times 2 \times 2 \times 125$

$2 \times 2 \times 2 \times 2 \times 5 \times 25$

$2 \times 2 \times 2 \times 2 \times 5 \times 5 \times 5$

Problems **23.-30.** We expect you to check your explanations with the textbook or internet.

31. $\frac{7}{11}$ **32.** $\frac{1}{2}$ **33.** 21 **34.** $\frac{5b}{7}$

35. $\frac{3 \times 31}{2 \times 3 \times 31} = \frac{1}{2}$ **36.** $\frac{2\times3\times3\times3\times3}{3\times3\times3\times7} = \frac{6}{7}$

37. $LCD = 2 \times 2 \times 7 \times 7 = 2^2 \times 7^2 = 196$

38. $LCM = x \cdot x \cdot x \cdot y \cdot y \cdot z \cdot z \cdot z \cdot z = x^3y^2z^4$

39. $LCM = 2 \cdot 3 \cdot 3 \cdot 3 \cdot 5 \cdot 5 \cdot m \cdot m \cdot m \cdot n \cdot n \cdot n \cdot n \cdot (x+y) \cdot (x+y) = 2 \cdot 3^3 \cdot 5^2 \cdot m^3n^4(x+y)^2 = 1350m^3n^4(x+y)^2$

40. $36 = 2^2 \cdot 3^2$ & $48 = 2^4 \cdot 3 \therefore LCD = 144$ **41.** $99 = 3 \cdot 3 \cdot 11$ & $121 = 11 \cdot 11$ & $66 = 2 \cdot 3 \cdot 11 \therefore LCD = 2178$

42. $LCD = 108$ $\frac{15}{108} - \frac{10}{108} = \frac{5}{108}$ **43.** $LCD = 2520$ $\frac{2205}{2520} - \frac{630}{2520} - \frac{490}{2520} - \frac{56}{2520} + \frac{2002}{2520} = \frac{3031}{2520} = 1\frac{511}{2520} = 1\frac{73}{360}$ **44.** $LCD = 84$

$\frac{31}{14} + \frac{74}{21} - \frac{37}{28} = \frac{186}{84} + \frac{296}{84} - \frac{111}{84} = \frac{186+296-111}{84} = \frac{371}{84} = 4\frac{35}{84} = 4\frac{5}{12}$

45. $909 = z - 11$

$+11 = \;+11$

$920 = z$

46. $p + 101 = 201$

$-101 = -101$

$p = 100$

47. $0.03d = 67.2$

$\div 0.03 = \div 0.03$

$d = 2240$

48. $\frac{a}{7} = 9$

$\times 7 = \times 7$

$a = 63$

49. $z - \frac{3}{8} = \frac{7}{24}$

$+\frac{9}{24} = +\frac{9}{24}$

$z = \frac{16}{24} = \frac{2}{3}$

50. $\frac{n}{.7} = \frac{3}{4}$

$\times .7 = \times .7$

$n = .525 = \frac{21}{40}$

51. $3.3d = 67.2$

$\div 3.3 = \div 3.3$

$d = 20.3636 ... = 20.364$

52. $a + 11.93 = 89.661$

$-11.93 = -11.93$

$a = 77.731$

53. $100.75 \div 25 = 4.03 = 4\frac{3}{100}$ **54.** $\frac{9}{5} \div \frac{27}{10} = \frac{9}{5} \times \frac{10}{27} = \frac{9\times10}{5\times27} = \frac{2}{3} = .66 ...$

55. $LCM = 2^2 \cdot 3^2 \cdot 5^2 = 900$ & *2700 is 3 times too big.*

56. $LCM = 2^3 \cdot 3^2 \cdot 5 = 360$ & *1440 is also 4 times too big.* **57.** *15 cars + 65 trucks + 73 SUVs + 5 tractors*

58. $5.25\,ft.$ **59.** $5ba$ or $5ab$ **60.** $113.25\,x^2y^3z$ *(Remember when terms are multiplied the order is irrelevant.)*

61. $14\frac{3}{8}xyz + 11.92x^2y^2z^2$ or $11.92x^2y^2z^2 + 14\frac{3}{8}xyz$

> The second answer is probably the better way to write the answer because the variables are in alphabetical order and the exponents are larger. Not an extremely important point.

62. $7x^3 + 2x^2 + 2x + 3$ *(The preferred order of the 4 terms is based on the largest exponent of the variable, x.)*

63. $1237.5\,ft.^3$ **64.** $\frac{15b^2(8+m)}{16+m}$ **65.** $\frac{11\,yd.^2}{2}$ or $5.5\,yd.^2$ **66.** $5x^2y^2$ **67.** $D = \frac{400}{1} \cdot \frac{mi.}{hr.} \cdot \frac{5.5}{1} \cdot \frac{hrs.}{1} = 2200\,mi.$ **68.** $A_{cir.} = \pi(1\,ft.)^2 = \pi\,ft.^2$ **69.** $V_{cube} = (3.5\,cm)^3 = 42.875\,cm^3$ **70.** $LCD = 2 \cdot 3^2 \cdot 5 \cdot 7 \cdot 17 = 10{,}710$ **71.** $LCM = x^2y^3z^4$

72. $LCM = 2^3 \cdot 3 \cdot 7 \cdot 11 \cdot 23 = 42{,}504$ **73.** $LCM = 180x^4y^2$ **74.** $\frac{33.5}{0}$ *Undefined No Solution* **75.** $\frac{14-65+75}{78} = \frac{24}{78} = \frac{4}{13}$

76. $\frac{17}{18} - \left(\frac{12}{15} - \frac{2}{15}\right)^2 = \frac{17}{18} - \frac{2^2}{3} = \frac{17-8}{18} = \frac{1}{2}$ **77.** *Commutative Property for Addition* **78.** *Symmetric Property*

79. *Transitive Property* **80.** *Reflexive Property* **81.** *Associative Property Multiplication* **82.** *Associative*

Property Addition **83.** *Commutative Property Multiplication* **84.** $\frac{3z(z-8)^2}{4y(m+4)(z-16)^3}$ Problems **85.-96.** The answers to all these questions can be found using the internet. **97.** $\frac{1000\ ml}{1\ L}=1=\frac{1\ L}{1000\ ml}$ **98.** $\frac{1\ yd.^2}{9\ ft.^2}=1=\frac{9\ ft.^2}{1\ yd.^2}$

99. $\frac{.76\ mi.}{1}\times 1=\frac{.76\ mi.}{1}\times\frac{5280\ ft.}{1\ mi.}=4012.8\ ft.$ **100.** $\frac{500\ in.}{1}\times 1=\frac{500\ in.}{1}\times\frac{1\ yd.}{36\ in.}=13.888\ldots\ yds.\ or\ 13\frac{8}{9}\ yds.$

101. $\frac{7.5\ km}{1}\times 1=\frac{7.5\ km}{1}\times\frac{1000\ m}{1\ km}=7500\ m$ **102.** $\frac{100\ oz.}{1}\times\frac{1\ lb.}{16\ oz}=\frac{100\ oz.\times 1\ lb.}{1\times 16\ oz.}=6.25\ lbs.\ or\ 6\frac{1}{4}\ lbs.$ **103.** 30.04

104. 3000 **105.** *Fact*: $100\%=1\ \therefore\ \frac{100\%}{1}=1=\frac{1}{100\%}$ & $0.78\%\times 1=\frac{0.78\%}{1}\times\frac{1}{100\%}=.0078$ & *Fact*: $\frac{10000}{10000}=1$ &

$\frac{.0078}{1}\times 1=\frac{.0078}{1}\times\frac{10000}{10000}=\frac{.0078\times 10000}{1\times 10000}=\frac{78\times 1}{1\times 10000}=\frac{78}{10000}=\frac{39}{5000}$ **106.** $95\frac{95}{100}=95\frac{19}{20}$ & $\frac{95.95}{1}\times 1=\frac{95.95\times 100\%}{1\times 1}=9595\%$

107. $\frac{7}{8}=.875$ & $\frac{.875}{1}\times\frac{100\%}{1}=.875\times 100\%=87.5\%$ **108.** $\frac{31035\%}{1}\times\frac{1}{100\%}=\frac{31035}{100}=310.35\ \&\ 310.35=310\frac{35}{100}=310\frac{7}{20}$

109. $3\frac{3}{4}=3.75$ & $\frac{3.75}{1}\times\frac{100\%}{1}=3.75\times 100\%=375\%$

110. $\frac{.0015}{1}\times\frac{10000}{10000}=\frac{15}{10000}=\frac{3}{2000}$ & $\frac{.0015}{1}\times 1=\frac{.0015}{1}\times\frac{100\%}{1}=.15\%$

FINAL TEST Part B:

1. Find the LCD for 16, 10, and 15. $16=2^4$ $10=2\times 5$ $15=3\times 5$ $\therefore$ $LCD=2^4\cdot 3\cdot 5=240.$ Next, convert all three fractions into equivalent fractions by dividing the LCD by each denominator and multiplying each of the original fractions by a special value equal to the number 1, which will be determined in three division problems. $\frac{240}{16}=15$

$\therefore 15=15\ \&\ \frac{15}{15}=1,\ \frac{240}{10}=24\ \therefore 24=24\ \&\ \frac{14}{14}=1,\ \frac{240}{15}=16\ \therefore 16=16\ \&\frac{16}{16}=1$ $\frac{7}{16}\times 1=\frac{7}{16}\times\frac{15}{15}=\frac{7\times 15}{16\times 15}=\frac{105}{240}$

& $\frac{7}{10}\times 1=\frac{7}{10}\times\frac{24}{24}=\frac{7\times 24}{10\times 24}=\frac{168}{240}$ & $\frac{7}{15}\times 1=\frac{7}{15}\times\frac{16}{16}=\frac{7\times 16}{15\times 16}=\frac{112}{240}$ $\frac{7}{16}+\frac{7}{10}-\frac{7}{15}=\frac{105}{240}+\frac{168}{240}-\frac{112}{240}=\frac{105+168-112}{240}=\frac{161}{240}$

We illustrated many of the steps required to simplify this problem. You are expected to write the solution using all the steps we indicated and a few additional steps. We will not illustrate the same degree of detail in the remaining solutions for this section of problems.

2. $LCD=120\ \therefore\ \frac{100}{120}-\frac{75}{120}+\frac{28}{120}=\frac{53}{120}$ **3.** $\frac{3\times 5}{2\times 2\times 2\times 2\times 2}\times\frac{2\times 2\times 2}{5\times 5}\times\frac{2\times 2}{3}=\frac{3\times 5\times 2\times 2\times 2\times 2\times 2}{2\times 2\times 2\times 2\times 2\times 5\times 5\times 3}=\frac{1}{5}$

4. $\frac{15}{8}\div\frac{25}{4}\times\frac{5}{6}=\frac{3\times 5}{2\times 2\times 2}\times\frac{2\times 2}{5\times 5}\times\frac{5}{2\times 3}=\frac{1}{2\times 2}=\frac{1}{4}$ **5.** $\frac{39}{8}+\frac{143}{20}-\frac{151}{24}=\frac{585+858-755}{120}=\frac{688}{120}=5\frac{88}{120}=5\frac{11}{15}$ **6.** $\frac{91}{120}\times\frac{8}{49}=\frac{13}{105}$

7. $\left(\frac{4}{25}\times\frac{1}{4}\right)+\frac{7}{30}=\frac{1}{25}+\frac{7}{30}=\frac{6+35}{150}=\frac{41}{150}$ **8.** $\frac{105}{360}+\frac{156}{360}-\frac{40}{360}+\frac{260}{360}=\frac{481}{360}=1\frac{121}{360}$ **9.** 0 **10.** $\frac{133}{2001}$

11. *Fact*: $36\ in.=1\ yd.\ \therefore\ \frac{36\ in.}{1\ yd.}=1=\frac{1\ yd.}{36\ in.}$ & $7.75\ yds.\times 1=\frac{7.75\ yds.}{1}\times\frac{36\ in.}{1\ yd.}=\frac{7.75\ in.\times 36}{1}=7.75\ in.\times 36=279\ in.$

12. *Fact*: $100{,}000\ cm=1\ k\ \therefore\ \frac{100000\ cm}{1\ km}=1=\frac{1\ km}{100000\ cm}$ & $10{,}540\ cm=0.10540\ km$ **13.** $\frac{3600\ secs.}{1\ hr.}=1=\frac{1\ hr.}{3600\ secs.}$

$\therefore\ 36{,}000{,}000\ secs.=10{,}000\ hrs.$ **14.** $\frac{5280\ ft.}{1\ mi.}=1=\frac{1\ mi.}{5280\ ft.}\ \therefore\ 19{,}800\ ft.=3.75\ mi.$ **15.** $\frac{1\ gal.}{4\ qts.}=1=\frac{4\ qts.}{1\ gal.}$

$3.75\ gals. = 15\ qts.$ **16.** $\frac{12\ in.}{1\ ft.} = 1 = \frac{1\ ft.}{12\ in.}$ ∴ $189\ in. = 15.75\ ft.\ or\ 15\frac{3}{4}\ ft.$ **17.** *Fact*: $36\ in. = 1\ yd.$

∴ $\frac{3.5\ yds.^2}{1} \times \frac{36\ in.}{1\ yd.} \times \frac{36\ in.}{1\ yd.} = 4536\ in.^2$ **18.** *Fact*: $100\ cm = 1\ m$ ∴ $\frac{30000\ cm^3}{1} \times \frac{1\ m}{100\ cm} \times \frac{1\ m}{100\ cm} \times \frac{1\ m}{100\ cm} = 0.03\ m^3$

19. *Facts*: $5280\ ft. = 1\ mi.$ & $60\ min. = 1\ hr.$ ∴ $\frac{5280\ ft.}{1\ mi.} = 1 = \frac{1\ mi.}{5280\ ft.}$ & $\frac{60\ min.}{1\ hr.} = 1 = \frac{1\ hr.}{60\ min.}$ *then*

$\frac{48\ mi.}{1\ hr.} \times \frac{5280\ ft.}{1\ mi.} \times \frac{1\ hr.}{60\ min.} = 4224\ \frac{ft.}{min.}$ **20.** *Fact*: $3\ k\&ks = 7\ l\&ns$ ∴ $\frac{3\ k\&ks}{7\ l\&ns} = 1 = \frac{7\ l\&ns}{3\ k\&ks}$ *then*

$25\ l\&ns = 25\ l\&ns \times 1 = \frac{25\ l\&ns}{1} \times \frac{3\ k\&ks}{7\ l\&ns} = \frac{25\ l\&ns\ \times\ 3\ k\&ns}{1\ \times\ 7\ l\&ns} = \frac{75}{7}\ k\&ns\ or\ 10\frac{5}{7}\ k\&ns$

FINAL TEST Part C:

1. $\frac{54.75\ ft.}{1} \times \frac{1\ yd.}{3\ ft.} = 18\frac{1}{4}\ yds.$ **2.** $\frac{787.78}{1} \times \frac{100\%}{1} = 78778\%$ **3.** $\frac{7992\ in.^2}{1} \times \frac{1\ ft.^2}{144\ in.^2} = 55.5\ ft.^2$

4. $\frac{120\ mi.}{1\ hr.} \times \frac{5280\ ft.}{1\ mi.} \times \frac{1\ hr.}{60\ min.} \times \frac{1\ min.}{60\ sec.} = \frac{176\ ft.}{1\ sec.} = 176\ \frac{ft.}{sec.}$ **5.** $\frac{50\ in.^3}{1\ min.} \times \frac{1\ ft.}{12\ in.} \times \frac{1\ ft.}{12\ in.} \times \frac{1\ ft.}{12\ in.} \times \frac{60\ min.}{1\ hr.} \times \frac{24\ hrs.}{1\ day} = 41\frac{2}{3}\ \frac{ft.^3}{day}$

6. $\frac{15{,}000\ l}{1} \times \frac{1000\ ml}{1\ L} = 15{,}000{,}000\ ml$ **7.** $\frac{3\ mm}{1} \times \frac{1\ m}{1000\ mm} \times \frac{1\ dam}{10\ m} = 0.0003\ dam$ **8.** $.875\% = \frac{.875\%}{1} \times \frac{1}{100\%} = .00875 =$

$\frac{875}{100000} = \frac{35}{4000} = \frac{7}{800}$ **9.** $\frac{1.78\ mi.}{1} \times \frac{1760\ yds.}{1\ mi.} = 3132.8\ yds.$ **10.** $\frac{3.75\ m}{1} \times \frac{100\ cm}{1\ m} \times \frac{1\ in.}{2.54\ cm} = 147.638\ in.$

FINAL TEST Part D:

1. $\frac{r^2(r+7)(r+2)}{r(r-3)(r+2)} \times \frac{r(r+5)(r+5)}{r^2(r+7)(r+5)} = \frac{(r+5)}{(r-3)} = \frac{r+5}{r-3}$ **2.** $LCD = (f-3)(f+3)(f-2)$ ∴ $\frac{1}{1} \cdot \frac{(f-3)(f+3)(f-2)}{(f-3)(f+3)(f-2)} - \frac{5}{(f-3)(f-2)} \cdot \frac{(f+3)}{(f+3)}$

$+ \frac{2f}{(f-3)(f+3)} \cdot \frac{(f-2)}{(f-2)} = \frac{f^3-2f^2-9f+18-5f-15+2f^2-4f}{(f-3)(f+3)(f-2)} = \frac{f^3-18f+3}{(f-3)(f+3)(f-2)}$ **3.** $\frac{m(m+5)(m+3) \cdot (m+4)(m-2)}{m(m+4)(m+3) \cdot (m-2)(m-2)} = \frac{(m+5)}{(m-2)} = \frac{m+5}{m-2}$

4. *The LCD in the numerator and the denominator is "y".* $\left(\frac{-t}{y} + \frac{t^2y}{1} \cdot \frac{y}{y}\right) \div \left(\frac{ty}{1} \cdot \frac{y}{y} - \frac{4t}{y}\right) = \left(\frac{-t+t^2y^2}{y}\right) \div \left(\frac{ty^2-4t}{y}\right) =$

$\frac{t(ty^2-1)}{y} \times \frac{y}{t(y-2)(y+2)} = \frac{ty^2-1}{(y-2)(y+2)}$ **5.** $LCD = (c-5)(c-5)(c-2)(c-2)$ $\frac{7}{(c-5)(c-2)} \cdot \frac{(c-5)(c-2)}{(c-5)(c-2)} -$

$\frac{2c}{(c-5)(c-5)} \cdot \frac{(c-2)(c-2)}{(c-2)(c-2)} - \frac{5c}{(c-2)(c-2)} \cdot \frac{(c-5)(c-5)}{(c-5)(c-5)} = \frac{7c^2-49c+70}{(c-5)(c-5)(c-2)(c-2)} - \frac{2c^3-8c^2+8c}{(c-5)(c-5)(c-2)(c-2)} - \frac{5c^3-50c^2+125c}{(c-5)(c-5)(c-2)(c-2)} =$

$\frac{-7c^3+65c^2-182c+70}{(c-5)(c-5)(c-2)(c-2)} = \frac{-(7c^3-65c^2+182c-70)}{(c-5)(c-5)(c-2)(c-2)}$ **6.** $\frac{(2x-1)(2x+3)}{(3x-1)(x-1)} \times \frac{(x-1)(x+1)}{(3x+5)(2x-1)} \times \frac{(3x-1)(3x+5)}{(2x-3)(2x+3)} = \frac{x+1}{2x-3}$

7. $LCM = (v-2)(v+2)(v-1)(v+1)$ $\frac{v}{(v-2)(v+2)} \cdot \frac{(v-1)(v+1)}{(v-1)(v+1)} + \frac{v}{(v+2)(v-1)} \cdot \frac{(v+1)(v-2)}{(v+1)(v-2)} + \frac{v}{(v-1)(v+1)} \cdot \frac{(v-2)(v+2)}{(v-2)(v+2)} =$

$\frac{v^3-v\ +\ v^3-v^2-2v\ +\ v^3-4v}{(v-2)(v+2)(v-1)(v+1)} = \frac{3v^3-v^2-7v}{(v-2)(v+2)(v-1)(v+1)} = \frac{v(3v^2-v-7)}{(v-2)(v+2)(v-1)(v+1)}$ **8.** $\left(\frac{(x+2)(x+3)}{(x-2)(x-3)} \cdot \frac{(x-2)(x+2)}{(x+2)(x+2)}\right) - \frac{6}{(x-3)} =$

$\frac{(x+3)}{(x-3)} - \frac{6}{(x-3)} = 1$ **9.** $\frac{(3y+1)(y-4) \cdot ((5y-2)(3y-4)}{(3y-4)(3y-4) \cdot (5y-2)(5y-2)} = \frac{(3y+1)(y-4)}{(3y-4)(5y-2)}$ **10.** $\frac{(d+5)(d-3)}{d(d+7)(d+4)} \times \frac{d(d+2)(d+7)}{(d+2)(d+5)} = \frac{d-3}{d+4}$

11. $LCD = (w-1)(w+1)$ $\frac{(w+1)}{(w+1)(w-1)} - \frac{(w+1)}{-(w-1)} = \frac{1}{(w-1)} + \frac{(w+1)}{(w-1)} = \frac{1+w+1}{w-1} = \frac{w+2}{w-1}$ **12.** $\frac{49}{(x+5)(x+5)} - \frac{7}{(x+5)}$

$LCD = (x+5)(x+5)$ $\frac{49}{(x+5)(x+5)} - \frac{7}{(x+5)} \cdot \frac{(x+5)}{(x+5)} = \frac{49-7x-35}{(x+5)(x+5)} = \frac{-7(x-2)}{(x+5)(x+5)}$ **13.** $84 = 2^2 \cdot 3 \cdot 7 \quad 92 = 2^2 \cdot 23$

$96 = 2^5 \cdot 3 \quad 100 = 2^2 \cdot 5^2 \quad LCD = 2^5 \cdot 3 \cdot 5^2 \cdot 7 \cdot 23 = 386{,}400 \quad \frac{21}{84} \cdot \frac{4600}{4600} + \frac{21}{92} \cdot \frac{4200}{4200} - \frac{21}{96} \cdot \frac{4025}{4025} + \frac{21}{100} \cdot \frac{3864}{3864} =$

$\frac{96600+88200-84525+81144}{386{,}400} = \frac{181{,}419}{386400} = \frac{60{,}473}{128{,}800} = \frac{8{,}639}{18{,}400}$ **14.** $LCD = (c+3)(c-3)(c+4) \quad \frac{3(c-3)}{(c+3)(c-3)(c+4)} +$

$\frac{5(c+4)}{(c+3)(c-3)(c+4)} + \frac{7((c+3)}{(c+3)(c-3)(c+4)} = \frac{3c-9+5c+20+7c+21}{(c+3)(c-3)(c+4)} = \frac{15c+32}{(c+3)(c-3)(c+4)}$ **15.** $LCM = (x-2)(x+2)$

$\frac{3x+7}{(x-2)(x+2)} + \frac{7}{-(x+2)} - \frac{-(x-1)}{-(x^2-4)} = \frac{3x+7}{(x-2)(x+2)} - \frac{7}{(x+2)} \cdot \frac{(x-2)}{(x-2)} - \frac{(x-1)}{(x-2)(x+2)} = \frac{3x+7-7x+14-x+1}{(x-2)(x+2)} = \frac{-5x+22}{(x-2)(x+2)}$

16. $\frac{25x^2y(5x-1)}{y(5x-1)(5x+1)} = \frac{25x^2}{5x+1}$ **17.** $\frac{rs}{1} \div \left\{\frac{r}{1} - \left[sr \div \left(\frac{s^3-r}{s^2}\right)\right]\right\} = \frac{rs}{1} \div \left\{\frac{r}{1} - \left[\frac{sr}{1} \times \frac{s^2}{(s^3-r)}\right]\right\} = \frac{rs}{1} \div \left\{\frac{r}{1} - \frac{s^3r}{(s^3-r)}\right\} =$

$\frac{sr}{1} \div \left\{\frac{r(s^3-r)-s^3r}{(s^3-r)}\right\} = \frac{sr}{1} \div \frac{-r^2}{(s^3-r)} = \frac{sr}{1} \times \frac{(s^3-r)}{-r^2} = \frac{-s(s^3-r)}{r}$ **18.** $\left(\frac{x-5}{(x-5)(x+5)} + x\right) \times \frac{(x+5)(x-3)}{x-3} =$

$\left(\frac{1}{x+5} + x\right) \times \frac{x+5}{1} = \frac{1+x(x+5)}{(x+5)} \times \frac{(x+5)}{1} = \frac{(x^2+5x+1) \times (x+5)}{(x+5) \times 1} = (x^2+5x+1) \times 1 = x^2+5x+1$

19. $LCD = 2^4 \cdot 3 \cdot 5 = 240 \quad 77\frac{170}{240} - 101\frac{232}{240} - 87\frac{177}{240} = -188\frac{409}{240} + 77\frac{170}{240} = -111\frac{239}{240}$ **20.** $\frac{(x^2+1)}{x} - \frac{x^3+2}{x^2} =$

$\frac{x(x^2+1)-(x^2+2)}{x^2} = \frac{x^3+x-x^3-2}{x^2} = \frac{x-2}{x^2}$

When writing the solutions to the previous 20 problems we indicated many steps, but we also skipped many steps. We wanted to lead you in the correct direction, but <u>you need to write your solutions as if you are explaining the solutions to students who have never solved these types of problems.</u> In all the addition and subtraction problems we indicated the "*LCD*" but we never went into detail how we determined the "*LCD*". We multiplied several fractions by fractions equal to the number <u>1</u>, but we never indicated how we determined these special fractions which equaled <u>1</u>. We did not use the one-big-fraction concept in any of our illustrations and we never emphasized either of the two new theorems which were emphasized throughout this textbook. When you solve the 20 problems in this last section of the final test you need to emphasize all the important steps which will help students understand how to solve all the problems when they attempt their homework problems. When you are the teacher and after you illustrate all the steps required to simplify the previous 20 problems, then illustrate the steps you want your students to write to simplify the problems and receive full credit in your class.

Short Autobiography: Timothy W. Young, Chartiers Valley School District, Bridgeville, Pennsylvania.

I was born in Altoona, Pennsylvania in 1949. Altoona is about 50 miles southwest of State College, home of Pennsylvania State University (Penn State). I graduated from Altoona Area High School in 1967 with approximately 1000 other students. I never considered myself to be brilliant academically, but I always did well in school, and I believe I graduated in the top 10% of my class. When I made my visit to the guidance counselor my senior year in the spring of 1967, the guidance counselor asked me what I was going to do after graduation. I told him I wanted to be a mathematics teacher and I was accepted at both Pennsylvania State University and Indiana University of Pennsylvania in their math education programs. The meeting probably lasted less than ten minutes, but I was satisfied when he said, "You have done well in all your math classes and IUP had a better reputation at that time for math education majors." So, I went to IUP. While at IUP, I obviously majored in Math Education, but I was in the band in the fall of my freshman year, then in the spring I made the freshmen baseball team which meant in the fall of my sophomore year, I needed to decide, whether I was going to play IUP baseball or be in the IUP Band. It was a tough decision, but I loved baseball. I never started on the baseball team and finally during my senior year when I knew I was going to do my student teaching during the spring semester I walked away from baseball.

If you know your history you should realize when I graduated from high school in 1967 the United States was involved in the Vietnam conflict, (it was a war by a different name). I was one of the few people in my group of high school friends who had good grades and the money to attend college. My father had a plumbing business located in Altoona and I had a full-time (part-time) job every time I had a break from college. We were not rich, but I was lucky enough to be able to afford college and not go to Vietnam right out of high school. Many of my classmates did go to Vietnam and around 20 of my friends either died or got wounded while serving our country.

During my four years in college, protestors and hippies were everywhere on many college campuses, but there were only a few protest marches while I attended IUP for four years. I was convinced when I graduated from college I would also end up in Vietnam. I figured if I was going to go to Vietnam, I preferred to be an officer, so I was in ROTC while attending IUP. I was not the top math student nor the top ROTC Cadet at IUP, but I was probably in the top 50% in both situations. I graduated from IUP in 1971 with a bachelor's degree in math education and a 2Lt. in the United States Army Engineers. I figured I would serve at least two maybe three years in the United States Army, but I was wrong. In the summer of 1971, the United States military was trying to pull out of Vietnam, therefore there was an excess of young Army officers and over half of the newly commissioned officers were ordered to go to their Basic Officers Course. Once I successfully completed my Engineer Officer Basic Course (EOBC), I had a choice (required) to either join the Army Reserves or the National Guard. I joined an Army Reserves unit in Altoona, since the company commander was the first to call me, after I visited several units.

After only 90 days in the military, I was a "90-day wonder," and boy, I had a lot to wonder about. I was discharged from the Army on December 6, 1971, and I had to wonder what I was going to do. I was lucky; I found a math teaching job at Tyrone Area Jr/Sr High School, located about 30 miles southwest of State College. I was without a full-time job for less than a month since I started at Tyrone on January 2, 1972, and I was still able to work part-time with my dad's plumbing business.

I quickly found out I was lucky to get into the reserves because my starting pay as a teacher was $35.00 per day and my pay for two weeks was $139.00 since the school district spread my pay over 9 months through August and then they had the gull to withhold taxes. Wow, what a wake-up event.

Tyrone School District treated me well. I became the Mathematics Department Head in 1978 even though I was not the most senior teacher, out of 9 math teachers I was 7th on the seniority list. Since

I was the Math Department Head, I felt it was important for me to teach every class offered in the curriculum for at least one year, so I would know what was expected in each grade level and each course. The administration must have thought I was doing something right. When I was teaching at Tyrone, the school was named Tyrone Jr/Sr High School, grades 7-12 in one building. I also coached cross country and softball for 8 years in the late 1970's and early 1980's. After my 11th year of teaching, I realized I needed to become a better teacher. The Principal, Neil Smith, never made any negative comments about my math teaching skills, in fact he was always positive about my teaching methods and procedures, but I realized after the 11th year of teaching, I was not doing as good a job as I expected from myself. When I did my self-evaluation in the summer, I realized too many of my students had earned C's when they should have earned B's, and the same was true about the number of students who earned D's and F's. I was missing something with the way I was teaching. At that point in my career, I made up my mind I was going to be a better math teacher and I had to become committed to doing better in the classroom and helping students "learn and remember" the procedures required to solve the problems and subsequently be better prepared for the math class they were going to take next year. I spent more time writing lesson plans and a lot of time thinking about how to teach different topics and sections in the textbook. I simply became obsessed with becoming a better teacher.

Also, around my 11th year as a teacher, I was progressing in my Army military career. I was a Captain in the Army Reserves, serving with the 458th Engineer Battalion (C)(C). There were 5 companies in the battalion, with the Headquarters and Headquarters Company located in Johnstown, Pennsylvania, and 4 other Engineer combat Companies located in western Pennsylvania. I needed command time if I was going to be promoted to Major.

The Battalion Commander, LTC Rodney Ruddock, called me into his office and made it clear that he wanted me to assume Company Command of the unit in Pittsburgh, Pennsylvania. After all, Pittsburgh was only about 100 miles west of Altoona, and during the past 7 or 8 months, there were

5-6 different temporary commanders. It was not something which I had much of a choice, even though there were two other units about 50 miles from Altoona which I had hoped to command. After 30+ months as the Company Commander of D Company, 458th Engineer Battalion, I did get promoted to Major and found a position with the Reserve Headquarters Command, 99th RSC, also located in Pittsburgh. I mention my command time as a company commander because it had a great influence on my future life decisions. I had been the leader of a 150+ man unit, which had experienced problems for several years. When I left this command, I felt I had accomplished something positive and left behind a unit that had experienced problems, and they improved significantly during my tenure.

A couple of years later, I decided I needed to consider becoming a Secondary School Principal. I attended IUP again and got my Principal's Certification while pursuing a master's degree. I was ready to be a leader in a high school or a middle school, although I preferred the High School atmosphere. I accepted the position of Principal at Glendale Jr/Sr High School, which is located about 20 miles northwest of Altoona. Glendale is a small rural school district with less than 500 students in grades 7-12. The parents, the teachers, the administration, and the school board treated me very well, but for financial reasons, it made sense to move closer to Pittsburgh.

After four years as the Principal at Glendale, Chartiers Valley School District offered me a position as Assistant Principal in the High School. Chartiers Valley School District is located less than 15 minutes southwest of downtown Pittsburgh. The address for the administrative offices is a Pittsburgh address, and the high school has a Bridgeville address.

In Pennsylvania, we do NOT have county school districts; we have local school districts throughout the county, sometimes, a school district will spread into two counties, and each local school district has its own school board, administrative staff, and teachers within the school district. During my first three years at Chartiers Valley Senior High School, I was an Assistant Principal, and when the High School Principal retired, the school board selected me to be the new high school principal. Chartiers Valley High School had between 1000 and 1100 students in grades 9-12. I consider Chartiers Valley School District an upper-middle-class school district with many students living in a Jack Nicklaus golf course development called The Club at Nevillewood and many students coming from less wealthy communities located in the school district.

I was blessed to be the Principal of Chartiers Valley High School. There were times when things seemed to be a problem, but every problem got solved and I feel confident that most of the students, teachers, parents, administration, school board, and support staff supported me and treated me with the upmost respect. I could not have found a better school district to serve as a principal and work.

When I was a young man, I used to ride motorcycles and when I was the Principal, I wanted to do something which would allow me to relax, clear my mind, and give me the feeling-of-freedom which I always experienced when I rode a motorcycle. So, on a Saturday afternoon in the fall of 1999, I decided I was going to go for a ride on my motorcycle just to relax and think. Unfortunately, while I was riding on a two-lane road near the Pittsburgh International Airport, I started to think about a problem which occurred the previous week and I crossed the center line on a long sweeping curve and hit a car head-on. It was my fault.

I spent 28 days in the hospital with serious left leg injuries, close to four months in a wheelchair, and around a year using crutches or cane. I was worn out and physically struggling getting around the school when a math teacher decided to retire. I approached the school superintendent and school board about the possibility of returning to the math classroom. The school board did not owe me any special privileges, but they did allow me to return to the math classroom even though I never taught in the Chartiers Valley School District. Once I returned to the classroom, I felt I owed the school district something and I tried to be the best secondary math teacher I could possibly become. I hope I succeeded, but that question can only be answered by the students I taught until I retired in 2009. Every year I was a teacher at Chartiers Valley High School, I constantly did self-evaluations focused on my teaching methods and how well the students learned and remembered the concepts and topics which I considered important in each class. Again, I hope I succeeded, and the students appreciated how much effort I put into my lesson plans and classroom lessons.

After I retired, I continually thought about better methods/procedures teachers could use to teach students in arithmetic and mathematics classes. I was fixated on determining what needed to be done and what could be done to improve math education in the United States, it became my passion. On June 19, 2012, I noticed an article on the front page of the Pittsburgh Post-Gazette titled (short title) "Formula written for math success" by Mary Niederberger. The newspaper article focused on the research findings of Dr. Robert Siegler a Professor at Carnegie Mellon University. Dr. Siegler had been involved with several research projects during his tenure at CMU and presently at the Teachers College, Columbia University, focused on students' understanding and knowledge with fractions and long division problems. Dr. Siegler, supported by his research, insists that these two arithmetic topics are key indicators to predict success in algebra and advanced mathematics courses. Two earlier research papers mentioned in the newspaper article involved a group of 3,677 children born in the U.K. when the students who were 10 in 1980 and sixteen in 1986 and the second research paper involved 599 children born in the U.S. when they were 10-12 in 1997 and 15-17 in 2002. Both studies reasoned that fraction and division knowledge of the students from the United States and the United Kingdom, likely were the strongest indicators of success in algebra and advanced mathematics courses. Dr. Siegler and his team conducted their own independent research on these two topics, but much of the research focused on fractions and later the research articles investigated all rational numbers. The research paper mentioned in the newspaper article was titled "Early Predictors of High School Mathematics Achievement." The article was published prior to the newspaper article in an edition of *Psychological Science* (Siegler, Duncan et. al. 2012). The findings in this research article simply verified early research findings. When I read the article in the paper, I immediately knew this man had the answers to many of my questions and beliefs which I wanted to tell parents when I was a high school math teacher and principal, but I could not because I did not have the proof to back-up my thoughts. I immediately contacted Dr. Siegler, he invited me to join him for lunch at CMU, then invited me to be a guest and attend his weekly research discussion group meetings at CMU. I accepted and attended his meetings along with other meetings at CMU for the next six years, until Dr. Siegler retired from CMU and took a similar position at the Teachers College, Columbia University.

Once I started to attend the research meetings, I listened and the more I listened to the young and experienced math researchers in the group discuss their research and research findings and at the same time I read between 150 and 200 research papers focused on math learning, I wished I was 22 again and ready to begin my math teaching career. I learned so much about problems students encounter when they are in elementary arithmetic classes, and I continually kept thinking about the problems students do not fully understand in arithmetic and how these same problems are the foundation of advanced math courses starting with Algebra. My main focus was to find the answer to the question, "How can teachers better teach these challenging arithmetic topics, so students learn and remember the concepts and procedures?" **This is the reason why I wrote this book/textbook.** If this textbook helps young inexperienced elementary arithmetic teachers and young inexperienced secondary math teachers be better prepared to help students learn and remember the concepts, rules, and procedures which are important in every arithmetic/math class they will teach, I have helped all students be more successful in elementary arithmetic and high school math classes. I want these young teachers to be prepared to effectively teach all students when they initially enter their first classroom and emphasize the same rules in arithmetic which are taught and required in algebra and other advanced math classes. My first dream is to help students still in college be prepared to enter their first arithmetic or math classroom and be successful. My **number one dream and passion** is to help young students understand the concepts, rules, procedures, and number sense for all numbers starting with natural numbers up to and including rational numbers before they enter an Algebra class. If this occurs, I am confident more students around the world will be more successful in algebra classes and all higher-level math classes.

Webpage: https://onethemostpowerfulnumber.com Email: twypitts1@gmail.com

One Last Important Teaching Statement, a statement which all arithmetic and mathematics teachers must always remember: **"If students do not practice solving problems after learning new rules and procedures, they will not "Learn or Remember" the newly introduced rules and procedures in 1-2 months."** This statement is a fact for over 99% of all students, the degree of practice required, varies from student to student.

When I taught low achieving math students in 9th-12th grade I frequently heard the following comment from over 50% of the students, "I do not do any homework!". This statement can be extended to mean, "I do not do any classwork either!" If you are the teacher and students make this comment, how are you going to proceed with the goal to have over 90% of your students' "Learn and Remember" the rules and procedures? If you are going to be a successful arithmetic or math teacher, you must find a solution to this problem.

The following plan is a solution which worked well for me. I decided I would not give homework or classwork to these students. I made every assignment a graded assignment, either a quiz or a test, and since it was just not practice or classwork the students tried to solve the problems. I tried to follow the four-step plan listed below as much as possible, but obviously there were days/weeks I had to modify my procedures.

1. On Monday, I would discuss a topic for the week.
2. Give a 15-point quiz on Tuesday, Wednesday, Thursday, and Friday. I called them quizzes and I always graded and recorded the grade for each quiz. To me it was not a quiz, it was a way to get the students to attempt to do the work.
3. Each quiz consisted of 10 review questions and 5 questions focused on the topic for the week. If all students were trying and working quietly, I would go around and help students get the correct answers especially for the new problems. Sometimes I would allow students to help each other in order to vary the process, but only if all students were working intently.
4. My goal was to get all the students to earn at least a "C" or better on all quizzes, initially with my help, and then without my help or with very little help. With time, over 90% of my students were successful.

Once the students experienced success, their attitudes and work ethic improved significantly. I also gave 100-point tests (25 problems) three times every nine weeks. Before the students took a 100-point test, I would give them a similar practice test worth 25 points. The day after a quiz or practice test, I always gave the students written solutions to all the problems for them to use as a reference and I would answer all questions regarding the quiz and test questions, then if time permitted, I would explain how to solve the most challenging problems and/or the most missed problems on either the quiz or test.

Acknowledgments and Influential Friends in my life

Thanks to the many people who have helped me along the way over the past 73 years.

Anna Jean Young and **Donald R. Young**: My mom and dad who taught me right and wrong and a work ethic. I was far from perfect, but with their help and guidance I was able to achieve at a reasonably high level. Thanks for being the greatest parents. I know it must have been a challenge for both of you, starting on day one.

Mr. Nicholas Luciano: My high school geometry teacher and because of him I became a secondary math teacher. I hope I lived up to your standards.

Dr. Marlin Hartman and **Dr. Doyle McBride**: Two of the most amazing math professors at Indiana University of Pennsylvania. Both professors helped me, guided me, and made a tremendous impression on me when I sat in their classrooms. Unfortunately, both are deceased but never forgotten in my mind. Doyle and his brother, whom I never had, were the handball champions when I was in college, and they would take on all challengers.

Mr. Neil Smith and **Dr. Mike Bonacci**: Neil Smith was the Principal at Tyrone Jr./Sr. High School for most of the 21 years when I taught math and Mike Bonacci was the principal at Chartiers Valley High School when I served as one of the Assistant Principals. Both individuals helped prepare me to be a quality principal by first respecting all students and parents, how to handle everyday problems, always be courteous and understanding with everyone even under the most stressful situations, generally develop excellent leadership skills, and develop a strong curriculum in the high school.

Dr. William Miller: The Superintendent at Tyrone Area School District during my first 21 years as a math teacher. Dr. Miller was a strong leader, stood up to the school board when they were wrong, and guided Tyrone School District in a positive direction for many years. As I look back on my career in public education, Dr. Miller is one of the three most influential individuals in my career. He was a rock, a leader, and a man of integrity in every situation he faced throughout his career.

Mrs. Carol Blundell: The Superintendent at Glendale School District where I was a principal for four years. A strong leader and a great person.

Frances Coledo and **Renetta Folk**: Two ladies I graduated with when I got my bachelor's degree, and both impressed me as two future outstanding math teachers. There were both brilliant, special people and they both made an impression in my life regarding what I hoped to be when I entered the classroom as a mathematics teacher.

Mr. Francis Bloom: My best friend, math teacher, and coworker in the 1970's, 1980's, and early 1990's at Tyrone Area Jr./Sr. High School. Fran started at Tyrone as a math teacher in the fall after I started in the previous January. We were both young and we both wanted to be good math teachers. We would sit and discuss the best ways to teach specific math topics to students at lunch time on a regular basis. I know Fran made me a better math teacher and I hope I helped him become a better math teacher. I always considered Fran the better mathematician and the better math teacher. He was a fantastic teacher and person. He retired when he was 60 years old and died a year later with cancer. If I were to dedicate this book to one special person, it would be Francis Bloom.

Mrs. Natalie Zamanski: Natalie was a special education teacher at Chartiers Valley High School with several years of experience when we co-taught one of the low-level prealgebra classes consisting of mostly 9th graders but also some 10th, 11th, and 12th grade students. Natalie was amazing and we complemented each other immediately with both academics and discipline. Natalie was not completely sold on my idea of teaching a new topic on Monday and giving 15-point quizzes on Tuesday through Friday. We did agree to refer to the quizzes as quizzes even though in our minds the quizzes were classwork, and we would both go around the classroom and assist any student who asked for help. Our goal was to get all the students to work, earn passing grades with our help, and over time convince the students that they could correctly solve the problems on their own. It was at this point that the students started to demonstrate real progress with both their math competency and self-esteem. The 15-point quizzes consisted of 10 review problems from the previous weeks and 5 new problems based on the information presented on Monday. We interleaved fractions, decimals, and percentages into 75% of all the problems on the daily quizzes/classwork assignments, especially the second semester after the students demonstrated an understanding of the relationship between fractions, decimals, and percentages. At the end of the year, Natalie made a comment to me which I will never forget, "She was not sure how my teaching methods would work during the year, but when the students took the final exam in late May she was amazed by the improvement which all students demonstrated. She knew students were learning and remembering how to solve problems better than in previous years, and she was amazed with the end results."

MG Rodney Ruddock: Other than my mother and father, I consider General Ruddock to be the most influential person in my life. I first met General Ruddock when he was a Major and the Executive Office of the 458th Engineer Battalion, Johnstown, PA. I followed in his footsteps until he was the Major General of the 99th RSC, which was an Army Reserve Command covering Pennsylvania, West Virginia, Virginia, Maryland, Delaware, and the District of Columbia. General Ruddock taught me more about leadership, honesty, and integrity than any person I know. A great man and a great friend.

Dr. Robert Siegler and his team of Math Researchers at Carnegie Mellon University (CMU) for over 40 years and now at the Teachers College, Columbia University. I also consider Dr. Siegler to be one of the three most influential individuals in my life, especially when it comes to math education. I already wrote a condensed version of my respect for Dr. Siegler, his work, and his team in the beginning of this textbook, when he was a professor at CMU. Here are the names of some of the great math researchers I met through Dr. Siegler: **Dr. Drew Bailey**: School of Education, University of California, Irvine: **Dr. Hugo Lortie – Forgues**: Senior Lecturer, Loughborough University, Department of Mathematics Education, UK: **Dr. Jake McMillan**: Associate Professor - University of Turku, Department of Teacher Education, Finland: and **Dr. David Braithwaite**: Assistant Professor, Psychology, Florida State University. All four of these gentlemen did post-doc work under the supervision of Dr. Siegler. All four are excellent math researchers and I have referenced their research frequently throughout this textbook. All four have moved on and proven to be leaders in the field of math research. I was always impressed with their comments during the research meetings and all four made me think about teaching arithmetic and mathematics differently.

Dr. Jing Tian: Dr. Tian received her doctorate from CMU and Dr. Siegler was her main advisor. Her thesis focused on percentages. Jing is presently a post-doc researcher in the Department of Psychology at Temple University. I got to know Jing when she was working on her Ph.D., and we became friends. Very intelligent young lady and a true friend.

Dr: Lauren Schiller: Dr. Schiller received her Ph.D. from the Teachers College, Columbia University in the spring of 2020. Her advisor was Dr. Siegler. After receiving her doctorate, she mentioned to Dr. Siegler that she was interested in doing some research on the number, 1. Dr. Siegler knew I had a special interest in the number 1, since I had written a short paper on the importance of the number 1, when I was attending meetings at CMU before Dr. Siegler retired and took a similar position at Columbia. Lauren and I talked on the phone and emailed each other many times in 2020-2021 to discuss her research. I referenced her research previously in this textbook. I find her research on the number 1, to be interesting and informative.

Mr. Brian S. Young and **Maj. Chad A. Young** (Ret. Army): Brian and Chad are the highlights of my life. Brian is a CFP/Business Owner in Maryland with offices in Hagerstown and Frederick, and Chad is a retired Major from the Army and presently a Jr. ROTC instructor in South Carolina.

Mrs. Randy C. Philson: Randy is my biggest supporter, teammate, proofreader, advisor, and wife for the past 15 years. She is a retired Elementary Teacher and Reading Specialist, which immediately qualifies her as a miracle worker. **Thank you for all your love and help, I would never have had the strength to keep going and complete this textbook without your constant encouragement.**

I am so blessed to know so many great individuals and consider many of them friends for the rest of my life. Just like every other person who has lived and walked on this earth there are thousands and probably tens of thousands of people who have influenced us and because of them we develop our own set of values and an understanding of right and wrong.

A tribute to all arithmetic teachers: k-3, teachers who lay the math foundation for the math skyscraper.

Imagine, it is a nice sunny day in August, the first day of school for 22 little 5-year-old students entering your classroom for the first time. The differences between the 22 students are great. These students do not have the same social skills, or the same knowledge regarding numbers, or the same knowledge about letters, words, and reading.

For the next four school years (k, 1, 2, and 3) four main teachers along with other specialized teachers will mold these 22 students into a small social group where they will learn to respect each other and make friends, this is one of the first goals. This is a challenge which somehow most of these teachers are the experts and masters.

A second, important goal for k-3 teachers is to start to teach students how to recognize and work with letters to form words and then how to read. The goal is to have all 22 students learn to read. Some will excel in reading and enjoy reading. Reading will not be easy for some of the other students, but great teachers cannot and will not be discouraged, and they will continue to help all 22 students improve and reach their maximum potential by the time they leave 3rd grade. Many parents consider this goal to be the most important academic goal in the early elementary grades and most parents are eager and willing to help their child learn to read at the expected grade level or higher.

The third goal is just as important as the first and second goals, but sometimes teaching arithmetic, does not get the same emphasize as goal number 2. There is a lot to learn in the first four years in school regarding natural numbers and whole numbers to include adding, subtracting, introduce multiplication and division facts, plus place an emphasize on magnitude and number sense.

Wow, these teachers are amazing, but if they fail, your child is behind and probably will remain behind for years to come. These are the most important teachers in your child's overall education career. The foundations they build are the keys to success for the remainder of your child's life.

Fourth grade through Prealgebra teachers build the first floor for the skyscraper to come.

Grades 4, 5, 6, 7, and/or 8 are by far the most important years in your child's education if your child is going to be successful in higher level math subjects, starting with Algebra in 6th, 7th, 8th, or 9th grade for over 90% of the original 22 students. Some students will excel in arithmetic and take algebra in 6th grade and some students may not take algebra until 9th grade or maybe never.

If your child is going to be successful in high school level math classes starting with Algebra, the most important prerequisite in arithmetic is a strong understanding of rational numbers which includes fractions, decimals, and percentages. The arithmetic teachers who teach the higher-level arithmetic classes prior to entering an Algebra class must be well prepared and master teachers, knowledgeable with all the teaching skills required to ensure their students master all the concepts, rules, procedures to work will all types of rational numbers. These teachers must be the best arithmetic teachers and not only be able to teach but also be knowledgeable about all arithmetic topics and problems students will encounter regarding advanced arithmetic topics. These teachers must know how to apply the arithmetic rules and procedures learned in these grades to solve advanced higher level rational expression (fraction) math problems.

I suggest, before any student enters their first algebra class, the math course taught the previous year is devoted to understanding the concepts, rules, and procedures involving all rational numbers. This means that 3 or 4 days per week the goal is to teach rational numbers. I specifically mentioned concepts, rules, and procedures, but in this arithmetic class the teacher must also teach number sense involving all sets of numbers to include rational numbers.

Do you realize fractions, decimals, and percentages are all forms of equivalent numbers with one exception? If you know the one exception you are ready to teach the arithmetic class indicated above. If you do not know the one exception, then you are not ready to teach a high-level arithmetic class focused on rational numbers. (Comment/Exception: All fractions can be written as a decimal or percent, but the opposite "converse" is not true.)

Secondary Math teachers, Algebra through Calculus and Statistics in high school, begin to build the first 10-20 floors of the math skyscraper, and things really become interesting or impossible if the students are not fully prepared.

The Secondary Algebra, Geometry, Precalculus, Calculus, and Statistics teachers can only build the first 10-20 floors of the math skyscraper if there is a solid foundation. If all students entering these classes are highly proficient with all arithmetic concepts, procedures, and common sense regarding natural numbers, whole numbers, integers, and rational numbers (fractions, decimals, and percentages) then these students are prepared to build the strongest math skyscraper imaginable. If a student enters an algebra 1 class with a weakness in one of these areas especially rational numbers, the math skyscraper will eventually collapse because of a weak foundation.

Imagine you are building a real skyscraper on a slab of 10-inch-thick concrete. You may be able to build a building consisting of one, two, or maybe three floors, but eventually if the building is built much higher the total structure will crumple and turn into a pile of rubble. You cannot build a skyscraper on a slab of concrete. This foundation is not designed to build a tall skyscraper. If you are going to build a skyscraper, there is a lot of design work, manual and equipment work, to build a foundation to support a 20-60 floor skyscraper, but without the foundation, the skyscraper can only consist of 2 or 3 floors.

The same is true when you build the math skyscraper. If students have not mastered the concepts, rules/procedures, and number sense regarding the sets of numbers indicated above then the high school portion of the skyscraper will either collapse or tetter on the brink of destruction and the students will struggle.

Suggestion, prior to permitting a student to enter an algebra 1 class, make sure the student masters all the rules, procedures, and number sense involving rational numbers. I suggest, students take an **advanced arithmetic** course prior to entering an Algebra 1 class, and the main objective of the course is to have students focus on rational numbers. A strong understanding of rational numbers is the number one indicator of success when students enter an algebra class and future success in advanced math classes.

College Professors build the skyscraper high into the clouds.

The math skyscraper will never be fully completed, it only gets higher and higher. The college professors reinforce the first 10-20 levels and they will continue emphasizing math, science, and technology, therefore, adding an infinity number of floors.

I am always puzzled about the lack of emphasize which universities and colleges place on higher level math courses. I had a dream when I was a high school principal which was, "Every student who received a diploma on graduation night as a minimum, could pass a basic Algebra 1 final test." I have a second dream about students who graduate from any university or college, "Students who receive a bachelor's degree, are proficient with both Calculus 1 and Statistics, and they can pass a college final test in both courses." Both dreams would place a standard on high schools, colleges, and universities, which cannot be meant. Thus, I simply dream.

When I was an invited guest of Dr. Robert Siegler's at Carnegie Mellon University with his math research team, I made the following comment, "When I was a high school principal, I wished every student who received a diploma had excellent communication skills to include reading, writing, speaking, and listening in order to get a job in the United States." One of the students on the CMU research team was a young Chinese lady, named Jing Tian, and she immediately said, "In China, they teach us if we can do math and science, we can get a job anywhere in the world." Her comment has remained in my mind ever since that comment was made, because in China they have one main educational goal: "The students will learn math and science." So simple and yet so powerful!

What is the number one educational goal in your local school district? Is it football, or basketball, or dance, or band, etc.? I will bet that less than 1 in 20 educational administrators would say math or science. They might say English or more likely they will state some basic general educational goal, such as, "To educate every student to reach their maximum ability." What a generic statement and goal. I like the Chinese goal to emphasize math and science, what about you? I am a dreamer, but I am also a realist when referring to educational goals.

Made in the USA
Coppell, TX
09 December 2023

25633953R00332